THE
HISTORY
OF
AMERICAN
METHODISM

THE

HISTORY

OF

AMERICAN

METHODISM

In Three Volumes

VOLUME III

ABINGDON PRESS
NEW YORK   NASHVILLE

Library of Congress Catalog Card Number: 64-10013

SET UP, PRINTED, AND BOUND BY THE
PARTHENON PRESS, AT NASHVILLE, TEN-
NESSEE, UNITED STATES OF AMERICA

THE WRITERS

THEODORE L. AGNEW, Professor of History, Oklahoma State University

WALTER W. BENJAMIN, Head, Department of Religion, Morningside College

EDWIN P. BOOTH, Professor of Historical Theology, Boston University School of Theology

RICHARD M. CAMERON, Professor of Church History, Boston University School of Theology

WILLIAM R. CANNON, Dean and Professor of Church History and Historical Theology, Candler School of Theology, Emory University

DOUGLAS R. CHANDLER, Professor of Church History, Wesley Theological Seminary

PAUL DOUGLASS, Professor of Government, Rollins College

BISHOP F. GERALD ENSLEY, Resident in the Iowa Area of The Methodist Church

WEBB GARRISON, Minister, Roberts Park Methodist Church, Indianapolis

JOHN O. GROSS, General Secretary, Division of Higher Education, Board of Education of The Methodist Church

BISHOP NOLAN B. HARMON, Resident in the Charlotte Area of The Methodist Church

LEONARD L. HAYNES, JR., Minister, Wesley Methodist Church, Baton Rouge, and Professor of Philosophy, Southern University

STUART C. HENRY, Professor of American Christianity, The Divinity School, Duke University

W. RICHEY HOGG, Professor of World Christianity, Perkins School of Theology

ARTHUR E. JONES, JR., Director of the Library and Professor of English, Drew University

BISHOP GERALD KENNEDY, Resident in the Los Angeles Area of The Methodist Church

BISHOP WILLIS J. KING, Retired, of The Methodist Church

DOW KIRKPATRICK, Minister, First Methodist Church, Evanston

MURRAY H. LEIFFER, Professor of Sociology and Social Ethics and Director of the Bureau of Social and Religious Research, Garrett Theological Seminary

GERALD O. McCULLOH, Director, Department of Ministerial Education, Board of Education of The Methodist Church

WILLIAM J. McCUTCHEON, Assistant Professor, Department of Religion, Beloit College

v

FREDERICK E. MASER, Minister, St. George's Methodist Church, Philadelphia

JAMES W. MAY, Associate Professor of Church History, Candler School of Theology, Emory University

ROBERT MOATS MILLER, Associate Professor of History, University of North Carolina

RALPH E. MORROW, Professor of History, Washington University

ARTHUR BRUCE MOSS, Minister Emeritus, John Street Methodist Church, New York City

BISHOP T. OTTO NALL, Resident in the Minnesota Area of The Methodist Church

J. ROBERT NELSON, Fairchild Professor of Systematic Theology, The Graduate School of Theology, Oberlin College

FREDERICK A. NORWOOD, Professor of History of Christianity, Garrett Theological Seminary

JAROSLAV J. PELIKAN, Titus Street Professor of Ecclesiastical History, Yale Divinity School

COEN G. PIERSON, John Clark Ridpath Professor of History and Chairman of the History Department, DePauw University

JAMES P. PILKINGTON, Personnel Manager, The Methodist Publishing House

J. MANNING POTTS, Editor, *The Upper Room*

MARTIN RIST, Professor of New Testament and Christian History, The Iliff School of Theology

LELAND SCOTT, Director, the Wesley Foundation, University of Arizona

LAWRENCE SHERWOOD, Minister, St. Paul's Methodist Church, Oakland, Maryland

DAVID C. SHIPLEY, Professor of Theology, Methodist Theological School in Ohio

GRANT S. SHOCKLEY, Professor of Religious Education, Garrett Theological Seminary

GEORGE A. SINGLETON, Editor, *The A.M.E. Review*

TIMOTHY L. SMITH, Associate Professor of History and Education, University of Minnesota

NORMAN W. SPELLMANN, Professor of Philosophy and Religion, Southwestern University, Georgetown, Texas

RALPH STOODY, General Secretary and Director, Commission on Public Relations and Methodist Information

CHARLES T. THRIFT, JR., President, Florida Southern College

FRANCIS C. WILSON, Executive Secretary, Communications Section, Board of Education of The Methodist Church

vi

THE CONTENTS

26. Structural and Administrative Changes 1
    NOLAN B. HARMON

27. The Missions of American Methodism 59
    W. RICHEY HOGG

28. Methodist Publishing in Historical Perspective, 1865-1939 129
    Sections 1-5, T. OTTO NALL
    Section 6, JAMES P. PILKINGTON

29. The Field of Education, 1865-1939 201
    JOHN O. GROSS

Part V. A Maturing Church in a Maturing Nation: 1919-60

Introduction 253
    GERALD KENNEDY

30. American Methodist Thought and Theology, 1919-60 261
    WILLIAM J. MCCUTCHEON

31. Methodism and American Society, 1900-1939 328
    ROBERT MOATS MILLER

32. The Story of Unification, 1874-1939 407
    FREDERICK E. MASER

33. United Methodism, 1940-60 479
    Sections 1-5, MURRAY H. LEIFFER
    "The Central Jurisdiction," WILLIS J. KING
    Section 6, J. ROBERT NELSON
    Section 7, RALPH STOODY

34. Methodism's Contribution to America 596
    JAROSLAV J. PELIKAN

35. American Methodism: An Experiment in Secular Christianity .. 615
F. GERALD ENSLEY

Appendix: American Methodist Hymnody: A Historical Sketch 631
CARLTON R. YOUNG

Bibliography 635
Index 651

viii

Illustrations

(Following page 342)

1. The beginnings of the Methodist Federation for Social Service
2. *The Child's Magazine*
3. *Sunday School and Youth's Library*
4. *Picture Lesson Paper,* 1877
5. *Pictures and Stories,* 1956
6. *Classmate*
7. *The Methodist Magazine and Quarterly Review*
8. The *Ladies' Repository* and *Together*
9. John R. Mott
10. G. Bromley Oxnam
11. McKendree Church, Nashville
12. The Strawbridge Church, Maryland
13. Old St. George's
14. St. Timothy's Methodist Church, Iowa
15. John F. Goucher and Earl Cranston
16. Unification: John M. Moore, James H. Straughn, Edwin Holt Hughes

chapter 26

STRUCTURAL AND ADMINISTRATIVE CHANGES

Functions of Boards

The Ministry

Annual Conferences

Growth of the Episcopacy

The Constitution

Lay Representation

THE PARALLEL GROWTH OF THE METH-odist Church with that of the United States has often been noted. The periods of great expansion for the nation were those of great expansion for the church. The throwing forward of the American frontier, with its final conclusion at the Pacific Ocean, was accompanied by a concomitant expansion of the Methodist Churches until they, too, touched the far-western shores. The Methodist Church thereby became, and now is, the most evenly distributed Protestant church in America. Its members influence, and in turn are profoundly influenced by, the attitudes and mores of each particular region or section of the nation in which they may happen to live.

The influence of the frontier and its effect upon the mind of both state and church was profound, and remained so well past the end of the century. William Warren Sweet holds that the increased emphasis upon discipline on the part of the churches was due to the "general laxness in morals and letting down of standards . . . inherent in pioneering." [1] Frontier work also called for a certain robustness on the part of the ministry, especially an itinerant one, and a tendency to adopt the practical at the expense of theoretical moves, both in churchly doctrine and in organizational procedures.

Noteworthy among the factors influencing both the church and the nation as they grew larger and larger was the dividing out, and in time the great proliferation, of the functions of government and of church into many adminis-

[1] *Religion in the Development of American Culture* (New York: Charles Scribner's Sons. 1952), p. 137.

1

trative departments—or "boards," as they came to be known in the church. In the government, the comparatively few departments—State, Treasury, War, etc.—with which the nation began, multiplied more and more as time went on. The departments themselves ramified enormously in many ways, and one cabinet post after another was added to the federal superstructure. In the Methodist Churches, likewise, it was found necessary, as numbers vastly increased, to have the church's special causes and various areas of work cared for by special boards, commissions, and committees. Each of these agencies was created to do a special task and empowered to care for a particular work of the church itself.

The ecclesiastical development here was natural and normal, all things considered. Starting at first with the Publishing House, or Book Concern, as the first corporate structure and entity of the connection, there came in time the need for a general agency to oversee missions, then one for education, and thereafter many types of corporate organizations, as the church, through its General Conference or even smaller bodies, might find need. The cry of "bureaucracy" was raised in the church, as it has been raised in the nation, as time went on. But a huge, vital organization such as The Methodist Church cannot possibly do its manifold work unless it does create and control, support and direct, respective and greatly needed agencies in various special lines of endeavor.

The boards in fact have become integral parts of the church's basic structure, not because of some parchment or charter granted them, but because they fulfill and will continue to fulfill an absolutely vital role in the life of The Methodist Church. They came into being in answer to a need which in turn grew as Methodism increased in numbers and effectiveness; and they will remain as long as the same needs persist, that is, as long as the church shall fulfill its manifold duty as a great ecclesiasticism.[2]

It is not part of this chapter to trace the development of the huge Board of Missions or that of Education or that of Publication—traditionally the major boards of the connection. Church Extension, however, as the missionary enterprise in the United States came to be called, gave opportunity for Methodism to move forward in a systematic and well-organized way toward the building of new churches and the taking of new territory. The Board of Church Extension of the Methodist Episcopal Church was formed in 1864; the corresponding board of the Southern Church, in 1886.

[2] Much of the material in this chapter is taken from the author's *Organization of The Methodist Church* (2nd rev. ed.; Nashville: The Methodist Publishing House, 1962). This quotation is from p. 217.

Other huge boards, such as the Board of Evangelism and the Board of Hospitals and Homes, were also destined to come into prominence by the middle of the twentieth century. It would be tedious to outline the history of each separate structure in each of the three Methodisms before these became The Methodist Church in 1939. The development of the activities of these and other important church bodies may be studied elsewhere. For missions there is the authoritative *History of Methodist Missions* by Wade Crawford Barclay—a monumental series of volumes which is in itself practically a history of American Methodism. Likewise, the field of education and the work of Methodism in it has produced a comprehensive literature. So have other boards and agencies been covered by appropriate bibliographies. It is our part here to note the effect of this development upon the general church, especially as this relates to the structural and administrative changes which came about during the last half of the nineteenth century.

It may be noted that the distinguishing mark of a "board," as Methodism uses this term, is that it is a legal corporation; this, almost without exception. Incorporation gives an agency of the church the power to transact business as a legal entity, receive bequests, hold property, sue and be sued, after the manner of any other corporate body. It is important that these functions inhere in the general church boards, as otherwise they could not carry on and do the work they have been created to do.

"Commissions," as this term has come to be commonly used in The Methodist Church, differ from boards in lacking legal incorporation— as a rule—and usually commissions work at some more or less temporary or specialized type of task. Occasionally, commissions which are seen to be conducting a continuing work of importance are given the power to organize and become regular boards. This happened in the case of the Commission on Evangelism, which in time became the Board of Evangelism, duly incorporated.

The boards are the continuing effective agencies of the church. When the first missionaries went out, they had to look back to the church at home for supplies, for their salaries, for medicine, and for help of various kinds. To whom were they to look? The bishops had scattered; the General Conference had adjourned. Local-church committees and friends proved entirely inadequate, and it was necessary that there be a headquarters group in the homeland which should continually care for, supervise, and support the missionaries in their far-flung outposts. Thus, in time, the huge Board of Missions came into being. It developed rapidly and, with able executives in charge, functioned not only as a sustaining power, but also as a promotional agency and an aggressive exponent of, and champion for, the world-wide missions of The Methodist Church.

Other boards have had somewhat similar origins. Each arose in answer to a need. They mediate and make continually effective the power of the church as this is to be applied to local situations.

At their beginning the boards and agencies of the church did not attain to the high degree of specialization they were to manifest as the years went by and their work increased. Specialization has, in fact, been the glory and at the same time the snare of the various departments and agencies of The Methodist Church. This church itself is centrally organized, with its well-integrated connectional character infusing all its departments. The separate boards are, of course, expected to oversee their own work wisely and well, but in order to do so, each board must in practice confine its attention to those matters under its own distinct charge. No board therefore can help too greatly in those phases of activity carried on by other and similar boards, and sometimes serious conflicts of interest and overlapping of work occur. However, interference on the part of one agency with another did not become a problem until the first quarter of the twentieth century had passed. But before Methodist union came about in 1939, however, there were readjustments which had to be made between the boards, with an occasional redefining of tasks called for and put into effect by the respective General Conferences. After union, it was found necessary to appoint a "Survey Commission" in 1948 which made a complete survey of all the agencies of the church and subsequently made recommendations which were put into effect in 1952. At that time there was a definite regrouping and reorganizing of the boards, a more careful delineation of their particular tasks, and a firm fixing of the respective headquarters.

The parallel development of the Methodist Episcopal Church and the Methodist Episcopal Church, South, was quite noticeable in their organization and structure, especially after the Civil War. This can be made clear by many illustrations. The parallel development of the respective episcopacies will be pointed out, as will the two churches' ways of meeting the special problems which the years pressed upon their episcopal establishments in almost the same way.

Both churches lost heavily, especially in membership, during the Civil War. The Methodist Episcopal bishops in their Episcopal Address of 1864 noted the loss of 50,951 members in the four years 1859-63. The church did, however, keep its connectional machinery functioning, its missionaries supported, and the broad field in the West open to its circuit riders.

The Southern Church as a connection, however, was almost destroyed. Bishop Holland N. McTyeire said:

The distresses of war were intensified by the impoverishment and confusion which follow invasion and defeat. The actual loss of members—not including colored—slightly exceeded one hundred and thirteen thousand. Hundreds of churches were burned, or dismantled by use as hospitals, warehouses, or stables. College endowments were swept away, and the buildings abandoned. Annual Conferences met irregularly or in fragments; the General Conference (of 1862) was not held; and the whole order of the itinerancy was interrupted. The Church-press was silent, and many of the most liberal supporters of the Church and its institutions were reduced to abject want.[3]

The same authority states that "in 1860 the number of white members (including 5,353 local preachers) was 542,489; in 1866 the number (including 3,829 local preachers) was 429,233. . . . In 1860 there were 2,458 effective traveling preachers . . . ; in 1866 the number was 2,116, and 114 admitted on trial." [4]

The whole changing structure of American life during the latter half of the nineteenth century forced almost identical changes in the attitudes and polity of the Methodist Churches. Immediately after the war ended, both churches saw the West as a promising field, and both sent forth missionaries and able ministers to oversee the field, build churches, and assemble congregations where they might. The increase of church membership compelled changes in organizational structure—as always happens when a small body grows to become a large one. The heavy immigration, especially in the North and Northwest, had to be reckoned with, and taken care of, by the Methodist Episcopal Church. Meanwhile, the Southern Church was rebuilding, getting its members back, and renewing its missionary fervor in foreign lands. Then came in such factors as the great growth of industrialism and its consequent effect upon society; rural life became greatly altered, and the enormous growth of the cities, with their "crowded ways of life," posed direct problems for the Methodist Churches. The increase of national wealth, and, as the century ended, the United States' becoming a pre-eminent world power, all brought profound changes and new challenges to the church. The effect of certain of these changes must be noted here, especially in connection with the structural and constitutional growth of Methodism.

With the cessation of the immediate tensions of the era of Reconstruction, the Methodist Episcopal Church, South, as well as the Methodist Episcopal Church, grew rapidly. In the Southern Church from 1870-74

[3] *History of Methodism* (Nashville: Southern Methodist Publishing House, 1883), p. 664.
[4] *Ibid.*, pp. 664-65. The figures are taken from P. A. Peterson, *Hand-Book of Southern Methodism* (Richmond: J. W. Fergusson & Son, 1883).

"there was an increase of 126,299, the largest gain which had ever been made during a similar period." [5] Succeeding years saw this great growth continue. The gain in the Methodist Episcopal Church was even more marked. The formation of the Board of Church Extension and the election of Charles C. McCabe as its executive secretary inaugurated a magnificent era of expansion. McCabe's appeal for individual gifts of $250 to erect new churches on the frontier was highly successful. The colorful McCabe, in order to get money for his projects, would occasionally lecture on the "bright side of life in Libby Prison." "And then how the people would turn out!" he said later. "I talked to them of Libby Prison and then of church extension. I let them in free and charged them for going out." [6] McCabe's famous slogan, "We are building two a day"—meaning churches on the frontier—was the answer to pessimism, and Methodists liked to feel it was the answer to the resurgent tide of agnosticism of that time, dramatized by the equally colorful agnostic, Robert Ingersoll.

1

Changes in the Ministry

Meanwhile, there had begun the great development of the city and urban growth throughout the whole country. For a time it appeared that the new and fast-growing cities were going to be lost to the Methodists for lack of aggressiveness. But early fears that the city might not be taken for Methodism were ill founded. During the 1880's the increase of church membership in the larger urban centers surpassed that in the church at large. In the Methodist Episcopal Church the "institutional church" was sponsored in certain of the large cities, as it was seen that the

proletarian masses who thronged the crowded, tenement-house, industrial sections of the large cities shunned the conventional type of Protestant religious services. . . . Wesley Chapel [in Cincinnati, in the last year of the century] maintained a kindergarten, a day nursery, a young ladies' benevolent society, a bureau of justice in which four lawyers gave their services free to the poor, a building association in which people were taught to save toward a home, and a visitation society.[7]

[5] The New Orleans Christian Advocate, January 20, 1876.

[6] Frank M. Bristol, The Life of Chaplain McCabe (New York: Fleming H. Revell Co., 1908), p. 120.

[7] Wade Crawford Barclay, The History of Methodist Missions (New York: Board of Missions of The Methodist Church, 1957), III, 66-67.

Metropolitan Temple, formerly Central Methodist Church of New York City, under the leadership of Dr. S. Parkes Cadman, made similar moves, and in Chicago in 1895 institutional church activities were carried on in connection with the Halsted Street Mission. Morgan Memorial in Boston in time became an outstanding institutional church.

This movement was promoted by the City Evangelization Union, an organization authorized by the General Conference of 1892. However, Wade Crawford Barclay observes: "With few exceptions, attempts made to establish institutional churches were discontinued after a brief period and secular agencies were developed to render the varied social services, without the aid of religion, that the Churches had failed to provide." [8]

But the city church, as such, grew, and its growth began to affect the practical working of the itinerant system. This it did in two ways: first, by the establishment of strong station churches which fixed the salaries of the pastors assigned them, and which by fixing above-average salaries often secured the type of minister they felt would be adequate to man their pulpits; and secondly, by the powerful pressure such churches exerted to keep popular ministers longer than the allotted time limit. Both these attitudes affected profoundly the itinerant system as it had from the first been carried on.

Support of the Ministry

It appears that up to and through the division of 1844, ministers were presumably paid out of a common fund with an equal allowance to each. Beginning in 1774, each preacher was to be allowed "six pounds, Pennsyl vania currency, per quarter, and his travelling charges besides." [9] The item of traveling expenses becomes quite interesting when we find that as late as 1848 the *Journal of the General Conference* explains that "horse feed, in case of those who are under the necessity of keeping a horse to attend to their appointments and duties in the ministry, is to be paid for as travelling expenses." [10]

The allowance of "six pounds, Pennsylvania currency," of 1774 became "eight pounds, Virginia currency" in 1778. Then in 1784 it was "twenty-four pounds, Pennsylvania currency." In 1800 the "annual allowance," as it was then termed, of traveling preachers became $80; in 1836, $200 for the married traveling, supernumerary and superannuated preachers, and the bishops. In 1844 the *Discipline* ordered:

[8] *Ibid.*, p. 68.
[9] *Minutes*, 1774.
[10] Pp. 128-29.

1. The annual allowance of the married, travelling, supernumerary, and su-perannuated preachers, and the bishops, shall be two hundred dollars, and their travelling expenses.

2. The annual allowance of the unmarried travelling, supernumerary, and superannuated preachers, and the bishops, shall be one hundred dollars, and their travelling expenses.

3. Each child of a travelling preacher or bishop shall be allowed sixteen dollars annually, to the age of seven years, and twenty-four dollars annually from the age of seven to fourteen years.[11]

This figure apparently held as the norm of what the general church intended in equalizing salaries and paying all preachers out of a theo-retical common treasury. But in 1816 the *Discipline* carried a provision putting upon the Quarterly Conference the duty of "making an estimate of the amount necessary to furnish fuel and table expenses for the family, or families, of preachers stationed among them." This at once began to push the matter of support over upon the local churches and the Quarter-ly Conferences, where it really belonged. In due time, by a process which will be obvious to anyone who has studied the ongoing of American life, the "fixing of the salary" by the local church came to make a great differ-ence between charges. For one thing, it was difficult to maintain a central disbursing office, and much easier for each congregation to pay its own preacher. Thus rapidly there came about the system which has been con-tinued to the present, that of allowing each charge to fix its own salary and pay its own minister directly, irrespective of what other charges pay. The effort to "equalize" all salaries has again and again been championed here and there in the church, but except in the case of a uniform salary for district superintendents in many conferences, American Methodism has not gone back to its earlier plan. It should be said here that in Eng-land the original plan has been continued among the Methodist ministers, though even there special allowances for special situations or family needs are provided.

The Time Limit and Ministerial Appointments

Since itinerancy is fundamental to Methodist polity, every regulation regarding it is of prime importance to the church. In the early days of Methodism the preachers changed sometimes as frequently as every three months, and certainly every six months. In the Minutes of 1794 there is this note: "The bishop and Conferences desire that the preachers

[11] "Of the Allowance to the Ministers and Preachers," p. 173.

would generally change every six months, by the order of the presiding elder, whenever it can be made convenient."

Even though many of the preachers were unmarried and could move quite frequently, a natural resistance to such constant changing immediately began to manifest itself. Where the preacher suited the people and they suited him, the tendency was, and always will be, for the relationship to be continued.

Until 1804, Bishop Asbury made all the appointments, changing men or leaving men placed as seemed best to him, with no word from the General Conference acting as directive, or even advice. But in 1800 there was in Albany a pastor by the name of Stebbins, who was very popular with the people, but whose continued reappointment for that special place, Asbury felt, would be a mistake. Pressure from Albany, however, was so strong that the bishop felt that he must keep Stebbins in the appointment there, even against his better judgment. Then certain of the ministers suggested that the situation would be taken care of if the General Conference itself would fix a definite time limit for each appointment. Asbury saw that this would "restrict the appointive power," as he put it, but he made no real objection. The 1804 General Conference, therefore, passed a resolution setting a two-year time limit beyond which a bishop could not appoint any man to any one place.[12] When the 1808 General Conference passed a Restrictive Rule forbidding the General Conference to "do away episcopacy, or to destroy the plan of our itinerant general superintendency," [13] the "plan" referred to already included a time limit beyond which a bishop could not continue a man in any one station.

In 1836 we find a regulation of the General Conference affirming that "it is a violation of a rule of discipline for a bishop to continue a preacher in a station or circuit for more than two years, notwithstanding the station may be divided into two or more stations or circuits." [14] The same conference, evidently troubled by what was considered the violation of the spirit of the time-limit regulation, held that "it is inconsistent with the genius of Methodism to continue a preacher for many years in succession in the same part of the work, and, therefore, the bishops are advised not to continue any preacher for many years in succession in the same city, town, or district." [15]

With the development of more and more station churches, and the es-

---

[12] *Journals of the General Conference, 1796-1836* (New York: Carlton and Phillips, 1855), p. 56.

[13] *Ibid.* (1808), p. 83.

[14] *Ibid.* (1836), p. 473.

[15] *Ibid.*

tablishment of parsonage homes in connection with these, and also with the growth in membership and the ongoing of time, there was increased pressure to obtain relief from the ironclad time limit of earlier years. In every Annual Conference there proved to be situations where it was clearly to the interest of the work for a man to be continued longer in a special situation than the law allowed.

The breakthrough on the time limit really came in the appointment of special editors, missionary secretaries, and men set apart for special missionary work. It was evident that men who manned such places had to be untrammeled as to time.

It should be noted that the two-year limit was changed to three in 1864 and to five in 1888 for regular preachers-in-charge. Eventually the time limit was removed entirely in the Methodist Episcopal Church.

In the Methodist Episcopal Church, South, a similar development occurred. The two-year regulation, in effect in the 1844 *Discipline,* became four years, as ordered by the General Conference of 1866. Here, as in the Northern Church, the Methodist Episcopal Church, South, found it necessary to except "the general editor, the general book steward and his assistants," and a number of other editors, together with "the 'corresponding secretaries of the foreign and domestic missionary boards,' etc."

In the Southern Church, up to the time of union, the four-year time limit held, but with a modifying regulation that a bishop might continue a preacher in one appointment more than four years with the consent of a majority of the district superintendents voting by ballot.[16]

The district superintendent, or presiding elder (as he continued to be called in the Methodist Episcopal Church, South), was, of course, always limited in his term of appointment, just as were other conference members. But it frequently happened that a district superintendent, finishing his term on one district, was immediately appointed to another; thus he was kept in the cabinet and in a powerful position in the making of conference appointments. In some Annual Conferences the same men continued to be appointed to district superintendencies for term after term, and while their immediate term on any one district might end, their position in the cabinet seemed to be fixed. To put an end to the "self-perpetuating cabinet," the General Conference in time fixed a limit upon the number of years a man might serve as a district superintendent. Legislation to this end was passed by the Methodist Episcopal Church in 1924; by the Methodist Episcopal Church, South, in 1938. The united church fixed the limit at "six years in any consecutive nine."

[16] *Discipline of the Methodist Episcopal Church, South, 1930, ¶ 122.*

2

The Methodist Episcopal Church and Separate Negro Annual Conferences

The Negro membership of the Methodist Episcopal Church and that of the Methodist Episcopal Church, South, took different ways in the course of Methodist development. Carter G. Woodson is authority for the statement that "between the separation of the northern and southern wings of the church in 1844 and the Civil War, the Negro members of the Methodist Church in the North asked for separate conferences. . . . The reason given was that the African Methodists, holding up to these Negro communicants the contempt with which they had been treated by their white superiors, caused large numbers of Negro Methodists to join the independent African churches." [17]

Elsewhere the author explains that the African Methodist Episcopal Zion Church was making definite inroads on the Negro membership of the Methodist Episcopal Church "because they could point with pride to men in authority in their church." [18] As there were no Negro Methodist officers "in authority" in the Methodist Episcopal Church at that time, Dr. Woodson's statement will be understood.

But the matter of separate conferences for their Negro membership did not impress the Methodist Episcopal General Conference of 1848 as expedient, and no move was made to create them. However, in 1852 the Negro Methodists of the Philadelphia and New Jersey Conferences were allowed to hold an annual meeting of the Negro Methodist pastors whenever the bishop thought it was all right.[19]

During the Civil War, Dr. Woodson, who was not a Methodist, affirms, "The Methodist Church was neutral if anything. . . . It did not try to get rid of its Negro membership and it made no particular effort to increase it." [20] The General Conference of 1864, however, did encourage colored pastorates for colored people wherever practicable.[21]

With the end of the Civil War and the organization of the Freedmen's Aid Society, there came a great resurgence of interest in, and work for, the Negroes of the South on the part of the Methodist Episcopal Church.

[17] *The History of the Negro Church* (Washington: The Associated Publishers, [1921]) , pp. 188-89.
[18] *Ibid.*, p. 192.
[19] *Ibid.*, p. 188.
[20] *Ibid.*, p. 191.
[21] *Journal of the General Conference of the Methodist Episcopal Church*, 1864, p. 487.

In 1872 the General Conference of that church called upon all its people to "support the Freedmen's Aid Society." This society had as a primary aim the founding of schools—the "establishment and maintenance of institutions of learning in the Southern States among Freedmen and others who have special claims upon the people of America for help in the work of Christian education." [22]

In pursuance of such plans, there came into the South the ministers and missionaries of the Methodist Episcopal Church following the victorious Northern arms. The Episcopal Address of the General Conference of the Methodist Episcopal Church in 1864 stated: "The progress of the Federal arms has thrown open to the loyal Churches of the Union large and inviting fields of Christian enterprise and labor. In the cultivation of these fields it is natural and reasonable to expect that the Methodist Episcopal Church should occupy a prominent position. She occupied these fields once. For nineteen years they have been in the occupancy of the Methodist Episcopal Church, South, to the wrongful exclusion of the Methodist Episcopal Church." [23]

In consequence of these moves and the organization of the Freedmen's Aid Society, nine new Negro conferences were organized in the states lying below the border. These moves, of course, were greatly disliked by the members of the Methodist Episcopal Church, South, whose people did not welcome the organization of such "northern" conferences in their midst, especially as the Negro membership of the Methodist Episcopal Church, South, was being set off about that time into a separate connection.

The tensions of the postwar era during which the Freedmen's Aid Society operated have, to a certain extent, prevented a proper recognition of the real progress made under the leadership of that organization. "It has been said," writes Beverly F. Shaw, "that perhaps never before in the history of the human race has the world seen the advancement of a people from slavery to citizenship in one or two generations. The rise of a people out of the depths of ignorance and superstition into any respectable place among the peoples of the world is usually the work of centuries." [24] Shaw lists as leaders and forward-looking men in bringing this about: Bishop J. M. Walden, the first secretary of the Freedmen's Aid Society; and other distinguished members of the Methodist Episcopal Church, including Bishops D. W. Clark, Edward Thomson, J. P. Newman, Gilbert Haven, J. C. Hartzell, Henry W. Warren, Willard F. Mallalieu, D. A. Goodsell, J. W. Hamilton, and Wilbur P. Thirkield. These

[22] *Discipline of the Methodist Episcopal Church,* 1888, ¶ 403.
[23] *Journal of the General Conference,* 1864, p. 278.
[24] *The Negro in the History of Methodism* (Nashville: The Parthenon Press, 1954), p. 151.

were "untiring friends of the Negro," states Shaw, who added to this list Bishop Charles B. Galloway of the Methodist Episcopal Church, South.

In connection with the work of the Freedmen's Aid Society, the Woman's Home Missionary Society of the Methodist Episcopal Church moved into the South to organize colleges and industrial homes. In the last two decades of the nineteenth century it came to maintain Thayer Industrial Home (affiliated with Clark College), Atlanta, Georgia; Boyland Industrial Home, Jacksonville, Florida; Brewster Hospital and Training School for Nurses in Jacksonville; Kent Industrial Home allied with Bennett College, Greensboro, North Carolina; New Jersey Conference Industrial Home, Morristown College, Morristown, Tennessee; E. L. Rust Industrial Home at Rust College, Holly Springs, Mississippi; Adeline Smith Industrial Home with Philander Smith College, Little Rock, Arkansas; Peck School of Domestic Science and Art, New Orleans, Louisiana; Eliza Dee Industrial Home, Samuel Huston College, Austin, Texas.

It should be noted that all the Negro conferences of the Methodist Episcopal Church were not organized among the newly freed Negroes of the Southern states, nor were they all organized with the idea of direct opposition to the Methodist Episcopal Church, South. The Lexington Conference can be taken as an instance. The Kentucky Annual Conference of the Methodist Episcopal Church had certain Negro members admitted on trial into that conference at Covington, Kentucky, in 1866. But these members in 1868 expressed the desire that a new Annual Conference might be formed to be composed of themselves. The right to do this was subsequently granted by the General Conference, and Lexington Conference, as it was called, completed its organization in 1869.[25] Its boundaries were outlined by the General Conference of 1872.

This conference grew in numbers and prestige until in 1947, Dr. David E. Skelton, its historian, was able to point out that 15 ministers—all slaves—had laid a foundation upon which had been built a membership of 1,500 in 1870, and 39,000 in 1947. The bounds of this conference were destined to stretch far beyond Kentucky, and eventually to take in a great Negro membership in such cities as Chicago and Detroit.

There were diverse views, even in the Methodist Episcopal Church, regarding the organization of these separate Negro Annual Conferences. Carter G. Woodson states that "some [Methodists] actually encouraged the Negroes in saying that, should the blacks go out and establish themselves independently of the whites, the latter would have more respect for them because of this exhibition of their self-reliance."[26] It was

---

[25] David E. Skelton, *History of Lexington Conference* ([Lexington], 1950).
[26] Woodson, *History of the Negro Church*, p. 190.

thought at this particular time that such separate conferences would be a much more effective way for the Negro membership of the church to carry on its own life and be a structural part of Methodism than to continue membership within the structural and disciplinary patterns of the already existing Annual Conferences. The fact that about this time also there were being organized German-speaking Methodist conferences, and those of other language groups in the United States, made it seem more natural for the Negro Methodists to be set off as conference entities by the General Conference during the later years of the nineteenth century.

In 1864 the Delaware and Washington (Negro) Conferences, respectively, were admitted to the Methodist Episcopal Church. So were others in time, and when union came about in 1939, there were nineteen such conferences in the connection, namely:

a) Atlanta Conference—the Negro work in Georgia not included in the Savannah Conference.

b) Central Alabama Conference—the Negro work in Alabama and West Florida.

c) Central West Conference—including Negro work in Kansas, Colorado, Nebraska, Missouri, and Iowa, and in certain sections of Illinois, and "all the Negro work in North and South Dakota and Montana."

d) Delaware Conference—Delaware, New Jersey, and New York State, excluding Buffalo and certain regions around New York City. This conference also included the Negro work on the Eastern Shore of Virginia, and all Maryland and Pennsylvania not included in the Washington Conference.

e) East Tennessee Conference—including that part of Tennessee not in the Tennessee Conference, certain sections of southwest Virginia, and certain counties in Kentucky.

f) Florida Conference—including the Negro work in Florida except the part lying west of the Apalachicola River.

g) Lexington Conference—Kentucky, Ohio, Michigan, Indiana, Illinois, Wisconsin, and Minnesota, except the sections of Illinois already assigned to the Central West Conference, and certain Kentucky counties— Whitley, Knox, Bell, and Harland.

h) Louisiana Conference—all Louisiana.

i) Mississippi Conference—all southern Mississippi.

j) North Carolina Conference—including all Negro work in North Carolina and the southern section of Virginia.

k) Savannah Conference—the Negro work in that part of Georgia not in the Atlanta Conference.

l) South Carolina Conference—all South Carolina.

m) South Florida Conference—the southern half of the Florida peninsula.

n) Southwest Conference—the Negro work in Arkansas and Oklahoma.

o) Tennessee Conference—the Negro work in that part of Tennessee west of and including the regions not taken in by the East Tennessee Conference.

p) Texas Conference—most of East Texas.

q) Upper Mississippi Conference—the northern part of Mississippi.

r) Washington Conference—Negro work in western Maryland, District of Columbia, West Virginia, that part of Pennsylvania lying west of the Susquehanna River, and that part of Virginia which is not included in the East Tennessee, the Delaware, and the North Carolina Conferences.

s) West Texas Conference—embracing the Negro work in that part of Texas not included in the Texas Conference.

The fact that the Methodist Episcopal Church, South, grew stronger and stronger after the hard times of what has been called the "tragic era" had passed; and the fact that the Colored Methodist Episcopal Church comprised, or largely comprised, the former membership adhering to the Southern Church, made something of a difference between the Negro conferences of the Methodist Episcopal Church and the conferences of the Colored Methodist Episcopal Church. The question of these separate Negro conferences of the Methodist Episcopal Church, many of them within the territory covered by the Methodist Episcopal Church, South, provided one of the great problems which had to be faced at the time of church union.

The bishops of the Methodist Episcopal Church continued to supervise the Negro conferences of that church. But as early as 1858 a Negro, Francis Burns, was elected bishop by the Methodist Episcopal Church for the work of that church in Africa. He had been born in the city of Albany, New York, and was converted at fifteen years of age. Thereafter he felt strongly that God had called him to preach, but refrained from doing so because he was "bound to his master until he was twenty-one." [27]

Burns finally became a local preacher and eventually, in 1834, sailed for Liberia with the Rev. John Seys, as a missionary teacher. In time he was elected to orders by the conference there. Upon his return to New York, he was ordained deacon and elder by Bishop Janes, and the General Conference of 1856 made provision for the election and consecration of a missionary bishop for the African work. "Accordingly,

[27] Matthew Simpson, ed., *Cyclopaedia of Methodism* (Philadelphia: Louis H. Everts, 1880), p. 147.

in January, 1858, the Liberia Annual Conference elected Mr. Burns as their first bishop, and he returned to the United States for ordination. This took place at the Genesee Conference, October 14, 1858, the services being conducted by Bishops Janes and Baker." [28] Bishop Burns went back to Liberia and there worked until, his health being impaired, he was advised to return home, and did so, but died in Baltimore within three days after his arrival.

The election of Francis Burns as a Negro bishop, even though a missionary bishop and for Africa, lent support to an increasingly insistent call which came from the Negro conferences of the Methodist Episcopal Church urging that bishops of their own race be elected to supervise them. The fact, as had been pointed out by Dr. Woodson, that other Negro churches had Negro bishops and executives in high position, while the Methodist Episcopal Church had none, gave weight to the demand that the church elect properly qualified Negro ministers to the episcopacy. In 1920, therefore, the General Conference decided that there should be two bishops elected from among the Negro constituents of the church, and that these should be general superintendents in the full sense of the term. Bishop Burns, it may be remembered, had been a missionary bishop. It was therefore recommended by the Committee on Episcopacy of the 1920 General Conference, in its Report No. 2, that there should be: (a) the election by this General Conference of two Negro general superintendents; (b) a separate ballot for the election of the Negro general superintendents. The report was adopted May 11.[29]

Under its directive, two bishops, Matthew W. Clair, Sr., and Robert E. Jones, were duly elected and took their places with the Board of Bishops.

Bishop Robert E. Jones was a native of North Carolina and had served as a general officer in the administrative boards of his church, and also as editor of the *Southwestern Christian Advocate,* before being elected a bishop.

Bishop Matthew W. Clair was a native of West Virginia and was elected to the episcopacy from the pastorate of the Asbury Church, Washington, D. C.

Subsequently, at the General Conference of 1936, Bishop Alexander Preston Shaw, a native of Mississippi, who had spent the most of his ministry as pastor of Wesley Church in Los Angeles, and at the time of his election was editor of the *Southwestern Christian Advocate,* was elected bishop.

[28] *Ibid.,* p. 148.
[29] *Journal of the General Conference of the Methodist Episcopal Church,* 1920, p. 455.

There seems to have been a general understanding that the assignment of these bishops should usually be to the Negro conferences of the church, though as general superintendents they were expected to travel at large and be accorded all the rights and privileges appertaining to their office. These men rendered excellent service in the Board of Bishops, and Bishops Jones and Shaw, who survived to be members of the Council of Bishops of The Methodist Church, became well known and highly regarded all over Methodism.

In the discussions previous to the final adoption of the Plan of Union, the question of the separate Negro conferences was of great importance, and their proper incorporation in the reunited church proved to be a point of much concern. During the discussions which were held between representatives of the Methodist Episcopal Church and the Methodist Episcopal Church, South, in the joint meetings of their respective Commissions on Union during the years 1914-18, many lengthy and informative viewpoints were presented. Eventually, under the Plan of Union, the formation of the Central Jurisdiction, in which these several conferences were combined, came about.

3

The Growth of the Episcopacy

The development of the Methodist episcopacy has been such a fundamental and constitutional feature of the life of The Methodist Church that an outline of this development will practically be a review of all major moves in American Methodist history. To study the full development through the period which this chapter endeavors to cover, it is necessary to mention briefly, first, the formative era of the episcopacy—and of the church—which closed in 1808. Then came a second period, when the episcopacy was put beyond the reach of General Conference control (though having a status greatly to be debated) until 1844, when episcopal Methodism divided. The third period, of which this chapter must particularly treat, covered the period during which the episcopacy of the Methodist Episcopal Church and that of the Methodist Episcopal Church, South, continued to develop along almost parallel lines, though with certain marked differences. This period was destined to come to an end in 1939 when the Plan of Union of The Methodist Church was adopted. This finally gave constitutional recognition to an episcopacy "of like plan, powers, privileges, and duties as now exist in The Method-ist Episcopal Church and The Methodist Episcopal Church, South." [30]

The Early Episcopacy

Methodist episcopacy originated not at all under such a name, but by virtue of the appointment by John Wesley of Thomas Rankin and later Francis Asbury to superintend the other preachers of Methodism in the American colonies. John Wesley himself was, of course, the father and director of all Methodist moves in Britain and elsewhere, and while he lived, his leadership was never questioned. He said that no one was ever going to call him a bishop, but also that he thought that he was as scriptural an *episcopos* as there was in Europe. He early began the practice of stationing or assigning his preachers to pulpits where they were to preach. This practice was continued on the American shores by Rankin and Asbury. These men were not bishops of the church and claimed no episcopal authority in making their assignments. Wesley simply felt that for the benefit of the work it would be necessary to "change the preachers" and to keep an itinerant ministry flowing through the chapels and societies in England which were "in connection" with him. He fixed the itinerant Methodist system firmly in the Large Minutes of the English connection, and in time saw it established in the United States.

But there was a difference between the English and American situa-tions. In England, Wesley's preachers were practically all unordained men, "lay" men, who made their living at some special trade or occupa-tion and preached on Sunday in the pulpits assigned to them—usually on large circuits. All, including even Wesley himself, considered these helpers entirely as laymen, nor could any of them be ordained unless and until a bishop of the Church of England should put his hands upon him and invest him with the requisite order—something English bishops proved unwilling to do.

Methodist itinerancy was a fairly simple system as it worked in Britain, with the lay preachers quite often able to live in their own residencies and make their travels on Sunday where they were assigned. But even then there was some revolt against being told where to preach. "This is shackling freeborn Englishmen," said some. "Who gave this man authority to reign over us?" [31] Wesley's terse answer was that he

---

[30] *Discipline of The Methodist Church*, 1939, ¶ 34.
[31] Harmon, *Organization*, p. 14.

had no authority over anyone except what that person gave to him; that if any man did not like the relationship, he could terminate it; but that if a preacher was to stay "in connection with him," such a person must "not mend our rules; but keep them." [32]

But in America, after the organization of the Methodist Episcopal Church in 1784, a different situation was presented from that which the Methodist societies in England had faced. These societies were all a part of the Church of England, or in loose connection with it; in America a new church had been formed, and that the ministry of that church, ordained by forms of ordination which were based on kindred forms in the Church of England, should be stationed by one man, called the "superintendent," brought on a tension which has not, after 175 years, yet subsided.

No other Protestant church had ever tried such an ironclad itinerancy. No other congregations—Baptist, Presbyterian, Congregational, or even Episcopal—had their ministers assigned them by the authority of one man. No other body of ministers submitted their own lives and that of their families to the will of one man. It was the power of the bishop to station ministers which was, and is now, the crux of the whole issue over episcopacy. For while there was a fight over the name "superintendent" versus "bishop," and questions asked regarding the meaning of this name; and a continuing discussion as to what John Wesley meant by empowering Thomas Coke to go to America, and *ordain* Francis Asbury as a *superintendent;* these became academic questions over against the undoubted fact that by whatever name a Methodist superintendent be called, he has always had the power (though this has come to be greatly limited through the years) to station ministers in the respective charges; and, from the point of view of the charge, to assign to people their pastor even though this may be contrary to the wish of either pastor or people. This is the nub of the whole episcopal controversy, as it has continued through the years—sometimes reaching a high boiling point, sometimes simmering away quietly, but always present.

Francis Asbury made a move of epochal import when for the first time he met Thomas Coke at Barratt's Chapel in Delaware. Coke told him that John Wesley had sent him, Thomas Coke, with two newly ordained Methodist elders, to ordain Francis Asbury as superintendent for "our brethren in North America." Asbury refused such an ordination until he could get the voted consent of the American preachers.

It was this unexpected stand of Francis Asbury, in asking for the consent of the American preachers, which marked the difference between

[32] *Discipline,* 1960, ¶ 1924.

English Methodist polity and that which developed in American Methodism. States Bishop Tigert:

Wesley never intended to originate an American General Conference. Upon this fact proper historical emphasis has not, as yet, been placed. . . . All the indications are that Mr. Wesley meant his superintendents to ordain whom they chose, and to be the sole ecclesiastical rulers, under himself, of both preachers and people in America. They were not to wait on the election of a Conference before they conferred deacon's or elder's orders. . . . Such was not the habit of the English Bishops or the law of the English Church. He, in turn, expected to name the superintendents with as much freedom as an English premier issues his congé d'élire to fill vacancies in the sees of the Church of England.[33]

It was the call of Asbury for a conference which became the genesis of the powerful General Conference of the Methodist Episcopal Church in America and marked a definite breach with the method of control which Wesley had exercised in Britain and continued to exercise as long as he lived.

Asbury, of course, was elected a superintendent by the Christmas Conference of 1784, and Dr. Coke was recognized likewise as a superintendent. It was Asbury, however, who made the appointments, and who began to establish firmly, by his own personal strength and consecration, the powerful, almost untrammeled "Asburian" episcopacy which became the pattern and fountainhead of all succeeding episcopal power.

Asbury followed out his original demand for an electing conference by making it clear thereafter that he and Dr. Coke, as general superintendents, felt themselves entirely under the control of the General Conference when it was called into session. In the Notes affixed to the Discipline of 1798, Asbury and Coke affirmed that they themselves were "entirely dependent on the General Conference."

But why, may it be asked, does the General Conference lodge the power of stationing the preachers in the episcopacy? We answer, On account of their entire confidence in it. If ever, through improper conduct, it loses that confidence in any considerable degree, the general conference will, upon evidence given, in a proportionable degree, take from it this branch of its authority.[34]

As it turned out—although Asbury's authority was questioned, and move after move was made in the attempt to modify the stationing power of the bishop—by his own strength and power, Francis Asbury "de-

[33] A Constitutional History of American Episcopal Methodism (Nashville: Publishing House of the Methodist Episcopal Church, South, 1916), pp. 191-92.
[34] P. 41.

veloped a doctrine of the episcopal office which was radically different from the main development of the [classic] doctrine. Asbury emerged as the natural leader among the early Wesleyan missionaries; he was selected as Superintendent by the Christmas Conference; and to the day of his death, he was master of every crisis." [35]

Earlier chapters of this history have narrated the attempts made to denature Methodist episcopacy during these formative years. There was the O'Kelly schism, largely motivated by the effort to allow the ministers to appeal their appointments to the Annual Conference when they felt themselves wronged. O'Kelly was defeated, and his people withdrew and formed a separate ecclesiastical connection. Later efforts to secure an elective presiding eldership also were defeated. Thus when 1808 came, and a delegated General Conference was created, the "episcopacy and plan of itinerant general superintendency," thereafter protected from General Conference action by the Third Restrictive Rule, was the episcopacy as Asbury had developed it up to that time.

It should be said that while Asbury was the first and in some ways the greatest of the Methodist bishops, and the Asburian episcopacy was destined to be the pattern and in some sense the directive for all subsequent Methodist bishops, Methodist episcopacy itself, in the mind of Asbury, was not an end in itself, but the instrument to reach a greater end, namely: to establish itinerancy. Itinerancy was the foundation, keystone, pillar, and roof of the whole Asburian polity. Asbury saw clearly that to make itinerancy work, especially in the newly freed American states where liberty was a catchword and where boundless freedom was in the very air, a powerful episcopacy would be needed. *Itinerancy,* not the establishment of episcopacy, was the main policy of Francis Asbury, and well did he accomplish this purpose. While he lived, he was the unquestioned leader and father of the Methodist Episcopal Church. In fact, Francis Asbury laid his mind upon American Methodism— certainly instructed its polity—even more than John Wesley did.

1808-44

The second period of American episcopacy began when, in 1808, "episcopacy" as it had developed to that time was safeguarded from General Conference action. "They shall not do away episcopacy nor destroy the plan of our itinerant general superintendency," was the Third Restrictive Rule. Under this rule, early Methodist bishops pro-

[35] J. Hamby Barton, "The Definition of the Episcopal Office in American Methodism" (Unpublished dissertation, Drew University, 1960), p. 34.

ceeded to guide the church and to claim for episcopacy itself a constitutionally established right which undoubtedly it had. Subsequently,
General Conferences took the position that while they could not destroy
episcopacy, they could greatly modify it, and indeed did so by various
enactments. Also, in time there came discussion as to what is meant by
the "plan of itinerant general superintendency"—whether this meant the
bishop or bishops themselves itinerating over the connection (which they
undoubtedly did), or whether it meant a bishop or bishops supervising
and stationing all itinerants, wherever they happened to be, anywhere in
the general connection. To a certain degree, both meanings have always
been involved.

Since the formation of the Methodist Protestant Church has been
treated elsewhere, it will not be necessary here to enter into the controversy over lay rights which eventuated in the organization of Methodist
Protestantism. It should be noted, however, that when the proposal allowing each Annual Conference to elect its presiding elders had been adopted
by the General Conference of 1820, there came to the fore a constitutional question as to the right of the General Conference to pass such a
measure. It was held by many that the elective eldership would destroy
or greatly impair the plan of superintendency which the conference of
1808 had said should be beyond the reach of the General Conference.

But what was constitutionality? Joshua Soule had by this very Conference
of 1820 been elected bishop, but he had refused ordination or consecration
to that office. He had written a formal letter to Bishops George and
Roberts saying that by this act "Episcopal government [is] greatly ener-
vated by a transfer of executive power from the Episcopacy to the several
Annual Conferences." [36] Bishop Tigert notes that Joshua Soule himself
had written the Third Restrictive Rule and felt himself well qualified to
pass upon its constitutionality. Soule's dramatic stand and Bishop William McKendree's powerful support brought to the floor another question, deeper and more important than that of Soule's own personal
opinion: Who was to say when an action of a General Conference was
constitutional or unconstitutional? William McKendree later commented
in 1822, in an address to the Baltimore Annual Conference: "Bishop
Asbury much regretted the lack of a constitutional tribunal in which
recourse might be had on such occasions. It was finally concluded that to
submit the subject to Annual Conferences was the safest, and happiest
experience." [37]

That the General Conference of 1820 suspended its resolution calling

[36] Tigert, *Constitutional History*, p. 340.
[37] Barton, "Definition of the Episcopal Office," p. 68, quoting from "an Emory
University manuscript."

for an elective presiding eldership, and that the succeeding General Conference of 1824 killed the measure, following a church-wide campaign against it by Bishop McKendree, in no wise settled the question. Who could determine the exact relationship of a bishop or of the episcopal power to the General Conference? The Methodist Protestant withdrawal in no way touched this matter, though it did draw away the "dissidents," as the polemic editors of episcopal Methodism then called them. But the question of episcopacy versus General Conference remained in abeyance. Then came 1844.

There were reasons why matters of polity should not then obtrude themselves too greatly upon the ongoing of the whole church. General Conferences meet only once every four years, and bishops even today are comparatively few when the vast size of Methodism in membership, churches, and institutions is taken into consideration. The whole formative era was one in which the church was growing magnificently.

Members were being added, and the old Methodist system, as the fathers of 1816 were even then reverently terming it, was functioning effectively—if multiplied numbers and influence mean anything (as they do). . . . In the marvelous growth of Methodism it was not the actions of General Conferences or debates over great issues which determined the progress of the church. Rather it was the preaching of the countless circuit riders, the testimony and work of the innumerable class leaders, the vital ministry of a growing church filled with evangelistic fervor, and the irresistible testimony of men and women that they had been redeemed from sin and found life sweet and purposeful. It was in church on Sunday, or in the class meeting at early candlelight, or in the fervor of camp meeting throngs, in the work of a happy exultant people, singing—sometimes shouting—that Methodism found its best expression. Its organization has played indeed a great part in its success, but perhaps not as much as the constitutional historian sometimes thinks.[38]

The Divided Episcopacy

In 1844 occurred the division of episcopal Methodism. Subsequently there were two branches of the church, each moving forward under Methodist bishops. In the Methodist Episcopal Church there was a Board of Bishops; in the Methodist Episcopal Church, South, a College of Bishops. And in spite of the somewhat different attitudes toward episcopacy which were taken officially by the two respective churches from 1844 until reunion in 1939, the development of the office in both com-

[38] Harmon, *Organization*, p. 30.

munions shows an amazing parallel. Neither church made any immediate change in the written regulations regarding episcopacy. The Methodist Episcopal Church, South, which might have been expected to strengthen by legal enactment its own position as set forth powerfully in the debates and the Southern "Protest" in 1844, did not do so, but kept in its first *Discipline* (of 1846) the exact language of the 1844 *Discipline* of the Methodist Episcopal Church.

Except for two important differences, the two churches met the special problems which the years pressed upon their episcopal establishments in almost the same way. Both inherited from the unbroken church the plan of having a Committee on Episcopacy in every General Conference. Both relaxed, little by little, the time limit on the pastorate. Both faced the problem of missionary bishops, or of a special superintendency for the foreign field, at about the same time, though each met it in a different way. The limitation of term for the presiding elder, or district superintendent, was in due time adopted by both churches, as was the age limit for the retirement of bishops. The question of "term episcopacy," or of electing a bishop for a definite number of years, arose to agitate both connections late in this period; and both churches were subjected to increasing, and eventually almost overwhelming, pressure on the part of local churches to the end that these local churches might have more direct control in making or unmaking their own pastoral appointments.

In the development of the episcopacy in both branches of the divided church, it can easily be seen that each branch swung at once to the extreme limit of its own proclaimed position. There had been uncertain differences over episcopal power and prerogative before 1844, but after that date the leaders in both churches saw that these differences should be made absolutely unmistakable. Certainly they both made plain *after* 1844 what they had argued about *in* 1844. For from the day of the division, and for many years afterward, all the ecclesiastical historians and apologists in either camp simply reiterated and reinforced the contention of their own particular fathers and brethren. What the Pecks and Hamlines had declared, the Neelys, Stevenses, and Buckleys of the Methodist Episcopal Church echoed with power and ability; and what the Winans and Pierces of the South had affirmed, the McTyeires, Tigerts, and Dennys were to restate with increasing fervor.

As was made clear in the chapter dealing with the division of episcopal Methodism, a fundamental difference regarding the episcopal office became the center of the controversy. Was the bishop an officer of the General Conference, as were book agents, missionary secretaries, and the like, who could be made or unmade by the General Conference as its will might desire? This was the position of the Northern delegations when the motion was made to depose Andrew, not for malfeasance in office or for any question affecting his character, but simply for the expediency of the work. Leonidas Hamline had said to the General Conference of 1844:

Our Church constitution recognizes the episcopacy as an abstraction, and leaves this body to work it into a concrete form in any hundred or more ways we may be able to invent. We may make one, five, or twenty bishops; and, if we please, one for each conference. . . . We may limit [his term] at pleasure, or leave it undetermined. But in this case is it *undeterminable?* Certainly not. The power which elected may then displace.[39]

It may be added here that after Hamline was elected bishop, and some thought in order to support this view of the episcopacy, he later "resigned" as bishop. While he gave his impaired health as the reason, there were those who felt that Hamline was simply illustrating the fact that a bishop could be a bishop for a brief term and then go back into the conference eldership and be perfectly in line with the theory which he had professed before the General Conference.

On the other hand, the Southern contention was, "Once a bishop, always a bishop." "To say that we can deprive a bishop of his office, and yet not censure him," said Benjamin M. Drake of the Mississippi Conference, "is to my mind absurd in the extreme." [40]

George F. Pierce of Georgia, who later became a bishop, in answering Jesse T. Peck of the Troy Conference, who later became a bishop himself, said that he was astonished to hear "that a bishop had no constitutional right to be a bishop." [41]

The Northern group and the Northern General Conferences, up to the time of union in 1939, maintained strongly that the bishop was in no sense one who belonged to a third ecclesiastical order, but was simply an officer of the General Conference set aside for certain administrative duties; and that his status, as well as his office, might be modified as the General Conference should determine.

The Southern position, on the other hand, was that Methodist episcopacy was a co-ordinate branch of the constitutional life of the church; that the power to elect did not give the power to depose, unless there should be charges of immorality or malfeasance in office. The deposition of Bishop Andrew by a majority vote in 1844 served to crystallize and

[39] Walter C. Palmer, *Life and Letters of Leonidas L. Hamline* (New York: Carlton and Porter, 1866), p. 156.

[40] *Report of Debates in the General Conference of . . . 1844* (New York: Lane and Tippett, 1844), p. 106.

[41] George G. Smith, *The Life and Times of George Foster Pierce* (Nashville: Hunter & Welburn, 1888), p. 131.

make more intense this feeling among Southern Methodists. As a consequence, the episcopacy of the South became practically, if not theoretically, set upon a higher pedestal than was the case in the North.

Had there been no division and no debate over episcopal prerogatives in 1844, the signs are not lacking that even so there would have been something of a difference between the Northern and Southern sections in the development of Methodist episcopacy.

The bishop through the years had come to occupy a proportionately stronger position in the South than in the North. . . . The very name "bishop" from Colonial times on, meant more in Virginia, for instance, than it did in Massachusetts. The social organization in the South also would be more friendly to the bishop as belonging to the traditional ruling class than could be expected in the more democratic North.[42]

Also with the great growth of the church and the election of more and more bishops, the matter of supervising the conferences came after a time to divide, not only physically, but psychologically also, the episcopacy of the church. Asbury always wanted the bishops to travel together, and they did so for a time. Thus superintendency was kept "general." As long as the church was small and there were at most three bishops, all under the tutelage of Asbury, any appointment made by one was understood to be made by all. But as American Methodism grew enormously, and as conference after conference was added to the connection, it was clear that no one bishop, or team of bishops, could oversee the whole work. It was quite natural, therefore, that after a time the bishops should agree on a division of their labor.

McKendree explained in 1816 that the three bishops—then George, Roberts, and McKendree himself—agreed among themselves to "attend the Conferences alternately, thus changing their work every year; and for the Bishop, whose turn it might be to attend a Conference, to be the responsible president of it; and the other Bishops, if present, to be his counselors." [43]

It should be noted that this dividing out of the work and superintending the conferences was put into effect by the bishops themselves, and has so remained their prerogative and duty to the present time. However, the genesis of the "area plan," as it later came to be called, with a particular bishop repeatedly supervising a particular conference or conferences, early began to shape up. Bishop Tigert held that part of the responsibility for the split between the North and the South in 1844 came about by reason of the division of the work of the superintendency

---

[42] Harmon, *Organization*, p. 41.
[43] Tigert, *Constitutional History*, p. 335, quoting McKendree's Journal.

(in 1820) —the superintendents who knew the North never came to the South, and vice versa. Bishop Hedding from 1824 to 1844 made but a single tour to the Southern conferences. Bishop Soule did not until 1831 make his first episcopal visitation to the North. The bishops perhaps unconsciously and gradually came to be sectionalized.

Again and again Roberts and Soule advanced as far north as the Baltimore Conference and returned again on their southern track; again and again George and Hedding came as far south as the Philadelphia Conference, and retreated into New York, New England, and Canada. . . . Bishop McKendree's plan of such an episcopal itinerancy as would make the superintendency truly general, failed, and great hurt came to the Church thereby.[44]

Leaving aside all theory, it came at length to be the official position of almost all Methodist authorities that the bishop in Methodism does not represent a third order in the sense of a spiritual or ecclesiastical grade, but remains a presbyter or elder who has been set apart for a special and highly important work in the church. In pursuance of this idea, the form for the Ordaining of Bishops in the Ritual of the Methodist Episcopal Church was revised in 1864, and the "Form of Ordaining Bishops" became the "Form of Consecrating Bishops."

This distinction was intended to prevent any assertion of episcopacy *jure divino*. In an ill-defined way, *order* was thought to appertain to the ministerial class sanctioned by scripture; *office* was a category derived from the exigencies of human organization.

Wesley in the *Sunday Service* had fixed upon *ordain* even though (or perhaps because) Anglican use commonly employed *consecrate*. *Ordain* is more scriptural, and *consecrate* in its etymology is more certainly related to *jure divino*. These were good reasons for Wesley to choose *ordain*, and contrary reasons for the Church to revert to *consecrate*. But the Methodist distinction between *order* and *office* over-ruled, and *consecrate* was fixed in the Ritual.[45]

The Southern Church in 1870 also made the change of "ordain" to "consecrate" in this office, and so the word was carried over into the Ritual of The Methodist Church in 1939.

Episcopacy in the Methodist Episcopal Church

In the development of the episcopacy in the Methodist Episcopal Church following 1844, Bishop Hamline's resignation in 1852 did, as we

[44] Tigert, *Constitutional History*, pp. 392-93.
[45] Barton, "Definition of the Episcopal Office," p. 125.

have indicated, serve to dramatize his idea of the ephemeral and temporary nature of the episcopacy. "The Committee on the Episcopacy recognized Hamline's act as symbolic of his doctrine; they therefore recommended his acceptance by the conference." [46] An alternate resolution giving him liberty to *retire* (instead of resign) as bishop, was "soundly defeated." Hamline's resignation was then accepted, and subsequently the Ohio Conference, from which he had been elected, received him as an elder and gave him the superannuate relation. This action, as Barton points out, as well as that deposing Andrew in 1844, confirmed the doctrine held through the Northern conferences that a bishop was simply an officer of the General Conference. It should be added that the Judicial Council of The Methodist Church decided, following unification, that a bishop "effective or retired" is not and cannot be a member of an Annual Conference.[47]

In further support of its theory of episcopacy, the Methodist Episcopal Church in 1864 made a further change in its Ritual, in the ceremony of investiture in the rite of episcopal ordination. Wesley had sent over, and Methodism in America up until 1864 followed, in the rite of ordaining of a bishop these words, which were to accompany the imposition of hands of the ordaining bishops:

Receive the Holy Ghost for the office and work of a Bishop [Wesley: "superintendent"] in the church of God, now committed unto thee by the imposition of our hands, in the Name of the Father, and of the Son, and of the Holy Ghost. *Amen.* And remember that thou stir up the grace of God which is given thee by this imposition of our hands; for God hath not given us the spirit of fear, but of power, and love, and soberness.[48]

In 1864 the Ritual was made to read: "The Lord pour upon thee the Holy Ghost for the office and work of a bishop in the Church of God now committed unto thee *by the authority of the Church* through the imposition of our hands, in the name of the Father, and of the Son, and of the Holy Ghost." [49] This change was to make it plain that there was no room for a doctrine of an independent institution of the episcopacy. The will of the church was to be lodged in the General Conference, as the source of all episcopal authority.

A further step in subordinating the episcopacy to the General Conference came in 1884, when Bishop Isaac Wiley, as chairman of a com-

[46] *Ibid.,* p. 124.
[47] *Decisions of the Judicial Council of The Methodist Church,* Decision 22, May 2, 1944, p. 47.
[48] *Discipline,* 1792, p. 263.
[49] *Discipline of the Methodist Episcopal Church,* 1864, p. 182. Italics mine.

mittee, endeavored to speak from the floor upon a particular measure. Bishop John Hurst, presiding, ruled that Wiley had a right to the floor; but Dr. James M. Buckley, the potent and tremendously influential editor of the *Christian Advocate,* challenged his right to speak. "We may invite him, but we cannot have him forced on us," said Buckley. "Bishop Wiley is not a member of this body." [50] Buckley's position was sustained.

Bishop Asbury had made motions during his presidency, but the action of the body in 1884 as just cited firmly established the practice that since bishops are not members of the General Conference, they may not speak on the floor except at the pleasure or invitation of the conference. In practice, bishops do appear before the General Conference for various presentations and the like, but this is by good-natured sufferance as well as for the practical reason that bishops do have important causes and reports to present which the body should hear.

In 1884 also, at the insistence of Dr. Thomas Neely (later bishop), a resolution was adopted reaffirming the "doctrine of the fathers of our Church" that the episcopacy is not an order but an office. The resolution went on to deprecate the idea that the episcopacy was a third order. "Even on the floor of this Conference," Neely exclaimed, thinking no doubt of the Southern contention, "has it been said: 'Once a Bishop, always a Bishop.' What new doctrine of apostolic succession is this? What heresy is this which for the first time creeps into and raises its head in this place?" [51]

Missionary Bishops

Enough has been said to indicate the Methodist Episcopal point of view regarding episcopacy. Along another line, but in support of the same conviction, a different type of move was made, in the electing of a different type of bishop to be known as a "missionary bishop," who was set apart for a special missionary area. We have already seen how this first came about in the election of Francis Burns in 1858 as a missionary bishop for Africa. How this occurred may be explained here in greater detail.

As mission churches developed in foreign lands, the need for a superintendency which could acquaint itself with local conditions, and reside with the native people, came to be more fully appreciated. In 1856 there

[50] *The Daily Christian Advocate* of the Methodist Episcopal Church, May 27, 1884, p. 179.

[51] *Ibid.,* May 16, 1884, p. 107.

came to the Methodist Episcopal Church a request from Liberia that a bishop be elected for that particular field. But how could a bishop be elected for one special area without destroying the "plan of general superintendency"? The General Conference of 1856 got around this by proposing a change in the Third Restrictive Rule which would read as follows: "They [the General Conference] shall not alter or change any part or rule of our government so as to do away with episcopacy or destroy the plan of itinerant general superintendency, *but may appoint a Missionary Bishop or Superintendent for any of our foreign missions, limiting his episcopal jurisdiction* to the same respectively." [52]

The amendment to the Third Restrictive Rule is indicated above by italics. It was passed by the General Conference of 1856 and sent to the Annual Conferences, which concurred in adopting it. So certain were the fathers of 1856 that the amendment would be adopted that they provided for the ordination of a missionary bishop between the General Conferences, when the restrictive rule should be changed. This, to the church, meant Francis Burns, who was elected in January, 1858.

The missionary bishop thus became a part of the episcopal economy of the Methodist Episcopal Church. Such bishops were elected by the General Conference of the entire church, but elected for one special field. In his field, each respective bishop would exercise full episcopal power, but could not claim such power in the homeland or outside his own area. He was, therefore, not considered a "general" superintendent, and in the Methodist Episcopal *Discipline* the names of the missionary bishops were listed separately from those of the regular bishops, until the General Conference of 1920. At that conference an issue was made of such listing, and there was considerable debate upon the whole matter of the status and privileges of missionary bishops. At that conference also, by special ballot, three effective missionary bishops were elected to be general superintendents of the Methodist Episcopal Church, and all effective bishops were thereafter to be listed in one roll in the *Discipline*.[53]

The missionary bishops of the Methodist Episcopal Church were men who in every respect gave the type of leadership and provided episcopal supervision of a high order in the lands to which they were assigned. They were, however, embarrassed by a certain anomaly which they sometimes felt, in that when Central Conferences, as the respective General Conferences of mission fields came to be called, would elect a bishop

[52] *Journal of the General Conference of the Methodist Episcopal Church,* 1856, p. 146. Italics mine.
[53] *Journal of the General Conference of the Methodist Episcopal Church,* 1920, pp. 337-38.

from their own body, as they were occasionally empowered to do, something of an overlapping of authority was threatened. Bishops elected by Central Conferences were amenable to their own empowering and ordaining Central Conferences, and in their conferences and areas enjoyed full episcopal power, as did also the assigned missionary bishops from the homeland. However, good spirit and organizational ability usually overcame the difficulties which such intertwined superintendencies might be expected to have. When, however, the Commission on Union finally drew up the plan of Methodist union which came into effect in 1939, it was unanimously agreed that the office of missionary bishop should not be perpetuated. Missionary bishops then living were allowed to continue in their honored position, but no new ones were provided for by the church.

The question as to whether missionary bishops might possibly be elected arose again at the General Conference of 1944. Dr. L. O. Hartman made a motion that missionary bishops be elected for administration in Central Conferences as need might arise. Dr. Hartman explained to the General Conference that neither he nor the conference itself knew whether or not it was possible for such a bishop to be lawfully elected. He asked, however, that his motion be passed so the Judicial Council could rule upon the matter. In an atmosphere of some uncertainty, the Hartman resolution did pass, but the Judicial Council, after reviewing the matter, declared that "there is no provision for the election of a Bishop by the General Conference. Since the General Conference cannot go beyond the clear powers granted in the Constitution, we must declare that it would be unconstitutional for the General Conference to elect Missionary Bishops." [54]

I was told by both Bishop John M. Moore and Bishop Edwin D. Mouzon, who served on the Commission on Union, that the bishops of the Methodist Episcopal Church—I remember their mentioning particularly Bishop William F. McDowell—stated that the plan of having missionary bishops had not worked out well, and that he hoped that in the Plan of Union this particular type of office would not be continued.

Development of the Area System

There came into effect in the Methodist Episcopal Church late in the century, and for a few years previous to union in the Methodist Episcopal

[54] *Journal of the General Conference of The Methodist Church,* 1944, p. 291.

Church, South, a division or grouping of the conferences known as "areas," each to be under a specially assigned bishop. The plan of general superintendency as this was put into effect by Asbury, who wished all the bishops to move together, has already been outlined. But as early as 1816, the bishops—McKendree, George, and Roberts—abandoned the Asburian plan, dividing out the conferences among themselves, and eight years later the General Conference itself recommended that the bishops meet annually to plan their work, suggesting that they divide the connection "into several episcopal departments, with one bishop or more in each department." [55]

Ezekiel Cooper, in supporting this resolution, moved that the plan of such division be made obligatory upon the bishops. However, the conference refused to adopt mandatory language here, making its resolutions advisory only. The bishops were, however, in agreement with the plan and divided the work in two divisions, with Bishops Roberts and Soule taking the western and southern conferences and Bishops George and Hedding the eastern and northern. Bishop McKendree's health did not permit him to travel. In 1826, George wrote McKendree that he thought that the arrangements made were to be carried through for a full four years, explaining: "I do sincerely think that I have neither strength of body or mind, at present, to undertake a continental superintendency." [56] Bishop George, it is said, did not want to take work that would make him serve in the slaveholding states.

In 1828 the General Conference recommended that "each of our bishops should, if practicable, be known in each of the annual conferences once in four years." [57]

Thus early, we can see that the plan of an itinerant general superintendency—a "majestic constitutional abstraction," as one authority pronounced it—proved to be unworkable, for the simple reason that if bishops are to make appointments for men and conferences, they must *know* those men and conferences. Desultory visits on the part of any one bishop, or frequent exchanges among bishops, certainly work against such a plan.

Methodism has always been opposed to a diocesan episcopacy—that is, one where the bishop settles down to supervise his own conference or area with scarcely more than a theoretical connection with the general

[55] *Journals of the General Conference,* 1796-1836, p. 302.
[56] Tigert, *Constitutional History,* p. 396. Bishop Tigert stated that he had the original copy of this letter.
[57] *Journals of the General Conference,* 1796-1836, p. 351.

church. Nevertheless, since the most important work of a bishop is to station the preachers and make appointments, it has long been clear that he does his best where he lives with, knows, and participates with his preachers and people in all matters affecting their work. In support of this idea, the Committee on Episcopacy of the Northern General Conference of 1864 affirmed: "The bishops ought, and therefore are hereby respectfully requested to so distribute their residences as to be the most accessible to and in the intervals of the conferences, to be able to oversee every part of our extended work so far as possible." [58]

In 1868 the General Conference went a step further and named the cities which they thought the bishops ought to occupy, asking the bishops to choose such places in order of their seniority. In 1884, when the General Conference was challenged as to its right to "fix episcopal residences," its Judiciary Committee, which had enormous prestige, affirmed that it "is . . . the opinion of the Committee that the General Conference has power to fix the residence of any of its Bishops in any part of the territory occupied by the Methodist Episcopal Church." [59] The General Conference adopted the report on May 9, 1884. Again in 1896 the General Conference decided that episcopal residences should be designated quadrennially and that bishops must reside in the cities to which they were assigned.[60]

Further steps were taken in 1900, and then in 1904 the General Conference fixed the residential cities but left the assignments—that is, manning these residences—to the bishops. In 1908 the General Conference requested the bishops to form groups of Annual Conferences around their respective residences. [61] In 1916 the Committee on Episcopacy firmly assigned the bishops to their residences,[62] and the conferences were then grouped by the bishops about their contiguous residencies. In 1920 the term "episcopal area" was first applied to such groups of conferences fixed about a particular residence, and when the respective groupings were arranged by the bishops, the resulting areas and assignments were formally approved by the General Conference.[63]

That the area plan was not unanimously approved by all the bishops is illustrated by the following excerpts from a reply from Bishop William Quayle in response to a letter sent by J. Ralph Magee (later bishop) to all bishops resident in the United States. This, together with extracts

[58] *Journal of the General Conference,* 1864, pp. 359-60.
[59] *Journal of the General Conference,* 1884, pp. 160, 369.
[60] *Journal of the General Conference,* 1896, pp. 380-81.
[61] *Journal of the General Conference,* 1908, p. 456.
[62] *Journal of the General Conference,* 1916, pp. 416, 482.
[63] *Journal of the General Conference,* 1920, pp. 461-64.

from other replies, appeared in an article by Magee in *Zion's Herald*, January 21, 1920, "Area Episcopal Supervision: Has It Succeeded?"

I have your letter and may say in preluditory word, that I am not now and have not been a devotee of the area. Some things it can do and many things it cannot do, and it certainly tends toward the provincializing of Methodism. It has a Protestant Episcopal rather than a Methodist Episcopal squint. It tends to keep a bishop busy being noisy so that the people may see from the frequency of his name being in print that he is a great worker. Whereas what is needed by the bishops and the rest of the ministers is noiseless effectiveness. In a word it would seem to make more of mechanism than of dynamics. I hold no brief for area supervision and do not feel called upon to justify the system. . . . We are at present in the church programmed to the point of nervous exhaustion, and if it is desired that a bishop add to the already overprogrammed preacher and church, a program of his, we shall go program mad. I have an idea that the brethren who are troubled about the bishop having no program are likely to be brethren under whose overprograms the church is now restive.

I should suppose a bishop should work quietly and unneurotically and without publicity as much as possible, and refuse to destroy the initiative of preacher and district superintendent and local church, by always seizing the initiative for himself. The power of initiative is the supremest power of the human soul and no system of church work should for a moment tolerate that this power of initiative should be pre-empted by church boards or church bishops. Really the Methodist Discipline is a sane and wholesome book and presents sufficient methods of church work to give a track for the church to run on, without the bishop or anybody else frothing around about more programs. . . .

The bishop who can make spirituality to be apparently the great design of the church and is not simply reduced to a maid of all work in financial matters . . . will render a superior service to the church of the present and the more glorious church of the future. Less mechanics not more machinery, and more divine dynamics—this is the need of this hour and all hours.

However, in spite of this and other objections, there did come about by slow stages in the Methodist Episcopal Church the area system and "presidential and residential superintendency." Let it be understood that the bishops themselves, then as always, had the right to divide out the conferences over which they would preside, and to assign themselves to the presidencies of the respective conferences and areas. This, however, was not allowed to be their right without challenge. At the General Conference of 1904, Thomas B. Neely brought in a motion to "assign bishops" to episcopal districts. Forthwith, the Judiciary Committee of that conference brought in a careful report (under the heading "Districted Episcopacy") which decided that the proposed plan of mandatory episcopal districts would be a "violation of the Third Restrictive Rule."

The 1904 Judiciary Committee, composed of distinguished jurists and judicially minded ministers, affirmed that

[this proposed change] looks to localizing, by territorial limitation, the itinerant superintendency of the Bishops—confining them for four years or more to districts which the Conference shall mark out. . . . By its operation, . . . the Bishops would at once be made local superintendents—exercising their powers of supervision over what in other systems is known as a diocese. . . . Consequently, . . . the labors of our General Superintendents might be wholly localized—the character of their itinerancy radically changed at the will of this body—thus entirely destroying the constitutional plan and the kind of episcopacy established by the fathers.[64]

A substitute was offered affirming that there is nothing in the constitution of the church to prevent the exercise of such power by the General Conference. The matter was made an order of the day, and after debate, the substitute lost and the conference adopted the committee's report.[65]

The General Conference, however, did adopt a plan by establishing a system which, on the one hand, provided for continuous local responsibility but, on the other, did not destroy the connectional mobility of the bishops. Under the particular plan put into effect by the Methodist Episcopal General Conference, the church was divided into four areas, and within these areas contiguous Annual Conferences were grouped together and placed under the care of a resident bishop. However, the presidency of the sessions of these conferences was not limited to the resident bishop, but was rotated among the several bishops assigned to the regional areas. The administration of the system was left to the Board of Bishops, who ruled that no bishop could preside over the same conference more than twice in a quadrennium.

It should be said here—before dismissing the area system as a feature of Methodist Episcopal economy—that with the growing influence of what came to be known as the "church program"—putting into effect all the various causes and moves and interests and work called for by the general church—the bishops were called upon more and more to be administrative officers, rather than *episcopoi* in the strict ecclesiastical meaning of that term. By 1939, bishops had found that there was much more of minute administration called for, and more unrelenting attention to be

[64] *Journal of the General Conference of the Methodist Episcopal Church,* 1904, p. 516.

[65] *Ibid.,* pp. 304, 315, 514-17.

given to all manner of details, than there was to presiding over conferences, making appointments, or making formal appearances upon stated
occasions. Bishops, in fact, were called upon more and more by the great
boards of the church, as these developed, to put into effect in their respective areas the particular causes and interests which the boards and
church agencies felt should be pressed. The progress of each episcopal
area came to be measured not simply by the former standards of evangelistic fervor, ingathering of members, building of new churches, and
the like, but by activity and advancement made in these, and in all manner of other worthy undertakings and promotional meetings. The program of the church in time thus came to rest heavily upon the bishops.

It has been mentioned that in the Methodist Episcopal Church, South,
while the area plan was slower in coming, come it did, for the same
reasons that brought it about in the Methodist Episcopal Church. There
was no thought that a bishop could ever be stationed by a General Conference of the Methodist Episcopal Church, South. But the College of
Bishops of the Southern Church was asked in 1918 to so group their
episcopal areas, with a resident bishop in each area, that they might provide continuous supervision and presidency for a quadrennium. I recall
hearing Bishop Warren A. Candler of Atlanta, Georgia, complain about
the 1918 request, by observing that the General Conference was simply
"telling the wife of a bishop what residence she might live in" but could
not prescribe for a bishop where he should live or how to manage his
time. The respective Methodist Episcopal churches went into union with
the area system established in each one, but with the matter of forcing
a bishop to reside in a definite locale left somewhat in the air. Good
judgment and good co-operation between both the bishops and the
Committees on Episcopacy, first of the General Conference and recently
of the Jurisdictional Conferences, have worked this matter out to general
satisfaction.

The Judicial Power of the Southern Bishops

At an early date, bishops as presiding officers were compelled to rule
from time to time upon matters of Methodist law. In 1840 this power
was frankly recognized and established by a disciplinary direction empowering the bishops to "decide all questions of law in an annual conference, subject to an appeal to the General Conference; but in all cases
the application of law shall be with the conference." [66]

[66] *Discipline,* 1840, pp. 27-28.

This regulation remained in every *Discipline* of the Methodist Episcopal Church and was carried over into The Methodist Church, where it remains today as ruling law. It should be said here that a bishop's ruling is always subject to an immediate appeal on a matter of parliamentary law, with the house making the decision; and that the right of appeal from a bishop's decision on a question of Methodist law was held to inhere in the whole conference in the days of the Methodist Episcopal Church, South, and not in an individual member thereof. It took a majority vote to appeal a bishop's decision—no one person could do it unless he had a majority with him.[67]

In 1854 the Methodist Episcopal Church, South, wrote in its *Discipline* an epochal pronouncement:

An annual conference shall have a right to appeal from such decision to the college of bishops, whose decision in such cases shall be final. And no episcopal decision shall be authoritative except in the case pending, nor shall any be published, until it shall have been approved by the college of bishops. And each bishop shall report in writing to the episcopal college . . . such decisions as he has made, . . . and all such decisions, when approved by the college of bishops, shall be either recorded in a permanent form, or published in such manner as the bishops shall agree to adopt; and when so approved, and recorded or published, they shall be authoritative interpretations or constructions of the law.[68]

Thus, ten years after the division of the church, there was lodged in the bishops of the Methodist Episcopal Church, South, the power to act as the final interpreter of Methodist law. There had been no such final interpreter in 1844, and thereby, as Southerners saw it, they were at the mercy of a majority vote of an all-powerful General Conference. Over against the General Conference, as the judge of the constitutionality of its own acts, the Southern Church thus placed in its College of Bishops the authority to act as a final court of appeals.

The General Conference of 1854 went further when it formally recognized the bishops "practically as well as theoretically a co-ordinate branch of the government of the Church." [69] A noteworthy resolution was introduced by W. A. Smith of Virginia, passed by the conference, and made an Appendix to the Restrictive Rules:

[67] Collins Denny, *A Manual of The Discipline of the Methodist Episcopal Church, South* (Nashville: Lamar and Whitmore, 1931), p. 44, citing a College of Bishops Ruling in 1891 and 1925.

[68] *Discipline of the Methodist Episcopal Church, South,* 1854, p. 50.

[69] *Journal of the General Conference of the Methodist Episcopal Church, South,* 1854, p. 253.

Provided, That when any rule or regulation is adopted by the General Conference, which, in the opinion of the Bishops, is *unconstitutional,* the said Bishops may present to the General Conference their objections . . . ; and, if after hearing the objections and reasons of the Bishops, two-thirds of the members of the Conference present shall vote in favor of the rule or regulations . . . , it shall have the force of law—otherwise it shall be null and void.[70]

Since this was passed by the General Conference as a simple statutory enactment, its validity was soon called into question. It was published as a part of the Restrictive Rules, but the General Conference of 1808 had not added it, nor had it been adopted by the body of traveling preachers which alone, it was universally conceded, had the authority to make constitutional changes. Therefore in 1866, W. A. Smith proposed to the General Conference that the provision be sent around to the Annual Conferences and voted upon as though they were changing a Restrictive Rule—which they were.

Some asserted that this measure simply recognized an inherent power already in the bishops—there by constitutional right—which needed no statutory or constitutional enactment to make it clear. Others held that it did need such enactment. The 1866 Conference put the matter off, and it was postponed indefinitely. But in the General Conference of 1870, Dr. Leroy Lee of the Virginia Conference, the chairman of the Committee on Episcopacy, brought in an able—and, as the fathers of that day contended, a statesmanlike—report which pointed the way out.

This report held that the power to veto an act of the General Conference was not inherent in the episcopacy—and secondly, that the General Conference did not in its own right possess the power of determining the constitutionality of its own acts, but that the church as a whole, through the constitutional action of the several Annual Conferences, could adopt the 1854 measure. Here follows the form in which it was passed and sent down to the Annual Conferences:

Provided, That when any rule or regulation is adopted by the General Conference, which, in the opinion of the Bishops, is unconstitutional, the Bishops may present to the Conference which passed said rule or regulation, their objections thereto, with their reasons; and if then the General Conference shall, by a two-thirds vote, adhere to its action on said rule or regulation, it shall then take the course prescribed for altering a restrictive rule, and if thus passed upon affirmatively, the Bishops shall announce that such rule or regulation takes effect from that time.[71]

[70] *Ibid.,* p. 356.
[71] *Journal of the General Conference of the Methodist Episcopal Church, South,* 1870, p. 287.

Voting on this resolution for the next few months, the members of the Annual Conferences agreed to it by 2,024 yeas to 9 nays, and the matter was declared law in May of 1871. The approval of this measure can be considered the high-water mark for any kind of Methodist episcopacy.

The adoption of this measure did not give the bishops a "veto power," as was often erroneously stated, but it did give them power to block, or check, what they considered unconstitutional legislation. A veto in American political parlance means the power to kill or suppress a measure not favored by the executive. The 1870 measure simply enabled the Southern bishops to "lay down an episcopal check," as Bishop Collins Denny once expressed it. Its effect, paradoxically, was to make constitutional whatever the bishops declared to be unconstitutional.

The action of 1854 and 1870 gave the episcopacy in the Southern Church a very great power. Equitably enough, however, in spite of the vast power given, there were only two instances—so Bishop Collins Denny told the Commission on Unification in 1918—when the Southern bishops used their power to check the General Conference.[72]

It is somewhat heartening, therefore, to record that the General Conference of the Methodist Episcopal Church, which had the right to determine all matters of constitutionality arising before it, never abused its privilege, all powerful though it was; and that the bishops of the Methodist Episcopal Church, South, having the right to sit in judgment on the acts of their General Conference, even those affecting their own interests, never abused their privilege."[73]

It may be added here that this power of the Southern bishops to pass upon the constitutionality of General Conference legislation was taken away in that church by the creation of a Judicial Council in the Southern Church just previous to church union. This, a constitutional move, was initiated in 1934 and came to fruition in 1938, when, as it turned out, the General Conference of the Methodist Episcopal Church, South, held its last session before church union. At the 1938 General Conference, however, the Judicial Council did function, and as I, the chairman of the Committee on Episcopacy, well recall, made an important decision affecting episcopacy at that particular time. But as the Southern Church was on the point of union with the Methodist Episcopal and Methodist Protestant Churches, and as a new Judicial Council was to be created for and by that body, the judicial power of the Southern bishops, and their

[72] See Horace M. Du Bose, *A History of Methodism* (Nashville: Lamar and Smith, 1916), p. 115.
[73] Harmon, *Organization*, p. 48.

acting as a "Bench of Bishops," or a Supreme Court of Methodist law, was practically coeval with the life of the Methodist Episcopal Church, South.

Bishops yet continue to decide questions of law in Annual Conferences under well-defined disciplinary regulations, and all their decisions must be reviewed and are reviewed by the Judicial Council before they may have final status as church law.[74]

Term Episcopacy

A strong move to establish what was known as "term episcopacy" came about late in the nineteenth century in both Methodist Episcopal Churches. This was the proposal that bishops should be elected for a certain term of years, not for life. As the plan was usually presented, it provided that the period for which a man was to be elected to serve as bishop should be fixed by the General Conference, and that after each man had concluded his term, he should be eligible for re-election. The proposal fitted in with the contention that bishops were not a "third order," but simply elders set apart for a special duty. It was therefore held by proponents of the measure that neither the episcopal office nor any of its essential prerogatives was impaired by such a limitation of tenure.

The great argument for term episcopacy was the undeniable fact that the church, in both episcopal branches, had from time to time made serious mistakes in selecting men for the bishopric. Persons who managed to impress one General Conference very greatly, and thereby be elected bishops, would absolutely fail to measure up subsequently in the heavy and varied duties of the great office into which they had been inducted. Since there was no recourse against this under Methodism's time-honored construction of its constitution, and since each bishop, whether able or mediocre, must be kept in charge of great conferences and of the entire work of the church until age retired him, it was said that term episcopacy would be the answer. If bishops should be elected for a term of years, it was argued, those who do not make acceptable bishops would not and should not be re-elected. The mistake of one electing conference would be corrected by another.

Also, proponents of the measure further argued that bishops them-

[74] Constitution, Division III, Article VII.

selves, knowing that they would be held accountable for their position and administration at each succeeding General Conference, would be more likely to give the church the very best they had, and in no way feel themselves beyond its command.

But this argument cut two ways. Eventually term episcopacy was defeated, not simply by conservatives, who objected to such a fundamental constitutional change, but by a practical-minded majority, who felt that it would vastly increase the unrest and excitement in the church if every bishop were compelled to stand for re-election at every quadrennial gathering. It was pointed out that if it were true, as was alleged, that men do scheme to be elected bishop, they would be much more involved if they were endeavoring to be re-elected at recurring intervals. If a bishop appointed as new district superintendents those who would be friendly to him in normal times, how much more would his inclination to do this be increased if he felt that he needed influential friends in the cabinet when the next election at General Conference came along! This reasoning had great weight.

In the Methodist Episcopal General Conference of 1888, the first serious proposal was made to secure term episcopacy. The Judiciary Committee had the pending measure referred to it as to its constitutionality. The committee brought out a strong report, affirming that "a lifelong tenure of office is one of the attributes of that episcopacy, originated by our fathers, and which the General Conference 'may not do away or destroy.' " [75]

A minority of the Judiciary Committee took exception to this, the majority report, and presented to the General Conference a contrary argument in which it was held that the Third Restrictive Rule guards the office of the episcopacy and its prerogatives but does not touch its tenure. "It is our opinion, therefore, that it is within the power of the General Conference, in its wisdom, to limit the term of office of Bishops to be elected, as it may deem best." [76]

But when the majority and the minority reports were presented, both were laid on the table, and neither one, for some unexplained reason, was taken up again by the 1888 Conference.

In 1924, thirty-six years after this, the fight for term episcopacy was renewed in the Methodist Episcopal Church, and the point was made

[75] Arthur Benton Sanford, *Reports of the Committee on Judiciary of the General Conference of the Methodist Episcopal Church* (New York: The Methodist Book Concern, 1924), p. 257.

[76] *Ibid.*, pp. 257-58.

that the 1888 body had never decided adversely to the principle of term episcopacy. But on this occasion there was a sharp debate and the measure was defeated.

In the Methodist Episcopal Church, South, as part of a powerful revolt against its very strong episcopacy, a campaign for term episcopacy almost succeeded in the years previous to church union. A written constitution had been proposed for the Methodist Episcopal Church, South, and was presented to the General Conference of 1930, and at length considered item by item. In considering one section, an amendment was offered, empowering the General Conference to limit the term of office for which any bishop might be elected. After a heated debate, the amendment was written into the proposed constitution. However, when that document had been "perfected"—as its opponents sarcastically put it—it was overwhelmingly defeated. Many who might have supported the proposed constitution, for the other statesmanlike proposals which it incorporated, were against it because it inaugurated term episcopacy in the Southern Church.

Four years later, in 1934, the "termites," as one of their leaders publicly stated that they were called, renewed their fight in the General Conference of the Methodist Episcopal Church, South. But again the Southern Church refused to admit that once a bishop, a man might be something else later on. "An ex-bishop, save the mark!" one irate antagonist exclaimed.

At this General Conference, it may be added, the newly created Judicial Council of the Methodist Episcopal Church, South, brought out a strong pronouncement as to the real meaning of episcopacy. This affirmed the time-honored Southern position. There the whole matter rested, waiting for church union, which, by that time, all saw was near at hand.

Term episcopacy has been adopted in some of the Central Conferences of The Methodist Church, notably that in Latin America. A somewhat different situation, however, prevails in Central Conference areas outside the United States from that within it, and term episcopacy may possibly mark one aspect of this difference.

It is no part of a historian's task to advance a theory regarding episcopacy, but no historian can record the action of The Methodist Church in America without seeing that theories regarding the episcopacy have had tremendous effect upon that church's history. Methodism emphasizes the office as a special administrative position, and not as a churchly order; but it also demands, and from the first has demanded, that men set apart for this office shall be invested as persons with tremendous power, and inducted into the episcopacy through an august ceremony which is almost an exact replica of the Church of England's episcopal ordination. The vows of the bishop-elect are exactly those of the time-honored episcopacy of the Church of England, and were so furnished by John Wesley to those who are to be ordained superintendents among the Methodists in America. Those who have felt that the substitution of the word "consecrating" for "ordaining" would obviate some of the implications here have failed to note the original office which Wesley sent over, or to give full weight to the disciplinary direction that a bishop is to be constituted by the laying on of hands of other bishops or by Methodist elders. "What is this direction for, as John Emory argued long ago, if not to certify that there is to be in the investiture of this man, as he goes into this office, something that is not to be temporary or ephemeral, but for life? To this day The Methodist Church has officially so regarded it." [77]

4

Development of the Annual Conference

The Annual Conferences as geographical and structural divisions of Methodism had their origin in 1796. Before that, there had been the general, widely scattered, but undivided body of preachers. But in 1796 certain contiguous districts, in which preachers lived, were taken together to form convenient administrative areas, and the Annual Conference as a geographic, a ministerial, and a churchly body came into being.

As the church grew, more and more conferences were called for; and as membership increased, these conferences themselves divided, and other new conferences were formed. The General Conference always has had the power to create Annual Conferences and to outline Annual Conference boundaries.

Since a preacher admitted to full connection in one Annual Conference is a member of the whole Methodist traveling connection, and potentially a member of any or every Annual Conference, the practice of trans-

[77] Harmon, *Organization,* p. 56.

ferring ministers across conference lines has always been carried out authoritatively by the bishops, as need might seem to direct.

In time, with the development of the strong city church, it came to be quite customary for bishops to man such churches with men who were known to be able to serve acceptably large churches, irrespective of such a man's original conference membership. In the Methodist Episcopal Church, it was not at all unusual to transfer a minister from a large church, as in Detroit or Buffalo, to one in Wilmington or Binghamton or Des Moines or any other comparable city; while in the South a similar practice prevailed. A preacher from a strong church in New Orleans could be transferred to Baltimore, or one from Richmond to the First Church in Memphis. Quite often the laymen of the churches involved made their will felt in asking for men they felt desirable, especially where these involved the leading appointments. This practice was often viewed with distaste by the members of the Annual Conferences within whose bounds such transfers would be stationed. Each conference liked to feel that it had within it ministers who could serve acceptably any of its churches; and when a minister was transferred in "over the heads" of the faithful rank and file of a particular conference, there were murmurings and unrest. This, together with the fact that each Annual Conference was compelled to adapt itself more and more to an intensive development of its own life and ministry in its particular area, caused in time the growth of a definite Annual Conference solidarity. This was not so much opposed to, or set over against, the authority, program, and plan of the general church, but was the way each individual conference played its part in the church as a whole.

The question as to how many ministers might be allowed to organize as a separate Annual Conference, and how Mission Conferences were to be organized and take their place as conferences in the general church, presented quite a problem, especially to the Methodist Episcopal Church. The General Conference of 1860 gave the bishops of that church authority to constitute the missions in India as a Mission Annual Conference "if in their judgment it will promote the interests of our missions in India." [78] This was not followed out during the quadrennium, but later on it was, and in December, 1864, under the presidency of Bishop Edward Thomson, the India Mission Conference was organized and became the first Mission Annual Conference in the Orient. However, full rights were not given to the Mission Conferences, especially the crucial one of being represented in the General Conference. But the

[78] *Journal of the General Conference of the Methodist Episcopal Church*, 1860, pp. 277-78.

General Conference of 1868 repealed all acts of former General Conferences restricting the powers of Mission Conferences, and the Liberia, Germany and Switzerland, and India Mission Conferences were declared to be full Annual Conferences, endowed with all the rights, privileges, and immunities of such conferences in the United States. Mission Conferences grew and in time became the nucleus of what are known in the church today as Central Conferences.

In 1884 the General Conference of the Methodist Episcopal Church first made provision for a "Central Conference," that is, a combination of Mission Conferences empowered to act together. The action read: "When in any of our Foreign Mission fields there is more than one Annual Conference or Mission, or more than one form of Methodism, it shall be lawful, either by order of the General Conference, or by a majority vote of all the Conferences or Missions wishing to unite, . . . to organize a Central Conference." [79] The first Central Conference of the Methodist Episcopal Church was convened in Bareilly on January 13, 1885, under the presidency of Bishop John F. Hurst. This was then called the Central Conference of India and Malaysia.

When the constitution of the Methodist Episcopal Church was adopted in 1900, it was provided that it was necessary to have twenty-five ministers to form an Annual Conference.[80] However, it was decided in 1904 that the status of an Annual Conference would not be "affected by the fact that its membership falls below the number required by the Constitution for the organization of an Annual Conference." [81]

In time, when the constitution of The Methodist Church was adopted in the Plan of Union of 1939, the Annual Conference was recognized as the "basic body" in the church. As such, it had reserved to it

the right to vote on all constitutional amendments, on the election of Ministerial and Lay delegates to the General and the Jurisdictional or Central Conferences, on all matters relating to the character and conference relations of its Ministerial members, and on the ordination of Ministers, and *such other rights as have not been delegated to the General Conference.*[82]

This last reservation gives to the present Annual Conferences a tremendous power.

---

[79] *Journal of the General Conference of the Methodist Episcopal Church,* 1884, p. 349.

[80] *Discipline of the Methodist Episcopal Church,* 1904, ¶ 46.2.

[81] *Journal of the General Conference,* 1904, p. 521.

[82] Constitution, Division II, Section VII, Article II. Italics mine.

5

The Question of a Constitution for the Church

Methodist authorities were for many years divided, and put different interpretations upon the exact meaning of the word "constitution," as this had to do with the Methodist Episcopal Church in America. It has already been made clear how there were differing points of view over the constitutional rights of the episcopacy, and how the Methodist Episcopal Church and the Methodist Episcopal Church, South, were divided bitterly in their respective interpretations. That there was no court of high appeal to settle this matter made the difference one of supreme import rather than simply an academic affair—especially in 1844, and to a certain extent in preparing for eventual reunion in 1939.

It is agreed that full power to create a church inhered in the body of the traveling preachers who came together in Baltimore in 1784. Bishop Collins Denny makes the point that "the first General Conference, by way of eminence called the Christmas Conference, was composed of traveling preachers only." (Coke said: "We had near sixty of them present. The whole number is 81." [83]) This same authority points out that while there were regulations in the *Disciplines* of 1792, 1801, and 1804, prescribing that the General Conference should be composed of "traveling preachers in full connection," yet these traveling preachers were not necessarily ordained, and "ordination was not a prerequisite to membership in the General Conference." [84] It was the undivided body of traveling preachers who up until 1808 held in their hands, and expressed by their vote at General Conference meetings, the complete sovereignty of the church.

When the General Conference of 1808 met, the official Minutes of the church showed that there were 516 traveling preachers. Of these, 240 are marked as "elders," and of these elders, five were supernumeraries and six were superannuates. Those preachers were members who had traveled four years from the time of their reception on trial by an Annual Conference, and were in full connection at the time the General Conference was held. "Those who met at the appointed time and place, whether many or few, constituted the General Conference, which then possessed original, unlimited, unrestricted powers." [85]

---

[83] *Extracts of the Journals of the Rev. Dr. Coke's Five Visits to America* (London: G. Paramore, 1793), p. 23.
[84] Denny, *Manual*, p. 14.
[85] *Ibid.*, p. 13.

When this body, meeting in the General Conference of 1808, created the delegated General Conference, it gave that conference full power to make laws except in certain particulars carefully outlined by six stated restrictions, which thenceforth circumscribed its powers. These Restrictive Rules, as has previously been noticed, subsequently played a tremendous part in Methodist history, but—who was to interpret or enforce them? No one had been constitutionally set apart to do so when 1820 came, and the elective presiding eldership was adopted by a majority of the General Conference; no one had been made arbiter in 1844, when Bishop Andrew was asked by the General Conference to desist from the exercise of his episcopal functions as long as his particular impediment as a slaveholder remained. It was sometimes asked what exactly was the constitution of the Methodist Episcopal Church in America—or did it have what could be called a constitution? The debate over the constitutionality of any particular matter always introduced the deeper question: What is the constitution? Methodist authorities proved to be greatly divided in their opinions as to the answer.

Bishop Collins Denny gives an able review of the main findings and consensus of opinion on this matter in his *Manual of the Discipline* (pp. 16-17).

He shows that in 1786 there was set forth the "organic law of the Church," as "the General Minutes of the Conferences of the Methodist Episcopal Church in America, forming the Constitution of the said Church." [86] In 1789 Thomas Morrell, chosen to answer William Hammett's attack on the church, published a pamphlet entitled "Truth Discovered." In that pamphlet he wrote: "It was written in our *constitution* [italics supplied] that no person shall be ordained a Superintendent over us without the consent of a majority of the Conference." [87]

Denny further cited Nicholas Snethen in his reply to James O'Kelly's *Apology;* Snethen said of an action of the conferences in 1787 that "the whole case was constitutionally carried through the Conference and voted by a fair majority." [88] Denny observed:

The fact that all changes at that time were made by a majority vote alone did not make the organic law of the Church other than organic. It is not the proportion of the vote necessary to adopt or to change a law that makes it organic, but the powers possessed by the body making the changes. From 1784 till the next General Conference met, that of 1792, changes in the organic law of the Church were effected by the bishops taking the proposed changes from Con-

[86] So reads the title page of the 1786 *Discipline.*
[87] Quoted in Tigert, *Constitutional History,* p. 234.
[88] Snethen, *A Reply to an Apology for Protesting Against the Methodist Episcopal Government* (Philadelphia: Henry Tuckniss, 1800).

ference to Conference till all preachers in the several Conferences had an opportunity to vote. . . .

In 1792 quadrennial General Conferences were made part of the organic law,
and General and Annual (then called District) Conferences were given separate
powers. Not until 1792 did "the conference" viewed as one body, though meeting
and voting at different times and in different places, cease to function. From
1792 through 1808 the General Conference alone changed the organic law; and
during those years the full sovereignty of the Church was lodged in the self-
sufficient, original, unlimited, unrestricted General Conference.[89]

In 1808, by the creation of a delegated General Conference, the preachers
in whom resided the sovereignty of the church, gave to this General Conference full powers to make laws for and govern the church completely,
with the exception of certain restrictions which were definitely written
and which ever thereafter have been known as the Restrictive Rules.
Later, the Supreme Court of the United States, in deciding the issue between the Southern and Northern groups over the Plan of Separation,[90]
regarded the organization of the church after 1808 as a constitutional
matter. The Supreme Court said: "Subject to these restrictions—the six
restrictive rules—the delegated Conference possessed the same powers
as when composed of the entire body of preachers. . . . In all respects
and in everything else that concerns the welfare of the Church, the
General Conference represents the sovereign power the same as before." [91]

But always there remained the question as to who might decide what
was constitutional. As has been shown above, in the Methodist Episcopal
Church, South, the College of Bishops, acting as a Bench of Bishops,
had the final say as to what was or what was not constitutional; in the
Methodist Episcopal Church, the General Conference itself acted as a
court, deciding the constitutionality of its own acts. The Methodist Episcopal General Conference did this usually through a Committee on
Judiciary, which was an extremely able body, so that when that committee
brought in its reports, the General Conference almost always adopted
them. Under the leadership of Judge Henry Wade Rogers, who acted
as chairman of the Committee on Judiciary in 1908, 1912, 1916, and
1920, this committee climbed to a lofty altitude in the esteem of the
church. Its "Reports," published by order of the General Conference, together with rulings by the Board of Bishops of the Methodist Episcopal
Church, furnished to The Methodist Church of today a body of solid
Methodist law which the Judicial Council of The Methodist Church
has seen fit to take for guidance in many instances. So have the "epis-

[89] Denny, *Manual,* pp. 26, 28-29.
[90] Smith *et al.* vs. Swormstedt, *57 U.S.* (16 Howard), pp. 288-313.
[91] *Ibid.,* pp. 307-8.

copal decisions" of the bishops of the Methodist Episcopal Church, South, been duly recorded, and in time accorded high authority upon all constitutional matters.

But the question as to what was the constitution of the church would not down throughout the whole of the last century, becoming acute, as we have said, first in 1820 when Bishop Soule refused election as bishop because he believed an unconstitutional action had been taken by the General Conference in voting for an elective presiding eldership. It was then that Bishop McKendree noted that there was no way to settle what was a constitutional matter, and stated that the bishops had "consulted together" and "agreed to recommend to the General Conference a *constitutional test* which should for ever settle these things." [92] But it appears that this measure, proposed by the bishops, did not eventuate in any definite action. However, that there *was* a constitution, all allowed.

Bishop Collins Denny quotes with approval Bishop S. M. Merrill of the Methodist Episcopal Church, whom he terms "one of the really great authorities on Methodist law," when Merrill held that:

The organic law of the Church, and the Constitution of the General Conference, are not the same. . . . There is a Constitution of the General Conference outside of or beyond the Restrictive Rules. We are surprised to find that there are yet living here, there, and yonder, individuals who believe that the whole Constitution of the General Conference is found in these restrictions. . . . If we assume that these six restrictions are the only Constitution, you may just as well obliterate the rest of the chapter. Suppose you had to organize a General Conference on these six restrictions. How would you go about it? Restrictions to what? On whom? On the power given to a General Conference previously described. What General Conference is that previously described? Not any General Conference or assembly of people that may call themselves a General Conference. This General Conference previously described and provided for, a General Conference consisting of just so many delegates as is described, of just such qualifications as are therein found, forming a quorum as therein described, meeting at just the time and place provided for, under just such a presidency as therein provided for—then that General Conference and no other has conferred upon it, not by itself, but by the whole Church at large, through this instrument which we call a Constitution—that particular General Conference and no other has conferred upon it power, sole power, to make rules and regulations for the Church under these limitations and restrictions. We thought that which constitutes is a Constitution. That which organizes is organic. [93]

[92] Robert Paine, *The Life and Times of William McKendree* (Nashville: Southern Methodist Publishing House, 1869) , II, 44-45.

[93] Denny, *Manual*, pp. 36-37, quoting *The Daily Christian Advocate,* the Methodist Episcopal Church, 1892, p. 75.

In time the consensus of Methodist authorities, including Bishops Merrill and Neely of the Methodist Episcopal Church and Bishops Tigert and Denny of the Methodist Episcopal Church, South, came to be that the whole section of the *Discipline* creating and setting up the General Conference (the section then entitled "Of the General Conference"), as well as the restrictions and the proviso relating to the amending of those restrictions—all of it was truly constitutional, and could be amended only by the due process therein provided. Indeed, the General Conference of the Methodist Episcopal Church in 1892 decided by the adoption of the so-called "Goucher Substitute" that the constitution of the church was in substance the section of the *Discipline* of 1808 ("Of the General Conference") "together with such modifications as have been adopted since that time in accordance with provisions for amendment in that section." [94]

In order to settle finally the question of the constitution and provide a formal document about whose intent there could be no question, the Methodist Episcopal Church adopted a rather brief but well-integrated constitution in 1900. This instrument was frankly recognized as a verbal alteration and positive restatement of Methodist fundamental law. As such it was referred to the separate Annual Conferences for their adoption, and the necessary process having been followed out, in due time this constitution was adopted and appeared first in the *Discipline* of 1900 of the Methodist Episcopal Church. It remained unaltered until 1939, when the Plan of Union, which was frankly called the Constitution of The Methodist Church,[95] was adopted by the Annual Conferences of the Methodist Episcopal Church, the Methodist Episcopal Church, South, and the Methodist Protestant Church in the same way.

The Methodist Episcopal Church, South, held to the 1808 General Conference section of the *Discipline*—and the amendments which had been added thereto by constitutional process—as its fundamental law. The Methodist Protestant Church began frankly with a written constitution, as the *Discipline* of their church was always entitled "The Constitution and Discipline of the Methodist Protestant Church." Today these former churches, now The Methodist Church, have a constitution, adopted as such by their respective constitutional processes, with a Judicial Council to interpret and settle all matters affecting constitutionality. The decisions of that body continue to define and explain its import and meaning in all moot matters which arise in the ongoing of the living church.

[94] *Journal of the General Conference of the Methodist Episcopal Church,* 1892, pp. 206, 228.

[95] Preamble to the Declaration of Union, II; *Discipline,* 1960, p. 8.

6

Lay Representation

Lay representation is so much a part of The Methodist Church of the present, and the tremendous worth of laymen in the Annual, Jurisdictional, and General Conferences of the church is of such high moment, that it is difficult to understand why this was so long in coming about. It must be remembered, however, that the first Methodist conferences, both in England and in America, were composed of preachers, and that the Methodist Episcopal Church in America was itself organized by preachers. As stated elsewhere in this chapter, the sovereignty of the church resided in the undivided body of traveling preachers, and this sovereignty was destined to remain with them until, in due time, both in the Methodist Episcopal Church and in the Methodist Episcopal Church, South, they admitted laymen to share in exercising it, in both the Annual and the General Conference.

The highly centralized administration and type of organization of The Methodist Church made it difficult—and in some respects yet makes it difficult—to decentralize to any degree without denaturing fundamental Methodist polity. John Wesley himself asserted: "As long as I live, the people shall have no share in choosing either stewards or leaders. . . . We are no republicans, and never intend to be." [96] On this side of the Atlantic, Asbury and Coke presided over conferences of ministers exclusively. In Coke and Asbury's Notes on the *Discipline,* the bishops wrote:

But it may be asked, Why are not delegates sent to these conferences from each of the circuits? We answer, It would utterly destroy our *itinerant plan. They* would be concerned chiefly, if not only, for the interests of their own constituents. They could not be expected, from *the nature of things,* to make the necessary sacrifices, and to enter impartially into *the good of the whole.* They would necessarily endeavour to obtain the most able and lively preachers for their respective circuits. [97]

The stewards themselves were appointed by the preacher in charge. It took a long time and quite a struggle to establish the right of the Quarterly Conferences to elect their own stewards. The whole church was of the preachers, by the preachers, and, said their opponents, *for* the preachers.

[96] *Letters,* to John Mason, January 13, 1790.
[97] *Discipline,* 1798, p. 34.

The first serious endeavor to denature some of the power of episcopacy was begun in 1792 when James O'Kelly introduced a measure allowing the ministers to appeal their appointments to the Annual Conference if they felt themselves aggrieved. This was defeated. Later on, the elective presiding eldership was championed strongly by some who had sympathized with O'Kelly, and especially by Nicholas Snethen, who had not, and whom once Asbury had called his "silver trumpet." In 1800, 1804, 1808, 1812, and 1816, the question of the appointment—or conference election—of the presiding elders was heatedly and repeatedly fought over. In 1820, as has been indicated elsewhere, the elective eldership did carry, but because of Bishop Soule's unexpected stand the measure was held in abeyance for four years, and then finally defeated. Thereupon, the Methodist Protestant Church organized.

Bishop James H. Straughn, president of the Methodist Protestant General Conference, 1936-39, and elected bishop by the Methodist Protestant delegation at the Uniting Conference in Kansas City in 1939, calls attention to the fact that up until 1820, the entire controversy for getting the church on a more democratic foundation had been a struggle within the clergy. "It had been a constant division led by such leaders as Garrettson, Bangs, Hedding, Pickering, Emory, Waugh, Snethen, Shinn, seeking liberalizing administration as opposed by Collins, Capers, Andrew, Roszel, Reed, Soule, on the side of episcopacy." [98] Bishop Straughn goes on to say that "until this time the voice of the laity had not been heard."

But in 1821 a Philadelphia layman named William S. Stockton began the publication of *The Wesleyan Repository,* a semimonthly periodical devoted to what was beginning to be termed "reform" in the church. *The Wesleyan Repository* became *Mutual Rights* after a time and was edited by S. K. Jennings, a physician. But with the organization of the Methodist Protestant Church and the publication of *The Methodist Protestant,* the official organ of that church, the immediate drive for laity rights in the Methodist Episcopal Church died down. "The church now could breathe more easily for a while. The more ardent reformers were gone, to be sure, but the agitation for lay representation had only quieted down. It was still in the blood stream of the church and eventually to become an integral part of its polity." [99]

Episcopal Methodism, however, went up to and through its epochal division in 1844 with no change in the matter of laity rights, although the years began to show the "incongruity of a Protestant church com-

[98] James H. Straughn, *Inside Methodist Union* (Nashville: The Methodist Publishing House, 1958), p. 33.
[99] *Ibid.,* p. 40.

posed of millions of loyal members and living in a democratic country who had no voice whatever in the management of their own beloved organization." [100]

In 1840 there came a renewed call for lay representation by "certain abolitionists," as James Porter called them in his *History of Methodism.* Of course, nothing happened, but by 1852 the protagonists of lay representation in the Methodist Episcopal Church had got a bit further. A committee of that year, headed by Dr. Matthew Simpson (at that conference elected a bishop), seriously considered the matter, but reported it "inexpedient so to alter the economy of our Church as to introduce lay representation into the General and Annual Conferences." Only three votes seem to have been cast against the Simpson Report.

But a little later, Matthew Simpson himself began to change. "The more Simpson thought upon the excellence of Methodist laymen, the more embarrassed he was by their exclusion from the councils of the church—and the more determined he was that they should be given a voice." [101] By 1856, Simpson expressed confidence that it would be only a matter of time until the General Conference should make the change, and he increasingly became the champion of lay representation. He himself was greatly censured for the leading part he took in bringing this about in the church. "In 1860 he persuaded the board of bishops to insert a paragraph on lay representation in their address to the general conference. He wrote the section himself—a fact which the delegates generally knew. 'We are of the opinion,' said the bishops, 'that lay delegation might be introduced in one form into the General Conference with safety, and perhaps advantage, that form being a separate house.' " [102]

As it turned out, since the Civil War was on, the people were "indifferent to ecclesiastical reform. The ministers opposed the change, 3,069 to 1,338, and the people likewise turned it down, 47,885 to 28,884." [103] In 1864 the bishops repeated the stand they had taken in 1860, but the conference itself took no action. Then came the election of Daniel Curry as editor of the *Christian Advocate and Journal,* and this able protagonist threw his full weight against the whole movement. "He was tall, with a slender but rugged frame, thin, somber face, and shaggy, overhanging brows. His mouth and chin were narrow but firm as lines made with a carpenter's rule, and his ideas were as set as the thin line of his compressed lips." [104]

[100] Harmon, *Organization,* p. 116.

[101] Robert D. Clark, *The Life of Matthew Simpson* (New York: The Macmillan Co., 1956), p. 277.

[102] *Ibid.*

[103] *Ibid.*

[104] *Ibid.,* p. 280.

This powerful editor went into action and attacked the whole movement as something of advantage to a "church aristocracy." He censured Simpson for being a partisan, holding that no one could do as a bishop what he might properly do as a man. But in 1868, as it turned out, the friends of lay delegation obtained an almost unanimous vote showing that the General Conference was ready to admit laymen. That body ordered that a plan for lay representation be put before all the members of the church, lay and clerical, for approval or disapproval. "There shall be held a general election in the several places of worship of the Methodist Episcopal Church, at which all members in full connection, and not less than twenty-one years of age, shall be invited to vote by ballot: 'For Lay Delegation' or 'Against Lay Delegation.' " [105]

However, since at that time laymen really had no other than an advisory vote, the ministerial ballot on the actual written plan, whereby the Second Restrictive Rule was to be altered so as to admit laymen, was the deciding factor. Bishop Simpson was glad to report to the General Conference of 1872 that 4,915 had voted for the proposed change, 1,597 against. After considerable discussion, the General Conference adopted a formal motion to concur with the action of the Annual Conference members in altering the Second Restrictive Rule as provided, and the constitutional majority was at once given.

There was considerable discussion through the rest of this quadrennium as to exactly what the church was voting on. It was argued that the lay people of the church had voted for the *principle* of lay representation, not upon a definite *plan*, as had the preachers. Meanwhile, Bishop Simpson began to work strongly through the conferences over which he presided, for the adoption of the General Conference measure.

The bishops were divided. Bishop Ames spoke against the measure in every conference he held. "Where Ames presided, lay delegation lost. . . . On the other hand, wherever Simpson conducted conferences . . . reform prospered. Southeast Indiana was 76 for, 4 against; Tennessee, 37 for, 0 against; Philadelphia, 142 for, 18 against; Vermont, 71 for, 14 against." [106]

The fact that the Methodist Episcopal Church, South, had voted in 1866 for lay representation cut both ways in influencing the electorate of the Northern Church at that particular era. Some thought the South had pointed the way; others were against anything the South was for. But as it turned out, when the quadrennium ended, lay delegates were seated almost without a ripple.

[105] *Discipline of the Methodist Episcopal Church*, 1868, Appendix, Section 44.
[106] Clark, *Life of Simpson*, pp. 285-86.

The plan of lay representation adopted by the 1872 General Conference provided for two lay delegates from each Annual Conference, except where a conference had only one clerical delegate; in such cases only one lay delegate was allowed. Lay and clerical members were to deliberate in one body, but they were to vote separately if such separate vote should be called for by one third of either order. In such cases both orders had to concur to complete the action. [107] It should be noted that this was lay representation *in the General Conference*. No layman was elected to the Annual Conferences of the Methodist Episcopal Church until 1900, when, with the adoption of the new constitution of that church, a "Lay Conference" was established. Even then members of the Lay Conference were never, strictly speaking, members of the Annual Conference, as membership in that body is usually understood.

Between the time of the seating of lay delegates in the General Conference and the creation of the Lay Conference in 1900, it was provided that there should be an "Electoral Conference" of laymen, which was to assemble on the third day of the session of the Annual Conference held previous to a General Conference. The Electoral Conference was to be made up of one layman from each circuit or station, and each must be over twenty-five years of age and must have been a member of the church for five years. The duty of the Electoral Conference was simply to elect lay delegates to the approaching General Conference.

The establishment of the formal Lay Conference in 1900 was simply a perpetuation of the old Electoral Conference, which, previous to that time, had met only once in four years. The Lay Conference after 1900 sat in parallel with that of the ministers and was established for the purpose of

"voting on constitutional amendments," considering and acting upon matters relating to lay activities, and such other matters as the General Conference might direct. One lay member from each pastoral charge was to be elected to the lay conference by the suffrage of all the lay members who were over twenty-one years of age. Clerical and lay members were to meet in united sessions for certain parts of their joint program, and to divide into separate bodies to carry on the specific task committed to each.[108]

Thus lay delegation came about slowly and by two successive moves in the Methodist Episcopal connection. In 1872 laymen were admitted to

[107] *Journal of the General Conference of the Methodist Episcopal Church,* 1872, pp. 44-46.
[108] Harmon, *Organization,* p. 119.

the General Conference; in 1900 they were admitted collaterally to the
Annual Conference by establishing in co-operation with each Annual
Conference a Lay Conference.

Bishop Neely said of the move of 1868:

The admission of laymen to the General Conference has been pronounced the
most remarkable instance of the voluntary relinquishment of power to be found
in the history of the world. The clergy were under no compulsion to give up the
authority they had from the beginning, and yet they voluntarily admitted the
laity into the supreme legislative body of the Church to share with them the
vast powers of the General Conference.[109]

Women's Work and Equal Representation

The story of the organization of women's missionary work has been
told elsewhere. In the organizational development of the church during
the past century, and well into the present one, there were repeated efforts
to secure for women "full laity rights" in the church. The seating of lay
delegations in the respective General Conferences served to implement
a growing demand that there should be equal lay rights on the part of
women members in both the Northern and Southern Churches. In the
lay Electoral Conferences, which the Methodist Episcopal Church provided for, which were to vote upon delegates to the General Conference,
five women were elected to membership in five different conferences.
Among these was Frances E. Willard, the temperance reformer, whose
membership was in the Rock River Conference. There was considerable
debate as to whether the women thus elected members by the Electoral
Conferences could be seated. They were not recognized as members by
the 1888 General Conference, but their rebuff stirred the church during
the ensuing quadrennium.

In 1892, while no woman had been elected as a General Conference
delegate, two had been elected as alternates. The Committee on Judiciary,
however, in giving an official definition to the words "laymen" and "lay
delegates," reported their judgment to the conference and held that
these words applied to men only.[110]

The ruling caused a storm. Dr. J. W. Hamilton, who was later to
become a bishop and who was a champion of women's rights, moved

[109] Thomas B. Neely, *The Governing Conference in Methodism* (New York: Hunt
and Eaton, 1892), p. 434.
[110] Sanford, *Reports of the Committee on Judiciary*, p. 62.

to submit to the Annual Conferences a proposition which would amend the Second Restrictive Rule so that this rule would state positively concerning lay delegates that "said delegates must be male members." Hamilton, who knew that this amendment would scarcely carry, knew that he would be in position, when it failed, to say that "laymen" therefore undoubtedly meant both men and women.

The Hamilton Amendment caused much confusion in the Methodist Episcopal Church during the quadrennium, and a number of Annual Conferences refused to vote upon it at all. The Colorado Annual Conference proposed an amendment which would affirm directly that "delegates may be [either] men [or] women." Only by a slim margin was this amendment defeated.

In 1896 four women were elected delegates to the General Conference. A stormy debate was brought on by their presence and the consequent effort to seat them. A compromise plan was finally worked out, but in the meantime the four women who had been elected delegates and whose names appear on the official roll had withdrawn, directly or indirectly, from sitting in the conference. But it is to be noted that the expenses of these women were paid, as were those of all other delegates.

The whole matter then was held in abeyance until 1900, since a new constitution was to be voted on by the Methodist Episcopal Church at that time. In this document "equal laity rights" were granted to women. Therefore, when the constitution was adopted by the whole church, all the measures for which the women had been contending were obtained.

It should be said here that the right of ordination was a question which came up later and, while allowed in time by the Methodist Episcopal Church, can scarcely be termed a "laity right."

The Methodist Episcopal Church, South, moved more slowly in giving rights to women. As late as 1914 there was a heated debate in the General Conference of that year as to the right of women to be elected stewards and to hold other representative positions in the church. The General Conference sustained its committee which had refused to concur in the memorial asking this. But in 1918 the General Conference approved the same proposal by a large majority. Forthwith, the bishops of the Southern Church laid down an "episcopal check," holding that the General Conference had exceeded its powers and contravened the constitution of the church by this piece of legislation. Whereupon the General Conference passed the measure again by the requisite two-thirds majority and sent it down to the Annual Conferences, which overwhelmingly voted in favor of the proposal (4,280 to 467). So it came about that at the General Conference of 1922 the bishops reported that "lay rights for women" had been written into the constitution of the Methodist Episcopal Church, South.[111]

Needless to say, women have proved able and efficient members of the conferences to which they have been elected, and, in the course of time, they were granted full rights in every way. The last bastion to be stormed was admission to the traveling connection in Annual Conference membership, and this was granted by the General Conference of The Methodist Church in 1956.

[111] *Journal of the General Conference of the Methodist Episcopal Church, South,* 1922, p. 62.

chapter 27

THE MISSIONS
OF AMERICAN
METHODISM

Background and Early
  Beginnings

Missionary Organization

Emerging Overseas Missions,
  1844-76

Overseas Missions,
  1876-1919

National Missions

B Y THE END OF WORLD WAR I, AMERICAN
Methodism had completed, with several minor exceptions, its overseas geographic expansion. On the threshold of new growth, the resulting churches were already intensively developing indigenous leadership. At the same time Methodism's national missions had completed their territorial outreach and had established the continuing pattern of their work.

For Methodist missions the nineteenth century began in 1819, with the founding of the Methodist Missionary Society, and ended in 1919, when the Treaty of Versailles was signed. Significantly, within the context of world history, mankind entered the twentieth century only at the time of World War I. Thus, in a word, what follows is the story of Methodist missions in the latter half of the nineteenth century.

In tracing the major outlines of this vast, complex, and multiform development, one can include few details. Those who seek the full story, meticulously detailed and documented, will find it in Wade Crawford Barclay's *History of Methodist Missions.*[1]

1

The Background

The missions of American Methodism can be understood adequately only in relation to those men—Wesley, Asbury, and Coke—who gave them initial impulse and shape and to those tides of

[1] (New York: Board of Missions of The Methodist Church), Vols. I-III, 1949-57.

history—ecclesiastical, social, and political—on which they were borne and of which, inevitably, they were a part.

The Founding Fathers

To James Hervey, an old friend critical of John Wesley's preaching on street corners in a parish district where resided a clergyman of the Church of England, Wesley wrote on March 20, 1739, "I look upon all the world as my parish."

That oft-quoted statement is important—not as a ringing call to missions in faraway lands (as Methodists have repeatedly and inaccurately used it), but as an index to Wesley's understanding of his mission in Britain.

The pre-Aldersgate Wesley who went to the Indians of Georgia thought of himself as—and was—a foreign missionary. He must be understood in this light.[2] The post-Aldersgate Wesley perceived with almost blinding clarity that England, itself a part of Christendom, was a prime field for missionary endeavor—Wesley's mission field! Wesley anticipated by two centuries the essential meaning of the Anglican Communion's call to national mission in the 1940's—"toward the conversion of England." People not in church cannot by pulpit preaching be won to Christ.

Parish comity and the revivalist's responsibilities when among another minister's congregation—not foreign missions—provide the setting for Wesley's bold declaration. With it, Wesley put all on notice that he would preach wherever he could and without regard for certain of the supposed niceties of "ministerial ethics." Wesley was a man with a mission—to revive true Christianity in England. When lives are to be saved, the burning heart dismisses irrelevant protocol.

To Wesley, Christendom was unique in heritage and potential destiny. But lacking vital and pure Christian faith, it could not fulfill its mission. Thus, aware of the decadent Christendom in whose midst he stood, Wesley came to see no difference between "home missions" and "foreign missions." Yet such was his theological perspective and his devotion to the mission to which he was called that he virtually denied the importance of missions among non-European non-Christians outside Christendom.

"The General Spread of the Gospel" (Sermon LXVIII), Wesley's only "missionary sermon" and one delivered late in his life, best reveals his attitude. A thorough revival of Protestantism would commend the "true understanding of the faith" and lead to its acceptance by all Christendom,

[2] Cf. Martin Schmidt, *The Young Wesley: Missionary and Theologian of Missions,* tr. L. A. Fletcher (London: Epworth Press, 1958).

including the Orthodox, Copts, and Roman Catholics. The resulting unity and concord would mirror, Wesley believed, that of true, primitive Christianity. Moreover, a Christendom thus revived and unified would produce an overpowering witness. Through it, in God's providence, men everywhere would accept the truth of the gospel.

Any major "foreign missionary" enterprise would weaken, in Wesley's judgment, the renewal already under way in Britain. To the extent that such would retard the transformation of Christendom, it would delay the decisive sign and witness of the gospel's truth to all nations.

Thus, in 1784 when Coke advanced his plan for a missionary society, Wesley's icy disapproval—for reasons theological, ecclesiastical, and personal—quickly killed that potentially notable project. But soon Coke's persuasive importunity won Wesley's approval for limited missions in northern Britain and Nova Scotia. The results a few months later displeased Wesley. Coke had convinced several of the ablest young men in Methodism to serve as missionaries outside England. Noting this, Wesley asked critically whether Coke should be allowed "to pick out one after another the choicest of our young preachers?" [3]

Despite this lack of enthusiasm Wesley—and the Wesleyan Revival— contributed in incalculable measure to the modern missionary movement. That vast enterprise began in 1793 when William Carey, the self-taught British Baptist cobbler, sailed for India. England's Evangelical Awakening was larger and broader than Methodism, but Wesley was its chief figure. That awakening so changed and quickened the religious temperament of Great Britain that when Carey issued his call to world mission, there emerged a steadily growing and continuing response. That was Wesley's greatest gift to missions.

Two lesser contributions, sometimes wrested from context and magnified unduly, need noting. First, Wesley's rejection of a rigid hyper-Calvinism and his insistence upon man's ability—any man, anywhere— to turn to God to be saved eventually compelled Methodists and some others to launch missions. Yet the reinterpretation and reinvigoration of Calvinism by Calvinists—most notably by the American Jonathan Edwards—released the missionary imperative inherent in the theology that most influenced Baptists, Congregationalists, Presbyterians, and those in the Church of Scotland. Indeed, in the fifty years following the publication of Carey's Enquiry (1792), most Protestant missions begun overseas came not from those motivated by Wesleyan thought but from Calvinists. Second, pietism in Germany, the Great Awakenings in America, and the Evangelical Awakening in England interpenetrated and shaped one

[3] Letters, to Peard Dickinson, April 11, 1789.

another. All three emphasized one major common element—conversion. To this emphasis Wesley contributed. From these closely interrelated movements—manifestations on three continents of the working of the Spirit—came modern Protestant missions.[4]

From a missionary perspective what Wesley had been for Methodism in Britain, Francis Asbury was for Methodism in America. Asbury volunteered for a mission in the colonies and in the regions beyond. To give himself completely to this vast endeavor, he intentionally remained unmarried. He was called to claim for the gospel those who were settling a new land. Before his death Asbury had come to see the importance of missions to Indians and to others, but with single-minded devotion he had given himself to one work—to the mission among those who advanced the frontier. Asbury's belief in the Methodist Church as a missionary agency did much to shape American Methodism's view of the task in its homeland.

With friends among the nobility, of independent means, and with a doctorate in civil law from Oxford, Thomas Coke was in many respects different from Wesley and Asbury. Driven out of his Anglican pulpit in 1776 because of his Methodist convictions, Coke, then twenty-nine, stood before the seventy-three-year-old Wesley to ask, "What shall I do now?" Wesley replied, "Go out and preach the gospel to all the world." Undoubtedly Wesley meant what he intended when he had made his similar statement in 1739, but Coke took the words literally. He never surrendered his "commission."

In 1784, nine years before Carey departed for India, Coke had sought actively to begin a Methodist mission in that land. In the same year, at the Christmas Conference, Coke's urging resulted in two missionary appointments to Nova Scotia and one to the West Indies. Within two years Coke himself had become the real pioneer of Methodist missionary expansion in the Caribbean. In 1805 he began Methodism's "home missions" in Britain. In 1811 he sent the first British Methodist missionaries to Sierra Leone, Africa. Coke spent his entire fortune initiating and maintaining missions overseas.

In 1813 he led a band of volunteers to establish a mission in Ceylon. Just short of the goal and in his sixty-seventh year, Coke died, but what was eventually to prove one of the most important missions in southern

---

[4] Cf. Johannes Van Den Berg, *Constrained by Jesus' Love: An Inquiry into the Motives of the Missionary Awakening in Great Britain in the Period Between 1698 and 1815* (Kampen: J. H. Kok, N.V., 1956), pp. 84 ff. See Also William Richey Hogg, "The Rise of Protestant Missionary Concern, 1517-1914," in Gerald H. Anderson, ed., *The Theology of the Christian Mission* (New York: McGraw-Hill Book Co., 1961), pp. 100-108.

Asia had been born. Coke's work led also to the founding in 1818-19 of the Wesleyan Methodist Missionary Society in England. Those who began the Methodist Missionary Society in the United States in 1819 were men who had been influenced by Coke.

Wesley understood his mission to be the revival of true Christianity in England and thence throughout Christendom. Asbury held his mission to be the winning of a new land—the settlers of which had had some background of Christian faith but were largely out of touch with it—to the gospel. Coke saw the world. He believed his mission to be, through the agency of Methodism, spreading the gospel to all mankind. To British and American Methodism Coke bequeathed awareness of still another dimension of mission than those already being furthered vigorously by both Methodisms in their respective homelands.

The Nineteenth-Century Setting

The "great century of Protestant missions"—as Kenneth S. Latourette has termed it—coincided with the peak of Western imperialism. The latter began on the eve of the sixteenth century when Spain and Portugal laid claim to territories in Asia, Africa, and the Americas. In the nineteenth century Britain held India, the Dutch controlled what is now Indonesia, and the European powers forced open China, Japan, and Korea. In the latter countries treaty concessions enabled missionaries to enter. Following the transfer of the Philippines from Spain to the United States in 1898, Protestantism was first introduced in those islands.

Largely in the latter part of the nineteenth century Africa was opened to Western European penetration. During the previous four centuries Western Europeans had taken Africans as slaves from the coastal areas. Livingstone began exploring the Zambesi only in 1852. Not until 1877 did Stanley traverse the length of the Congo River. The Berlin Conference of 1885 established boundaries and ground rules for the European powers in Africa.

Surfeited with scientific miracles, mid-twentieth-century man can scarcely realize with what awe his grandfather in 1900 looked upon that era's unprecedented scientific and technological advance. In 1800 man's travel was still limited to a horse or oxen and to the sailboat. By 1900 man could travel rapidly by train or steamboat anywhere in the world. Air flight was a reality. Under the seas 170,000 miles of cable linked every continent for instantaneous communication. Largely blank on the interior until 1877, the map of Africa was now completely filled in.

What had come to pass in a few decades was unique. Throughout the world the Western nations held dominant power. Men everywhere viewed Western might and technology with wonder. In the non-Western world those with the keenest and most venturesome minds avidly sought Western education—the magic key to Western accomplishment.

Among Western Christians, those sensitive to the signs of the times saw unparalleled opportunity which called for a great missionary response. In an unexampled outpouring of life and substance Protestantism rose to the challenge. American Methodism was in the vanguard. It also shared consciously and unconsciously in the inevitable involvement in Western imperialism.

In their nineteenth-century world-wide outreach Protestant missionaries were vigorous evangelists. They preached, they sought to convert both individuals and groups, and they translated the Bible. Moreover, since Protestants deem it important that everyone be able to read the Bible, missionaries found themselves increasingly involved in teaching people how to read—in educating them. Missions meant schools. Concerned with the whole gospel, missionaries looked upon man in his wholeness and saw the totality of his needs. That often meant, among other considerations, medical care. The Christian medical missions that resulted spurred the rise of modern nursing, special treatment for lepers and the blind, and women's medical training. Protestant missions influenced the life of man everywhere. In all this, American Methodism's missions played an important role.

The Missionary Society and Its First Missions

Early American Methodism was a missionary movement. Its founders and leaders so regarded it. Yet before his death in 1816 Asbury was making what for him was an unaccustomed distinction between "preachers" and "missionaries." Unlike the preacher the missionary volunteered his services for a particular area, was thus consulted and given some choice in his appointment, and was meant "to break up new ground." That distinguishing definition mirrored a profound transformation in American Methodism. What had been viewed initially as a mission was now becoming a settled church with pastors *and also* with missions and missionaries.

Those who believed most strongly that Methodism was a missionary movement were those most convinced by 1816 that Methodism also needed a missionary society. A small group—most of them had been missionaries in Canada and among the Indians—they were Coke's heirs. Some churches had sent missionaries to Asia and Africa. Others had sent missionaries among the Indians. Methodism had done neither. These men knew the importance of Methodism's frontier missions among settlers. They also saw Methodism's other—and as yet unmet—missionary responsibilities. A special society would direct attention to and help meet these needs.

Nathan Bangs was the chief figure in creating in 1819 what one year later became the Missionary Society of the Methodist Episcopal Church. From several quarters opposition to the new society was formidable. Many argued that a church which was a mission needed no missionary society. Yet the society grew slowly. Volunteers were rare. The society had only advisory and auxiliary powers. It could claim only spare-time attention from its officers until 1836, when Bangs became the society's full-time corresponding secretary. With headquarters in New York and a large annual meeting, the society quickly came to rely upon its board of managers. Thus emerged "the Board."

The first period of American Methodist missions—as aided and encouraged by the Missionary Society—ended in 1844. Even before the society's founding and quite apart from it, John Stewart, a mulatto, became Methodism's first missionary to the American Indians. In the Ohio Conference James B. Finley, the perceptive and missionary-minded presiding elder who encouraged Stewart, also provided timely and authoritative support for the then-unknown William Nast, father of all German Methodist work. In another area Martin Ruter, president of Allegheny College, left that post to begin in 1837 the Texas Mission.

Methodism began numerous small missions among Indians in the North and South. Many were abandoned, and most achieved only limited results. Continuing lack of a studied, over-all policy for Indian missions and the yearly appointment of new men to a demanding task that required mature insight and long experience among Indians ill served the cause of a responsible and effective Methodist mission to America's aborigines. Facing a financial crisis in 1841 and 1842 and with other considerations in mind, the society recalled Jason Lee in 1843 and in 1845 liquidated his Oregon Indian Mission. The General Conference of 1844, ready to explode on the urgent question of separation, refused to hear Lee. Broken-hearted, he died the following year.

One mission overseas—that in South America—was begun in 1835-36. The same depleted mission treasury that was finally determinative for Lee led to its hasty abandonment. Most of the work had been among the English-speaking foreigners there.

On the eve of the 1844 division, American Methodism had some 360 missionaries in the homeland but a bare handful in its one overseas mission—that in Liberia. Begun in 1833 by that amazing and undaunted tubercular, Melville B. Cox, the mission flourished briefly. Cox had spent more time on his ocean voyage than he did in Africa. He had planted well in his four months in Africa before death claimed him. His blazing faith attracted others, but by 1844 the mission was slipping into a lethargy from which it was not rescued until William Taylor's arrival in 1884.[5]

2

Missionary Organization

Methodist division was followed in 1845 by a similar division among Baptists and by the final split in 1861 between the Presbyterians. Among Methodists the first visible result for missions was the creation of roughly parallel missionary administrative machinery in the two churches. The second was competition. Baptists and Presbyterians repeated this process.

In the Northern and Southern Churches the passing of decades brought integration of missionary endeavors into the whole life of the church. The General Conferences increasingly recognized their jurisdiction over the missionary societies.

The Northern Church

By 1872 the General Conference was electing the board of managers for the Missionary Society. Meanwhile, many were convinced that Methodism was overemphasizing home missions to the detriment of foreign missions. Among others, Stephen Olin and Bishop James M. Thoburn argued for two missionary societies—one for home and one for foreign missions. Yet repeated memorials to General Conference for two agencies regularly met defeat. The Christian mission, it was argued, is one and ought not to be divided. But what is true theologically may neither evoke response to the fullness of that truth nor in its outworking be administratively practical. Thus, pressure for administrative division continued. By 1907 the work and administration of national missions were separated from those of foreign missions.

In 1906 the charter of the Missionary Society was amended. Henceforth that body was designated the Board of Foreign Missions of the

[5] Full details of these early beginnings are to be found in Barclay, *History of Methodist Missions* I, 203-5, 318-57; II, 113-285.

Methodist Episcopal Church. The General Conference of 1908 adopted the new board's constitution.

To speed the growth of new churches the General Conference of 1864 had created a "General Church Extension Society." One of its chief functions was to raise capital funds and then to lend money to new congregations for erecting their buildings. The link between church extension and home missions roots in the conception of Methodism as a missionary movement. Thus, in 1907, the Board of Home Missions and Church Extension came into being with headquarters in Philadelphia.

A new pattern of organization was also to be seen overseas. The first Mission Annual Conference was authorized for Liberia by the General Conference of 1836. The new body had the same "rights, powers, and privileges" as any Annual Conference, except that it could not elect delegates to General Conference nor could it receive funds from the Book Concern. In 1864 all overseas missions of sufficient strength were made Mission Annual Conferences, and two further limitations were added to the 1836 definition: first, powers of the Mission Annual Conference were exercised only "with the concurrence of the presiding bishop"; and second, these bodies could not vote on constitutional changes proposed in the *Discipline*. These restrictions produced so much objection that in 1868 all former Mission Annual Conferences were made Annual Conferences. The General Conference of 1884 reaffirmed the action of 1868. Yet through changing circumstances, by the final decade of the century some of the overseas Annual Conferences established earlier became Mission Annual Conferences. By 1900 there were outside the United States four missions and seven Mission Annual Conferences. The latter were bound by the restrictions in effect in 1864, except that these conferences could now receive Book Concern funds. By 1920 there were outside the United States and its territories twenty-eight Annual Conferences, thirteen Mission Annual Conferences, and seven missions. In view of the more restricted use of the word "mission" by many denominations in this period and later, one notes that Mission Annual Conferences involved both missionaries and nationals as equal members.

In addition to Mission Annual Conferences, the church after 1856 created missionary bishops, who were appointed to overseas conferences. Elected by the General Conference, they could exercise episcopal jurisdiction only in the areas to which they were elected. In 1920 they were recognized as general superintendents of the whole Methodist Episcopal Church and achieved equal status with other Methodist bishops. In 1939 no provision was made in The Methodist Church for the election of missionary bishops. Yet 1944 legislation enabled the General Conference to allow a Jurisdictional Conference to elect a bishop beyond its specified number in order to provide episcopal oversight for mission areas outside the United States. One group of bishops did resemble in many respects the earlier missionary bishops, namely, those elected after 1939 by Central Conferences. These men could be elected for a specified term; in the Council of Bishops they had the privilege of the floor but no vote.

The Southern Church

What was later to be called the Board of Missions of the Methodist Episcopal Church, South, began in 1845 in Louisville, Kentucky. The General Conference of 1846, enlarging the scope of the work and establishing the new agency with a constitution, entrusted home and foreign missions to the board of managers of the Missionary Society of the Methodist Episcopal Church, South. Working with the bishops that board chose areas of work, selected missionaries, and raised funds. From its original headquarters in Louisville, Kentucky, the Board of Missions in 1856 moved to Nashville, Tennessee.

The General Conference of 1866 provided for a Board of Home Missions in Nashville and a Board of Foreign Missions in Baltimore. The division was expensive and seemed to offer few advantages. As a result, the two agencies were consolidated in 1870 in Nashville. Annual Conference Missionary Auxiliaries took responsibility for missions within their boundaries. Yet belief that home missions were being neglected led in 1910 to creation of the Department of Home Missions under the Board of Missions.

The Southern Church also had Mission Annual Conferences, which differed from those of the Northern Church chiefly in the provision that each could elect one ordained voting delegate to the General Conference. The Southern Church did not provide for the election of missionary bishops as the term was used by the Northern Church.

Women's Societies

In large measure the voluntary missionary society was a creation of the nineteenth century. Also new in that era was the sending of women as missionaries. With several exceptions (for example, under Boniface during the eighth century in Germany) women missionaries were unheard of until the nineteenth century. Then, as married Protestant pastors and laymen took their wives with them on overseas missionary assignments, these women were thrust into a missionary role. By the second half of the century single women were volunteering and being accepted for service overseas.

By 1910 more than half the Protestant missionaries were women. By the same year, of the somewhat more than one thousand medical doctors serving as Protestant missionaries, one third were women. Moreover, in the nineteenth and twentieth centuries women have probably provided the major means for supporting overseas missions. This new undertaking for women may well have had large influence upon the character of modern missions, perhaps most fully in the development of medical, educational, and social welfare work. Methodist missions fully reflect this recent development in missionary outreach.

THE NORTHERN CHURCH

Earliest among the Methodist women's agencies, the Woman's Foreign Missionary Society of the Methodist Episcopal Church (W.F.M.S.) took form in Boston. In that city were Dr. and Mrs. William Butler, Methodism's first missionaries in India. On furlough from India, Mrs. Edwin W. Parker spoke in the church Butler served. Before leaving Asia she had been urged to enlist the interest of American women in Christian work among Indian women. To her Boston audience Mrs. Parker explained India's customs and how in India only women could reach other women with the gospel. The result was an invitation to the Methodist women of Boston to meet—and act! A heavy downpour on March 23, 1869, limited the gathering in Tremont Street Church to eight persons. Undaunted, they formed the W.F.M.S.

With the interdenominational Woman's Union Missionary Society, organized in 1860, and the Woman's Board of Missions (Congregational), begun in 1868, as precedents, the founders of the W.F.M.S. determined to support women missionaries and national Christian teachers in foreign lands. Five weeks later the society's first issue of the *Heathen Woman's Friend* appeared. In 1896 it became the *Woman's Missionary Friend*. The W.F.M.S. was under way—and it grew rapidly.

Convinced of the need for a separate agency to support women missionaries the officers of the W.F.M.S. carried on, undeterred by criticism, opposition, and the pressure of the Missionary Society to become a money-raising auxiliary. The General Conference of 1872 approved the society and its constitution, and twelve years later acknowledged the W.F.M.S. to be part of the church and subject to governance by the General Conference. The women were delighted. And the jeremiads of the critics proved to be the precise opposite of what actually happened. As the W.F.M.S. prospered, every increase in its income was matched by a corresponding increase in the Missionary Society's income. By 1919 the

Woman's Foreign Missionary Society proved to be outstanding in medical and educational missions.

The Woman's Home Missionary Society of the Methodist Episcopal Church (W.H.M.S.) began largely through the efforts of Jennie Culver Hartzell. Wife of the Rev. Joseph C. Hartzell (later missionary bishop in Africa), who had been appointed from Illinois to New Orleans in 1869, Mrs. Hartzell ministered in that city to Negro women. Her first call was to help a young Negro woman dying in a house of prostitution. Other calls from similar quarters and the plight of many in surrounding areas convinced Jennie Hartzell there was work in America that only women missionaries could do.

Little by little, through a decade, support grew for Mrs. Hartzell's endeavors. When the General Conference of 1880 did nothing to further their hopes, some fifty women met in Cincinnati's Trinity Methodist Church, heard Mrs. Hartzell, and in July, 1880, formed the W.H.M.S.

In 1877 Rutherford B. Hayes had gone into the White House. His wife, Lucy Webb Hayes, a graduate of Ohio Wesleyan and an active Methodist, agreed to become president of the W.H.M.S. No mere name lender, she served energetically. Her influence, prestige, and concern greatly aided the society. The General Conference of 1884 that made the W.F.M.S. an agency of the Northern Church did the same for the W.H.M.S.

THE SOUTHERN CHURCH

In the South several local women's missionary societies had been formed before 1844. With the founding of the Southern Church local, conference, and regional societies emerged. Most of these began in the 1870's.

Then from China Mrs. J. W. Lambuth appealed for an unmarried woman to help there in a girls' school. In 1877 Miss Lochie Rankin, already a teacher in a Tennessee Indian school, eagerly responded. Her action galvanized the scattered and separated women's missionary societies in Southern Methodism. In May, 1878, their representatives met in Atlanta and, with General Conference authorization, began what was later to be known as the Woman's Board of Foreign Missions of the Methodist Episcopal Church, South (W.B.F.M.) In 1880 the board began publication of the *Woman's Missionary Advocate*. Local missionary societies made up the member units of the Woman's Foreign Missionary Society, which in turn conducted its overseas operations through its administrative agency, the W.B.F.M.

In 1886 Miss Lucinda B. Helm became general secretary of the Woman's Department of Church Extension. Miss Helm traveled widely and became convinced of the need for larger home-missionary outreach by and among women. Thus was begun in 1890, with General Conference approval, the Woman's Parsonage and Home Mission Society. In 1898 this became the Woman's Home Missionary Society with the Woman's Board of Home Missions (W.B.H.M.) serving as its administrative agency. Miss Belle Harris Bennett was its president.

Belle Harris Bennett holds a unique position in the growth of women's missionary endeavors in the Southern Church. Active from young adulthood in the service of her church and impressed with the need for the special training of new missionaries before their going overseas, she conceived, raised money for, and brought to completion what in 1892 became the Scarritt Bible and Training School in Kansas City, Missouri. In 1924, two years after her death, the Scarritt College for Christian Workers was re-established in Nashville, Tennessee.

Miss Bennett did not serve on the Scarritt staff. She was, rather, an organizer and an able executive with vision who traveled through the entire church. Working always without salary, she founded the Wesley Community Houses and the Bethlehem Centers and also filled responsible posts in interdenominational bodies. Concerned with the total mission of the church, she was the logical choice to head the Woman's Missionary Council.

In 1910 the Woman's Board of Foreign Missions and the Woman's Board of Home Missions were merged into the Woman's Missionary Council. Until her death in 1922 Miss Bennett served as president. As with its counterparts in the Northern Church, the work of the Woman's Missionary Council expanded steadily.

Methodist Protestant Missionary Organizations

The several missionary structures of the Methodist Protestant Church claim separate treatment, since in their founding and functioning they were so closely interrelated.

The first General Conference of the Methodist Protestant Church in 1834 created a Board of Foreign Missions. At the time, "foreign" meant anything on the western frontier. Yet during the next four and one-half decades relatively little outreach developed.

New missionary interest and vigor entered the church in the 1870's, when Methodist Protestant women of Baltimore and Pittsburgh organized missionary societies. Those in Baltimore contributed to missions of the Northern Church, and those in Pittsburgh contributed to the interdenominational Woman's Union Missionary Society. So meaningful was one donation to Miss Elizabeth M. Guthrie, then in Japan under the

W.U.M.S., that on her return she related to the women of Pittsburgh how their gift had enabled her to take two little Japanese girls—who would otherwise have been sold by their parents—and support them in school. The result of her report was the founding in Pittsburgh in February, 1879, of the Woman's Foreign Missionary Society of the Methodist Protestant Church. The General Conference of 1880 made it an official agency of the church.

That General Conference also formed a new Board of Home and Foreign Missions. This agency joined with the Woman's Foreign Missionary Society to send Miss Guthrie to Japan. She died in San Francisco en route, but almost immediately Miss Harriett Brittain, who had had twenty years of service in India under the W.U.M.S., offered herself and was sent to Japan. The Rev. and Mrs. F. C. Klein followed in 1883. Later a mission was begun in India in 1906, and then one in China in 1909.

The General Conference of 1888 created a Board of Foreign Missions and a Board of Home Missions. Specially organized by 1900 to support the latter board, the women in 1916 developed the Woman's Home Missionary Society.

3

Emerging Overseas Missions, 1844-76

Between 1844 and 1876 American Methodism began its missions in Asia's two largest nations, China and India, and in South America's colossus, Brazil. Methodism also took root on the European continent. From 1844 on, Methodist missionary organizations steadily proliferated, and missionary growth is continuous. Except for the mission to South America, those developments originating before 1876 will be listed here, and their growth charted through 1919.

American Methodism's two largest overseas mission fields—in population and assigned missionary resources—were China and India. In China the Northern Church, the Southern Church, and the Methodist Protestant Church were all represented. In India, except for a small mission begun in 1906 by the Methodist Protestant Church, the work was developed entirely by the Northern Church. To the work begun in China in 1847 and in India in 1856 American Methodism had soon committed half its missionaries. Within those years Methodism also rooted itself in Germany. The following pages trace the outgrowth of these beginnings.

China

China holds 25 per cent of the world's people. With its population and ancient, high civilization, China by 1919 had drawn to itself with magnetic force from all churches the largest single concentration of Western Christian missionaries in the non-Western world.

Proud—and distrustful of the Western "barbarians"—China had tried to limit her dealings with aggressive Western traders to particular periods of the year on several offshore islands. Dissatisfied with these restrictions, smarting under treatment as unequals, and unwilling to accept China's ban on the importation of opium, the British launched against China in 1839 the "Opium War." In the resulting treaties of 1842 and 1844 China ceded Hong Kong to the British and opened five major port cities to foreign trade and residence.

The Chinese resented these concessions, and their outbursts of anger brought further European military action. The ensuing treaties of 1858 and 1860 gave to foreigners travel rights throughout China and to missionaries permission to seek the conversion of Chinese. China had been opened at gunpoint to an unwanted Western incursion.

Protestant missionaries entered China's port cities only after 1844 and penetrated the country after 1860. Although a nonbelligerent, America shared in all treaty rights. After the Opium War, America signed her treaty with China in 1844—the year of Methodist division. To the two resulting Methodist bodies China seemed to beckon strongly.

Methodist work in China by 1919 was vast. The Northern Church entered China in 1847, the Southern Church in 1848. The latter confined itself to the central eastern coastal area in the territory surrounding Shanghai and Soochow. The Northern Church, beginning to the south in Foochow, extended its work widely—northward to Peking and westward to the Chengtu-Chungking area. In 1909 the Methodist Protestant Church began its continuing work in China to the far north, in Kalgan, by taking over an American Congregationalist mission.

The first two missionaries to China from the Northern Church, Judson Collins and Moses White, began their ministry in Foochow in 1847. In 1848 Charles Taylor and Benjamin Jenkins brought Southern Methodism to Shanghai.

From the Southern Church came, among others, J. W. Lambuth in 1854 and Young J. Allen in 1860. The American Civil War greatly hindered the missions of the Southern Church. By 1866 only Lambuth and Allen remained in China.

A man of rare ability, Allen began the *Review of the Times* in Chinese in the 1870's to enable Chinese officials and scholars to learn Western ideas. In 1882, to meet the need for English-speaking Chinese in important posts, he founded the Anglo-Chinese College in Shanghai. Before the Revolution of 1911 Allen was one of three or four Westerners eagerly sought out by young Chinese intellectuals and reformers, such as Sun Yat-sen, for counsel. Allen served China's government, edited church papers, and advanced Christian education.

J. W. Lambuth became superintendent of his mission. His son, Walter R. Lambuth, was born in Shanghai, obtained a B.D. and an M.D. in the United States, and returned in 1877 to begin the first organized medical mission in China of the Southern Church. Walter R. Lambuth also opened the mission of his church in Japan, then became a missionary executive, and later was elected to the episcopacy. As a bishop he initiated the mission of the Southern Church in the Congo.

Laura Haygood, known throughout Atlanta for her effective missionary endeavors there, went to China. By 1900, steadily supported by Young J. Allen, she had built the McTyeire School in Shanghai into an outstanding institution for Chinese young women.

The Northern Church spread widely and had as its outstanding pioneer in west and central China Vergil C. Hart. Another prominent figure was Spencer Lewis. Bishop James W. Bashford, who was in China from 1904 to 1910, gave the church statesmanlike episcopal leadership.

The W.F.M.S. took the lead in systematically developing notable Christian medical work. Dr. Lucinda Combs, China's first woman medical missionary, began her work in Peking in 1873 and was soon joined by Dr. Lenora Howard. Called in to treat the wife of Viceroy Li Hung-Chang, Dr. Howard won Madame Li's friendship and respect. Subsequently remarkable opportunities opened for medical expansion and for training Chinese women as doctors. Among the best known of these devoted and respected Chinese Methodist women physicians were Mary Stone, Ida Kahn, Hu King-Eng, and Li Bi-Cu.

The Boxer Uprising of 1900 disrupted some missions. In that anti-Western upheaval no American Methodist missionary lost his life. But Chinese Christians, including many Methodists, suffered grievously and many were killed. In the two decades following, colleges and universities were built. Hwa Nan College for women, begun in 1914 under Miss Lydia A. Trimble in Foochow, graduated its first class with B.A. degrees in 1921. Ginling College for women was begun interdenominationally in

1915, in Nanking, with the support of the W.F.M.S. The Southern Church in 1901 began what became Soochow University.

The Northern Church sped the emergence of some of China's great union (that is to say, interdenominational) universities. In 1910 its Board of Missions joined with other missions to found West China Union University in Chengtu. The Methodist Nanking University, begun in 1889, merged in 1910 with other institutions to become the University of Nanking. Fukien Christian University emerged in 1916 from a union of several colleges. Yenching University (until 1928 Peking University) resulted from a 1916 merger of colleges. Cheeloo University in Tsinan began interdenominationally in 1917.

Among prominent Chinese Methodists was Charles J. Soong. An orphan lad, he ran away to sea, eventually was put ashore at Wilmington, North Carolina, and came under the care of a Southern Methodist minister. Converted, he was graduated from Duke and Vanderbilt Universities. In 1885 the North Carolina Conference appointed him a missionary to China, where in 1886 he became a charter member of the new China Conference of the Southern Church. With an education equal to that of his American colleagues, but given subordinate status and a lower salary, he left the mission. Yet Soong and his wife remained loyal Methodists and reared their children in the church.

The Soongs had a remarkable home, and in it Sun Yat-sen found solace and encouragement. They reared an outstanding family. One daughter married Sun Yat-sen. One married H. H. Kung. The other, Mei-ling, married Chiang Kai-shek, and helped him to achieve a Christian faith. The one son, T. V. Soong, became the guiding financier of the Chinese Nationalist Government.

By 1919 Methodism had been firmly planted and was growing. Chinese Christians held posts of major leadership, and through them came most of the Methodist outreach. Some of those best known internationally came into prominence after 1925. Among them were Dr. Y. C. Yang, president of Soochow University, Dr. Wu I-fang, president of Ginling College, Dr. T. C. Chao of Yenching, and Bishops W. Y. Chen and Z. T. Kaung.

India

From 1498, when Vasco DaGama reached India, the Portuguese began a long period of control over some of India's major coastal areas. From the outset they encouraged Roman Catholic missions. The Dutch, French, and Danes were not long in laying claim to certain other Indian territories. Undaunted by all protests, the British early in the 1600's began their trading and colonizing ventures that led by the eighteenth century to British dominion over much of India.

The East India Company allowed Anglican chaplains for the British people in its territories but resolutely opposed any missions. Thus, William Carey had to begin his work in Danish-held Serampore. At twenty-year intervals Parliament reviewed the East India Company's charter. When it came up for renewal in 1813, William Wilberforce led the fight—and won partial victory—for missionary freedom. Now British missionary societies could enter India. In 1833 the battle was even more intense, the victory more sweeping. From that year anyone from anywhere—trader or missionary—could enter India. Once again British imperial power had opened a great Asian nation to Western incursion.

Methodists from Britain had early begun work in India. James Lynch, one of Coke's group who arrived in Ceylon in 1814, became India's first Methodist missionary. In Ireland in 1824, Lynch met and talked with the young William Butler. Years later William Butler, American Methodism's first missionary to India, declared that he had received the missionary spirit from Lynch. Through Lynch and others Coke's influence carried to Butler.

The Southern Church never undertook work in India, but in 1847, the year of entry in China, the Missionary Society of the Northern Church voted to begin a mission in India. Yet despite numerous appeals, no one responded. Finally, late in 1855, the Rev. William Butler volunteered. A year later he was in India.

Butler had joined the Irish Methodist Conference in 1844. Shortly after his arrival in the United States in 1850 he published a *Compendium of Missions,* reflecting his major interest. Of scholarly bent, with a family, and thinking himself too old, he had initially refrained from responding to the India appeal.

Butler settled in Bareilly, east of Delhi. His assignment was to begin a mission, to go only to those Indians who had not heard the gospel, and to use preaching as his chief method to gain converts. For Indian Methodism "The Butler Era" (1856-64) was a period of concentration—intensive cultivation of a limited area.[6]

Butler had scarcely arrived when in 1857 the Sepoy Mutiny broke all around him. He fled temporarily, but afterward moved Methodism's headquarters to Lucknow.

Convinced that the missionary's basic task is to train an indigenous clergy—then leave, Butler moved decisively. He recruited, built churches,

---

[6] Cf. Marvin H. Harper, *The Methodist Episcopal Church in India* (Lucknow: The Lucknow Publishing House, 1936).

and raised money without reference to the Missionary Society. From the General Conference of 1864 he won Mission Annual Conference status for his work. Butler insisted that Indian pastors be admitted to Annual Conferences as full and equal members with missionaries.

Butler attracted strong men. Among those who came to India under him were Edwin W. Parker, James W. Waugh, James M. Thoburn, and John T. Gracey. By 1864 Indian Methodism comprised thirty-five missionaries, four ordained Indian clergy, and eleven local preachers, who served twelve Indian congregations, sixteen schools, two orphanages, and one publishing house. Judging his work accomplished, Butler returned to America in 1864 and later undertook a similar task in Mexico.

Indian Methodism's second period sharply contrasted with the first. The years from 1865 to 1920 saw vast numerical growth and unplanned geographic expansion. Two men dominated the era—James Mills Thoburn and William Taylor. Born in Ohio of Irish immigrant parents, Thoburn was graduated from Allegheny College. In 1859 he went to India to win that land for Christ. Thoburn's unbounded zeal could not abide comity's restrictions. With marked capacity for leadership, he quickly came to the fore and reversed Butler's policy of concentration. In 1888, at fifty-two, he became a missionary bishop. William Taylor furthered Thoburn's policy of expansion.

After the Sepoy Mutiny many educated Hindus became suspicious of missionaries. As a result missionaries turned increasingly to the depressed classses and outcastes, among whom many found in Christianity the route to a better life. Moreover, recurring plagues and famines—the results of which were alleviated by Christian orphanages, food relief, and medical work—drew many to the Christian faith. When Thoburn reached India, there was a bare handful of Methodists. When he retired in 1908, there were more than 200,000. Ninety per cent had become Christians between 1888 and 1908.[7]

Meanwhile, the women had been active. Its founding initially pointed the W.F.M.S. toward India, and its first two missionaries, Isabella Thoburn (sister of James M.) and Clara Swain, M.D., arrived in Bareilly in January, 1870. The first qualified woman doctor in Asia, Dr. Swain opened a hospital and soon began medical training for women. Isabella Thoburn spent her life in Lucknow educating girls and young women. She opened a college that in 1895 gained government charter. When she died in 1901 of cholera, the institution took her name. The first Christian

[7] Cf. J. Waskom Pickett, *Christian Mass Movements in India* (Cincinnati: The Abingdon Press, 1933).

college in Asia for women, Isabella Thoburn attracted students from all India and from other Asian countries.

In 1878 Lilavati Singh, a homeless waif, came seeking admission to Miss Thoburn's school. She was taken in. Eventually she worked her way through high school and college. When Miss Singh addressed the Ecumenical Missionary Conference in New York in 1900, four thousand people jammed Carnegie Hall to hear her. Impressed by her eloquence and ability Benjamin Harrison declared, "If I had given a million dollars to foreign missions, I should count it wisely invested if it led only to the conversion of that one woman." [8] From 1903 to 1907 Miss Singh was assistant principal of Isabella Thoburn College. Given a year of study in the United States, she was to become principal in 1909. But before her return she died. Her grave is in Elgin, Illinois.

The work of the W.F.M.S. in India expanded rapidly through women well prepared and highly trained. By 1900 nearly one fifth of those who had reached India under W.F.M.S. auspices were medical doctors. Most of the others were teachers. In addition to other educational interests the W.F.M.S. also supported from its founding in 1915 the interdenominational Woman's Christian College in Madras. Under the W.F.M.S. institutional medical work flourished. Besides Clara Swain Hospital in Bareilly, Ellen Thoburn Cowen Memorial Hospital (1910) in Kolar, and small clinics, Methodist women supported the Vellore Christian Medical College, founded in 1918 by Dr. Ida Scudder.

The Leper Colony at Chandag owed much to the remarkable Mary Reed. Serving women in Indian cities from 1885, Miss Reed contracted leprosy. Convinced that God had led her into a ministry among lepers and that her leprosy had been arrested by the petitions of hundreds who were praying for her, this radiant and energetic woman worked at Chandag from 1891 to 1943. And there she died at eighty-nine.

In the winter of 1905-6 in Dhulia, northeast of Bombay, two women of the Methodist Protestant Church began an orphanage. There that church continued its efforts in India, and in the early 1920's built a hospital. Edith Lacy, M.D., who arrived in 1927, was its first physician.

William Taylor's four years in India deserve attention. Late in 1870 and at Thoburn's invitation Taylor arrived in India. From his first sermon he set a new course for Indian Methodism.

Taylor was unique. Landing in San Francisco in 1849 with his wife and tiny children, this tall Methodist quickly became a commanding religious figure in California. Eschewing church support during his seven years there Taylor provided for himself.

To meet the debt—for which he had become responsible—on a sea-

[8] *Ecumenical Missionary Conference* (New York, 1900), I, 47.

man's mission, Taylor wrote a book on his California experiences. Wherever he went, he sold copies. Later, sale of his books supported him and some of his missions. In 1856 he began an evangelistic tour of the eastern United States and Canada. By 1862 he was in Britain. Then he proceeded to Australia, where his street preaching is said to have resulted in the conversion of thousands. In 1866 Taylor was in South Africa. His revivals marked the first vigorous expansion of the British Methodism already in that area. Campaigns in England, Europe, and the British West Indies ensued before Taylor's India period. Later he planted Methodist missions in South America and then worked for twelve years in Africa! This was the man who reached India in 1870.

From 1856 to 1870 Methodism in India had concentrated on the Indians. Any ministry to English-speaking people was incidental to the major task. Taylor changed all this. He judged that Methodism's revivalistic approach would produce the largest results among inactive English-speaking Christians already in India—the British in government, commercial, or military service and the Anglo-Indians. His plan was to revitalize the nominal Christians—mainly of Anglican or Roman Catholic background—and enlist them in winning India's masses. They would be self-supporting. Taylor saw that Christian Westerners overseas must witness to their faith. He seems not to have seen that any real penetration of the gospel would have to come through Indians and the languages of India.

Taylor went everywhere. He preached for all denominations that would accept him, and in the process aroused widespread opposition. When pulpits were closed to him, he preached in the streets. He organized his converts into Methodist societies. In Bombay, Bangalore, Madras, Calcutta, and elsewhere, English-speaking Methodist congregations grew. Taylor's work resulted eventually in several new conferences.

Taylor left in 1874 to join Dwight L. Moody in London. But what of his four whirlwind years in India? He spread Methodism across that land. He organized many self-supporting English-speaking churches, and became Methodism's apostle to the Anglo-Indians. He won some notable adherents. The saintly George Bowen of Bombay, a Congregationalist missionary for twenty-three years, saw the worth of Taylor's work and espoused it—in his own way—in 1872. The young engineer William F. Oldham, born in India of Roman Catholic parents, attended a Taylor meeting to make sport, but was converted and became one of Methodism's best-known missionary bishops. On the whole, Taylor's revivals renewed hundreds; his flagrant breaches of comity angered many more; but his efforts had little direct influence on the Indian population.

Taylor's work explains Methodism's geographic extent in India. But

Methodism's remarkable expansion among Indians resulted from vigorous attention given to outcaste groups, first by Thoburn and later by others. In Uttar Pradesh (then the United Provinces), on the Northern Gangetic Plain and India's most populous province, there were in 1900 about 109,000 Indian Christians. Of this number 96,500, or 88 per cent, were Methodists. Almost all had come from the lowest caste or outcaste groups.[9]

By 1914 American Methodist missions were found throughout India, but 80 per cent of the members were in the North, the fruits of mass movements among the depressed classes. This membership then constituted the largest church in India resulting from American missionary auspices and was exceeded in size only by the Roman Catholics, the Syrian Christians, and the Anglicans.

Methodism's mode of missionary operation came in for strong censure. No believer in geographic comity, Thoburn held that Methodism should move in where it wished and proceed in harmony with other Christians already at work. At the third Decennial Missionary Conference at Bombay, 1892-93, Methodists encountered vigorous criticism for disregarding comity and for receiving as members many already under discipline in other denominations. The German historian Richter accused Methodists in India of "recklessly intruding" on others' work.[10] Indeed, Methodism became involved in so many controversies on comity that in 1912 the Central Conference in India agreed that because of earlier undisciplined expansion Methodism should henceforth exercise the utmost caution and follow a policy of concentration.

To provide an education for young men the church began in 1889 Lucknow Christian College. Yet because of its constituency in India Methodism concentrated on primary and secondary schools rather than, as in China, devoting large resources to higher education. This background helps to explain the growth and importance of the Lucknow Publishing House. Its books for the newly literate and others proved an important part of Methodism's mission.

Among notable figures in Indian Methodism after 1910 were Jashwant Rao Chitambar and E. Stanley Jones. Taught in Sunday school by Isabella Thoburn, first graduate of Lucknow Christian College, and challenged to serve the church by John R. Mott, Chitambar was Indian Methodism's most powerful preacher. He was a linguist, writer, administrator, and man of prayer, and in 1930 became Methodism's first Indian bishop.

[9] Julius Richter, *A History of Missions in India*, tr. Sidney H. Moore (Edinburgh: Oliphant Anderson & Ferrier, 1908), p. 234.
[10] *Ibid.*, p. 212.

E. Stanley Jones was teaching at Asbury College when the Board of Missions of the Northern Church wrote to ask if he would go to India. After an inner struggle he agreed. He arrived there in 1908 and within a few years demonstrated his unusual ability to convey the gospel to India's intellectuals. Missionary, writer, and world evangelist, Jones came into greatest prominence after 1920. Yet by that year, and in India, the course of his life had been set.

By 1919 India's Methodist Church had become and was to remain the largest body overseas begun by American Methodist missions. In the years following it experienced further rapid growth, largely through mass movements from the depressed classes.

Europe

Until the end of World War I American Methodism was represented in Europe only through the Northern Church. The missionaries—always few in number—were usually nationals returning to their homelands. The Board of Missions also on occasion supported missionary endeavors undertaken by the tiny new European Methodist Churches in other European countries. Thus by 1919 American Methodist missions had been felt directly or indirectly in Germany, Norway, Sweden, Denmark, Finland, Russia, Yugoslavia, Bulgaria, Lithuania, Latvia, Estonia, Austria, Hungary, Switzerland, France, Spain, and Italy. The Southern Church began work in Belgium, Czechoslovakia, and Poland after World War I.

Although a tiny minority, Methodism took a firm hold in Germany and Scandinavia and from there spread elsewhere on the continent. Some of the earliest Methodist growth in Europe rooted in British Methodism.

Methodism entered Germany through the spontaneous activity of German laymen converted under Methodism in England or America who then returned to their homeland. As they told curious friends and neighbors about their own transformation, some of these responded and determinedly began Methodist societies. Thus, Christoph Gottlieb Müller returned to Germany in 1831 after his conversion in a London Methodist society and watched the repeated account of his religious experience produce new Methodists.

Meanwhile in the United States, through William Nast's pioneering efforts, Methodism spread among German immigrants.[11] When these wrote to families across the sea about their new-found faith, they elicited requests for Methodist preachers there. In 1849 the Board of Bishops of the Methodist Episcopal Church sent the first missionary from America

[11] For the story of German-American Methodists, see chapter 22.

to Germany. He was Ludwig S. Jacoby, a German-born immigrant converted under Nast. Müller had already begun several congregations in southern Germany and welcomed Jacoby's efforts to the north in Bremen.

A young farm boy, Ehrhardt Wunderlich, converted in Dayton, Ohio, returned to Saxony and to his brother's farm in 1850. Wunderlich converted his brother Friedrich, and both became founders of Methodism in eastern Germany. Ludwig Nippert and Heinrich Nuelsen, both German-born, were among others appointed by the Board of Missions to Germany. German Methodism confronted sharp opposition, but it grew steadily. In 1897 the British Wesleyan Methodist Church and the American Methodist Episcopal Church united in Germany. In 1912 Bishop John L. Nuelsen, son of Heinrich, went to Europe to supervise all continental Methodism. By 1914 German Methodists totaled nearly 30,000.

In Switzerland the first Methodists pointed to British origins. The small but vigorous Methodist Church in Switzerland by 1919 had sprung from the preaching of Methodists from Germany in 1856.

In Austria and Hungary Methodism began in 1870, when Christian Dieterle went there from Germany. When Baroness von Langenau, widow of the Austrian ambassador to Russia, became a Methodist, her patronage facilitated the hitherto restricted work. Initial ties were with British Methodism, but supervision was given to American Methodism. In 1900 Otto Melle from Dresden began work in Hungary, and in 1911 the Mission Conference of Austria-Hungary resulted.

The Yugoslavia Mission Conference began at the end of World War I. It resulted largely from efforts of German Methodists supported first from the United States and then from Switzerland and Germany.

In the nineteenth century Russia contracted with German craftsmen to work there. One of these men, Heinrich Ramke, went to America, became a Methodist, and with missionary zeal returned to Russia in 1893. There he organized a Methodist society. Beginning in 1889 Finnish Methodists also worked in Russia. American Methodism supported a missionary of German descent in St. Petersburg (Leningrad) from 1907 into the 1920's.

Methodist missions in Scandinavia relate to a ship bought by the Missionary Society in 1845, rechristened the "John Wesley," and berthed permanently at a New York City river pier. Widely and popularly known as the "Bethel Ship," it had as its missionary-captain O. G. Hedström. A Swedish sailor stranded in New York, Hedström was converted, became a Methodist preacher, and served the Bethel Ship from 1845 to 1875. Swedish immigrants entered America through New York City, and many sought out the Bethel Ship. It was instrumental in developing a strong Scandinavian Methodism in the North Central United States.

Norwegian Methodism began on the Bethel Ship, where Ole Petersen, a Norwegian sailor, was converted in 1846. Visiting Norway in 1849 he told family and friends about his new Christian life. A year later, in the United States, Petersen became a lay missionary among Norwegians in Iowa. Meanwhile, those among whom he had spoken in Norway appealed to America for a preacher. Ordained in 1853, Petersen went under mission board appointment to Norway. Methodism grew there, and in 1856 the Danish-born Christian Willerup, who in America became a Methodist, went as superintendent. In 1876 the Norway Annual Conference was organized.

The first Methodist preaching in Denmark seems to have been done by Boie Smith, a Dane converted on the Bethel Ship. Subsequently, Willerup was sent from Norway in 1858 to Denmark. Six months later in Copenhagen the first Methodist society emerged, and from its spreading influence came in 1911 the Denmark Annual Conference.

Methodism first entered Sweden in 1826 from Britain but soon dwindled. Methodism's second entry occurred when John Peter Larson (or Larsson), a sailor converted on the Bethel Ship, returned to his homeland in the early 1850's. He aroused great interest, and in 1854 the Missionary Society aided him. In 1855 it appointed him a lay missionary. Other Swedes, most of whom had had contact with the Bethel Ship, returned to their homeland as lay preachers and organized and led Methodist societies. Liberalization of Sweden's religious laws in 1873 made possible three years later the Sweden Annual Conference.

Two Swedish-speaking Finnish brothers converted on the Bethel Ship returned to Finland in 1866 and began to preach. With help from Sweden the work they initiated grew and by 1887 was spreading among the much larger Finnish-speaking population. By 1923 Finnish Methodism had two Annual Conferences.

In several European countries Methodism entered in small force, convinced that Protestant witness was required. Thus, in part at the invitation of Congregationalists, American Methodism went into Bulgaria in 1857 and began the Bulgarian Mission Conference in 1892. American Methodism entered France in 1907, but eventually turned over several congregations to the Switzerland Annual Conference and merged most of the others with the French Reformed Church. In Spain Francisco Albricias opened his first Model School for children in 1897 and began conducting Methodist worship. In 1919-20 he offered two schools to the Methodists, and they became the nucleus of the small Spain Mission. American Methodism began work in Italy in 1873. Eight years later the Italy Conference was formed.

Methodism began mainly among German-speaking people in Lithuania in 1904 and in Latvia in 1912. With Methodism's entry into Estonia in 1921 outreach in these three countries was designated the Baltic and Slavic Mission.

As a result of its determination to help meet physical need in Europe after World War I, the Southern Church after consultation with the Northern Church in 1920 began relief work in Belgium, Czechoslovakia, and Poland. Response in Belgium to these endeavors led in 1922 to the Belgian Methodist Mission, which nine years later became an Annual Conference. In 1932 the few American missionaries then in Belgium were withdrawn. Belgian Methodism in 1959 counted somewhat less than 2,700 members.

Work in Czechoslovakia arose in similar fashion, and the exodus of some two million Czechs from the Roman Catholic Church in eight years following World War I aroused hopes that Protestant bodies would gain new adherents. Yet despite the fact that the church had strong preachers, Methodism in Czechoslovakia by 1959 had a constituency of some 6,600, with less than 2,100 full members.

Southern Methodist relief centers in Poland often resulted in the formation of small Methodist congregations. On the eve of World War II, the Polish Conference had thirteen congregations and more than 1,100 members. Twenty years later it had twenty-seven ministers and was conducting a highly popular English-language school that enrolled 3,000 students.

4

Methodist Missions Overseas, 1876-1919

Geographically speaking, most of Methodism's overseas outreach had its origins between 1876 and 1919. Although in a few instances (Japan, Brazil, Argentina, and Mexico) these missions originated somewhat before 1876, they had their major growth after 1876 and thus are treated as belonging to this second major period.

East Asia

In East Asia the Northern Church, the Methodist Protestant Church, and the Southern Church in that order entered Japan. In Korea only the Northern Church and the Southern Church developed missions.

JAPAN

Western traders and Roman Catholic missionaries first entered Japan in the mid-sixteenth century. Yet within a few years Christianity was forbidden, and Japan sealed itself off against European contact.

By the mid-nineteenth century the westward movement of the American frontier to the Pacific Coast generated a momentum of interest that thrust the United States across the Pacific and involved this nation actively and increasingly in Asian affairs. To facilitate commerce and establish effective international political relations, the United States sent Commodore Matthew G. Perry to Japan in 1853 to "open" that nation. The necessary accord was signed early in 1854, and Japan soon signed treaties with other Western nations.

In 1868 Japan embarked upon an unprecedented period of rapid westernization. Aware of what was happening in Asia and elsewhere, Japanese statesmen became convinced that in a world where Western nations held power and achieved their will, Japan could gain power and respect in only one way—by westernizing itself. Japan's government and army followed the Prussian model, its new educational system the Anglo-Saxon pattern. Industrialization proceeded apace. Because it was the religion of the West, many leading Japanese commended Christianity as a religion for Japan.

Related to this entire adaptive process—the aim of which was power— was the Sino-Japanese War of 1894-95. In what was primarily a struggle for control of Korea Japan won a major victory. The peace treaty recognized Korean independence, but after centuries of Chinese dominance Korea was to come increasingly under Japanese control. Russian penetration of northern Korea brought on the Russo-Japanese War of 1904-5. Once again Japan won a decisive victory—this time over a Western power —and among other treaty rights received Korea virtually as a protectorate.

In its own eyes Japan had become the equal of the Western nations. Yet when these refused to grant Japan equal status, that land experienced a strong anti-Western reaction. Industrialization continued. The transformation within a single generation was unparalleled. But only Japan's outward appearance and actions had changed. The Japanese soul remained largely what it had been.

The change in Japan's pattern of life was brought about by intellectuals, professional people, and the well-to-do. These were the urbanized national leaders. As in all such massive modifications of culture the cities changed first. The rural areas changed very slowly. From the upper-middle class—those seeking rapid westernization for their country—came those who embraced Christianity. Few others did. All Protestantism in Japan must be seen against this unique background.

As soon as the first treaties were signed, several of the larger American Protestant bodies entered Japan. The Southern Church in 1858 determined to begin a mission there, but the Civil War long delayed this action. The Northern Church arrived earlier through the efforts of Robert S. Maclay. Maclay had begun his missionary career in 1848 in China. In 1870, with a statesman's vision, he had urged the Missionary Society to enter Japan. Two years later, while on furlough, he again pressed his point. This time the society concurred and appointed Maclay to begin the mission. This he did in 1873. In 1874 the W.F.M.S. entered.

The Methodist Protestant Church in 1880 determined to begin its first overseas mission. That enterprise was launched in the same year with the arrival in Japan of Miss Harriett Brittain, a missionary of the church who drew her support from the Woman's Foreign Missionary Society. In Yokohama she began schools and Sunday schools. In 1883 the Board of Home and Foreign Missions sent its first ordained missionary to Japan, the Rev. F. C. Klein. The first congregation, with twelve members, was organized in 1886 in Yokohama. A year later Klein moved to Nagoya, where he and his wife laid foundations for outreach that came to include a boys' school, a girls' school, and another congregation. In 1891 work began in Shizuoka, midway between Yokohama and Nagoya. The mission grew steadily but never claimed more than a few missionaries. By 1919 there were nine Methodist Protestant missionaries in Japan, with eighteen congregations embracing a total membership of nearly 2,100. The Methodist Protestant Church confined itself to developing schools at the primary and lower secondary level.

In 1886 the Southern Church sent the James W. Lambuths and O. A. Dukes from China to begin work in Kobe, with Walter R. Lambuth, M.D., to superintend the mission.

In part by happy accident and in part by agreement the several Methodist bodies, including the Methodist Church of Canada, effectively covered much of Japan. Although lacking any co-ordinating agency, they co-operated well. This co-operation and the unique situation then existing in Japan facilitated the creation in 1907 of the Japan Methodist Church—the first autonomous church resulting from American Methodist missions. The Methodist Protestants did not enter the union.

Christianity in Japan had a burst of growth from 1883 to 1889. A nationalistic reaction in the following decade slowed the rate of growth. After 1900 Methodism and other churches grew slowly but steadily. Those who came into the faith were business and professional men, government workers, and the well educated. This helps to explain the high caliber and ability of Japanese Christian leaders. The churches largely failed to reach the common people, but the numerically small Christian community had considerable influence on Japanese life.

With the Japanese government's early insistence upon universal education the churches could concentrate on Christian education of high quality. Among the outstanding Methodist schools was Tokyo's Aoyama Gakuin, begun in 1883 with a gift from John F. Goucher of Baltimore. Begun in 1889, Kwansei Gakuin honors Walter R. Lambuth as its founder. In 1912 it added college courses, and twenty years later became a university. Woman's Christian College of Japan, begun interdenominationally in Tokyo in 1918, from the outset enlisted W.F.M.S. support. It was the first college for women in Japan. Hiroshima Jo Gakuin, begun in 1886 by the Southern Church, had Miss Nannie B. Gines as its president for more than three decades. It began college level instruction for women in 1920.

From its beginning Methodism in Japan produced an unusually able leadership. The first convert was the Hon. Sen Tsuda, pioneer of scientific agriculture in Japan. Equally noteworthy was American-educated Sennosuke Ogata, who became acting president of Aoyama Gakuin in 1907.

No one surpassed the brilliant and able Yoitsu Honda. Of the samurai class, he became a Christian in 1872. Honda could have achieved high place in the national government, but in 1874 he chose to become a Protestant minister. In Hirosaki he organized a union church and became a fast friend of John Ing, the resident Methodist missionary. When Ing left in 1876, he asked Honda and the congregation whether they preferred to remain a local, independent group or to become Methodists and have world-wide ties. Honda chose Methodism, and his interest in Christian unity led him to become primarily responsible for bringing together the three Methodist bodies that in 1907 formed the Japan Methodist Church. That church elected him its first bishop.

First chairman of the Japan Y.M.C.A., one of seventeen Asians at the World Missionary Conference, Edinburgh, 1910, and frequently chairman of interdenominational bodies, Yoitsu Honda holds a place of honor in the history of Christianity in Japan. Dead at sixty-five of typhoid, he was succeeded in 1912 by Bishop Hirawa. Some years later Honda's nephew, Yoshimune Abe, became a bishop.

Formation in 1907 of the Japan Methodist Church did not end the sending of missionaries to Japan. They came as before, but did not organize and oversee churches. Their efforts were wholly contributory to the development of the Japan Methodist Church. By the end of

World War I, Japanese Methodism numbered some 25,000 baptized members.

OKINAWA

After centuries of varying ties with China and Japan, the Ryukyu Islands in 1879 were made a province of Japan. Sending Japanese pastor-missionaries to Okinawa, largest of the islands, the mission of the Northern Church in Japan began work in the Ryukyus in 1892, although there had been earlier contacts. With its independence, the Japan Methodist Church did not carry the work, and it remained the responsibility of the American mission. Henry B. Schwartz, the first American missionary, settled there in 1907. A decade later another came. Results were limited, and on the eve of World War II all Protestants in Okinawa numbered less than one thousand.

KOREA

Three great countries—China, Russia, and Japan—surround Korea. Under Chinese hegemony for centuries, this strategic peninsula came increasingly under Japanese influence. In 1910 Japan annexed Korea. A religious, cultural, and military bridge between the mainland and Japan and dominated by its larger neighbors, Korea has had an unhappy history.

After several fruitless attempts by the United States and others to force their way to Seoul, an American naval officer in 1882 negotiated a treaty through Chinese Viceroy Li Hung-Chang, then in charge of Chinese-Korean relations, by which, among other privileges, the United States was given access to Korea. Treaties between Korea and other Western powers soon followed.

Through the efforts of John Ross, a Presbyterian missionary in Mukden who had translated the New Testament into Korean, some Koreans had had a portion of the Bible for nearly a decade before 1884, when the first Protestant missionaries entered Korea. When they arrived, they found Shinto, Buddhism, and Confucianism already present. They also discovered Shamanism, a religion of spirit worship and exorcism, to be the real religion of Korea's multitudes.

Despite its initial unpromising appearance, Korea proved to be a land in which Christianity could take root and grow vigorously among the masses. That expansion has continued unabated, but Korean Protestantism has suffered from grievous internal quarreling, much of it related to biblical and theological interpretation, some to political differences, and some to problems of authority in the church.

The history of Christianity in Korea since the mid-1880's has been predominantly one of Protestantism, and that largely of the Presbyterian and Methodist Churches. The two began with numerical equality, but the Presbyterians outgrew the Methodists.

Appointed to survey the Korean situation for the Northern Church, Robert S. Maclay reached Seoul in 1884. He gained permission for Methodist educational and medical missions. Meanwhile, John F. Goucher, impressed by a Korean delegation in the United States, gave $5,000 to begin a Methodist Korean mission. He wisely stipulated that an able clergyman and a medical doctor be sent.

William B. Scranton, M.D., and his wife, and the Rev. and Mrs. Henry G. Appenzeller went to Korea in 1885. With them was Mary F. Scranton, widow of a Methodist minister and mother of the young doctor. She went as a W.F.M.S. appointee to begin work among Korea's women. With Japan as their advance base, the Appenzellers reached Korea but were turned back because of political turmoil. Scranton then went alone, made contact with a Presbyterian physician in charge of a government hospital —appointed because he had saved the King's nephew—in Seoul, and was welcomed to the staff. From this advantageous position Scranton soon purchased land near the American legation and the Presbyterian mission. Thus began the mission of the Northern Church in Korea in the summer of 1885.

Scranton opened a dispensary, his mother the first girls' school in Korea. Beginning with only one ten-year-old girl, and after several major transformations, this school eventually grew into Ewha Woman's University. Appenzeller started the first Protestant school for boys in Korea. The first convert came in 1886 from the Japanese legation.

From the outset Methodists and Presbyterians co-operated. Horace G. Underwood of the Presbyterian Mission and Appenzeller formed an outstanding interdenominational team. With several others they organized a Bible Committee in 1887 and produced translations together.

In part because of official restrictions on evangelism, in the mission's first years only medical work grew rapidly. Among those physicians who arrived early was Rosetta Sherwood. In 1892 in Seoul she began what eventually became the Lillian Harris Memorial Hospital—and also married William J. Hall, M.D., who died of typhus two years later. After some time in the United States Dr. Rosetta Sherwood Hall returned to Korea and opened a woman's hospital in Pyengyang. Pioneering in work for the deaf and blind, she began in 1928 the Woman's Medical Institute in Seoul to give women medical training.

By the early 1890's Methodist missionaries were spreading throughout Korea, with medical work usually opening the way. Schools were begun, and Bible translation and the printing of Christian materials proceeded apace. An 1893 arrival, Lulu E. Frey, began teaching in Ewha School; in 1906 she became principal, and was the person most responsible for developing Ewha College in 1910. Ewha University emerged in 1945.

Through invitation from Baron T. H. Yun, the Southern Church entered Korea in 1895. A member of a political group that wanted Korea to westernize, Yun had earlier been driven from his homeland, and went to Shanghai. There, under the tutelage of Young J. Allen and A. P. Parker, he became a Christian. Later he studied at Emory and Vanderbilt Universities and while in the United States made a gift to the Southern Church to start an industrial training school in Korea. With a more favorable political climate in Korea, Yun was recalled from his teaching position in Shanghai's Anglo-Chinese College to become a cabinet minister. While in that post, he invited the Southern Church to enter Korea. The first missionaries, already with China experience, were C. F. Reid, C. T. Collyer, and Mrs. Josephine Peel Campbell.

The Presbyterians had begun Chosen Christian College (now known as Yonsei University). In 1915 both Methodist Churches joined the Presbyterians to strengthen what then became a union institution. Similarly the Methodists joined with the Presbyterians in 1913, thirteen years after its founding, to support Severance Union Medical College.

The Bible Committee, begun by Underwood and Appenzeller, completed its New Testament translation in 1900. With help from the National Bible Society of Scotland, the American Bible Society, and the British and Foreign Bible Society, the same interdenominational body published its Old Testament translation in 1910. Wide circulation of the Scriptures was a major factor in the highly fruitful evangelism that followed.

The appearance of the New Testament—Koreans immediately found meaning in the striking political parallels between Korea then and Palestine nineteen hundred years earlier—and the formation of Bible classes throughout Korea resulted from 1905 to 1910 in revival and rapid growth. In 1907 the two Methodist Churches organized the Union Biblical Institute, which in 1910 became the Methodist Union Theological Seminary. At the suggestion of the Southern Church the co-operating missions launched in 1909-10 the Million Movement ("a million souls for Christ"). Yet from 1911 to 1919 the churches grew slowly. In 1920 they began another period of striking advance.

Many have noted the rapid growth of the Korean church. Without wealth, it has been largely self-supporting. With the evangelistic imperative widely felt, it has been self-propagating. Indeed, the overwhelming majority of Korean Christians have come into the faith through the lay witness of other Koreans. In 1920 Korean Methodism counted more than

25,000 members. As the second thirty-five years of Korean Methodism were to show, this was only a beginning.

Southeast Asia

Through the Northern Church, and principally by extension from its mission base in India, American Methodism entered Southeast Asia. In the period here under survey, work in Burma, Malaya, Singapore, Sarawak, West Borneo, Sumatra, Java, and the Philippines was begun. With the Philippines a major exception, most of these beginnings by 1919 were numerically small. Methodism most frequently developed among immigrant Chinese and Indians in these areas.

BURMA

A Buddhist land, Burma through British administration was tied closely to India. Among the predominant Burmans the Christian gospel made little progress. Most Christians came from among minority hill people such as the Karens, the Kachins, and the Shans. Christian work also developed among the Chinese and Indian population. The churches emerging from American Baptist missions in Burma accounted for more than 80 per cent of Burma's Christians. Most of the remainder were Anglicans. Relatively speaking, the Methodist group was minuscule.

Because of the Tamils and Telugus—people from South India—in Rangoon, the South India Conference initially took responsibility for Burma. Invitations came from Indian converts there, and Rangoon first appeared as an appointment in 1878. At first James M. Thoburn asked William Taylor to send a missionary to Rangoon. Then in 1880 and under Thoburn's direction the newly appointed J. E. Robinson built a strong English-speaking congregation in Rangoon. In 1881 the W.F.M.S. began a girls' school. In 1887 William F. Oldham succeeded Robinson as supervisor in Burma, taking up residence in Singapore, then part of the Burma District.

In 1886, when the Bengal Conference was organized, it included the Burma District. Only in 1900 did non-English-speaking work begin in Burma. In the following year the Burma Mission Conference was organized. Its growth was limited, its constituency diverse. Within two decades it included a Chinese, an English, an Indian, and two Burmese Districts.

MALAYA AND SINGAPORE

Singapore became a great naval base and the strategic island head-quarters from which Britain watched all its Far Eastern and Pacific

interests. Its population included more Chinese than Malays and held a
sizable Indian minority.

The South India Conference in 1884 appointed William F. Oldham as
missionary to Singapore. He and Thoburn arrived early in 1885 and
began a self-supporting church among English-speaking people. Oldham
soon opened a school for Chinese boys. It flourished from the outset.
He also began schools for the children of English residents and for
Tamil boys. At Oldham's urging the W.F.M.S. agreed to conduct a
mission in Singapore. Miss Sophia Blackmore, an Australian recruited by
Oldham, was the first appointee. In 1887 she started a school for Tamil
girls, a year later one for Chinese girls.

Captain William G. Shellabear, commanding officer of the Royal
Engineers in Singapore, met the Oldhams in 1886, began to attend the
Methodist church, and participated in its work. Returning briefly to
England he resigned his commission, married, and having been made a
missionary—by Thoburn's action—of the American Methodist Society,
returned to Singapore in 1890. Shellabear was a rare find—an able
linguist, skilled in Malay, a man of administrative ability, and a warm
and convinced Christian. While in England, and at Oldham's suggestion,
he had learned how to operate a printing house. He then brought with
him to Singapore sufficient equipment to establish a mission press and
began *The Malaysia Message* in 1891. Shellabear found his major work
in producing Christian literature for the Malays and overseeing the
mission press. He left Southeast Asia in 1919 for reasons of health and
between 1921 and his death in 1947 held teaching posts at Drew Theological Seminary and the Kennedy School of Missions in Hartford.

From Singapore Methodist work spread to the Malay Peninsula—to
Malacca, Kuala Lumpur, Ipoh, and other cities. Thoburn in 1893
organized the Malaysia Mission Conference. That body became the
Malaysia Annual Conference in 1902 and came also to include missions
in Java, Sumatra, West Borneo, and Sarawak. Except for Sarawak, which
remained in the Malaysia Conference, these fields in 1918 became the
Netherlands Indies Mission Conference.

WEST BORNEO, SUMATRA, AND JAVA

Dr. H. L. Emil Leuring from the German Methodist Conference
arrived in Singapore in 1889 and preached among the city's German
residents. Early in 1890 he and Benjamin F. West, M.D., both members
of and authorized by the Bengal-Burma Conference of the Methodist
Episcopal Church, traveled to Pontianak, West Borneo, then went 250
miles inland on the Kapuas River to Dyak territory. West and Leuring

returned to Singapore—West by way of China for language study—and served there among the Chinese. In 1891 the conference again commissioned Leuring to open a mission in British North Borneo (Brunei); but convinced it was impracticable, he resumed his work in Singapore.

A Methodist mission in West Borneo, then under Dutch control, was begun in 1906 and continued for some years, usually with one missionary dividing his time between Pontianak and Singkawang. Each city had an Anglo-Chinese school and a Chinese church. Shellabear in 1914 pointed to Muslim efforts to convert the Dyaks inland, but his voice was unheeded.

In 1893 Benjamin F. West traveled in Sumatra, and in 1894 two W.F.M.S. missionaries from Singapore went there selling Christian literature. West went again to Sumatra in 1897, and was followed in 1904 by the Rev. George F. Pykett, an Englishman who served the American Methodist Malaysia Mission from 1891 to 1932 as an outstanding educator. Pykett's visit in Medan in northern Sumatra resulted in the opening of a school for Chinese. When the school soon closed, its Indian business manager, S. S. Pakianathan, went to Palembang in southern Sumatra and opened two schools. In 1910 two Chinese opened a school and a church in Medan, and two years later the Rev. William T. Ward arrived. Methodism took root among Medan's Chinese. In 1919 the Rev. and Mrs. Mark Freeman were appointed the first Methodist missionaries to Palembang.

Methodist missionaries in 1905 entered Djakarta (Batavia), then Buitenzorg, and in 1909 Soerabaya, on Java. The mission was mainly among the Chinese and included schools and churches, but an approach was made to the Muslim Malays.

In 1922 North Sumatra became a separate mission. Three years later the North Sumatra Mission Conference was formed, and in 1927 Methodist work in Java was transferred to Sumatra. In 1929 what had been the Netherlands Indies Mission Conference and the North Sumatra Conference became the Sumatra Mission Conference.

SARAWAK (NORTHWEST BORNEO)

Methodism in Sarawak had an unusual beginning. Uong Nai Siong, a Chinese Christian familiar with the Pilgrims' migration to American shores, decided to venture in Borneo a similar project with Chinese. From the Rajah of Sarawak he gained permission for his settlement. The majority of these Chinese were Methodists from Fukien. The first years in Borneo were exceedingly difficult. Half the colony of one thousand died. Yet in 1902, when the peripatetic Benjamin F. West touched briefly in Sarawak, he discovered Chinese local preachers at work. In 1903 James M. Hoover, already having served among the Chinese in Penang, went to Sarawak and there spent his life among the Chinese. The mission among the Ibans (Sea Dyaks) was only beginning at the time of Hoover's death in 1935.

PHILIPPINE ISLANDS

The United States received the Philippines from Spain in 1898. Under Spanish rule for nearly 350 years, the Philippines were largely Roman Catholic, but held also 500,000 Muslims. American Protestants sent missionaries to the islands beginning in 1899. Although separation of church and state prevailed under American rule, Protestant missionaries and Filipino pastors frequently encountered harassment and occasionally physical harm. Much more important in influencing Protestantism's slow growth was the massive social pressure exerted by the dominant culture against the acceptance of the Protestant faith.

At the urging of a Methodist layman in Manila, Bishop James M. Thoburn visited that city in March, 1899. He licensed his host, Mr. W. A. Prautch, as a local preacher and made arrangements with an army chaplain for holding Methodist worship. Five months later the Rev. Nicolas Zamora, a convert, was put in charge of the earliest Methodist work in the Philippines. In February, 1900, the W.F.M.S. sent the first missionaries. In 1901 Homer C. Stuntz became superintendent of the mission.

The Evangelical Union of the Philippines, a Protestant co-ordinating body, came into being in 1901. Through it comity agreements were reached that assigned Methodists to Manila—with others—and to the area north of Manila on Luzon. Initially the Philippines were a district of the Malaysia Conference, but in 1905 they were designated the Philippine Islands Mission Conference. Three years later that body became an Annual Conference.

For several reasons the first missionaries were transferred to other fields, and in 1902 W.F.M.S. work was temporarily interrupted; but from 1903 it was continuous. In that year Miss Winifred Spaulding opened a Bible training school for women that within a few years became the Harris Memorial Deaconess Training School. In 1906 the Mary J. Johnston Memorial Hospital in Manila opened its doors to women and children. Rebecca Parish, M.D., was its founder.

The Florence B. Nicholson Bible Seminary in 1907 became a union project with the merging of the Presbyterian Ellinwood Bible School. As the United Brethren, Disciples of Christ, Northern Baptists, and Congregationalists later joined in support of this enterprise, it became in 1919 the Union Theological Seminary.

In Manila especially, Methodism developed "dormitory work." Here were Christian living quarters for young people attending high schools and the University of Manila. This notable Christian service to students resulted in many conversions.

In the first two decades of the new century much Methodist preaching took place in the open air, but often on Sunday morning large theaters became the locale for Methodist worship. Eventually Methodist chapels were erected. Many Filipinos became pastors, and to them is due the major spread of the church. Yet among some, discontentment grew, and several established independent churches. Among the early preachers the energetic evangelist Felipe Marquez was best known.

By 1920 Methodism in the Philippines counted nearly 60,000 members and probationers. A Domestic Missions Society had been founded that within a short time organized four new congregations and supported their pastors. The importance of the locally established Methodist publishing house was increasing. Most impressive of all was the steady growth of all Protestant churches.

Latin America

Spain and Portugal, the two great Iberian powers, conquered Latin America in the sixteenth century. Those who colonized the area were seeking wealth and power, not religious freedom. Accompanying them were Roman Catholic missionaries. They spread their faith widely.

Three hundred years later there erupted the Latin American wars of independence. In 1800 Portugal still held Brazil, Spain the rest of Latin America. But within three decades the countries between the Rio Grande and Cape Horn had won their freedom.

Iberian Catholicism—very different from the Catholicism of France, Germany, or the United States—to a profound degree shaped the life and culture of Latin America. Yet Christianity in Latin America cannot be understood apart from the rise of radical atheism among the intelligentsia and widespread anticlericalism in the second half of the nineteenth century. Moreover, Roman Catholicism in Latin America has existed at an appallingly low level of vitality and effectiveness. It has depended upon Europe and North America to supply many of its priests. In some areas it still is but a thin veneer over a continuing paganism. It was, and remains, so thinly staffed that in many areas it could offer no ministry at all.

Much more needs to be said, but this is a minimum background for understanding the entrance of American Methodist missions into Latin America. Most Protestant missionaries there came from the United

States, and denominations most widely represented were the Presbyterians, Lutherans, Methodists, and Baptists. After World War I, Pentecostalism—imported and indigenous—had the most rapid growth.

To bring the picture of Latin American Methodism into focus, one can say that after 1844 the Southern Church planted in Northern Mexico, Brazil, and Cuba; William Taylor initiated—and the Northern Church later developed—Methodism in Bolivia, Chile, Peru, Panama, and Costa Rica; and the Northern Church inaugurated missions in Southern Mexico, Argentina, and Uruguay.

ARGENTINA AND URUGUAY

Five years after abandoning the original mission in Argentina, the Northern Church in 1847 appointed Dallas D. Lore to Buenos Aires. For seven years he was, in effect, Protestant chaplain to the English-speaking foreign community.

In 1851 the Board of Managers enunciated its policy: to establish work in every large Latin American city with a Protestant population; to help educate the Protestant children; to provide—through these missions—Roman Catholics with an example of "pure, simple Christianity" and "thus gradually win them to embrace it."

Lore's successors were G. D. Carrow and William Goodfellow. During Goodfellow's tenure (1857-69) two important developments occurred. First, a substantial immigration—about one-third Protestant, and with many Waldensians—from Europe was under way. Goodfellow and the three other Methodist missionaries moved rapidly to aid the Protestant immigrants. Second, at Goodfellow's urging, preaching in Spanish began in 1867. John F. Thompson first undertook this task.

Thomas B. Wood, president of Valparaiso College in Indiana before going as a Methodist missionary to Argentina in 1870, was appointed in 1872 acting United States consul at Rosario, Argentina. In that post he became well known and was widely appreciated. For several years he taught in the National College. In 1877 Wood went to Montevideo, Uruguay, and that year also founded El Evangelisto. For eleven years he edited this first Protestant paper in Uruguay and also from 1878 to 1887 was mission superintendent. From 1889 to 1891 Wood served as president of the Buenos Aires Theological Seminary. For the next quarter century he served in Peru.

At Wood's suggestion the W.F.M.S. began in 1874 educational work in Argentina. Other notable undertakings grew in Buenos Aires. Soon providing materials for all Spanish-speaking countries in Latin America the Methodist publishing house in Argentina was begun in 1883. In 1885 the Libreria La Aurora (Union Evangelical Bookstore) was opened;

this also produced and distributed Protestant books throughout Latin America.

The Methodists and Waldensians in 1884 founded a theological training school. Moved from Uruguay to Argentina in 1887, it became the Buenos Aires Theological Seminary. In 1919, with the co-operation of the Disciples, it became the Union Evangelical Theological Seminary.

Both nationals and immigrants from Latin Europe became effective missionaries. In Uruguay Juan Correa and Carlos Lastrico, won by Correa, traveled widely despite imprisonment and opposition. The remarkable Francisco G. Penzotti, an Italian immigrant and a convert to Methodism, went in 1879 as a missionary to the Waldensians in Uruguay, but eventually as an evangelist covered all South America. His name is linked with the winning of religious freedom in Peru.

From 1881 to World War I a small mission functioned in Paraguay. From Montevideo the Methodists also pushed northward in 1885 to Porto Alegre in southern Brazil. The schools founded there flourished. By 1920 the Methodist constituency in Argentina and Uruguay numbered 7,200.

BRAZIL

Following the American Civil War many Southerners migrated to Brazil. In 1867 the Southern Church appointed Junius Newman to Rio de Janeiro to minister to these overseas Protestants. Newman built a congregation, and his daughter began a school. Then, in 1874, the Southern Church voted to conduct a full mission in Brazil. John J. Ransom, the first missionary, arrived in 1876 in Rio de Janeiro. The Northern Church sent Juan Correa from Porto Alegre to help him. In 1900 the Northern Church transferred what it had already begun in Brazil to the Southern Church, so that all Methodists in Brazil could be one.

Through the years missionaries from the Southern Church came to Brazil, but an extraordinary trio arrived in the early 1880's. For the next fifty years Methodism's growth in Brazil reflected their able leadership. James F. Kennedy came in 1881, J. W. Tarboux in 1883, and H. C. Tucker in 1886. Bishop Granbery in 1886 surveyed what was being done and organized the Brazil Annual Conference. Kennedy, Tarboux, and Tucker were the three charter members.

Begun in 1890 to train ministers, Granbery College (later Granbery Institute) by 1919 had prepared more than half the Methodist pastors in Brazil. The People's Central Institute (adult education, mothers' training, and later medical and dental clinics) in Rio was started in 1906 by Tucker. In 1919 the Brazilian Methodist publishing house took form in São Paulo. Bennett College, named for Belle Harris Bennett, was opened in 1921 by Martha H. Watts. An outgrowth of earlier schools, the Porto Alegre Institute was begun in 1923 to do for southern Brazil what Granbery Institute was doing for the Rio area. By 1919 Brazil was the largest field of the Southern Church in Latin America and counted some 10,000 Methodists.

MEXICO

The Northern and Southern Churches entered Mexico in 1873. Yet the Southern Church already claimed an adopted congregation in Mexico. As a result of reading the Bible, Sosthenes Juarez had organized in Mexico City in 1865 a Protestant church, and on Bishop John C. Keener's invitation associated his congregation in 1871 with the Southern Church.

Of wider influence for the Southern Church was Alejo Hernandez. Already training for the priesthood, this well-to-do young man disliked what he saw in the Roman Church and left it. In the Revolutionary Army he became an atheist. Yet reading a Protestant tract aroused his curiosity and led him to Brownsville, Texas, where he experienced a profound Methodist conversion. Once ordained he went to the Mexicans in southern Texas.

Serving in Mexico City in 1873-74 Hernandez was stricken with polio. J. T. Daves, the first regularly appointed missionary, followed him and there joined Juarez and J. E. Mota. Others came. The Central Mexico Mission Conference was organized in 1886, and by 1892 claimed nearly 3,000 members.

The Southern Church also developed work—closely associated with the West Texas Conference—across northern Mexico. In 1885 this became the Mexican Border Mission Conference and stretched from the Gulf of Mexico to the Pacific Ocean. Within seven years the Northwest Mexican Conference with some 650 members was created from the Mexican Border Mission Conference and gave the latter more compassable limits. Between 1900 and 1910 Methodism here made steady progress. Indeed, between 1910 and 1914 the Southern Church contributed more money to this field than to any other. But the revolutionary uprising of 1910-18 slowed the work and brought a considerable loss of members.

In 1914 many of the co-operating mission boards in the United States met in Cincinnati for comity planning and there reallocated territory in Mexico. The Southern Church turned over its work in the Mexico City area to others—mainly to the Northern Church—and kept its two northern conferences. In 1918 it joined its missions in Mexico with its Mexican outreach in Texas, New Mexico, and California.

The Northern Church voted in 1872 to enter Mexico. Bishop Matthew Simpson appointed William Butler, founder of the India Conference, to begin and superintend the mission. Through an amazing stroke of good fortune, Butler in Mexico City in 1873 purchased a huge building, originally a monastery. It served the mission well. His son, John W. Butler, and Charles W. Drees, both of whom had prepared by studying Spanish at Boston University, were the first missionaries. Butler established the Mission Press in 1875, began publishing in 1877 *The Spanish Christian Advocate* (succeeded by the interdenominational *Christian World* in 1919), initiated theological training in 1875, and saw to it that schools and orphanages were begun. The theological training class begun in 1875 in Puebla became in 1917 the Union Theological Seminary in Mexico City. Methodism grew steadily.

The W.F.M.S. built and staffed schools and orphanages. The widely known Good Samaritan Hospital in Guanajuato began in 1891. Levi B. Salmans, with a decade of evangelistic service in Mexico, founded the hospital the year he received his medical degree. Salmans started Mexico's first modern nurses' training school and continued to enlarge the hospital until his retirement in 1927.

The most important work was done by Mexicans. Some of the pastors were former Roman Catholic priests. Of these, two of the ablest were Trinidad Rodriguez and Augustin Palacious. The latter had been assistant chaplain to Maximilian. Among others who served the church were Dr. Marcellino Guerrero, P. F. Valderrama, and B. N. Velasco. The mission expanded, but not without occasionally severe and bloody persecution. Through 1887, among all Protestants in Mexico, fifty-nine missionaries and Mexican pastors had been violently done to death. Methodism's first Mexican martyr was Epigmenio Monroy. A convert and a local preacher, he was slashed to death in 1881 by a mob for whom, during the process, he prayed. Two of the companions attacked with him also died. The able preacher Conrado Gamboa was shot through the lung and his companion killed by assassins. Amazingly, Gamboa recovered and served eight years more.

By 1919 the Northern Church counted nearly 9,200 members in Mexico, the Southern Church 5,100. These two groups, which united to form the Methodist Church of Mexico in 1930, gave Mexico the largest Methodist population in Latin America.

CHILE, PERU, BOLIVIA, COSTA RICA, AND PANAMA

In the history of Methodist missions Chile, Peru, Bolivia, Costa Rica, and Panama hold one thing in common—their Methodist beginnings relate to William Taylor.

Directed to South America by an old friend, William Taylor became convinced in 1877 that God's will for him meant opening missions on South America's western coast. The bishops would not support his plan because, among other reasons, he refused to allow the fruits of his missionaries' labor to come under the Board of Missions' jurisdiction. Yet this, and the widespread failure of his work in India to achieve self-support, left him undaunted. Taylor determined to begin self-supporting missions in South America.

Taylor's "South America Period" extended from late 1877 to early 1883. In those years he made three trips to South America. For nearly five months in 1877-78 he was in Peru and Chile. He spent one day in Panama. His second trip in 1880 took him—with Justus Nelson, who in Para (today called Belem) began a church that continued until his retirement in 1926—for a few weeks to northern Brazil. His third trip in 1883 took him briefly to Chile.

Reduced to bare essentials, Taylor's plan was to visit the English-speaking foreign colonies; pledge these people to raise money to begin a school and pay a teacher; recruit a teacher-preacher-missionary from the United States; and allow this person to support himself as a teacher, start a church as a preacher, and evangelize as a missionary. Taylor recruited women, but he did not envision their becoming preachers.

Taylor readily obtained his pledges in South America. Meanwhile, he had a student at Boston University gathering volunteers. He sent his first group from New York in 1878; but because Taylor had received only part of the money pledged for passage, the group traveled steerage and underwent no little suffering. That first sailing symbolized the way in which most of Taylor's so-called self-supporting missions in South America were to be conducted. From the beginning, these encountered major difficulties. From a few persons there came heroic response, but the majority were ill fitted for what confronted them. When there were deaths or resignations, Taylor sent new recruits.

In the majority of cases Taylor paid the missionary recruits' outgoing passage; sometimes he could give them a small amount to help establish their work. But all understood that there would be no salary, return passage, or medical care provided. On reaching their assignments the missionaries all too often found that those who had agreed under Taylor's persuasive power to support schools had changed their minds. With pluck and determination most of these missionaries managed for a while. But, traveling in the United States, Taylor was far away. His missionaries could not reach him when they needed him, and he gave no studied or direct supervision to the work he had so grandly launched.

Taylor had the unusual ability to become immediately self-supporting and influential anywhere in the world. His mistake was to suppose that others—without his gifts—could easily do the same. Poor morale plagued Taylor's missionaries, and many returned home. Relationships with the Northern Church and with its Missionary Society frequently posed acute problems. Judged by Taylor's announced intentions, the project was a failure.

Yet some of Taylor's missionaries gave magnificent accounts of themselves. From the labors of several there came permanent results, as in Chile, where all property developed by Taylor's recruits was offered to and accepted by the Missionary Society of the Northern Church in 1893, including Iquique English College and Santiago College. The latter had sprung in 1880 from efforts of the able Ira H. LaFetra and his wife.

Taylor sponsored the first attempts to root Methodism in Bolivia, but nearly thirty years later, in 1906, the Rev. Francis M. Harrington founded the first Methodist congregation in La Paz. By 1919 there were thirty-four missionaries at work in Bolivia with a Methodist constituency of eighty-five people.

In Chile Taylor's first missionaries laid some important foundations. Later, in 1888, the Rev. and Mrs. Goodsil F. Arms went to Chile under Taylor's auspices and there served with distinction. In 1919 the mission purchased a large acreage and made it into a model farm and training center. At the time Chile had nearly 5,000 Methodists.

In Peru a Methodist agent of the American Bible Society, Francisco G. Penzotti, was arrested in 1890 and imprisoned for eight months. His case became a *cause célèbre,* and the court's decision in his favor established a large measure of religious freedom. Thomas B. Wood, earlier in Argentina and Uruguay, came to Lima in 1891 as presiding elder. Other missionaries followed. Wood's daughter, Miss Elsie Wood, also arrived in Peru in 1891. Under the W.F.M.S. she began a school in Callao in 1891 and in Lima in 1892. From the latter came the widely known Lima High School. Work was begun in the Andes at Huancayo in 1905 by national pastors, and in 1914 they were joined by North American missionaries. The Andino Institute, founded in 1914, provided primary and secondary schooling. By 1919 there were 1,000 Methodists in Peru.

William Taylor sent John E. Wright of the Wisconsin Conference to Costa Rica in 1881. He and his wife began a school, but for reasons of health soon left for California. The much-traveled Penzotti also visited Costa Rica in 1886 and 1891. In 1917, on the basis of an interdenominational survey and recommendation, Methodist work began in Costa Rica with the appointment of the Rev. Eduardo Zapata from Mexico. Within two years several missionaries came from the United States.

In Panama the churches begun by his missionaries in 1878 were given in the early 1890's by William Taylor to the British Methodists. In 1906 the Northern Church entered Panama and began the school that later became the Pan American Institute. Both Methodist churches and schools were for whites only. No other congregation then in Panama was segregated. Before World War I a school for West Indian Negroes was begun, and some work was initiated in the Chinese colony. In 1921 Methodism in Panama and Costa Rica was united in the Central American Mission Conference. The two countries together then mustered a total of 400 Methodists.

CUBA

The Southern Church found missions in northern Mexico a natural extension of those among Mexican-Americans north of the Rio Grande. So, too, missions begun among Cuban-Americans in southern Florida by the Florida Conference in 1874 elicited interest in reaching to Cuba. That became possible after the Spanish-American War. As a result of a preliminary survey, George N. MacDonnell went to Havana in 1899. Soon Methodism was represented throughout the island. The Cuban Mission, organized in 1907, became a Mission Conference in 1919 and an Annual Conference in 1923. The W.B.F.M., from its entry in 1900, concentrated on secondary education for young women. By 1920, some 4,700 Cubans held membership in the Methodist Episcopal Church, South.

Methodism entered the Philippines in 1899. It began to take root in Latin America in 1847. By 1919 Methodism had been present in those Latin American countries where it had its largest membership for more than twice as long as it had been in the Philippines. Yet by 1919, with more than 400 Methodist missionaries, all Latin America had a Methodist constituency—members, probationers, and baptized children—of somewhat less than 43,000. At the same time, with only 51 Methodist missionaries in the islands, the Philippines had some 60,000 Methodists.

The Philippines and Latin America had the same background of three and one-half centuries of Iberian Catholicism. Throughout Latin America there was a dislike for and distrust of the Yankee colossus to the north. But in the Philippines and in Cuba there was a generally good feeling toward America. Since the Protestant missionaries came from the United States, this was undoubtedly a factor. Yet one cannot help conjecturing to what extent an American administration in the Philippines may have created a climate more favorable for conversion to Protestantism. To be seen whole, the picture must show the growth pattern for all Protestantism in the Philippines and in Latin America to the present. Nevertheless, the contrasts evident by 1919 are thought-provoking.

Africa

By 1890 the imperial powers of Europe—Britain, France, Portugal, Belgium (Leopold II personally held the Congo from 1878 to 1907), and Germany—were well entrenched in Africa. The only nations there free of Western domination were Ethiopia and Liberia. The latter had been created an independent nation by Americans for the repatriation of ex-slaves, and its situation was altogether unenviable. The Americo-Liberians lived along the coast and nominally ruled the country, but were unable to exercise jurisdiction over the indigenous population from whom came frequent forays and disruptive warfare.

Portugal held Angola and Mozambique, closed its eyes as late as 1910 to slavery in Angola, and—despite its widely publicized policy of considering "assimilated" a Negro African who managed to achieve a Western education—provided an altogether unenlightened administration. In the adjoining Congo Leopold and his favored friends pursued a policy of "forced labor." The atrocities resulting from "recruiting" reluctant Congolese evoked such a cry of shock and outrage from the American and European governments that Leopold transferred the Congo to Belgium in 1907. In the Union of South Africa and in what was to become Northern and Southern Rhodesia, British power was dominant.

In Africa, until the arrival of the Southern Church in the Congo in 1914, all American Methodist outreach came from the Northern Church.

LIBERIA

Melville Cox's death and his stirring cry, "Let a thousand fall before Africa be given up," brought forth in 1833 the Liberia Mission. It built upon the first Methodist society begun there in 1822 by resettled Negroes from America. The mission suffered from weakness, neglect, and lack of policy. From 1857 to 1884 a few American Negro missionaries went to Liberia, but no white Methodist missionary made the journey. Monrovia Seminary, a high school, seemed to be closed as much as it was open. Projects were begun and then dropped. Between 1879 and 1883 the W.F.M.S. sent several missionaries, but then withdrew.

By 1884 the state of the mission in Liberia produced acute embarrassment in the Northern Church. Indeed, in no small measure its degenerating weakness helps to explain William Taylor's election to the episcopacy in 1884. Although highly controversial, Taylor bore the reputation of persuasive power and dynamic action. If anyone could rectify and strengthen the Liberian mission, argued many, Taylor could. For these Taylor's election brought joy.

Taylor spent little time in Liberia, but his administration there was vigorous. He brought new missionaries with him, established several self-supporting missions, and sent missionaries to the indigenous people. A persistent blight ruined his plan for coffee plantations that would make the entire mission financially self-sufficient. Yet his self-supporting missions in Liberia achieved their goal, and in 1893-94 he transferred these to the Missionary Society.

In many respects Taylor's work in Liberia was perhaps the best in his whole amazing career. When in 1896 the General Conference retired Taylor, it appointed to succeed him the sound and able administrator Bishop Joseph C. Hartzell. Like Taylor, he also had responsibility for American Methodism—at the time only the Northern Church was there —throughout Africa.

Taylor gave new vigor to the Liberian Conference. Between 1900 and 1920 that body had its strongest growth. In 1900 it numbered 2,900 members; by 1910, some 5,600; and by 1920, 9,200. Indeed, among the indigenous population during World War I a revival movement reached such proportions that the Methodist Episcopal Church was unable to provide sufficient instruction for those who sought admission. Many entered other churches. The revival largely reflected the amazing fruits of William Wade Harris' preaching. Harris was an independent Liberian evangelist.

In 1896 the old Monrovia Seminary became the College of West Africa. Dr. Alexander P. Camphor, a Negro from Louisiana, served as its president from 1896 to 1908. As a delegate of the Northern Church, Camphor attended the Edinburgh Conference in 1910, and in 1916 was elected a bishop. Assigned to Liberia, he died there within three years.

WILLIAM TAYLOR IN AFRICA

William Taylor was never happy with the Missionary Society. He judged it to be too restrictive. As a responsible agency of the church it had to act prudently. As an individual Taylor could begin missions wherever and however he chose. As already noted, he did. The varied results included demoralized withdrawal and heroic response, fiascoes and Methodist extension. To the Methodist bishops and the Mission Board Taylor was an independent Methodist organizing irregular and non-recognized Methodist missions. In the attempt to clarify an anomalous and utterly confused series of relationships, it was finally announced by a committee appointed by the Missionary Society to interview Taylor that those holding membership in Methodist Annual Conferences, but continuing in Taylor's missions, would have to locate (to give up Annual Conference membership and, in effect, retire from the active ministry). With one exception Taylor's men located. Taylor did too.

In 1882 Taylor asked the South India Conference to locate him. It did, but the next year it also elected him lay delegate to the General Conference of 1884. Taylor was in Latin America when the news reached him, and he hurriedly returned to the United States. That General Conference—as had the conference of 1880—faced the problem of the Liberia Mission. In 1880 Taylor had put the picture in totally new perspective when he boldly declared that strategically Liberia was the wrong base for a mission to Africa. What Methodism needed, he proclaimed, was a bishop for all Africa—a man like David Livingstone. To many in the conference of 1884 Taylor seemed to be the man of the hour. Despite attempts to delay the action the conference elected him missionary bishop for Africa. Nominally a lay delegate, Taylor suddenly became a bishop commissioned to plant Methodism throughout Africa.

Taylor's election implicitly involved sanction for his missionary methods. Yet Taylor knew his earlier relationship to his South American missions could no longer be maintained. Consequently he gathered some of his friends and financial supporters. They created the Transit and Building Fund Society of Bishop William Taylor's Self-support Missions with headquarters in New York. The new body's president was William Taylor. To new missionaries the society provided transit (one way) and a small building fund. Its policies were Taylor's. In 1888 General Conference legislation laid the groundwork for the rapid absorption of Taylor's society and the "regularizing" of his self-supporting missions. Thus ended what was, in effect, Northern Methodism's second missionary society.

Although given episcopal supervision of Liberia, Taylor really went to Africa to throw a chain of self-supporting missions from coast to coast across that continent. Taylor did not fully realize this ambition; but in trying, he placed missions in northern Angola, of which the remaining ones became the nucleus for continuing Angola Methodism. He launched a series of missions—all of which quickly disappeared—northeastward from its mouth along the Congo River; and in Mozambique he took over a Congregational mission and appointed the founder to American Methodist mission work there.

Before leaving America Taylor had recruited thirty missionary volunteers, some of whom had children. He sailed for Africa in December, 1884, held his first conference in Liberia on January 29, 1885, and by March 20 was in Luanda, Angola, ready to plant mission stations inland toward the Congo. He trekked eastward with his recruits, saw them begin their

work, and returned to Luanda. Then he sailed to Europe to confer with
the rulers of Belgium and Portugal concerning his missions in their
African territories.

Taylor returned with more volunteers in 1886. From the mouth of the
Congo they moved inland to a point fifty miles northeast of Leopoldville.
Taylor's ultimate objective was to push southward from there to the
southern Congo.

An eager pioneer, Taylor lacked knowledge of what Africa required
of those who would be effective missionaries there. Frequent deaths and
more frequent resignations depleted his missions, but additional volunteers seemed ready to fill vacated posts. Yet—not always. The important
mission in Angola's capital, Luanda, closed soon after it opened in 1885.
It was briefly reopened, then closed—and remained closed until 1902.
From then it has had a continuous existence.

In 1885 Taylor formed the Congo Mission with two districts, Angola
and Upper Congo. Later, in 1897, Bishop Hartzell convened the first
Congo Mission Conference; at this time he discovered only two barely
existing outposts in the Congo and a considerable depletion of forces in
Angola. In the latter country, due to the shrewd farming skill and
granite-like faith of two New England brothers, Samuel J. and William
H. Mead, the mission at Malange was flourishing.

During his African episcopacy Taylor planted Methodism on Africa's
east coast. In 1873 Erwin H. Richards had begun work in Mozambique
under the American Congregationalists. When that mission decided to
withdraw, Richards was reluctant to leave those among whom he was
ministering. In 1890 Taylor arranged for purchase of the mission property
and on Christmas Eve gave Richards a Methodist appointment as the
first member of the Inhambane District, in the Liberia Conference. Taylor
then sent four additional missionaries to aid Richards. The latter effectively developed the mission which in 1896 came under the Missionary
Society and into the Congo Mission Conference. Taylor was retired in
1896 and died six years later.

ANGOLA

In 1896-97 Bishop Joseph C. Hartzell had to consolidate what Taylor
had begun and integrate it in the Methodist connectional system. When
in 1897 he convened the first session of the Congo Mission Conference in
Angola, Hartzell discovered that most of those present had been in
Angola since 1885. For these he immediately began arranging furloughs.
Hartzell's administration was greatly appreciated.

In 1899, with the appointment of Cora Zentmire, the W.F.M.S. entered
Angola. Within months Miss Zentmire died. Her successor, Josephine

Mekkelson, also died shortly after her arrival. Susan Collins, daughter of a former slave, then came and served from 1902 until her retirement in 1922. Others followed.

As a matter of administrative necessity Hartzell in 1902 organized in Angola the West Central Africa Mission Conference. In 1920 that body became the Angola Annual Conference.

The day after Angola established its law in 1914 allowing non-Roman Catholic bodies to build churches, the Hartzell Methodist Church was begun in Luanda. Six years later Angola Methodism had 1,300 members.

MOZAMBIQUE

With Richards as superintendent Hartzell in 1901 organized in Mozambique the East Central Africa Mission Conference. The church in Mozambique grew steadily and by 1910 had organized its own home missions society. In that same year the Rev. Pliny Keys began at Cambine the Bodine Training School (later Central Training School) soon called "Tuskegee in Africa."

Mozambique's young men in increasing numbers were working in the mines of the adjoining Transvaal. The Methodist mission followed and extended its ministry to the Johannesburg area of South Africa. This work begun in 1920 was limited to the young men from Mozambique temporarily there as miners. In 1924, however, the Central Mission Press was transferred from Cambine to Johannesburg and soon, as printer for other churches also, became an all-Africa agency.

The enabling act of the 1912 General Conference made possible in 1915 organization of the Portuguese East Africa Mission Conference. In 1920 that body, embracing work in Mozambique and the Transvaal, became the Southeast Africa Mission Conference with 7,100 members.

SOUTHERN RHODESIA

In October, 1897, Bishop Hartzell rode across the Mozambique border into the Southern Rhodesian town of Umtali. Struck with the magnificent location and surroundings he exulted, "Here is to be the chief center of American Methodist missions in East Africa." [12] The Beira-Salisbury Railway was just then nearing completion. A steep incline made it impracticable to bring the railway into Umtali, so Umtali was moved ten miles to the railway. The abandoned town site became Old Umtali.

Hartzell negotiated with Cecil Rhodes's British South Africa Company in Rhodesia and in England, and received in 1898-99 from the company

[12] Annual Report of the Board of Foreign Missions of the Methodist Episcopal Church, 1902, p. 53.

Old Umtali with 13,000 acres of land. The gift was then worth at least $100,000. On this acquisition Hartzell envisioned creation of an agricultural and industrial center for training Africans. Old Umtali became Methodism's largest mission station.

The first American Methodist missionaries in Southern Rhodesia were the Rev. and Mrs. Morris W. Ehnes in 1898. A year later came the Rev., and Mrs. James L. DeWitt and Mrs. Anna Arndt. In 1900 John M. Springer went to Rhodesia and took charge of the Umtali Industrial Mission. Soon Bible translation, schools, an orphanage, and an experimental farm were under way. In 1904-6 Springer was pioneering new work to the north of Umtali. Slow but steady growth continued.

In 1915 the Rhodesia Mission Conference was set off from the East Central Africa Mission Conference. In 1931 it was made an Annual Conference. Limited funds in the period 1912-15 brought some retrenchment, but by 1920 Methodists in Southern Rhodesia numbered 4,600.

THE CONGO

In 1907, ten years after the last vestiges of Taylor's missions in the Congo had disappeared, the Rev. and Mrs. John Springer, traveling northward from Rhodesia, explored the southern Congo. Based in Luanda, Angola, from 1910, Springer saw the imperative need for Methodist missions in the Congo. Chiefly at his urging Methodism entered the Congo in 1911. In 1912 Springer visited Kapanga and there had a mission house built. By June, 1914, Arthur L. Piper, M.D., and his wife were living in it. Meanwhile, Springer had left Angola and settled at Kambove in the Congo. Recognizing the importance of Elisabethville, which then had no other Protestants in it, Springer, then a superintendent and later to be a bishop, had work begun there in 1917. Two years earlier Hartzell had established the Congo Mission. In 1917 Bishop Eben S. Johnson organized the Congo Mission Conference.

The Southern Church also began a mission to the north on the Congo River. As a boy, Walter R. Lambuth had read of Robert Moffatt and David Livingstone. In 1891, after serving in China and Japan, he offered himself for a mission on the upper Congo. His Mission Board was not ready. But in 1910 the Southern Church decided to survey possibilities in the Congo. Lambuth, recently elected a bishop, was sent. Eager to have the Colored Methodist Episcopal Church co-operate in any African missions, the Southern Church asked Professor John Wesley Gilbert of Paine College to accompany Lambuth. Late in 1911 the two men arrived in the Congo, and in February, 1912, they reached the village of Chief Wembo-Nyama. The chief received them well, and they promised to begin a mission. With full co-operation from the nearby Southern Presbyterian mission, the Southern Church opened its station in 1914 in Wembo-Nyama. The first Annual Conference met in 1922.

In 1920 the two Methodist bodies had 41 missionaries in the Congo and a total membership of 600 persons.

NORTH AFRICA AND MADEIRA

Work in the Portuguese-held Madeira Islands, four hundred miles west of Casablanca, began in 1898 under Bishop Hartzell. The islanders welcomed a small Methodist congregation in their midst. A port of call for naval vessels, Madeira frequently had a heavy influx of seamen. Through World War I much Methodist work there was on behalf of sailors. In 1920 Madeira became part of the North Africa Mission but was later to be linked with other conferences.

Several American Methodists who stopped in Algiers in 1907 became convinced that a Methodist mission under Hartzell's supervision should be started in North Africa. The conviction bore fruit with the establishment in 1908 of a mission in Algeria and Tunisia. In 1913 the North African Mission Conference emerged. In 1909 the W.F.M.S. agreed to support two English women who had already been missionaries there for nearly two decades. The W.F.M.S. sent its first American missionaries to Algeria in 1922. By 1920 Methodists in Muslim North Africa numbered about 200 and in Madeira perhaps 300.

5

The Maturing of Mission-planted Churches

This rapid survey of Methodism's overseas missionary outreach inevitably raises one question. To what degree of maturity or independence had the so-called "younger churches" achieved by 1919?

The question of maturity—whether applied to men, nations, or churches—can bring forth only a relative answer, for degrees of maturity are expressed in many different ways, in different situations, and always in relation to one of several standards. Was American Methodism "mature" in 1784 by virtue of its independence? Indeed, was mid-twentieth-century American Methodism "mature" as judged by its attitudes toward the churches it had founded overseas, by its relationships with other denominations, by its approach to the major problems of mankind? Was it "mature" in faith and in prophetic insight?

For years a favorite measuring rod for the maturing strength of "younger churches" was the threefold norm of self-support, self-government, and self-propagation. These seem self-evidently simple and adequate, but they are not. Moreover, recognition of interdependence and willingness to act accordingly may be a sign of much greater maturity than insistence upon independence. There are other criteria. An Asian church evidences one form of maturity when it conducts its own national missions. Does its sending missionaries overseas indicate greater maturity?

The above simply points to the complexity of assessing maturity. One further word of caution: American Methodism's overseas missions grew during the heyday of Western imperialism. The analogy of the imperial mother country and the scattered overseas dependent colonies very naturally has suffused much Protestant missionary thinking. Whether in relation to new churches this analogy is justified is open to serious theological question. Nevertheless, the issue of maturity and independence persists. How, for example, did Methodism in Japan by 1919 demonstrate its maturity vis-a-vis American Methodism? Here one criterion only is examined, namely, degrees of organizational independence.

As evidence of the maturity of Methodism overseas, organizational structure that reflects growing strength and ability to achieve some measure of self-sufficiency may be one useful measure. Three organizational patterns have evolved—the Central Conference, the affiliated church, and the independent church. In the writer's judgment no one of these is superior to the others, and no one essentially represents either greater strength or greater maturity. Instead, each appears to be a useful device fitted to its own national or cultural setting.

Central Conferences

ORIGINS IN INDIA

William Taylor's efforts in India produced the South India Conference. J. M. Thoburn and E. W. Parker were concerned that Methodism in north India and in south India should not, because of wide geographic separation, drift apart. From their efforts to keep both geographic segments of Indian Methodism closely related there met in January, 1880, a "United Conference." It elected its own president and perpetuated itself by instructing the North India and the South India Conferences to elect delegates to its future sessions. Several months later Thoburn presented to the General Conference a memorial for a delegated conference in India. The motion met defeat. Nevertheless, the Second Delegated Conference of the Methodist Episcopal Church in India met in July, 1881. It dealt with all-India matters, approved a General Board of Publication and a Board of Education, and took other actions.

At the General Conference in 1884 the Committee on Missions had a request from Japan to unite the missions of the Northern Church and the Methodist Church of Canada. Meanwhile, Parker and Taylor, as individuals, also presented a memorial to that committee for "a Subordinate General Conference in India." The committee could not approve the proposed union in Japan but recommended the creation, wherever certain conditions were met, of Central Conferences. These would have power to supervise "the Educational, Publishing, and such other Connectional interests and work as may be committed to [them] by the Annual Conferences or Missions; but never in contravention of the Book of Discipline, or Rules of the General Conference." [13] The General Conference agreed and voted to constitute a Central Conference in India and to authorize one for Japan.

Eventually India's Central Conference was composed of many more than two Annual Conferences. Indeed, within fifteen years of its founding it included delegates from Annual Conferences and missions in Burma, Malaysia, and the Philippine Islands. Thus it came to be known as the Central Conference of the Methodist Church of Southern Asia.

ENLARGED POWERS AND GROWTH

Through the years the General Conferences enlarged the powers of Central Conferences until in 1928 they were authorized to elect their own bishops. Thus, the Central Conference of Eastern Asia (China) in 1930 elected John Gowdy and Wang Chih-P'ing bishops of the Methodist Episcopal Church. Several months later India's Central Conference elected J. R. Chitambar as bishop.

The Southern Church made provision for Central Conferences as voluntary regional bodies, but none emerged.

By end of the World War II, among the Methodist Churches related to the General Conference held in the United States, there were six Central Conferences and three Provisional Central Conferences. India's Central Conference dated from 1884, China's from 1897 (restructured in 1941 after unification). Except for Liberia, which was not present by reason of its distance and which was under different episcopal supervision, Methodism in Africa south of the Sahara held its first Central Conference in 1921. This later became a Provisional Central Conference and included the work of the Southern Church in the Congo. The Northern European Central Conference (Scandinavia) began in 1924.

---

[13] *Discipline*, 1884, ¶296. This legislation is essentially what Parker had drafted for the committee.

The Central European Conference, begun in 1925, became the Central and Southern Europe Provisional Central Conference in 1939. The Latin America Central Conference had emerged before 1928. The Germany Central Conference was organized in 1936. Methodism in the Philippines established its Central Conference in 1944. The Provisional Central Conference for Southeastern Asia had also been formed by the end of World War II.

Affiliated Autonomous Churches

THE METHODIST CHURCH OF BRAZIL

Aware that some of its overseas churches desired greater autonomy, the Southern Church in 1926 established a Commission on Nationalism under the Board of Missions. After correspondence with that commission, Methodists in Brazil in 1930 memorialized the General Conference of the Southern Church for sufficient autonomy to elect bishops and revise the *Discipline*. The result in August, 1930, was the Methodist Church of Brazil. The churches on the two continents maintained organic affiliation through a Central Council, composed equally of Brazilians and missionaries, and exchanged nonvoting delegates to the respective governing conferences. The Methodist Church of Brazil chose to elect its bishops quadrennially. The first was J. W. Tarboux, succeeded in 1934 by a Brazilian, César Dacorso.

THE METHODIST CHURCH OF MEXICO

Needing autonomy and desiring unity, the two Methodist conferences in Mexico—one belonging to the Northern Church and one to the Southern Church—memorialized their respective parent bodies to create a single church. Thus arose in July, 1930, the Methodist Church of Mexico. That autonomous body, which also quadrennially elected its bishops, and the two mission boards concerned established a Council of Co-operation.

THE KOREAN METHODIST CHURCH

With the 1926 collapse of unification efforts in the United States, the Korean offspring of the two American Methodisms memorialized their parent bodies to allow them to form a single Methodist Church. The Koreans were outspokenly frank. Having two Methodist Churches in Korea called "for constant defense before non-Christians." United, they could evangelize more effectively. Thus in December, 1930, came the Korean Methodist Church. It too elected its bishops quadrennially and formed a Central Council that facilitated ties with the American churches.

Independent Methodist Churches

In 1828 the Methodist Episcopal Church agreed to the creation of the Methodist Church of Canada. In 1870 the Southern Church established the Colored Methodist Episcopal Church. Both were autonomous and independent denominations.

These were the precedents when, in 1907 in Japan, the Northern and Southern Churches and the Methodist Church of Canada agreed to the independent Japan Methodist Church. For Japan this action was not unusual. Thirty years earlier the Congregationalists had taken a similar step, and in 1877 five groups, including American and Scottish Presbyterians and the Reformed, created the United Church of Christ. The 1887 Anglican-Episcopal merger resulted in the Holy Catholic Church. Seen against its background, Japanese Methodist union came relatively late.

With the union Yoitsu Honda was elected the first bishop. The Japan Methodist Church met the needs of Japan's unique situation, invited and welcomed missionaries from overseas, and within a decade had more than doubled its membership.

6

Methodism's National Missions

As was true in other denominations, Methodists to about 1890 designated missions in America "domestic," from then to about 1940 "home," and after that "national." In the larger framework the scope of American Protestantism's national missions has been vast. Moreover, the number of persons serving those missions has probably been consistently greater than those going overseas as missionaries. American Methodism has reflected both these factors.

Methodism has always had more "home" than "foreign" missionaries. And, too, national missionaries were concentrated among numerically smaller groups than were those who served overseas. In other words, the ratio of missionaries to non-Christians was much higher in Methodism's national missions than in its overseas missions. Without attempting to tabulate statistics, one can cite substantiating examples. The Missionary Society of the Northern Church alone supported, in whole or in part, some 3,000 national missionaries in 1874. As late as 1919 it had only 70 per cent of that number overseas. In 1919 the Southern Church had, statistically speaking, three missionaries in the United States for every two overseas. Moreover, the three uniting churches in 1939 had a national missions staff of nearly 5,600 and an overseas staff of less than 1,500.

On the comparative basis of missionary personnel alone, Methodism's national missions would seem to warrant more space than has been devoted thus far to overseas missions. Yet for three reasons their story is here highly compressed. First, statistically speaking, until 1919 the United States was the world's most fruitful mission field. Here in the "great century" Protestant missions achieved their largest numerical gains. A major part of Methodism's story in America recounts missionary outreach. Thus, much in these volumes stands as necessary amplification of these pages. Second, and without contradicting the first, in the degree to which Methodism's national missions were conceived as special outreach among minority groups, their numerical results—with missions among Negroes a notable exception—were seldom proportionately equal to those of similar missions overseas. Third, Methodism reflects much of the homogeneity of American life, and the results of its national missions have increasingly become part of the central story of American Methodism. But the fruits of Methodism's overseas missions have maintained their quite separate histories. They have modified and been modified by the different cultures in which they are growing. They are producing in Asia, Africa, and Latin America the leaders increasingly engaged in building new nations. Accordingly, national missions are here allotted a relatively brief space.

What are national missions? To this important query no answer is here attempted. What at first may seem a simple question involves a theological discussion on the nature of the church. More important for these pages is to discover what late-nineteenth-century American Methodism regarded as national missions.

One basic fact must be noted. From early in the country's history the dominant elements in America regarded the United States as a Protestant, white, Anglo-Saxon nation. Methodism in large measure accepted and reflected this view.

Exceptions can be cited, but by 1850 Methodism's national missions were generally seen as reaching those who were "different"—non-white, non-Protestant, or non–Anglo-Saxon. On this basis missions were largely to those regarded as underprivileged or as handicapped by language, color, or physical infirmity. Among English-speaking white people of

Protestant heritage a Methodist preacher organized a *church*. Among others he began a *mission*.

From another point of view, Methodism's national missions included those forms of evangelism and service in which long-term supplemental aid (personnel and funds) would be needed because the leaders of those among whom work was undertaken were not sufficiently trained and because the economic level of the people was too low to support the institutional structure deemed necessary for them in the American culture. National missions also involved "opportunity projects." In these the stimulus of outside leadership and/or funds—as in the case of much "church extension"—was seen as enabling self-supporting work to come into being.

Conference Missions, New Areas, Church Extension

Conference missions in the Northern and Southern Churches figured prominently in Methodism's outreach. These were usually directed to destitute areas within or adjacent to conference boundaries. Where, as on the frontier, population was sparse or where, as in many cities, people were living at subsistence level, conference-supported mission preachers were the only answer. By 1880 conference missions had begun to decrease in the Northern Church, but for another half century in the Southern Church they loomed large in importance.

Expansion of both churches in new areas and on the westward-moving frontier was designated missionary outreach and was supported accordingly. The Southern Church had pushed westward into New Mexico, Arizona, California, Oregon, Colorado, and Montana, before the Civil War. That conflict disrupted such expansion, and by 1919 the Southern Church counted somewhat less than 30,000 members in the West and Northwest.

Closely related to development of churches on the frontier is what Methodism calls "church extension." By the end of the Civil War growth in newly opening areas of the country clearly required the support and resources of the entire denomination. The Northern Church organized its General Church Extension Society in 1864. The Southern Church created its Board of Church Extension in 1882 with headquarters in Louisville, and the Methodist Protestant Church in 1888 added that responsibility to its Board of Home Missions. These agencies sometimes granted funds as a gift but more often made loans for erecting parsonages, churches, and related buildings. Church extension had its largest growth after 1919.

Missions to Minority Groups

Methodism's major outreach in its organized national missions came among minority groups. These included Indians, Negroes, immigrants, the indigent and handicapped in cities, and mountaineers.

INDIANS

To 1919 the Northern and Southern Churches continued missions among the Indians. The Northern Church conducted these from New York to California and Oregon and by 1921 had forty-one missions with seventy workers, fifteen of whom were Indians.

In Oklahoma, despite resettlement there of the Five Civilized Tribes, white members in the Southern Church soon considerably outnumbered Indians. What had been an Indian mission became the Oklahoma Conference. Unfortunately a racial line was drawn, and Indians were so neglected that they requested the church to renew its missions among them. Thus was organized in 1919, with nearly 2,700 members, what later became the Indian Mission Conference of Oklahoma.

Beginning in 1887 J. J. Methvin of Macon, Georgia, extended the work of the Southern Church among Indians far beyond the Five Civilized Tribes in Oklahoma. By 1919 the Northern and Southern Churches had nearly 13,000 Indian members about equally divided between them.

NEGROES

Convinced that the needs of 3,500,000 freed slaves were too much for the churches to cope with, the General Conference of the Northern Church in 1864 asked Congress to create a Bureau of Freedmen's Affairs. In 1865 Congress established the Freedmen's Bureau. To this agency the Northern Church gave strong support, but most of its work with Negroes was channeled through its Freedmen's Aid Society.

From the end of the Civil War the Northern Church organized Negro mission conferences in the South. The presence and outlook of missionaries from the North produced friction. By 1919 the Northern Church was clearly aware that a long period of major Negro migration from the South to northern industrial centers was under way and that responsibilities for service among Negroes in the North would increase.

The missions of the Southern Church among Negroes were conducted largely through the C.M.E. Church. The two bodies founded Paine College in 1884, and in 1901 the W.B.H.M. began to share in that project. The Southern Church also helped to support other educational endeavors and missionary preachers of the C.M.E. Church. Mary DeBardeleben in 1912 began the first Bethlehem Center in Augusta, Georgia.

The Northern Church was widely active through the former states of the Confederacy. It regarded its work not as competing with but as supplementing the missionary outreach of the Southern Church in its home territories. Indeed, by 1920 between Delaware and the Rio Grande the Northern Church had twenty Negro and seventeen non-Negro conferences, with some 3,800 ordained ministers and an even larger contingent of local preachers. Among its nearly 850,000 members in the area were more non-Negroes than Negroes. The Northern Church owned and maintained in the South seventy-three schools, many of them high schools, some colleges and medical schools. It conducted two hospitals. Surprisingly, somewhat more than one fifth of the total property value of the Northern Church was to be found in the Southern states.

NON—ENGLISH-SPEAKING IMMIGRANTS

European immigrants to the United States for the most part came through the port of New York. The majority settled in northern industrial cities or in the farmlands of the northeastern and north central states. Yet a large number, among them Germans, Italians, Greeks, and people of French background, moved into the South.[14]

The extensive German migrations, the growth of strong German-American churches, and the resultant missions to Germany have been noted. But also before the Civil War the Southern Church began a mission in Texas' large German settlement. That work flourished, and in 1918 the German Mission Conference became part of the West Texas Conference.

Wide-spread missions among Scandinavians in the north central states, as seen earlier, resulted from uncounted conversions on the Bethel Ship in New York. Numerically smaller than the German-speaking bodies, the Scandinavian conferences by 1900 held some 13,000 members and had helped plant Methodism in Scandinavia.

By 1890 the Northern Church had begun missions among Italian immigrants in Philadelphia, New York, Boston, New Orleans, Chicago, and other cities. By 1921 these missions to Italians—from Maine to California—were the most extensive it was then conducting among foreign language groups.

Often overlooked is the fact that by 1920 more than 200,000 Italian immigrants had come to the states in which the Southern Church was operating. It developed missions among Italians in New Orleans, in the Birmingham area, in Florida, in Kansas City, and elsewhere.

Several missions of the Northern Church among French-speaking people in Louisiana had dwindled away, but in 1885 it began new missions in

---

[14] The detailed story of Methodist bilingual conferences is told in chapter 22.

New Orleans and elsewhere in French-speaking enclaves. By 1900 these had largely disappeared, for their members were absorbed in English-speaking churches. The French Acadians and Creoles in Louisiana claimed the attention of the Southern Church, but few missionaries—and often none—adequate for the task could be found. Those missions remained small.

The Northern Church also conducted missions among immigrants of Bohemian (Czechoslovakian), Portuguese, Spanish, and Jewish background. The Southern Church conducted a highly successful mission among the Czechoslovakian people in Texas, some of whose ablest representatives returned to their homeland after World War I to introduce Methodism there. Through the ministry of the Syrian immigrant Charles Assaf, the Southern Church in 1921 began a small mission among the Syrians and Greeks in and northward from New Orleans.

Spanish-speaking immigrants from Latin America were to be found in the Southwest from Texas to California. Many were present in Florida. By 1900 New York also claimed a substantial Spanish-speaking population. The Northern Church organized Spanish-speaking congregations in California in the 1880's and in Brooklyn, New York, in 1893. By 1919 it had also started missions among Spanish-speaking Americans in New Mexico and Arizona. Among these were two groups: first, those whose forebears had lived in the territory when Mexico held it; and second, those migrants who streamed over the border from Mexico in search of work—most of them agricultural laborers—and those who came seeking political or economic refuge.

The Southern Church carried major responsibility for the Spanish-speaking Americans in the Southwest. The Lydia Patterson Institute in El Paso, Texas, begun in 1913 by J. F. Corbin, trained Methodists for Spanish-speaking missions north and south of the Rio Grande. By 1919 Texas held some 400,000 and New Mexico, Arizona, and California 400,000 more Spanish-speaking people. Most were nominally Roman Catholic, but as with so many immigrants from Latin America and Italy large numbers had no attachment to the church, and among the men many were agnostics or atheists.

During the latter half of the nineteenth century a small but steady stream of immigrants flowed from Cuba to Florida. Many settled and became cigar makers. The Southern Church in 1874 began its missions—never large—among Cubans in Tampa and Key West. From these beginnings came in 1899 the larger mission in Cuba.

Immigrants from the Far East entered the United States mainly through San Francisco, and America's heaviest concentration of Asians was on the Pacific Coast. By 1920 the Japanese in America numbered

111,000, the Chinese 62,000, the Filipinos 5,600, the Indians (mainly Hindu) 2,500, and the Koreans 1,200. Almost from the outset Asians encountered bitter antagonism and often suffered from mob action. "The Yellow Peril" and "Send the Chinese Home" were anti-Asian rallying cries.

Methodism inaugurated its Pacific Coast missions among the Chinese two decades after the first Chinese immigration. Otis Gibson, a former China missionary of the Northern Church, began that work in San Francisco in 1868. The Woman's Missionary Society of the Pacific Coast, founded in 1870 by Methodist women there, contributed greatly to missions among Chinese, Japanese, Koreans, and others. In 1893 it became part of the W.H.M.S.

Most of the initial migration from China had consisted of men; the importation of women began soon after. The more fortunate became wives. Others became prostitutes or servant-slaves. Many were children and young girls. For these the W.H.M.S. and the W.B.H.M. built refuge homes and schools.

By 1920 the Northern Church had missions among Chinese, Japanese, and Koreans in New York, Boston, and Philadelphia. Among them it also conducted missions in many states west of the Mississippi, but had its largest work on the Pacific Coast. There, in time, emerged the California Oriental Mission.

Methodism ministered to the first Japanese arrivals in 1877 in San Francisco. Kanichi Mieyama was one of the earliest to seek instruction from Otis Gibson, and became an outstanding evangelist. Work among the Japanese grew so rapidly that in 1893 the California Conference formed a Japanese District. These new and vigorous Methodists raised money to send Mieyama to Hawaii in 1887 to present the gospel to Japanese immigrants there. In 1940 the Pacific Japanese Provisional Annual Conference was formed.

MORMONS

Brigham Young and his followers settled in 1847 in what became Salt Lake City. Thenceforth the Church of Jesus Christ of Latter-day Saints (Mormons) played a dominant role in Utah's history. In 1855 the Missionary Society of the Northern Church voted funds for a mission in Utah—which meant among Mormons. Believing in a revelation committed to Joseph Smith by the Angel Moroni, practicing polygamy, and engaging in baptism for the salvation of those already dead, the Mormons, so Methodists believed, needed evangelical missions. Yet not until 1869-70 did Methodists enter Utah, and they began to make progress only in 1882 with the arrival of Thomas C. Iliff. The W.H.M.S. aided, and by 1900 the Utah Mission had some 1,100 members with more than 2,000 children in Sunday schools. It met major resistance from the Mormons.

In 1920 the Utah Mission frankly acknowledged a twofold purpose: first, to evangelize and educate; second, to force Mormons to modify their view of "evangelical truth." In 1939 Methodism's Utah Mission numbered 2,700 members and was the largest body in Utah's Protestant community, which included Baptists, Presbyterians, Congregationalists, and Episcopalians.

Urban, Rural, and Mountain Missions

CITY MISSIONS

Shortly after the 1844 division, both Methodist bodies began to see needs in great cities not being met by churches there. Migration from rural areas, immigration from overseas, the establishment of ghettos, the development of slums, the problems arising from industrialization, child labor, "latch-key" children of working parents, human derelicts, sailors temporarily in port—these and other concerns elicited a special missionary ministry.

By the turn of the century the industrialization of the South with giant textile mills and iron and steel manufacturing brought the problems of New England and Pittsburgh to North Carolina and Birmingham. Coal and lead mines in the South reproduced the human problems seen in northern mining districts. What was being done, for example, in the Industrial School, Lincoln Street Community Church, Chicago, and in Stewart House, Gary, was paralleled by the Textile Industrial Institute in Spartanburg. Among their other services, these institutions taught illiterates how to read and provided further general education along with new trade skills. The women of the Southern Church took special responsibility for work among seamen in the burgeoning Gulf ports.

Even before World War I the downtown church, surrounded by the unchurched and with its original members in the suburbs, was seen to be a major, growing problem. To help meet the need, the Northern Church founded in 1912 its Department of City Work. It steadily increased in importance.

GOODWILL INDUSTRIES

Just after the turn of the century young Edgar J. Helms began the Goodwill Industries. Hoping to be a missionary in India, he was assigned instead to Boston's Morgan Memorial Methodist Church. To the indigent and handicapped he brought the used clothing, furniture, and other articles he was able to gather in Boston's Back Bay section. They repaired these items and sold them at low prices. What began in a Methodist church basement grew to become a nation-wide interdenominational Christian social-service undertaking. It has always had strong Methodist support. Goodwill Industries of America aids each local and autonomous Goodwill Industries.

Goodwill's motto, "Not charity, but a chance," across the years meant aid and encouragement for thousands. On the average, of those employed in Goodwill Industries probably 33 per cent were physically handicapped, 25 per cent were unemployable elsewhere because of advancing age, and 15 per cent were emotionally unstable or mentally ill. Through Goodwill others obtained temporary employment when it was desperately needed. Goodwill Industries included occupational training and the teaching of new skills.

RURAL MISSIONS

By the second decade of the twentieth century the Northern and Southern Churches were aware that many country, village, and small-town churches had entered a period of decline and ineffectiveness. In the North the majority of Methodist churches were in villages and small towns. In the South more than 85 per cent of Methodism's congregations belonged to circuits in country districts.

Although specific aspects of the problem varied from North to South, two major factors faced both churches: the shift of the rural population to urban centers and low-salaried ministers more often absent than present because of responsibilities in other churches on the circuit. The result—an impoverished program and a decaying church.

In 1916 the Northern Church in reorganizing its Board of Home Missions and Church Extension established five departments, one of which was the Department of Rural Work. In 1936 this became the Department of Town and Country Work. Major advance here came after 1919.

MOUNTAIN MISSIONS

In the extensive Appalachian Highlands and in the Ozark Mountains the church encountered the isolated mountaineeer. Cut off from the tides of American life, people in these mountain regions by 1919 were still following ancient and crude patterns of agriculture. They were impoverished, illiterate, and were constantly disease-infected.

A minority among them were religious. Of these, one group gave itself to highly emotional—often frenzied—religious expressions. Another group followed what might be called the stern logic of an uninformed rationalism founded on Calvinism. For example, missionary societies and church organs, because they are not mentioned in the Bible, were held to be of the devil. Yet the majority of mountain folk had simply lost contact with whatever religious heritage they had had.

The Northern and Southern Churches conducted missions among these people, mainly through providing schools, settlement houses, and medical clinics. Among others Ferrum Training School (1914) in Virginia, Hiwassee College, begun before the Civil War in Eastern Tennessee, and Young Harris College in Georgia were schools maintained by the Southern Church. An outstanding achievement was Pittman Center in Tennessee. This rural community center, with a large outreach, begun in 1920-21 by the Northern Church, developed—where mountain feuds were common—education, vocational training, medical facilities, and local Methodist churches. A similar enterprise in Tennessee was the John A. Patten Community Center.

DEACONESS WORK

For Methodism the work of women officially recognized and appointed by the church for Christian service appears to have begun in Germany. German Methodism included the deaconess as part of the church's missionary outreach as early as 1868. In 1888 the General Conference of the Northern Church officially recognized the Methodist Deaconess Movement. James M. Thoburn, with an eye to the needs of Indian women, urged the church to sponsor deaconesses. In 1889 he took three of them to India. Isabella Thoburn on her second furlough served as house mother for the Chicago Deaconess Training School. In 1889-90 she helped to begin in Cincinnati the Elizabeth Gamble Deaconess Home and Training School and also Christ Hospital, which was under deaconess management.

The number of deaconesses in the United States grew steadily. In 1890 the Northern Church had three, all working in India. Three decades later it had nearly 900. The Southern Church also provided for deaconesses. The one essential difference between the deaconess and other women workers in the church was that she held membership in the Deaconess Board of an Annual Conference. Her relationship with the conference was much the same as that of the ordained minister. Deaconesses served in any work to which they were appointed—in administrative or editorial posts, as teachers in church-related schools, as a pastor's aide or as the congregation's special missionary, and in social service and missionary posts (orphanages, settlements, district nursing, immigrant work, and vocational schools). In all this the deaconesses may be regarded as part of the church's home missionary staff.

Educational and Medical Work

Medical and educational institutions were also a part of the missionary outreach in America. Methodism's contribution to education is a large one, but in national missions most of the medical and many of the educational institutions were developed by women. Among schools and colleges begun by the W.B.H.M. were Sue Bennett College, a high school and teachers' training school in Eastern Kentucky named for the sister of Belle Harris Bennett and begun in 1897; Brevard Institute, founded in 1895 in North Carolina; and the Vashti Industrial School in Thomasville, Georgia, begun in 1903. Bennett College in Greensboro, North Carolina, begun in 1885 and widely known for its training of Negro young women, was a striking instance of W.H.M.S. efforts in higher education.

Among the important medical centers founded by the W.H.M.S. were Brewster Hospital for Negroes in Jacksonville, Florida (1886); Sibley Memorial Hospital in Washington, D. C., for all who needed medical care there (1895); the Methodist Deaconess Hospital in Rapid City, South Dakota, serving the needs of what was then still the frontier (1912); the Methodist Deaconess Sanitarium in Albuquerque for tuberculars (1912); Holden Hospital, begun earlier but in 1916 established in Carbondale, Illinois; and Methodist Hospital in Los Angeles. The Southern Church built few hospitals until the 1920's.

Outpost Missions

ALASKA

Methodism began its work in Alaska when in 1886 J. H. Carr, a local preacher, and his wife arrived in Unga to begin a mission. In 1888 the W.H.M.S. instituted its Bureau of Alaska Work and two years later was building the Jesse Lee Memorial and Industrial Home at Unalaska in the Aleutians. Agnes Soule, under W.H.M.S. auspices, was the first missionary there.

In 1897 the Northern Church formally established a mission in Alaska and sent a missionary. By 1920 Methodism in Alaska stretched from Ketchikan to Juneau and Skagway, to Seward, Fairbanks, and Nome and out to Unalaska. It ministered to whites, Indians, and Eskimos. The Presbyterians, Episcopalians, and other Protestant bodies also conducted missions in Alaska. By 1940, after both had had roughly a half century in Alaska, the Methodists and Presbyterians could each point to only one self-supporting church. There was no self-supporting Episcopal congregation.

HAWAII

At the request of Hawaii, and with the strong conviction that Hawaii would serve American interests in the Pacific, the United States annexed the Hawaiian Islands in 1898.

Congregational missionaries had planted Christianity in Hawaii early in the nineteenth century. In time their descendants controlled the islands' major financial and commercial interests. By the 1880's Hawaii's increasing need for a larger labor force drew thousands of immigrants from Japan, China, Korea, and the Philippines.

In 1855 several English and American Methodists formed a class in Honolulu and met regularly with a preacher appointed from the California Conference. But interest dwindled, and all Methodist property was sold in 1862. Methodism's second entry came in 1887, when Japanese Methodists in California sent and supported missionaries from among themselves to Hawaii's new Japanese immigrants. When these efforts bore fruit—and not least of all because of financial difficulties—the California Conference transferred the work in 1892 to the Hawaiian Board, an agency of the Hawaiian churches in co-operation with the Congregational Board in Boston. Yet the Japanese Methodists in Hawaii refused to acknowledge the transfer and continued to meet as Methodists. The California Conference officially resumed a mission in 1893, when it sent two more Japanese missionaries.

In 1904, by General Conference action, the Hawaiian Mission became a home missionary project. By 1921 there were in Honolulu two Japanese Methodist Churches and a Korean and a Filipino Methodist Church. Methodism in Hawaii grew very slowly, and as late as 1955 numbered less than 3,800 members.

PUERTO RICO AND THE DOMINICAN REPUBLIC

The United States received Puerto Rico in 1898 from Spain. With American rule came complete religious freedom on the island and an incursion of Protestant missions from the mainland.

Methodism entered Puerto Rico in 1900, with the transfer of Charles W. Drees from Uruguay to Puerto Rico. He opened the first Methodist Church in San Juan, and within months other Methodist missionaries began arriving. In 1902 the W.H.M.S. inaugurated several projects, one of which eventuated in the George O. Robinson School for Girls in Santurce. When the several Protestant churches in Puerto Rico concluded a comity agreement, Methodism was assigned an area running north and south through the center of the island and including the important cities of San Juan, Ponce, and Arecibo.

As an outgrowth of its Puerto Rican mission, the Northern Church in

1920 joined with what are now the Evangelical United Brethren Church and the United Presbyterian Church in the U.S.A. in the Board for Christian Work in the Dominican Republic (in 1920 Santo Domingo). Outreach early included a church, a hospital, several schools, and community service.

7

Retrospect and Prospect

With a few exceptions—for example, Hong Kong and Taiwan—American Methodism by 1921 had largely achieved its geographic outreach. Methodism was to grow strongly in India, but achieved a more rapid growth rate in Korea. It expanded steadily in Latin America and swiftly in Africa.

By 1921 the 99,000 American-related European Methodists outnumbered the 42,500 in Latin America. The smallest group—nearly 23,000—was in Africa, with Liberia, Mozambique, and Southern Rhodesia accounting for all but 2,000 of that number. Some 218,500 were in East and Southeast Asia, with China supplying more than 101,000. India alone with its 405,500 American-related Methodists outnumbered the combined totals of all other lands. Of the 790,000 Methodists outside the United States and related to American Methodism through its overseas missions, about 37,000 were associated with the Southern Church, about 3,500 with the Methodist Protestant Church, and the remainder with the Northern Church. Because the Southern Church statistics appear to list only church members, rather than including preparatory members and baptized children, its figure should be doubled to make it more nearly comparable to the "constituency" figure given for the Northern Church.

By way of comparison, by 1921, of American Methodism's nearly 2,300 overseas missionaries, some 1,675 were concentrated in Asia—in lands with ancient civilizations and high religions. More than 1,165 (over half the total) were in China and India. Elsewhere, some 400 were working in Latin America; 170 (31 of them in the unproductive Muslim North) in Africa; and 33 in Europe. Of the total number of missionaries, 1,846 served under the Northern Church, 432 under the Southern Church, and the others under the Methodist Protestant Church.

One notes also that by 1921 the proportion of Methodist missionaries overseas—allowing for all the yearly variations—averaged about 48 per cent single women, about 50 per cent married couples, and somewhat less than 2 per cent single men. Thus, in any given year, of the Methodist missionaries overseas from 67 to 75 per cent were women. To be precise, by 1921 women composed 69 per cent and in 1938 nearly 74 per cent of the total. In this and in other factors Methodism mirrored the trends in American Protestant missions.

Table I shows the geographical distribution and denominational make-up of American Methodism's missionary force overseas on the eve of union. The total number of missionaries in 1938 was considerably smaller than it had been two decades earlier, but the geographical distribution was proportionately similar. Although in 1960 there were only twenty more missionaries than in 1938, the proportional geographic distribution had shifted.

Table I

Geographic Distribution of Foreign Missionaries in 1938
(Methodist Episcopal Church, Methodist Episcopal Church, South, Methodist Protestant Church) [15]

Area	M.E.	M.E.S.	M.P.	Total
Asia				
1. Japan	51	65	5	121
2. Korea	63	61	—	124
3. China	265	87	5	357
4. Philippines	26	—	—	26
5. Malaya	64	—	—	64
6. Sarawak	2	—	—	2
7. Sumatra	15	—	—	15
8. Burma	25	—	—	25
9. India	330	—	4	334
Asia Total	841	213	14	1,068
Africa				
10. Algeria	17	—	—	17
11. Tunisia	1	—	—	1
12. Liberia	12	—	—	12
13. Angola	15	—	—	15
14. Congo	15	41	—	56
15. S. Rhodesia	32	—	—	32
16. Union of South Africa	2	—	—	2
17. Mozambique	17	—	—	17
Africa Total	111	41	—	152

[15] Reconstructed from the *Christian Advocate*, May 19, 1938, as reprinted in John R. Mott, *Methodists United for Action* (Nashville: Board of Missions of The Methodist Church, 1939), p. 33.

Area	M.E.	M.E.S.	M.P.	Total
Latin America				
18. Cuba	—	34	—	34
19. Mexico	15	21	—	36
20. Central America	4	—	—	4
21. Brazil	—	68	—	68
22. Uruguay	9	—	—	9
23. Argentina	17	—	—	17
24. Chile	15	—	—	15
25. Bolivia	24	—	—	24
26. Peru	18	—	—	18
Latin America Total	102	123	—	225
Europe				
27. Bulgaria	3	—	—	3
28. Italy	1	—	—	1
29. Poland	—	8	—	8
Europe Total	4	8	—	12
Combined Total	1,058	385	14	1,457

To provide perspective on the number of missionaries at home and abroad immediately prior to unification Table II is printed below. As it indicates, when compared with Table I, almost four times as many were then engaged in national missions as in overseas missions.

Table II
Missionaries and Deaconesses in National Missions, 1938 [16]

Methodist Episcopal Church
Board of Home Missions and Church Extension 2,550
Woman's Home Missionary Society 890
                                                    _____
                                                    3,440

Methodist Episcopal Church, South
Board of Missions 234
Annual Conference Boards of Missions 1,737
Woman's Missionary Council 166
                                                    _____
                                                    2,137

Methodist Protestant Church
Board of Missions 15
        Combined Total 5,592

[16] Mott, *Methodists United for Action*, p. 32.

Thus is drawn in all too brief detail the picture of American Methodism's missions as they were in the United States and overseas at the end of World War I.

The four decades ahead were to produce many instances of rapid growth. They were to speed the rise to prominence of first-class national leadership in the non-Western churches. They were also to bring in 1939 unification of the three bodies of American Methodism—a union eagerly desired and accomplished, in greater or lesser degree, earlier in Japan, Mexico, and Korea. Increasingly, the question of uniting with other Protestant churches was to come to the fore. And once again the Japan Methodist Church led the way when, at the beginning of World War II, it entered and remained permanently in the *Kyodan*, the Church of Christ in Japan. As Methodism was to discover, mission and unity are opposite sides of one Christian coin. Mission leads to unity.

The decades already past held their own meaning. In 1844, except for a handful in Liberia, there were virtually no Methodists outside the continental United States who had sprung from American Methodist missions. Seventy-five years later, in 1919, there were approximately 800,000 who, humanly speaking, had received the gospel through Methodism's agency. The statistics point to major growth, but they are coldly impersonal. What lies behind them—human loneliness and separation from family (especially of missionary parents from their children), dedication of life, willingness to endure persecution for new-found faith, joyous service to others, uncertainty and belief—cannot be measured. But these imponderables are what really matter, for in ways that pass human understanding they are caught up in and made part of the abiding and eternal purpose of God.

chapter 28

METHODIST PUBLISHING IN HISTORICAL PERSPECTIVE

1865-1939

Growth of the
   Publishing Programs

Books

Church Papers

Sunday School
   Literature

Men Who Built
   the Programs

I F METHODISM, OUTGROWING ITS EARLY immaturity of thinking and working, came of age in the bitter controversy over slavery, it reached a greater maturity in the testing times of Reconstruction.

Here were the freedmen, to be cared for and to be prepared for the full responsibilities of citizenship. It was not easy to look after the moral and intellectual needs of a people emerging from slavery; and while the government was ready to give some leadership, this was primarily a task for the churches. Methodists, both North and South, were ready and willing.

There were other problems, only a little less difficult. As always in wartime, the country suffered a moral breakdown, and it came in spite of the idealism that found expression on both sides in such songs as "The Battle Hymn of the Republic." A period of luxury, extravagance, speculation, and intemperance followed. Immigration from overseas, the westward move to the frontiers, industrialization, and the growth of the cities brought new problems.

Methodists would have done better if they could have faced these as a reunited church. Yet it must be remembered that there were no dividing differences of theology, and this helped mightily in healing the wounds left by the war between brothers.

129

1

The Story of Three Ventures, 1866-1900

It was in such a sticky complex of problems, with all the bitterness that often boils up out of religious zeal, that the publishing enterprises, North and South, were doing their work at war's end. It was good for them that there was no waning of religious idealism to go with the religious enthusiasm that persisted on both sides of the Mason-Dixon line.

The Publishing House in the Postwar South

The economic plight of the South was desperate. When the 1866 General Conference met at New Orleans, the first since 1858, it heard that church membership had been depleted by a third and hundreds of church buildings had been destroyed. Homes were gone. Businesses were wiped out. Farms abandoned. Almost everyone was poor, and many were hungry. (Subscription rates of the *South Carolina Christian Advocate* had jumped to $5 a year in 1863, $10 in 1864, and $20 in 1865, when the paper had only two pages a week.)

That first postwar General Conference was a brave and determined one. It determined to launch out on new plans for the Board of Missions, and to re-establish the Publishing House.

The delegates read again the words of John B. McFerrin, editor of the Nashville *Christian Advocate* in 1855, when he made a plea for support of the publishing program. He suggested that Methodists thereby would be helping "in disseminating among the masses a sanctifying and enlightening leaven, in elevating the standard of public morality, in erecting a barrier against the assaults of Popery, infidelity, intemperance and every evil thing, in securing to our country a yet more exalted position among the nations of the earth, and in hastening the reign of the Prince of Peace." [1]

This statement was made soon after the Southern Church received, after long-drawn-out court procedures, a settlement of its share of Book Concern assets and debts, and started its publishing house on a permanent basis. A remodeled sugar warehouse at Nashville, Tennessee, became the plant, and there were installed "three Adams presses of different sizes, a sheet press, a book press, a smasher [for book binding], two or three

[1] The Nashville *Christian Advocate*, September 13, 1855, p. 2.

standing presses, three embossing presses, cutting machines and other necessary materials." [2]

This was the building that Federal troops occupied in February of 1862 and turned into a government printing office. When it was handed back at war's end, it was in wretched condition. The machinery had been worn out or destroyed. Much of the stocks of paper and ink and other materials had been used. "There was practically nothing left except the walls and the roof," wrote Bishop Horace M. Du Bose.[3] And claims for damages were not settled until 1898.

With a courage that is hard to understand at this distance, the Southern Church determined to make a new beginning. The old building was remodeled. The bookstore was refitted. Needed equipment was found for the publication of the Nashville *Christian Advocate*. The General Conference of 1866 had recommended reduction in the number of periodicals and tighter control over depositories; and these changes were made.[4]

Book agent McFerrin, who had come back from the chaplaincy with the Confederate armies to devote to the publishing business his skill at handling men, materials, and money, was elected secretary of the Board of Domestic Missions, and A. H. Redford was named his successor.

Twelve troubled years followed. Lack of capital, failure to win church-wide backing, and inability to collect overdue debts put the Publishing House in such a sad state that the 1870 General Conference debated closing the whole operation. Finally, the delegates decided to keep the headquarters at Nashville (as over against Louisville, which made a strong plea for a move and a fresh beginning) and to abolish as a luxury the office of financial secretary.[5]

To make matters worse, in 1872 fire destroyed part of the old building. The office of the book editor and the composing and stereotyping rooms were demolished by flames and water. When book editor T. O. Summers saw the damage, he commented in a predestinarian vein: "The Lord would not have permitted so great a calamity to happen to me, if he had not intended to over-rule it for good; so I submit without murmuring." [6] Those in charge of publishing found a new site and authorized the book agent to issue bonds to pay for a new building. But when this was completed, the north wall bulged, making the whole structure unsafe. The wall had to be torn down and rebuilt.

[2] Book Committee Minutes, Methodist Episcopal Church, South, June 7, 1854.
[3] Du Bose, *A History of Methodism* (Nashville: Lamar and Smith, 1916), p. 152.
[4] *Journal of the General Conference of the Methodist Church, South*, 1866, pp. 71, 83.
[5] *Journal of the General Conference*, 1870, pp. 303-4.
[6] Diary of T. O. Summers, quoted in O. P. Fitzgerald, *Dr. Summers, A Life Study* (Nashville: Southern Methodist Publishing House, 1885), p. 270.

At the 1874 General Conference Southern Methodists faced the fact that their publishing venture was on the verge of bankruptcy. But they looked at the responsibility of providing Christian literature and determined to keep the presses turning.

The decline continued. The circulation of all periodicals fell off. Book sales were at the lowest ebb since 1866. Debts could not be collected because of a business depression that engulfed the nation. Liabilities came to exceed assets by more than $45,000.[7] All sales were put on a cash basis, and the College of Bishops solicited funds from the whole church.

By 1878 there was a complete report for the General Conference. The conference accepted it, attributing whatever shortcomings there were to injudicious expenditures on the building, faulty construction that required expensive repairs, a disastrous fire, excessive and unwise credit policies, high rates of interest and discount, large salaries paid to some employees, and general depreciation in values because of pressure for money.

The General Conference, instead of re-electing Redford, called McFerrin back to straighten things out. He and the Book Committee were given full authority to liquidate the business, if they thought it necessary. The devoted McFerrin was then seventy-one years old, but he accepted the tough assignment. When the election was unanimous, he sat in his chair and wept.[8]

His problem as book agent was to buy time. First, he asked all employees to accept reduced salaries. He persuaded creditors to extend credit on overdue accounts. He developed what came to be known as "McFerrin's Bond Scheme," a plan for raising $300,000 in bonds running for thirty to forty years and secured by a mortgage on all the property of the Publishing House. He went from Annual Conference to Annual Conference selling the plan, enlisting the support of the ministers and lay people, and hoping and praying for better days.

When the bonds had been sold, payments of wages and salaries in full were resumed, creditors were paid off, many of the old Redford bonds were bought up, the credit of the House was restored, machinery and other needed equipment was purchased. New books of standard quality came from the presses.

When McFerrin died in 1887, as he was approaching his eightieth year, it was clear that he had worked a miracle in saving a bankrupt book business. All the bonds would be retired before their maturity date, and a plan had been devised for repaying the $16,619 that Redford

[7] *Journal of the General Conference,* 1878, p. 143.

[8] O. P. Fitzgerald, *John B. McFerrin* (Nashville: Publishing House of the Methodist Episcopal Church, South, 1889), p. 359.

was judged, on careful accounting, to owe the Publishing House. Best of all, the Southern Church had the best-equipped publishing house in the South.

In reviewing this story of defeat turned into victory it is important to remember the political and social confusion of the times. There was widespread corruption in government on all levels. Judges, as well as votes, were bought. Laws went through legislatures and were signed with no other purpose than to create great private fortunes. Prominent political figures were guilty of chicanery and devilry that eventually brought some of them disgrace, but many escaped.

The Methodist editors cried out against such political goings-on, even as they did not hesitate to condemn blacker corruption in business. Across the nation there were defalcations of one kind and another, wildcat selling, speculation that smelled to high heaven, and railroad projects that were crawling with fraud. Pious men were guilty of impious actions. It was a day when "making a fast buck" was almost unrestrained by public laws or private morals. Many of the guilty ones were church members, but there were few preachers to cry out, "Thou art the man!"

The Book Concern in the North

Although the war did not wreck the Book Concern in the North as it did the Publishing House in the South, many setbacks came. First, the fighting postponed until 1869 the purchase of a new building authorized by the General Conference of 1860. That conference also proposed a change of policy so that the bishops would no longer be paid from proceeds of the book business in violation of the Sixth Restrictive Rule. This rule, a part of the Methodist constitution, provided that all profits be devoted to the relief of worn-out preachers and the widows and orphans of preachers.

There was remarkable growth in net capital, sales, and profits in both the New York and Cincinnati houses from 1861 to 1872, but no corresponding increase was made in payments to conferences for pensions. The New York agency was incorporated as the "Methodist Book Concern," and the Western Book Concern, in Cincinnati, was authorized to get a new act of incorporation. The Western branch was also given permission to publish the *Southwestern Christian Advocate* at New Orleans.

In spite of wartime shortages many tracts and a few books continued to pour from the presses. *Golden Hours,* a magazine for young people, was started in 1869. But probably the most significant venture was the

development of the Sunday school literature that was to become later
such an important part of the publishing program.

An article published in the *Western Christian Advocate* in 1863 declared that "any church which fails properly to bestir herself in the cause
of liberal education will fall behind and lose the influence with the
public mind which she would otherwise exert." Because the ministers
were the leaders of Methodism, the editor continued, "the ministry must
be more intelligent than the masses of the people, or it will fall into
merited contempt." [9]

Educational standards had been improving from the very start of the
church, but the publishers never forgot the admonition of the 1816
General Conference: "In the opinion of this Conference, it is expedient
for the managers of the Book Concern to publish more small books and
fewer large ones." [10]

Between 1868 and 1872 there were widespread rumors of fraud in
the operation of the publishing interests in the North, as well as in the
South.

In 1868, when John Lanahan was elected junior agent in New York,
he discovered irregularities in several departments. The son of a former
assistant sold the Book Concern all of its paper, amounting to $100,000
a year. Paper houses sold him the supplies, and he resold to the
Book Concern at a substantial profit. Other alleged frauds in payment
of wages, in inventories, in purchase of inks and leathers totaled some
$300,000.

When Lanahan disclosed these conditions, the Book Committee was
summoned and he was directed to present evidence. There were both
majority and minority reports from the committee, with only the minority
favoring Lanahan. Both reports were sent to the Annual Conferences,
and they, too, voted against the junior agent.

Lanahan was brought to trial before the Book Committee and the
bishops, charged with official misconduct, neglect of official duty, ir-
responsibility, untruthfulness, and insubordination. But the charges
were dismissed, largely through the influence of the bishops.

Controversy between Lanahan and the senior agent, Thomas Carlton,
followed. Lanahan appealed to the civil courts and was suspended again,
this time for taking church affairs into other than church courts. The
trial found him guilty, and he was removed from office, but the bishops
refused to concur.

The 1872 General Conference heard the reports of falsification, "prac-

[9] July 1, 1863, p. 204.
[10] *Journals of the General Conference*, 1796-1836 (New York: Carlton and Phillips,
1855), p. 171.

tices in the bindery, by which the Book Concern has suffered loss," and other "irregularities in the management of the business." But the conference concluded that there were no "reasonable grounds or proof to justify an assumption that any Agent or Assistant Agent is, or has been, implicated or interested in any frauds which have been practiced in the Concern." [11]

These sad events had a good sequel: they brought laymen into the church's book business, with the hope of introducing better business methods.

In 1869, with the Missionary Society, the Book Concern had bought a five-story building at 805 Broadway in New York, at the then-extravagant price of $1,000,000. It served until 1890, when an eight-story structure was erected at 150 Fifth Avenue.

In 1870 the Western Book Concern also occupied new quarters. Depositories were opened from time to time in various cities as the church moved westward. Indeed, church journals had much to do with this expansion. A single instance was Jason Lee and his reading in a church paper the story of the Indians journeying across the mountains to St. Louis in quest of the "white man's book." And soon Jason Lee was on his way to Oregon.

Methodist Protestant Publishing After the War

While the Methodist Protestants did not suffer precisely as did the two larger bodies of Methodists during the war that divided the nation, they had problems. And their publishing enterprises were almost stopped.

The Methodist Protestant Book Concern was never large, yet its products were of a high order. In the early days there was a well-defined plan to promote the program of democratizing (some said "Americanizing") Methodism. Other denominations had to depend on effective organization to achieve and preserve unity. This one, comparatively small in numbers and with a definite purpose, achieved unity largely through the persuasive power of its editors. According to J. Minton Batten, "They attained their most notable success by developing periodicals which typed the life, thought and practice of the church. No American denomination of like strength has produced such an able succession of editors of church papers." [12]

The denomination divided in 1858 over the slavery issue, and con-

---

[11] *Journal of the General Conference*, 1872, p. 367.
[12] Batten, *The History of the Methodist Publishing House* (Nashville: Personnel and Public Relations Division of The Methodist Publishing House, 1954), p. 186.

tinued divided until 1877. During this period each church had its own publishing agency and its own periodicals. The paper serving the Northern and Western conferences was the *Methodist Recorder;* it moved to Pittsburgh in 1871 and emanated from a parsonage there. This headquarters was known as the "Pittsburgh Book Directory."

The other publishing enterprise centered at Baltimore and printed the *Methodist Protestant.* Since it could not be circulated beyond the Federal lines during the war, its subscriptions declined. The book business was almost completely destroyed. This location was known as the "Baltimore Book Directory."

When the church reunited, the General Conference decided to maintain the book centers in both Pittsburgh and Baltimore as a means of serving the forty-four conferences.

In the period from 1877 to 1896 the Methodist Protestants issued a constantly increasing volume of Sunday school literature. E. J. Drinkhouse, editor of the *Methodist Protestant,* worked hard to convince the church that it ought to have its own religious education materials. Finally, Methodist Protestant helps on the International Sunday School Lessons were issued.

Pertinent here is the comment of N. S. Albright, as quoted by F. A. Archibald in *Methodism and Literature:*

> The question of Lesson Helps involves in their preparation a broad Christian scholarship, a spirit of catholicity in harmony with the prevalent spirit of unity among Christians, and a clear view of the varied wants of the several departments of Sunday-school instruction.
>
> They [lesson helps] present the catholic faith from our Methodist standpoint. . . . They are none the less Christian and catholic for being positively Methodistic; for Methodism is an insistence not so much upon non-essentials of creed as upon the essentials of Christian life.[13]

There were problems, of course, revolving around Sunday school methods. The question-and-answer plan of teaching was deeply entrenched. As late as 1890 the bishops of the Methodist Episcopal Church, South, urged the advantages of catechetical instruction. But as early as 1880, the Committee on the Relation of Children to the Church reported to the Methodist Protestant General Conference: "The infant children of our members, upon receiving baptism, shall be enrolled as probationary members of our Church, and shall be taught and watched over as lambs of the flock, with a view to their confessing Christ pub-

---

[13] N. S. Albright, "Our Sunday School Lesson Helps," *Methodism and Literature,* F. A. Archibald, ed. (New York: Phillips and Hunt, 1883), pp. 201-2.

licly, as soon as their knowledge and experience shall enable them to do so." [14]

Periodicals in the Postwar Era

These years in which the nation was being rebuilt found the churches laying a strong emphasis on reading, and on good reading. There was some reversion against the sentimentality of such papers as *The Ladies' Repository*, with a sweetness-and-light approach that before the Civil War had appealed to the sheltered second-generation daughters of pioneers. Nevertheless, with some variation in approach, the magazine continued for thirty-five years. *The Southern Ladies' Companion* was published for awhile about the middle of the century.

These papers changed their "escapist" slant in the starkly realistic days of the war and after, and they added a note of moralism.

The same note could be found in the reviews that flourished after the war. In 1847 *The Quarterly Review* had been founded by the Southern Church, but it was suspended during the conflict. In 1870, A. T. Bledsoe's *Southern Review* became the official review of the denomination, and in 1879 it resumed the original name. The Northern Church's *Methodist Quarterly Review*, retitled in 1885 *The Methodist Review*, continued to flourish. It had many distinguished editors, and a multitude of readers beyond the limits of the denomination.

Regarding this periodical, which brought the values of theological insights to bear on current problems, W. F. Whitlock wrote:

It has always been most aggressive in the work assigned to Reviews. Its pages uniformly contain a very concise, vigorous, and elaborate treatment of living, current questions. Its circulation has shown that our ministers and people have not been inattentive to subjects requiring laborious investigation and varied learning. Its editorial management has been characterized by keen insight, ripe scholarship, and a broad catholicity; and its contents, spirit and influence have compelled recognition from sources the least willing to bestow it.[15]

---

[14] *Journal of the General Conference of the Methodist Protestant Church*, 1880, p. 56.
[15] *The Story of the Book Concerns* (Cincinnati: Jennings and Pye, 1903), p. 200.

2

Moving into a New Century

As the twentieth century began, the Methodist publishing interests in
the North were providing a literature that made Methodists. Editor
James M. Buckley of the New York *Christian Advocate,* on the occasion
of the opening of the Methodist building at 150 Fifth Avenue, wrote:
"Perhaps the greatest work accomplished by Methodist literature has
been to counteract the natural tendencies of strong religious emotion to
fanaticism." [16]

The Northern Church's Program

During the twenty years that marked the end of the nineteenth century, there occurred an enormous popularity of religious books and
periodicals. From 1888 until 1900 the Book Concern of the Methodist
Episcopal Church made new sales records and invested large sums in
real estate and equipment.

The General Conference of 1904 ordered a committee on the unification
of Book Concern enterprises in the East and West, and the next General
Conference made plans for this union. The incorporation was under
the name "The Methodist Book Concern," with responsibility for producing and circulating the various publications of the church.

The General Conference of 1924 emphasized the purpose of the Book
Concern and pointed out the "objects and purposes" as then contained
in the *Discipline* (paragraph 379) : "The promotion of Christian education; the dissemination of moral and religious literature; the spread
of Christianity by the publication, sale and distribution of moral and
religious literature; the transaction of such business as is properly connected with book publishing, making and book-selling." The stipulation
was that the produce was to be applied for the benefit of the preachers,
their wives, widows, and children.[17]

Teaching material came to the forefront in the early 1900's. In 1908
the Book Concern co-operated with other Protestant denominations in

---

[16] Address printed in memento volume *Centennial of the Methodist Book Concern
and Dedication of the New Publishing and Mission Building* (New York: Hunt and
Eaton, 1890) , p. 78.

[17] *Journal of the General Conference of the Methodist Episcopal Church,* 1924, pp.
607-10.

the preparation of the Graded Lesson Series. The success of the venture surprised even the publishing agents. In 1910 they reported: "These lessons are meeting with great favor wherever introduced. The material of this series is prepared by persons who justly rank among the foremost Sunday-school experts of the land." [18]

These early years of the century were marked by expanding sales and large dividends for conference claimants. During the quadrennium 1908-12 the New York House "published from original manuscripts 128 volumes, imported 42 volumes in sheets; purchased in sheets from outside publishers 40 volumes; also published four different sets of church and Sunday-school requisites, making a total of 294 distinct publications." [19] Payments to conference claimants increased from $240,000 in 1904-8 to $370,000 in 1908-12.

In 1916 the matter of reducing the number of *Advocates* came up again, but the General Conference rejected a plan for combining the three published at Chicago. Again in 1920 the problem of consolidating the *Advocates* was discussed and shelved.

The General Conference of 1924 ordered the *Advocates* to publish "from six to ten pages of uniform matter, exclusive of advertising," [20] and this was to be prepared by a contributing editor. Halford E. Luccock was named. A secretary of good literature was ordered for each charge, to promote circulation of books and papers.

In 1924 the total sales of the Methodist Book Concern since 1844 and the division of the church were listed at $142,000,000.[21] For the 1921-24 quadrennium the conference claimants received $1,125,000.[22]

The building and dedication of a beautiful new plant at Dobbs Ferry, New York, came in 1927.

The General Conference of 1932, as an economy measure, discontinued *The Methodist Review*. Begun in 1818 it reached its zenith in the halcyon days of the reviews immediately after the Civil War.

A merger of the *Advocates* was ordered, providing for the publication of the *Christian Advocate* as a national weekly, with six regional editions produced at five separate editorial offices scattered from New York to San Francisco.

[18] Homer Eaton and George P. Mains, Annual Report on the Methodist Book Concern in New York City, *The Methodist Yearbook*, 1911, p. 82.
[19] *The Methodist Yearbook*, 1913, p. 89.
[20] *Journal of the General Conference*, 1924, p. 606.
[21] *The Methodist Yearbook*, 1925, p. 25.
[22] *Ibid.*, p. 13.

Southern Publishing in the New Century

The end of the nineteenth century and the first years of the twentieth brought new opportunities, too, for the Southern Publishing House. Immediately after the heroic work of McFerrin, sales increased and improvements were made in all departments. The bonded indebtedness was decreased, a sinking fund was created to take care of all outstanding bonds, and distribution of profits was made to conference claimants. With the best-equipped printing plant in the South, the Publishing House was producing materials that won wide acclaim.

Book depositories, set up in the postwar years, were discontinued as unprofitable. The book agent recommended that a plan for selling books and pamphlets from meeting to meeting and house to house be adopted to increase sales. Annual Conferences were to have their own plans for colportage, employing colporteurs to do the job of more widely disseminating the word of God and placing literature in the hands and homes of the people.[23] But this program did not produce the expected results, and it was abandoned after 1906.

Despite the depression years of the 1890's, especially the panic of 1893, the Publishing House continued its expansion. The General Conference in 1894 heard a report of the agents:

> Many private fortunes were swept away, promising enterprises came to grief and loss; banks were suspended and broken; railroads were wrecked and placed in the hands of receivers; and the commercial interests and activities of the land received a shock from which, even now, they are but slowly recovering. . . . The fact that under conditions so unfavorable our Publishing House not only maintained its credit unimpaired, but pushed forward the great work beyond the lines of its former success is quite enough to cause Southern Methodism to "thank God" and take courage! [24]

In March of 1898 the church received the news that Congress had approved a long-delayed bill for paying the war claims for damage to the Nashville plant during the Civil War. The amount was $288,000. The General Conference of 1898 heard the news gladly, and ordered expansion.

This expansion continued as a branch was set up in a rented house in Dallas. In 1901 a book agent went to Shanghai, China, to investigate the advisability of opening a Methodist Publishing House there. A joint

[23] *Journal of the General Conference of the Methodist Episcopal Church, South,* 1890, p. 249.

[24] *Journal of the General Conference,* 1894, pp. 230-31.

effort with the Northern Church, this was another step toward Methodist reunion.

Back in 1890 the agents had been authorized to translate, publish, and sell materials for the dissemination of religious knowledge in Mexico and Brazil.[25] This had been the beginning of the process of using foreign-language publications on the mission field. The Board of Missions gladly joined in this venture. The Spanish literature met with an immediate response.

The settlement of the war claims against the federal government brought severe criticism to the Publishing House. Church papers accused the publishing agents of unethical conduct in pressing the claims. Actually, the church had been working for more than thirty years to get a settlement. Finally, E. B. Stahlman, an attorney, was hired to obtain the most favorable terms possible, with the agreements that he would receive 35 per cent of the amount collected.

Senator Pasco of Florida, who was sponsoring the bill in the Senate after the House had passed it, heard a rumor being circulated that Stahlman had been promised a 40 per cent commission. The senator wired the publishing agents. They authorized him to deny the story, and their statement was read on the Senate floor. The erroneous impression got around that no commission at all was being paid. When it became evident that this was not the case, a storm of criticism inside and outside the church ensued. The College of Bishops addressed a letter to the Senate's presiding officer which said: "If the Senate, by affirmative action, declares that the passage of the bill was due to such misleading statements, we will take the proper steps to have the entire amount returned to the government." [26] This quick and forthright action brought complete exoneration for the church.

Criticism, however, continued for some time. There was a demand in the General Conference of 1902 that the church "retire from the printing business as speedily as possible," abandoning plans for a new plant and office building. The practice of selling nonreligious items also came in for censure.

A new era in Publishing House history followed that General Conference. D. M. Smith and A. J. Lamar were elected publishing agents. Smith, a layman, knew the House thoroughly; Lamar, a minister, knew the church. An innovation which came that year was the establishment of a circulation and advertising department.

Except for the usual wartime difficulties experienced when America

[25] *Journal of the General Conference*, 1890, p. 99.
[26] Du Bose, *History*, pp. 189 ff.

entered World War I, the period between 1905 and unification was one of relatively great success for the Southern Publishing House. In 1906 the property on the Nashville public square was sold and a new building erected at 810 Broadway. This structure, which became the headquarters location of the Publishing House following unification, until 1924 housed both offices and the printing plant, as well as offices of other Southern Methodist boards located in Nashville. In 1922 an acre of ground was acquired at 815 Demonbreun Street for the erection of a new printing plant. This was completed in 1924, and forms the core of what today are the property holdings of the Methodist Publishing House in Nashville.

Steady growth in production, sales, and appropriations to the Annual Conferences characterized the Southern House in the thirty years leading up to unification. Indicative of this is the fact that appropriations to conference claimants rose from $2,000 in the early quadrennia of the century to more than $100,000 a year in the 1920's. Annual sales increased from less than $500,000 in 1900 to more than $2,100,000 in 1922. Throughout the 1920's, and even during the depression years of the 30's, annual sales ranged between $1,500,000 and $2,000,000. When unification of the publishing interests came about in 1940, the Southern Publishing House was in the best financial condition of any of the three houses. Ironically, after decades of struggle even to keep its doors open, to the Southern House in 1940 fell the responsibility of putting the unified publishing interests of Methodism on sound financial ground.

The publishing venture in the Methodist Episcopal Church, South, went on from one success to another. The plan for lifting literary standards and distributing books more effectively through Cokesbury Press (described later) was one of its chief contributions to the publishing program at the time of unification.

Immigration and the Publishing Program

Immigration, which was one of the trying problems of the nineteenth century, helped Methodism by bringing to the growing country many Germans and Scandinavians. *Der Christliche Apologete* went back to 1839, and by 1884 the Methodist Episcopal Church was ready to order a German translation of the *Discipline. Den Kristelige Talsmand* was published for Norwegians from 1877 to 1922. In 1889, *Vidnesbyrdet* was added for Norwegian and Danish newcomers to the Pacific Coast. The *Talsmand* was followed by *Evangelisk Tidende,* published from 1922 to 1940, when it became the *Gospel Advocate,* in English.

To indicate something of the contents of these publications, here is a sampling, taken from editor Christian Treider's prospectus for 1899: "God's Providence in Nature," "The War with Spain and Its Lessons," "Missionary Activity in India," "The Marriage of Christians to Ungodly Persons," "Mormonism," "Conditions in the Philippines," and "Preachers' Salaries."

The significance of these papers, which the publishing houses printed, is indicated by these words of Arlow W. Andersen, who said of *Talsmand* (as he might have said of the Swedish *Sandebudet* too) : "Through this weekly visitor a thinly dispersed minority of a major denomination, in an English-speaking land, found an invaluable bond of union and spiritual guidance." [27]

Distribution of Published Materials

Clearly, the success of the publishing ventures in the three churches that became in 1939 The Methodist Church was not merely in the writing and editing and printing, but also in the distributing of books, tracts, and periodicals. The purpose was never to make money, but rather to furnish religious reading matter. The leaders steered a middle course between two extremes—publication at actual cost, with abundant reading materials at such a low figure as to defy competition, and publication at the average market rate, with the largest possible return to ministers, their widows, and orphans, in accordance with the Sixth Restrictive Rule.

The key man in the distribution of Methodist materials was always the preacher. In 1820 he was allowed 37½ per cent discount on purchases for his own use and liberal commissions on the books he sold. Often a preacher made twice as much in commissions as he gained in salary. In 1889 it was stated that "three-fourths of the products of the Methodist Book Concern have reached their destination, directly or indirectly, through the agency of Methodist preachers. The people still look to them for their reading matter, as well as for their Sabbath instruction, and the preachers still feel the need of the press as their most potent ally in their work." [28]

[27] Paper read at the North Central Jurisdiction Historical Society meeting, Chicago, July 5, 1957.
[28] Sandford Hunt, "Centennial of the Methodist Book Concern," *The Methodist Review*, March, 1889, p. 228.

Writing in 1889, at the centennial of the Book Concern, Sandford Hunt, publishing agent of the Northern Church, said: "It required the heroism of a Methodist preacher's faith in a divine call, to grapple with the difficulties and overcome them. . . . The occasion required men who were profoundly convinced of the necessity of a literature which would build up in Christian faith those who were placed under their charge, and with whom the profits of the business were a secondary matter." [29]

Paying deserved credit to the pioneers and urging on his contemporaries a similar concern for "dispersing" books and periodicals, Henry C. Jennings, also a Northern publishing agent, said in 1902: "The old Methodist preachers never thought of this work as undignified or unministerial; it was to build up the people in righteousness, and there was a unity and strength about our Methodism from this cause as from no other. The same could be done today, if not in the same way, reaching the same end." [30]

In 1867 Abel Stevens wrote of the Methodist Book Concern:

The diffusion of popular literature and the creation of a taste for reading among the great masses of the denomination, has been incalculable. . . . If Methodism had made no other contribution to the progress of knowledge and civilization in the New World than that of this powerful institution, this alone would suffice to vindicate its claim to the respect of the enlightened world.[31]

3

Of Making and Selling Books

The Growth of the Publishing Program

"Take care that every Society be duly supplied with Books," John Wesley told his British preachers, and his advice was heeded on this side of the Atlantic as the first American itinerants started their journeys on "the long road." [32]

Books were placed first in the statement which defined the purpose of the Book Concern: "To advance the cause of Protestant Christianity by

[29] *Ibid.*, p. 220.
[30] *Northwestern Christian Advocate*, June 4, 1902, p. 9.
[31] Stevens, *History of the Methodist Episcopal Church* (New York: Carlton and Porter, 1867), IV, 463 ff.
[32] *Discipline*, 1785, p. 20.

disseminating religious knowledge and useful literary and scientific information in the form of cheap books, tracts, and periodicals." [33]

The first titles to come from the presses of Methodist publishers in America were reprints of books written in England, most of them by John Wesley and his contemporaries. The first book officially published in America was Wesley's translation and condensation of *The Imitation of Christ*, a devotional classic by Thomas à Kempis. Wesley's title was *The Christian's Pattern*. After that came a hymnbook, the *Discipline*, Baxter's *Saints' Everlasting Rest*, and Wesley's *Primitive Physic*, a book of remedies that, though now curious and amusing, went through some thirty editions while its writer was still living and is still in print.

The scope of the books was soon broadened to include books of sermons, books about the Bible, theology, general and church history, preaching, and moral theology. Gradually, and cautiously, a number of books in the field of general literature were introduced, but it was well toward the end of the nineteenth century before Methodist presses published anything that was not strictly Methodist. At this time, although the word "ecumenicity" was still an obscure one found only in the larger dictionaries, church union was in the air.

The catalogue issued by the Book Concern in 1795 contained the works of Wesley, Fletcher, and Garrettson; Asbury's *Journals;* the hymnbook; the *Discipline;* and *The Arminian Magazine*. Historians say that the first book agent combined in himself the functions of manager, buyer, stockkeeper, salesman, entry clerk, bookkeeper, packer, and shipping clerk.

At Cincinnati, during the early years of the Western Book Concern, *Vindication of Methodist Episcopacy,* by Nathan Bangs; *Treatise on Divine Providence,* by Bishop Sherlock; and a Scripture catechism and primer were the first books reprinted, but these the book agent handled on his own financial responsibility. It was not until 1836 that the General Conference officially asserted to such practice with this directive: "They [the agents] shall have authority to publish any book in our catalogue, when in their judgment and that of the Book Committee, it shall be deemed advantageous to the interests of the church, provided that they shall not publish type editions of such books as are stereotyped in New York." [34] This action was taken when, much to the surprise of Easterners, there developed considerable demand for books in the West.

The type of books published was not greatly changed during the years that saw the startling expansion of the churches. Even in times of stress

---

[33] *Discipline of the Methodist Episcopal Church, South,* 1855, p. 251.
[34] *Journals of the General Conference,* 1796-1836, p. 488.

the publishers brought out new books. The years of the financial panic
in the early 1870's found the list in the New York catalogue lengthened
with such costly and standard works as these: *History of the Methodist
Episcopal Church,* by Stevens; *Freedom of the Will,* by Whedon; *Treatise
on Homiletics,* by Kidder; *Meditations of the Actual State and Essence
of Christianity,* by Guizot; and *Commentaries on the Evangelists,* by
Whedon.

From the very start the publishing interests of Methodism were directly identified with the preacher. The cause that was closest to
his heart was benefited by the distribution of books and periodicals.
His pocketbook was helped, too, by his commissions and by his pension—
money for which came, at least in part, from the sale of books.

Before the Methodist Book Concern came into being in 1789, the
profits from books sold by the preachers were turned over to the conference. Such funds were used to make up the deficiencies in the preachers' allowances and in the relief of worn-out preachers. When the Book
Concern was organized, its profits were earmarked for the same purpose,
and in 1808 this plan was written into the Sixth Restrictive Rule.

Henry C. Jennings, publishing agent, commented:

> It must have meant a great amount of industrious work producing the profit
> on these books, many of which were small, selling for only a few cents a copy.
> It must have been a very small profit that was made, and it is safe to say that
> no generation of our Methodist people have ever bought or read the same pro-
> portion of religious books and pamphlets as were literally consumed by the
> people of that first generation in this country. It is, of course, a certainty that
> there were almost no other books.[35]

The circuit riders took seriously their job of distributing books. Sometimes this occupied as much of their time as preaching. They pored over
their books as they rode along, until the figure of the lonely horseman
riding with a book tucked under his arm, or held before him as he
strained his eyes to make out the type on its pages, became the symbol
of the traveling preacher.

Joseph Tarkington, one of the early itinerants in the West, wrote in
his autobiography:

> Undershirts and drawers were not then known in pioneer society; and only
> one handkerchief (a red and yellow silk bandanna, though often it was cotton)
> and an extra pair of socks. This gave ample room in the saddlebags for a Bible,

---

[35] Jennings, *The Methodist Book Concern* (New York and Cincinnati: The Methodist
Book Concern, 1924), p. 265.

hymn book and *Discipline,* and a copy of Fletcher's *Appeal* or Wesley's *Sermons,* but hardly ever both at once; leaving room, ordinarily, for an assortment of books for sale.[36]

It was appropriate that the profits from the sale of books as well as magazines should come back to the itinerants. "Without these legmen, who checked constantly on subscriptions which had expired, sold the quotas of books which their presiding elders had sent them, and made the business of the Book Concern their business as well, the entire system would have been a failure." [37]

The bishops also supported the plan of distributing books and the growing program for developing publishing houses of size and prestige. Other denominations tried to copy Methodism, but, as the editor of the *Western Christian Advocate* wrote in 1840, "It would be . . . impossible for them to . . . invent any other plan which can at all equal . . . in exact order and efficiency" the one that Methodism had developed along with its itinerant system.[38] This plan continued through the Civil War and long after. Young ministers were expected to have both an ability to preach and a zeal for selling books and magazines.

The church papers were widely used to advertise books published by the Book Concern, and such advertisements were carried without charge. One of them, in the *Western Christian Advocate* in 1897, was cast in the form of a reading notice. Under the heading "A Typographical Gem" it said: "At about Easter time, there will issue from the press of Curtis and Jennings a volume entitled *From a Cloud of Witnesses,* by Dr. Davis W. Clark. It will be gilt-top, rough edges, wide margin, printed in two inks, and bound in blue and gold. The subject matter will be worthy of such a setting." [39]

The success book publishers enjoyed in the latter years of the nineteenth century began to waver in the early 1900's. It was the predicament not only of denominational publishers but of all booksellers. People were reading periodicals rather than books, which were confined more and more to public and circulating libraries. There was little interest in the building of personal and family libraries.

In 1903 W. F. Whitlock, chairman of the Book Committee of the Methodist Episcopal Church, wrote:

[36] *Autobiography of the Reverend Joseph Tarkington,* ed. by T. O. Godwin (Cincinnati: The Methodist Book Concern, 1899), p. 8.

[37] Millard George Roberts, "The Methodist Book Concern in the West, 1800-1870" (Unpublished dissertation, University of Chicago, 1947), p. 220.

[38] *Western Christian Advocate,* January 24, 1840, p. 159.

[39] *Ibid.,* February 17, 1897, p. 194.

The books of the Methodist press are becoming less accessible to the people. There is an unbridged chasm between the publishing house and the proper constituency. The fathers bridged this chasm, but their sons and successors leave it wide open. Moreover, issues of denominational houses do not so easily enter into the general trade. To bring our publishing houses and patrons into closer touch is now a problem seeking solution.[40]

Various new plans were proposed, and the old ones were carefully assessed. Depositories had been set up in the days when transportation was still slow and uncertain. The assumption was that such centers in the midst of the territory served would create local interest, as well as make possible better service in filling orders. But when transportation improved, the function of the depositories changed. They became interested in the miscellaneous book trade, and there they bumped into competition with the growing department stores. To the General Conference of 1896 the book agents of the Western Concern recommended that the depositories close out their general stocks and keep their shelves exclusively for publications of the church.[41]

In the early 1920's publishing leaders in the Methodist Episcopal Church, South, devised another plan. They saw that their press was publishing books about Methodism, its doctrines, history, government, and leaders. Many of the books, while well written and valuable, could not possibly pay their cost. "The publishing house was making an effort to preserve the literature of the church, even at financial sacrifice," a report to the church said.[42] But the books were not getting the circulation they deserved.

Many of the best writers were forsaking this field because they could not depend on an adequate circulation for their books. Many of the textbooks used in the Conference Course of Study were issued by commercial houses or by houses of other denominations. There were few books for the training of church school teachers. Even the catalogued songbooks were out of date.

The result of the study was a plan for a department in the Publishing House, which would seek the best in Christian literature from all sources and sell to all markets, not only within the church but among all Christian groups at home and abroad. This new idea was launched in 1923 as "Cokesbury Press," harking back to the college that bore the names of both Thomas Coke and Francis Asbury. The colophon, or emblem, that

[40] *Story of the Book Concerns*, p. 90.
[41] *Journal of the General Conference of the Methodist Episcopal Church*, 1896, p. 593.
[42] *Fifteen Years and an Idea, A Report* (Nashville: Cokesbury Press, 1938), p. 22.

served as its trademark was a pioneer circuit rider, book clutched in hand, mounted on his horse. Around him was a pair of circles, symbolizing the world parish of Methodism, and the words, "Cokesbury Press—Good Books."

The first publication was *The Cokesbury Hymnal,* of which more than a million copies were sold in two years.[43] Another early book was John Trotwood Moore's novel, *Hearts of Hickory.* Still another title that made a notable record was Toyohiko Kagawa's *Song from the Slums.*

An aggressive program of advertising and selling accompanied these plans for attracting prominent authors. So successful was this venture that Cokesbury survived the dark days of the depression and came to unification with a strong record "in the black."

Meanwhile, the Book Concern of the Northern Church was reaching out in much the same way through Abingdon Press. E. Stanley Jones's *Christ of the Indian Road* was translated into some thirty languages, and was succeeded by other best sellers. Church leaders such as Bishop Francis J. McConnell and theologians such as Professor Harris Franklin Rall, as well as novelists such as Gene Stratton Porter, were soon writing for the Methodist press.

Book Manufacture

The growth of the Methodist publishing program was, through the years, paralleled by advancement in techniques of the mechanical departments. Although at the very beginning of the Book Concern the products were printed and bound on contract, the organization was but little more than thirty years old when the beginnings of its present large manufacturing operation were first manifest.

Reasoning that the House could more economically and conveniently manufacture its own materials, Nathan Bangs in 1821 installed a bindery in the Wesleyan Academy building, 14 Crosby Street, New York City. On September 20, 1824, he introduced printing presses. From these beginnings the Methodist printing establishment so grew that by the end of the century, both in the North and in the South, Methodist printing operations were among the most highly respected in the trade.

The significance of the printer in the hierarchy of Methodist publishing is early shown by the listing of the name of "Azor Hoyt, Printer," along with the names of the editor and publishers, on the mastheads of the first New York *Christian Advocates.* In fact, the printers had wide

[43] *Ibid.*

privilege and heavy responsibility in these early days, as indicated by the
following incident: Apparently without the knowledge and consent of
the agents, Hoyt in 1828 ordered a new press installed for the *Advocate*
that would "print both sides of a sheet of paper . . . without turning the
sheet." The results, however, proved unworthy of the risk. So far below
standard was the printing of one issue, and apparently so great the
confusion that resulted from the experiment, that the marvelous new
device was scrapped and Hoyt lost his job. Offended by what he considered unfair treatment, Hoyt went into the printing business on his
own and issued an edition of the official Methodist hymnbook, in competition with the Book Concern and at a lower price. Further complica-
tions followed. Names were called. Editorials written. Hoyt sued the
Concern for libel and won.[44]

This awkward situation, brought about by one printer's desire for
progress, did not, however, inhibit change in the printing operations—
when change was for the better. From the handpresses of the 1820's, which
could produce two hundred sheets an hour, printed on one side, the
Book Concern came to use in rapid succession steam-powered presses
(1831); double-cylinder presses (1840); four-cylinder rotary presses
(1877); rotary perfecting presses (1890); and electrically run presses
(1898).[45]

Other aspects of book manufacture in publishing houses of Methodism
kept pace with that in the industry as a whole. The unillustrated, simply
bound volumes of the early 1800's were replaced by the elaborate tomes
of the Gilded Age. Perhaps the acme of fancy book manufacture in the
nineteenth-century plants of the Methodist houses was the Exhibition
Bible, produced in 1893 by the Southern Publishing House for the
World's Columbian Exposition in Chicago. Designed to show the
mechanical attainments in bookmaking in the Southern states, it won
a medal for specific merit. When open, the Bible, now on display at the
Publishing House in Nashville, measures 23 by 40 inches; when closed,
23 by 17 inches. It is 6 inches thick, has 836 pages, and weighs 60 pounds.
Printed in letters of pure gold on genuine sheepskin, each page is il-
lumined, different colors following on borders of successive pages. The
case binding inside and out is of Russian leather intricately tooled in
gold and colored leathers. The front is heavily embossed with a Maltese
cross interset with scenes from Solomon's temple. The inside of the case
depicts Christ before the Doctors. While of course not exactly typical, this
Bible indicates the heights that could be attained by Methodist book-
makers in their first seventy-five years of printing.

[44] The New York *Christian Advocate*, September 9, 1926 (Part II), pp. 1114-15.
[45] *Ibid.*, pp. 1113-16.

Methodist Publishing and Its Audience

Many Methodist books through the years have been of substantial and lasting value, giving the lie to the canard that an evangelistic people, with an interest in feeling as well as thinking, cannot produce great literature. Great literature is great largely because of its emotional content. Fervent faith and ardent zeal have characterized Methodist literature from its start with John Wesley.

Furthermore, Methodism has had a well-balanced literature. It has kept the theological, biblical, doctrinal, historical, biographical, and devotional in proper relationship to one another. For this, the absence of any serious theological controversy in Methodist ranks has been partly responsible. Whitlock expressed it well at the turn of the century:

> Methodist literature has the true elements, many of the most commendable elements of English literature; elements that distinguish English from Continental literature. For example, it has an aversion to extremes of opinion; it revolts from excesses; opposites are well balanced in it; it never surges this way and then that, as if the church had run wild for want of mental ballast. . . . The same theology and morality have been taught in our schools of learning, fostered by our pulpits and press, and sung in our hymnology.[46]

Nevertheless, Methodist literature has been a popular literature, a literature designed for all the people. It has been written and printed for the people of the cities and of the countryside, the sophisticated centers as well as the rough-and-ready frontiers. The writing has been clear, even when subjects were profound. It has sought to make the truths of the gospel plain to plain people. To quote Whitlock again, "It has sought to advantage the many, rather than to gratify the pride of the few." One of the bishops wrote:

> The wisdom manifested in the preparation and publication of a literature for the people merits the highest consideration. The secular press seeks the popular ear, and its subject matter and methods of presentation do not always contemplate the instruction and elevation of the reader, but too often his mere temporary entertainment. . . .
> A popular literature is in circulation; and if the Church desires to be heard; to stimulate the good and counteract the bad, it must adapt its teachings to the needs of the great populace. It is the office and function of the Church to furnish reading-matter that will deal with the realities of daily living, that will

[46] *Story of the Book Concerns,* pp. 186-87.

set forth the legitimate results of virtue and industry, and that will secure attention to the great and grand problems of human existence and destiny.[47]

Never have the goals been stated better. Through the years Methodism's publishing leaders have steered a course midway between the two
extremes—publication at actual cost, producing abundant reading matter at such low figures as to defy competition, and publication at the
average market rate, providing the largest possible dividends for the
Annual Conferences. But much of the way the publishers were striving
hard to keep out of bankruptcy.

4

Literature for Teaching Children

Even prior to the formal organization of the Methodist Episcopal
Church, the question had been raised at conference: "What shall be
done with the children?" The reply: "Meet them once a fortnight, and
examine the parents with regard to their conduct toward them." [48]

The early interest in children as more than "little adults" in long
clothes (and thoughts to match) was followed by the development of
the Sunday school as a training center for the children of the church and
as a missionary institution for the care of neglected children in the community. The trend in the first two of these directions is well known.

Sunday schools were formed early, although this institution was not
formally recognized in the Discipline until 1828, when a beginning was
made in supplying books and tracts for children. These constituted the
start of the Sunday school literature which was to form such a large part
of the Methodist publishing enterprise.

The Sunday School Union was organized in 1827 and was recognized
by the General Conference of 1828. The Sunday School Advocate was
first published in 1840, and in 1860 the Sunday School Journal, designed
especially for teachers, appeared. For a time the first paper published
stories for children, helps for parents, and "Letters on Sunday School
Instruction" for teachers. Classmate, which has had a long and distinguished career, was introduced for older pupils in 1873.

In the Southern Church the General Conference of 1846 ordered the

---

[47] Ibid., pp. 188-89.
[48] Minutes, April 28, 1779.

publication, at Charleston, South Carolina, of a Sunday school journal. It was the first publication in a long list. Later, in 1869, the *Sunday School Visitor* was added. A paper for children, the *Visitor* was for many years an important publication and a forebear of much that characterizes the present children's periodicals.

Any account of these beginnings must mention *Golden Hours,* which was voted by the 1864 General Conference of the Methodist Episcopal Church and launched in 1869. Although discontinued in 1880 because of lack of support, it met a real need during its eleven-year span of service.

The growth of Sunday school papers was rapid in all three of the major branches of Methodism. The number of copies printed was truly astounding. In 1850 the Methodist Episcopal Church had 514,000 persons connected with the Sunday schools and distributed 75,000 papers— or one for every seven pupils. In 1888, it had about 2,000,000 teachers and pupils in the schools, and was distributing approximately 3,000,000 papers—or more than one and a half for each pupil and teacher. The increase in the schools had been fourfold; the increase in the papers, fortyfold.[49]

Only a little less rapid, because of financial stringency, was the growth of Sunday school literature in the Southern Church. Despite practical obstacles, the problem of keeping pace with the needs was always before the leaders. In 1876 International Lesson Helps were approved for inclusion in the literature of this church.

As early as 1874 the *Methodist Protestant* began to convince church leaders that they should develop their own religious education materials. By 1884 the Pittsburgh Directory was publishing *Our Morning Guide* (a four-page weekly) ; *Scholars' Quarterly* (thirty-two pages) ; *Our Teachers' Journal* (a sixty-four-page quarterly) ; *Bible School Leaf* (a monthly) ; and *Our Children* (a four-page weekly).[50]

At the same time the Baltimore Directory was issuing a series of helps covering the International Lessons. In 1884 the two centers reached an agreement by which all material in this field was to be published in Pittsburgh.

The Northern General Conference of 1892 took some forward steps in publishing for Sunday schools. The *Sunday School Advocate* was made into a weekly paper. *Classmate* was doubled in size. The *Picture Lesson Paper* was ordered printed in colors. The *Epworth Herald,* which had become the organ of the Epworth League, established in 1889 and recog-

---

[49] *The Methodist Review,* March-April, 1889, p. 229.
[50] *The Methodist Protestant* (Centennial Edition) , May 16, 1928, pp. 39-40.

nized by the General Conference of 1896, began its rapid circulation climb.

The Southern General Conference of 1894 established the Epworth League as an official organization and ordered the Publishing House to begin the *Epworth Era*. The same conference gave orders for a wider range of Sunday school periodicals. By 1906 the Methodist Episcopal Church, South, was circulating these papers: *Children's Visitor* (successor to the *Sunday School Visitor*), *Our Little People, Sunday School Magazine, Intermediate Quarterly, Senior Quarterly, Junior Lessons* (a quarterly succeeding *Illustrated Lesson Paper*), *Home Department Quarterly,* and *Olivet Picture Cards*. All of these publications carried the International Uniform Lessons. By 1910 *Primary Teacher* (for workers with children), *Boys and Girls* (a story paper for older children), and *Adult Student* had been added.

Improvements in teaching materials came thick and fast. In 1908 there were 3,429,915 teachers and pupils in the Sunday schools of the Methodist Episcopal Church, and these materials were being published: *Sunday School Journal and Bible Student's Magazine; Adult Bible Class and Teacher-Training Monthly; Senior Berean Lesson Quarterly; Illustrated Berean Lesson Quarterly; Berean Intermediate Lesson Quarterly; Lesson Leaf; Boys and Girls' Quarterly; Shorter Junior Lesson Quarterly; Berean Primary Teacher; Bible Study Home Department Quarterly; Classmate; Sunday School Advocate for Boys and Girls; Picture Lesson Paper; The Leaf Cluster; Berean Lesson Pictures; Berean Beginners' Lessons; Large Picture Cards; and Golden Text Cards.*[51]

This expansive literature was thought inadequate in 1908, and new ventures were launched. The Book Concern co-operated in the Graded Lesson Series which was being developed by several denominations together. This was a pioneer attempt to offer a complete system of religious instruction for everyone, from childhood to young manhood and womanhood. Succeeding years brought further developments—the group graded and closely graded lessons that were designed to suit the individual needs of various age groups. Finally came the lessons for small schools without the resources or leadership of the larger schools in the strong city churches.

As might be expected, the development of Sunday school literature was accompanied by a lively controversy over the religious welfare of the child. Back in 1848 John McClintock, editor of *The Methodist Quarterly Review,* had written to Stephen Olin, declaring that he thought pernicious the habit of "baptizing infants and then treating them as if they were heathen, until the breath of a revival comes over to convert them, in-

---

[51] *The Methodist Yearbook,* 1909, pp. 4, 87.

stead of holding them as initiated into the church, as our standards do, and training them up for her service, and God's." [52]

Historians have pointed out that while Methodist doctrines made clear the Methodist support of infant baptism, and the *Discipline* clearly stated that the "baptism of young children is to be retained in the church," there was, prior to 1856, no statement that put the stamp of theological approval on infant baptism. Many Methodists, along with Congregationalists and Presbyterians, thought that children, even though baptized in infancy, were living in bondage to sin until they were converted. The attitude of the church was confused, and the confusion was often based on differing interpretations of Wesleyan theology.

The General Conference of the Methodist Episcopal Church in 1856 helped greatly by stating: "We hold that all children, by virtue of the unconditional benefits of the atonement, are members of the kingdom of God and, therefore, graciously entitled to baptism"; and, "We regard all children who have been baptized, as placed in visible covenant relation to God, and under the special care and supervision of the church." [53] Furthermore, the conference gave specific direction for the religious nurture and instruction of children preparatory to reception into full membership.

This position neither stated nor implied that it was necessary for a child to go through a conversion experience before being regarded as a Christian; but there was a long period of heated controversy before this idea fully prevailed and it was thought that a child, in a Christian home and church environment, might so naturally become a Christian as to be unable to say just when conversion occurred. Nevertheless, most Methodists were sure that the child needed a definite commitment, for becoming a Christian calls for a spiritual awakening, whether gradual or sudden, a deliberate choice, and a genuine sense of God's indwelling presence. This was one of the compelling ideas behind the development of teaching methods and curriculum in the growth of the Sunday school movement.

The years of the Civil War brought some slowdown in both North and South, but the Sunday schools were not long in regaining lost ground, and even lengthening their previous stride.

John H. Vincent, who had become general agent of the Sunday School Union in 1866, was elected editor of Sunday school publications of the Methodist Episcopal Church in 1868. He believed in applying to Sunday

[52] Letter to Stephen Olin, October, 1948; quoted in George R. Crooks, *Life and Letters of the Rev. John M'Clintock* (New York: Nelson and Phillips, 1876) , p. 201.
[53] *Journal of the General Conference of the Methodist Episcopal Church,* 1856, pp. 133-34.

schools the advanced methods of the public schools, and this conviction soon showed up in the curriculum materials. He was clearly committed to enriching religious experience with spiritual and intellectual vitamins. He stood squarely for educational evangelism. And, specifically, he proposed to make the Sunday school a church school, reflecting the purposes of the church, and maybe even improving on them.

The second issue of the *Sunday School Journal* following Vincent's election as editor carried "four versions of a lesson," each adapted to a different age group of a fully organized school. A hint about the popularity of this idea is glimpsed in the fact that the *Journal's* subscription list shot up from 23,000 in 1868 to 58,000 in 1872.[54]

In 1868 the Sunday School Union established the Normal Department that Vincent had advocated for the training of teachers, and in 1873 the Sunday School Union approved the project of a teachers' assembly at Chautauqua Lake in New York. The first purpose of this movement, which was to achieve widespread popularity as a means of adult education, was to develop interest in training teachers for the Sunday schools. Within a dozen years there were twenty-one different Chautauqua organizations, reaching thousands of people.

The development of teaching materials was a natural accompaniment of this interest in teaching methods. From 1845 to 1865 the curriculum materials had been of various types, with "question books" based on the Bible as the most common. Catechizing was a popular method of instruction. As a part of opening or closing exercises, pupils were catechized each Sunday. And the pastor asked the questions, often formulating some of his own. There was a trend, furthered by Vincent, to make the Sunday school the church school. As Wade Crawford Barclay described it, "Vincent desired to lift the Sunday school to the level of the church, to supplement the church by making its compass broader, deeper, and all embracing." [55]

Nevertheless, new movements were on foot. In 1865, at an interdenominational institute in Chicago, Vincent proposed introducing a uniform system of lessons for all the schools. He developed a pilot series for Chicago Sunday schools, and it became the forerunner of the International Uniform Lesson system. Although teaching aids and methods were different for the four age groups into which the schools were divided, the same scripture was used for all.

The battle for graded lessons had to be waged on a different front, and

---

[54] *Journal of the General Conference*, 1872, p. 549.
[55] Barclay, *The History of Methodist Missions* (New York: Board of Missions of The Methodist Church, 1957), III, 98.

that, too, was a long battle. Unquestionably, the Uniform Lessons, a distinct advance in their day, delayed the development of fully graded lessons suited to the varying needs of young children and adolescents, just as the Akron plan for church buildings gave future church architects a hard time.

The use of graded materials meant that there had to be a periodical to interpret the whole matter of grading. This was the reason for publishing the *Graded Sunday School Magazine,* which was issued jointly by the Methodist Episcopal Church and the Methodist Episcopal Church, South. Later, the Southern Church withdrew its sponsorship and started the *Sunday School Standard. Pilgrim Magazine* of the Congregational Church, *Sunday School Standard,* and *Graded Sunday School Magazine* were merged to form *Church School,* which was published by the Graded Lessons Syndicate that included several denominations.

The creative venturing continued as the church school program developed. When Sunday morning classes were brought into combination with Sunday evening programs for youth, appropriate changes were made in the papers, especially *Epworth Herald* and *Highroad.*

Some years before this, in 1900, Bishop Charles Galloway wrote:

> The Sunday school has passed its apologetic period. Its right to live has been demonstrated by the spiritual achievements it has wrought, by the marvelous history it has written. Its first suggestion and initial development was as a moral police institution. Its avowed purpose was to restrain the depredations of ragged hoodlums upon personal property and their shameless desecrations of the holy Sabbath.[56]

A new emphasis on the family brought the launching of the *Christian Home,* resulting from the sincere effort to make the home a school of religion and a close partner with the church. The magazine was edited so that a class of parents could use it regularly as a part of their course of study.

When unification came in 1939, the three churches were ready to move forward with one purpose and one approach to the varied opportunities of Christian education. And the publishing houses were ready to play their indispensable part.

---

[56] John F. Hurst, *History of Methodism* (New York: Eaton and Mains, 1903), V, 880-81.

5

Papers That Molded Methodist Opinion

Like John Wesley, Francis Asbury set much store by the printed word. His saddlebags bulging with tracts and periodicals, the Prophet of the Long Road is reported to have made the famous statement that "the propagation of religious knowledge by means of the press is next in importance to preaching the gospel." [57]

The beginnings of Methodist church papers, however, are not to be attributed solely to a pious desire to spread the gospel. The trend away from established churches in the colonies put the denominations on their own, and this brought a denominational self-consciousness that slanted everything, missions and evangelism included.

Historians of the period have called this a "drawing-in" movement. "This turning inward of the denominations related itself to the religious press in two ways: the trend was being promoted and extended by the periodicals, and at the same time it produced more journals of a distinctly denominational character to maintain it." [58]

The religious climate changed markedly during the period of expansion that was brought to a halt in mid-century by the Civil War, yet the character of the church papers changed but little. They remained polemical and critical. For example, the *Northwestern Christian Advocate,* starting in 1853, had these words in its first editorial:

We can never suffer the doctrines of our church to be challenged in our columns, or our *Discipline* to be assailed. But to any contribution that evolves, teaches and enforces the former, or even professes improvements in the latter, we shall never feel at liberty to close our columns. We fear nothing, but hope everything from freedom of speech. . . .

We shall never be found a stickler for things morally indifferent, magnifying the "mint and anise," canting and pandering to a fossilizing conservatism, sneaking into the coverts of non-commitalism, or mounted on a hobby of ultra-progressionism. We shall never be found so visionary as to hope to escape censure, so accustomed to it that it will not grieve us, or so reckless as intentionally to deserve it.

Of the persons who have a right to be heard in our pages, of the suitableness of their cogitations to promote truth and righteousness, we are to be the judge. [59]

---

[57] Jennings, *The Methodist Book Concern,* Flyleaf; see also George P. Mains, *Francis Asbury* (New York: Eaton and Mains, 1909) , p. 80.

[58] Ralph Stoody, "Religious Journalism: Whence and Whither?" (Unpublished thesis, Gordon College of Theology, 1939) , pp. 97-98.

[59] February 5, 1853, p. 1.

This forthrightness was not unique with the paper published at Chicago; all of them, North and South, had it. They were developed by a school of writers who knew that their readers did not have access to the stiff and starched papers of the Atlantic seaboard. The church was bringing into the lives of its humble people a spirit of honest inquiry and heroic consecration.

At the same time, the Methodist publications did more than anything else to win for the new church a standing equal to that of older churches imported from abroad. Though humble, the editors and their writers were not ignorant men. They had a profound knowledge of the Bible and an understanding of human nature. They helped their preacher-readers to discuss doctrines with other ministers and with lay people. And as a result, Methodists were able to hold their ground against Calvinists, Universalists, Unitarians, and others. Furthermore, the papers, despite the large number of them and the divisions they propagandized and fostered, developed a solidarity among Methodists that even the divisiveness of the Civil War could not destroy. After many years, this homogeneity led to reunion.

It is true, of course, that Methodist papers had much to do with lifting up and sharpening the issues back of the division of Methodism in 1844. Until 1842 the editors, restless under pressure from the bishops, nevertheless refrained from a full-scale debate. Then it could be held back no longer, and white-hot idealism on both sides brought steaming arguments as Methodists opposed Methodists. For both sides slavery was a moral issue, while there was nothing immoral about name-calling. The war itself was a sacred crusade.

This is not to say that the church press agreed with the conduct of the war. In 1863 the *Western Christian Advocate* carried an article saying:

We are not at all satisfied that affairs have been well managed in that department [the Southwest]. There seems to have been blundering from the beginning of the effort to reduce Vicksburg. . . . It is certain that men enough, with the right kind of generalship, can take Vicksburg. . . . *Celerity* is what we want, and what we have most wanted from the beginning, and yet our Generals that have this gift are laid aside. Why is it thus? [60]

During the postwar years the *Advocates* printed detailed arguments about the policies on which the Northern Church based its reconstruc-

[60] April 8, 1863, p. 108.

tion plans. For example, the New York *Christian Advocate* in 1872 carried an article discussing the pros and cons of developing "colored conferences," while it announced that there were already three—Washington, Delaware, and Lexington:

> The conciliation of Southern white people cannot be secured permanently by flattering their prejudices. Their contempt, rather than their confidence, will be increased by any compromise of principle on their behalfs. And every thing like an adjustment of our church organization to the level of their old slavery platform they would instinctively detect and stigmatize as contradicting our profession in favor of freedom and equality for all men.[61]

Religious idealism and patriotic zeal walked hand in hand, especially in the North. The unofficial *Zion's Herald* was probably the most outspoken, but many *Advocates* were not far behind. Such statements as this, in a letter from the front published in *Zion's Herald* in 1864, were not unusual in praising the Negro soldier:

> The government little realized what a terrible blow was struck at the rebels, and what a good thing was done for the freedmen when the war-school was opened to them. This is indeed the black man's university. Hitherto they have had the entire national government against them. But when they get the soldier's uniform on, their muskets in hand, then they breathe freely. An unearthly inspiration seems to come down on them; with God and the government both on their side, they can contemplate the strangulation of the rebellion with the coolness of Samson, who slew the lion that warred against him. . . . And who, that truly reads the character and aspirations of the freedman, as well as God's providences concerning them doubts that they . . . are to be the giants of this land? That their bayonets are to be the Northern man's protection in trade and travel through the sunny South! . . . Mr. Editor, are you prepared to admit that God intends to make the Africans real benefactors to the nation? . . . In seeking out his own freedom, the freedman is called to render aid to the government, without which, in all probability, the nation would have failed of victory.[62]

The same paper added in 1868:

> One barrier still remains—our colored ministerial brethren have not yet been welcomed in our churches as regular pastors. They are warmly received and enjoyed as occasional preachers and revivalists, but they have never yet been recognized as regularly stationed ministers. Till this is done much remains undone. We cannot receive these churches into our communion unless we admit

---

[61] April 4, 1872, p. 106.
[62] August 3, 1864, p. 122.

their ministers to our Conferences. . . . Could we treat their pastors like our other preachers, every difficulty would vanish.[63]

Equally frank on other subjects, and equally willing to take on opponents inside or outside the church, the editors thundered their invectives. In fact, Methodist opinions on the moral issues during the remainder of the century may be seen by sampling the church press. It was influencing opinions and forming them. In 1873 the *Northwestern Christian Advocate* had an editorial on "Venality in High Life," and by life of that kind the editor meant public life in its higher echelons. He scorched and blistered men in high places, just as his predecessor ten years earlier had had his say on "Relieved Generals," complaining about the disgraceful fact that some generals were off on long rests while their unskilled subordinates took over the commands. "They are too valuable to be cooling their spurs, and coddling their scabbards in costly idleness." He warned: "The country will not endure to be taxed to support men in idleness." [64] And this was wartime, with its clear dangers.

There was liquor, against which Methodists had stood since the days of John Wesley. Methodist journalism reinforced the pulpit in striking out boldly against drinking habits. When *Zion's Herald* wanted to say the worst it could against President Andrew Johnson and his reconstruction policies, it blistered him in these words: "He strolled like a drunken circus manager from East to West and West to East, making speeches incoherent in every particular save one—a detestable hatred to the ideas and purposes of the North." It labeled him as "the execrable libertine, drunkard and tyrant." [65]

That was in 1868. The same stinging words about alcohol could be read in all Methodist publications. The Prohibition Party was formed in 1869, and in 1874 a convention of Christian women organized the Woman's Christian Temperance Union with a Methodist, Miss Frances E. Willard, as its warlike, if winsome, leader.

Prohibition sentiment grew to such an extent that *Zion's Herald* unquestionably spoke for many when it declared, in 1895, that "prohibition, like total abstinence in its sphere, is the safe and effectual remedy for traffic in intoxicants. But it requires to be enforced. What restrictive statute does not? In many states public opinion has not yet been educated up to prohibition." [66]

[63] January 30, 1868, p. 56.
[64] *Northwestern Christian Advocate*, February 4, 1863.
[65] March 5, 1868, p. 109.
[66] January 9, 1895, p. 27.

Prize fights were frowned on. The editor of the *Western Christian Advocate* wrote of prize fighting in the state of Nevada in 1897:

That rotten borough Nevada, deserves to be unfrocked of Statehood. She has sold her birthright, and her civic honor, for a mess of pottage. There is no analogy between the prize-fight which, for a price, she permits upon her soil and the Olympic sports. The former is vulgar, demoralizing, inhuman, . . . degrading to the last degree to participants and spectators alike.[67]

Gambling was another evil against which the church press battled. In 1860 *Zion's Herald* attacked the practice of betting on the outcome of elections. Reminding its readers that New York State had a law disqualifying any voter who wagered on an election, the paper said: "Would it not be well for other states to pass a similar law? At all events, it is high time something was done to stop this disgraceful gambling in the liberties of the people." [68]

In 1878 the *Wesleyan Christian Advocate* protested that some towns were spending more money for race tracks than for sidewalks. And when Alabama permitted a lottery with proceeds going for the rebuilding of the state university, the *New Orleans Christian Advocate* quoted Bishop McTyeire as saying, "Better its walls should never rise from their ashes; better its foundations were sowed with salt and plowed up, than by such means it should be helped." [69]

In an article on "What Harm Is There in Card-Playing?" a writer in the *Western Christian Advocate* in 1899 spoke out against "the harm of handling the tools of the gambler, learning the methods of using these tools, of coming under the influence of the tendency towards the tricks and trickery that commonly go with the use of these tools, of entering even the outer circle of the kind of people who use such tools." [70]

Stage plays and even novels were condemned by Methodists. *Der Christliche Apologete,* which the General Conference established for German Methodists, said in 1860: "The true task of the Christian is to sympathize with and help those in need. But those who shed tears over the tragedies in the theater aren't so likely to help those in trouble in real life. The theater may not lead to ruin, but it is no help in leading a Christian life." [71]

Repeatedly, dancing was condemned by the bishops and by the General Conferences. In 1872 the General Conference of the Methodist

[67] March 10, 1897, p. 301.
[68] November 28, 1860, p. 191.
[69] September 15, 1866.
[70] February 22, 1899, p. 232.
[71] April 22, 1860, p. 54.

Episcopal Church listed as evidence of "imprudent conduct" such diversions as "dancing, playing at games of chance, attending theaters, horse races, circuses, dancing parties, or patronizing dancing schools, or taking such other amusements as are obviously of misleading or questionable moral tendency." [72] And the church papers did their share of scolding on such subjects.

The Christian Sabbath was the subject of much discussion, especially when the immigrants came with strange new ideas about the profanation of Sunday, as practiced in Europe. In 1898 the *Western Christian Advocate* published an article with the title, "Bicycle-Riding on Sunday," in which the writer quoted a "liberal-minded Congregationalist" who had said that "the Sunday paper and the Sunday bicycle are the greatest modern enemies of the Christian Sabbath." Even the *Chicago Daily Herald* held that "properly used, the bicycle is as harmless as a wheelbarrow; but the part it is being made to play in the matter of Sunday recreation is wholly and indefensibly vicious." [73]

The editors did not overlook public infringements of the sanctity of the Sabbath. The *Methodist Protestant* declared in 1900:

To the members of the Maryland legislature we want to say this: The moral sentiment of Baltimore, the people who are the strength of the city, the people who obey the law, and have to pay the bills for the prosecution of those who violate it, are a unit in favor of perpetuating the Christian Sabbath. It is the saloonist, and the gambler, the greedy tradesman, and the conscienceless money-grabber who want the law repealed. [74]

The General Conference of the Methodist Protestants in the same year added to the list of proscribed Sunday occupations: "Buggy riding, letter writing, novel reading, social visiting, and the most baleful feature of our modern civilization, the open saloon." [75]

When William E. McKinley, a Methodist, was elected president of the United States, and an expensive inaugural ball was planned, John L. Dyer, "the snow-shoe evangelist," wrote an article in the *Western Christian Advocate*. There he suggested that it might be a sin for a Methodist to attend a $60,000 party while there were so many poor and needy people around; and whether it was a sin or not, "it would certainly be against the Rules of our Church to participate in such a ball."

[72] *Journal of the General Conference,* 1872, p. 380.
[73] *Western Christian Advocate,* August 10, 1898, p. 1013.
[74] February 21, 1900.
[75] *Journal of the General Conference of the Methodist Protestant Church,* 1900, p. 61.

Nevertheless, "many of our people insist on acting for themselves, irrespective of the Rules. To their Master they must stand or fall." [76]

On the subject of participation in war there was a changing attitude. During the Civil War there was little disposition to look upon killing as wrong. Methodist writers in the North thought that nothing short of total war should be waged against the South, and those in the South felt the same way about the North.

In 1863 the editor of the *Western Christian Advocate* argued for more troops: "If our advice would do any good, we would urge the Government to hurry up measures for putting into the field at least half a million of men under the Conscription Act of the last Congress. Why should we be always outnumbered at all points by the enemy, when we have it in our power to put twice as many soldiers in the field as they can." [77]

The passing of the years brought new honors for the veterans in both blue and gray. In 1897 the Nashville *Christian Advocate* gave two full pages to a report of the Confederate reunion in that city when thirty thousand gray-coated heroes marched to "Dixie's" stirring measures and shouted themselves hoarse at the sight of their old comrades and tattered battle flags. The *Western Christian Advocate* commented on this bit of journalism by its Southern contemporary: "The *Advocate* could not have made a better use of the space." [78]

Nevertheless, there was a developing conscience on the morality of imperialism and the part war played in it. Concerning some issues of the Spanish-American War, the editor of the New York *Christian Advocate* wrote in 1898, in an editorial headed "The Lust of Conquest":

It is a cause for regret that the President of the United States has committed himself so earnestly to the annexation of Hawaii as to make it almost necessary, in the estimation of many of his congressional constituents, to enter upon this course. It has been a great stimulus to all other schemes of territorial aggrandizement.

Once entered upon, we may be sure that it will be carried to the last extent. One of the greatest evils resulting from one act of folly, in individuals or in nations, is the necessity, under the color of consistency and under the impulse of force developed, of an indefinite number of acts of equal or greater folly. Rarely are men or nations willing to acknowledge in the face of the world that their past acts were unwise. [79]

[76] February 17, 1897, p. 194.
[77] April 8, 1863, p. 108.
[78] July 14, 1897, p. 865.
[79] May 26, 1898, p. 839.

The varied social problems of the century's last decades looked worst in the bulging cities. The westward expansion was matched by the march from villages and towns into the centers of population to man the machines of the new industrialism. This accelerated migration, stimulated by the Civil War, was like that of the British working people into the cities at the start of the industrial revolution, and Methodism was not so well prepared as it had been under John Wesley's early tutelage. Besides, there was the growing stream of immigrants from Europe, with different cultural backgrounds. Many were Roman Catholic and many Jewish. Most of these newcomers settled in the industrial cities, and many Methodists wanted to keep them there.

An article in the New York *Christian Advocate* in 1898 commented: "Every candid observer knows that we have not kept pace with the other strong Churches in the cities, and notably in the greatest cities. In the smaller cities, in the towns, and in the country we do not lose our members to other denominations. Our church is 'established' in such localities. But as the cities grow larger, the denominational bond appears to grow weaker." [80] The same article indicated that if Methodists coming into the cities from the country continued to be Methodists, Methodism would lead other Protestant groups.

Apparently neglected was the fact that middle-class Methodism, starting as a movement of the common people—on the American frontier as well as in England—had lost something of the common touch. It was developing the "middle-class mind." It forgot the "pit out of which it was digged," and this forgetfulness found expression in worship that was more formalized, evangelism that was more educationalized, and a ministry that was more institutionalized.

Methodists did not welcome the newcomers crowding into the slum areas of the teeming cities. The fact that many were Roman Catholics presented one barrier, although there were others. The church papers were not reticent in speaking out against Roman Catholic practices, especially when they seemed to compound the social problems.

An example is this statement in the *Western Christian Advocate* in 1897: "Romanists could not do a more impolitic thing than to urge the appointment by this country of a minister accredited to the Pope. We do not recognize the Pope's temporal power, and would be the last people to seek its restoration. The suggestion is so offensive that we are unable to believe it has substantial foundation. . . . An American minister to the Pope! What an opportunity for political suicide!" [81]

[80] H. A. Buchtel, "The Church and the City Problem," November 3, 1898, p. 1778.
[81] April 21, 1897, p. 481.

The Scandinavians and Germans who came into the rural areas as well as the cities were subjects of evangelistic movements. As is well known, Methodism moved to Germany, Sweden, Norway, and Denmark as a result of beginnings among immigrants in America. Not so well known is the fact that excellent church papers were started among these groups and lasted until their merger with the so-called "English" conferences.

Nevertheless, Methodism was aware of its failures in the cities—and this despite the development of some strong city churches, as well as the Goodwill Industries movement, which determined to "save the waste in men and things" as it worked through the sheltered shop. The growing gulf between Methodism and the laboring classes was glimpsed by the bishops of the Northern Church, who said in 1888:

Have we lost our love for them or the aggressive spirit which carries the Gospel to their homes and hearts? Have we forgotten our mission as we have increased in wealth? Nothing is more alarming to the philanthropist and the patriot than the alienation of the laboring people from the evangelical churches. . . . If we have given too much attention to the rich, or cherished too much regard for social position, or have in any wise neglected the poor, we have departed from the spirit of our calling.[82]

Methodism had begun to encounter what has sometimes been known as Wesley's Law:

Wherever Riches have increased . . . the essence of Religion . . . has decreased in the same proportion. Therefore I do not see how it is possible, in the nature of things, for any revival of true Religion to continue long. For Religion must necessarily produce both Industry and Frugality. And these cannot but produce Riches. But as Riches increase, so will Pride, Anger, and Love of the world in all its branches.

How then is it possible that Methodism, that is, the Religion of the heart, though it flourishes now as a green bay-tree, should continue in this state? For the Methodists in every place grow diligent and frugal: consequently they increase in goods. Hence, they proportionately increase in pride, in anger, in the desire of the flesh, the desire of the eyes, and the pride of life. So, although the form of Religion remains, the spirit is swiftly vanishing away.[83]

Through these eventful years the relationship between politics and religion occupied many writers. For example, John G. Woolley, a Methodist layman, wrote in *Zion's Herald* in 1895:

[82] *Journal of the General Conference,* 1888, p. 58.
[83] "Thoughts Upon Methodism," *The Arminian Magazine,* 1787, p. 156.

Politics is diurnal, Religion is eternal. Politics has "ups and downs," Religion has no downs. Politics is discouraging, Religion is everlasting sunrise, seeing which the regenerate soul cries, "God's in his heaven, all's right with the world." But all is not right with the world, nor will be, until politics and religion shall be the same thing.[84]

There was many another to agree that monopoly, suffrage, franchise, money, and labor were becoming moral and religious questions at the turn of the century. But this interest was stepped up when Walter Rauschenbusch and others awakened the social conscience of whole denominations.

Significantly, the Social Creed of the Federal Council of Churches was really an adaptation of the Methodist Social Creed. Methodists, especially in the Methodist Episcopal Church, were in the vanguard of the social gospel movement, even though the best-known leaders were Congregationalists, Episcopalians, and Unitarians.

The church papers did their share of commenting. The editors were prophets, thundering jeremiads.

In 1908 the bishops of the Methodist Episcopal Church said:

We hold the right of those working men who desire to do so to form labor unions for the advancement of their interests, as we hold the right of individual laborers who prefer to do so, to keep control of their own labor. . . . The church and the trades Unions should seek each other's help for the uplift of mankind. . . . By so much as a capitalist is selfish, miserly, exacting, oppressive, the Church has business with him. She cannot throw him off and away until the last day of his desiccated and shrunken life brings him before God.[85]

Such statements strengthened the editors. A few years before, they had had their moments of hesitation, even timidity. The *Western Christian Advocate* said in 1887:

It is clear now as ever that the only possible satisfactory solution of this difficult problem is such mutual concession as will commend itself to the enlightened judgment of the people. Neither party should demand what will imperil the rights and interest of the other. There is a middle ground of equity where both can meet, and by righteous dealing become friends and allies, and to that middle ground they must come at last.[86]

Yet the same paper in the same year had shown sympathy for the Hazelbrook Coal Company's miners, evicted from their houses because the

[84] July 10, 1895, p. 435.
[85] *Journal of the General Conference,* 1908, p. 136.
[86] May 25, 1887, p. 321.

company owned them, and forced to trade at the company stores because management owned them, too.

Richard M. Cameron reports that *Advocates* in the South had less to say than those in the North, because the tendency toward urbanization and industrialization had less headway in the South. The *Wesleyan Christian Advocate,* commenting in 1878, warned the cotton weavers of Lancashire to accept a reduction of wages rather than depend on charity. And the *Richmond Christian Advocate* grumbled because Northern outsiders were sowing seeds of discontent among "poor white" mill workers who were putting in longer hours for the same wages paid Northern workers.[87]

Wall Street was a popular subject of derogatory cartoons at the turn of the century. The manipulations of the stock market began to draw critical fire, but the church press was slow to get into the fray. As early as 1878 the *Wesleyan Christian Advocate* objected to dealing in futures and on margins. But generally the Methodist church press was not alive to the sins of big business until after Theodore Roosevelt's "trust-busting" campaigns and the social awakening that unearthed the social gospel out of the eighth-century Hebrew prophets and the New Testament.

Sentiment against war did not enter the social gospel movement until after the close of the "war to end war." Previously, imperialism was regarded as a part of manifest destiny. The words of President William McKinley, given to his fellow Methodists, offer evidence:

I walked the floor of the White House, night after night, and I am not ashamed to tell you, gentlemen, that I went down on my knees and prayed to Almighty God for light and guidance more than one night. And one night late it came to me. . . . There was nothing left for us to do but take them all, and to educate the Filipinos, and uplift and civilize and Christianize them, and by God's grace do the very best we could by them as our fellow men for whom Christ also died.[88]

In 1898 the New York *Christian Advocate* had opposed entering the war with Spain over Cuba. But after the declaration of war had been made, the editor supported it, even while he deplored the certain results that it would have on political and social reforms. On the other hand, the *Richmond Christian Advocate* declared: "The President has uttered the word. There is war. Let us maul well the Spaniard, but never

[87] *Methodism and Society in Historical Perspective* (Nashville: Abingdon Press, 1961), p. 297.

[88] Charles and Mary Beard, *The Rise of American Civilization* (New York: The Macmillan Company, 1927), II, 375-76.

forget to settle with Congress that coerced the country into war." [89]

The sweep of idealism, and idealistic pacifism, that followed the "war to make the world safe for democracy" carried the church papers with it. It persisted until it was swallowed up in disillusionment that brought rearmament and the second world conflict.

Methodists were conscious of world problems. In 1933 the editor of the *Northwestern Christian Advocate* paid his respects to the matter of Philippine independence under the title, "The Flag Comes Down—and How." He noted the gains to the sugar barons and the dairy business. He doubted that "giving" independence was as unselfish as it looked. He said:

We haul that flag down, not because we think our wards fully competent to exercise themselves in the arts of commerce and self-government, which we taught them, but because, with cold-blooded directness, a few American exploiters say they are inconvenienced by the very goods we have encouraged our wards in the Pacific to produce for export in this country. "Manifest destiny" has surrendered to sugar and oil and economic determinism.[90]

Thus the church editors wrestled with the social problems of their day. The editor of the *Quarterly Review* of the Methodist Episcopal Church, South, probably summarized well when, in 1914, he looked ahead:

The church and the social movement must be wedded, not divorced. There is need, on the one hand, for a quickened social conscience in the Church; and, on the other, for the Christianization of the social movement. Let the Church be brought closer to the real problems of humanity, that humanity, with its cry for social justice, may see the Church its friend and champion, and that the tremendous moral dynamics within the Church may be released for lifting those burdens that are grinding men and women and little children to despair.[91]

The struggle against Communism lay in the future, and the churches had not yet been called upon to draw clear distinctions between Christian and Communist doctrines of man.

[89] April 28, 1898.
[90] February 2, 1933, p. 99.
[91] *Quarterly Review*, January 14, 1914, pp. 118-19.

6

Personalities and Publications

While it is erroneous at any given time to equate organizations and the persons who comprise them, it cannot be denied that over a period of years, and to a certain degree, such an equation evolves. When considering what the Methodist publishing interests were in the middle and late years of the nineteenth century, one must first consider what Methodism itself was, and what society as a whole was. But those individuals who occupied positions of authority and leadership with the publishing interests during the period must not be overlooked, for undeniably the men themselves influenced the organizations that came together in 1940 and are today known as the Methodist Publishing House. To what extent their influences are still felt today it is hard to say. Would, for instance, there have been a Methodist Publishing House had not John Dickins and Ezekiel Cooper been willing to invest their own savings in the enterprise at its inception? Would the Methodist Publishing House be in the printing business today had not Nathan Bangs opened a bindery in New York in 1821? Would the Southern House have survived the rigors of financial debacle in the Reconstruction days following the Civil War had not John B. McFerrin stumped the South with his bond scheme that was its salvation? Who can say? Yet the fact remains that these men, because of what they were, because of the convictions they held, took these actions; and the history of the Methodist Publishing House was written accordingly.

In the course of the years covered by this chapter, in the publishing houses of the three branches of Methodism considered, many personalities brought influences to bear. Some men are more influential in a year than others are in a lifetime, but it nevertheless becomes necessary because of space limitations to establish a criterion for selection of those to be mentioned here. In this case, it shall be length of service—men who served notably for long periods in posts of distinction.

Men of the Southern Church

With Methodist publishing, as with other enterprises, enduring fame seems always to attach itself to the founding fathers. When one thinks of the Methodist Book Concern, his thoughts naturally incline to the men of the early years—John Dickins, the initiator; Ezekiel Cooper, the nurturer; Nathan Bangs, the developer; Martin Ruter, the pioneer. Decisive, often bold, action was the role of these, and so they overshadow to a great degree men who came later, capable though these successors were.

To another chapter in this history of Methodism, however, belong the names mentioned above. By the time the Civil War ended, the event of the founding of the Methodist Book Concern had receded into the dimming past. By comparison with other American institutions, the Methodist Book Concern in 1866 was already old, well established, and prospering.

The real drama in Methodist publishing of this era was being enacted south of the Mason-Dixon line, where the Publishing House of the Southern Church, if not actually in its birth throes, was in its infancy and struggling for survival against almost overwhelming odds. Barely begun at the time the war broke out, it was forced to cease operations altogether from 1862 until 1865, while Nashville was occupied by Federal forces and the property of the House commandeered for government printing. The end of the war found the enterprise with its organization and physical properties wrecked, and its constituency reduced to poverty.

JOHN B. MCFERRIN, EDITOR AND AGENT

The name that rises above all others during these years is that of John B. McFerrin, who was agent from 1858 until 1866, and who was called back to the job in 1878 when the House faced financial failure. Born in Rutherford County, Tennessee, in 1807, the son of a soldier-farmer converted to Methodism and become preacher, John Berry McFerrin grew naturally into the Methodist ministry. Educated in the country academies of the day, and somewhat possessed of the fighting spirit that characterized the pioneer times of his boyhood, McFerrin in 1840 became editor of the *Southwestern Christian Advocate,* a paper published at Nashville. Significantly enough, his first duty was to pull the paper out of debt, a role he later played so well in behalf of the Southern Publishing House.

His editorial work extended over a period of eighteen years, during many of which he maintained close contact with the church as a traveling minister throughout the South. When the Nashville *Christian Advocate* was begun in 1846, McFerrin was elected to the editorship, and continued in this post until becoming book agent in 1858. In this election the church again placed McFerrin in charge of a debt-ridden enterprise, and again his diligence in cultivating the support of the church reduced the indebtedness. When Nashville fell to Union forces in 1862, McFerrin and his family, on the advice of the retreating Confederate General Sidney Johnston, refugeed south. For most of the time until April, 1865, he rode as a chaplain with the Confederate forces, being present at the battle of Atlanta and at later battles in Middle Tennessee near Nashville. At the end of the war, when he returned to Nashville, his first act was to secure, in personal interview with President Andrew Johnson, release of the Federal-held property of the Publishing House. Together with one Richard Abbey, who had remained in Nashville and at least in touch with the House throughout the war, McFerrin resumed publication of the *Advocate* and such other affairs of House management as the times would allow.

Because of declining health McFerrin was not elected agent when the General Conference met in 1866. Instead, A. H. Redford received this post, while McFerrin, who had served in his early ministerial years as a missionary to the Indians, became secretary of home missions. In 1870, when the foreign and domestic departments were combined into one board, McFerrin was named missionary secretary. Again, his first task was freeing the society from debt, incurred during the war and owed to Dr. Thomas Carlton, senior agent of the Book Concern in New York and mission secretary for the Northern Church. Until 1878 McFerrin continued in this post, his last act as secretary being to recommend the forming of a woman's missionary society.

At the time of the General Conference of 1878, the affairs of the Publishing House were in a sad state. Unwise management had caused it to become so heavily involved in debt that sale of the property and abandonment of the whole enterprise seemed to many the only solution. In a last effort to save the House, the General Conference returned to the job of agent the best debt-liquidator in its ranks. Although seventy-one at this time, McFerrin engineered a sale of bonds that raised $300,000 in two years to extricate the organization from its plight. In order to accomplish this feat, the old man literally covered the South, making his appeal in conference after conference. Despite his well-advanced years, McFerrin was twice again elected agent by the General Conferences of 1882 and 1886, and at his death left the House in the best financial condition it had enjoyed up to that time. When he died in 1887, Bishop Holland N. McTyeire, in McFerrin's funeral sermon, recalled:

I never doubted that the bonds would go and the House be saved. . . . Who saw and heard can ever forget that dramatic scene, in which he represented the Bishops and superannuated and other preachers and their wives, and the official members, all assembled in the Public Square of Nashville, and the crier, with "one, two, three—l-a-s-t call" swinging down his hammer upon the Publishing House of the Methodist Episcopal Church, South? Those who heard and laughed and wept said, "No, that must never be;" and they took the bonds.[92]

So John B. McFerrin saved the Publishing House of the Southern Church, which, at a later date, was itself to play so large a role in saving the publishing interests of a newly united Methodism.

T. O. SUMMERS, EDITOR

No student of Methodism can long pursue the subject without becoming aware of the name and influence of Thomas Osmond Summers, the most prolific author-editor of the Southern Church in its earlier years. Until 1878 when, at his request, he was relieved of the editorial duties of the Nashville *Christian Advocate,* it could be said that at least editorially he had guided the destinies of the entire program of publishing in the Southern Church.[93]

From the start of the Southern Publishing House in 1854, T. O. Summers served as book editor, and as such was editor of the *Quarterly Review.* At the General Conference of 1866, with the financial affairs of the church in such serious straits, Summers was asked to assume also the editorship of the Nashville *Christian Advocate.* (The *Quarterly Review* had ceased publication during the war.) Although in 1874 Summers was elected professor of systematic theology at Vanderbilt University, he continued serving as book editor.

Biographers characterize the man as primarily a theologian, which evidently is correct, for it was the theology of Methodism that brought him into the church. Born in England in 1812 and reared in a strictly Calvinistic environment, he left the Presbyterian Church shortly after coming to America. (Orphaned, and almost alone in the world, he came to this country at the age of fifteen.) While still a youth he encountered Methodism in the eastern states; and its Arminian theology was the answer to his prayers. Had he been by nature or training less interested in theology, doubtless he would never have so questioned his Presbyterian teachings as to seek out Methodism.

Summers committed himself to the Methodist ministry in Maryland, and followed the path of the circuit rider in Virginia and later in Texas. A student by nature, he assiduously trained himself in the courses then required by the church, which was his only formal training beyond what he received during his childhood in England.

[92] Fitzgerald, *John B. McFerrin,* p. 441. Much in this sketch was taken from McFerrin's journal, quoted liberally by Fitzgerald.
[93] Information on Summers' life is from O. P. Fitzgerald, *Dr. Summers, A Life Study.*

Through Methodism Summers was introduced to the South, and his loyalties ever lay with that section. Especially was he fond of Alabama, where he held pastorates and where he found his future wife. When the church split in 1844, he sided with the Southern faction, maintaining to the end of his days that the South's was the "constitutional side of the question."

That Summers had much in common with John Wesley is borne out by the scope and type of editorial duties to which he devoted himself. Following what seems today a peculiar (but was then an accepted) practice, Summers issued a multitude of "revised" volumes ranging in subject from *The Bible in Many Tongues* to *The Art of Printing* and the *Life and Times of Charlemagne*. Many of the "revisions" were published with the name of T. O. Summers in place of the original author, and only the alert scholar or librarian can distinguish between books actually written by Summers and those that were revisions of the works of others. In the words of G. B. Winton, a later editor of the Nashville *Christian Advocate,* "His was not an original mind. . . . It was editing that especially suited his taste." [94]

In addition to its theology, the warm spirit of Methodism in its early years appealed to Summers; thus, second only to his interest in its theology was his interest in its hymnology. He was chiefly responsible for a hymnbook published for the Southern Church in 1846 that was widely popular and long recognized as a good hymnal. As editor of such official publications as the *Hymnal,* the *Discipline,* and the *Book of Worship,* Summers for many years exercised considerable influence over the character of the Southern Church. In fact, to a large extent he alone is credited with the retention of a certain liturgical formality about Southern Methodism in an age when primitive crudeness was the prevailing preference.

Of things Methodist, Summers held nothing dearer than Vanderbilt University. Pedantic, scholarly, loquacious on subjects in which he was interested, Summers was a born teacher, and persisted in this calling even after growing so weak of body that he had to be carried to his classes in a chair. It was he who dubbed the Vanderbilt Theological School the "School of the Prophets." *Schola Prophetorium* he had carved over the doorway of the university's famous old Wesley Hall.

Although never strong of body, Summers attained the age of seventy-one. Because of what it reveals of the rigors of an early Methodist circuit rider's life, a freak accident that occurred in Summers' early years and was the cause of much trouble for the rest of his life is worth considering.

[94] Nashville *Christian Advocate,* April 17, 1925, p. 499.

In his youth on the circuit, apparently because of the exhausting requirements of constant travel, preaching, and studying, Summers became afflicted with sleepwalking; and one night while thus engaged he fell from a second-story bedroom window. So extensive were his injuries that for a time it was thought he would die. And he never recovered completely. In addition, poor eyesight, sadness in his personal life—the loss of three children, one by illness and two in unusual accidents—and the fact of personally experiencing the rigors of life in the South during the Civil War took their toll. Despite all his afflictions, and even despite having much of his life's work consumed in the fire that destroyed the Publishing House in 1872, Summers, retaining some of his early teachings of predestination, held to his conviction that God had a good purpose behind all things.

In 1882, while serving in his usual post as secretary of the General Conference, he suffered the beginnings of his final illness. Dying several days later while the conference was still in session, he was buried on the campus of his beloved Vanderbilt University. His grave is there now, alongside those of Bishops Joshua Soule, Holland N. McTyeire, and William McKendree.

O. P. FITZGERALD, EDITOR

Oscar Penn Fitzgerald, who edited the Nashville *Christian Advocate* from 1878 until 1890, brought to the official organ of the Southern Church a popularity it had never before enjoyed.[95] His facile and consistently witty and humorous style gave the paper a light, agreeable quality that was important to Methodism in years when extreme bitterness characterized relationships between the Northern and Southern branches of the church. That it won favor with its readers is indicated by an advertisement that appeared in 1883 proclaiming that the *Advocate,* with 25,000 subscribers, had the widest circulation of any newspaper in the South.

Although a man of strong conviction, Fitzgerald's stock in trade was his wit. Typical was his handling of a situation in which the New York *Christian Advocate* berated Southern Methodism. C. H. Fowler, its editor, had written several articles of exceeding strength and bitterness against his Southern brothers. In return Fitzgerald reproduced in his paper the most vicious of the articles, making no other comment than the words of the caption—"Fowl, Fowler, Fowlest." [96] Again, in his

---

[95] Nashville *Christian Advocate,* August 11, 1911, p. 1001.
[96] *Ibid.*

volume of reminiscences entitled *Sunset Views,* Fitzgerald headed the chapter on his genealogy "Blood Will Tell, But Not All."

Born in North Carolina in 1829 and baptized into the Methodist Church when but two days old, Fitzgerald was forced by pecuniary necessity to leave home at the age of fourteen and go to work. He became a printer's apprentice and remained in newspaper work during the remainder of his youth and his early manhood. Feeling himself, as he put it, "always within the arms of the church," he joined the Georgia Conference and was first assigned as minister to a colored congregation. From this charge he went to Andrew Chapel in Savannah—"dreamy, delightful, seductive old Savannah," as he was later to write.[97]

Like many Southern Methodist leaders of the period, Fitzgerald early in his ministry went as a missionary to the West Coast, arriving in "red hot California," as he termed it, only six years after the Gold Rush began. He remained there for twenty-three years—minister, editor of the *Pacific Methodist,* and superintendent of public instruction for the state. In the last of these positions, to which he was elected by popular vote, he was instrumental in the beginnings of an institution that has since become known as the University of California at Berkeley.

Writing was Fitzgerald's forte. Best at devotional meditations and vignettes of life as observed in the Old South and the New West, he was considered during his lifetime a peer of Bret Harte and Mark Twain. The latter, living in California at the same time as Fitzgerald, is reported to have remarked that Brother Fitz, as he was called, was "trying to show the members of a Southern church the Southern way to a Southern heaven." [98] Whether or not such was the case, Fitzgerald on more than one occasion was nearly the victim of mob violence because of his stanch and outspoken allegiance to the Confederacy.

A wonderful command of the English language and a marvelous sense of humor, much of it directed at himself, make his *California Sketches,* first published in 1878 and remaining in print for years, lively reading even in the present age. While editor of the Nashville *Christian Advocate,* he introduced a page of naturalist features—animal stories from his own pen and from contributors that are in the best tradition of native American humor and the tall tale. These helped popularize the *Advocate,* especially as family reading, and are important foreshadowings of this aspect of present periodicals.

Like so many of the early editors, North and South, Fitzgerald was

[97] Fitzgerald, *Sunset Views* (Nashville: Publishing House of the Methodist Episcopal Church, South, 1906), p. 114.

[98] Nashville *Christian Advocate,* August 18, 1911, p. 1033.

elected to the episcopacy. Beginning in 1890 he served as bishop from Maryland to California. After his death on August 5, 1911, the lovable old bishop was for weeks eulogized in pages of the Nashville *Christian Advocate*. Tributes were paid by members of other denominations as well as by his fellow Methodists. Each remarked the wit, geniality, and sweet Christian spirit that caused Fitzgerald to be known as the "St. John of Methodism."

A. L. P. GREEN, BOOK COMMITTEE CHAIRMAN

Although A. L. P. Green was never an editor, an agent, or a bishop, his was an important role in the life of the Southern Publishing House in the first quarter century of its existence.[99] For all but four of the twenty years from 1854 until his death in 1874, Green was a member of the Book Committee. From the time of the division of the church, he was a major figure in Southern Methodist affairs. One of the three men appointed by the Southern Church to visit the General Conference of the Methodist Episcopal Church in 1848, he was the central figure in the negotiations, and later the lawsuit, that resulted in the division of the Book Concern property. On this money the Southern House was established, and to Green is chiefly attributed the choice of Nashville as the site for the establishment.

Born in Sevier County, Tennessee, in 1806, he went into the ministry at the age of eighteen. Prior to coming to Nashville in 1831, he served circuits in Tennessee, Arkansas, and Alabama.

In two respects Green was a contradiction of the usual idea of the Methodist minister of his day. Although a traveling minister in the fullest sense of the term, he maintained a home in Nashville for forty-three years. For many years after his death the family home, "Greenlands," a three-hundred-acre farm outside Nashville, was the rallying point of the large Green connection. More unusual than this, perhaps, was the fact that Green was a man of some considerable wealth. Not dependent on his preacher's salary, he for many years returned most or all of it to the church.

As a preacher he is chiefly remembered as one of the early ministers of Nashville's historic McKendree Church. In later life he was treasurer of Vanderbilt University, a post from which he retired in 1874. As a major figure in affairs of the Southern Church from the time of its establishment, he championed the cause of lay delegation to the conferences and lay involvement in church matters.

[99] For a full account of Green's life and work see William M. Green, *Life and Papers of A. L. P. Green, D. D.* (Nashville: Southern Methodist Publishing House, 1877).

JAMES D. BARBEE, AGENT

James D. Barbee, book agent of the Southern Church from 1886 to 1902, was paradoxically one of the most genuinely beloved and most widely criticized men in the annals of Southern Methodism. Senior agent at the time of the war settlement claim controversy, Dr. Barbee was personally blamed by many for blotting the escutcheon of the church.

Oddly enough, Barbee was one of the few early agents who brought to the job no especial acumen for business affairs. A successful career of more than thirty years in the pastorate and the office of presiding elder was the record on which his election to the agency was based. So inadequate did he feel to guide the House that he requested the Book Committee to elect as junior agent a layman with business-school training and experience to assist him with the management.

First and foremost a preacher, Dr. Barbee's success as an agent is attributed by one biographer more to his spirit than his method.[100] And successful he was in many respects, despite his finally requesting the General Conference not to consider him for re-election in 1902. The criticism to which his office had been subjected during the preceding quadrennium made him feel it would be a mistake that he be continued in the job.

The years of Barbee's agency were the first during which the House experienced any real financial solidarity; the first, in fact, when the House was in a position to appropriate any money for conference claimants. These years saw the laying of the first really sound foundations of the Southern Publishing House.

Barbee came to be discredited by many because of the wording of one telegram. This cast a shadow on his integrity that, however unfair, persists to some extent even down to the present. He was at the time, and continues to be, a victim of the age's demand for brevity of statement. Any situation, regardless of complexity, which cannot be disposed of in a word or two is likely to be suspect. Such was the case of Barbee.

Born in Alabama in 1832 and afforded scant formal education, Barbee was a self-taught man. After setting aside desires to be a physician or a lawyer, he entered the ministry in 1852 and held pastorates for thirty years in Tennessee and Alabama before becoming pastor of McKendree Church in Nashville—then one of the most prominent churches in Southern Methodism. From this post he was elected book agent.

The event which brought criticism to Barbee as agent occurred in 1898. On the eve of the Senate's passing of the bill to pay the Southern

---

[100] See H. M. Du Bose, *Life and Memories of Reverend J. D. Barbee* (Nashville: Publishing House of the Methodist Episcopal Church, South, 1906).

House for damages incurred during the Civil War, there arose a feeling among the senators that, if rumors were true, the Publishing House was paying too large a fee to the lawyer employed to present the case. Although the arrangements the House had made with its lawyer had no bearing on the justice of the claim, the case was about to be prejudiced. A wire was sent to the agents asking them to confirm or deny by return wire the rumor that the lawyer was to receive 40 per cent of the funds to be awarded. The agents wired back that this was not true; and indeed it wasn't. The fee had been set at 35 per cent. After the passage of the bill, the amount of the fee came to light. Some of the members of the Senate felt that the agents had been deliberately misleading. Investigations both by the church and the Senate ensued. In both, the agents were exonerated. But the stigma remained.

That Barbee was not censured by those with whom he was most closely associated is attested to by the fact that the day he left his office after the conference of 1902, all the employees gathered, with tears streaming down the faces of many, and presented him with a purse, made in the bindery of the plant and crammed full of gold coins and bills.

Born in poverty, his life harassed by family illness, generous to a fault, Dr. Barbee never amassed even enough to make his last years debt free. This in itself belies the feeling some have expressed that his conduct in the war claim matter was merely that of a shrewd businessman.

From 1902 until his death on December 5, 1904, Dr. Barbee was superintendent of the Nashville district.

ELIJAH EMBREE HOSS, PREACHER, EDUCATOR, EDITOR, BISHOP

Elijah Hoss played a prominent role in affairs of the Methodist Episcopal Church, South, for nearly half a century. Editor of the Nashville *Christian Advocate* from 1890 to 1902, when he was elected bishop, he brought to this official organ of the Southern Church a vitality that placed it in a position of leadership before unequaled.[101]

A born fighter, great-grandson of the famous Revolutionary War hero John Sevier, Hoss consistently during his lifetime was a champion of causes. These ranged in order and type from the stand taken early in his career that the Northern Church had no right to confiscate and hold pulpits in established Southern churches during and after the Civil War, to the advocacy of the church's right to complete control over Vanderbilt University. His conviction in the first of these matters grew out of firsthand experience with just such a situation in Knoxville, Tennessee, where

---

[101] See Isaac P. Martin, *Elijah Embree Hoss, Ecumenical Methodist* (Nashville: Parthenon Press, 1942).

he served his second assignment as pastor. His stand on the Vanderbilt matter, concerning a university where he had occupied a chair for five years, colored and affected the last thirteen years of his life. On both issues he stood out for what he believed to be the right of the church. Both issues were ultimately settled by the courts of the land. The Supreme Court of the United States ruled in favor of Bishop Hoss's position in the earlier issue. The Supreme Court of Tennessee ruled against Bishop Hoss and his colleagues in the latter. The Southern churches were ultimately returned as places of worship for their rightful congregations. Vanderbilt University, begun by the Methodist Episcopal Church, South, became a private institution devoid of church control.

A native of Tennessee, born in 1849, Hoss joined the church at the age of eleven. Early declaring his intention to enter the ministry, he was sent by his parents to Ohio Wesleyan University in 1866. Union sympathizers, though stanch Southerners and slaveholders, the Hoss family felt that Elijah would encounter political ideas more in keeping with their own at the Northern university than he would in his own section. Two years in Ohio, however, convinced Elijah that he was more Southern than Northern. He returned to finish college at Emory and Henry in Emory, Virginia, and on graduation entered the ministry in the Holston Conference of the Methodist Episcopal Church, South, rather than going into the Methodist Episcopal Church—as earlier might have been presumed to be his natural course.

Prior to being elected editor, Hoss served pastorates in the South and on the West Coast, and held professorships and presidencies of Southern Methodist colleges.

During Hoss's years as editor of the Nashville *Christian Advocate,* the difficulty broke concerning the settlement of the war claims held by the Southern Methodist Publishing House against the United States government. With the possible exception of the Vanderbilt controversy, no issue caused more heated debate in the ranks of the church. Editor Hoss strongly supported the actions of the agents in the matter and the right of the church, again, to receive payment for damages to Publishing House property during the Civil War. While deploring the sending of the telegram, Hoss editorially presented his reasons for supporting the general actions of the House management in such a way that even at a distance of many years they must be judged classic for their clarity and good sense.

While editor of the *Advocate,* Hoss first embarked upon the ecumenical activities that were to be characteristic of the remaining years of his life. Delegate to the Second Ecumenical Methodist Conference, which met in Washington, D.C., in 1891, Hoss addressed that body on the subject of the church newspaper, an indication of his standing as editor even after only a year in the job. In 1894 he was fraternal messenger to the Canadian Methodist Church; in 1900 fraternal messenger to the Methodist Episcopal Church; in 1903 fraternal messenger to the Brazilian Wesleyan Conference; in 1915 messenger for all of Methodism to the Australian Methodists. For four years after 1905 he was bishop in charge of the work in Brazil. In 1910 and again in 1915 he visited the Orient and the work there, for which he had volunteered his services as a missionary in 1871. During his years as bishop Hoss was responsible at various times for Methodist conferences throughout the central South and the Southwest as well as for the work in Brazil.

No activity of his life in the episcopacy stands out so obviously as does the role he played in the Vanderbilt controversy that swept the entire church and section. In the case that, at least popularly, was identified as a struggle between religion and secularity, Hoss was undisputedly the central figure on the side of the church in opposition to Vanderbilt's Chancellor James H. Kirkland, the man to whom much of the present greatness of the university is attributed. In some circles Hoss emerged, though defeated, as the strong and devoted champion of the church's rights; in others he was considered "earnest, sincere, prejudiced and passionate." [102]

Death came to Bishop Hoss at the age of seventy during the influenza epidemic of 1919.

DAVID M. SMITH, FIRST LAY AGENT IN THE SOUTH

In the North and in the South, Methodist publishing for many years was almost solely the responsibility of the ministry. In this sense it paralleled the attitude of the whole church, which did not for generations admit laymen to its conferences or to positions of supervisory responsibility in general church affairs.

When the Southern House was established in 1854, there was created the office of financial secretary, a job filled by a minister, but a minister who had first been a businessman. Richard Abbey held the post throughout the war, remaining alone in Nashville to defend the House against the ravages of fire and sword. To his tireless energy and legal skill was attributed whatever success the House had in coming through the war at all.

From time to time, as the years went on, in addition to the agents the

[102] Edwin Mims, *A History of Vanderbilt University* (Nashville: Vanderbilt University Press, 1946), p. 301.

Southern House employed a business manager. In 1886, when James D. Barbee was elected agent, he requested the Book Committee to fill this position, feeling that he as a minister was weak in the area of financial management. The man chosen for the post was David M. Smith, a young businessman from Arkansas who had come to Nashville to attend school and who had taken a position with one of the town's leading firms. Smith was an active Methodist who organized the Men's Bible Class at McKendree Church during Barbee's pastorate there. Too, he was the son-in-law of Dr. W. G. E. Cunnyngham, an early Sunday school editor.

In 1890 the General Conference named Smith assistant agent, and in 1902 elevated him to the post of senior agent, which job he filled until his retirement in 1922. From 1922 until his death in 1931 he was agent emeritus. The Nashville *Christian Advocate* for August 14, 1931, said of Smith: "He was conservative in time of financial panic; he was progressive when indications warranted advances."

His contribution was that of cautious management in a time when caution was necessary, with result that a sound foundation was laid for growth in coming years and the example set for navigating troubled waters of financial difficulty such as characterized the 1930's.

JOHN JAMES TIGERT, III, BOOK EDITOR

When a "wretched little accident" caused the untimely death of John James Tigert, III, in 1906, the Southern Church mourned the loss not only of one of her youngest bishops, but also one of her brightest scholars, preachers and writers.[103] En route to preside over his second conference after his election to the episcopacy six months earlier, Tigert in the course of a meal swallowed a small bone, which, becoming lodged in his throat, caused blood poisoning, and brought about his death seven days later.

Thus was abruptly ended a lifetime that in less than fifty years had included the pastoral ministry, professorship at Vanderbilt University, book editorship of the Southern Church, and, in 1906, the episcopacy.

John J. Tigert was born in Louisville, November 25, 1856, of Methodist parentage. He early declared the ministry his vocational intention. Educated at Vanderbilt University, where he subsequently became professor of philosophy, Tigert spent a number of years in the pastoral ministry in Kentucky and Missouri before being elected book editor in 1894.

A scholarly man, he was author or editor of twenty-two publications, from his first *Handbook of Logic*, published in 1885, to *The Christianity*

[103] See the Nashville *Christian Advocate*, November 30, 1906, pp. 3-5.

of Christ and His Apostles (1905). Perhaps his best known were the *Constitutional History of American Episcopal Methodism* (1894) and *Theism: A Survey of the Paths That Lead to God* (1901).

During his lifetime the Northern and Southern branches of Methodism began to make real progress toward unification, and Tigert was an important figure in such undertakings as the *Standard Catechism* adopted by both churches.

Administrators of the Northern Book Concern

A review of the history of the Methodist Book Concern, both in its New York and Cincinnati locations, from the end of the Civil War until the 1920's, reveals a stability of management that bespeaks the well-established condition of the enterprise. Because of this, the history of the Concern during this period, while nonetheless significant, is less colorful than that of earlier periods or than that of the Southern House during these crisis-ridden years.

Between 1852 and 1922, a group of men in positions of top management in the Concern had careers ranging from seventeen to twenty-four years in length. No one can be associated with any endeavor for so long without leaving his stamp upon it.

THOMAS CARLTON

For the most part, all of these men—six of them ministers—made their outstanding contributions as business managers. In chronological order, the first of these was Thomas Carlton, senior agent in New York from 1852 to 1872. A native of New Hampshire and an ordained minister of the Genesee Conference, Carlton guided the affairs of the Concern during the period when it became firmly established as a major American publisher. No longer merely a struggling, debt-ridden church enterprise, it began during these years to diversify its activity, publishing an impressive list of hardbound (and handsomely bound) volumes, as well as a variety of church papers and Sunday school materials. The catalogues of the Concern for these years are, in themselves, arresting volumes, setting forth an amazing number and range of titles of surprising scope.

Although he made, without question, a major contribution to the publishing program of the church and had many admirers throughout church ranks, Carlton, in his last quadrennium, suffered much criticism as the result of a fraud charge brought against his administration by John Lanahan, for a time junior agent. Although Carlton himself was exonerated by the 1872 General Conference, he was not re-elected. Dr. Reuben Nelson at that time became senior agent, and a layman was elected to the post of junior agent.

JOHN M. PHILLIPS

The story of John Milton Phillips, the man to whom fell the honor of being the first layman to head the publishing activities of the Northern Church, has a surprisingly modern twist. He was in a sense an organization man, whose whole career centered in the Methodist Book Concern, and was the first to rise from a lowly position in one location to the head man in the home office. And this in 1872.

Orphaned at the age of fifteen and left with the responsibility of rearing a younger brother, John Phillips began his career with the concern in Cincinnati as office boy and general factotum.[104] His father, a minister, had been the assistant editor of the *Western Christian Advocate,* so doubtless the Concern adopted a parental attitude toward the boy, little more than a child himself, who suddenly found himself in a father's role. This part of the story is truly of the mid-nineteenth century, almost Dickensonian.

Like the Horatio Alger heroes the young pauper did indeed apply himself with diligence to the task at hand, and in his manhood reached the highest rung of the ladder in the Cincinnati branch of the Concern, as accountant and guardian of the organization's business affairs. In addition, he became president of the Union Central Insurance Company and the Farmer's Fire Insurance Company, both Cincinnati firms. An active Methodist layman, he was elected a delegate to the Northern Church's first General Conference at which laymen sat. The General Conference in 1872 elected Phillips to the post of junior agent in New York, with Reuben Nelson as senior agent. In addition to the fact of his lay status this elevating of Phillips was for the times surprising, because in those days the Eastern and Western branches of the business were almost separate enterprises, and transfer of personnel from one to the other was a practice all but unknown.

When Nelson died in 1879, Phillips became senior agent and served until his death in 1889. Characterized as a quiet and unassuming man, who knew the "entrails of the business," Phillips brought to his post as publishing agent thirty years' experience with the Concern and at the end of his career was lauded as an "efficient, safe, unobjectionable officer," genuinely admired for his ability and his humility. At the time of his death the New York *Christian Advocate* said, "Little has been

---

[104] For a biography of Phillips see W. V. Kelley, "John Milton Phillips," *The Methodist Review* (Northern), January, 1889, pp. 66-75.

done or organized on a large scale in Methodism for a quarter of a century without receiving the benefit of his unobtruded counsels and harmonizing spirit." [105]

HOMER EATON

Homer Eaton, who served as publishing agent from 1889 until his death in 1913, is distinguished as having the longest career in the office and as being the first general agent of the Book Concern following unification of the Eastern and Western branches.[106] Born in Vermont in 1834 of Methodist parentage, Eaton entered the ministry in 1857 and joined the Troy Conference. First of all a preacher, he served eight years on the Book Committee and one year as chairman before being elected agent upon the death of John Phillips. In the quarter century of Eaton's administration the growth of the business was unprecedented.

SANDFORD HUNT

When Reuben Nelson died in 1879, Sandford Hunt was elected to serve as agent with John Phillips, thus beginning a seventeen-year career with the publishing interests of the church. Born in western New York in 1825 and educated at Allegheny College, he served as pastor and presiding elder before his election to the agency. Prior to this he had been on the Book Committee. When Phillips died in 1889, Hunt became senior agent. He occupied this position until 1896, when he died unexpectedly in a Cincinnati hotel where a meeting of the Book Committee was about to begin. Characterized as a conservative, quiet, patient man, he was remembered in the Book Concern for the knowledge he possessed of the organization's history and his clarification of its objectives.[107]

GEORGE PRESTON MAINS

The man elected to fill the vacancy created by Dr. Hunt's death stands apart somewhat from other agents of this period as being not only a sound businessman but also a scholar, with an intellectual bent to theological and philosophical matters. Considered for his day quite liberal, George Preston Mains served well as publishing agent from 1896 until 1916. At the time of his death, it was written of him that "his personal faith . . . remained serene and confident, though he would not have expressed it in traditional forms at all points." [108]

[105] February 14, 1889, p. 97.

[106] *Homer Eaton*, a memorial volume published by the Methodist Book Concern (New York and Cincinnati, 1913).

[107] H. C. Jennings, *The Methodist Book Concern*, pp. 91-92. See also the New York *Christian Advocate*, February 20, 1896, pp. 113, 120.

[108] New York *Christian Advocate*, September 18, 1930, p. 1123.

Born in Newport, New York, in 1844, and a graduate of Wesleyan University, Mains joined the New York East Conference and spent twenty-five years in the pastorate before becoming agent. During his administration the publishing interests of the church enjoyed one of their most active periods, to which he strongly contributed by his knowledge of the literary market. Himself an author, he wrote such books as *Modern Thought and Traditional Faith* and *Some Moral Reasons for Belief in the Godhead of Christ.* Retiring from the agency in 1916 at his own request, he lived until his death in 1930 at the home of a daughter in Southern California, where he was the center of a large circle of Methodists.

JOHN M. WALDEN

In Methodist publishing, as is often the case in life generally, men who excel in one area are also outstanding in others. Like Nathan Bangs, many of the early agents, while heading the Publishing House or Book Concern, doubled in important positions with the missionary endeavor of the church. The senior agent in New York usually served concurrently as treasurer of the Board of Missions. And the same was true in the South.

Typical of such versatile and energetic personalities was John Morgan Walden, book agent in Cincinnati from 1868 until 1884, when he was elected to the episcopacy.[109] Just as Nathan Bangs excelled in numerous and widespread activities of the church in the early years of the nineteenth century, so Walden was outstanding in the middle and later years. And in many respects Walden was to the Western Book Concern what his contemporary John B. McFerrin was to the Publishing House of the Southern Church. Both saw the publishing enterprises through troubled times of indebtedness and both ended their labors as agent with the respective houses on financial footings much improved if not absolutely sound. Also like McFerrin, Walden won fame as a Methodist personality for work that was entirely aside from his career with the publishing interests.

Of his many accomplishments, John Walden is probably best known as the founder of the Freedmen's Aid Society of the Methodist Episcopal Church, which had its inception in 1866 and continued active in support of schools throughout the South for many years. Early in his life, as a newspaperman in Kansas, Walden, born in conditions of pioneer poverty so typical of the age, sympathized with the abolitionists. It is interesting to note that Walden, while publisher of a small newspaper espous-

[109] Information on Walden is from David Hastings Moore, *John Morgan Walden* (New York; Methodist Book Concern, 1915).

ing the cause of "Free Kansas," became one of the founders of the Republican Party. Concern for those who had been slaves carried over into his years in the ministry, when he served in many offices and finally as president of the Freedmen's Aid Society. Throughout his life he was also an active champion of temperance, the second of the big social causes embraced by episcopal Methodism in the 1800's.

True to his times in so many respects, Walden became a Christian and a Methodist by way of a typical brush-arbor revival in rural Ohio. As the result of an unstable childhood—homeless from the age of ten, and so subject to all manner of influences in his formative years—Walden as a youth manifested the religious skepticism of Tom Paine, whose *Age of Reason* came to the boy's hands through an acquaintance. Walden early showed an interest in the arts, acquired through association with a book peddler, which for a time seemed certain to lead him into a career on the stage. It was during this time, however, that he became converted in the Methodist revival that changed his life. He enrolled at Farmer's College (where he was a classmate of Benjamin Harrison), went into newspaper work, and thence to the role of local preacher. He turned to the ministry as his lifework in 1858 and was ordained in the Cincinnati Conference.

During his lifetime, and in biographies published since his death in 1914, Walden's capacity for work and his ability to comprehend detail stand out as his dominant characteristics. He was known as the best businessman in Methodism, and like so many was referred to as a "walking encyclopedia." He was indeed the prototype of the self-made man whose brilliance was the brilliance of loyalty and toil.

HENRY C. JENNINGS

Henry C. Jennings, the agent who began the movement that led to consolidation of the Eastern and Western sections of the Book Concern in 1912, filled this important position in the Methodist Book Concern during one of its most fruitful periods. A Methodist minister, son and grandson of Methodist ministers, Jennings was elected publishing agent of the Western Methodist Book Concern in 1896. Until 1900 he was the resident agent in Chicago. In 1900 he became senior agent in Cincinnati. From 1913 until his retirement in 1920 he was general agent, responsible for the total Book Concern operation.

Born on December 21, 1850, in Fremont, Illinois, Jennings was only a child when the death of his father necessitated his going to work. Converted in a revival, educated in the log cabin schools of Methodism, he attended Northwestern University for a time. Upon entering the ministry, he joined the Minnesota Conference in 1871, was ordained in 1873, and served as pastor of churches in Minnesota until elected publishing agent.

During the years of his official connection with the Book Concern it grew steadily, achieved unquestioned financial stability, and appropriated before-unequaled sums for the conference claimants. Expansion of the Sunday school literature program characterized Jennings' years as agent, as did development in the graphic arts and progress in the printing departments. While he was general agent Abingdon Press was established as the book publishing division of the Concern.

Although the Book Concern was the primary field of church service to which Jennings devoted his life, he was a man of wide influence in the general affairs of the denomination. He was a delegate to seven General Conferences, and was the only person up to that time ever elected a delegate twice without ballot and by acclamation. He was also a member of the Epworth League Board of Control for the first seven years of its existence.

Jennings' outstanding characteristic as agent was his ability as a business administrator. So good was he in this respect that it became the telling argument that kept the General Conference of 1908 from electing him to the episcopacy. If he were elected bishop, it was argued, no replacement could be found for him in the leadership of the Book Concern. At the time of his death he was hailed by the church as "a far seeing executive with a genius for independent action." [110]

EDWIN R. GRAHAM

In the annals of Methodist publishing, Edwin R. Graham, agent from 1904 to 1921, stands out as being primarily a bookman. Typical of what has since been the background of Publishing House executives, Graham, while himself a layman, was the son of a Methodist preacher. In his young manhood he was employed by the Western Methodist Book Concern. From there he went to a position with the Boston publisher Houghton, in the sales department of Riverside Press.

Because of this experience in the book field, the General Conference of 1904 elected him agent in Cincinnati. When the Western and Eastern branches of the Concern united, Graham was elected one of the three agents. After eight years in charge of the business in Chicago, he moved to New York in 1916 to head the operation at 150 Fifth Avenue.

His obituary in the New York *Christian Advocate* at the time of his

[110] Addresses Given at the Funeral Services of Reverend Henry C. Jennings, D.D., First Methodist Episcopal Church, Oak Park, Illinois, November 9, 1927. See also the *Western Christian Advocate,* November 17, 1927, p. 1102, and the New York *Christian Advocate,* November 17, 1927, p. 1388.

death in 1921 stated that "Dr. Graham's equipment was that of a business man."[111]

Born in Ohio, educated at Baldwin University, Graham married a daughter of the parsonage. When ill health foretold death, he returned to his farm in Richwood, Ohio, and died in February, 1921, at the age of sixty-seven.

Editors of Publications for the Methodist Episcopal Church

Because of the nature of the publishing enterprise, which involves not only the publication but also the sale of materials, the Methodist Publishing House throughout the years has been the center of debate concerning its main purpose. Is its primary function the publishing of items to aid the church in the preaching of the gospel? Or does it primarily serve as a source of income for the church's retired ministers? Clear though the *Disciplines* through the years have given the answer, time after time the question has arisen, and time after time the church has affirmed the *Discipline:* The chief purpose of the institution is publishing and distributing, the monetary aspect is secondary. Because the organization for most of its history has been supported not by the benevolent contributions of the church but by income from its own labors, the financial aspect cannot be discounted as irrelevant. Yet it must be said, in the final analysis, that prime importance attaches itself to what issues from the Publishing House presses, not what comes into its treasury. Those who have served as editors could in a sense be termed "keepers of the flame," for they have established the criteria for what the church has published.

At the beginning of the Book Concern, the agents themselves served as the book editors. And in the Northern Church up until 1904 the book editor's job carried with it also editorship of *The Methodist Review.* Outstanding in the period covered by this chapter were Daniel D. Whedon, book editor and editor of the *Review* from 1856 to 1884, and William V. Kelley, book editor from 1892 to 1904 and editor of the *Review* from 1892 to 1920.

DANIEL D. WHEDON

Typical of the editors of the period, Whedon came to the editorship from the schoolmaster's desk. One of the early college graduates of Methodism, he taught Greek and mental philosophy at Wesleyan University

[111] February 24, 1921, p. 236.

before entering the pastorate. Born in Onandaga, New York, in 1808, Whedon was reared in the Presbyterian Church, although his mother and one of his brothers were Methodists. A voracious reader, he graduated at the age of twenty from Hamilton College. Although always religiously inclined, Whedon during his formative years went through a period of religious doubt springing in a measure from his rejection of the Calvinistic doctrine of necessity to which he had been early exposed.[112] Converted by a Methodist preacher during the period of the great revivals, he joined the New York Conference on trial in 1834, but not until 1842 did he decide to give up university life for the pastorate. At this time he transferred to the Troy Conference and was appointed to Pittsfield, Massachusetts. Preaching, however, was not his forte, so he returned to teaching, accepting a professorship at the University of Michigan, where he won fame throughout the West.

Although at the outset an apologist for slavery as an inherited institution, he so strongly opposed its extension into free territory that he became quite outspoken on the matter, and as a result found it to his best interest to leave the University of Michigan and return East. He opened a private school at Ravenswood, New York, and in the ensuing years won recognition as a writer and speaker, thus establishing a reputation in the eastern states paralleling that he had earned in the West. Plagued by deafness and thus not effective as a pastor, he was nevertheless recognized by the church for his intellectual prowess, and so in 1856 was elected book editor and editor of the *Review*. Throughout his life Whedon was a stanch advocate of the Arminian position and is probably best remembered for his book *Freedom of the Will,* published by the Book Concern in 1864, and for Whedon's *Commentary,* published between 1860 and 1885. When he died in 1885, he was hailed as the man who had been the brain of the Methodist Episcopal Church for nearly a quarter century.

WILLIAM V. KELLEY

From 1893 until 1920 the editorship of *The Methodist Review* was in the hands of William V. Kelley, the son of a Methodist preacher, who began his career teaching school. A graduate of Pennington Seminary and Wesleyan University, Kelley entered the pastorate at the age of twenty-four and had an established reputation as a preacher when elected to editorship of the *Review.* Characterized by Lynn Harold Hough as a "Christian humanist," [113] Dr. Kelley was rigid in his judgment of

---

[112] D. A. and J. S. Whedon, "Biographical Sketch," *Essays, Reviews, and Discourses,* by D. D. Whedon (New York: Phillips and Hunt, 1887), pp. 7-49.

[113] New York *Christian Advocate,* December 22, 1927, p. 1555.

writers. Exasperated by the likes of Mencken, indignant with the likes of Whitman, he was a scholar, insistent on precision of style in writing. Retired at his request in 1920, he lived in Maplewood, New Jersey, until his death in 1927.

DANIEL CURRY

Of all products of the American press, none has been more consistently influential than the newspaper. From the days of Benjamin Franklin until the advent of television, the daily or weekly tabloid knew no real rival as the prime source of information for the American mind. This has been especially true of the religious press, and particularly true of the Methodist press. At first primarily a frontier and then a rural denomination, Methodism has kept in touch with the world through its church papers. Often these journals, whose columns were devoted almost as largely to secular as to religious items, were the only contact between the isolated home and the centers of civilization, and so were widely popular. Needless to say, the influence of their editors was considerable.

Although for many years the *Western Christian Advocate,* published in Cincinnati, was an important voice in the Methodist Episcopal Church, no paper ever really challenged the lead early set by the *Christian Advocate,* published in New York.

In the years between the Civil War and unification, three editors stand out as especially influential because of the length of their tenures. The earliest of these is Daniel Curry, who was born in 1809 and died in 1887. Although others were editors of the *Advocate* for periods as long or longer than that during which Curry served, Curry is notable not only for his twelve years as *Advocate* editor but also for the fact of his editorship of the *Ladies' Repository* and *The Methodist Review.*

Born in New York and educated at Wesleyan University, Curry was first a teacher at the Troy Conference Academy at Poultney, Vermont. In 1839 he became a professor at the Georgia Female College at Macon, and in 1841 was admitted on trial to the Georgia Conference. Full connection was accorded him in 1843, and he was assigned to a pastorate in Savannah. Because of the slavery issue, he returned to the North in 1844, transferred to the New York Conference, and in 1848 became one of the founders of the New York East Conference.

Primarily a teacher, not a preacher, Curry left the pastorate to become president of Indiana Asbury, from which post he was elected *Advocate* editor in 1864. He served in this capacity until 1876, when he became editor of the *Ladies' Repository.* From 1884 until 1887 he was book editor and editor of *The Methodist Review.*

Characterized as a contender whose contentions were not always upheld by the church, Curry was nevertheless widely influential as an edi-tor; [114] and while his arguments were often voted down on the floor of the General Conference, he invariably and successively was elected to position of higher rank.

JAMES M. BUCKLEY

The dominant *Advocate* personality in the period following the Civil War was James Monroe Buckley, who served as editor from 1880 until 1912, when at his request he was retired, to become editor emeritus.[115] Born in Rahway, New Jersey, and reared by his widowed mother and her parents, Buckley was educated at Pennington Seminary and Wes-leyan University. Although attracted to teaching and the law, Buckley in his early twenties determined to devote his life to the pulpit. Ridden with tuberculosis, which had claimed the lives of his mother, father, and brother, Buckley, on entering the ministry, declared his de-sire to preach the gospel of Christ "as a dying man to dying men." The will to live, however, caused him to leave the pastorate for a time in order to cultivate his health abroad. Careful exercise and proper climate restored his health, and he returned a cured man, to take up pastoral duties in Detroit.

Characterized as a religious newspaperman, a Greeley of Methodism, Buckley was strong for social reform. Because of the precarious condition of his own health in his early years, he always harbored an interest in the medical profession, and to an editorial written by him in the *Advo-cate* is attributed the founding of the Methodist Hospital in Brooklyn. As did most Methodist leaders of the time, Buckley championed the tem-perance issue; and he was one of the first churchmen to manifest an in-terest in insanity and other psychological disturbances, foreshadowing the current role of the pastor as counselor. Although a man of unusually broad interests for his day, Buckley was by modern standards a religious conservative, and at the time of his death was acclaimed for having held Methodism to its anchors midst the theological cyclones of the late nineteenth and early twentieth centuries. While not quite the bishop-maker he was termed by the secular press, Buckley was of great in-fluence in the General Conference. Of his writings, aside from those in the *Advocate,* the best known is his *History of Methodism in the United States,* published in 1897. In 1920, eight years after his retirement in 1912, he died in Madison, New Jersey.

---

[114] *Ibid.,* August 25, 1887, p. 545.

[115] See George Preston Mains, *James Monroe Buckley* (New York: The Methodist Book Concern, 1917).

JAMES R. JOY

The third of the long-time editors of the New York *Christian Advocate* was James R. Joy, who served in the post from 1915 until 1936, when he retired. Immediately after graduating from Yale in 1885, Dr. Joy entered service with John H. Vincent, then editor of Sunday school publications. Later he became assistant to Dr. Buckley, and then in 1915 editor of the paper. Born in 1863, Dr. Joy lived until 1957. After his retirement he served as librarian of the Methodist Historical Society in New York City.

JOHN H. VINCENT

In the history of Methodist publishing, the late nineteenth and early twentieth centuries might be characterized as the years of the Sunday school publications. While the Sunday school movement had begun about forty years before the Civil War, the refinements in teaching methods and materials characteristic of the present program did not become manifest until the last two decades of the 1800's. Prior to this time the Sunday school had for the most part been devoted entirely to Bible instruction with no particular continuity or unity. The earliest Sunday schools, of course, had taught general subjects—the "three R's"—but as public education became more general, the schools in the churches concentrated on the Bible. Methods and topics, however, varied from church to church, from Sunday to Sunday.

When considering Methodist Sunday school publications, the name that rises above all others is that of John Heyl Vincent, Sunday school editor from 1868 to 1888. Never before had the Sunday school occupied so important a position in the life of the church as it did during these years. Following the editorships of Daniel P. Kidder, whose chief contributions had included organizing the Sunday school movement of Methodism for the purpose, among other things, of gathering statistics and initiating leadership training conferences; and Daniel Wise, who had carried forward the unifying work begun by Kidder; Vincent, with his Chautauqua movement, put the Sunday school in the "big time." Lacking college training, yet believing strongly in education, Vincent became the leader of millions like himself, and what he began as a training school for Sunday school teachers became the first widespread institution of adult self-education in America. By accident of birth Vincent was a Southerner, having been born in Tuscaloosa, Alabama, February 23, 1832.[116] While he was still a child, however, his family returned to their native Pennsylvania, where Vincent was reared. His family connections

---

[116] For a life of Vincent see Leon H. Vincent, *John Heyl Vincent* (New York: The Macmillan Company, 1925).

on his father's side were all Presbyterian; his mother's family were Lutherans. In Alabama the Vincents had become Methodists, the father being especially active as a Sunday school superintendent. Thus John Vincent was reared in the Methodist Episcopal Church. After completing his secondary education, he became a teacher himself, specializing for a time in "Singing Geography," a fad by which students learned places and peoples by means of tuned rhymes. In 1850 he was licensed to exhort and later became a local preacher. For a time Vincent was a student at the Newark Wesleyan Institute in Newark, New Jersey, and in 1853 became a member of the New Jersey Conference.

While minister at Camptown, New Jersey, he began the venture that later grew into Chautauqua. Believing that the Bible would better be understood if seen in historical and geographic perspective, he began in Camptown a project known as the "Palestine class." Designed primarily for adults of both sexes, but largely attended by the ladies, the Palestine class was almost entirely a course in the geography and history of the Holy Land. Rather gimmicky (the several groups within the class, as it grew, bore the names of certain areas, and the students were "citizens" of these areas, until on completion they became "citizens" of the whole country) the first classes were enormously popular, and their success in Camptown was repeated in other places as Vincent moved from church to church.

The primary justification of the Palestine class was training of Sunday school teachers, but as an end in itself it became an important part of Vincent's churches both in the East and later when he transferred to the Rock River Conference. In Galena, Illinois, especially did Vincent win popularity, and there he became a friend of Ulysses S. Grant, whose appearances at Chautauqua in later years were great drawing cards.

While pastor in Rockford, Vincent had the opportunity of taking a European tour and visiting the Holy Land, which increased his zeal for the Palestine classes. But in Chicago, as pastor of Trinity Church, he ran into a situation where Sunday school activity was more or less at a standstill. The result was that he joined an interdenominational group zealous for the betterment of Sunday schools in general. Having conducted the first Sunday School Institute at Freeport, Illinois, several years earlier, Vincent was instrumental in starting a Sunday school magazine for the Northwest—which was an early effort toward the publishing of uniform Sunday school lessons. So prominent had he become in promoting institutes for the training of teachers and in designing methodical lessons to take the place of the haphazard ones so long in use that in 1866 he was sent to New York to be general agent of the Methodist Sunday School

Union. His job was to be the promotion of Sunday schools in general and teacher training in particular.

In 1868 a reorganization of certain departments of the church resulted in Vincent's being elected editor of *The Sunday School Journal,* corresponding secretary of the Sunday School Union, and superintendent of the Department of Sunday School Instruction. When the International Sunday School Convention was held in Indianapolis in 1872, Vincent was made chairman of a committee of five to draw up outlines of what were the first International Sunday School Lessons.

The desire to hold a large-scale Sunday School Institute led to the first meetings at Chautauqua Lake, New York. Held in the summer of 1874, the institute lasted only two weeks, and was aimed directly at teacher training. But all the forces of fate were too much in accord with the venture for it to be left at that, and soon the "season" was extended to several months. Thousands, of all denominations, flocked to Chautauqua Lake for "self-culture," while still other thousands remained busy at home the year round, improving their minds by reading the publications and books prescribed by the Chautauqua Literary and Scientific Circle.

The great story of Chautauqua can only be viewed here briefly; suffice it to say that it is generally recognized as the primogenitor of that sacrosanct and very worthwhile American pastime formerly called "self-culture"—and now "adult education."

In 1888 Vincent was elected to the episcopacy and in 1900 became resident bishop in Europe. After his retirement in 1904, he took up residence in Indiana, moving to Chicago after the death of Mrs. Vincent in 1909. There he died in 1920. At the time of his death the Chicago *Evening Post* said of him:

> Bishop Vincent will be remembered by America chiefly because he founded one of the distinctive features of its life—the Chautauqua movement—And whatever the supercilious may say of Chautauqua, or however the movement itself may at time have strayed from its higher aims, beyond cavil it has brought millions of Americans, in towns and rural communities, into contact with the richer and finer things of the soul and the spirit. Bishop Vincent helped America. He believed in God and in man, and was the friend of both.[117]

DAN B. BRUMMITT

Thirty-seven years in editorial positions of publications of the Methodist Episcopal Church distinguishes the career of Dan B. Brummitt. Guided into the ministry as a student at Baker University, English-born

[117] *Ibid.,* p. 313.

Dan Brummitt successively became editor of *The Epworth Herald,* the *Northwestern Christian Advocate,* and the *Central Christian Advocate.*

A member of the Rock River Conference, Brummitt held pastorates in Kansas and Arkansas before becoming an assistant on *The Epworth Herald* in 1901. In 1912 he became editor of the *Herald,* which post he vacated in 1924 to become editor of the *Northwestern Advocate.* In 1932 he became editor of the *Central Advocate,* published in Kansas City.

An enthusiast for unification, which took place in Kansas City in 1939, Dr. Brummitt spent his last hours on earth preparing the special unification issue of the *Central Advocate.* Death came suddenly on April 5, 1939, when he suffered a heart attack in the lobby of a Kansas City hotel, where he had gone to complete hospitality arrangements for the forthcoming Uniting Conference.

Born in 1867 in Batley, England, Brummitt came to America with his parents at the age of fourteen. After graduation from Baker he went to Drew for theological training, and entered first the teaching profession. While working on a college paper he got his first taste of the journalistic career that was to be his life work. At the time of his appointment to the editorship of the *Central Advocate* the incumbent editor wrote, "Dr. Dan Brearly Brummitt is a student of choice English style, a purist in literary form, a trip hammer in blows that pulverize. He is a front bencher in international circles, in interdenominational councils, in those reforms which lie close upon the soul and spirit of Methodism." [118]

WILLIAM NAST

Just as Francis Asbury took Methodism to the American pioneers, so William Nast carried Methodism to the German immigrants who came to America in the middle years of the 1800's. Himself a native German, Nast came to America to start a new career after having become religiously disillusioned in his studies for the Lutheran ministry. Leaving seminary, his belief sorely affected by the rationalistic teaching of Baur, he emigrated to the United States, where, as a tutor in a Baltimore household, he first encountered Methodist preaching. Attracted to it, yet restrained by his earlier experience, Nast for a time entered a communistic society—then a socialistic one. As these did not bring the peace sought for, Nast left and became an instructor in Greek and Hebrew at Kenyon College in Gambier, Ohio. At Gambier he surrendered himself completely to Methodism, became a minister, and accepted the post of city missionary in Cincinnati.

His success as a preacher at first was not overwhelming. Then, like

[118] *Central Christian Advocate,* June 2, 1932, p. 2.

Wesley, he began to write, to edit, to translate—until finally he became almost *the* German Methodist Church in America. In 1839 he began *Der Christliche Apologete* at Cincinnati and remained its editor for fifty-three years. Of the 410 German Methodist books and 700 tracts published by the Book Concern during his lifetime, the larger part were totally or partially his work.

His obituary, carried in the *Western Christian Advocate* at the time of his death in 1899, said, "German Methodism, in 1835, consisted of William Nast. In 1899 it has 1,062 Churches; 821 preachers; 88,000 members." All was attributed to William Nast, the father of German Methodism.[119]

Methodist Protestant Personalities

It has already been pointed out that because of the nature of the Methodist Protestant Church, the heaviest responsibility for retaining the identity of the loosely organized denomination lay with the editors of its periodicals. Devoid of the cohesive central setup characteristic of episcopal Methodism, the Methodist Protestant Church of necessity had to rely on the individual commitment of its congregations and members to certain ideas and ideals. The persistence of the Methodist Protestant point of view was of prime importance, and the denomination's periodicals were, in a sense, the guardians of this trust.

Three editors during the years covered by this chapter are outstanding for the contribution they made in this area.

EDWARD J. DRINKHOUSE

The power of a single Methodist sermon brought Edward J. Drinkhouse, for many years editor of the *Methodist Protestant,* from the German Reformed Church of his forefathers and into the Methodist ministry.[120] Though first aligning himself with the Methodist Episcopal Church, he shortly withdrew to the Methodist Protestant, with whose form of government he felt more compatible, and in which he held a position of leadership until his death in 1903.

Born in Philadelphia in 1830, Drinkhouse joined the Maryland Conference of the Methodist Protestant Church in 1850, and, except for several years spent recovering his health in California, served most of his years in and around Baltimore.

[119] *Western Christian Advocate,* May 24, 1899, pp. 641 ff.
[120] *Minutes of the Maryland Annual Conference,* Methodist Protestant Church, 1904.

A profound preacher, logical and earnest in his presentation of scriptural truth, he was a natural choice for the editorship of the *Methodist Protestant* when that post became vacant in 1874. That he was of a studious disposition is indicated by his study of medicine while living in San Francisco. Though he never practiced the profession, he was graduated from Toland College in San Francisco with an M.D. degree.

While editor of the *Methodist Protestant* he began publishing the Bible School Series of Sunday school lessons, which he maintained without compensation until the General Conference of the church put them under the Board of Publication and an editor was elected for that special work.

Of all his editorial endeavors, Drinkhouse is best remembered as the recorder of the history of the Methodist Protestant Church. For eighteen years, while editor of the paper, he gathered material for this work, which he began when relieved of the editorial duties of the *Methodist Protestant*. Having during his lifetime pledged most, if not all, of his fortune to the support of the Book Concern, he made the church heir to his estate after his death. Of his vital interests, none was more evident than that in ministerial education, in support of which cause he often used his pen while editor of the *Methodist Protestant*. During the closing years of his life he was president of the board of governors of Westminster Theological Seminary.

F. T. TAGG

F. T. Tagg, editor of the *Methodist Protestant* from 1892 to 1916, was one of the leaders of the Methodist Protestant Church for more than half a century. Born in Carroll County, Maryland, in 1845, he joined the Maryland Conference at the age of twenty-five, and two years later was ordained an elder. After serving churches in Virginia, Maryland, and Washington, D.C., he was elected secretary of the church's Board of Foreign Missions, and served in that position for eight years prior to becoming editor of the paper.

Essentially a preacher, Dr. Tagg preached somewhere nearly every Sunday morning during the years of his editorship. In 1921 he was chosen as the first minister to preach a radio sermon from Baltimore. As an editor he brought to the *Methodist Protestant* a standard of excellence that gave it high rank among religious journals. The financial affairs of the church never being very strong, it was said of him at the time of his death that "he received a salary far below the worth of either his service [as editor] or the labor it cost him." [121]

[121] *Minutes of the Maryland Annual Conference,* Methodist Protestant Church, 1924.

The first of Methodist Protestantism's foreign missions secretaries, he developed in the church a missionary consciousness and organized this important branch of its work upon a substantial basis. He introduced the idea of Children's Day, which was an important event in all three branches of Methodism in the late nineteenth and early twentieth centuries.

Retiring from the editorship of the *Methodist Protestant* in 1916, he spent the remaining years of his life in preaching as opportunity afforded. Saddened in his last years by the death of his wife and, soon after, the untimely death of his son, Dr. Tagg died June 18, 1923, and was buried in Centerville, Maryland.

F. T. BENSON

Frank T. Benson, who succeeded F. T. Tagg as editor of the *Methodist Protestant,* remained in the post from 1916 until his death in 1929. During the years of his editorship the paper enjoyed "an unparalleled" circulation.

Born in 1862, the son of the Rev. B. F. Benson of the Maryland Conference, Mr. Benson was reared in the Methodist Protestant Church and educated in its schools. He received the B.A. degree from Western Maryland and the B.D. degree from Westminster Seminary.

While editor of the *Protestant,* Mr. Benson took strong editorial stands on moral issues. The writer of his obituary says that his editorials "furnished his readers with history, old and new, doctrines, dead and living, church programs, wise and unwise, modern foes and friends of the Gospel, so that none should be led away from the faith of the fathers." His Editorial Briefs were "rich and racy epigrams which gripped the thought and fired the spirit." [122]

During the years of his editorship the printing plant operated for the paper was equipped with modern machinery, a bit of progress credited to Mr. Benson.

Men Who Molded Methodist Publishing

The twenty-six men treated in this section represent the manpower of Methodism's publishing interests from the time of the Civil War up to unification. To them alone, of course, cannot be wholly attributed the history of Methodist publishing during this period. But the responsibility of leadership was theirs.

[122] *Minutes of the Maryland Annual Conference,* Methodist Protestant Church, 1929.

To this task they brought not only the characteristic commitments of the churches they represented, and under whose surveillance they performed their duties, but they brought also their own convictions, the knowledge gained from their own experiences, their own hopes and motivating impulses. They were men. And the desire to present them as such, as more than mere names listed with titles and dates, explains the inclusion of certain details of their lives that might be considered somewhat extraneous to a history of Methodist publishing.

From all walks of life came these leaders of the Methodist publishing program. Pioneers, immigrants, the highborn and well educated, the poor and self-instructed, most of them preachers with the varied backgrounds of the aristocrat, the farmer, the tradesman, the teacher. Each gave of himself; and the aggregate of their combined strengths and weaknesses accounts to a great extent for the successes and failures of Methodist publishing in a period covering nearly three quarters of a century.

chapter 29

THE FIELD
OF
EDUCATION

1865-1939

Development of
  Educational Institutions

Effects of the Civil War

Financing and Control

Theological Education

I N THE FIRST DECADES OF THE NINE-
teenth century the foundations for
many of America's best-known colleges
were laid. A traveler from England, who
visited all parts of the United States during the 1830's, said: "Some of these colleges are literally springing up in the
desert, and are putting themselves in
readiness to bless generations that shall
be born! It is impossible not to feel that
the influence they exert must be amazing
in extent." [1]

Twenty-four institutions of higher
education established between 1800 and
1830 became permanent. Seventeen
were denominational schools, and seven
were state or semistate institutions. None
of them was Methodist.

After Cokesbury, Methodism's first
college, was destroyed by fire in 1795,
Bishop Asbury, discouraged by the
failure of the venture, commented in his
Journal that "the Lord called not . . . the
Methodists to build colleges." Methodist
work in higher education halted for a
quarter of a century. Before 1830, however, the church founded several academies such as were then popular in the
eastern part of the nation. In secondary
education Methodist efforts were especially successful. In 1860 the Methodist Episcopal Church, South, had under
its direction 106 academies or preparatory schools.

To say the least, the Methodist Episcopal Church during its first forty-six
years was not ready to open colleges and
universities. Methodist members be-

[1] Andrew Reed and James Matheson, *A Narrative of the Visit to the American Churches*
(New York: Harper & Brothers, 1835), p. 139.

longed largely to the underprivileged classes and were the unlettered, forgotten men and women of their time. Unlike the Pilgrims of New England, who counted among their members before 1640 some one hundred university graduates, including John Harvard, the first American Methodists had no college graduates within their fellowship. A permanent educational program had to wait, therefore, until the church could raise up leaders who were able to capture the minds and hearts of the people.

At the 1820 session of the General Conference a resolution was passed that called for the establishing of a literary institution in every Annual Conference. This in time was accepted by all the conferences. During the 1840's and 1850's the founding of Methodist colleges became a crusade. The peak of the movement was reached in the 1850's. The Methodist *Almanacs* and General Conference *Journals* list two hundred colleges founded between 1835 and 1860. Every forward advance of the church was followed by a call for an indigenous college. By 1865, Methodists had started schools in thirty-three of the thirty-four states.

Another enactment of the General Conference of 1820 enabled a bishop to appoint a minister to be the president of an educational institution. This made possible many quasi-Methodist schools. When such an appointment was made, the conference often approved the institution and encouraged Methodist people to patronize it. Some of these institutions were privately owned. This arrangement explains in part the long list of Methodist schools.[2] It has been estimated that the Methodist churches between 1784—the founding of Cokesbury—and 1939 had connections in one way or another with at least a thousand schools.

When the three branches of Methodism united, the Methodist educational institutions had narrowed down to nine universities, nine theological schools, sixty-seven colleges, twenty-seven junior colleges, seventeen secondary schools, and five schools with special classifications.

Some colleges founded by Annual Conferences did not survive because of their limited finances, denominational competition, unfavorable location, natural catastrophes, and internal dissensions. Donald G. Tewksbury, in his *Founding of American Colleges and Universities,*[3] lists a total of 182 colleges in the United States started before the Civil War which were able to maintain a legal existence up to 1939. The book includes thirty-four Methodist colleges which were established before 1865 and continued to exist up to 1939. These are included in Tewksbury's list of permanent colleges. By "permanent" Tewksbury means the institutions which were started prior to 1865 and were in existence in

---

[2] See A. W. Cummings, *The Early Schools of Methodism* (New York: Phillips and Hunt, 1886), p. 428.

[3] (New York: Bureau of Publications, Teachers College, Columbia University, 1932).

1939. The Methodist colleges on the list are given in Table I. (Asterisks indicate dates when existing institutions came into Methodist hands.)

Table I

(Giving Present Name, Location, and Charter Degree Date)

1. Randolph-Macon College, Ashland, Virginia, February 3, 1830
2. Wesleyan University, Middletown, Connecticut, May 26, 1831
3. Allegheny College, Meadville, Pennsylvania, March 24, 1817 (1833) *
4. Dickinson College, Carlisle, Pennsylvania, September 9, 1783 (1834) *
5. McKendree College, Lebanon, Illinois, February 9, 1835
6. Emory University, Atlanta, Georgia, December 10, 1836
7. Wesleyan College, Macon, Georgia, December 23, 1836 (1839) *
8. DePauw University, Greencastle, Indiana, January 10, 1837
9. Greensboro College, Greensboro, North Carolina, December 28, 1838
10. Emory and Henry College, Emory, Virginia, March 25, 1839
11. Ohio Wesleyan University, Delaware, Ohio, March 7, 1842
12. Centenary College of Louisiana, Shreveport, Louisiana, February 18, 1825 (1845) *
13. Baldwin-Wallace College, Berea, Ohio, December 20, 1845
14. Lawrence College, Appleton, Wisconsin, January 15, 1847
15. Taylor University, Upland, Indiana, January 18, 1847
16. LaGrange Female College, LaGrange, Georgia, December 17, 1847
17. Albion College, Albion, Michigan, February 18, 1850
18. Northwestern University, Evanston, Illinois, January 28, 1851
19. College of the Pacific, Stockton, California, July 10, 1851
20. Wofford College, Spartanburg, South Carolina, December 16, 1851
21. Duke University, Durham, North Carolina, November 21, 1852
22. Willamette University, Salem, Oregon, January 12, 1853
23. Illinois Wesleyan University, Bloomington, Illinois, February 12, 1853
24. Cornell College, Mount Vernon, Iowa, February, 1854
25. Hamline University, St. Paul, Minnesota, March 3, 1854
26. Columbia College, Columbia, South Carolina, December 21, 1854
27. Iowa Wesleyan College, Mount Pleasant, Iowa, January 25, 1855
28. Wheaton College, Wheaton, Illinois, February 15, 1855
29. Central College, Fayette, Missouri, March 1, 1855
30. Birmingham-Southern College, Birmingham, Alabama, January 25, 1856
31. Upper Iowa University, Fayette, Iowa, April 5, 1856
32. Mount Union College, Alliance, Ohio, January 9, 1858
33. Baker University, Baldwin, Kansas, February 12, 1858
34. Adrian College, Adrian, Michigan, April 16, 1839 (1859) *

In compiling this list, Tewksbury accepted the date for the founding of each institution as the one on which the legal right to confer degrees was granted to the institution.

This classification excludes some Methodist colleges claiming founding dates before 1865. A few schools existed as academies and became colleges at later dates. One such is Lycoming College, which grew out of Williamsport-Dickinson Academy, founded in 1812. Southwestern University in Texas dates its beginnings from the time a charter was granted by the Republic of Texas in 1840.

Wheaton College was associated with the Wesleyan Methodist Church until 1861, and was then taken over by the Congregationalists. Upper Iowa University became an independent college in 1928. Taylor University in Indiana was discontinued as a Methodist institution by the University Senate in 1900. In 1939 there were eighteen permanent institutions in the Northern branch of the church, twelve in the Southern branch, and one in the Methodist Protestant Church.

1

Characteristics of Schools (1865-1939)

The seventy-five-year period between 1865 and 1939 was one of the most creative and expansive in the history of education. During that time millions of dollars from public funds were directed to public institutions. Generally, public education became accepted as an obligation for all the states in the union. With the enactment of the Morrill Act by Congress in 1862, tax-supported institutions of higher education were able to expand their work in agriculture and industrial education. It was also a time when many private fortunes were given to establish private universities and colleges, including Johns Hopkins, Leland Stanford, Vassar, and Wellesley.

In this period a large number of the educational institutions founded by the Methodist Episcopal Church were coeducational. In the Methodist Episcopal Church, South, separate educational institutions for men and women were the rule. In some schools classified as coeducational, women did not take the same courses as men. These schools had what was called a "ladies' course," which put high emphasis upon literature, art, and language.

Before the 1890's, the curriculum of the Methodist colleges adhered to classical subjects, languages, and mathematics. This commitment to the classical program inherited from the revered past was seriously challenged during the last years of the century and the era before World War I. The election of Charles William Eliot to the presidency of Harvard University in 1869 marks the opening of a new epoch in higher education in America. Under Eliot's leadership the long reign of the classical disciplines in higher education began to give way to a new and more utilitarian emphasis.

Student life during the latter half of the nineteenth century stands in wide contrast to that of the twentieth century. There was little of the gaiety and self-important luster associated later with the social life and extracurricular activity of twentieth-century educational institutions. A puritanical Methodism frowned upon all social behavior that could be considered lax. Literary societies occupied an important place in the ongoing program of the institutions. Indeed, they were educational instruments, and in some colleges the literary societies had better libraries than the colleges themselves.

The period between 1858 and 1939 witnessed the rise of the intercollegiate student religious societies. These, and later the Y.M.C.A., made possible effective Christian-fellowship campus groups. The movement was inspired by the nineteenth-century religious awakening. One important feature of these religious societies for college and university students was Bible-study classes. The Bible did not become a required part of the students' curriculum in church-related colleges until around the opening of the twentieth century. Religious societies and the Y.M.C.A. made it possible for students in the tax-supported universities to study the Scriptures.

There also emerged during this period a strong missionary emphasis resulting in the organization of the Student Volunteer Movement. In the colleges of the United States during the college year of 1886-87 more than 2,200 students volunteered for foreign missions. Educational institutions in all three branches of Methodism made significant contributions to the foreign mission fields.

In the opening decades of the twentieth century the tax-supported institutions continued the expansion started at the close of the Civil War. By 1930 there were 250 such institutions with more than 500,000 students. Church leaders now saw that the students in state and independent institutions of higher learning needed special consideration by the church. Without it a large portion of these students would be graduated from American universities without having had careful religious nurture.

The Methodist Episcopal Church pioneered in making provision for student work under direct church auspices. The outstanding approach to this work was made at the University of Illinois, at Urbana, where the term "Wesley Foundation" was first used. The program as developed vested the care of the Methodist students enrolled in a state school with the Foundation and made its financial support the responsibility, not of the church in the university center alone, but of the Annual Conference of the state in which the university was located. The Urbana idea grew and in a comparatively short time became a pattern for student work among other denominations. The first Wesley Foundation in the Methodist Episcopal Church, South, was established at Austin, Texas. By arrangement with the Methodist Episcopal Church to use the name of Wesley Foundation, uniform terminology for this work was established before the union of the churches. It should be noted that the union of all Methodist student work was well under way prior to unification.

The last decade of the nineteenth century witnessed the rise of the accrediting associations for higher education. These organizations set up standards for accrediting a college's educational program. Failure to meet these standards in time eliminated many church colleges. On the other hand, the quest for the improvement of their educational plans as outlined by the accrediting association proved helpful to many colleges in raising needed endowments and providing better plants. Through the rigid demands made by these associations, standards of excellence in academic work became fixed.

One major development in the improvement of higher education during the first thirty years of this century was the establishment of the General Education Board by John D. Rockefeller. Between 1902 and 1940, this board appropriated for educational work about $250,000,000, most of which was given to colleges and universities as challenge money.

Up until 1939, forty-seven universities and senior colleges related to Methodism received grants amounting to $19,599,353 from the General Education Board. The conditional promises made by the Board encouraged greater support from Annual Conferences and local constituencies. The General Education Board attached no strings to its gifts that required a college to compromise its denominational ties.

In the midst of this upsurge of America's effort to improve its work in higher education, World War I began. War was declared by the United States on April 6, 1917. This brought unrest and losses in enrollment to all the colleges. Students left not only to join the armed forces but also to work in agricultural production, factories, and munitions plants. Many colleges lengthened their vacation periods during the summer to give more time for productive work. The service flags which hung in the colleges bore witness to the number of students who had entered the services.

The war brought to the colleges of the nation the most critical problems they had known since the War Between the States. They not only had heavy losses in enrollment, with corresponding decreases in income, but unprecedented increases in operational costs, particularly for fuel and food. To "prevent unnecessary and wasteful depletion of the colleges," the Department of War established in 1918 the Student Army Training Corps. In addition to helping to sustain the educational work of the nation, its aim was to prepare the large body of young men in colleges for military service and to mobilize and develop the brain power of the young men of the country. Methodist colleges and universities shared in this special program with the government. At the close of the war these colleges, along with most schools, had unprecedented increases in enrollment. The Student Army Training Corps gave thousands of young men their first experience with college life. Increases in enrollment after the war ranged from 10 to 60 per cent.

Following the war Methodist colleges and universities, along with others in the United States, began a program for the enlargement of the educational plants and the increasing of endowments to meet the increased responsibilities. The decade of the 1920's was one of the most prosperous in their history. However, in the 1930's, during the national depression, enrollment sharply declined from the all-time high which followed World War I. During this time income from all sources was reduced, including church support. The colleges had to economize in every possible way to keep open during this time. The federal government set up the National Youth Administration to help stabilize enrollments.

Methodism in many instances did not have clear-cut policies for relating the church to its institutions. Often the only tie with their church was through the appointment of Methodist clergymen to serve as presidents. The charters of several institutions had been drawn to make them self-perpetuating, making it possible for a board of trustees to alter the relationship of the institution to the church. This has been done in several instances.

The loosening of the ties between the church and some of its institutions goes back to 1905, when Andrew Carnegie established a pension system for retired professors in universities, colleges, and technical schools in the United States. One qualification for participation in the program was freedom from denominational control. In some instances changes were made in the charters and bylaws to qualify for these benefits. The Carnegie pension plan proved in time to be a mirage to the institutions. The increase in the number of teachers to participate in it was greater than anticipated. Later, a modified program called the Teachers Insurance and Annuity Association was opened to all schools without any restrictions.

It will not be possible in the sections that follow to give much more than an outline of Methodism's educational work. The years covered were strategic ones. The renaissance of higher education which began at the close of the Civil War found Methodist leaders alert to the importance of a vital educational system. That the three branches of Methodism possessed the strongest list of Protestant schools in the nation in 1939 is due to their foresight and courage.

2

Higher Education in the Methodist Episcopal Church

The educational work of the Methodist Episcopal Church after the division in 1844 was, with certain exceptions to be noted later, confined to the northern and western parts of the nation. Its history furnishes many contrasts to the same work in the Methodist Episcopal Church, South. Only one of its colleges, Dickinson College at Carlisle, Pennsylvania, had any direct contact with the war. Lee's army, on its way to Gettysburg, occupied Carlisle for several days. The town was shelled, and the college was hit in two or three places. The damage, however, to the town and the college was small. This stood in contrast to Chambersburg, Pennsylvania, a neighboring city, which was burned by the Confederates.

At the end of the Civil War, in 1865, the southern part of the United States faced bankruptcy, and its educational work was in a disorganized, chaotic position. The North, however, stood in a position for an unprecedented growth in wealth. The opening of the West for settlement and the expansion of industry in the North and East opened the way for the period known as the "Gilded Age." Furthermore, the work in the Northern Church was spread across the continent. It was composed of many diverse elements, such as industrial, agricultural, and even linguistic. Methodist work among German and Scandinavian immigrants was confined almost entirely to the Methodist Episcopal Church.

While none of the northern colleges closed during the Civil War, their enrollments were greatly reduced. Student enlistments in the Union Army in some schools took half or more of the students. Methodist Episcopal schools furnished many generals, colonels, and other officers in the Union Army. After the war, colleges promptly rebuilt their enrollments by offering special inducements, such as free tuition to veterans.

The 1864 General Conference of the Methodist Episcopal Church, in anticipation of the reconstruction work needed at the end of the war, set 1866, the hundredth anniversary of the founding of American Methodism's first society, for the raising of $2,000,000 for "those institutions and agencies to which the church has been most indebted for its efficiency." This call enabled the colleges to enlarge their service and lay the foundations for the endowments which later were to stabilize their finances. New institutions founded as a part of the Centenary celebration included Drew Theological School, Centenary Collegiate Institute, and Centenary Biblical Institute at Baltimore. The latter was for the "education of . . . pious young men, especially colored, for the ministry." [4]

Two other developments of the decade of the '60's were quite significant in the church's program of education: the chartering of the Board of Education and the founding of a loan fund to help Methodist students enroll in Methodist colleges. The Board of Education was chartered by the state of New York in 1869.

Higher Education for Negroes

The end of the war furnished the spark for the opening of one of the most dramatic missionary and educational movements in the life of the Methodist Episcopal Church. Emancipation brought into freedom four million slaves who were illiterate and unprepared for citizenship. The close identification of the Methodist Episcopal Church with the Union placed it in a strategic position to take the lead in Negro education. This was to be done through the Freedmen's Aid Society. This agency became the dominant one of the Methodist Episcopal Church for missionary, educational, and social work among the Negroes, and probably the most effective among many such organizations founded after the Civil War.

[4] Matthew Simpson, ed., *Cyclopaedia of Methodism* (Philadelphia: Louis H. Everts, 1880) , p. 176.

At the outset, it was concluded that missions among the Negroes would fail without schools. Fortunately, the Freedmen's Aid Society linked education with evangelism. In order to provide for the fullest development of the vocational, educational, and religious needs of the freedmen, high emphasis was placed upon education.

Across the South several institutions still exist that bear the names of the persons who were important in establishing colleges for Negroes: I. W. Wiley, R. S. Rust, Clinton B. Fisk, and D. W. Clark. These men, with John M. Walden, Alonzo Webster, and Joseph C. Hartzell, are listed among the nation's most creative leaders of the post–Civil War years for the advancement of Negroes.

The Freedmen's Aid Society began with a tremendous display of enthusiasm and creative imagination. During the first year, fifty-nine schools were founded. These were distributed as follows: Tennessee, seventeen; Georgia, eleven; Alabama, four; Kentucky, three; Louisiana, nine; Mississippi, one; Arkansas, one; Virginia, three; South Carolina, eight; North Carolina, two. Strategic locations were carefully selected for these schools. In 1868 the society reported that its schools were placed in towns "containing the largest ignorant and degraded population." The first students ranged in age from seven to seventy years. Most of the schools began with the basic elementary studies, and moved upward from that level to include courses designed for the preparation of Negro teachers.

By 1869 eight schools of collegiate grade had come into existence. These were: Central Tennessee College (later called Walden University), Nashville; Clark University, Atlanta; Claflin University, Orangeburg, South Carolina; Baker Institute, Charleston, South Carolina; Huntsville Normal School, Huntsville, Alabama; Shaw University, Holly Springs, Mississippi; Union Normal School, New Orleans, Louisiana; Thomson University, Franklin, Louisiana. Central Tennessee College opened a medical department in 1875 with eight students. From that beginning grew Meharry Medical College, one of the nation's best-known colleges of medicine for Negroes. Shaw University in Mississippi, later called Rust College, began in 1866, and Claflin and Clark Universities in 1869.

It should be noted that these schools were called universities, not colleges. By 1875 the society had fourteen "universities" in the South, with departments of theology, medicine, and law. The law schools never succeeded and in time were closed, and efforts were concentrated on the preparation of ministers, teachers, and physicians.

The first educational work of the Freedmen's Aid Society among Negroes encountered many obstacles. Some of the communities were hostile to it. Teachers were accused of being "spoilers," carrying the "New

England Gospel." [5] A leading Southern Methodist, Dr. Atticus G. Haygood, author of *Our Brother in Black,* helped to set the climate in favor of the schools. He was genuinely appreciative of these teachers and of their work. "Suppose," he said, "these Northern teachers had not come, and that nobody had taught the negroes, set free, and citizens! The South would have been uninhabitable by this time [1881]." [6]

Fires were frequent, and always there was need for money to meet expenses. The fifty-nine schools reported in 1867 were not expanded. In fact, Negro educational institutions have made progress through elimination, consolidation, and upgrading. Their aim was to educate leaders for the Negro people. As rapidly as possible, elementary work was turned over to trained Negro teachers, so that the schools could concentrate upon the higher levels of education.

Negro education from the outset was the responsibility of the whole church. Support came from annual offerings made on the Sunday nearest Lincoln's birthday. (In the Plan of Union the second Sunday in February became Race Relations Sunday.) During the first forty years of the Freedmen's Aid Society, $8,000,000 was contributed by the church in special offerings.

Most of these schools were aided by concerned friends of the Negro in the North. Claflin University owes its origin to a gift made by Governor Lee Claflin of Massachusetts, who was one of the founders of Boston University. Elijah Gammon, a superannuated minister in the Rock River Conference, through a gift opened the way for the theological school which bears his name.

The years between 1920 and 1939 were most significant ones for the Methodist educational institutions that serve Negro youth. Fortunately, they recognized that their continuation demanded a realignment of plans if they were to continue as parts of the educational program of the areas they had served. In making the changes they were encouraged by substantial grants from such foundations as the General Education Board, the Rosenwald Fund, and the Slater Fund. Some schools were recipients of large gifts from Mr. and Mrs. Henry Pfeiffer, Christian philanthropists of New York. Clark College became a part of the University Center at Atlanta. Bennett College, a coeducational college, became a senior college for women. In this change the Woman's Home Missionary Society of the Methodist Episcopal Church assumed responsibility for much of its support. New Orleans University was consolidated with Straight College, a Congregational school, to form Dillard University.

[5] Nashville *Christian Advocate,* January 31, 1867, p. 1.
[6] *Our Brother in Black* (Nashville: Southern Methodist Publishing House, 1881), p. 150.

Flint Medical School was closed, but the Goodridge Hospital was named
Flint-Goodridge Hospital and continued as a part of Dillard University. By concentrating all medical work at Meharry Medical College
in Nashville, generous aid was given by the Rockefeller Foundation to
make it the most important institution of its kind in the United States.
Morgan College in Maryland was turned over to the state in 1939 and
is now a tax-supported college. Funds derived from the sale of the plant
formed an endowment for the support of the Morgan Christian Center.

A significant indirect testimony of the influence of the Methodist
Episcopal Church's educational work among Negroes came out in the
book *Who's Who—Sixty Years of American Eminence*. It showed that
23 per cent of all Negroes who had achieved notable places of leadership and had biographies in *Who's Who in America* were Methodists and
53 per cent of them were members of the Methodist Episcopal Church.
The Negro membership of the Methodist Episcopal Church never exceeded 300,000 [7]—less than any of the Negro Methodist churches. The
high percentage of leaders furnished by the Northern Church is unquestionably due to the church's concern for education.

Colleges in the West

By 1865 there was a Methodist educational institution in every state
east of the Mississippi River except West Virginia. The Methodist Episcopal Church was in the vanguard of the western movement. Pioneers
moved into the virgin country and began, as someone said, to make it
a "fit place to raise children." The church and school were potent influences in bringing stability and civilization to the vast region west of
the Mississippi that now forms the center of America's agricultural life.

The institutions founded by the Methodist Episcopal Church in the
new West included Iowa Wesleyan College, the first college in Iowa,
founded in 1842—four years before Iowa became a state and thirteen
years before there was a state university. Baker University was founded
three years before Kansas was admitted to the Union. Hamline University and Lawrence College both antedate the admission of Minnesota and Wisconsin to the Union. The University of Denver was an outpost of Christian civilization in the Rocky Mountain region twelve years
before Colorado became a state. Willamette University, founded as
Oregon Institute in 1842, seventeen years in advance of the admission of

---

[7] Cedric A. Larson, *Who's Who—Sixty Years of American Eminence* (New York:
McDowell, Obolensky, 1958), p. 220.

Oregon, was the first institution of higher learning west of the Rocky Mountains. The University of the Pacific (originally chartered as California Wesleyan College, and renamed the College of the Pacific in 1911) was founded in 1851, two years after the discovery of gold and eighteen years before the establishment of a state university. It had the first college of liberal arts and the first medical school in California.

The 1880's were marked by a veritable epidemic of colleges in the new western states. With the opening of new territories and the forming of new conferences, educational institutions were established. The Methodist Episcopal Church was in the vanguard of this movement. The directive of the General Conference of 1820 for each Annual Conference to have a literary institution within its own bounds was zealously followed.

All the schools experienced periods of travail when their continuation was doubtful. Most of the Annual Conference histories relate stories of acute financial crises in their colleges. The solicitude of the preachers in the Annual Conferences for the well-being of their colleges explains more than any other thing the preservation of the church's educational work against the heavy odds faced.

Methodist educational institutions have been started in every state west of the Mississippi except Nevada, Arizona, Utah, and Wyoming. Gooding College in Idaho was a casualty of the depression, and Montana Wesleyan at Helena, Montana, suffered severe damage from an earthquake in 1932. The latter institution moved from Helena to Billings, where it united with the Presbyterian and Congregational colleges to form one Protestant college for Montana. Methodists since 1939 have united with the Presbyterians in operating Westminster College in Utah.

Secondary Schools

The first successful educational efforts of American Methodism, as previously noted, centered upon literary academies. Bishop Asbury favored academies and took the lead in starting them. It would be difficult to ascertain how many academies the Methodist Episcopal Church has supported. A list published in 1886 showed eighty-four academies previously owned and operated by the Methodist Episcopal Church.[8]

In 1922 there were thirty-nine academies, thirty-two for white students and seven for Negro students. Of the thirty-two white schools, twenty-four were in the Northeast. At the time of union, in 1939, fourteen academies remained and ten of them were in the northeastern sec-

---

[8] Cummings, *Early Schools,* pp. 426-27.

tion. The public high school did not get under way until the end of the first quarter of the century, and private academies continued to be needed to provide the educational opportunities for youth desiring secondary work. However, the movement for public high schools spread rapidly, and many of the academies had made transitions to junior-college status by 1939. In this way The Methodist Church has been able to conserve some of the efforts put into its secondary schools. It might be well to note here that most of the academies that have lived are the ones which had substantial endowments.

Extension of Education in the South

It was expected at the time of separation in 1844 that the Methodist Episcopal Church would confine its work to the northern states. However, beginning in 1848, it started to develop some work in the South, particularly in those regions which opposed slavery. Some Annual Conferences of the Methodist Episcopal Church were in existence in the South at the outbreak of the Civil War. At the end of the war in those sections where the population was sympathetic to the Union, the Methodist Episcopal Church opened a vigorous program. In 1880 the General Conference of that church extended the Freedmen's Aid Society's work to include the education of the southern white people. Most of the institutions operated by the Methodist Episcopal Church were in the Appalachian Mountain area. With Chattanooga as the center, it undertook to develop a chain of well-equipped, efficient secondary schools that would furnish college-preparatory courses to the youth, sometimes called "mountain whites," in the Appalachian Mountains.

The work among the white people in the South never reached the proportions of the educational work done with the Negroes. Opposition within the church itself was voiced by many influential leaders. The institutions related to the Methodist Episcopal Church that had been firmly established in the South by the time of union in 1939 were: the University of Chattanooga, Chattanooga, Tennessee; Tennessee Wesleyan College, Athens, Tennessee; Snead College, Boaz, Alabama; and Union College, Barbourville, Kentucky.

The Woman's Home Missionary Society of the Methodist Episcopal Church, organized in 1880, wielded an important influence in the church's educational work with southern white people and Negroes. In its comprehensive program for missionary work it placed a strong emphasis upon education. At the time of union it had five schools ministering to Negroes that offered grade- and high-school work and four in-

stitutions serving the southern mountain area, two junior colleges and
two elementary and secondary schools. It also maintained a dormitory
on the campus of Tennessee Wesleyan College, Athens, Tennessee, for
the teaching of home economics and religion.

Universities

Many educational institutions established by the Methodist Episcopal
Church were called universities. Of forty-two senior colleges listed at
the time of union, twenty-one were called universities. Only six, however,
of the twenty-one had been classified as universities by the University
Senate: American University, Boston University, Northwestern University, Syracuse University, the University of Denver, and the University of Southern California.

Some of the schools called universities in their early years actually
did the work of a university, having, along with a college of liberal
arts, one or more other schools such as law, medicine, and theology.
With the raising of standards by accrediting agencies most of these "universities" reorganized their work to offer only liberal-arts studies. In general, fifteen "universities" listed in 1939 were only senior colleges. And
most of them had no plans beyond that.

The six institutions which were classified as universities in 1939 owe
their rapid development to the cities in which they were located. Large
cities opened the way for professional and graduate schools. Unlike the
first university in the Methodist Episcopal Church, South, there was no
church-wide plan made by the Methodist Episcopal Church for one central university. However, when locations are studied, one can see that
they were wisely selected for service to the church and nation. When
these six were joined in 1939 by the three distinguished universities of
the Methodist Episcopal Church, South, Methodism possessed the most
important list of Protestant-related universities in the nation. Legal ties
which relate them to the church vary from university to university and
from region to region. Generally the ties may be described as moral and
historical, rather than legal. The agreement between the University of
Southern California and the Southern California Annual Conference
concerning the election of trustees was altered by mutual consent of the
university and the conference in 1928. Such actions have been taken by
several schools supposedly to increase financial support from non-Methodist sources.

Northwestern University, founded in 1850, became the university for the great Northwest. In the first fifty years of its life it was closely associated with all of the church's educational work. It is said to have furnished 10 per cent of the church's foreign missionaries in the latter part of the century. All its presidents up until 1890 were Methodist ministers, and three were elected to the episcopacy.

American University was established in Washington, D.C., with the hope that it would become the "head and crown of the educational system of our common Methodism." It opened in 1914. The idea did not win from all parts of the church the support needed for such an undertaking. The potential for a great national Methodist university in the nation's capital was there, but prior to 1939 it had not taken hold.

Boston University, incorporated in 1869, became one of the most creative forces among the nation's universities. Under the progressive leadership of one of Methodism's able educators and scholars, William Fairfield Warren, it pioneered in lifting the standards of professional work in medicine and law. The theological school formed the nucleus of the university. The influence it has exerted upon the religious and educational life of the church and nation has been far out of proportion to its size. At unification, sixteen of the Methodist Episcopal educational institutions had graduates of Boston University as their chief administrators.

Syracuse University was founded in 1870. Its roots go back to Genesee College at Lima, New York. Its beginning years called for great sacrifices, but these were not evaded by the people who wanted the church to have a school in some central and accessible location. Its school of forestry became one of the best known and respected in the nation. In 1939, Syracuse ranked sixteenth in size among the universities of the nation.

The University of Denver operates upon the foundation of a school chartered by Methodists in 1864, Colorado Seminary. One of its founders, Dr. John Evans, was appointed by President Lincoln to serve as the first governor of the Territory of Colorado. Evans, for whom the city of Evanston, Illinois, was named, also was influential in the starting of Northwestern University.

The wisdom of the church leaders in choosing a location for a university has never been more evident than in locating the University of Southern California at Los Angeles. In a comparatively short time it became one of the most influential privately owned universities in California.

The University Senate

It has been previously noted that the General Conference of 1868 made provision for a Board of Education. It was designed to be a permanent institution of the church and to act as the perpetual custodian of the educational interests committed to it. The hopes of this organization's exercising a wide connectional influence, however, were not immediately realized. For years its work was confined to administering the Student Loan Fund. The need for an active, highly organized body became more apparent as the church's concern for its educational institutions deepened.

In a report to the General Conference of 1892, Dr. C. H. Payne, secretary of the Board of Education, expressed regret that "not one of the schools founded by the church fathers between 1789 and 1819 or during the first third of the nineteenth century became permanent." He also cited the fact that no fewer than 84 institutions directly related to the Methodist Episcopal Church and 58 other Methodist schools with quasi connections, making a total of 142, had ceased to exist or had lost all Methodist relationship by 1884.

In response to the recognition that Methodist schools were dwindling, it was felt that some drastic move to tighten supervision should be made, to prevent the waste and loss of educational effort which had been going on through the nineteenth century. The immediate answer given to this by the 1892 General Conference at Omaha was provision for the University Senate. This body, made up of practical educators, would know the problems connected with the church's institutions and could evaluate their ability to meet them. It could also offer counsel and guidance in developing plans for strengthening their work. The University Senate has prevented some waste of the church's educational dollars by insisting upon the schools' observing sound academic and business practices.

The University Senate became the first accrediting agency founded in the United States. It antedates the North Central Association of Schools and Colleges by three years. Myron F. Wicke in his *Brief History of the University Senate of The Methodist Church* says: "The history of American education can be traced in the actions and studies of the University Senate. In educational principle and practice, the Senate was usually in the vanguard." [9]

The standards set forth by the University Senate became the ideals to-

[9] (Nashville: Board of Education, The Methodist Church, 1956), p. 12.

ward which all the institutions related to the Methodist Episcopal
Church aspired. Approval by the University Senate meant to Methodists
that an institution was worthy of support and patronage. One of the
most significant acts of the University Senate was to include English
Bible in the course of study for Methodist institutions. This was the beginning of the effort to establish Bible as a part of the curriculum of
Methodist universities and colleges.

In 1912 the University Senate published an answer to the perennial
question: "What is a Methodist college?" It defined a Methodist educational institution as

one which, frankly declaring that it is under the auspices of the church and
distinctly claiming that it aims to plan and conduct its work so as to serve the
Kingdom of Christ as represented by the life of the Methodist Episcopal Church,
shall have the recognition and support of some conference, mission conference,
or mission; the endorsement of the Board of Education and official classification
by the University Senate.[10]

The power of the University Senate over the educational institutions
was augmented by the authority it had to qualify an institution for student loan funds. The withholding of such help vitally affected the standing of a Methodist school with its constituency.

Standards and Financing

A study of higher education in the Methodist Episcopal Church after
1900 shows that there were six new senior colleges established; twenty-
two that were on the list in 1900 were discontinued by 1939. Seven of
these discontinued schools had consolidated with other colleges. Three of
them were schools supported by German-speaking conferences. Two became private, independent schools. Of the six new senior colleges started
since 1900, two were Negro colleges and four white; two of the white
schools did not survive until 1939. As standards were raised by all the accrediting agencies, including the University Senate, the chances of survival for institutions unable to meet them decreased.

TOWARD RAISING ENDOWMENTS

Out of this period of apparent defeat for Methodist educational work
came another aggressive move of the Board of Education. In 1908, when
it began studies to determine the needs of the Methodist colleges, it

---

[10] *Ibid.*, p. 10.

found only four of its institutions with $1,000,000 or more in endowment. It announced that at least $30,000,000 should be raised for productive endowments for the colleges and universities. The General Conference of 1912 was asked to designate 1916, the 150th anniversary of the organizing of the first Methodist society in America, as an Educational Jubilee year, and to urge the churches to unite in making that year a great educational anniversary. A far-reaching financial program was projected to help standardize all the institutions, free them from debt, and enable them to achieve the educational efficiency expected of Christian schools.

Seventy-two schools, many of which were secondary institutions, joined in the campaign. At the end of the intensive campaign, in 1918, a grand total of $35,708,000 was reported to have been raised in cash and subscriptions.

The success of this first united effort in campaigning opened the way for a continuation of special drives by individual colleges. This was the period when the General Education Board was offering special grants on a matching basis. The total given by this Board to thirty-four colleges and universities related to the Methodist Episcopal Church up until 1939 was $13,675,944. The tangible results of the twenty-five years of special campaigning and efforts to raise funds for the universities and colleges may be seen in a comparison of the reports of 1914 and 1939. In 1914 the combined endowments of forty-three senior colleges and universities was $20,461,359.[11] In 1939 the combined endowments for forty-eight senior colleges and universities was $86,610,447.

THE STUDENT LOAN FUND

The Children's Day program of the Methodist Episcopal Church came out of the 1866 celebration of the "Centenary of Methodism." The second Sunday in June was set aside to be the day for the presentation of the interests of Christian education. The collections taken in the Sunday schools on Children's Day formed the Student Loan Fund of the Board of Education. This has been administered for the benefit of young Methodists whose personal resources were insufficient to enable them to secure higher education.

Children's Day as observed in the Methodist Episcopal Church also had a wide influence both in creating sentiment favorable to the Methodist educational institutions and in inspiring young people to go to college. In practically every state of the union, Methodists lead in the total percentage of students attending educational institutions—church-

[11] *Christian Student*, February, 1914, p. 32.

related, Methodist-related, and tax-supported. This, without doubt, is due to the continuous emphasis Methodists have put upon the work of Christian higher education. By 1939 the fund had become the largest loan fund for college students held by any Protestant church. Up to 1939 a total of 55,651 loans had been made to students, amounting to $8,284,390.

THE EDUCATIONAL ASSOCIATION SURVEY

Another progressive move, launched in 1928 by the Educational Association of the Methodist Episcopal Church, called for a scientific study of member institutions. The General Conference approved the plan and asked the Board of Education to carry it out.

Thirty-five senior colleges and eleven secondary schools participated in the study. It covered every area of an educational institution's organization. Each institution was given a complete statement of findings and a list of recommendations for the improvement of its administration. A composite volume of 715 pages, *The Liberal Arts Colleges*, drew together from all the schools the salient facts in the study. These reports make up the most exhaustive study of higher education up to that time. Each school, with its own study, had before it a blueprint of what it needed to do to strengthen its work. It can be added that the attitude assumed by the institution toward its study had much to do with its progress or decline.

The survey aided in eliminating secondary schools that, with the coming of public high schools, had no further mission. Most of them were in the southern mountain section. Several of the more promising ones were urged to become junior colleges. The supplementary aid given by the survey doubtless accounts for the fact that only five of the senior colleges in the Northern Church had not been accredited by their regional association in 1939.

At unification the following institutions were associated with the Methodist Episcopal Church:

Universities	VALUE	ENDOWMENT	INDEBTEDNESS
American University	$ 3,239,301	$ 806,600	$ 445,331
Boston University	6,124,220	4,235,072	920,537
Northwestern University	16,460,000	31,608,000	2,187,000
Syracuse University	8,649,869	4,323,765	852,000
University of Denver	1,731,374	2,429,151	13,823
University of Southern California	9,449,467	1,455,549	55,000
	$45,654,231	$44,858,137	$ 4,473,691

Schools of Theology	VALUE	ENDOWMENT	INDEBTEDNESS
Boston University School of Theology	$ 354,300	$ 901,456	$ —
Drew Theological Seminary	1,960,732	4,173,650	—
Gammon Theological Seminary	280,550	595,868	3,227
Garrett Biblical Institute	500,000	930,000	—

(The figures given for Gammon and Garrett are for the year 1942-43. The figures for 1939 were apparently not reported.)

	VALUE	ENDOWMENT	INDEBTEDNESS
Iliff School of Theology	167,000	228,813	—
School of Religion, University of Southern California	See University of Southern California		

	VALUE	ENDOWMENT	INDEBTEDNESS
	$ 2,482,032	$ 5,668,919	$ 5,681

Colleges	VALUE	ENDOWMENT	INDEBTEDNESS
Albion College	$ 1,611,123	$ 1,390,931	$ —
Allegheny College	1,786,390	1,407,770	207,557
Baker University	602,217	1,217,887	54,824
Baldwin-Wallace College	1,614,804	1,545,397	86,510
Bennett College	1,075,671	354,155	4,500
Brothers College, Drew University	765,566	1,017,234	53,000
Claflin College	550,000	158,606	4,816
Clark University	453,816	538,000	—
College of Puget Sound	900,084	1,128,620	40,000
College of the Pacific	929,778	555,593	306,128
Cornell College	1,114,449	1,842,069	—
Dakota Wesleyan University	553,796	296,342	98,969
DePauw University	2,969,157	5,172,200	—
Dickinson College	1,449,500	1,308,824	57,650
Dillard University	907,053	73,597	—
Evansville College	697,352	446,940	117,000
Hamline University	902,736	1,774,373	20,000
Illinois Wesleyan University	1,007,229	1,151,122	6,500
Iowa Wesleyan College	734,786	403,633	—
Kansas Wesleyan University	381,623	103,000	—
Lawrence College	2,084,638	1,137,248	87,337
MacMurray College for Women	1,693,138	732,648	—
McKendree College	268,000	264,770	46,000
Morningside College	406,028	329,678	290,483
Mount Union College	990,909	1,216,890	35,000
Nebraska Wesleyan University	629,557	814,765	132,704
Ohio Northern University	890,713	192,369	185,634
Ohio Wesleyan University	3,236,095	3,633,354	239,000
Oklahoma City University	702,990	95,000	334,929

(In the 1930's Oklahoma City University was controlled by both the Northern and Southern churches. The figures reported do not agree.)

Colleges	VALUE	ENDOWMENT	INDEBTEDNESS
Philander Smith College	177,490	200	9,645
Polytechnic-Intermountain College ..	168,400	98,725	4,000
Rust College	173,409	21,736	6,470
Samuel Huston College	323,750	10,658	5,600
Simpson College	555,242	1,272,836	100,000
Southwestern College	610,585	576,954	179,489
Union College	330,788	290,932	20,719
University of Chattanooga	1,455,000	753,432	124,000
Wesleyan University	5,471,707	5,998,064	—
West Virginia Wesleyan College	384,544	289,965	209,674
Wiley College	343,887	600,274	8,754
Willamette University	909,475	1,517,219	—
Wesley College (affiliated with University of North Dakota)	—	18,900	—
	$42,813,475	$41,752,910	$ 3,076,892

Junior Colleges

	VALUE	ENDOWMENT	INDEBTEDNESS
Bethune-Cookman College ....$	900,000	$ 78,026	$ 7,659
Cazenovia Junior College	547,220	240,126	164,054
Centenary Junior College	550,242	27,091	—
Evanston Collegiate Institute	215,000	36,101	3,285
Green Mountain Junior College	513,742	59,251	50,300
Morristown Normal and Industrial College	555,000	52,071	6,682
Snead Junior College	277,380	110,100	—
Tennessee Wesleyan College	424,145	106,750	35,000
Tilton Junior College	450,000	344,628	127,000
Vermont Junior College	273,365	146,619	27,000
Williamsport-Dickinson Junior College	646,164	317,089	45,119
	$ 5,352,258	$ 1,517,852	$ 466,099

Secondary Schools

	VALUE	ENDOWMENT	INDEBTEDNESS
Baxter Seminary ....$	185,185	$ 100,000	$ —
Cazenovia Seminary	See Cazenovia Junior College		
Drew Seminary for Young Women ..	296,216	7,750	—
East Greenwich Academy	177,000	80,215	—
Gilbert Academy	271,000	40,981	331
Jennings Seminary	238,305	11,300	—
Kents Hill School	261,260	210,774	70,225
Montpelier Seminary	See Vermont Junior College		
Pennington School	691,500	1,637,192	11,856
Snead Senior High School	See Snead Junior College		

Secondary Schools	VALUE	ENDOWMENT	INDEBTEDNESS
Tilton School	See Tilton Junior College		
Wilbraham Academy	355,147	311,808	59,228
Williamsport-Dickinson Seminary	See Williamsport-Dickinson Junior College		
Wyoming Seminary	513,050	1,000,000	—
	$ 2,988,663	$ 3,400,020	$ 141,640

Commercial School			
Port Arthur College ....$	165,620	$ —	$ 47,110

Negro Professional Schools			
Flint-Goodridge Hospital of Dillard University ....$	455,675	$ —	$ —
Meharry Medical College	2,220,000	739,699	—
	$ 2,675,675	$ 739,699	$ —

Training Schools			
Chicago Training School (Affiliated with Garrett) ....$	—	$ 337,134	$ —
Kansas City National Training School	515,000		—
	$ 515,000	$ 337,134	$ —
Grand Total	$102,646,954	$98,274,671	$ 8,211,113

3

Education in the Methodist Episcopal Church, South

The Methodist educational movement in the South began at Abingdon, Maryland, where the American Methodists founded their first college. All the schools founded by Bishop Asbury were in southern states. After the General Conference of 1820 requested each conference to establish a literary institution, Virginia responded by chartering Randolph-Macon in 1830. Between the time of the first General Conference of the Methodist Episcopal Church, South, in 1846 and the unification of three Methodist denominations in 1939, a total of 261 schools that called themselves colleges had been related to the Southern Church in some fashion. In 1939, a total of forty-five institutions of collegiate grade which were under the auspices of the Methodist Episcopal Church, South, entered into the united program of higher education of The Methodist Church.

The Civil War was fought almost entirely in the southern states. It laid waste the whole economic life of the South. Property values declined 48 per cent. Investments made in Confederate bonds were completely wiped out; not a single bank or insurance company was left solvent. The situation at the end of the war was described in the 1909 annual report of the church's General Board of Education:

The whole school system was destroyed. The wealth of the South, together with the flower of southern manhood and southern genius, passed away. The soldiers returned to find their once kept farms devastated, their homes in ruin, their wives and children in poverty and rags, and their state, county, and municipal governments in the hands of ignorance and vice. . . . A whole generation grew up with practically no school advantages.[12]

In no other sphere of the church's activity was there such complete prostration as in education. The continuance of colleges in the South, especially for men, was impossible during the war. With the exception of Wofford, every Methodist college for men closed. Ten institutions were completely destroyed. Most of the colleges suffered severe losses in their physical plants. This was especially true of colleges where the campuses were occupied by the Union armies. Even in the buildings used for hospitals, soldiers did not show respect for property. Before education could be resumed, buildings had to be rehabilitated. The main building of Pacific Methodist College in California was burned by a mob following the assassination of President Lincoln.

Most of the small endowments held by colleges were wiped out. Investments had been made not only in Confederate bonds but also in other forms of securities needed for the war. The $100,000 left by Benjamin Wofford, for the institution that bears his name, had been invested in 8 per cent Confederate bonds. Randolph-Macon sold all its stocks that did not pay an interest of more than 6 per cent and invested the returns in Confederate state bonds.[13]

At the 1866 session of the General Conference in New Orleans the Committee on Education reported the results of the war upon the church's educational work. This report stood in contrast to the optimistic one

---

[12] For conditions in Virginia, see Richard Irby, *History of Randolph-Macon College* (Richmond: Whittet & Shepperson, [1899]), pp. 164 ff.
[13] *Ibid.*, p. 147.

made in 1858, which had pointed proudly to the multiplication of Southern Methodist schools and colleges "from the Pacific to the Atlantic
Oceans, and from her Northern boundary to the Gulf of Mexico." [14]

The report of 1866 said that the four years of war had

created an irreparable chasm in the improvement of the youth of the Southern
States. Professors, teachers, students, were withdrawn from the seats of learning; their halls were vacated; text-books and apparatus were abandoned, endowments lost, and patrons impoverished. . . . It will require, however, our
united strength to restore [our institutions] to their previous efficiency. But
we must meet the emergency with an unfaltering purpose, and rise with determined might to the difficult yet hopeful task which lies before us.[15]

The educational policies of the Methodist Episcopal Church, South,
which generally prevailed before the war continued as the guiding principles for education during Reconstruction years. According to these
policies, the church's work in education was maintained for the perpetuation of Christianity. While all the colleges claimed to exist for the diffusion of culture among the people, generally they were proudly Methodist and their denominational accent was strong. The church set the
religious atmosphere of the colleges and academies. Revivals were held
at regular intervals, and the presidents of the institutions included in
their annual reports the number of students converted. The bishops in
1870 expressed appreciation for the schools and said that they were "unequivocal in their Methodism."

Because of the autonomous nature of the Annual Conferences, little
outside guidance was received for their educational work. Colleges multiplied more rapidly in the church than its ability to support them. The
only source of financial help available was through annual offerings
taken in local churches. Most schools were small and the mortality among
them high. It seems, as one historian said, that the Methodist practice of
placing churches near the homes of the people was adapted to its educational program. In order to put its institutions within reach of its people,
therefore, the church established more than it could successfully maintain. Wesley's plan of locating Kingswood in a rural region apart from
the urban temptations was followed through the South. Consequently,
the twentieth century dawned upon an educational system with the
church's schools located in villages and hamlets instead of in promising
cities. The moving of several such rural institutions to growing cities
helped them to attain prestige and strength.

[14] *Journal of the General Conference of the Methodist Episcopal Church, South,*
1866, p. 133.
[15] *Ibid.*

Secondary Education

The history of Southern education following the Civil War obviously begins during the Reconstruction period. As "conquered provinces," the Southern states were in the hands of Federal officials and soldiers, rather than under locally chosen officials. These out-of-state leaders determined the government's policies, and in particular the educational work. The inability of the Southern states to have a satisfactory system of public education prompted the Methodist Episcopal Church, South, to set up schools for its people.

Dr. Thomas O. Summers, editor of the Nashville *Christian Advocate,* believed that the church could be the schoolmaster of the South. In 1872 he wrote that the "three great Protestant Communions—Baptist, Methodist, and Presbyterian—are competent to take this matter in hand. They can educate all the children in the South." [16]

This same view was held by Bishop Holland N. McTyeire, who gave what has been called a "grudging support to public education." He said:

> I take the ground that the Church has a distinct duty and function to educate. I take this ground because the Church can do it better and cheaper than any other organization, and turn out better work. I have not been hopeful of our public school system. . . . The public school may supply the need of mere intellectual training, but omits that higher training—the culture of the moral faculties. . . . I must liken public schools to soup houses in great cities. The poor are abundant, and as we don't want them to starve to death, we establish soup houses. . . . So with the public schools; for those who want no religious education, for the poor who would have no education but for these public schools, we say go there and learn something. . . . Within fifty years I prophesy that our Church will have a school wherever we preach the word.[17]

During the 1870's most of the Annual Conferences projected plans for a program of secondary education. The Holston Conference opened high schools in each of the presiding elders' districts. The principals of these district high schools were chosen by the Annual Conference. The bishops in 1874 urged the General Conference to form an educational system that would include district high schools. It accepted the recommendation and resolved that "as far as practicable, Southern Methodist schools be established in every District of our work, provided that they be strictly

---

[16] Nashville *Christian Advocate,* November 30, 1872, p. 8.
[17] Address at Pacific Methodist College, printed in the New Orleans *Christian Advocate,* November 21, 1872.

tributary to, and, in no case, in conflict with our colleges, male or female, or any other of our institutions of a higher grade." [18]

This interest in high schools continued until the last decade of the nineteenth century. Between 1860 and 1920, 187 academies were started by Annual Conferences of the Methodist Episcopal Church, South. In addition, 162 academies were related to the church through the appointment of Methodists as their principals or headmasters.

The academies had a significant relationship to preparatory education in the Southern states. Prior to 1900 there were fewer than a hundred public high schools in the entire South. Sentiment began to rise throughout the South for public schools. The attitude of the church toward public education began to be favorable in the 1880's. The Episcopal Address of 1882 made it clear that the church should not interfere with the work of public education.

Higher Education

The condition of higher education in the South between 1865 and 1880 is reflected in some statistics gathered at random from across the South. The University of Alabama had been burned, and when it reopened in 1873 had only 53 students; in 1875, only 111. Most of these students were in the preparatory department. The University of North Carolina had 80 students in 1870. At Wofford College no catalog was published between 1861 and 1871. The salaries of the professors between 1865 and 1876 at Wofford were fixed at $1,500. Between 1865 and 1870 about 40 per cent of this amount was paid to the professors, and between 1871 and 1878 about 75 per cent was paid.[19] The three professors who reopened Emory College in 1866 received only about $200 for their first six months of teaching.[20]

This general condition continued throughout the South until near the end of the century, when an industrial economy began to replace an agricultural one. The South, its leadership realized, could not progress as long as it clung to an agrarian way of life. The solution to its problems was to be found in science, industry, and popular education. Cotton spinning was the first form of manufacturing to gain a place of prominence in the South. By the end of the nineteenth century five eighths of the na-

[18] *Journal of the General Conference of the Methodist Episcopal Church, South,* 1874, p. 507.

[19] David Duncan Wallace, *History of Wofford College, 1854-1949* (Nashville: Vanderbilt University Press, 1951), p. 69.

[20] Henry M. Bullock, *A History of Emory University* (Nashville: Parthenon Press, 1936), p. 151.

tion's cotton mills were in the South. Iron, lumber, mining, and tobacco industries soon shared with cotton in the boosting of southern economy.

As a result of the industrialization of the South, per-capita wealth grew and the whole region became more cosmopolitan in outlook and practice. Economic recovery in the South, however, did not produce during the nineteenth century outstanding philanthropists such as were found in the North. The largest gifts to Southern Methodist colleges in this period came from two New Yorkers: Cornelius Vanderbilt and George I. Seney. The limited resources held by the church for education made it difficult for its colleges to keep able faculty members. The lack of educational stability likewise operated against their attracting large gifts.

Between 1860 and 1899 the Methodist Episcopal Church, South, founded 104 colleges in the Southern states. At the time of union only sixteen of this number continued as educational institutions; three of the sixteen (Morris Harvey at Charleston, West Virginia; Vanderbilt at Nashville, Tennessee; and Asbury College at Wilmore, Kentucky) are now privately supported. Because of the scarcity of preparatory schools most of the college work of this period consisted of secondary studies.

The Vanderbilt Controversy

In the 1870's the church's first successful effort in university education was launched with the founding of Vanderbilt University. Shortly after the division in 1844 the Southern Church accepted Transylvania University at Lexington, Kentucky, as a central university. Its location and limited funds made it impractical for a church-wide institution. It was abandoned in the 1850's. Immediately after the war the idea of a central university was revived. The General Conferences of 1866 and 1870 refused to endorse the plan, since a theological school was to be included as one of its schools. Instead, the General Conference of 1870 recommended biblical chairs in the existing colleges.

Leaders of the movement, such as Bishop Holland N. McTyeire, refused to be defeated by the opponents of professional education for ministers. They united the liberal forces of seven Annual Conferences, and in January, 1872, twenty-seven representatives met at Memphis, Tennessee, and projected plans for a university to be called Central University of the Methodist Episcopal Church, South.

This historic gathering, known as the Memphis Convention, fixed $1,000,000 as the amount needed to finance the undertaking. It agreed, further, that the university should not open until $500,000 was obtained.

The opponents of theological schools saw in this a plan to circumvent the General Conference decision against theological education. Bishop McTyeire, in spite of the opposition and the impoverished condition of the South, carried on; and when prospects seemed darkest, a northern capitalist, Cornelius Vanderbilt, offered the necessary $500,000 for the university.

Without question, Vanderbilt University became the most potent force in the educational awakening of the South. Through the endowment Mr. Vanderbilt had provided, the university was able to set up the highest academic standards of any institution in the South.

Its leadership in scholastic ideals was reflected in the upgrading of education in other colleges. Its professional schools—medicine, law, dentistry, pharmacy, and engineering—provided new leadership in many depleted areas. Its theological school furnished for forty years just about all the professionally trained ministers of the Methodist Episcopal Church, South. It also furnished to the mission fields served by the church their foremost missionaries. All the church's colleges were enriched by teachers educated at Vanderbilt. Between 1875 and 1914, Vanderbilt demonstrated that a church's educational program is incomplete without an influential university.

Vanderbilt University, especially through the leadership of Chancellor James H. Kirkland, exerted a most salutary influence upon the South's program of higher education. Because of inadequate facilities and inability to pay ample salaries, Southern colleges had not done the kind of work expected of first-class colleges. Schools had multiplied not only in the Methodist churches, but in all the denominations. In 1884 six southern states were trying to maintain sixty-seven colleges for men. Kirkland and several members of Vanderbilt's faculty called a meeting of representatives from sixteen Southern colleges on November 6, 1895, to consider the organization of an accrediting association for higher education in the South. As a result, the Southern Association of Schools and Colleges was formed, with ten institutions as charter members, three of which were Methodist schools. This organization has been a most important factor in elevating standards of scholarship in all institutions of higher learning in the South.

Vanderbilt University became an independent institution in 1914. It is generally assumed that it broke its relationships with the church. Such a conclusion is not justified. For a period of at least ten years relationships between the administration of the university and some church leaders were strained. These church leaders believed that the chancellor wanted Vanderbilt to be independent of the church and had designs for that purpose. The chancellor, however, denied that this was his intent. He held, along with some members of his board of trust, that the administration of a university was more complex than that of a small church college. Furthermore, he was concerned about the failure of the church to take seriously the financial needs of the university. When the twentieth-century fund was launched in 1898, a goal of $300,000 was set for the theological department. Less than $30,000 was raised, and most of this amount came from Nashville and the Vanderbilt faculty. Church and university relationships continued to grow more tense. In order to clarify some questions about the powers of the board of trust, the General Conference of 1906 appointed a commission "to inquire into and determine the present relationship of Vanderbilt University to the Methodist Episcopal Church, South." The decision of the commission was to become operative when its report was presented to the bishops.

The commission, made up of five lawyers, concluded that the university board of trust was not a self-perpetuating body and that the General Conference could fill vacancies on the board; that the seven conferences mentioned in the original charter, not Mr. Vanderbilt, had founded the university; and that the bishops, by virtue of the church's being the founder, possessed visitorial powers. The commission interpreted visitorial powers to mean that the founder of a charity could take it over if it was not being administered in harmony with the giver's intention. The commission declared that a violation by the board of trust of previous agreements, made at the time of its founding, would return the university to the General Conference.

The report of this commission was given to the university's board of trust. It did not accept it in totality but did recognize the "ownership of the church in the university" and voted to "cordially receive" the report. This statement, however, was not satisfactory to the commission. It requested, with the concurrence of the General Conference then in session at Asheville, North Carolina, that the board of trust meet there and formally approve the report. The chairman of the board, Bishop Hendrix, held that the previous action of the board of trust meant it had accepted in principle the commission's report. The General Conference adopted the commission's report and elected three persons to the board of trust. This latter action was designed to test the validity of the commission's report in the courts. The bishops, therefore, were directed to "take whatever steps they may deem necessary to maintain the claims of the church."

The university's board refused to recognize the three trustees elected by the General Conference, and the bishops, following the mandate given by the General Conference, filed a suit against the university board of trust. In February, 1913, the Chancery Court of Tennessee decided in favor of the bishops, affirming that the General Conference had the exclusive right to elect members of the university's board of trust, and that the bishops had general visitorial power over the corporation as provided in the Memphis resolutions. The university dissented and appealed the case to the Tennessee Supreme Court.

The Supreme Court of Tennessee overruled the Chancery Court. Its decision vested control of the university with the board of trust, recognized Cornelius Vanderbilt as the founder, and denied visitorial powers to the bishops. The charter, the court said, formed the contract between the church and the university. The court also held that the board of trust's right to elect its members was contingent upon confirmation by the General Conference or its agent, the General Board of Education.

The court's decision did not please either the church or the university. At the General Conference of 1914, meeting in Oklahoma City, this matter was the most important item of business. The whole church had been stirred by the controversy. Feelings were intense. Many delegates were ready to break all ties with the university. Another sizable group wanted to seek an amicable solution.

The majority report of the committee which had been appointed by the General Conference to consider the matter bowed to the decision of the court and recommended to the General Conference that it give up all its rights in the university and return the school to the conferences which had originally held it. The committee called also for the appointment of a commission of sixteen members to make plans for two new universities—one east of the Mississippi River and one west of it. A minority report from dissenting members of the committee declared that the court's decision did not represent the real equities in the case and refused to accept it as a just one. However, it pointed out that since the court held that control of the university was with a board of trust, the church's power to confirm members enabled it to determine the personnel of the board. Because of vacancies and expirations, a new board could be named in less than one quadrennium if the present one refused to recognize the church's rights in the university. It also noted that all the rights the church had ever exercised previous to 1910 had been preserved in the court's decision.

When final action came, after several days of heated discussion, 151 members voted to sever all relations with the university, and 140 voted to keep the university. By a majority of only 11 votes, a member of the minority group, President Henry Nelson Snyder, said, "Methodism tossed away in a fever of blinding emotionalism the richest opportunity for educational service ever given to an ecclesiastical body in the South." [21]

[21] Henry Nelson Snyder, *An Educational Odyssey* (New York and Nashville: Abingdon-Cokesbury Press, 1947), pp. 194-95.

The Commission of Sixteen, authorized by the General Conference, found that it would not be possible to transfer to the conferences the control they originally held over Vanderbilt. The whole question was therefore dropped—after a final protest from the commission—and the church turned to other educational ventures.

While the General Conference of 1914 debated the future status of Vanderbilt University, many of the members of that conference were talking about the church's need for at least two more universities. The two reports before the General Conference dealing with the Vanderbilt issue both pointed toward the establishing of two new universities—one east of the Mississippi River and one west of it. The majority report, which was adopted, provided for a commission with power to establish "an institution or institutions" of university grade. The minority report, while still clinging to the hope that Vanderbilt could be saved for the church, gave similar authority to the General Board of Education. The conviction that the church now needed at least two more universities became fixed. One member of the Commission of Sixteen appointed by the General Conference, Bishop Warren A. Candler, said that the commission was given the greatest task that had "ever been laid upon any committee in the history of our Church in the last fifty years." It had the opportunity "to do more than repair the loss of Vanderbilt—the opportunity to save our whole Church, and, in a measure, the entire South from the ruinous effects of secularized and Godless culture." [22]

Other Universities

The Southern Methodist University at Dallas, Texas, was founded in 1911 by Texas Methodists. It was promptly offered, after the General Conference of 1914, to the education commission as the university west of the Mississippi. The commission accepted the university with the condition that the ownership and control would be in perpetuity with the Methodist Episcopal Church, South. The university opened in 1915.

On July 14, 1914, less than two months after the General Conference had adjourned, Asa Candler of Atlanta offered $1,000,000 toward the founding of a university at Atlanta, Georgia. This opened the way for a university east of the Mississippi River. The proposal was made in a letter that contained one of the strongest statements for the work of

[22] Alfred M. Pierce, *Giant Against the Sky* (New York and Nashville: Abingdon-Cokesbury Press, 1948), p. 131; quoting from Thomson's Emory History Scrapbook, Emory University Library.

Christian higher education ever published. No doubt with the memory of the Vanderbilt episode in his mind, Mr. Candler wrote:

I see no way by which such religious education can be supplied, without institutions of learning owned and controlled by Churches. . . . I cannot agree for a moment that the best type of religious education is that which some claim is propagated in an unwedded state, outside any and all churches, by institutions which are subject to neither civil nor ecclesiastical authority, and which acknowledge no responsibility to the people whom it proposes to educate. . . . I desire that whatever I am able to invest in the work of education shall be administered by the Church with a definite and continuous religious purpose.[23]

This institution, Candler further stated, must follow the tradition firmly established in Methodist institutions of being church-related yet not sectarian. Methodist history in the work of education, he wrote, "justifies me in believing that it will use what I entrust to it in a liberal and catholic-spirited manner; for in all of its institutions of learning it has on occasion engaged Christian men of other denominations . . . , and it has never used its schools for the purpose of proselyting the sons and daughters of other Churches."[24] Emory College at Atlanta was made the liberal arts division of the new Emory University.

The charters of these two new universities stated that they belonged to the church and charged the corporations to administer and hold their properties for the benefit of the church.

In 1924 James B. Duke and his brother, Benjamin N. Duke, proposed a plan for establishing a Christian university. The institution chosen for the foundation of the university was Trinity College, the strongest liberal-arts college in the Methodist Episcopal Church, South, having then property and endowment valued at approximately $6,000,000. Trinity College had been generously supported by the Duke family. The Duke brothers announced a $40,000,000 gift, the largest gift ever made to the work of Christian education in the United States, and there was brought into existence, in a comparatively short time, Duke University, an institution now recognized as one of America's great universities.

The magnificent gift from the Duke family inspired many other large gifts to educational institutions related to the Southern Church. In 1925 twenty-two colleges of this church reported over $3,000,000 in gifts for new buildings and endowments.[25]

[23] *Ibid.,* p. 134. For the full text of the letter, see pp. 133-36.
[24] *Ibid.,* p. 135.
[25] *Christian Education Magazine,* November, 1925, p. 7.

Mission Schools

The recognition of education as a means of advancing the kingdom of God brought the missionary motive into the church's educational program. Schools, mostly elementary and secondary, were founded in some isolated rural sections, in the Appalachian Mountain region, among textile workers, in the new West, and among Mexicans and Indians. Paine College, the church's outstanding missionary effort among Negroes, was founded in 1884 through the joint efforts of the Methodist Episcopal Church, South, and the Colored Methodist Episcopal Church.

In this phase of the church's educational work the Board of Missions and the Woman's Board of Home Missions were very active. The Board of Missions carried responsibility for a school for the employees of cotton mills in South Carolina. The women's group started Scarritt College, the church's foremost college for the training of Christian workers, in Kansas City in 1892. In 1924 it was moved to Nashville, Tennessee. After Scarritt College for Christian Workers moved to Nashville, it joined in a co-operative operation with Vanderbilt University and George Peabody College for Teachers. Outstanding developments of this plan were the Joint University Library, the elimination of unnecessary duplication of courses, and the free interchange of work on all levels.

Standards and Financing

The proliferation of the church's educational efforts continued to be a concern to educational leaders as the demand for integrity in academic work grew. Obviously the large number of educational institutions in the church indicated that there were only a few that could be listed as first class. The church, however, was helpless between the pressure of local interests and the autonomy of Annual Conferences. Since 1865 there had developed all over the church educational institutions beyond the ability of the church to support.

This waste of educational energy disturbed intelligent leaders. The failure of the church to maintain properly many of the institutions under its patronage had weakened its influence and called into question its competence as an educator. The editor of the Nashville *Christian Advocate,* on April 17, 1886, urged that the church "make denominational control commensurate with denominational responsibility for schools called Methodist schools."

THE BOARD OF EDUCATION

The answer to this problem seemed to be in the church's having a General Board of Education. Such a board was created by the 1894 General Conference. It was given the authority to determine the educational enterprises that were to receive financial aid from its funds; to gather statistics; "to prepare, publish, and distribute tracts and other documents calculated to advance the cause of Christian education"; and to "have control of all our work on behalf of the Colored Methodist Episcopal Church in America." It was asked to seek to increase the endowments of the educational institutions; to strengthen, systematize, and correlate the work being done; and, finally, to originate new institutions where they could be "judiciously established and maintained." The location of the Board of Education in Nashville put it under the direct influence of Vanderbilt University, and its chancellor, James H. Kirkland, who for many years had called for quality in educational work. It immediately set itself to establish some uniformity of standards for all educational institutions under church auspices. The board called for fewer colleges and higher standards of scholarship and said that it should "give no endorsement to the deluding diplomas of a counterfeit college."

THE EDUCATIONAL COMMISSION

In 1898 the General Conference enacted legislation creating an Educational Commission made up of ten practical educators appointed quadrennially by the College of Bishops. This body was given the right to set educational standards classifying the schools and colleges of the church. The commission's work in enforcing high standards obviously accounts for the reduction of the number of colleges in the church.

POLICIES

In 1898 the General Conference set up a plan for a "twentieth-century fund," which was the first distinctly connectional educational campaign to be made by Southern Methodists. An awareness of the limitations of educational institutions and their need for modern equipment had spread through the church. Colleges of the nineteenth century were not prepared to meet the responsibilities of the twentieth century. In 1897 the forty-six collegiate institutions of the Southern Church reported a combined endowment of $2,210,895. The financial goal set for the twentieth-century fund for educational institutions was $1,500,000. Subscriptions reached $2,031,948, of which $1,411,511 was actually paid. Vanderbilt University received from this fund only $28,282. Obviously the interest of the church continued to be in the Annual Conference colleges and not in a central university.

The Southern Church through the years had urged separate educational institutions for men and women. Of the 171 schools listed between 1850 and 1900, more than half were for women. Wesleyan College of Georgia was the first school of collegiate grade in the United States to confer degrees upon women. Randolph-Macon College for Women, chartered in 1893, soon became one of the leading colleges for women in America. During the last decade of the nineteenth century a change of policy toward coeducation came, and one strong coeducational institution was considered preferable to two weak institutions.

ACADEMIC FREEDOM

Educational institutions in the Methodist Episcopal Church, South, have had good records in giving to teachers the freedom required for sound academic work. This has demanded courage on the part of both the administration and the trustees. A situation at Trinity College in North Carolina in 1903 did much to clarify the rights of professors to take positions opposite to existing public opinion. Professor John S. Bassett of Trinity College published an article that endeavored to give an objective appraisal of the Negro problem in the Southern states. There were many who challenged the right of a professor to express such opinions and called for Bassett's immediate removal from Trinity.

This episode gave Trinity the chance "to show that it is the home of free thought and free speech" and to settle once and for all the position of Trinity College with respect to academic freedom. The board of trustees in session on December 2, 1903, refused to accept Professor Bassett's offer to resign.

The document adopted, clarifying the board's position on academic freedom, belongs in the list of great declarations on the rights of all institutions to be free in the pursuit of truth. One statement in it related this whole matter to the church: "Trinity College is affiliated with a great church whose spirit and doctrines are tolerant and generous, and a due-regard for the teachings and traditions of this Christian society requires us to exercise our judgment in harmony with its spirit and doctrines." [26]

During the 1920's, when anti-evolution laws were passed or proposed in ten states, liberalism again was challenged. The educational association of the Methodist Episcopal Church, South, went on record as op-

[26] Paul N. Garber, *John Carlisle Kilgo* (Durham, N.C.: Duke University Press, 1937), p. 278.

posed to all legislation that would interfere with the proper teaching of scientific subjects in American schools and colleges. This was not a popular thing at the time, but it did help protect the rights of freedom in a threatening period.

THE CHRISTIAN EDUCATION MOVEMENT

Church support for current operations of educational institutions in general came from the Annual Conferences of the Methodist Episcopal Church, South. Unlike the Methodist Episcopal Church, it did not include higher education in its Centenary Campaign. Following the Centenary Campaign, the Southern Church instituted the "Christian Education Movement" in a church-wide appeal for its colleges. The quotas given to the Annual Conferences totaled $33,580,300—an amount estimated as necessary for getting the existing schools accredited. A total of $17,554,077 was pledged, of which about 50 per cent was paid. In 1927 there were ninety-nine schools listed as being related to the Methodist Episcopal Church, South. At the time of union forty-nine of these had ceased to exist. These forty-nine schools which were closed during the 1930's, however, received from the Christian Education Movement $1,687,244.53. The fifty schools that were in existence at the time of union received a total of $4,923,966.29.[27]

FINANCING

Benevolent support in the Methodist Episcopal Church, South, never became as centralized as in the Northern Church. Annual Conferences had their own programs, and apportioned specific amounts of the offerings to their own projects. In some conferences not over 35 per cent of the total benevolences went to the general program of the church.

Despite discouragements, the General Education Board never overlooked the importance of an educational system worthy of the church. It recognized that many small colleges with limited clientele and with little prospect for accreditation had served their day. Between 1925 and 1935, in a campaign for a creditable system of higher education, it pointed out that one strong college in each state would be more in keeping with the church's ability for support. Consolidations, with the projected goal of one single four-year coeducational college, were completed in Arkansas, Mississippi, and Missouri. The mergers in these states not only reduced costly duplications of effort but also opened the way for substantial help from foundations.

[27] See *Christian Education Magazine*, August, 1928, pp. 26-28.

By setting their academic houses in order, many conference colleges received substantial grants from the General Education Board, founded by John D. Rockefeller. Prior to 1939, fourteen universities and colleges of the Methodist Episcopal Church, South, were given $5,897,550 for increasing their endowments, constructing new buildings, and enriching their teaching resources. The accredited colleges became stronger despite the obstacles brought by the nation-wide depression in the 1930's.

At unification the following educational institutions were associated with the Methodist Episcopal Church, South (1939-40 figures):

Universities	VALUE	ENDOWMENT	INDEBTEDNESS
Duke University	$27,445,078	$34,795,100	$ —
Emory University	5,285,661	5,313,909	—
Southern Methodist University	3,475,131	2,400,241	327,635
	$36,205,870	$42,509,250	$ 327,635

Senior Colleges			
Athens College	$ 548,000	$ 200,000	$ —
Birmingham-Southern College	2,027,500	615,510	—
Centenary College	842,692	503,040	—
Central College	1,987,304	1,305,801	375,811
Columbia College	525,829	468,521	78,395
Emory and Henry College	548,127	381,817	215,799
Florida Southern College	506,283	521,000	36,696
Greensboro College	645,784	496,385	—
Hendrix College	868,463	1,025,025	—
Huntingdon College	781,487	398,232	154,240
Kentucky Wesleyan College	470,729	80,150	11,984
LaGrange College	250,500	250,661	—
Lambuth College	232,500	12,505	52,720
Lander College	402,135	221,088	76,391
McMurry College	404,414	78,457	34,053
Millsaps College	872,266	753,896	5,730
Morris Harvey College	33,836	269,384	33,065
Oklahoma City University	658,435	106,650	326,638
Randolph-Macon College	642,504	1,075,411	79,091
Randolph-Macon Woman's College	1,994,658	1,246,130	88,500
Scarritt College	992,486	182,239	40,826
Southwestern University	1,103,517	690,383	1,000
Texas Wesleyan College	502,772	147,482	—
University of San Antonio	488,510	11,000	40,000

Senior Colleges	VALUE	ENDOWMENT	INDEBTEDNESS
Wesleyan College	1,867,931	497,293	404,860
Wofford College	753,675	789,796	50,894
	$20,952,337	$12,327,856	$ 2,106,693

Junior Colleges			
Andrew College	$ 220,841	$ 41,200	$ 4,810
Blackstone College	492,044	43,225	19,478
Brevard College	255,066	63,662	161,794
Emory Junior College (Valdosta)	320,440	200,000	—
Emory Junior College (Oxford)	445,663	—	—
Ferrum Training School	297,291	35,000	17,500
Hiwassee College	157,666	82,608	8,165
Lindsey Wilson Junior College	127,424	4,813	4,988
Lon Morris College	277,435	102,466	48,603
Louisburg College	388,647	58,758	55,000
Martin College	143,780	48,000	4,168
Reinhardt College	248,000	10,000	—
Sue Bennett College	330,000	—	—
Textile Institute	225,055	20,000	—
Weatherford College	174,616	71,184	5,785
Young Harris College	227,837	111,150	—
	$ 4,331,805	$ 892,066	$ 330,291

Academies			
Holding Institute	$ 600,000	$ —	$ —
Randolph-Macon Academy	389,778	—	218,217
Vashti School	155,570	—	—
	$ 1,145,348	$ —	$ 218,217
Grand Total	$62,635,360	$55,729,172	$ 2,982,836

4

Higher Education in the Methodist Protestant Church

In 1939, at the time of union, there were five educational institutions related to the Methodist Protestant Church: one seminary, three

senior colleges, and one junior college. In 1916 the endowment of all
the schools was around $150,000.[28] In 1940 it totaled $1,143,249. The
value of all the college buildings and equipment in 1916 was about
$500,000, but in 1940 it exceeded $3,247,500. The oldest college of the
Methodist Protestants, Adrian College, was formerly a school of the
Wesleyan Methodist Church.

Another college, West Lafayette, located on the outskirts of West
Lafayette, Ohio, was chartered in 1899. It was said of this school that in
each of the sixteen years there its expenses exceeded its income. It
was ordered to be merged with Adrian College by the General Conference of 1916.

The institution of the Methodist Protestant Church with the largest
resources at the time of union was Western Maryland College. It was
established as an academy at Westminster, Maryland, in 1865. Plans were
envisioned at that time for a college. The school opened its doors for
college students on September 4, 1867. It received its charter on March
30, 1868.

Western Maryland College also has a relationship to the state of
Maryland which is unique. Since 1878 this institution has received a
number of scholarships paid by the state for young people who plan to
teach in Maryland's public schools. As far as the state has been concerned,
there has been no interference with the operation of this program. But
in the 1940's the state of Maryland made a study of its educational facilities. This study recommended that additional teachers' colleges be
founded and that the scholarship program be discontinued. However,
the state has never carried out these measures.

The third senior college related to the Methodist Protestant Church
was located at High Point, North Carolina. A substantial gift was made
by a prominent Methodist Protestant leader there. He offered $100,000
provided that the Methodist Protestants in North Carolina would raise
$300,000. The offer came during the 1920's, and the campaign itself did
not succeed. The city of High Point, however, was interested. It raised
$100,000 and donated fifty acres of land for the institution. The school
opened at High Point on September 15, 1924.

High Point College had a large debt on all its property which handicapped its work for many years. Its location in North Carolina in the
midst of thriving Methodist Protestant churches assured its success. At
the time of union its property was evaluated at $886,553, on which there
was an indebtedness of $210,490.

[28] *Handbook,* Department of Educational Institutions of the Board of Christian
Education, Methodist Protestant Church, p. 6.

Another college, called Westminster College, under the Methodist Protestant Church, was located in Collins County, Texas. It was founded in 1895 by two graduates of Western Maryland College. It was the only institution of higher learning fostered by the Methodist Protestant Church in the section of the nation west of the Mississippi River. In 1902 it was moved to Tehuacana, Texas and took over the plant that had been occupied by the Presbyterians' Trinity University before it moved to Waxahachie. For fourteen years Westminster College operated as a senior college, but the standards for a senior college were too difficult for it to meet. In 1916 it became the "first school in [Texas] to be officially accredited as a Junior College." [29]

The territory that supported it consisted of Texas, Oklahoma, Arkansas, Louisiana, and Mississippi. These conferences were small. The Methodist Protestants were widely scattered, a great majority of them being tenant farmers.

In 1896, Methodist Protestants took the initiative in starting a university in Kansas City, Kansas. From the outset this project was plagued with heavy debt and inadequate income to care for current operations. In 1913 a merger with Campbell College, a United Brethren institution, was effected with the hope that the enlargement of the constituency would enable the schools to continue. The merger failed to bring the new life that was anticipated. In 1924 plans were set in motion to discontinue the school.

The depression years were very hard ones for all the colleges connected with the Methodist Protestant Church. In a report made to the Board of Christian Education in 1936 the secretary of the Department of Institutions wrote:

No words can describe the anxieties, the distracting discouragements, the depressing educational problems and the incessant uncertainties. Had it not been for a steadying faith and sustaining confidence in the indispensable character of the service rendered, presidents and teachers would have given up long ago. Endowments are insufficient, buildings and equipment are inadequate, the financial support from the church is limited, while the gifts from alumni and other friends are far below what is reasonable to expect. In spite of these deficiencies and due principally to the heroic sacrifices of administrators and faculties, these splendid institutions have not only survived, but they have recovered much lost ground and seem destined to continue their growth and progress.[30]

[29] Olin W. Nail, *History of Texas Methodism, 1900-1960* (Austin, Texas: Capital Printing Company, 1961) , p. 75.
[30] Second Quadrennial Report, Department of Educational Institutions, 1936, p. 6.

The educational institutions of the Methodist Protestant Church were handicapped in their growth because of the small and scattered membership of that church. The total membership of the Methodist Protestant Church at the time of union approximated 200,000. Since a senior church-related college needs a church membership of at least 100,000 members to give it the stability and support needed, the record of Methodist Protestants in the development of their educational institutions is exceptional.

Of all the Methodist Protestant schools Western Maryland was most favorably located. It was in the conference having the largest membership. At unification it was the only fully accredited school of the denomination. It had established itself as one of the important educational institutions on the Atlantic seaboard. Adrian College was the institution of the Middle West. High Point, a new institution, had hardly started when the nation was plunged into the financial crisis of 1929. Because of problems inherited from the depression, High Point College, along with Adrian, was struggling for existence at the time of union. With the help of their former constituencies and the enlarged support brought by unification, these two schools have been fully accredited, and their financial foundations are more secure.

The story of Westminster Theological Seminary is told in the section on theological education. But here it should be said that twenty years after union, this institution furnished united Methodists the foundation for one of the most important developments in theological education in the history of Methodism. Methodist Protestants took pride in its "school of the prophets." It gave strong emphasis to training for the pastoral ministry.

The educational institutions related to the Methodist Protestant Church in 1939 were:

Schools	VALUE	ENDOWMENT	INDEBTEDNESS
Adrian	$ 337,086	$ 152,709	$ —
High Point	886,553	4,900	210,490
Western Maryland	1,775,561	917,940	154,000
Westminster Seminary	175,100	67,700	5,000
Westminster Junior College	3,247,500	—	5,000
Grand Total	**$ 6,421,800**	**$ 1,143,249**	**$ 374,490**

5

Theological Education in the Methodist Churches

At the close of the Civil War there were two Methodist theological schools—the Methodist General Biblical Institute at Concord, New Hampshire (which later became the Boston University School of Theology), and Garrett Biblical Institute, Evanston, Illinois—both related to the Methodist Episcopal Church. In 1939 there were nine—five related to the Methodist Episcopal Church, three to the Methodist Episcopal Church, South, and one to the Methodist Protestant Church. The total enrollment was 1,167.

The Conference Course of Study

At the time of union the main door of entrance to membership in an Annual Conference was through the historic four-year Conference Course of Study for traveling preachers. Graduation from a theological school could be substituted for this. The rule governing "admission into full connection" in the 1940 *Discipline* required satisfactory knowledge of the Conference Course of Study, but provided that this requirement

shall not . . . prevent the admission into Full Connection of one who, while a student in any College or Theological Seminary of The Methodist Church approved by the Authorized Standardizing Agency, or other College or Evangelical Theological Seminary of equal rank, has been for the proper length of time regularly appointed as Pastor in a Circuit or Station under the appointment of the District Superintendent.[31]

As late as 1939 more than half of all ministers who joined Annual Conferences on trial had no professional training in theological schools. The Asbury axiom, "The saddlebags are the best school for traveling preachers," continued long after the automobile had replaced the circuit rider's horse. Legislation calling for seminary graduation as the regular qualification for conference membership and the making of the Conference Course of Study the exception was not enacted until the General Conference of 1956.

The General Conference of 1844 vested full control of the Course

[31] ¶ 216.

of Study in the bishops. In that year the first uniform course was announced for all Annual Conferences. Each Annual Conference appointed one of its members to examine candidates in each of the subjects in the course. No formal academic education was required as a preparation for the ministry in these early years. Just before the Civil War a prospective minister, if he were twenty or over, was urged by the editor of the *Western Christian Advocate* to "enter with all speed upon his work. It will require seven years to go through college and many lose their religious fervor and are diverted from the ministry." [32]

Theological Schools

Increasingly the intellectual disparity between the ministers and the people they served became a matter of concern. Methodism's influence with the educated and more cultured classes demanded a ministry equal in ability to that of other churches. This growing interest in ministerial education caused the bishops of the Methodist Episcopal Church in 1856 to warn the church against allowing the movement to develop apart from the General Conference. This General Conference gave approval for theological education for its ministers.

The General Conferences of the Methodist Episcopal Church, South, of 1866 and 1870 rejected proposals for the founding of a theological school. Previously, in 1854, the General Conference of the Methodist Episcopal Church, South, had refused to approve departments exclusively for ministerial training in its colleges, since they in turn might ultimately become theological departments. A writer in the *Southern Christian Advocate*, January 5, 1855, thought those who promoted such departments were assuming a most fearful responsibility: "Our time-honored and God-honored plan is to be abandoned. The circuit or station is no more to be considered the best trainer of young men for the itinerant ministry."

The first two seminaries of the Methodist Episcopal Church were called "biblical institutes." This name in itself reflects the early opposition of Methodists to instructing their ministers in "theology" or "divinity." [33] The Centenary Educational Fund, projected in 1866, provided aid for the two existing biblical institutes and for the establishment of four more, one of which was to be on the West Coast and another at

[32] September 28, 1853.
[33] Richard M. Cameron, *Methodism and Society in Historical Perspective* (Nashville: Abingdon Press, 1961), p. 239.

Cincinnati. The latter never was established. The one in the Middle Atlantic states was made possible through Daniel Drew's gift.

Behind the advance movement for theological education in the Methodist Episcopal Church was John Dempster, the son of a Methodist preacher who had been sent to America by John Wesley. Both schools founded before the Civil War were the result of Dempster's leadership.

Dempster's influence also was directly felt in the founding of the third theological institution in 1867. Daniel Drew, whose gift made the seminary possible, had been a parishioner of John Dempster's before he left the pastorate to give full time to the Newbury Biblical Institute of Newbury, Vermont. Drew's name appears prominently in Dempster's subscription book.[34] Drew helped to acquire ninety-five acres of land at Madison, New Jersey. This new school, it should be noted, was part of the expansion program projected in connection with the celebration of the hundredth anniversary of American Methodism. It opened November 6, 1867.

In 1866 the bishops of the Methodist Episcopal Church, South, noted that there had arisen even during antebellum days a demand for "more culture in the pulpit." In the Episcopal Address to the General Conference, they urged upon the church the propriety and necessity of taking some steps to establish a theological institute. Conservative elements vigorously opposed theological education and discouraged gifts for such an institution. Bishop George Pierce said: "It is my opinion that every dollar invested in a theological school will be a danger to Methodism. Had I a million dollars I would not give a dime for such an object." [35] The conference, however, while declaring that a theological school was impractical, did authorize "biblical schools" at certain colleges until a theological school was feasible.

When it became clear to the advocates of a theological school that favorable action by the General Conference was not possible, liberal leaders united to achieve their end independently of the General Conference and founded a university. This institution became Vanderbilt University, and its theological school became the first to serve the Methodist Episcopal Church, South.

In spite of the Northern bishops' admonition, it may be seen that theological education in both churches, while theoretically a concern of the whole church, owes its existence to efforts independent of the General Conference.

Clark University, a school founded by the Freedmen's Aid Society in

[34] Cummings, *Early Schools*, pp. 378-79.
[35] Bard Thompson, *History of Vanderbilt Divinity School* (Nashville: Vanderbilt University Press, 1958) , p. 2.

1869, opened a theological department in 1872. Through a substantial gift made by the Rev. Elijah H. Gammon, of the Rock River Conference, in 1883 a separate building was erected for the school of theology on the campus of Clark University. This institution was named Gammon Theological Seminary and has been the leading theological school for the education of Negro ministers, not only of the Methodist Episcopal Church but of all Negro Protestant churches.

Other theological schools founded by the Freedmen's Aid Society included one at Central Tennessee College, Nashville, Tennessee, and another at Claflin University, Orangeburg, South Carolina. After a few years of service, the theological work in these institutions was discontinued.

The Freedmen's Aid Society of the Methodist Episcopal Church also included educational work among southern white people in the Appalachian Mountain sections. It founded the University of Chattanooga and between 1892 and 1910 operated a school of theology there.

The Methodist Protestant Church, like other parts of Methodism, felt the rising concern for an educated ministry. The Maryland Annual Conference of the Methodist Protestant Church in 1881 authorized the organization of a school of theology at Westminster, Maryland, which was to be separate from Western Maryland College. A campus of seven acres was obtained, and a seminary building was erected immediately. The school was opened in the autumn of 1882 with Dr. Thomas Hamilton Lewis as principal. In 1884 it became a project of the General Conference, with that body electing a board of governors. The school was incorporated as Westminster Theological Seminary.

As part of its mission, the school included courses for the training of laymen for religious leadership in various fields of Christian service. Up until 1939 its graduates numbered about five hundred. Without question, graduates of this school occupied most of the important pastorates and connectional offices of the Methodist Protestant Church. Throughout its history Westminster Theological Seminary had to struggle because its income was inadequate for the responsibilities committed to it.

The Norwegian-Danish Theological Seminary was established on a permanent basis in 1886, and the Swedish Theological Seminary in 1870. Both were located in Evanston, Illinois, where the Swedish Seminary had moved in 1875. As their names imply, they were primarily intended to provide theological education for the ministers of the Scandinavian-language conferences. German-language seminaries, all of them at the collegiate rather than the graduate level, at various times rendered service in Methodist ministerial education at South St. Paul, Minnesota; at Berea, Ohio; at Enterprise, Kansas; and at Warrenton, Missouri.

With the growth of Methodism on the West Coast, it became evident that a theological school would be needed to train ministers in that section. This was part of an educational program connected with the Centennial of American Methodism, but had not been carried through. In Chicago at the time of his death, John Dempster had in his possession tickets of passage by steamer around South America to Berkeley, California, to open a theological school to serve the western section of the church. Dempster himself was not to share in this achievement. In 1887 the Maclay College of Theology was opened. In 1894 this theological school was moved to the campus of the University of Southern California in Los Angeles, continuing its institutional independence for some years. In 1922 it became the Southern California School of Religion on the Maclay Foundation.

The Iliff School of Theology was established in Denver, Colorado, in 1892, to serve the Rocky Mountain region. William Seward Iliff, the layman whose gift made the school possible, was one of the potent leaders in the political and economic development of the West. The plan for the school and the original gift was devised by his sister, Elizabeth Iliff Warren, the wife of Bishop Henry White Warren.

The need for a trained ministry in the Pacific Northwest caused Willamette University in 1906 to ask the Rev. Henry D. Kimball to open a college of theology. In 1907 Kimball School of Theology was incorporated as separate from the university. It offered a three-year course leading to a degree of Bachelor of Divinity and a three-year course for persons who had not graduated from college. At one time the school made plans to move to Seattle, Washington. These failed to mature, and the board of trustees decided to close the school at the end of June, 1930.

The loss of Vanderbilt was a serious blow to the educational interests of the Methodist Episcopal Church, South. However, the General Conference of 1914, meeting in Oklahoma City, Oklahoma, acted to provide at the earliest possible time the establishment and maintenance of a biblical school for the teaching and training of young men for the ministry. As a result of this action the Candler School of Theology was opened in 1914 in the Wesley Memorial Church, Atlanta, Georgia. In 1916 the school moved to the campus of Emory University. A theological school to serve the church west of the Mississippi River was opened at Southern Methodist University, Dallas, Texas.

The Indenture of Trust creating Duke University was signed on December 11, 1924. The first purpose for this university, as stated in the indenture, was the training of ministers of the gospel. The Divinity School was the first of the graduate schools organized.

Doctrine

As Methodism matured, there was an increased interest in giving to the Methodist ministry a broad training in theology along with the rudiments of knowledge.

Up until the early part of the twentieth century generally, the bishops served as the keepers and defenders of the Methodist faith. With the coming of theological schools, the bishops of the Methodist Episcopal Church were given supervision "to the end that the church may be protected from unwarranted assault." They were also counseled neither to nominate nor to confirm any professor "concerning whose agreement with our doctrinal agreements they have a reasonable doubt." Professors in the schools were admonished to avoid "all occasion of misunderstanding of their doctrinal attitude both in their oral teaching and in their publications and that they counsel their pupils to carefully avoid statements which would disturb the faith of those to whom they minister." [36]

At the turn of the century professors who had studied abroad brought to the theological schools new insights into the Bible which were sometimes called "higher criticism." In 1895, Professor H. G. Mitchell of the Boston University School of Theology, a teacher of Old Testament, who had studied in Germany under German scholars, came under criticism for his liberal views on the book of Genesis. Some students in his classes took the initiative in calling the attention of the bishops to his "heretical views." After a study of the case the bishops decided not to confirm Dr. Mitchell as a member of the faculty of the school of theology.

This action raised a question about whether the bishops should investigate and report upon charges of erroneous teachings in theological schools or confirm appointments to their faculties. As early as 1899, President Warren of Boston University had questioned the wisdom of this relationship to the administration of the school. The proper appointing authorities of schools, he held, were the most competent to judge the qualifications of their faculties. He contended that bishops acting as a board of review lacked the intimate understanding needed for such decisions. The 1912 *Discipline* (¶ 206) indicates that the bishops were relieved of acting as a board of investigation on teachings in the theological schools, and the 1924 *Discipline* (¶ 458.5) was the last one

[36] H. G. Mitchell, *For the Benefit of My Creditors* (Boston: Beacon Press, 1922), p. 250.

to carry provision for confirmation by the bishops of faculty personnel in the theological schools.

Theological Schools in 1939

When the three churches were united in 1939 to form The Methodist Church, nine theological schools entered into the union. These were: Boston University School of Theology; Drew Theological Seminary; Duke University Divinity School; Candler School of Theology; Gammon Theological Seminary; Garrett Biblical Institute; Iliff School of Theology; Southern Methodist University School of Theology (later renamed the Perkins School of Theology); Westminster Theological Seminary (now Wesley Theological Seminary). (The University of Southern California School of Religion was not in 1939 accredited by the University Senate, nor was it a member of the Association of Methodist Theological Schools. This standing was achieved in 1946.)

At the time of union the endowments of these ten schools were valued at $6,081,781. Income from the church for current operations was $159,173. Years of inadequate income had resulted in their inability to render the services needed. The schools did furnish to the united church solid foundations for larger growth and development. In less than two quadrenniums after union, plans had been set in motion for the greatest advance in theological education the Methodists had ever known. That story, however, belongs to the twenty-five years following Methodist unification.

V

A
Maturing
Church
in a
Maturing Nation

1919-60

A Maturing Church in a Maturing Nation

THERE ARE DANGERS ASSOCIATED WITH REMINISCING, AND A MAN OUGHT to be aware of them. But when the period under discussion is roughly the span of his own lifetime, he can hardly think of it in other than personal terms. In 1919 I was twelve years old and at the beginning of that stormy, exciting, terrifying period called the teen age. This section of *The History of American Methodism* begins several years before 1919 and comes down to the present. If this division is proper, then The Methodist Church and I matured during the same period.

World War I had ended and the world was safe for democracy. I remember Armistice Day, 1918, very clearly, for I sold enough papers to make me wealthy according to my standards. Warren G. Harding was elected the twenty-ninth president of the United States in 1920, and we were back to normalcy and corruption. Not many realized that something had happened in the world that destroyed an era and opened a new chapter in our history. We found it out gradually, and it can be said that prophetic voices of Methodism and other churches warned and foretold.

New ages are born so quietly that the majority of people are not aware of what is happening. Isolationism was dead, but the Senate did not know it. The carefully worked out balance of power had been destroyed, and an unwise treaty had been forced on Germany. But it was not apparent to most Americans that we had prepared the soil for an evil growth called Hitler. As happens after nearly every war, we were anxious to go back to prewar conditions and shed our world obligation. But this was no longer possible, for the United States had emerged as the main world power. Like it or not, we were now involved with all mankind in the most practical way.

Yet most Americans clung to the idea that nothing fundamental had changed. We were still anxious to get back from Europe and mind our own affairs. The oceans were still our defense on east and west, and there were friendly nations to the north and south. Under the guidance of George Washington's warning about entangling alliances, we were more than ready to regard the war as a closed chapter and get back to our regular life. The churches as institutions continued to think of "foreign" missions. While they all believed in brotherhood, no one had an idea that this was more than a general and distant ideal. Indeed, our

253

missionary passion cooled and our giving declined. Like many a generation before us, we did not come to terms with reality gladly, and we tried
to believe that nothing much had changed.

It was a scientific age, and it affected our theology profoundly. The
Methodist theological seminaries, at least in the North, were for the
most part dominated by the liberal spirit. Here and there a conservative
voice was heard and respected because of its quality, but for the most
part our mood was liberal. Never as theologically rigid as some communions, Methodism found it easy to adjust to the spirit of experimentation and action. There was a tendency to adjust our religious thinking
to the spirit of the age, and in some quarters there was a feeling that
religion could exist only by the consent of science.

Down in Tennessee a young professor named Scopes defied a state law
and introduced his students to Darwin's theory of evolution. In a famous
trial that was both pathetic and shameful, William Jennings Bryan
fought for the literal interpretation of the Scriptures against Clarence
Darrow's attacks in the name of science. The trial revealed that a new
attitude toward biblical study had finally reached these shores.

It seems almost too much to absorb when I think that both the atomic
and space ages have been born in my lifetime. The news of the first
atomic explosion over Hiroshima reached me in August of 1945 while I
was teaching at Iliff School of Theology in Denver. Some years later I
stood on my patio in Los Angeles and saw the first Russian sputnik in
the sky. Almost at once people began to speculate as to what would
happen to Christianity if we found other living creatures on other
planets.

There were terrible strikes after the First World War and a bitter
fight between labor and capital. There was a tragic depression in the
1930's when many a man wondered if our economic system could endure.
There came a Second World War in the '40's, with mass bombings and
slaughter. Christianity was forced to consider its social implications and
preach a social gospel which was as old as Amos, who lived in the eighth
century B.C. The Methodist Church was one of the strong voices proclaiming that men do not live in a vacuum and that society as well as
the individual's personal affairs must come under the rule of God.

From the time of the Second World War, and partly as a result of it,
a new movement has swept across the churches, including Methodism.
It is called neo-orthodoxy, although the term is too general and covers
many differing theologies. In general it is a return to the general orthodox positions of the Christian church while maintaining the critical
methods and some of the spirit of liberalism. It differs from fundamen-

talism, which too often is obscurantist and reactionary. It is a rediscovery of the transcendence of God and the sinfulness of man. Neo-
orthodoxy is usually critical of human effort and insistent that only God
can accomplish man's salvation. It has been a restoring of the balance—
a swinging of the theological ship back on to the main course.

In more recent times there is apparent in Methodism a desire to
recover its own Wesleyan theology. Indeed, some of our theological
professors are insisting that we are more theological than we thought
and that John Wesley was something more than an itinerant preacher
and organizer. There are signs that an extreme neo-orthodoxy has run
its course and we are beginning to remember some liberal emphases
which must not be lost. This makes it a time of promise for a theology
which is both existential and absolute.

There is a renewed interest in the doctrine of the Holy Spirit, which
sparked the great Methodist revival of the eighteenth century. Certainly
a pessimistic hopelessness is not for us, and I do not think we will ever
go back to a shallow confidence in action only. Great movements begin
sometimes when great men of the past are rediscovered, and there are
signs of a rebirth of interest in John Wesley. Christian experience and
even Christian perfection may become doctrines seriously regarded and
preached once again. I believe that one sign of our maturity is a serious
and critical view of theology and a new sense of Methodist responsibility
to make its contribution in this field.

If you ask a man who knows the Protestant churches to define a distinguishing mark of Methodism, he will likely speak of its social concern.
We inherited this from our founder, who could find no holiness in the
Bible that was not social. The Methodist Federation for Social Service
was organized in 1907, and the Methodist Social Creed was adopted by
the General Conference of the Northern Church in 1908. In 1909 the
Federal Council of Churches (now the National Council) used that creed
as the basis of its own statement on social matters.

There have been pressure groups to silence the voices of prophetic
preachers and we have been through such periods as McCarthyism. But
Methodism, often by the prodding of the women's groups, has been in
the forefront of the battle against social sin. There was much in the
Prohibition Movement that we must now regret, but the motive was to
set men free from the destruction of alcohol. Any man who observes the
broken homes, the ruined lives, the killed and the maimed struck down
by drunken drivers, will not be ashamed of a church which maintains
the struggle against alcohol.

As a seminary student I heard a man say that the trend was in the
direction of socialism and that in fifty years we would see much social

welfare legislation. He was wrong only in his timing. We are a long way from the rugged individualism of the beginning of this period. Unions have grown rich, and prove the gospel's contention that sin and the abuse of power are not confined to one segment of society. After seventy-five years of effort the Nineteenth Amendment was passed, and women in all the states could vote. Labor legislation affecting children, women, minimum wages, hours of work, and safety conditions has been continuous. The Social Security Act was passed in 1935 and has been broadened from time to time up to the present. In all of this the Methodist churches were not insignificant factors.

The social emphasis sometimes is decried by men who think the church should "mind its own business." But that is precisely what the Soviet government of Russia believes. The whole genius of the doctrine of separation of church and state is to free the state from hierarchical domination and allow the church to pronounce the gospel's judgment on all our affairs. Anything that has moral and human effects is the business of the church.

The Russian Revolution, which began in 1917, has been another of the great new facts of our time. It has influenced profoundly the United States, and we have tended to blame everything bad in the world and in our country on the Soviet Union. We have not halted the spread of Communism in the world, and we know we are confronted by the toughest and most ruthless foe we have faced. It is all the more frustrating because our usual military and economic weapons have not won us a victory. Perhaps we are beginning to see at last that this conflict is of the mind and spirit. I believe that according to our faith, so shall the end be. America's spiritual and moral life is being tested as never before in history. This conflict has brought the church to judgment.

This has been a period of great emphasis on education. The Methodist Church has raised its standards for the ministry and it has endeavored to improve its teaching in its church schools. We have moved away from the mass evangelism appeals of the past, and we have grown suspicious of revival meetings which were primarily emotional. This has resulted in both gains and losses, as we are beginning to realize.

Our heritage is from Oxford University, and we have built colleges and universities in great number. Much of our missionary endeavor has been aimed at the establishment of educational institutions which were not sectarian and sometimes did not even carry the Methodist label. This spirit, which has been somewhat quiescent in recent years, seems to have come alive again, and several new colleges have been founded within the last decade. Methodists are doing a better job in supporting their educational institutions.

At the same time, we are beginning to be aware that education and evangelism are partners and not rivals. There has been a rebirth of evangelistic passion, and churches are more aware of their responsibility for training members to witness to their faith. Our growth has not kept pace with the nation in recent years, and we are forced to re-examine our attitudes and our methods. I am in hopes that this is resulting in a new combination of educational excellence and evangelistic fervor. Once again, we do not have to find something new but only recover something old, for one of the church's perennial tasks is to restore lost balances and recover neglected elements.

We have widened the concept of Christian vocation. Young people have been attracted to social work and welfare programs in our cities. Particularly during the '30's, Christian youth saw in these more secular efforts an opportunity to make their Christianity practical. I do not think we are so sure as we once were that the Kingdom can be entered through these doors. We have been brought back to the realization that activity which is not theologically grounded and spiritually motivated does not accomplish many lasting results. But one of the things which makes American churches relevant is their concern for the physical environment of people.

I thank God that I have lived through the period of Methodist Reunion, and just to think of these past years lifts up my heart. In 1939, when it was achieved, I was a pastor in California. In 1942 I was in Nebraska, serving under a former bishop of the Methodist Episcopal Church, South. In 1948 I became a member of the Council of Bishops, and I have had the opportunity of seeing The Methodist Church from three main viewpoints. In moments of irritation some may have wondered if union was worth it. I have never had any doubt but that God shaped it and he willed it.

Back of the Uniting Conference in Kansas City there was long and patient work by leaders and committees representing the three main branches of American Methodism. There is a picture of the three elder statesmen of the three Methodisms clasping hands, and it is still an inspiration to us. It seems obvious now that we belong together, and I cannot conceive any issue dividing us again.

William Warren Sweet, eminent church historian, said this was the largest and most significant union ever achieved in world Protestantism. One can imagine that it would involve some problems. One man said that the North was not as smart as the South had thought, and the South was not as pious as the North had thought. The Methodist Protestants had to overcome their suspicion of episcopacy. From all of us a good deal of patience was demanded. But each branch had something very precious in the Methodist heritage which it had preserved and which we all needed.

Union is one of the most encouraging signs of our maturity. At a time when the nation became the leader of the free world, in the providence of God, Methodism became one church again. I speak as a member of the former Methodist Episcopal Church when I say that the South has strengthened our fellowship immeasurably, and the Methodist Protestants have reminded us of things we must not forget. To sit with my brethren in the council and face seeming impasses has been a common experience during these recent years. But I watched these impasses melt away as men of good will and large vision found the way for us to stay together and move ahead. Now we are ready to strengthen our World Methodist Conference.

The jurisdictional system is not perfect and will probably need revision from time to time. But the idea of maintaining our regional character is good. We are too big and too varied to have just one center. We are able to keep our machinery from destroying our spirit by giving to the jurisdictions local authority and responsibility. It has enabled us to keep our sharp witnesses without finding the lowest common denominator of ten million Methodists.

The Second World War changed the world even more than the First World War. In the period between the wars many Methodist preachers and laymen were pacifists. Many changed their minds when they saw Hitler riding to what looked like victory. The Methodist Church has had to fight for the legal rights of its members who are conscientious objectors. But this is its position, and state officials have seen the point. We claim the right of conscience for every one of our members, and while the great majority of our men accepted military service as their conscientious duty, we also stand by those who for conscience' sake cannot do so.

I have been much impressed by the high quality of the military chaplains in general and of Methodist chaplains in particular. They are men who have accepted their positions as ministries, and they have pride in their calling. One does not find any body of men representing The Methodist Church with greater devotion. We support a strong peace movement, and world peace is one of our important concerns. There are vast differences on this and other questions before us, but Methodism views war as sin and claims the right to preach the ways of peace to all nations including our own.

Our official positions do not always coincide with our practices in all places. We oppose segregation by authority of the General Conference, and our statements are clear and precise. We accept as the law of the land the 1954 decision of the Supreme Court, outlawing segregation. We practice segregation in many places, and some of our people are violently opposed to integration as a principle. But the trend is toward bringing our actions into harmony with our pronouncements. These are difficult days for some Methodists, and we have had more than our share of brave witnesses and courageous prophets. When the whole record is written, The Methodist Church will be noted as one of the strong forces making for brotherhood.

Even before the final victory was achieved in World War II, President Roosevelt called fifty nations together for the setting up of a successor to the League of Nations. This was the United Nations, which has achieved some notable victories. At the same time it has been under constant attack during the period of the cold war. Most people know that it is only one world, and that some world organization is necessary to keep the peace. Many of the United Nations programs are secular copies of the church's missionary programs. John Foster Dulles, sometime secretary of state, was of the opinion that the churches had played an important part in defining the purpose and spirit of the United Nations.

Methodism is ecumenical in its spirit and in its practice. We recognize the ministries of other churches. We welcome all to our communion tables. We take our clue from John Wesley: "Is thy heart right, as my heart with thine? Dost thou love and serve God? It is enough. I give thee the right hand of fellowship." We pay our share of the expenses of the National Council of Churches and of the World Council of Churches. We have a permanent Commission on Church Union to pursue all possibilities which may appear.

I think it needs to be said, however, that Methodism has a strong sense of responsibility to maintain its own witness. It will not welcome an invitation to forget its heritage in order to preserve a theory of the ministry. There will be other unions in the future, and The Methodist Church may be involved in some of them. Because of our activism or practicality many Methodists will have to be convinced that the work of the Kingdom of God can be better done through a union, or they will take a dim view of it.

Because of rapidly shifting and growing population one of the great issues before us now is the inner city church. At the same time, we must minister to the great suburban areas which surround the cities. We have been a rural and small-town people, but now we must learn how to maintain and make vital our witness in the centers of great metropolises. We are aware of the situation, and we are at last putting our minds to dealing with it. Methodist leaders are beginning to say that there will be no further retreat from the cities. We will learn to stay where we are and serve the community where we are. This involves many problems such as support, transition population, and program. This is a hard situation. But there can be no retreat, and we shall face it realistically or perish.

Methodism grew faster than other churches because it followed the people and was not afraid of frontiers. We shall have to use different methods, but the rapid growth of the nation demands that we adapt our itinerant spirit to the modern situation. This is a restless generation, forever moving about, so that we must learn how to evangelize a procession. Well, we have been a restless church, forever on the move and forever invading new sections of life. I doubt that any church is better equipped by heritage and spirit for the facing of these days than The Methodist Church.

The election of the first Roman Catholic president of the United States marked a dividing line in American history. It made sharp and clear what has been the situation for some time, namely, that this is not so much a Protestant country as a pluralistic one. The real religion for many is a sort of secularistic Americanism with vague spiritual overtones. Certain pressures are already appearing out of the new situation, the most serious one being the drive for government aid to parochial schools. It is now clear that radical changes in the nature of the American society are desired by some and may be brought about unless strong opposition is mustered.

The Methodist Church does not desire to be merely an anti-Catholic force. It must, however, oppose further weakening of the doctrine of the separation of church and state. It must champion the public school system and maintain the essential unity of a pluralistic society. This will not be an easy role to fill, but its prophetic voices must be raised and its spirit of freedom must be made manifest. In the years ahead there are few things more important than to challenge monolithic institutions which would encroach on the individual's liberty, both at home and abroad.

We have been called the typical American church. We were the first church to be organized on American soil. We have been shaped by this land, and we have had a part in shaping it. Our spirit has been affirmative and hopeful. We believe in the sinfulness of man, but we believe in the redeeming power of the gospel. Our hymns have been sung by a thousand campfires and in a thousand cathedrals. We are a church of the people, and although there is a wide divergence of thought among us, we are of one spirit. In these difficult and often terrifying times, we join hands with all churches and all our Christian brethren as we seek to serve Him who alone can redeem the times.

chapter 30

AMERICAN METHODIST THOUGHT AND THEOLOGY*

1919-60

Theological Trends

Major Methodist Theologians

Creators of Popular Piety

Concern for Wesley

IN ORDER THAT THE READER MAY MORE easily discern the development of Methodist theology in America since 1919, it is necessary to portray the backdrop against which this theology can be adjudged. The period 1919-34 signifies the dominance of evangelical liberalism throughout the United States, with small but vocal conservative and "fundamentalist" reaction to this prevailing ethos. In the early decades of the twentieth century sensational advances in science, especially in the fields of evolutionary geology and biology, created new issues for America's theologians. The intensified discussion between religion and science centered upon the evolutionary biological theory of Darwin, which appeared to be in direct conflict with the Christian faith, particularly at the crucial point of the origin of the human race. By the 1920's, the evolutionary theory had been generally accepted by America's theologians, who had adapted their theological positions to it.

The general acceptance of the historical-critical method of investigation caused the whole of Christian history— biblical and postbiblical—to submit to criticism intended to be scientific both in method and in spirit. The assessment of man's origin as evolved from lower forms of life contradicted the biblical story of the Adamic origin. Many historical-critical scholars discarded as unacceptable the biblical stories of the Creation and the Fall as God's verbatim description of the origin of man, but retained

* This chapter is based on the author's dissertation (Yale Divinity School, 1960): William J. McCutcheon, "Theology of the Methodist Episcopal Church during the Interwar Period, 1919-1939."

261

them as elements of early Hebrew folklore. Creedal affirmations and doctrinal formulations, including biblical statements, were acknowledged to
be but human interpretations of religious experiences and thus subject
to continual restatement.

Behaviorism, which had been introduced in 1914 with the publication
of J. B. Watson's *Behavior—An Introduction to Comparative Psychology*,
counted among its devotees religious educators who devoted their attention to the observable and predictable aspects of personality. The
meaning of man was observed within the framework of empirical events
and measured against the data of psychology, sociology, and anthropology, rather than from a theological perspective. No responsible churchman could ignore the impact of these new scientific conclusions:

> Along with such visible evidence of scientific achievement has grown up a
> new set of ideas, so demonstrable and so effective both for theological explanation
> and practical consequence that everything is being tested by them. As a result
> one preemptory challenge now brings all our thinking to heel: "Is it scientific?"
> No area of human life has been more deeply affected by this question than
> religion. The men of faith might claim for their positions ancient tradition,
> practical usefulness, and spiritual desirability; but one query could prick all
> such bubbles: "Is it scientific?" That question has searched religion for contraband
> goods, stripped it of old superstitions, forced it to change its categories of
> thought and methods of work.[1]

"Only Yesterday" carried its theological symbols in Harry Emerson
Fosdick and William Adams Brown, who assumed the mantle of leadership in the "modernizing" of Christianity and stressed the development
of personal character and the realization of social righteousness.[2]

1

1919-34—Rampant Liberalism

In his authoritative and conclusive study, "Methodist Theology in
America in the Nineteenth Century," Leland Howard Scott depicts the

---

[1] Harry Emerson Fosdick, "Yes, But Religion Is an Art," *Harper's Magazine*, January, 1931, pp. 129-30. Copyright, 1931, by Harper & Brothers. Reprinted by special permission from *Harper's Magazine* and Dr. Harry Emerson Fosdick.

[2] Cf. H. Shelton Smith, *Changing Conceptions of Original Sin* (New York: Charles
Scribner's Sons, 1955); John Dillenberger and Claude Welch, *Protestant Christianity*
(New York: Charles Scribner's Sons, 1954); and C. F. H. Henry, *Fifty Years of Protes-
tant Theology* (Boston: W. A. Wilde Company, 1950).

unitive element of this tradition as its continuing concern for the personal relevance of universal redemption. The most significant Wesleyan contribution to American Protestantism, he holds, is the doctrine of gracious ability, the belief that man's essential freedom and moral dignity are dependent upon God's redemptive grace.[3] Nevertheless, Scott notes the subtle century-long drift in the Methodist theological tradition from this emphasis upon man's freedom within the context of God's redemptive grace, to a doctrine of the will's freedom of contrary choice. In support of this thesis, Scott notes the gradual decline in emphasis on radical conversion, the witness of the Spirit, the moment of entire sanctification, and the eschatological urgency of salvation, which were displaced by the ascendancy of the doctrine of practical holiness. This emphasis on practical holiness in turn nurtured and encouraged an interest in the doctrine of the will. At the end of the century, Scott concludes, "redemptive grace was no longer the supremely unitive element in Methodism's doctrine of man." [4]

In the Centennial issue of the New York *Christian Advocate* of September 9, 1926, John A. Faulkner of Drew Theological Seminary noted this same trend and placed 1879 as the year in which the tradition-shattering process picked up special momentum.

> The new theory of atonement by Dr. Miley in 1879, the revolutionary series of little books by Dr. Bowne in 1898-1900 (gathered into *Studies in Christianity* in 1909), the almost complete passing of the emphasis on holiness and perfect love, of which the first note was the remarkable book of Dr. J. T. Crane (father of the novelist Stephen Crane) in 1874, the substitution of the "liberal" Baptist divine's book on Theology (Dr. W. N. Clarke) for our own Dr. Curtis' in 1916 in the Course of Study for Preachers, and the many recent books and articles by Methodists of a radical or Unitarian trend—these are signs of a disintegration of that solidarity of testimony which was at once our glory and the spring of our world-wide conquests.[5]

Although the disintegration to which Faulkner refers must be seen in the context of his own conservatism, the accuracy of his observations is underlined by the fact that at the beginning of the 1920's, with the exception of Faulkner, every major theologian in the Methodist Episcopal Church considered himself an evangelical liberal.

Such liberals relied heavily upon the results of the theological leadership of Schleiermacher, Ritschl, and their interpreters in America, William Newton Clarke and Lewis Stearns. They sought to retain as

[3] (Unpublished dissertation; Yale University, 1954), chapter X.
[4] *Ibid.*
[5] "One Hundred Years of Episcopal Methodism," New York *Christian Advocate,* September 9, 1926, p. 1124.

their primary responsibility the essential message of Christianity, while at the same time they were dedicated to reason, an open mind, and the currents of modernity. The credo of liberalism in the twenties bore witness to a metaphysic which stressed the immanence of God, the goodness of man, and man's freedom of will and inherent capacity for altruism. Such a credo included a concept of growth and continuity which expressed the idea of progress and envisioned the chief functions of the church to be ethical preaching and moral education with less emphasis upon ecclesiology, and a lack of interest in the questions of the sacraments and worship. The note of authority in religion shifted from revelation to that of religious experience, with the feeling of absolute dependence given the honored seat of authority.

Creators of Popular Piety Among the People Called Methodists

The members of the episcopacy generally reflected the prevailing mood of liberalism of the time. Undoubtedly, Francis J. McConnell assumed the theological mantle for his colleagues. To him has come the acclaim of Reinhold Niebuhr, who praised "Bishop M——— . . . the most glorious figure in American church life." [6] McConnell as an apologist and social critic defended the Christian faith within the philosophical framework of personalism. Borden Parker Bowne is reported to have said, "McConnell was my greatest student and ablest interpreter." [7]

Beginning with the concept of life as ultimate reality and meaning based upon the personal values, McConnell attacked both Calvinistic doctrines of divine sovereignty and humanistic skepticism as represented by H. G. Wells. He thought of God as absolute in his independence of anything outside himself, while insisting, however, that God's power is relative and limited to the greatest that human personality can conceive. McConnell stated that no longer could churchmen declare that God is sovereign and man's eternal salvation depended on his obediently following a prescribed and determined way. "It might be nearer the truth to say that in some choices God has no way. He waits for men to choose and then adjusts himself to the outcome." [8]

In Southern Methodism, Bishop John Monroe Moore in like manner indicated his allegiance to and dependence upon liberal theologians and

---

[6] *Leaves from the Notebook of a Tamed Cynic* (Chicago: Willett, Clark & Colby, 1929), p. 193. A personal letter dated January 14, 1960, from Professor Niebuhr affirmed that this reference was to Bishop McConnell.

[7] Charles M. McConnell, "Francis J. McConnell," *motive*, May, 1957, p. 21.

[8] Francis J. McConnell, *Public Opinion and Theology* (New York: The Abingdon Press, 1920), p. 57.

especially upon Borden Parker Bowne. Bishop Edwin Du Bose Mouzon cautiously placed himself—and Methodism—as mediating between the fundamentalists and the modernists, favoring the latter and their "living, dynamic theology." Bishops Horace Mellard Du Bose and Warren Akin Candler represented the more conservative voices in Southern Methodism. In 1923-24, Du Bose edited and contributed to *The Aftermath Series,* twelve booklets in which foes of higher criticism wrote on Pentateuchal dating and authorship, and the blood atonement and bodily resurrection of Jesus Christ (the latter two by Du Bose). Writing in professional journals, Du Bose delineated a constructive biblical science based upon the nature of objective truth in revelation as against a subjective restatement of its original divine disclosure. He also declared that coherency in biblical literature was demanded, as such a motif was sufficient in itself to establish the claims of tradition, independent of the inductive methods of certain critical schools of the past.

Methodism in this period possessed many of the greatest preachers of the country and provided the largest number of Beecher lecturers of any single denomination. Frequently heard from its pulpits were sermons based upon such themes as: the reality and reasonableness of Christianity as the "way of living according to the principles of Jesus and in fellowship with him"; the Christlike God, which emphasized the "God and Father of our Lord Jesus Christ"; the redemptive power of sacrificial love made evident in Christ's death; Christian experience interpreted in terms of moral union with Christ; intense moral passion for social justice and the realization of the kingdom of God among men.[9] Significantly, the "Christian hope" supplanted the "doctrine of Last Things," and the "doctrine of election" became almost extinct.

Such men as Merton S. Rice, William L. Stidger, Lynn Harold Hough, Albert Edward Day, Roy L. Smith, Paul Bentley Kern, Halford E. Luccock, and Ernest Fremont Tittle are representative of this great line of splendor. Each of these men carried his own unique contribution into his pulpit, but all pronounced the general themes of the dominant liberalism. Tittle well epitomizes the theology of the Methodist pulpit in the 1920's. As an evangelical liberal he believed that God was the source of value whose nature was Christlike. He believed that "Jesus was so much like God that he could with perfect propriety and profound truth declare, 'He that hath seen me hath seen the Father.'" [10] Tittle urged men to believe in man as well as God, for "faith in man supports

---

[9] Gerald Birney Smith, ed., *Religious Thought in the Last Quarter-Century* (Chicago: University of Chicago Press, 1927), p. 194.

[10] Ernest Fremont Tittle, *The Foolishness of Preaching* (New York: Henry Holt and Company, 1930), p. 83.

faith in God and faith in God gives meaning and justification to faith in man. Let faith in man be completely lost and faith in God is likely to cave in." [11]

Nowhere could one better gauge the impact of liberalism than in the field of religious education. The authors of *The Story of Methodism* have noted the tremendous changes in the life of the church since 1870 and found none greater than the new emphasis upon training of the young.[12] William S. Bovard, correspondence secretary of the Board of Sunday Schools, reported to the 1924 General Conference the seven outstanding educational gains in the church: (a) Evangelistic passion and educational process are now more closely linked than ever before. (b) Scientific principles and tested methods in general education are finding application in the particular field of religion to the great advantage of Christian character and conduct. "By this alliance the Christian revelation is having a fuller chance at the life it came to save than at any period of the Christian era." (c) Denominational colleges and universities and Wesley Foundations are establishing departments of religious education in which educational courses in religion are given rating equal to that of courses in other departments. (d) Religious-education literature is improving in educational quality. (e) A new type of church building, designed with an educational emphasis, is being built. (f) The demand is growing for a correlated, if not unified, program of religious education in the local church and community. (g) The Christian witness is resting primarily upon childhood training. The report continued:

We have long understood that individual character is not conferred independently of one's own efforts, but is an achievement wrought out in continuous cooperation with the Divine Spirit. We are coming to see that a Christian world must likewise be achieved if we are to have one. It is not to come by divine fiat without regard to the spiritual capacities of mankind. The mission of the church whether in America or in India may be defined with a good degree of adequacy as the business of growing a Christian world. With such a conception it is not difficult to see the prime importance of nurture, instruction and training.[18]

Bovard summarized the function of religious education when he stated:

It is undoubtedly true and happily so that the reliance of the church upon external authority and specific rules of conduct is giving way to a faith in the

---

[11] *A Way to Life* (New York: Henry Holt and Company, 1935), p. 26.
[12] Luccock, Hutchinson, and Goodloe, *The Story of Methodism* (Nashville: Abingdon Press, 1949), pp. 452-58.
[18] *The Daily Christian Advocate*, May 13, 1924, pp. 319-21.

inner integrity of the soul that knows God as a personal reality and a faith in the perennial power of Christian ideals. In this critical transition of authority in religion it is our solemn duty as a board of religious education to arouse the teaching capacity and kindle to a flame the spiritual devotion of the church, in order that the on-coming generation may have an adequate personal experience of God and a life-controlling faith in the practicability of a world order such as Jesus taught and for which he gave his life.[14]

George H. Betts's *How to Teach Religion* was widely circulated throughout the church. It exemplified the methodology taught by Methodist Betts in the Northwestern University Department of Religious Education. Basing his approach upon the evangelical-liberal notion of Christian nurture, Betts listed a code of action for youth, to help them maintain the great fundamental virtues whose value had been proved through ages of human experience. The purpose of education was "to lead the child to make such ideals his habit of life and action, so that at last they may govern his conduct and become an inseparable part of his character." [15] This code of action illustrates the degree to which the impetus of the religious-education movement in Methodism had turned toward character development:

> I will respect and care for my body.
> I will keep good-natured, cheerful, and responsive.
> I will take pride in work and thrift.
> I will be honest and speak the truth.
> I will be obedient to the rules of my home and to the
>   laws of the country.
> I will be courteous and kind.
> I will show courage and self-control.
> I will be dependable and do my duty.
> I will love and enjoy nature.
> I will each day turn to my Heavenly Father for help,
>   strength, and forgiveness.[16]

Conservative Reaction

Such dominance of liberalism within the church caused some consternation among the conservative leaders. One such voice was that of John Alfred Faulkner, professor of church history at Drew Theological Seminary. He had been ordained in 1883 and had served pastorates till

[14] *Ibid.*, p. 321.
[15] *How to Teach Religion* (New York: The Abingdon Press, 1919), p. 100.
[16] *Ibid.*, pp. 95-100.

his appointment to the Drew faculty in 1897. He expressed his thoughts in few books, but chose to write extensively in the organs of the church, *The Methodist Review* and *The Christian Advocate*. His writings were polemics against what he thought was the modernizing of the church and apologies for what he considered the essential beliefs of Christianity in general and Methodism in particular.

In contrast to De Lagarde, Wernle, and Renan, Faulkner credited Paul with a sympathetic understanding of the gospel, and portrayed him as a witness to the belief in Jesus as the Messiah. He also argued against the liberals who found the significance of Jesus in his setting forth of principles. In so doing, he took to task Harnack's assertion that the whole of Jesus' message could be reduced to God as Father and the noble human soul as capable of union with him. Faulkner declared that Christianity was not and could not be a set of principles, or teachings, or even allegiance to such principles. It was rather a witness to the life, death, and resurrection of Jesus Christ.[17]

Faulkner's most significant critique of liberalism came in *Modernism and the Christian Faith,* published in 1921. He juxtaposed Ritschl and Wesley and defended the latter as a theologian primarily concerned with salvation and not value-judgments. Faulkner stated the Bible to be divinely inspired because of its very nature as a history of salvation, as a record of the fullness of the life of God ultimately revealed in Jesus Christ, as well as its consolatory tone and high moral level. He stressed the primary importance of the person of Christ as attesting to the real miracle of his being and the revelation of God. He simply stated that the Virgin Birth and the Resurrection were to be proclaimed as essential parts of the original witness of the apostolic church and recorded Bowne's lack of rejection of the Virgin Birth, noting: "It is certainly a matter of gratification that an assailant of 'orthodoxy' so violent as our learned philosopher should yet have believed in the miraculous birth. But I cannot go with him that it is unimportant or independent of divinity of Christ and incarnation." [18] To deny either the Virgin Birth or the Resurrection was to remit the divine dimension of the act of God in Christ. Faulkner concluded this work with a defense of the New Testament doctrine of the Last Things and rejected the universalism of Schleiermacher.

Faulkner displayed his general disillusionment toward liberalism in the pages of *The Christian Advocate*. The following "Creed of Jesus,"

---

[17] "Was Paul After Jesus?" *The Methodist Review,* July-August, 1920, pp. 572-82.
[18] *Modernism and the Christian Faith* (New York: The Methodist Book Concern, 1921) , p. 301.

reprinted from the China *Advocate* in 1925, occasioned his outburst:

He believed in God so naturally that He never tried to prove His existence, but took it for granted like the air He breathed or the food He ate.

He believed in His own mission, which was to give men life abundantly.

He believed in the fact of sin, and man's redemption from it by repentance and faith.

He believed in Heaven and Hell, and taught that men make their choice between right and wrong.

He believed in the possibility of Human Brotherhood, based on the oneness of human need and dependence.

He believed in the capacity of mankind to learn and accept the greatness of the abundant life.

He believed in the fact of immortality and took it for granted, as He did the existence of God, never arguing about it.

He believed in the seriousness of life, without being gloomy or ascetic, and He taught that life should be measured, not by pleasure, but by its joy in service.

He believed that prayer is a necessity for a full-grown life and taught the need of it without arguing about its meaning.

He believed in His own teaching so much that He commanded it to be taught to every nation and laid upon the Church as a last and binding commission.

What do you think of the creed of Jesus? Can you find a better one for yourself? [19]

John Alfred Faulkner felt so, and on October 1, 1925, he replied to the above creed, stating that all but two statements were equally the creed of every devout Jew of Jesus' time as well as most of the finer pagans.

Would you, then, allow me to supplement these ten with a few items of Christ's creed which really distinguished Him from His contemporaries, and which alone made Him the founder of the Christian religion and thus of our mission in China.

He believed that He was the Forgiver of sins and acted repeatedly on that creed.

He believed that He was the Restgiver for all weary and heavy laden.

He believed that He came to give His life a ransom for many.

He believed that His blood sealed the covenant of salvation.

He believed that He was the Eternal Son of the Father.

He believed that that Father sent Him to be the Saviour of the world.

He believed that that salvation was (not simply through faith in God which the Jews and many pagans believed but was) through faith in Himself.

He believed that after His ascension He would give the Holy Spirit for the world-wide mission.

[19] New York *Christian Advocate,* September 10, 1925, p. 1103.

He believed that it was the function of that Holy Spirit to see to it that all truth necessary for salvation should be preached and recorded by the disciples.

He believed that baptism and the Lord's Supper should be set in the Church as perpetual witnesses of Himself.

What do you think of the creed of Jesus? Can you find a better one for yourself? [20]

This same polemic against liberalism in general, Faulkner directed against the liberal theologians within the Methodist Episcopal Church in particular. He dictated that Methodism had a task to play in the theological patterns of the day, but that it needed first to redefine those items of belief essential to its message. Quick to allay any doubts that he could be labeled "fundamentalist" because of allegiance to any particularly worded phrases or doctrine, he discounted as non-essential any specific theories as to the Trinity, Christology, biblical inspiration, original sin, atonement, eschatology, or the method of conversion. He then declared that Methodism was basically an evangel as against a creed; a movement to tell of the good news of salvation through faith in Jesus Christ. In an article in *The Methodist Review* of 1925, Faulkner stated what he considered to be the essentials of this evangel: the deity of Christ, the active agency of the Holy Spirit, the divine inspiration of the Bible as a means by which men may know about God's acts, an honest recognition and dealing with sin, the possibility of eternal loss, justification by faith alone, the doctrine of perfect love and assurance of the Spirit, and an understanding of the Atonement which adheres to the objective value of Christ's work. "With moral influence we can adorn the fringe of a sinful world with pretty sentiments, but if we plunge into its fearful iniquities to rescue men and women from its hells we shall need to follow the example of our fathers with a firmer grasp on the Sword of the Spirit which is the Word of God." [21]

Harold Paul Sloan, prominent pastor of the New Jersey Conference, led the attack upon the entrenched liberalism within the church. Dismayed at the intrusion of liberal thought into the Conference Courses of Study, he spearheaded a drive which culminated in memorials from thirty Annual Conferences to the 1920 General Conference demanding an investigation of and amendment to the present Course of Study. Partial victory was celebrated by new appointive powers given to the Board of Education and the granting to the bishops power to amend and approve the books, which were to be prescribed as in "full and hearty

[20] *Ibid.,* October 1, 1925, p. 1209.
[21] John A. Faulkner, "What Are the Essentials of the Methodist Message?" *The Methodist Review,* July, 1925, p. 589.

accord with those doctrines and that outline of faith established in the constitution of the church; and that the Discipline, with some special emphasis upon the Articles of Religion, and the standard sermons of John Wesley, fifty-two in number, recognized as standards in American Methodism, shall be included in the conference course." [22] This victory was extended four years hence when General Conference delegates voted to allow any member of the church at large to examine the lists of the books nominated for the Course of Study.

The conference course of study issue, however, did not abate with the conclusion of the 1924 General Conference. The course of study itself grew in magnitude and serviceability. In 1926 the Commission on the Conference Course of Study noted that this "largest school for preachers" now enrolled 2,500 ministers in correspondence school. In Annual Conferences, boards of ministerial training enlisted men in the courses of study, drawing their membership largely from the 3,500 supply pastors of the church. Members of the boards served with bishops, professors, and noted church leaders in summer schools of theology, precursors to present-day pastors' schools. In 1924 the Commission began a series of schools meeting during the post-Christmas period chiefly, though not exclusively, for chairmen of Annual Conference boards of ministerial training and deans of summer schools. This "annual college of preachers" attracted the leading professors of the church, bishops, and outstanding church leaders who lectured on Christian doctrine and the Methodist heritage. In 1930 the lectures were printed in booklet form and distributed throughout the church.

Between the 1924 and 1928 General Conferences the conservatives within the Methodist Episcopal Church actively concentrated their power against the leaders of the course of study through the Methodist League for Faith and Life. The League was organized February 3, 1925, at St. Paul's Church, Wilmington, Delaware, by sixteen ministers and laymen, including Clarence True Wilson, noted Prohibition leader, and Harold Paul Sloan. These men credited the growth of modernism in Methodism as the basis and occasion for the formation of the League. Its purposes were to "meet this Modernist current and drive which is threatening Methodism as the Unitarian drive did Congregationalism a hundred years ago." [23]

Speaking as president of the League, Harold Paul Sloan made continuous attacks against the books of the course of study during the mid-years of the 1920's. The official publication of the organization, *The Call to Colors* (which later merged with *The Bible Champion* to become

[22] *The Daily Christian Advocate,* May 20, 1920, p. 391.
[23] Pamphlet, "The Occasion, Basis, Growth, and Purpose of the League."

The Essentialist), was the chief outlet for these attacks. Of the books listed for study, thirteen were blacklisted by Sloan as failing to conform with Methodism's constitutional standards. He felt that these works represented the "new theology," which was naturalistic, and concluded that "we do not believe that Professor Rall can persuade the church to substitute his opinions for the positive declarations of the Lord Jesus Christ." [24] Sloan displayed his greatest concern over these books as the means by which a thousand men yearly were inaugurated into the Methodist ministry.

Sloan's attack centered upon the inadequate Christology of the leaders of Methodism, which seemed, in his opinion, to lead to an insipid Unitarianism. Harris Franklin Rall of Garrett and Edwin Lewis of Drew bore the main brunt of his charges. He charged that Rall had no place for the Virgin Birth, the bodily resurrection, nor any concept of propitiatory atonement. "Perhaps the best effort to express Modernism constructively and fundamentally is to be found in the volume by Edwin Lewis of the Methodist Seminary, *Jesus Christ and the Human Quest*." [25] Sloan proceeded to criticize Lewis as Socinian in his doctrine of salvation and Monarchian as to his doctrine of Christ's person. "Professor Lewis has sacrificed the Theanthropic Person and offers to faith once more a little Unitarian Christ." [26]

The opening of the 1928 General Conference was keynoted with an Episcopal Address, the substance of which was a forewarning against all would-be heresy hunters. Allowing for a breadth of opinion within the church, the bishops cautioned against any polemical haranguing which would prove divisive. They concluded with a declaration that any such disagreement within the church would be handled according to due process of church procedure. "We cannot recognize any authority, however assumed, for ecclesiastical judgment and censure except as provided in our law, nor can we recognize the right of any other than those having official authority to demand an answer in case of alleged or suspected heretical teaching." [27] A few days later Harold Paul Sloan, armed with a petition of 10,000 signatures from 522 churches in 41 states, read the preamble charging "flagrant disloyalty to Methodist doctrinal standards in seminaries, pulpits and Sunday-school literature." [28] Amidst his appeal that the investigation committee report back,

---

[24] Harold Paul Sloan, *Historic Christianity and the New Theology* (Louisville: Pentecostal Publishing Company, 1922), p. 37.

[25] Harold Paul Sloan, *The Christ of the Ages* (New York: Harper & Brothers, 1928), pp. 121-22.

[26] *Ibid.*, p. 128.

[27] New York *Christian Advocate*, May 10, 1928, p. 580.

[28] *Ibid.*, p. 581.

the delegates drowned out his voice and refused to take heed of his cries during the remainder of the sessions and in the ensuing years.

Two cases involving doctrinal issues in the local parish reached the floor of General Conference. The Reverend Mr. William Shipman of Indianola, Iowa, had refused to ask a probationer about his subscription to the doctrine of Scriptures as set forth in the Articles of Religion. The residing bishop had ruled in favor of the constitutionality of the question and received the support of the conference. The second occasion involved the "retirement" of the Reverend Mr. J. D. M. Buckner of Aurora, Nebraska, who insisted, against his bishop and district superintendents, that he had been forced to retire because of his liberal views. *The Christian Century* and Buckner's son publicized the negative decision as another instance against an evangelical liberal, but without recording any reversal of judgment.

The fundamentalist controversy elicited much less disturbance in Southern Methodism. Bishop Mouzon attacked fundamentalism, as did Bishop John Monroe Moore. On the other hand, voices critical of liberalism were raised by Bishops Candler, Denny, and Du Bose, the latter of whom joined Harold Paul Sloan's staff in 1931.[29]

The fundamentalist-modernist controversy generally did not create much furor within Methodism. Reasons for this lay partly in the fact that the central governing body met only every four years and was not in session in 1925, the climactic year of the Scopes trial. Moreover, Methodism had no strong personality who spoke with force for the fundamentalist position. But perhaps it was true largely because as Donald Burton Meyer concludes: "Theologically, the principle of the personal experience of the individual as the only test of faith left Methodism open on the one hand to dilution of its testimony, depriving it of a clear tradition of witness, while on the other hand left it, of all the major denominations, least susceptible to the polarization of the fundamentalist-modernist controversy." [30]

Major Methodist Theologians

EDGAR SHEFFIELD BRIGHTMAN

The faculty of the Boston University School of Theology in this era consisted of men who were profoundly influenced by Borden Parker

[29] On Southern Methodism and the fundamentalist controversy, cf. Stewart Cole, *The History of Fundamentalism* (New York: Harper & Brothers, 1931); Norman F. Furniss, *The Fundamentalist Controversy, 1918-1931* (New Haven: Yale University Press, 1954).

[30] "The Protestant Social Liberals in America, 1919-1941" (Unpublished dissertation, Harvard University, 1953), p. 51.

Bowne. Edgar Sheffield Brightman was appointed to the chair of philosophy at Boston University Graduate School in 1919. Six years later he was appointed as the first occupant of the Borden Parker Bowne chair of philosophy. Brightman had studied at Brown and Boston Universities under Bowne, as well as in Germany under Adolf Harnack, Georg Wilhelm Friedrich Lasson, and Wilhelm Hermann. Bowne's impression was dominant, and Brightman maintained the personalist tradition at Boston University throughout the next thirty years.

Brightman described his theological stance as one of "rational empiricism," by which he meant that religion must be based on all conscious experiences. Under Professor John Miller Dow Meiklejohn at the University of Königsborg, he learned to revere reason as the ultimate judge of all experience.

My contention is that there is nothing about life which makes it desirable to have bad reasons for believing truths, or which allows us to believe any proposition without reason. In so far as life claims the right to be deliberately illogical, that is, inconsistent or incoherent, it is claiming the right to do wrong. The cause of religion, as well as the cause of philosophy, stands or falls with the cause of reason. Without sane persons in a sane universe, there is no sound basis for faith.[31]

Brightman's concern for religion was paramount throughout his entire academic career. His dissertation dealt with "The Criterion of Truth in Albrecht Ritschl's Theology." Brightman defined religion as "characterized by the feeling of dependence on a personal God and dominated by the will to coöperate with God in the conservation and increase of values." [32] His methodology of religion included both faith and reason, the former being defined as trust, confidence, and devotion and the latter as analysis, synthesis, and synopsis.

Each is an approach to the deepest reality of the universe. There is no *a priori* ground for regarding them as mutually exclusive. The object of faith gains nothing by being unreasonable; the object of reason is not necessarily untrustworthy. . . . Faith presupposes reason and reason faith. . . . Just as faith needs reason, so also reason needs faith. If reason is to interpret the real world, it must exercise a certain amount of trust in the unseen,—trust in the best hypothesis that has been found to explain the facts, and trust that the same rational order prevails in the entire cosmos.[33]

[31] Edgar S. Brightman, "Religion as Truth," in Vergilius Ferm, ed., *Contemporary American Theology*, First Series (New York: Round Table Press, 1932) , pp. 59-60.
[32] *An Introduction to Philosophy* (New York: Henry Holt and Co., 1925) , p. 321.
[33] *Ibid.*, p. 324.

Brightman was concerned to outline a path of reason and coherence for the "finding of God." He stressed the divine immanence and stated that God revealed himself in abundant evidences: the rationality of the universe, the emergence of novelties, the nature of personality, the existence of values, the validity of religious experience, and the ultimacy of systematic coherence.[34] It was quite obvious to Brightman that a God who is to be a Savior God and who will command respect will be a reasonable God. "If the Supreme Being were to be thought of as self-contradictory or incoherent or as failing to observe some of the facts and relations in the universe, such a Being could not be regarded as God." [35] Brightman argued that it would then follow that a reasonable God was to be approached through the use of reason.

Brightman also devoted himself to the questions of the nature of God and the problem of God. In a series of volumes written for the Y.M.C.A. Graduate School, he argued that the unity of the self implies a cosmic unity, in like manner as experience of purpose implies a cosmic function, or as the effort of the will to achieve its end implies a cosmic cause, or as personal reason implies cosmic law. Beginning with these presuppositions, Brightman concluded that there must be a common ground between human personality and its cosmic environment and the Infinite Being, the source of all human values.

To call God personal is to hold that the functions of conscious personality are present in him to the highest possible degree. Those functions are feeling, thought, and will. If we approach God through feeling, he is our comfort. If we approach him through thought, he implies a criticism of our entire civilization. If we approach him through will, he is the principle of cosmic progress.[36]

Brightman proposed the idea of a finite God in several of his works and taught that all evidence pointed to this conviction. "The God revealed in experience, then, is a God powerful enough to lead the world toward higher and higher levels, yet, if we are to believe the evidence of experience, not powerful enough to do it without great difficulty." [37] He believed God was also limited by the very time process itself. The real changes that take place within time, when men turn from self toward God, also register change in God himself. The problem of God for Brightman is focused upon theodicy, on the problem of evil. His personalistic unity precluded any dualism which would place the source of evil outside the nature and will of God. The divine consciousness contains, in

---

[34] *The Problem of God* (New York: The Abingdon Press, 1930), p. 148.
[35] *The Finding of God* (New York: The Abingdon Press, 1931), p. 55.
[36] *Is God a Person?* (New York: Association Press, 1932), p. 55.
[37] *The Finding of God*, p. 115.

every experience, both form and content, freely chosen activity, and unchosen passivity. God always chooses that which is of highest purpose but does not always experience immediate achievement and realization. The eternal nature of God contains a principle of delay and suffering within itself. This principle of delay is designated by Brightman as the "Given" and defined by him as the uncreated total complex of eternal factors within the nature of God with which the eternal creative activity of his perfectly good will must deal. Every choice of God, then, is limited by human freedom, the time process, and by the eternal necessities of reason which prohibit contradictions, as well as by the eternal and uncreated nature of divine experience. "Yet we may say that the content of this experience is such that it both renders necessary eternal pain in God and also renders possible the kind of triumph over pain that the inexhaustible good will of God achieves." [88]

ALBERT CORNELIUS KNUDSON

In 1921, Albert Cornelius Knudson succeeded Henry Clay Sheldon as professor of systematic theology. Prior to that date, Knudson had studied at Boston, Jena, and Berlin under such stalwart teachers as Bowne, Wendt, Harnack, and Kaftan. Following his appointments to Iliff School of Theology, Baker University, and Allegheny College, Knudson was appointed in 1905 to the chair of Hebrew and Old Testament exegesis at the Boston University School of Theology. In 1926, Knudson received the appointment of dean in addition to his teaching position, and he held this post until 1938.

Knudson has described his intellectual development as beginning with the philosophy of Josiah Royce, Jacob Gould Schurman, and Edward Caird. These men offered him a type of thinking that transcended the current common-sense realism. It was under the personalism of Bowne, however, that this trek came to its culmination. He found in Bowne one whose thought matched his own longings.

What Bowne did for me was first to clarify the field of thought, to mark out its great highways, and to show where each led. Then he laid bare with extraordinary lucidity the grounds of faith, and gave me an insight into the conditions of a sound metaphysic that has guided me in all my subsequent thinking. The year spent with him was a veritable *Aufklärung*. It brought me a mental relief and an intellectual illumination that may be described as akin to a redemptive experience. [89]

[88] *Ibid.*, p. 119.
[89] Albert C. Knudson, "A Personalist Approach to Theology," in Vergilius Ferm, ed., *Contemporary American Theology*, First Series, p. 223.

Knudson claimed that the profoundest change in the history of modern philosophy of religion was the shift from Platonism to personalism. In the Lotze-Bowne personalism, he discovered and proclaimed what he considered to be the "most thoroughgoing philosophical expression that Christianity has yet received." [40] Indeed, it was his purpose to unite into one discipline this philosophy and theology. He scorned those who taught the absolute disjunction of philosophy from theology, stating that nothing could replace the philosophical foundations of religious faith and that only a theistic metaphysics could meet the needs of Christian belief.

Having established personalism as his base of philosophy and implicitly the standard by which to judge all subsequent theological doctrines, Knudson explored the two fields of his profession. He published four books in the field of the Old Testament and within them developed the prevalent historical-critical anaylsis of the Bible. However, Knudson was most influential in the field of systematic theology, an area in which he taught for over twenty-five years. His intimate contact with students who later reigned in leadership posts in the churches and educational institutions and the widespread distribution of his writings have made him in this period one of the most influential theologians in the Methodist Episcopal Church. In addition to colleges and universities of the church which were staffed with Boston-trained men, professors in the church's seminaries offered courses in theology using his texts as basic readings.

A glance at the Table of Contents of *The Doctrine of God* reveals the methodology of Knudson. His first concern was to lay the philosophical basis for his later theological discussion of the attributes of God, the nature of man, and redemption through Christ. In his Foreword, Knudson declared personalism as the only adequate philosophical base of religion and theology. Then he discussed the three valid sources of authority in religion: revelation, reason, and experience. Revelation is described as that communication from the Divine found in the insights of the prophetic types of religion. In defense of the proposition that reason is a source of religious knowledge, Knudson insisted that without reason faith would remain an inarticulate, unsystematized, and inchoate emotion incommunicable to the modern world. In addition, Knudson insisted that reason might also establish the truth of Christian faith, as the process of systematizing calls for a certain amount of rational evaluation just as truly as a formal defense does.

The third source of religious experience, Knudson grounded in the

[40] *The Philosophy of Personalism* (New York: The Abingdon Press, 1927), p. 247.

theory of an immanent mental principle, as did his teacher Bowne. He insisted that such offered the only adequate foundation for an empirical defense of the Christian faith. To the criticism that such a position placed the source of religious knowledge and authority in man rather than in God, Knudson rejoined that since man's capacity for God was God-given, there would be no cause for it to be regarded as exclusive of the Divine Spirit. Such a God-given capacity could not be made a barrier between God and man, and hence there was no conflict between a theory of religious a priori and the New Testament doctrine of divine grace.

In stating his doctrine of God, Knudson discounted the humanistic approach of Henry Nelson Wieman and rejected William James's and H. G. Wells's narrow conceptions of a finite, growing God. After discussing the classical arguments for the existence of God, Knudson affirmed his belief in such an existence of God based upon the implied necessity of a Supreme Intelligence beyond the intelligent self and the intelligible world. For Knudson, God was not absolute in the sense that he is wholly other, *deus absconditus;* he was limited in his power from his prior decision to create man with freedom and now must so live within this limitation. Neither does divine omnipotence mean that God can do the nondoable; it means that he can do all things that are possible. Nor is there a distinction between God's ability and his willing; there is no transcendent reserve of divine power. God cannot act contrary to his nature, but receives direction from his nature, which is love. As such, the nature limits his will, for without such direction, God would be sheer emptiness or random power.

Knudson held that the uniqueness of Christian theology lay in its doctrine of the Trinity. He stated that God in the totality of his being was a unitary person, and hence there was little justification of speaking of three Persons in the Godhead. "The personality *of* God would seem to exclude the other ideas of personality *in* God." Knudson, however, did not wish to relinquish the religious values attendant to the orthodox theory and thus marked out the ways in which these values were preserved in the newer personalism, without the absurdities of the sharp distinctions within the being of God. He suggested that the Trinity could be seen as a revised Sabellianism wherein Father, Son, and Holy Spirit were as eternal manifestations of God's essential nature, or it could also be seen as a symbol of the richness of the idea of God. Knudson felt, however, that the most important newer insight concerning the doctrine of the Trinity was to be found in personalism's stress upon the unique ethical relationship between Christ and God and its emphasis upon the Christlikeness of God. "If this conception of God is granted, we have the heart of the Trinitarian doctrine and for practical purposes need nothing more." [41]

Knudson began the second volume of his systematic theology, *The Doctrine of Redemption,* by denying any radical distinction between time and eternity. He noted that the sharp disjunction of the two by Karl Barth was theoretically possible but metaphysically impossible, for in actuality "a dependent being implies an independent being upon which it is dependent. And so it is with the relation of time to eternity." [42] Knudson then insisted that a temporal world implied an eternal God upon whom the world depends, and "if we are to trust God in the full Christian sense of the term, we must think of him as present and immanent in the world." [43] Knudson prized the dignity and the sacredness of the human personality as the most fundamental and distinctive doctrine of the Christian faith. Basing his understanding of man upon modern anthropological studies that discredited the traditional orthodox picture of a pristine Adam, Knudson cited hypotheses to show that the growth of spiritual life consisted of accomplishment and achievement. Adamic man was created *imago dei,* that is, with the capacity to grow to perfection in knowledge and moral character. This perfection reached its ultimacy in Jesus Christ. In his *Doctrine of Redemption,* Knudson most often quoted with approval the Tübingen-trained successor to Albrecht Ritschl at the University of Göttingen, Theodore Haering, and specifically on this point: "One may still continue to use the figure of the divine image of man, but if so, it should be reinterpreted so as to mean nothing but man's 'destiny to become a child of God in the kingdom of God, or the capacity necessary for the realization of this destiny.' " [44] Knudson also insisted upon the metaphysical freedom of the individual amidst all the impulses which surround him. "What gives to man his unique worth is his sense of responsibility, his conviction that he is the captain of his own soul, the determiner of his own destiny. . . . The whole Christian conception of the supreme worth of man rests on the assumption of his freedom." [45] This indeterminism was necessary to ensure permanently the moral life in its fullest integrity, and for Knudson it offered the only justification for the testing of human wills. This metaphysical freedom is an act of grace, and as such belies any funda-

---

[41] *The Doctrine of God* (New York: The Abingdon Press, 1930), p. 427. Cf. Claude Welch, *In This Name,* chapter II, for an illuminating discussion of Knudson's doctrine of the Trinity.

[42] *The Doctrine of Redemption* (New York: The Abingdon Press, 1933), p. 31.

[43] *Ibid.,* p. 32.

[44] *The Doctrine of Redemption,* p. 89, quoting Theodore Haering, *The Christian Faith,* tr. John Dickie and George Ferries (London: Hodder and Stoughton, 1913), I, 394.

[45] *The Doctrine of Redemption,* p. 160.

mental division between the human and the divine. This personalistic anthropology represents a transition from a category of "being" to that of "doing" in the relation of man to God, and thus stresses the moral will as the condition of fellowship with God. Commenting upon this note of Knudson's thought, Robert E. Chiles points out that "prevenient grace which was said to exist in all men [by Wesley] here ceases to be distinguished from the human nature with which it strives, and man's part in salvation, in terms of free personal agency, is magnified. A growing tendency throughout the history of Methodist theology in America is thus fulfilled." [46]

Knudson declared the doctrine of original sin to be extrabiblical and insisted that the Bible defined sin rather as disbelief in God and selfishness toward neighbor. Man is redeemed from his self-centeredness by Jesus Christ, whose uniqueness does not abide in the nature of his person, nor in any forensic act performed for man, but in his superlative sense of oneness with God, his feeling of complete dependence upon God, and upon his creative work in founding the kingdom of God. The efficacy of the death of Christ is experienced by man, who sees in his cross an example of the love of God which awakens in him a sense of gratitude and a responsive life of love and obedience. Faith, according to Knudson, is the seeking of divine assistance toward the realization of the ideals of selfless love.

In the concluding chapters of *The Doctrine of Redemption,* Knudson pictured the Christian church as one of the promulgators of the kingdom of God through its dissemination of ideals of social reform. The Christian hope rested in the continuation of personal existence after death and the possibility of eternal satisfaction coupled with moral growth.

HARRIS FRANKLIN RALL

The theological scene at Garrett in this period was dominated by Harris Franklin Rall, professor of systematic theology. Professor Rall had prepared for this post through study at Yale, the University of Berlin, and the University of Halle. Following his sojourn in the German university atmosphere, Rall returned to New Haven to spend an additional year in study at Yale. He then entered the parish ministry and served churches in Connecticut and Maryland. After eight years as president of Iliff School of Theology, Rall exchanged his administrative tasks for a chair of systematic theology at Garrett in 1915. He filled this post until 1945.

In an article in *The Methodist Quarterly Review* of 1925, Rall delineat-

---

[46] "Methodist Apostasy: From Free Grace to Free Will," *Religion in Life,* Summer, 1958, p. 446.

ed the historic position of Methodist theology, assigning its unique significance to John Wesley's conception of religion itself. Rall denoted Roman Catholicism as a doctrine of the church, Calvinism as a doctrine of God, and Methodism as a doctrine of religion. He proclaimed Methodism's unique note to be the revival of the "central question that has come to the fore at every great religious epoch, not the question of this doctrine or that point of ritual or organization, but of the nature of religion itself, of the true relation of man and God." [47] The uniqueness of Methodism was its stress on the individual over the institutional and on righteousness over ritual. Rall cited precedence for this in the prophets, Jesus, Paul, Augustine, and Luther. He then summarized Wesley's conception of religion as follows: "Religion is man's life in personal fellowship with God, known in conscious experience, received by the grace of God through his Spirit, lived in holiness of life and especially in that spirit of love which forms the Christian fellowship and issues in Christian service." [48]

Rall stated that in this conception of religion one finds not only the distinctive notes of the Methodist heritage, but also the bases for a continuing Methodist theology: free grace, religion as conscious experience, and an emphasis upon moral living.

Rall professed to be an evangelical liberal whose passion was to present what he believed to be the crucial center of Methodism—the saving act of God in Jesus Christ available to all men through prevenient grace —in terms meaningful to the scientific world-view of the times. Max Reischle and Martin Kähler encouraged Rall's thinking along the lines of seeing religion as a distinctive interest of man. "They showed that a concern for values did not exclude metaphysical reality, but that through the realm of values one makes the surest approach to the realm of the real. Standing alike against the speculative and the dogmatic, they made plain the place of faith as personal trust and ethical venture and its centrality in religion." [49]

Rall subsequently centered his theology upon personal trust and ethical venture and attempted to demonstrate that the Christian faith had the power to instill meaning in personal living even in the midst of the turbulent times. The title of his first book, A Working Faith, indicates the pragmatic emphasis of his theology. Man's needs and the assurance

[47] "Making a Methodist Theology," The Methodist Quarterly Review, October, 1925, p. 581.
[48] Ibid., p. 584.
[49] Harris Franklin Rall, "Theology, Empirical and Christian," in Vergilius Ferm, ed., Contemporary American Theology, Second Series (New York: Round Table Press, 1933), p. 248.

of a higher power capable of satisfying these needs represent the heart of Rall's religious faith. In his doctrine of anthropology Rall stated that man has the inherent capacity for religion, an undying thrust toward moral ideals, is rational, and is born with impulses to which God and the good can appeal; "otherwise, man could make no response to God, Christian nurture would be an impossible dream, and we should have to go back to ideas of sacramental magic or irresistible grace." [50] Jesus Christ is depicted as the source of inspiration for personal trust in God. His moral mastery is based upon his being truly human and "wholly open to God, [having] no will but God's will, no desire but God." [51] His moral lordship consists of exhibiting to men what human life really is—or could be—and his life stands as an inspiration leading men into the fellowship of forgiveness with God. "He has given men the courage to believe in a God of mercy who seeks men in their sin." [52]

Rall limited his scope in *The Meaning of God* (1928) and forwent any idea of a complete treatment of a philosophy of religion. He urged his readers to turn to other contemporary volumes which would fill out his position.[53] He wrote that God would have meaning for democratic America only after the absolutist theory of the sovereign God had been dismantled and replaced by the picture of God as immanent, democratic, and indwelling. The conception Rall had of God as "wholly other" was merely that he was that higher power that can satisfy the basic needs of man. His stress fell on the "God Who is Near." Rall credited modern theology with a new appreciation of science and the assistance it had given to bringing God closer to man through the evolutionary concept of God as Creator of a dynamic and developing world. In this period, with its emphasis upon democracy, he wrote and lectured upon the democracy of God, who upheld those qualities inherent in democracy: sacredness of human personality, responsible freedom for man, solidarity of fellowship, and faith in man's decisions.

Rall insisted that theology also center in social relationships as well as in personal trust. The source of this ethical venture was the indwelling of the Holy Spirit, whose presence created personal fellowship. Where there is love and truth in the world, there is the indwelling Spirit. Rall

---

[50] *The Coming Kingdom* (New York: The Methodist Book Concern, 1924), p. 33.
[51] *The Meaning of God* (Nashville: Cokesbury Press, 1925), p. 107.
[52] *Ibid.*, p. 111.
[53] *The Meaning of God*, p. v. Cf. Clarence Augustine Beckwith, *The Idea of God* (New York: The Macmillan Co., 1922); A. Seth Pringle-Pattison, *The Idea of God in the Light of Recent Philosophy* (New York: Oxford University Press, 1920); William Ernest Hocking, *The Meaning of God in Human Experience* (New Haven: Yale University Press, 1912); William Ritchie Sorley, *Moral Values and the Idea of God* (New York: The Macmillan Co., 1918).

upheld the intimate relationship of Christianity and democracy and concluded that the former had much to offer the latter in its ideals of life, in its concept of equality among men, and in its moral dynamic. Rall evidenced awareness of the increasing number of criticisms against the evangelical liberal doctrine of Christian ethics, and especially was he cognizant of those who taught the interim ethic proposed by Albert Schweitzer which suggested that the ethics of Jesus were merely spoken for a short interval until his return from heaven. In 1920 he singled out those who were teaching the premillennial return of Christ and in most vigorous terms stressed that Jesus' ethic speaks precisely to the human situation NOW! Persons living in ethical relations can now sense living communion with God.

The following statement deserves to be quoted in entirety, as it well expresses the general attitude of Methodist theologians, pastors, and laymen, as well as Rall, toward social concern.

This, then, is our social faith:

I believe in the God of righteousness and mercy who is working in His world for the good of man.

I believe in the Kingdom of God on earth as the goal of life, where all sin and wrong shall be overcome, where the will of God, which is the life of men, shall be done in all the earth, in court and mart, in factory and mine, in Church and home, and in the soul of man.

I believe in men: in men whom God trusts—all men, and not the few; to whom belongs government; for whom God made the earth; whose welfare is the test of business and State and Church.

I believe in justice as the great social principle of man, as the great purpose of God. "Righteousness and justice are the foundations of His throne."

I believe in the spirit of Christ as the light of men: the spirit of purity that has sworn enmity to all that defiles and destroys; the spirit of love which reverences all men as children of God, which craves all men for fellowship, which alone can bind men together; the spirit of service in which each gives himself to his brother and spends his life for the whole. And I believe in Him who makes men new, who transforms the life of men by giving them the spirit of love and purity and service, which is Christ.[54]

Rall's influence was felt throughout the church, especially among the numerous pastors who had studied under him. While at Garrett, Rall endeared his thought to hundreds of laymen in the Chicago area through his leadership of study groups. For many years he was secretary of the Commission on Course of Study and was very influential in the final

[54] Rall, *A Working Faith* (New York: The Abingdon Press, 1914), pp. 192-93. Used by permission.

selection of recommended books for study (including his own *New Testament History* and *Modern Pre-Millennialism and the Christian Hope*). He was an active lecturer in the summer schools, the Evanston College of Preachers, and throughout the churches. Two of his books were published in the Methodist Church's *Kingdom of God Series,* a series of books approved by the Committee on Curriculum of the Board of Sunday School of the Methodist Episcopal Church. One book, *New Testament History,* was in the Bible Study Textbook Series for use on the college level. His social awareness was felt through the Methodist Federation for Social Action, of which he was secretary.

EDWIN LEWIS

Edwin Lewis joined the faculty of Drew Theological Seminary in 1916 as instructor in Greek and theology. He was to teach at Drew until his retirement thirty-five years later. During half this time he was an avowed evangelical-liberal theologian. He recommended to his readers for further study the volumes of Knudson, Brightman, and Rall. In 1927 he wrote that there was no better single volume available on theology than William Newton Clarke's *Outline of Christian Theology.* He nurtured his liberalism upon the thoughts of the personalist-idealists, especially A. Seth Pringle-Pattison. It was into the stream of British idealism that Lewis found himself carried. His major writings in the 1920's and early 1930's abound with reaffirmations of the liberal-personalistic-idealistic thought of Bowne and Pringle-Pattison. His channeling of this stream was enormous through his years as professor at Drew, his numerous lectureships throughout the church, including those of the Evanston College of Preachers, and the summer schools. His leadership increased because of his editing the *Abingdon Bible Commentary,* which became a standard reference book on the shelves of thousands of ministers. He was also known throughout the church through his writings in the *Adult Bible Class,* the senior educational publication of the Methodist Episcopal Church, as well as through his writings in professional journals and books.

In an introductory chapter to C. L. Drawbridge's *Common Objections to Christianity,* Lewis offered a yardstick by which to measure his theological thinking. In reviewing Christian thought to ascertain the place of skepticism and doubt, Lewis stated that "the defence of Christianity must finally rest—in the possibility of moral certainty arrived at through inward experience." [55] Lewis' theological stance until 1933 centered on these two focuses: the beginning of the quest of a man in the inward

---

[55] Cyprian L. Drawbridge, *Common Objections to Christianity* (New York: Samuel R. Leland, 1931), p. xiii.

experience of the mind and idea, and the postulation of a supernatural power which in turn granted the assurance of moral certainty.

Throughout all his writings Lewis resounds the themes resonant in the evangelical-liberal theologians of the day: God is pictured as Father, the efficacy of the Atonement is determined by its value, the return of Christ is seen in his influence upon individual lives, and the Virgin Birth and Resurrection are discredited if not discounted. Also, he concluded the necessity of the complement of reason and faith in order to comprehend the fullest certainty of God. Reason points the way to the supernatural, and faith confirms what reason, by virtue of its limitations to the visible, the measurable, and the thinkable, cannot affirm. Lewis' theological system was a personalistic-idealistic viewpoint similar to that of Knudson and Brightman. In *Jesus Christ and the Human Quest,* Lewis demonstrated his dependence upon British idealism in his attempt to locate the foundation of the Christian religion in the very nature of man. Personality is the highest value in the universe, and all data must be measured against this standard. The key to the universe is found in fact, idea, and relation, and there is in human nature that which answers to all three facets of reality. The laws of nature are the facts which are related to life beyond that of the physical limitations by the use of an idea which has its correlate in the universe. Thus, for Lewis, the beginning point of theorizing was man, or the seat of the idea. The inward experience of man is that of end-seeking activity, and this alone affords the permanent basis of religion. Within human nature are found individuality, sociality, and, most important, ideality or the power to conceive an ideal and give it certain value, then to allow it to control human activity. Out of this ideality grows a demand for an end of absolute worth or value in which all the above will be realized and satisfied.[56] Lewis further stated that man in his basic need conceives of value based upon that which gives to him the fullest achievement and happiness. Within the nature of man there is a supernatural need. Man is so constituted to "get beyond" the confines of the universe to satisfy this basic need, and he gives to this satisfying agent the highest value. That which is good is so only in relation to humanity and by this virtue is the highest good in the universe. Lewis stated that this, then, is the human quest—to satisfy the need for the supernatural that is basic within human nature. For the Christian believer, the quest must center in Jesus Christ. "If the completion or fulfillment or redemption of human nature can be shown to be thus dependent on him, we shall have all the reason

---

[56] *Jesus Christ and the Human Quest* (New York: The Abingdon Press, 1924), chapter II.

we ever can have or ever need to have for assigning to him the place of absolute lordship and finality." [57]

The completion and fulfillment of human nature did so reside in Jesus Christ, as evidenced by his moral character. "He achieved moral goodness without a flaw, and his achievement becomes at the same time a revelation of the nature of God and of the supreme purpose of God in the world." [58] Thus it appears that man knows the nature of God through Jesus Christ, as he attained the values subscribed to satisfy man's basic natural need for the supernatural and his need for a controlling end of absolute value. Lewis claimed of Jesus Christ that in such a man God was manifest in flesh. He asserted further that God "is in every man in some sense, and according to that divine indwelling the man is able to do this or that work. God was in Plato—to make him a philosopher; in Shakespeare—to make him a poet; in Bach—to make him a musician; in Jesus Christ—to make him the supreme exponent of the religious life, the Author and Finisher of faith, the world's all-sufficient Saviour and Lord." [59]

Every man is a son of God in God's plan and purpose, *"and in the realization of that sonship he does to that extent realize himself."* [60] Thus the full Sonship came to Jesus, because he was able to realize his sonship in the highest degree. This properly entitled him to be called the True Man, and his disclosure of the nature of God as being personal, rational, and ethical enabled him to be called True God. Lewis contended that such a revelation of God shows that he is a purposive God, a fatherly God, an approachable God, a God in complete relationship with man, a suffering God, a God of holy love, and an all-sufficient God. "The Christian religion is interested in God mainly as to his purpose with human life, and it believes that with respect to that purpose he is *utterly adequate."* [61] This adequacy is superlatively expressed in Jesus Christ, whose uniqueness lies in his total God-consciousness and his total utilization of the possibility already regnant in man's nature. It was at this point that Harold Paul Sloan and other conservatives in the church brought their heaviest fire. They charged Lewis with an inadequate view of the nature of Christ. A bitter exchange of letters ensued between Lewis and Sloan on this issue. Sloan criticized Lewis, saying that all Lewis pictured was an "extraordinary human life

[57] *Ibid.*, p. 30.
[58] *Ibid.*, p. 96.
[59] *A Manual of Christian Beliefs* (New York: Charles Scribner's Sons, 1927), p. 97.
[60] *Jesus Christ and the Human Quest*, p. 102.
[61] *A Manual of Christian Beliefs*, p. 22.

through whom God finally succeeded in getting Himself into complete expression." [62]

Man's dependence upon Christ is of such a nature as to have him see his shortcomings and the relative distance between Christ and his life. But Christ's life also gives man the hope that with the new knowledge of God secured through his ministry of moral goodness, man shall inwardly experience moral certitude and moral goodness. Christianity rests its defense on these grounds. The task of the church, for Lewis, is that of professing the possibility of this inward experience of moral certitude along with all other means of extending the kingdom of God. Its apostasy would consist in adhering to anything less than this.

WILBUR FISK TILLETT

Wilbur Fisk Tillett, long-time professor of theology at Vanderbilt University, can be regarded as the outstanding theologian of the Methodist Episcopal Church, South. Gilbert T. Rowe of Duke and Franklin N. Parker of Emory (Southern Methodist University was in its infancy and could boast no major theologian) bore their influence upon a limited number of graduates of their schools, while Tillett accomplished this and more through his writings. Earlier Tillett had written upon the doctrine and polity of the Methodist Episcopal Church, South, and in 1902 his great volume, *Personal Salvation,* which achieved a ninth edition in 1930 in addition to three translations.

In his MacConnell Lectures at Scarritt College in 1923, Tillett presented a survey of the grounds of theistic and Christian belief. He commenced by noting the pronounced transference of emphasis from the transcendence to the immanence of God, which "could not fail to result in a reinterpretation of God and of nature and the supernatural." [63] Hailing this, he declared that "both reason and revelations compel us to think of God as omnipresent and immanent. . . . By virtue of his immanence he is everywhere and all the time active, and what we call the laws of nature and of life are but an expression of his power and ceaseless activity." [64] Stating his position as that of a theistic evolutionist, Tillett defended Christianity as the epitome of man's religious quest, insisting that in this supremely ethical religion that bears Christ's name could be found the only adequate and satisfactory answer to the question, "What is religion?"

Tillett devoted the concluding lectures to noting the varying paths that lead to God: nature, giving evidence of the existence of a divine

[62] Sloan, *The Christ of the Ages,* p. 127.
[63] *The Paths That Lead to God* (New York: George H. Doran Co., 1924), p. 63.
[64] *Ibid.,* p. 68.

Creator; science, which led men to believe that nature could not be explained on any other hypothesis than that of an intelligent Governor of the Universe; evolution, whose note of continuity in creation affirms a Creator and Sustainer; man, the clearest path to God, demonstrating the affinity between intelligibility of the universe and the intelligence of humankind; philosophy, which sees that religion has reason in it and back of it in all that it teaches and enjoins; reason, which establishes conclusion, and attains to certitude in all realms of thought and study; the Bible, which renders to men what history proves nature and reason cannot supply, an altogether worthy and satisfying conception of God and proper guidance in rightly relating themselves to him; Christ, who stresses foremost the fatherhood and love of God ("The first and greatest service which Christ rendered to the human race by his teachings was— and this is a truth which we must needs utter and repeat over and over again—to reveal God as a Father and to make him lovable") ;[65] the church, which leads man through brotherhood to God; the creeds, which bind the churches together; experience, the best teacher.

It is, we repeat, through experience alone that men can really know God; and the revelation that creates a vital and enriching religious experience and makes God real is not so much the revelation which God made to some man in the past and which was recorded in the Bible as that other revelation that is being continually made in the heart which makes of the man who receives it a living epistle that may be known and read of all men.[66]

GILBERT T. ROWE

As editor of *The Methodist Quarterly Review,* Gilbert T. Rowe exerted influence through his occasional contributions to the "Editor's Table." In the April issue of 1925, Rowe wrote an essay, "Methodism and Progress," in which he noted Methodism's alignment with the best philosophies of the day and opined that Methodism's flexibility to these new thoughts was due to its "creedless condition," making it possible to accommodate freely and appropriate new thoughts at will. The progress of Methodism was attested in its pronouncements upon progressive revelation, ethics, liberal Christology, and anthropology. "In the center of Methodist theology is a doctrine of man, which recognizes human ability and freedom, and consequent accountability and responsibility." [67]

Rowe, teaching at Duke University, also formerly book editor of the Methodist Episcopal Church, South, wrote but two books, the first of

[65] *Ibid.,* p. 270.
[66] *Ibid.,* p. 509.
[67] "Methodism and Progress," *The Methodist Quarterly Review,* April, 1925, p. 342.

which continues his thought of the previous journal article. Describing Methodism as "Christianity in earnest," Rowe noted its entrance into history one hundred years too soon—all the churches were only now beginning to interpret religion in the Methodist way!

Rowe concluded his analysis of Methodism's meaning as culminating in the witness of the Spirit, which rested upon the universality of the Atonement and salvation by faith. "These are the three golden links in the unbreakable chain of primary Methodist theology." [68]

In his 1927 Quillian Lectures, Rowe confessed his dependence upon James Lee, D. C. Macintosh, Henry Nelson Wieman, and Canon B. H. Streeter. Declaring his purpose as a defense of scientific treatment of religion, Rowe claimed that Christianity "rests upon native capacities, impulses, and desires of humanity, and that Jesus Christ is the fulfillment of all religion—not only that which appeared in Israel as the immediate background of Christianity, but also that which appeared among all other peoples, especially in the Graeco-Roman world." [69] Rowe also leaned upon Alfred North Whitehead's *Religion in the Making,* quoting from it and kindred publications on scientific religion. "And it is high time that religion should become scientific, if its teachers are to hold the respectful attention of thinking men." [70] He thus encouraged the necessary use of the scientific method, which he felt Jesus and John Wesley had used in their day.

2

1934-39—Liberalism Reappraised and Partially Abandoned

The decline of the prevailing temper of liberalism came in the 1930's. Professor Henry Van Dusen pictured the year 1932 as one which marked a mounting distrust of the evangelical-liberal theology and the introduction of the "most arresting and baffling single characteristic of the contemporary religious mind—*a renascent supernaturalism.*" [71] The

---

[68] *The Meaning of Methodism* (Nashville: Cokesbury Press, 1926), p. 157.
[69] *Reality in Religion* (Nashville: Cokesbury Press, 1927), p. 18.
[70] *Ibid.,* p. 114.
[71] "Theology in the United States in 1932," *Yearbook of American Churches,* 1933, pp. 31-32.

supernaturalism to which he refers is but one of a complex of forces which had ignited the European theological scene. As early as the Franco-Prussian War of 1870, Jacob Burkhardt envisioned an age of individual *Fuehrers* and usurpers. Miguel Unamuno in Spain and Gabriel Marcel in France raised a radically existential critique of bourgeois ideologies. The appearance of Søren Kierkegaard's *Works* in German facilitated this trend. Another Christian corollary to this trend can be discerned in Albert Schweitzer's *Quest of the Historical Jesus* (1906), "with its resounding judgment that a century of European biblical scholarship, for all of its brilliance and ingenuity, was a colossal failure." [72] A very different critique was that of Paul Tillich and Georg Wünsch, who led an attack on the "bankruptcy of capitalist civilization, the hopeless blindness of the bourgeoisie, the tragic involvement of the Church in this diseased structure, and the uncritical participation of Christian thinkers in the prevailing ideology." [73]

In the field of theology, the "Luther renaissance" presented another movement of major significance. Swedish theology provided a "constant ferment during the era of transition, especially through its insistence that Christian theology and ethics be grounded in an understanding of God's self-giving love and of Christ's victory over sin, death and the devil." [74] One man, however, must be specially credited with awakening the heart, conscience, and mind of the Continental churches. Karl Barth exploded his *Römerbrief* in 1918 and 1921, and proclaimed man's dependence "but, with the opposite implication from Schleiermacher, also God's utter transcendence." [75] The "crisis" or "dialectical" theology became a major conditioning factor of the Christian thought of Europe. "It was from this quarter, too, that there came the peremptory—and not exactly tactful—demand that 'America must listen.' " [76]

The year in which Van Dusen wrote his assessment of current theological thought evidenced the great impact of Continental thought upon American theologians. As early as 1928, Douglas Horton had introduced Barth to English-reading Americans with his translation of *Das Wort Gottes und Theologie*. Between the years 1931 and 1934 several additional books were added to this inaugural volume.

---

[72] Sydney E. Ahlstrom, "Continental Influence on American Christian Thought Since World War I," *Church History*, September, 1958, p. 262. Used by permission of the author and publisher.

[73] *Ibid.*

[74] *Ibid.*, p. 263.

[75] *Ibid.*

[76] *Ibid.*

The Rediscovery of John Wesley

One contact point bridging Continental theology to American religious thought had to do with the recovery of the Reformation tradition. For Methodism, John Wesley was the logical focus for such concerns. During our period of study John Simon completed his authoritative five-volume biography of John Wesley (1934). A concomitant renewed interest in the Methodist heritage was awakened on this side of the Atlantic. A check of American Wesleyana in the twentieth century indicates an increase in books published, from four in the first decade to nine in the fourth. In the 1930's no fewer than four major American publications centered upon the life and theology of John Wesley.

In 1935, Professor George Cell of Boston culminated twenty-five years of intensive study of Wesley with the publication of *The Rediscovery of John Wesley,* one of the first modern theological attempts to remove the anti-Calvinistic interpretation of Wesley. Cell, throughout the monograph, stated that the true and proper interpretation of Wesley must be seen against a backdrop of sympathy for, and not antagonism to, the faith of the Reformers and specifically Calvin. He pictured Wesley as the third member of the Reformation trinity, whose message was justification by faith alone, a saving faith which transcends free will, and the operation of the continuing grace of God in and through the Holy Spirit. Wesley was pictured as the theologian of the revival, for whom the essentials of the faith were simply belief in original sin, justification by faith, and holiness of heart and life.

Maximin Piette's study—John Wesley: *Dans l'Evolution du Protestantisme* (1925) —was translated into English in 1937. Almost half of the volume is devoted to tracing the development of the Protestant movement until the entrance of Wesley in the eighteenth century. Piette interpreted the Aldersgate experience as a stage of spiritual development in Wesley's intense inner struggle for faith. Indeed, Piette traced the life of Wesley from a dual perspective of spiritual struggle and moral endeavor. In contrast to Cell, he insisted that Wesley was no doctrinal innovator but rather a saint with a passion to remedy the moral evils of the time. Piette endeavored to make it abundantly clear that Wesley was doggedly attached to the doctrines of the Church of England. Wesley interpreted the Thirty-nine Articles as he wished, as was the custom of the day, and substituted Arminianism for the Calvinism which others wished to read into them. Instead of attempting to ally Wesley with the Reformers, he tried to show the affinity of the "Patriarch of the movement" not to the past, but to the future and to the emphasis on religious experience by Schleiermacher. "We must recognize, however, that religious experience, so dear to the founder's heart, has still retained its place in the Methodism of the twentieth century." [77]

In 1936, Umphrey Lee contributed a third volume to the growing number of American Wesley studies with his interpretation of the relation of Wesley to modern religion. In large measure, Lee concurred with Piette's conclusion, especially as to the meaning and significance of the Aldersgate experience and the anti-Calvinistic note in Wesley. He underscored the pragmatic nature and existential framework of Wesley's thought and attempted to show that Wesley's theology centered in a God whose nature is love, whose sole determination is to confront man.[78] Referring directly to Cell, Lee credited Wesley with teaching a God-centered, God-given religion that was not peculiar to any one historic tradition but was common property of the historic church. Lee cautioned that to force Wesley to center his theology upon a God who is completely objective would be untrue to one who expressed his belief in a God who is both transcendent and immanent and in man as a child of God. Lee concluded with words of caution in accepting the old unworthy ideas of God—"aristocratic doctrines of the elect, . . . a fanatical shutting up of the grace of God to those who can pronounce theological shibboleths or to those who belong to certain cults"—and rather encouraged continued belief in the liberal God of Wesley's God-centered religion.[79]

He saw the affinity of Wesley to modern liberal religion in the context of a common emphasis on Christian experience. This modern emphasis, stated Lee, saved Christian apologetics from sterility and inaugurated investigation into the psychology of religion and the primary place of religious experience in religious education. He noted that the Methodist Church stood in the forefront of the discussion and practice stemming from this modern emphasis. As Wesley's teachings had been relevant for the past generations exulting in spiritual freedom and in the employment of their emotions in religions, so he felt that they also would be relevant for a time that criticized these overemphases and at the same time retained the centrality of Christian experience.

In 1939, Bishop McConnell took leave of his administrative duties long enough to pen a popular life of Methodism's founder. In his Index, McConnell took notice of the work of Lee in two places but did not mention either Cell or Piette. The prime motive of Wesley, according to the bishop, was to spread scriptural holiness through the land through

---

[77] Maximin Piette, *John Wesley in the Evolution of Protestantism*, tr. J. B. Howard (New York: Sheed & Ward, 1937), p. 477.

[78] Umphrey Lee, *John Wesley and Modern Religion* (Nashville: Cokesbury Press, 1936), pp. 171-72.

[79] *Ibid.*, pp. 318-19.

the societies. McConnell cited the three foes of Wesley as antinomianism, or living above the law; mysticism; and Calvinism, defined as planned life without freedom of choice. In regard to this last enemy, McConnell stated that there was much within Calvinism that Wesley accepted, such as the teaching that man's life was planned by God throughout and that there was a stern divine plan for the universe. The issue between Calvinism and Wesley centered upon free choice of man. Indeed, McConnell declared the cornerstone of Wesley's theology to be the very same foundation as his own—the moral character of God and the dignity of man. Wesley developed his thought vis-à-vis the inhuman God of Calvin, for the "God of Calvin was not moved by any moral claims that at all suggested the humane or the human." [80] McConnell also stated that Wesley "would not cloak the barbarity of God's sending men to eternal doom without moral fault of their own by calling the divine decrees mysterious." [81]

The bishop underscored the importance of such an understanding of God in the present hour when Calvinism was being brought to the fore once again, although under another name. He scorned the notion of removing the rationality of man's actions, so that the sole duty of the Christian was to discover what God wants and then blindly to do it. He then stated that if this dictatorial concept of God reigned, the idea of producing a moral idea of God was estopped. "We can have an adequate God, adequate to individual and social tasks, and at the same time a God of moral love. This it was for which Wesley contended." [82] With equal vigor McConnell portrayed Wesley as a warrior against all who would deny men the measure of freedom which would make the choice real.

Crisis Theology and Creators of Popular Piety

Another contact point is that of direct influence of the "dialectic" or "crisis" theology associated with the name of Karl Barth. "Crisis theology" is most closely associated with the discovery of the existential posture of Søren Kierkegaard and the implications of his thought upon Karl Barth, Emil Brunner, Rudolf Bultmann, and others. Essentially a reaffirmation of Reformation theology, "crisis theology" stressed the total sovereignty of God as One wholly other from man yet actively, in love and judgment, involved in man's affairs. That which disallows

[80] Francis J. McConnell, *John Wesley* (Nashville: Abingdon Press, 1939), p. 144.
[81] *Ibid.*, p. 145.
[82] *Ibid.*

man's acknowledgment of the intention of his creation is his sin. Crisis theology declared that God's revelation is found uniquely in Jesus Christ, as attested to in the Bible, and that he alone provided the means by which man can be reconciled with God. As such, the crisis theologians had called to judgment liberal optimism about man and human values and the attempt to build a theological system toward the source of such values. They had called for a re-examination of the person and place of Christ, the existential state of man, and the nature and mission of the church.[83]

Ernest Fremont Tittle in his 1925 Ayer Lecture presented a reasoned and sympathetic analysis of Barth's thought, willingly accepting it as a corrective of flamboyant liberalism, while at the same time rejecting it as akin to despotic authoritarianism. E. Stanley Jones concluded that Barthianism was curative if taken in small doses. He argued that God was present both in revelation of himself and in the spiritual and ethical aspirations and longings of men. Halford Luccock remained an unrepentant liberal, stating: "To me there seems to be much more genuine hope for faith along the way of the examination of values in human experience, than by the way of Barthianism with its dogmatism, its disparagement of reason, its aloofness from crucial human struggles." [84] Lynn Harold Hough, dean of Drew Theological Seminary, in his numerous "Forest Essays" promulgated a Christian humanism which disallowed a conclusion that "human nature is just the refuse of the universe until it is remade by God. If you think too poorly of men, you make them incapable of receiving the grace of God." [85] Albert Edward Day witnessed direct knowledge of the "dialectical movement" and judged his theology closer to that of Brunner than that of Barth. Bishop Du Bose exhibited great enthusiasm about Barth's treatment of Christ's divinity but was perplexed about his separation of the Word of God from the literal Bible. "I think that there can barely be a less important outcome of the Barthian movement than that it shall prove to be a halfway house from the destructive criticism of the last century to the orthodoxy of the fathers." [86]

Much space and attention was given in the denominational press to Barth's conflict with the German authorities and his subsequent departure for Switzerland. As early as May, 1929, Oscar L. Joseph, prominent

[83] Cf. William Hordern, *A Layman's Guide to Protestant Theology* (New York: The Macmillan Co., 1955), especially chapter 6.
[84] *Christianity and the Individual in a World of Crowds* (Nashville: Cokesbury Press, 1937), p. 69.
[85] "The Fourth Decade," *Christian Century*, February 15, 1939, p. 213.
[86] Horace M. Du Bose, "The Barthian Theology," *Christian Faith and Life*, April, 1933, p. 163.

Methodist, reviewed Barth's *The Word of God and the Word of Man* in *The Methodist Review*. Joseph urged his readers to secure the book, but cautioned: "The earnestness and genuine ability of Barth do not, however, excuse the exaggerations and contradictions of his agitated utterances, which are rhetorical rhapsodies that make more of hysteria than of history." [87] Joseph concluded that "where he [Barth] magnifies the sovereignty of God without relating the divine transcendence to the divine immanence, he is more akin to the heretic Marcion. He is asking too much to cut loose from Schleiermacher, Ritschl, Harnack, Wernle and Bousset and follow his random speculations." [88]

From its inception in 1932 as the successor to *The Methodist Review*, *Religion in Life* featured reviews on the movement and also numerous articles whose writers had been influenced by the Continental reformers. The New York *Christian Advocate* offered, on the other hand, very little by way of introduction to the movement or in the matter of articles and reviews about it. In 1933 a Pennsylvania pastor wrote a close-up portrait of Karl Barth, in which he prophesied that men would be responsive to his "clarion call of a soul that has searched deeply and found." [89] The following year the sole reference to Barth's theology appeared in an extended quotation from Albert Schweitzer's original Hibbert Lecture wherein he criticized Barth on his divorce of religion from the world. Schweitzer had analyzed Barth as merely reflecting the dissonant spirit of the age and in reality having made religion not ethical. In his defense of freedom of religion against the state, Barth demonstrated the falsity of his theory, so the Lambaréné doctor concluded.[90]

Georgia Harkness was both a creator of popular piety and a theologian of the Methodist Episcopal Church in this decade. Her philosophical and theological stance during the the entire period was that of evangelical liberalism. She expressed her indebtedness to William E. Hocking, D. C. Macintosh, and Edgar S. Brightman, "who first clarified my religious thinking and gave it what in general outlines is likely to be its permanent structure." [91] She classified herself an unrepentant and unashamed liberal whose views in 1939 were basically those expressed in her first book of ten years before: *Conflicts in Religious Thought*. This

---

[87] *The Methodist Review*, May, 1929, p. 470.

[88] *Ibid.*, pp. 469-70.

[89] John Wesley McKelvey, "Karl Barth, Teacher—A Close-up," New York *Christian Advocate*, June 22, 1933, p. 583.

[90] Editorial, New York *Christian Advocate*, November 15, 1934, p. 915.

[91] Georgia Harkness, *The Resources of Religion* (New York: Henry Holt and Company, 1936), p. viii.

book reveals merely the thoughts of personalism reinterpreted for the lay and college mind. The function of religion was that "it adds new meaning to all the values of life, and it affords to the religious spirit an unique enrichment." [92]

She confessed that she would not retreat one step from her position of 1929 in *Conflict;* nevertheless she added to this that which is absent from her earlier treatment. Since her first writing her thinking had become more Christocentric. "Whatever other grounds of faith may be adduced, it is 'through Jesus Christ our Lord' that the Christian finds God with life-transforming power. . . . Only in Christ is revelation ultimate and unequivocal." [93] It had become also more Bible-basic—her approach to the reality of God in her Mendenhall Lectures of 1940 is through the biblical description: Creator, Judge, Redeemer. In this decade Miss Harkness also experienced a new understanding of the function and mission of the church.

Within the decade Miss Harkness displayed no radical theological transformation but more correctly a spiritual pilgrimage. The trek was, in some measure, from philosophical objectivity to personal commitment. In the midst of the journey Miss Harkness accepted the Barthian note as a corrective of her liberalism but not as a substitute. In her six books published during this time there are but two critical statements about Barthianism. Both center in rejection of what she perceived as the juxtaposition of God's sovereignty and man's moral freedom. She stated that there can be no religious revelation without the free agency of a Divine Being, but neither can there be such a revelation without the free acceptance of it by a human spirit. "Karl Barth's theory of God's complete transcendence and man's helplessness breaks down, I believe, at this point." [94] Noting that the doctrine of predestination had pretty largely died an inglorious death, she predicted Barth would revive it, although it largely went "against the grain" of belief in God's respect for human personality. "To say that man cannot save himself is a position both empirically and theologically defensible: to say that God saves men either contrary to, or in the absence of, human volition is to defy all that we know of human and divine nature." [95]

[92] *Conflicts in Religious Thought* (New York: Henry Holt and Company, 1929) , p. 15.
[93] "A Spiritual Pilgrimage," *Christian Century,* March 15, 1939, p. 349.
[94] *The Resources of Religion,* p. 143n.
[95] Harkness, *The Recovery of Ideals* (New York: Charles Scribner's Sons, 1937) , p. 192.

Crisis Theology and the Major Methodist Theologians

EDGAR SHEFFIELD BRIGHTMAN

It is also necessary to record the specific responses of the major theologians of the church—Brightman, Knudson, Rall, Lewis, Rowe—in whose writings were reflected the influence of Barth, on the one hand, and the criticisms of the crisis theology on the other, in order to indicate the directions as well as the general spirit of Methodist theology at this time. Edgar Brightman in the 1930's deepened his allegiance to idealistic personalism. He wrote in 1939 that his thought had undergone a radical shift in the past decade from an emphasis upon the rationalistic and a priori facts in religion toward an emphasis upon the empirical, which included all items of experience. Concomitant with this shift was a heightened appreciation of Hegel, a new social consciousness, a reinterpretation and renewed consecration to personalism, a need of church reformation, and a growing conviction of God as the finite controller of the Given.[96]

Nowhere is this shift toward empiricism more noted than in Brightman's presidential address before the eastern division of the American Philosophical Association in 1936. Brightman argued for an empirical approach to religion in answer to the quest for the reality of God. He rejected the classical arguments for the existence of God as being based upon selective a priori principles. The proper approach would include all the facets of experience.

Personal experience, apprehended as completely as possible, analysed as thoroughly as possible, tested as experimentally as possible, and then grasped synoptically as a system or totality—that is the basis and method of metaphysics. That is the process of all verification. That is the empirical approach to God. If truth about God is to be found, it must be through such an empirical approach.[97]

Throughout the 1930's, Brightman criticized Barthianism and its associated influences. In 1930 he labeled Barth and Niebuhr as champions of a new deism, and at the close of the decade he declared: "Barth's thesis, we must assert against Mackintosh, is so utterly alien to the demands of philosophical reason, of historical science, of comparative religions, and of sociology that his influence is a tribute to his brilliant pen and per-

[96] Brightman, "From Rationalism to Empiricism," *Christian Century*, March 1, 1939, pp. 276-79.

[97] "An Empirical Approach to God," *The Philosophical Review*, XLVI (1937), 155.

sonality acting on a despairing age rather than an evidence of the inherent truth of his ideas." [98]

Brightman's judgments against Barth can be found scattered throughout the pages of his book *The Finding of God,* published in 1931. In the Preface he stated that God must be the Supreme Reason and that the approach of the book was to treat all forms of irrationalism as dangerous to religion. "Devout Barthianism is one of the subtle perils of the present; it cuts off religion from the rest of life and its inevitable outcome is a head hopelessly divided from the heart." [99] The danger implicit in Barthianism, according to Brightman, was that it would not in the long run have the desired effect of leading men to the biblical revelation, because, he felt, upon such a skeptical foundation only a skeptical superstructure could be built, which would lead to the end result of doubt and atheism.

The second reason set forth by Brightman for the failure of Barthian pessimism is that it did not have an adequate understanding of the necessity of human experience in the divine-human encounter. Brightman centered his attack at this point on the Barthian rejection of the prominence of the wholeness of experience. He declared that Barth ignored the basic teaching of the Bible that man is created in the image of God and that there is covenant between God and all flesh upon the earth. In reply to the Barthian emphasis on the absolute sovereignty of God, Brightman countered that the highest religious consciousness is more than being "laid hold of." "It would be both unreasonable and irreligious merely to lie passive until the Divine snatches you up and redeems you." [100]

Brightman continued that to posit God as utterly separated from human experience offered no hope in the human search for God. "If this view were wholly true, it would be difficult to see how, in the absence of all evidence and reason, belief in God ever arose. Here, then, is an unnecessary difficulty. We should not search with the hypothesis that search is useless." [101] Brightman concluded: "It seems to me utterly false to the empirical principle to regard any one item of experience, such as the Christian revelation, as being so privileged as to be exempt from testing by the rest of experience. . . . Men as different as Wieman and Knudson talk language that I can understand; but much European Christianity is to me a speaking with tongues." [102]

[98] Review of H. R. Mackintosh's *Types of Modern Theology,* in *Christendom,* Winter, 1938, p. 138.
[99] *The Finding of God* (New York: The Abingdon Press, 1931), p. 11.
[100] *Ibid.,* p. 27.
[101] *Ibid.,* p. 29.
[102] "From Rationalism to Empiricism," pp. 276-77.

ALBERT CORNELIUS KNUDSON

With the publication of Knudson's *Doctrine of Redemption* in 1933 there came to perfection within Methodism a theological system based upon the personalism fostered by Borden Parker Bowne. Its influence was great throughout the church and its seminaries as late as the 1950's. The only additional work in this era by Knudson was the publication of his 1937 Fondren Lectures, in which he reiterated his earlier defense, that there is in all men this native category of religious reason which assures any receptivity of a "revealed" truth of the Christian faith. Hence, there is no absoluteness to the claims of Christian experience, but merely a matter of difference in degree from other religious beliefs.

No other Methodist theologian wrote more explicatory and critical analyses of Barthianism than did Knudson. The alertness he exhibited is indicated in his knowledge and summary of the development of Barth's thought throughout the decade. In 1928, he listed among the positive teachings of Barthianism its summoning the church to a renewed understanding of the sovereignty of God; the pride, presumptiveness, and destiny of man; the centrality of revelation for the Christian faith; and the deeper study of the Word of God.

It is in this field, in my opinion, that the chief significance of the Barthian theology lies. Barth will hardly become another Schleiermacher, inaugurating a new theological era, as some of his admiring friends predict. . . . But however unclear, inconsistent, paradoxical, and even erroneous his utterances may be, they clothe a message of prophetic power.[103]

In 1935 Knudson wrote that Barthianism and humanism were fermented amidst the disillusionment following World War I and had a common starting point in philosophical skepticism. *"A theology which feeds on philosophical skepticism will perish thereby."* "It will run its course, and for a time serve an important function as a theological stimulant; but after that it will be laid aside as an interesting and brilliant but temporary revival of theological irrationalism." [104] More specifically, Knudson ascribed his lack of interest in the new theology and its significance as due to the internal contradictions within Barth's initial understanding of the theological problem. Knudson reported that he found nowhere in Barth's writings any evidence that the Word of God could be apprehended without religious experience. He berated

[103] Knudson, "The Theology of Crisis, II," *The Methodist Review,* July, 1928, pp. 559-60.
[104] "Humanism and Barthianism," *Religion in Life,* Winter, 1935, pp. 30-31.

Barth for building his theological system vis-à-vis the place of experience, while doing so upon his very own experience!

Knudson was among the first theologians in America to take cognizance of the newer trends in European theology. In 1928 he wrote full-length scholarly critiques of Barthian theology in both *The Methodist Review* and the *Christian Century*. In the latter he entitled his article "German Fundamentalism," but quickly qualified this by acknowledging Barth's acceptance of historical criticism of the Bible. On the other hand, he justified the use of such a title on the grounds of Barth's dogmatic opposition to modern theology. Throughout the 1930's, Knudson repeatedly criticized Barth's teaching of the central ideas first noted in 1928. These shortcomings were especially noted in the principal areas of how God made himself known (revelation); how man knows God (epistemology); man's understanding of God (theology), himself (anthropology), and Jesus (Christology).

Revelation: In opposition to Barth's teaching of the absolute qualitative difference between time and eternity and the miraculous act of revelation, Knudson insisted upon the actual emergence of the eternal into time, or at the least, an actual congruity between the temporal manifestation and the eternal reality. Even revelation defined as miraculous, he urged, must be received within the temporal line. Knudson also insisted that the doctrine of divine immanence disproved the discontinuity between God and man. Even the attempted use of paradox still did not explain this bald contradiction of metaphysical dualism between human and divine.

Epistemology: Knudson understood Barth and Brunner to state that faith was not found in willing, feeling, or knowing, but in a negation of everything human—a "leap into void." He decried this definition of faith and noted its affinity to the qualitative difference of time and eternity—certainly no teaching of Paul. He charged that Barth read back into the Bible the teaching of philosophical positivism and skepticism. "Faith does not imply pure passivity on our part. It is not a 'vacuum,' as Barth says. It is a profound ethical conviction. . . . What gives to it its unique value is its essentially moral character." [105]

Theology: Knudson credited Barth in his attempt to restore the sovereignty of God, but declared that his theology in reality posited an Unknown God with the biblical attributes of righteousness and love so submerged that their biblical lineaments were often lost.

Anthropology: Knudson interpreted Barth as having stated that the cause of sin in life was not volitional, but was due to man's very

---

[105] "Faith and Ethics," *Evanston Series*, 1935-36, p. 96.

finitude. This equation of finitude with sin, Knudson retorted, is excluded in the doctrine of creation. The fundamental errors of Barth's anthropology were two: Barth failed to note the picturesque and devotional use of theological language and hence had forced liberalism into an unfair rigidity. He also drove an unwarranted cleavage between traditional preaching of sin and repentance and modern preaching of ethical idealism.

Christology: To Barth's teaching that Jesus Christ is the unique Word of God, Knudson replied that if the starting point of theology is to be that of qualitative difference, then Jesus becomes a mere symbol. Rather, he asserted, his value is not as he points to the unknown, but as he is an example of one who has as a mere fact of history "mediated to us the knowledge of God, and his name has, furthermore, become so closely associated with that of Deity that for us the experience of the Living Christ is the experience of God himself." [106]

In 1935 the editors of *Zion's Herald* arranged an anniversary edition in honor of Borden Parker Bowne. Knudson contributed "Bowne and Barth," in which he demonstrated their basic similarities as evangelical Christians, fellow believers in grace, and apologists against the humanism of the day. He then acknowledged their differences. From a commonly held belief in divine grace, each built divergent metaphysical conclusions: Barth gave no place for human freedom in the Arminian sense or for any independent insight into religious truth, while Bowne held that such power must be attributed to man or he would not be a responsible being. Thus, Barth rejected natural theology and divine immanence ("by this he ruled out nine-tenths of Bowne"), while Bowne taught that philosophy could be religiously helpful. Consequently, Knudson felt, Barth's teaching of predestination and election led to a paralyzing of evangelism and missionary endeavor. "During the twenty-five years since his [Bowne's] death, several new systems of thought have arisen, but none of them nor all of them together have rendered any important aspect of his teaching obsolete. In their essential principles his philosophy and theology are as valid and significant for our day as they were a quarter or half a century ago." [107]

HARRIS FRANKLIN RALL

In 1936, Harris Franklin Rall published *A Faith for Today*, and in 1941 he was awarded the Bross Fiftieth Anniversary Prize for his book *Christianity*, a revision of his 1931 Taylor Lectures given at Yale. Both

---

[106] *The Validity of Religious Experience* (New York: The Abingdon Press, 1937), p. 227.

[107] "Bowne and Barth," *Zion's Herald,* March 27, 1935, p. 297.

these volumes reiterate the thought already analyzed as within the evangelical-liberal tradition. The themes in the former reproduce in large measure the earlier themes of Rall. There is a pronounced belief that the essence of the Christian religion is in the indwelling of the Holy Spirit in the lives of men. In juxtaposition to the idea of God's relation to the world as that of dualism or "wholly other," Rall defends the idea of God who is still transcendent yet not apart from the world. God does not work through the Bible, organization, or creed, but "as indwelling Spirit, as a divine life working in history and human experience. Christianity is the religion of the living God, but he is a God who works patiently, slowly, from within, not in a 'direct action' that is external, irresistible, and absolute." [108]

Professor Rall welcomed the Barthian theology as a corrective of insipid liberalism; however, he cautioned those who would see in Barth a new messiah, that "Barth does not have the solution of our problems (his theology ends in Calvin's), but we need him to see better what those problems are." [109] Rall's criticism of the movement centered in two probing queries: how does the "wholly other" reveal himself to man, and how is the saving relationship maintained between God and man? "Barth's emphasis upon God is one thing, his doctrine of God is another. . . . The emphasis is not as with the prophets and Jesus upon the ethical, but primarily upon the metaphysical. Characteristic is the fact that it is death rather than sin that is most stressed." [110] Rall viewed Barth's doctrine of God as dualistic and stemming from Hellenistic rather than Hebraic philosophy. But he insisted that Barth never resolved the dilemma of how revelation takes place within this dualism. "So far from being of aid here, through his conception of God and the world, he tends to make incredible the revelation which he asserts, and in no case shows how that revelation enters human life." [111]

More critical than this, yet allied with it, was the piercing criticism Rall directed toward Barth in his undercutting of the basis of the Christian salvation. Rall believed that the heart of the God-man encounter was the saving act of God toward man, and he was critical of all systems which failed to note this central motif. His prime question always was: Does this doctrine speak against or in any way slight the saving act of God? If so, it cannot and must not be believed. Rall determined that Barthianism was such a doctrine.

[108] Rall, *A Faith for Today* (New York: The Abingdon Press, 1936) , p. 43.
[109] *The Garrett Tower,* January, 1933, p. 14.
[110] "The Idea of God in Recent Literature," *Religion in Life,* Winter, 1932, pp. 66-67.
[111] *Christianity* (New York: Charles Scribner's Sons, 1941) , p. 152.

Barth, I fear, has no adequate answer for our questions. It is well for the preacher to say God, but we must go farther. How can we know God? How can we be sure of him? How does God move in his world? How does he enter savingly into our life? Here Barth fails us. His teaching is more calculated to emphasize our need than to meet it. It is not a theology that Wesley could have taken to his colliers, or that we can use with common folk in our churches, or that will meet these pressing questions of the modern mind. It is well to lift up God, especially in this day when man has been so satisfied with himself. But the Christian evangel proclaims not only the God high and lifted up, but the God who draws near. In his effort to stress the first, Barth has set such a gulf between man and God that he cannot give place to the second.[112]

Rall reviewed Barth's *Credo* and noted that "especially should those in the Methodist tradition see how his position rules out large areas in that gospel of Christian experience, of saving help, and transforming power for which the Methodist movement in particular had stood." [113] To this end is quoted in entirety a paragraph by Rall from "Which Way Theology" printed in the *Garrett Tower* in 1935, in answer to many student and alumni queries:

Are we going back to Calvin by the way of Barth? No. A divine determinism that fixes every event, including the fall of man and the damnation of the non-elect, a God who is arbitrary will and authority before he is moral goodness, the denial of human freedom and responsibility—we are not ready for these. We are not ready for Karl Barth: for the dogmatism that marks his method, for the agnosticism that leaves God finally unknowable, for the dualism that sets God and man so sharply against each other that God cannot really enter into human life, that rules out a real doctrine of the indwelling and transforming Holy Spirit and denies Methodism's insistent belief in salvation as moral renewal, nor for its assertion that religion has no message for the social order and can furnish no power for its renewal.[114]

GILBERT T. ROWE

Writing in the Summer, 1935, issue of *Religion in Life,* Gilbert T. Rowe reviewed *Jesus and the Word.* He classified Bultmann as more radical than Barth in both biblical criticism and theology, yet closest to modern scholars trying to cope with the difficulties thrust upon theology by science and modern philosophy. He reflected that after Barth and Brunner, "it is a relief to turn to Bultmann and follow him as he undertakes to recover the gospel as it was actually presented in the New Testament, and to ascertain wherein the permanent pertinence of that

---

[112] "The Teaching Ministry and Evangelism," *Evanston Series,* 1933, p. 50.
[113] *The Garrett Tower,* November, 1936, p. 14.
[114] January, 1935, p. 1.

gospel lies." [115] Rowe also accepted the "three B's" (Barth, Brunner, Bultmann) as a healthy corrective to theology, but warned against Bultmann's exaggeration of exercise of the will "to the point of destroying reflective thought and aesthetic appreciation," and Barth and Brunner's emphasis upon "the omnipotence of God and the reality of eternity very near to the utter destruction of man and the meaninglessness of time." [116] He suggested that the "way out" lay neither in the direction of a return to Calvin and Luther nor in humanism's gospel of man as his own savior, but " on into a future which must produce a better church and formulate a better theology than the world has ever yet had." [117]

EDWIN LEWIS

If it can generally be said of the other Methodist theologians that any change within their thought was evolutionary and that they remained within the context of evangelical liberalism, albeit realistic; it can likewise be asserted that the shift of theological stance of Edwin Lewis was of a radical nature. Lewis himself characterized this shift as that from "philosophy to revelation." The focuses that had previously been central to this theological stance—namely, the beginning of the quest of man in the inward experience of the mind, and that the idea was thus postulated to a supernatural satisfaction which granted assurance of moral certainty —these focuses were replaced by one central and dominant note—the revelation by God in Jesus Christ; and thus Lewis' theological stance became immovably Christ-centered. In 1939 he wrote:

Some ten years ago I was made to realize with a force that I had never even remotely felt before that the biblical doctrines of God the Creator and God the Redeemer, with all that was implied in these, were wholly central to Christianity and indispensable to its perpetuation, and that they could be held true only on the ground that they had been "revealed." [118]

Lewis criticized his own earlier attempts in *Jesus Christ and the Human Quest* and *Manual of Christian Beliefs* to portray Christ as the highest possible manifestations of God within the milieu of humanity. He confessed the first fears which caused his theological revolution were the implied conclusions warranted by such an approach which would be damaging to the essentials of the Christian faith. He concluded that the Christian faith could not be based upon any a priori and also that the demands of the Christian faith included belief in God who was

[115] "Bultmann as a Barthian," *Religion in Life,* Summer, 1935, p. 448.
[116] *Ibid.,* pp. 453-54.
[117] *Ibid.,* p. 454.
[118] "From Philosophy to Revelation," *Christian Century,* June 14, 1939, p. 762.

"*different* not only from his creation but also from man himself (the truth in *totalier aliter*, 'the wholly other')." [119] These demands intensified in Lewis through his constant immersion into the Scriptures in his work on the *Abingdon Bible Commentary* in 1926-29. He stated that he literally ate and slept with the Bible. In his work as editor he read many of the manuscripts, did all the proofreading, checked all scriptural references, and prepared the Index of forty-two two-column pages. Through this involvement in the Scriptures, Lewis forcefully came to see that "the Creator appeared as the Redeemer." The truth of such an assertion could come only by revelation. "Creation and the incarnation are alike acts of God, and each has its meaning because, and only because, they have been disclosed to us." [120]

The first publication by Lewis after this discovery of the centrality of revelation was *God and Ourselves* in 1931. This was a summary of prevailing naturalism, which proffered little place for Christian revelation. In this book Lewis brought under criticism all such naturalism but yet did not emerge as a champion of the exclusiveness of Christian revelation initiating solely from God and finding a response of faith in men. He spoke continuously of the co-operative endeavor of revelation as man's discovery and God's initiation. "All that we mean by civilization, and eventually by the kingdom of God, is but the exhibition of this cooperative principle on an everwidening scale." [121] In his defense of theism, he dwelt at length on the sovereignty of God as the most rational and ethical justification for belief in God. He listed the following men as those who had not yet bowed to Rimmon: W. E. Hocking, William Inge, William Temple, Seth Pringle-Pattison, Albert Knudson, Francis Leighton, B. H. Streeter, Karl Heim, A. E. Taylor, and Karl Barth.

The final break with the past came for Lewis in April, 1933, in his review of *Re-Thinking Missions*, edited by William Ernest Hocking. This book, a composite work of laymen representing seven denominations, reviewed the waning missions program of the church. The motive of missionary endeavor, as set forth by the commissioners, was to seek with other people a fuller knowledge of the love of God, expressed in those principles learned through Jesus Christ, and compounded with those elements in the non-Christian religions which were in kindred with the teachings of Jesus. The centrality of Christ was affirmed by the fact that his life was supremely given to manifest the true meaning of religion in the midst of the severest tests.

Lewis stated that his personal admiration for Hocking still did not

[119] *Ibid.*, p. 763.
[120] *Ibid.*
[121] *God and Ourselves* (New York: The Abingdon Press, 1931), p. 234.

prevent him from attacking the book. "The threads that were still binding me to my former compromises were broken—not without some 'sadness of farewell'—and I went a way I could no longer evade." [122] Lewis' attack centered, not upon what was denied by the commissioners, but what was omitted by them. He understood them to state that Christianity, with superlative features, was but one among many religions "but in nowise entitled to claim or to practice absoluteness or exclusiveness: rather, while it has something to give, it must also be willing to receive." [123] Lewis railed against this equivocal approach and argued for the absolute claim of the Christian evangel.

But, after all, the claim that in Jesus Christ God did something that he had never done anywhere else, and that what he did unites with an aggressive divine grace on the one hand and the tragedy of human sin on the other hand, and that Jesus Christ was not simply a supremely religious man and the first Christian but rather a fresh and original manifestation of the Creative Will, so that yesterday, today, and forever he is *the* Lord of *Christians* because he is the means of their deepest experience, and that it is through him alone that God purposes—and has eternally purposed—to reconcile all men to himself, meaning, to achieve the complete divine-human unity—this claim is not merely a matter of formal literary expression, but it is of the very substance or essence of Christianity.[124]

Beginning with this article, Lewis was to receive responses from men within and without the church. Hazen Werner, who was later elected bishop, wrote in gratitude to Lewis that this article put courage into the hearts of all in the pastorate "who are feeling the impact of these present-day disillusionments." [125] S. Parkes Cadman also expressed his appreciation for Lewis' forthright stand. There were also letters received which showed a decided distaste for the "new Lewis." District Superintendent Jesse Lacklen insisted that the present-day call included not so much dillydallying over the manner of theology, but more on the acts of love and deeds of kindness performed across the church. In addition, he expressed his disappointment that such a mainstay of the church would be "in company with Sloan and Machen even on one issue." [126] In the same year Lewis added his voice to those liberals who declared

---

[122] "From Philosophy to Revelation," p. 764.
[123] "The Re-Thought Theology of Re-Thinking Missions," *Drew Gateway*, April, 1933, p. 4.
[124] *Ibid.,* p. 5.
[125] Personal letter, Hazen Werner to Edwin Lewis, May 17, 1933.
[126] Personal letter, Jesse Lacklen to Edwin Lewis, May 5, 1933.

the bankruptcy of the modern church. His chief concern was the apostatizing by the church of the central New Testament message of, not a mere man who once lived and died, but "a Contemporary Reality, a God whose awful holiness is 'covered' by one who is both our representative and his, so that it is 'our flesh that we see in the Godhead,' that 'flesh' which was historically Jesus of Nazareth but is eternally the divine Christ whose disclosure and apprehension Jesus lived and died to make possible." [127] Lewis pleaded for a re-enthronement of Jesus Christ which would cause the church to affirm its belief in God's love and sacrificial presence in all the life and work of Jesus Christ; in Christ as the meaning of God, who emptied himself in human form ultimately upon the cross; in the Spirit, who will bring upon the hearts of man the impact of what God has done in Christ; and the church, the redeemed community carrying the mystery of the Incarnation until that day when God shall be all in all, in the Kingdom, the Christianizing of life everywhere. "O Church of Christ *everywhere,* on the avenue, down the side-street, in the town-square, at the country cross-roads, would that thou believedst as thou should!" [128]

Lewis received letters in commendation of this stand from Bishops Leonard, Lowe, Cushman, and Welch in distant China, and from ministers and professors. The most heartfelt letter is that of S. H. Shutleff, serving a parish in Madison, South Dakota. He sadly recounted the immediately preceding period as one of drought for Methodist ministers who had no gospel to preach. "They worship at the sign of the question mark, think any enthusiasm bad form, and the only word in their religious vocabulary is adventure." Then he lauds Lewis: "My, oh me! But you really did tell 'em. And how! Your article in the current number of *Religion in Life* is the most straight from the shoulder utterance along lines of religious thought, that I have read for many a day. And you really dared to use the word—'apostasy.' " [129]

C. F. H. Henry has called Lewis' next publication, *A Christian Manifesto,* the "trumpet call to Neo-Orthodoxy." Lewis felt compelled to write this volume, but only after much hesitation in the midst of his own theological revolution. Noting that something had happened within himself, he set down the meaning of this radical change. The title was chosen with a great degree of aptness. A manifesto, as defined by Webster, is a public declaration showing the intentions of the one who issues it. Lewis' publication is really a broadside proclamation rather than a

[127] "The Fatal Apostasy of the Modern Church," *Religion in Life,* Autumn, 1933, p. 487.
[128] *Ibid.,* p. 492.
[129] Personal letter, S. H. Shutleff to Edwin Lewis, October 23, 1933.

systematic and reasoned apologia for Christian revelation. Addressing himself to the American churches at large, Lewis called for a halt to the retreat before modernism and challenged the churches to thwart the emptiness and shallowness of its claims. He advocated the throwing off of the old shackles of crude expressions and outdated dogmatics and urged a retention of the truth that brought forth such affirmations. The central truth, Lewis proclaimed, was the saving act of God in Christ, and that the time had come for the churches to reaffirm a Christocentric message. The days of dependency upon a metaphysic that attained its precision at the expense of ignoring the deeper meanings of the faith by the Christian theology were called to be ended. "Better a complete testimony and incomplete intellectual articulation than complete intellectual articulation and an incomplete testimony." [130] This complete testimony would be

the message of original Christianity—the message of God's atoning and redeeming love for a lost world, the message that puts a new value on every human soul and gives to it a new meaning, the message that transforms a fallen and sin-doomed creature into a potential son of God, a potentiality that becomes actualized according as by faith Christ is formed anew in the believer's life.[131]

Throughout the volume Lewis reiterated themes of the neo-Reformation—the equation of Christianity with supernaturalism, the insistence upon the reliability of faith-judgments and not logic-judgments in matters of faith; the doctrine of man totally incapable of seeking after and knowing God except by the agency of the Holy Spirit; the plight of man born sinner without the redemptive revelation of God in Christ; the insistence upon the total sovereignty of God; the adequacy of the atonement from the divine grace and not divine omniscience. Amidst these themes, which were stressed in somewhat oratorical fashion throughout the book, Lewis at one point directed his attention to his own Methodist Episcopal Church and chastened the leaders who had led the church in its modern apostasy. He lashed out at the schemes after schemes and drives after drives that had plagued his denomination and had confused many as to the true nature and function of the church. The highest folly, he cried out, was to nurture the church according to the standards of the world. Noting that the bubble of the church had now burst, he conjectured: "The huge thing was mostly air—and the church may be grateful if it has escaped going so completely flat as the world it sought to imitate." [132]

[130] *A Christian Manifesto* (New York: The Abingdon Press, 1934) , p. 156.
[131] *Ibid.*, p. 215.
[132] *Ibid.*, p. 202.

As the nature of the manifesto was such a broadside, it was received with equal temper and judgment. Some declared that Lewis had "gone Barthian," "had passed his creative period and had become senile and conservative" (he was fifty-three) ; others said he was "slipping back into orthodoxy." Former students and followers were dismayed by this reversal of Lewis. Lamenting Lewis' reversal, Norman Twiddy noted others who also feared that the "revolt against humanistic tendencies and against naturalism has swung you too far back to the 'abandoned dugouts.' " [133] Lewis also encountered a series of letters from John Versteeg, a prominent Ohio Methodist pastor who noted that in a recent conversation one of the bishops, "referring to you, said to me that whenever a man gets ready to take a mental nosedive, he credits the Lord with the idea." Versteeg then sadly concluded that it was an alarming tragedy to see Lewis moving farther and farther from the issues of life. Noting the need of the church for Lewis, he said: "That is why some of us get alarmed when you appear to speak in terms of a Barthian automation." [134]

Among the more prominent adverse critics of this book was Jonathan B. Hawk, associate editor of Adult Home Publications, Department of Church School Publications, the Methodist Episcopal Church. He stated that he could not follow Lewis in this new-found Barthian-Calvinistic tendency.

If I had to admit that man's nature was essentially sinful, I could certainly not accept any redemption that might be offered. I could not bring myself to trust a Creator who had made me essentially wicked and then found it necessary to redeem me from that wickedness before he could count me worthy of his grace and to the ultimate life which we Christians think he is going to give us. [135]

Rall in his review of the book questioned "whether this demands the recurrence to old theological forms such as Barth is using? Dr. Lewis tends that way." [136] He also questioned some of the pronounced emphases of Lewis—holiness necessary to God while mercy remains optional; man's sinful status due not to his choice but to his "creatureliness"; the whole notion of God as "wholly other," breaking in from without in the Incarnation. "Surely these doctrines and speculations are hardly of the essence of the gospel demanding place in a manifesto to our day." [137]

[133] Personal letter, Norman Twiddy to Edwin Lewis, September 3, 1934.
[134] Personal letter, John Versteeg to Edwin Lewis, no date.
[135] Personal letter, Jonathan B. Hawk to Edwin Lewis, October 16, 1934.
[136] *The Garrett Tower*, November, 1934, p. 14.
[137] *Ibid.*

The most famous criticism of the book came from Bishop McConnell, who initially congratulated Lewis for the book, which stated so clearly the fundamental trustworthiness of the scriptural revelation while yet maintaining the fallibility and error of human channels through which this revelation comes. Then the bishop strongly criticized Lewis on three specific points: There were certain overexact statements of some truths which are better hinted at than boldly proclaimed; an example is that McConnell assured his readers that there is no attempt on the part of Lewis to pave the way to hell with children's skulls, a conclusion possible from the book's overstatement of man's sinful nature. There was an overemphasis on the divine sovereignty; McConnell questioned the unlimited power attributed to God by Lewis and asserted that God had no right to unlimited exertion of his power, unless he was willing to undertake to discharge the obligation thereby assumed. The bishop also insisted that modern people would not accept damnation to God's glory.[138]

One person who was especially eager to read McConnell's review was Harold Paul Sloan, who stated that in the past the bishop had always given penetrating and constructive reviews. After having read the criticisms of the bishop, Sloan reread the book and declared: "The bishop has totally missed the majesty and power of this book's burning message. Here is a book that is vibrant with the authentic voice of the Triune God calling the Church back to its essential mission; and Bishop McConnell, raising questions almost irrelevant, seems to have missed the roll of its divine thunder." [139] Sloan thereupon praised Lewis and in his exuberance marked the publication of the *Manifesto* as the beginning of a new epoch in Christian theology. Commendatory letters were also received from Bishop Titus Lowe and future Book Editor and Bishop Nolan Harmon, Jr. The editor of the *Advocate* in his review stated with alacrity that none need fear that the book is a mere record of surrender, a Radical turned Tory.

It does not repudiate the social gospel; it shows that its only hope of fulfillment is in the capture of the individual soul by the vitalizing forces of personal religion. It will hearten a host of discouraged and defeatist Christians, and unless we are greatly mistaken, it will raise a standard to which a new generation of Christian men and women may repair, a standard which is the sign of conquest.[140]

[138] Francis J. McConnell, "A Christian Manifesto," *Religion in Life*, Autumn, 1934, pp. 614-18.
[139] New York *Christian Advocate*, November 29, 1934, p. 962.
[140] Editorial, New York *Christian Advocate*, August 23, 1934, p. 708. Italics mine.

The sole remaining publication by Lewis in the 1930's was his Fondren Lecture of 1939, *The Faith We Declare.* The contents follow somewhat the same lines as those of the *Manifesto. A Philosophy of the Christian Revelation,* published in 1940, is an admixture of a rational defense of the existential nature of revelation to the Christian faith and of proclaiming a manifesto reminiscent of the book of 1934. This in part explains why, as Randolph Crump Miller noted in review of the book, "In spite of the great things he says about revelation, the incarnation, the church, and the sin of man, his argument fails to convince at a point he considers vital." [141] Lewis affirmed here that Christianity had a metaphysics of its own, derivable from the biblical faith, but understood in such a way as to correspond with the structure of human existence. The entire book was a defense of revelation in its claim of the fact of God, the meaning of God, and the purpose of God being given in Christ as they are given nowhere else. Lewis was quick to denote the error of Barth in limiting the revelation of God at the one point only in Christ and the historical preparation for his advent. Lewis contended that "to ignore outside of one narrow stream the fact of creation, the fact of history, the fact of man's own distinctive nature, especially his reason and his conscience, the fact of ethical activity, and the fact of universal religion, is to weaken rather than to strengthen the case for revelation in Jesus Christ and in all that of which he was the climax." [142]

Nevertheless, Lewis with equal veracity defended the uniqueness and the centrality of the revelation of God in Jesus Christ. Indeed, the whole story essential to the integrity of the entire Christian message had to do with the knowledge of God and of his activities which it claimed had been given in a special way, through God's revealing his nature and purpose through Jesus Christ. The sole message within the whole variety of the biblical message was *"God in Christ for the salvation of the world."* [143] The revelation cannot be proved as a logical theorem, but must be accepted by faith. Lewis explained further what he means by the separation of faith and reason, developing the argument to show that a propositional statement—"Here is a Man on a Cross—is rationally inescapable; but the proposition—This Man on a Cross is the Son of God, giving himself for me agreeably to the will of God—is not. On its behalf I must choose as it calls forth my assent." Thus the elements of revelation cannot be proved by reason, as this is beyond the claims of reason, al-

[141] *The Churchman,* January 1, 1941, p. 20.
[142] *A Philosophy of the Christian Revelation* (New York: Harper & Brothers, 1940), p. 3. Used by permission of the publishers.
[143] *Ibid.,* p. 49.

though revelation is rational. Rather, reason points to the necessity of such a revelation, and when it is accepted, life becomes meaningful.

Lewis portrayed the revelation in Christ in its organic whole and thus insisted upon the "Supreme Acquiescence" to believe the literal Virgin Birth and the Resurrection. He declared that believing in these facts of the Christian revelation was in no way dependent upon science any more than is the fact of the Christian revelation of the Fatherhood of God or the Incarnation of the Eternal Son as Jesus Christ. Considering all the objections to the contrary, Lewis contended one may yet still say:

> Nevertheless, I believe, and I believe primarily because of the intrinsic nature of Christianity; because ultimately it must stand or fall as an organic whole; because part fits into part with an astonishing exactitude; and because when the living whole is disintegrated, the fragments that are left, useful though they may still be, and acceptable for certain purposes, lack not only the intellectual cogency of the whole, but also, and more seriously, its moral power and its spiritual majesty.[144]

It is at this point that an adverse criticism is expressed by Reinhold Niebuhr, who, on the whole, lauds the work as an approach which measures the problem of human existence at a depth unknown to the modern culture. However, he stated that here Lewis "is a fundamentalist because he finds it necessary to nail down the 'revelation' which both fulfills and negates the aspirations of human culture with a 'fact' and therefore believes in the Virgin Birth. This is a pity." [145]

There is also a suggestion in this book which later developed into an integrated interpretation of the biblical message. His insistence upon the sinfulness of man and his moral blight is repeatedly interpreted in a metaphysical dualism of good and evil which, he declared, is perhaps the most accurate way to express the content of the Christian revelation. He painted in bold strokes his theory of God contending against the evil forces of the universe and also saw in the wholeness of the revelation of God in Christ a constant battle with the demonic forces which culminated in the Cross. Here Lewis was laying a foundation in behalf of metaphysical dualism, which he clearly enunciated in his 1952 Southwestern Lectures.

It can be readily observed from the above analysis of Lewis' thought that he was greatly affected by the Continental movement in theology. Throughout the decade in reviews and articles Lewis pleaded for a hearing on behalf of Barth and associates. In review of H. R. Mackin-

---

[144] *Ibid.*, p. 185.
[145] New York *Herald Tribune* (Book Review Section), November 17, 1940, p. 30.

tosh's *Types of Modern Theology,* he concurred with the author's judgment of the importance of the Barthian movement. "With that judgment only those will disagree who, in strange fatuity, have emptied out of Christianity all its wonders and glory because they have forgotten that 'the foolishness of God is wiser than men.'" [146] His judgment as to the need of the American churches to hear and listen to Barth was stated in review of the *Resurrection of the Dead and the Communion of the Holy Spirit*: "One could ask for nothing better than that the Church of Christ in America should be habituated to such preaching as that of Barth and Thurneysen." [147] Lewis' familiarity with Barth and the Continental theologians came from firsthand knowledge of their works. As early as 1932 he presented a lecture on Barth at Drew University, "Main Emphases in the Theology of Karl Barth." Later, unbeknownst to Lewis, this was serialized in *The Christian Century* in issues of January 18 and 25, 1933. Lewis then wrote a third article in criticism of Barth in the issue of March 22, 1933, "Where Is Barth Wrong?" In the initial lecture on Barth, Lewis showed appreciation for the clarion call issued by the Swiss pastor. Half the lecture is devoted to recounting the main outline of the "crisis theology"—the help Barth received in his new understanding from Kierkegaard and the Reformers; Barth's attack on liberalism, and Schleiermacher in particular; his keynote on revelation and the transcendence of God. Lewis concluded with specific analyses of the crisis theology, which he characterized as a theology of an eschatological dimension, wholly dependent upon the revelation of the transcendent God through his Word. Lewis asserted that this theology was revolutionary in nature, a call of judgment upon all the churches and its ministries, and an assault on comfortable liberalism. The power of such a theology is epitomized by Lewis as striking the deathblow to all human pride and schemes, and forces the hearer to an awful state in the proclamation of the Word. "A preacher who can read Barth without being driven to his knees in a deep heart-searching must have become so inexpressibly callous that he could remain unmoved even if Christ Himself should suddenly meet him in the way." [148]

Lewis' familiarity with the Continental theology is nowhere more apparent than in his 1940 book, *A Philosophy of the Christian Revelation.* Chapter 19, "The Rising Tide of Faith," devotes twenty-two pages to heralding the new voices being raised in the church. However, to

[146] "Mountain Peaks of Religious Thought," *Christian Century,* November 3, 1937, p. 1360.

[147] *Drew Gateway,* January, 1934, p. 9.

[148] Lewis, *Main Emphases in the Theology of Karl Barth* (pamphlet, "A Lecture Delivered in the Chapel of Drew University, October 27, 1932"), p. 14.

speak of familiarity is not to speak of uncritical adherence. Lewis jokingly referred to his being called a Barthian. He noted that when someone mentioned the Word of God, sovereignty, transcendence, the moral plight of man, unmerited grace—he was automatically a Barthian. He confessed appreciation to Barth but felt his kinship closer to Brunner, although he felt that the most promising movement on the then current scene was neo-Thomism. His appreciation for Barth, expressed in an article of a symposium, "How Barth Has Influenced Me," stemmed from Lewis' work on *The Abingdon Bible Commentary*. At that time Lewis was still a disciple of idealistic philosophy associated with Pringle-Pattison. "What therefore Barth chiefly did for me—and it was a great deal—was to help me find the courage, at an important period of my life, to throw off the shackles of mere contemporaneity and keep my mind 'exposed' to the Bible in the effort to determine the nature and the significance of the Christian faith." [149]

Lewis specifically objected to Barth's theology in three main tenets:

The wrong use of a right principle. Lewis criticized Barth for his position on the exclusive and absolute qualitative metaphysical difference between the temporal and the eternal. He insisted with Barth that the eternal and the temporal as mere categories are antithetical, but he also insisted that, but for the eternal there would be no temporal, and but for the temporal the eternal might just as well not be; it must be held that the eternal includes the temporal that is its antithesis. "The conceptual riddle gives way to the spiritual solution. What cannot logically be, actually is. The far God is the near God." [150]

Inevitable authoritarianism: Lewis noted Barth's utter rejection of the above points and all allowance for kinship between God and man, which made his whole theology dependent upon man's utter moral helplessness and God's revelation. This leads inevitably to an absolute authoritarianism of revelation centered in the men who received it and recorded it in the Scriptures. Lewis contended that the response of faith called for by Barth was not to the revelation as such but to the word of men as bearers of the Word of God. It was Lewis' view that there was no doubt as to the veracity of the revelational significance of the experience of the men of the Bible, but in effect we must know it for ourselves and not merely rest on the testimony of others. The teachings of the men of the Bible are true, but this statement can only be made by one as a confession of personal faith, experience, and encounter.

[149] "How Barth Has Influenced Me," *Theology Today,* October, 1956, p. 358.
[150] "Where Is Barth Wrong?" *Christian Century,* March 22, 1933, p. 385.

The passing of Jesus: Lewis charged Barth with one of the most glaring cases of religious apriorism in the history of theology. Barth's Christology, he felt, was Docetic to the degree that he presents a *seeming* in lieu of a *reality*. Lewis charged Barth with being hampered by his a priori metaphysics which caused him to misread half the New Testament in the interests of this metaphysic. In addition, he said, "it is also to ask us to substitute the abstract for the concrete, the speculative for the factual, the obscurities of a deft dialectic for the certainties of past and present experience." [151]

This study of the influence of Continental theology upon Methodism leads to the conclusion that some Methodist leaders in the years 1934-39 reflected an awareness of the movement. George Cell, Umphrey Lee, and Bishop Francis J. McConnell contributed various interpretations of Wesleyan theology in their participation in the rediscovery of John Wesley. Albert Knudson and Edgar Brightman openly rejected the Barthian movement as representing a rejuvenation of Calvinism and a return to irrational determinism. Harris Franklin Rall failed to be convinced of the movement's soteriological bridging of the gulf between the sovereign God and helpless man. Gilbert T. Rowe cautiously rejected the basic teachings of the new theology. Edwin Lewis alone among the major Methodist theologians was receptive to the "dialectical" movement and, although never becoming a "Barthian," reiterated the central themes of that movement, thereby indicating its influence upon his thought.

3

Since 1939—Methodist Theology Today

Issues first introduced in the mid-1930's were sharpened in the following decades, and to this upsurge was added an ecumenical concern and involvement with a renewed interest in ecclesiology, which in turn caused a sharper theological awareness of the particular denominations entering into the conversations. One additional factor of equal importance to the changing scene was the emergence of a generation of younger theologians who were able to see the new issues and speak to

[151] *Ibid.*, pp. 386-87.

them outside the framework of an inherited tradition needing to be defended.

It is especially significant that 1939 marks a turning point for Methodist theology, as this year culminated some seventy years of fraternal felicitations between the two branches of American Methodism. Unification brought with it an end to countless hours of administrative details, and allowed for the possibility of sharing disparate heritages that stemmed from a commonly held source. Accompanying such historical perspective was an increased interpenetration of leadership, South and North.

Popular Piety Among Methodists

Whereas, in reviewing events in past history, the historian is obligated to measure new notes against a discernible pattern of theology, when analyzing the contemporary scene he can only present the apparent trends. Such is the case of the contributions of Methodist leaders to the molding of the present theological ethos. On the level of popular piety E. Stanley Jones, Clovis Chappell, and Ralph Sockman emerged in the late 1930's to influence much of popular religious thought in America. Bishop G. Bromley Oxnam arose as the prophetic successor of Francis J. McConnell. Bishop Gerald Kennedy popularized the thought of such men as Rall, while recently Bishop F. Gerald Ensley reiterated Bostonian personalism out of his previous training. The Episcopal Address of 1960 reminded the people called Methodists of their theological heritage and urged a thoroughgoing re-examination of it to proclaim more adequately the gospel to this age.

Indicative of the involvement of Methodist laymen in the theological renaissance was the increasing number of pamphlets, booklets, and articles concerning the Methodist heritage. In 1949-50, during the Advance for Christ and His Church—"From Crusade to Conquest"—the church published and distributed packets of eight books which surveyed the basic elements of Methodist belief.[152] Also, indicative of the reawakened interest in lay theology was a series of articles directed to laymen by Methodist theologians as printed in the *Christian Advocate*.[153]

---

[152] *Our Faith in* Series: (*God, Christ, The Bible, Love, Prayer, Immortality, The Holy Spirit, The Kingdom of God*).

[153] Cf. "What Do Methodists Believe?" Series, beginning April 14, 1955, *Christian Advocate*. Cf. "We Believe" Series, beginning September, 1961.

Neo-Wesleyanism

As noted above, the impact of ecumenical conversations caused church leaders to examine more closely the very nature of the church as well as the constituent parties and heritages of the conversations. The theological reinterpretation of Methodism began with the simple yet acute realization that Methodism *had* a theological heritage to reinterpret! Contrary to Wilhelm Pauck's alleged remark, that "no denomination has shaped the *un*theological character of American Protestantism as decisively as the Methodists have done," American Methodism since 1939 has recaptured Wesley's theological orientation and American Methodism's unique theological witness. This concern was reflected in the Bishop's Message of 1958, which, in the face and fear of "neo-orthodoxy," advocated a return to Wesleyan theology—a call for a "neo-Wesleyanism." Professor Frederick Norwood of Garrett, a participant in the recovery of Wesleyana, has performed yeoman's service in his recent publication on Methodist historiography.[154] *Motive*, the magazine of the Methodist Student Movement, devoted its entire May, 1957, issue to the Methodist heritage. In addition, the church's press has contributed countless articles and promotional materials emphasizing the rebirth of Wesley and the Methodist history. Noteworthy in the Wesleyan revival is the attention given to the American Methodist theological heritage. A significant movement toward this renewal of the Wesleyan heritage is found in the Wesley Society, an informal movement within the church, begun in 1955 by Professors Hildebrandt (Drew), Shipley (Garrett), and Cameron (Boston). Its hope is to be a generator toward a redefinition of the contribution Methodism may make to the family of churches at large.

The recovery of Wesley's theology itself heightened with the increase of dissertations and book publications. Noteworthy among Wesley studies is William Cannon's *Theology of John Wesley*, in which Cannon examines the theological thought of Wesley against the backdrop of eighteenth-century theology. The first half of the book he devotes to the development of the Wesleyan doctrine of justification by faith. He concludes with several chapters relating various theological ideas which arise out of the first part of the book. Cannon thus claims that the basis of Wesley's theology was his understanding of the means whereby man is saved—i.e., by faith. He also concludes that Wesley so interpreted this indispensable act of faith by man as a beginning point in the Chris-

---

[154] "Methodist Historical Studies, 1930-1959," *Church History*, December, 1959; March, 1960.

tian life and thus opened a way toward moral perfection and holiness.

A second important analytical study of Wesley's theology is that of John Deschner, *Wesley's Christology*. Written in acknowledgment of indebtedness to the theological faculty of the University of Basel, and especially Karl Barth, this book attempts to delineate a fresh view from which to judge Wesley: his vision of Jesus Christ. Deschner argues that his intention is to "be faithful to Wesley's own center, to concentrate on the point where the unity of his theology is most clear, and thereby to serve the exegesis of the Wesleyan writings and the reformulation of the Wesleyan message in the present day." [155] Wesley's Christology is traced through traditional categories: Christ's person, his states, his work, and his role as prophet, priest, and king. It is not unique but part of the ecumenical stream of christological tradition. What is here offered are the characteristic emphases and tensions of Wesleyan Christology presented as a branch of Protestant orthodoxy.

Another significant publication is that of Colin Williams in 1960, *John Wesley's Theology Today,* wherein Williams attempts to analyze Wesley's theology in the light of the current ecumenical trends. After stating Wesley's teachings on such topics as original sin, repentance and justification, the doctrine of the church, and eschatology, he notes the distinction in Wesley between doctrines essential for unity (doctrines in creeds) and those essential to the nurture of Christians in fellowship (distinctive for Methodists). Of the latter he notes Wesley's teachings upon grace free for all and in all, assurance of God's love, the gift of perfect love in this life to all believers, an experience of fellowship not dependent upon acceptance of Methodism's distinctive emphases. Williams prophesied:

> It is true, of course, that what is needed is not a Methodist scholasticism which turns Wesley into an orthodoxy. It is vital that the important Methodist emphases should be related to the contemporary biblical and theological dialogue, and that Methodists should be prepared to hear every word that proceedeth out of the mouth of the living God as he speaks from all the traditions in which he has made his presence manifest. It is in the midst of the ecumenical encounter that the present theological task of the Church must be performed.[156]

Significant not alone as a contribution to Wesleyan studies but also as a concentrated selection of Wesley's theological thoughts is the *Compend of Wesley's Theology* (1954), edited by Robert W. Burtner and Robert E. Chiles. The *Compend* attempts to bring together under the

---

[155] *Wesley's Christology* (Dallas: Southern Methodist University Press, 1960), pp. 4-5.
[156] *John Wesley's Theology Today* (Nashville: Abingdon Press, 1960), p. 206.

groupings the thoughts of Wesley as found in his thirty-plus volumes, some of which were not easily available or were out of print. The breadth of coverage indicates the alertness of the editors to the newer trends in theology as well as to the interest assumed in its reading public.

An important appraisal of neo-Wesleyanism by a parish minister was that of Chester Pennington of Hennepin Avenue Methodist Church, Minneapolis, Minnesota, who in 1948 presented a dissertation to the faculty of Drew University, entitled "The Essentially Wesleyan Form of the Doctrine of Redemption in the Writings of Emil Brunner." Speaking under the auspices of the Wesley Society prior to the convening of the General Conference at Denver, Colorado, in April, 1960, Pennington partly responded to a message from the Council of Bishops issued in 1958, which suggested the emphases of neo-orthodoxy and neo-Wesleyanism. After a brief, thorough, and sympathetic analysis of the former, he noted the affinities between Wesley and these contemporary affirmations. He suggested that Wesley also rebelled against rationalism, moralism, and optimistic humanism and stressed that only God, through his grace received by faith, could alter the situation. He confessed that such a statement by him might seem strange, as he had always defended human freedom, but he now saw this very freedom as a gift of God's grace. Pennington concluded that Wesley sought to recover the authentic New Testament faith, while neo-orthodoxy is attempting to communicate this same New Testament faith. In distinguishing between neo-orthodoxy and neo-Wesleyanism, and in noting that the latter is not a mere rehash of the former, this perceptive minister saw Wesley's and Methodism's distinctive accent as the work of the Holy Spirit. He urged that such a reworking of this note be interpreted in terms of depth psychology. Noting that such a reinterpretation of hope in contemporary theology might be Methodism's unique contribution to other churches, Pennington suggests: "The sounding of this word, which our founders took to be one of their distinctive accents in their time, may be the reason for which we have been called to be a part of the Church Universal in this age." [157]

The Younger Theologians

Methodism's theological leaders of the former era continued to teach and write after 1939. At Boston, Albert Knudson retired in 1943 and

[157] "Neo-Wesleyanism, Neo-Orthodoxy and the New Testament," *Religion in Life*, Autumn, 1960, p. 539.

died ten years later. In his books he defended personalism, especially
against the "theological irrationalism" associated with the name of
Karl Barth. Edgar Brightman continued to lecture and was actively
preparing a book for publication when he died in 1953. His proclamation of personalism, as Knudson's, became a defense of it before the
onslaughts of Kierkegaardian motifs.

Rall continued to teach at Garrett until 1945, when he officially
retired, although he was seen and heard there for many years following.
His theological stance differed little from the earlier period, as he re-
emphasized the soteriological thrust necessary for a living theology.
Taking into account man's need for salvation, he insisted upon the
centrality of man's empirical and experiential involvement in his quest
for meaningful faith as well as its outline in ethical decisions.

At Drew, Lewis continued to teach until 1951, retiring after thirty-
five years of provocative teaching. He died in the winter of 1959. After
1940 he published several books which further explicated his new understanding of theology inaugurated in 1934 with *The Christian Manifesto*.
Perhaps his most notable contribution in these years was his characteriza-
tion of God as Creator in struggle with discreativity. In *The Creator and
the Adversary*, his *confesso fidei* of the Christian faith in terms of an
eternal conflict, Lewis urged the abandonment of metaphysical monism,
arguing against it and implicitly against personalism and Brightman's
noting of the Given within the nature of God. He felt that it failed
to take into account the propensity and reality of the Adversary and
evil. Lewis viewed creation as a strife between creativity and discreativity,
insisting that creation was only explicable on the basis of God's self-
disclosure as creative power. Through his holy love he sought the increase of good, albeit hindered by an alien power which laid a burden
of suffering—ultimately in the final battle between the Creator and the
Adversary: the Cross—both on the Creator and his creation. The
demonic, pictured as entirely passive until creativity begins, will be defeated in that the Creator has more power to bestow and had given it
in Jesus Christ and his resurrection.

The brevity of these summaries should in no way belittle the continuing contributions of these major theologians. Nevertheless, since
World War II, new issues in the form of ecumenics, ecclesiology, existentialism and philosophical linguistics, "demythologizing," and the
relation of Christian thought to culture (the arts, psychology, etc.)
have caused their voices to appear hollow as from a distant age. To

confront these newer trends, there arose new voices within Methodism.[158] Harold DeWolf, Paul Schilling, and Peter Bertocci have become the torchbearers for the idealistic personalism of Knudson and Brightman.

Assuming the position of professor of systematic theology at Boston University in 1946, DeWolf has cast a suspicious eye toward all theological thoughts other than those allied with personalism. His first depiction of contemporary theology, *The Religious Revolt Against Reason,* charged neo-orthodox theologians, in their rejection of reason and its right to judge between truth and error in affirmations of Christian belief, with bringing forth dire misunderstandings of reason's function in theology. He defended the place of reason as being structurally necessary and inevitable for knowledge and explication of God, even in the seeming rejection of it by the neo-orthodox theologians! In the conclusion of his book, he approvingly quoted from Brand Blanshard:

"Start with the assumption that what God says must at least make human sense, and we know what to think when some dervish from the desert or from Berchtesgaden raises his voice to claim guidance from above. Start from the assumption of Kierkegaard, Barth and Brunner that revelation must needs be an offence to our understanding, and what is to prevent us also from becoming blind followers of the blind?"[159]

DeWolf opined "toward a solution" of theology in 1953 in *A Theology of the Living Church.* Exhibiting keen awareness of contemporary theology, he proposed his solution within the methodology of comprehensive coherence, and reason dependent upon experience. His second presupposition detailed evidences for theism, including causal law, objectivity of abstract truth, human adaptations, and the objectivity of moral ideals and the ability to choose the coherent instead of the incoherent. DeWolf then developed within a liberal perspective the themes relevant to the church's life: revelation ("any activity of God by which truth is disclosed to human persons"), the Bible, natural theology (he noted the progressive development of ethical monotheism,

---

[158] On recent trends and theologians on the American scene, cf. Daniel Day Williams, *What Present-Day Theologians Are Thinking* (rev. ed.; New York: Harper & Brothers, 1959); David Soper, *Major Voices in American Theology* (Philadelphia: Westminster Press, 1953); and Sydney Ahlstrom, "Theology and the Present-Day Revival," *The Annals of the American Academy of Political and Social Science,* November, 1960, pp. 20-36. Ahlstrom especially notes the current scene and succinctly portrays six diverse trends operative in the United States. Unfortunately, he does not include idealistic personalism; perhaps he feels this is on the decline and does not warrant being designated a "trend." If so, I concur.

[159] *The Religious Revolt Against Reason* (New York: Harper & Brothers, 1949), p. 163.

whose evidence includes those listed above under theism, as well as the biblical testimony), the doctrine of God (transcendent because "according to the evidence of the Bible, religious experience, and philosophical considerations alike, it seems that God transcends the world"; immanent, "since God is the ground of logical, moral and causal law, whenever our thoughts are true and right they conform to God's own thought"), anthropology (man created *imago dei* suggests a spiritual being, a sense of moral obligation, a longing for union with God, and an aspiration to goodness), immortality (defended as a conservation of the experience of true value), Christology (noting pitfalls in identifying Jesus as God, affirming Jesus' responsiveness because of God's grace fully within him), a doctrine of the Holy Spirit (defended as modified Sabellianism or one mode of divine manifestation), and ecclesiology (the church presented as a *koinonia* or fellowship).[160]

Indicative of DeWolf's theological stance is his selection to write the liberal perspective in theology as part of a trilogy for laymen.[161] In this short book he defends freedom of inquiry, natural theology, and argues on behalf of empirical coherence. In his concern to indicate the interdependence of reason (philosophy) and faith (theology), DeWolf unfortunately appears to be fighting a straw man within the bailiwick he has chosen for the battle arena! He gives scant indication of awareness of the two prevalent philosophical stances—existentialism and philosophical linguistics—yet criticizes neo-Reformation theologians for their hesitancy to accept philosophy (idealism) in *rapprochement* with theology.

Will Herberg, professor of Judaic studies and social philosophy at Drew University, delineated the theological scene at Drew in 1960—especially among younger theologians.[162] He noted five main tendencies among the faculty: the first from members of the biblical department (Bernhard Anderson, Howard Kee, Lawrence Toombs, Robert Funk) who see biblical theology as a theology of recital of the mighty acts of God. George Kelsey was the exponent of a realistic social theology which is as "Augustinian as it is Niebuhrian." In Gordon Harland and especially John Dillenberger, the neo-Reformation (or the misnamed "neo-orthodoxy") theology finds its articulate spokesmen. The fourth tendency, still so formative that Herberg hesitates even to label it a

---

[160] *A Theology of the Living Church* (New York: Harper & Brothers, 1953).

[161] L. Harold DeWolf, *The Case for Theology in Liberal Perspective;* William Hordern, *The Case for a New Reformation Theology;* Edward J. Carnell, *The Case for Orthodox Theology* (Philadelphia: Westminster Press, 1959).

[162] "Some Comments on the Theological Scene at Drew," *Drew Gateway*, Winter, 1961.

tendency, is a "theology of the imagination," which would suggest that the imaginative faculty in man allows for religious understanding. In its embryonic stage, this theology was being nurtured by Stanley Hopper, dean of the graduate school, a student under Brightman and Knudson at Boston and Edwin Lewis at Drew, and Ray Hart, a youthful instructor from Yale. The fifth tendency centered in Carl Michalson, Edwin Lewis' successor and one of the church's outstanding younger theologians.

A prolific writer, Michalson has ranged in his writings from books dealing with personal crises to interpretations of contemporary Japanese theology. His major interest has been confined to the modern philosophy of existentialism and its relation to Christianity. Indicative of such concern are two publications dealing with the subject from different perspectives. In 1956, Michalson edited a series of articles originally presented as lectures comprising the fifteenth series of lectures in Christian biography delivered in Craig Chapel of Drew University. In this volume Michalson introduces the term "existentialism" and hazards to define it as a "way of life which involves one's total self in an attitude of complete seriousness about himself." [163] He is quick to qualify this statement by assuring his readers that existentialism deals with the involvements of living rather than the speculations of thinking. To exist is to realize that man can be nothing and to discover that such a declaration can be made only after a deep introspective search into one's own being. Michalson concludes that existentialism allies itself with Christianity in clearing the subterfuge of contemporary society and "nurses an aching void, keeps the wounds of man open until an authentically healing agent can be applied." [164]

Whereas in this book Michalson merely involves his personal theological position implicitly, in *The Hinge of History* he purposely directs his thought toward an existentialist approach to the Christian faith. That is, he here attempts to say *"what it means that Christianity is historical."* [165] World history is characterized as paratactic, or as a series of events which cannot be explained by what precedes them. Michalson's thesis is that biblical history—with the uniqueness of Christ at the center—supplies the "hinge" linking together mere factual events. Existential history has as its task to point up the paratactic structure in history as eschatological history points to Jesus Christ as the hinge to such history.

[163] *Christianity and the Existentialists* (New York: Charles Scribner's Sons, 1956), p. 3.

[164] *Ibid.*, p. 21.

[165] *The Hinge of History* (New York: Charles Scribner's Sons, 1959), p. 11.

The God who is experienced as the absent God in existential history is experienced as the present God in the eschatological history which the Christian proclamation heralds. The God and father of Jesus Christ is a God whose reality is not simply being but being there for us; not simply an *ousia* but a *parousia,* a presence. That makes the Christian life a life lived in a history which has a future because it is lived *coram deo,* in the presence of God.[166]

Herberg has said of Michalson: "He is the most 'Continental' of the Drew theologians, yet many have claimed to detect a familiar 'Methodist' note in his thinking." [167]

The theological leadership at Garrett upon Rall's retirement fell into the hands of Gerald O. McCulloh, who continued to teach from his Bostonian personalism, using as basic texts those of Knudson. McCulloh was succeeded by Edward Ramsdell, coming from Vanderbilt, where, in 1950, he had published a noteworthy and exceedingly perceptive book, *The Christian Perspective.* His position there set forth was one of mediation between the personalistic theism of Brightman and Knudson, which he shared, and the position of Brunner, Aulen, and Niebuhr, which he had come to appreciate. Noting that the overbearing question for Christian theology was one of meaning any thinker finds in the facts of man's humanity as limited by and relative to the perspective in which he views them, Ramsdell argued for synopsis and the coherent whole which, by recognition of the above limitation, would deny an absolute rational perspective. Faith and reason, hence, are not vis-à-vis, but the former knows the gift of God and is grateful, while the latter sees that by that gift life is made whole. The question for theology is not one of rationality, but of perspectives of rationality; not faith versus reason, but faiths which define divergent perspectives of reason.

William Hordern, a Canadian by birth, succeeded Ramsdell in 1957. In that year he published the popular book noted above wherein he traced the Protestant theology until its current expression in Tillich, Niebuhr, and others. The effects of this book have been widespread in the church through its use as a study guide among laymen and college faculty.

In *The Case for a New Reformation Theology,* Hordern acknowledges his indebtedness to Ramsdell. Hordern criticizes natural theology for possessing no other models (worlds) with which to compare this cosmos, hence arguing that it cannot say much of significance. Reiterating Barth's position that man can only receive a posteriori knowledge of God, Hordern insists that revelation of God as saving-God establishes

---

[166] *Ibid.,* p. 141.
[167] "Some Comments on the Theological Scene at Drew," p. 82.

its own criteria (*sola Scriptura*), on the one hand, and affords a base for its defense (Christ is Lord) on the other. Also, anticipating Methodist readers, he urges that the neo-Reformation theology is neither unethical nor anti-ethical, but a-ethical, with a new response of faith active in love as a motivation, not of hope of reward or fear. Hordern is obviously greatly influenced by the linguistic-analysis philosophers, such as Wiggenstein and Zuurdeeg.

Outstanding among the younger Methodist theologians is Claude Welch, whose training centered at Yale University. In his first publication of note, *In This Name*, Welch perceptively stated that the Trinity was grounded in Jesus Christ and that it is not arrived at by relating this revelation with other revelations, but should be taken in and of itself as the self-revelation of God. Such statements immediately acknowledge an awareness, if not dependence, by Welch upon the thinking of Karl Barth.

More recently, after study in Germany, he published *The Reality of the Church,* a book which indicates his awareness of the problems in ecumenical theology as well as the leading theologians and their attempts to meet these problems. Welch indicates his indebtedness to the World Council of Churches 1952 Lund Report in his considerations of Christ and the Holy Spirit in the study of the church. In this book Welch insists that the tension between the humanness in the church (*congregatio*) and the church as the *corpus Christi* (*convocatio*) be maintained. The church is analogous to the Being of Christ, both human and a servant. Its life consists of recollection and expectation, and as such, it is an eschatological community. However, he goes to great lengths to insist upon the reality of the church as a social embodiment of God. "And, if the unity has its essential reality in Jesus Christ himself, we must yet interpret this in some relation to the historical process." [168]

The range and depth of Albert C. Outler's influence upon the church is almost immeasurable. Outler has largely concentrated his writings in the fields of psychology and ecumenical theology. To the former he directed his attention in *Psychotherapy and the Christian Message,* published in 1954. Intending the small book to be an essay in clarification between these two disciplines, he noted the basic misapprehensions of the practitioners each toward the other. Psychotherapy is hailed as a significant opportunity and challenge to Christian thought and examined closely as to its basic presuppositions about life, its meaning and goals. In thus defining the points of alliance and conflict between this "most

---

[168] *The Reality of the Church* (New York: Charles Scribner's Sons, 1958) , p. 63.

important of the modern sciences of man and what I believe is the truest wisdom about the nature and destiny of man," [169] Outler caustically examines the basic areas of the self and its freedom, the human quandary and possibility, and the ordering of life.

In 1957, Outler published his Richard Lectures at the University of Virginia under the title *The Christian Tradition and the Unity We Seek*. Several danger signals are pointed out which could end the ecumenical covenant—insistence upon "pure doctrine," insistence by churches that they now possess the fullness of the Body of Christ, a furtive and fresh beginning by "free churchmen" who will want to obviate ancient quarrels, or the depth of stubbornness of difficulties prompting us to resignation and the decision that the present divisions appear more tolerable than the struggle for unity. Against such desultory approaches, Outler succinctly argues that the current ecumenical quest for unity can be marked off by its close connections with the Christian sense of history, and incisively, that it "has been providentially led to recover the priority of Christian community over the principle of 'pure doctrine'—and thus has been enabled to make mutual recognition of Christians as Christians the *precondition* of ecumenical work rather than the *goal*." [170] From this a third theme or claim there emerges: the ecumenical movement has managed to restore "the ancient and crucial distinction between *the* Christian tradition which supplies our common Christian history, and the Christian traditions which have often contributed to our divisions and our separate histories as 'churches.'" [171] Outler concludes that within this great new fact in contemporary Christianity—the ecumenical movement—that which really matters is that it be diversity-in-unity and that such unity should center "in our common loyalty to God's 'tradition' of Jesus Christ and to the Spirit's 'traditioning' of Jesus Christ in the Church." [172]

Ecumenical Involvement

Welch and Outler have spearheaded theological penetration of the pressing questions of ecumenical theology: the reality and the unity of the church. Awareness of concerns generated by ecumenical encounters

[169] *Psychotherapy and the Christian Message* (New York: Harper & Brothers, 1954), p. 9.
[170] *The Christian Tradition and the Unity We Seek* (New York: Oxford University Press, 1957), p. 10.
[171] *Ibid.*
[172] *Ibid.*, p. 134.

have stimulated all the minds of Methodism's younger theologians. Of particular interest have been the attempts to delineate the peculiar Methodist theological contributions to such encounters. Methodist theologians since 1939 have played an increasingly larger role in ecumenical theology. They suggest that the note of nineteenth-century American Methodism might be raised: gracious ability. That is, as Outler has said, a salient theological motif which forms at least a part of the Methodist heritage is the "doctrine of prevenient grace as the claim of God on *all* his human creatures, which manifests itself in the incipience and ordeal of *self*-hood and in the characteristic discovery of faith that *God has already been being gracious to us,* and this prevenience of grace is the actual power that leads men to the threshold of the Gospel!" [173] *Ergo,* Methodism says we are already "on the way," and urges the precondition of recognition of Christians as Christians already, rather than seeing this as a goal toward which to move. Christians *need not* take the first step again!

That Methodism has a vital theological heritage, none will deny. That Methodism must mold itself into one dogmatic voice in theology, none will encourage or affirm. That Methodism must engage in the current ecumenical conversations, thereby becoming conscious of its theological heritage, all would hope for. The call to theological maturity and witness presents a challenge we dare not evade. Methodists share with Albert Outler the desire for a theological reconstruction in The Methodist Church,

that Methodists should come again to the firm grip and the constant interpretation in living of these great motifs of God and God in Christ, and God's grace, and man's response and man's blessedness. And this seems to me to be one of the most important prospects in contemporary theology: that a way be found that is true to the deep historic springs of the Christian tradition, and yet that does not fall into what seems to me to be the increasingly restrictive confines of the Calvinist revival. This way is open to Methodists if they will seek and walk in it.[174]

[173] Albert C. Outler, "The Methodist Contribution to the Ecumenical Discussion of the Church" (mimeographed sheet, n.d.).

[174] "Methodist Doctrine" (mimeographed lecture; Yale Divinity School, 1950), p. 7.

chapter 31

METHODISM
AND
AMERICAN
SOCIETY

1900-1939

Temperance

Immigration

Race Problems

The Labor Movement

The Social Gospel

Effects of
  World War I

I N 1900 THE UNITED STATES HAD EMERGED but recently and triumphantly from what John Hay termed our splendid little war with Spain. In 1939 there erupted in Poland a war of staggering magnitude and little splendor; twenty-eight months later the United States was a participant. The four decades bracketed by the Spanish-American War and the Second World War were for the American people ones of challenge and hope, tension and progress, growth and, above all, change. The America of 1900 was confident, unified, innocent, and secure, yet scarred with grave economic and social injustice. The America of 1939 was less optimistic, less purposefully united, aging, and anxiety-ridden, yet measurably more democratic politically, socially, and economically. In the opening forty years of the twentieth century America's wealth, population, and power mounted arithmetically. However, internal and external challenges mounted geometrically, and as mid-century approached, the American people found neither physical nor spiritual peace in their new riches and world authority.

Methodism in 1900 shared many of the characteristics of American society. By every statistical measurement, the Methodist bodies were the largest, wealthiest, and most powerful of all Protestant denominations. Despite a curious slackening of growth in the last years of the century, despite a perceptible cooling of evangelical ardor and decline of church discipline, and despite the erosion of faith under the assaults of science and scholarship and the sabotage of a pervasive materialism, Methodism faced the new century in confidence. After all, the nineteenth had been a great century for world Christianity and a glorious age for American Methodism. In truth, the American nation and the Methodist churches had marched to greatness together. Herein lay the peril. To be sure, in 1900 the danger of persecution by a powerful state, such as in a Communist or Fascist society, was nil in the United States. Yet the danger of being subtly enveloped and smothered by American society was great, precisely because unrecognized. In 1900 the identification of church with nation, of Christianity (and more especially evangelical Christianity) with Americanism, was fearfully complete. By the time of unification this old identification had been broken. Consequently Methodism no longer enjoyed the status of favored partner in the American enterprise. Paradoxically, this very loss of temporal power made possible for Methodism a new freedom and inner strength.

In this chapter an attempt will be made to relate Methodism's involvement with the course of American society in the years 1900-1939; to note how the Methodist churches contributed to the shaping of this course and were in turn molded by it. And how, in the process, the people called Methodists sought for their beloved church the fulfillment of its own unique destiny.

The story is much too full to be told in detail. Thus, this chapter of necessity will concentrate on several matters that, it is to be hoped, will illuminate the larger kaleidoscopic scene.

1

The Temperance Movement

"Methodism is Christianity in earnest," is an oft-repeated phrase sweet to the followers of Wesley and acknowledged respectfully by others. And on no public issue in the twentieth century has Methodism been more in earnest than on intemperance. Toward liquor Methodism's spirit in 1900 was Garrisonlike—"as harsh as truth, and as uncompromising as justice" —and without hypocrisy Methodists could repeat the old abolitionist's vow: "I am in earnest—I will not equivocate—I will not excuse—I will not retreat a single inch—and I will be heard." [1] Soon distillery executives were mournfully warning one another to "realize that the entire Methodist Church is a solidified, active, aggressive and obedient unit in

[1] William Lloyd Garrison, *Liberator,* January 1, 1831.

this warfare on our trade," [2] and a report to the 1908 Northern General Conference could state matter-of-factly: "The Methodist Episcopal Church is a temperance society." [3] What John Barleycorn's friends and foes alike knew to be true has not eluded the recognition of scholars. Historians of Methodism and of organized religion generally, students of American social history, and muckraking champions of "personal liberty" have all praised, blamed, or merely soberly recorded Methodism's leadership in the prohibition movement. Without this leadership and without Methodism's evangelical zeal, social passion, and organized muscle, it is doubtful if the Eighteenth Amendment would have attained even the "experimental" stage. Since the temperance crusade is a twice-told tale, and inasmuch as all observers acknowledge Methodism's crucial participation, it is unnecessary to narrate once again this important chapter in Methodist and American history.

However, if a narrative account is inappropriate, an analytical assessment is not, for no other single issue provides such illumination of Methodism's involvement in, estrangement from, and accommodation to American culture. In a very real sense and in its larger outlines, the prohibition movement reflects and reveals Methodism's hopes and fears, powers and limitations, victories and failures. Inextricably enmeshed in the prohibition struggle were issues of rural-urban strain, ethnic tension, Protestant-Catholic controversy, church-state relationship, adjustment of means to ends, individual redemption and social reform, the elation of success and the frustration of failure, and finally reconciliation to living with an intolerable situation without succumbing to despair.

Relevance to Methodist Beliefs

To begin with, "the temperance movement was in many respects the *characteristic* Methodist battle of the century, the one which most fully enlisted the interest and enthusiasm of the church and the one in which Methodism rendered one of its largest services to the nation," [4] because of its relevance to Methodist doctrines of sanctification and perfection. Men *are* made new in Christ Jesus. It *is* God's purpose that men be blessed, that they grow in grace and stature, that they become perfect in love. Those who see God, as Nels Ferré tells us, are a people who are clean unto the Lord. They are pruned trees which bear much fruit. They bear the fruit of the Spirit. Twentieth-century Methodists reaffirmed Wesley's

[2] Quoted in *The Daily Christian Advocate,* the Methodist Episcopal Church, May 4, 1936, p. 62.
[3] *The Daily Christian Advocate,* the Methodist Episcopal Church, May 27, 1908, p. 6.
[4] Halford E. Luccock, Paul Hutchinson, and Robert W. Goodloe, *The Story of Methodism* (2nd ed.; Nashville: Abingdon Press, 1949), p. 465.

faith that nothing short of perfection, Christlikeness in thought, word, and deed, can measure God's loving purpose for us.

Methodists knew that liquor thwarted God's purposes for man. Scarred personalities, rotted bodies, wasted lives—how God must weep, Methodists believed, to see this end to beings of eternal dignity and worth, created in his image and called to be his sons! Holiness of life is a gift of God, but it is also the task of man, and Methodists deemed the subjugation of liquor an integral part of this task. Much has been said of the compulsion driving men to seek refuge in the bottle; it is further necessary to recognize that their theology compelled Methodists to fight the good fight against that which cut men off from the purposes of God.

Methodists were further compelled to support prohibition out of faithfulness to the injunction to be their brothers' keepers, or, to use a less pejorative image, to be their brothers' brothers. They shunned the hospitable offer of an occasional "cheering cup," not because of the sinfulness of a single toddy, but because by practicing total abstinence they hoped to give strength to their brothers. Imbibers were fond of pointing out that alcohol in moderation made life sweeter and fairer; the only abuse lay in excessive use. Methodists acknowledged that perhaps moderate drinking was possible, but that nevertheless millions of weaker, more disturbed, more emotionally desperate and spiritually destitute brothers were crushed by liquor. Thus, must not the true Christian, though personally in control of his habits, forgo the momentary pleasure of a highball in order that his brother be not destroyed?

Nor were Methodists deceived by the boast that has returned to mock countless decent twentieth-century Americans: "I can hold my liquor. I can quit any time I want. Drink will never get the best of me." Scientific studies merely confirm what Methodists already had good reason to believe: *Every* man is a potential alcoholic; *every* man who drinks is capable of slipping beyond the point of no return. On this matter, as usual, Mr. Dooley cut through much nonsense in answering Mr. Hennessy:

"I don't believe in this here prohybition," said Mr. Hennessy. "Th' man who dhrinks moderately ought to be allowed to have what he wants."

"What is his name?" asked Mr. Dooley. "What novel is he in?" [5]

Importance in the Social Gospel

If Methodism's commitment to prohibition owed much to the theological doctrine of Christian perfection and the command to bear one another's

---

[5] Quoted in Virginius Dabney, *Dry Messiah: The Life of Bishop Cannon* (New York: Alfred A. Knopf, 1949), p. 130.

burdens, it was also indebted to the social gospel. Methodists rightly insisted that the problem of alcohol was neither a personal nor a parochial affair, but a problem as deep as human nature itself and as wide as the nation, if not the world. "All the woes of perdition lurk in the barroom," warned the Northern bishops in 1912. "All that conspires against decency of living, peace of home, good of country, progress in achievement, honor in men, purity in women, and hope in humanity, has there its haunt." [6]

To support the fact that prohibition was an integral and legitimate element of the social gospel, it may be observed that those Methodists most sensitive to the sins of society—plutocracy, slums, corruption, exploitation of labor, lynching, war, and all the rest—were the very ones most outraged by the abuses of liquor. Nor was this fact unique to Methodism. With the exception of the Protestant Episcopal, all the churches which had been permeated by the social gospel were also officially committed to prohibition. "Thus if one does not posit an element of left-wing, populistic, social-reform feeling in their prohibitionism," wrote Professor Paul Carter, "one would have considerable difficulty in explaining how the Social Gospel could have arisen in these churches at all." [7]

Psychological Motivation

A fourth point to be underscored, because it is one where prohibitionists are particularly vulnerable and their critics singularly savage, is motivation. The familiar charge goes something like this: Prohibitionists were hatchet-faced, blue-nosed, sour-visaged, lank-haired kill-joys weaned on grape juice and teethed on persimmons; their wives, mustachioed matrons who somehow attained formidable proportions on a diet of water-cress sandwiches and prune whip. These old ladies of both sexes were motived, as H. L. Mencken sneered, by the haunting fear that someone, somewhere, might be happy. Revealed a whiskey trade journal:

The professional prohibition organization is backed mainly by the Methodist Church, and that Church is opposed to allowing men any of the joys of living and any of the luxuries that go to make life worth while. If that Church had its way, all that would be left to the workmen would be to labor hard six days in

---

[6] *The Daily Christian Advocate,* the Methodist Episcopal Church, May 4, 1912, p. 100.
[7] *The Decline and Revival of the Social Gospel: Social and Political Liberalism in American Protestant Churches, 1920-1940* (Ithaca: Cornell University Press, 1956), p. 33.

the week, go to prayer-meeting on Wednesday night, and suffer the ordeal of hearing dry Methodist sermons two or three times on Sunday.[8]

These absurd charges are to be expected from brewers and their pitchmen and need not be taken seriously. Far more damaging is the fact that eminent scholars have accorded prohibitionists the same harsh treatment. Professor Richard Hofstadter termed prohibition a "ludicrous caricature of the reforming impulse, of the Yankee-Protestant notion that it is both possible and desirable to moralize private life through public action." It "was a pseudo-reform, a pinched, parochial substitute for reform which had a widespread appeal to a certain type of crusading mind." [9] Hofstadter's critical assessment has been echoed by scores of distinguished students. In truth, it is difficult to find an outstanding secular social scientist who is favorable toward prohibition. Not only so, but of greater significance, it is rare to discover such a commentator sympathetic toward the motives and character of the prohibitionists.

Is this popular picture, sanctioned by scholars, fair? Methodists know that it is not. With their bishops they could say, We "fought liquor, not because it has made men happy, but because it has made men unhappy." [10] Liquor is not life, but the enemy of life.

As to the character of the prohibitionists, were they indeed cranky professional moralists, village vigilantes, local busybodies, prudish Pecksniffs, as countless commentators from Max Lerner to Philip Wylie have insisted? Were they driven to the suppression of liquor because, by throwing themselves into this crusade against "sin," psychic tensions—especially sexual ones—were eased, as Professor Oscar Handlin and other students have implied? Perhaps the best and certainly the best-humored answer to such an "exposé" of Methodist reform zeal was given by the *Northwestern Christian Advocate:* "As the lady from Europe was told, who had spent three weeks in a thorough study of American women's clubs, 'Why, you don't know the half of it, dearie!' " [11] Was Frances E. Willard really psychopathic? Was Jane Addams suffering hallucinations, due to inner strains, when she saw hundreds of saloons and no churches in one blighted Chicago area? Are the W.C.T.U. bows of white ribbon actually subject to interpretation in terms of Freudian symbolism? Was Bishop James Cannon, Jr., unbalanced because he was deeply moved when, going to conduct the funeral service of an infant child, he found that the

---

[8] Quoted in "The Secret Is Out," New York *Christian Advocate*, January 27, 1916, p. 105.
[9] *The Age of Reform* (New York: Alfred A. Knopf, 1955), p. 287.
[10] Quoted in Carter, *Decline and Revival of the Social Gospel*, p. 57.
[11] "We Are Discovered at Last," March 25, 1926, p. 267.

besotted father had taken the clothes from the little corpse and exchanged them for whiskey, and was lying in a drunken stupor on the floor
by the infant?

No, it simply will not suffice to dismiss these Methodist crusaders as
frustrated cranks. To be sure, as all men and all reformers, they knew
subjective anxiety. But to discount entirely the very real suffering
wrought by liquor and cavalierly to ignore idealistic motives of charity
and love is to do an injustice to countless warmhearted, sweet-tempered,
self-effacing men and women. It is unnecessary to cite the self-sacrificial
careers of the Clarence True Wilsons and Frances Willards to enforce this
point. All many readers need do is to glance across the room or down
the corridor of memory to realize that the cartoon caricature of the fanatical dry is just that—a caricature far removed from the reality of loving
and beloved human beings.

The Question of State Control

There is also the question of coercion. Many personally temperate
Roman Catholics, Protestant Episcopalians, Lutherans, Unitarians, and
other Christians believed the ravages of liquor should and could be
checked through self-discipline and individual restraint. Christian ethics,
they argued, depended upon moral choice. Virtue lay in self-control in a
condition of freedom. No stars were added to a man's crown if he remained sober because the state made it impossible or unlawful to be
otherwise. Prohibition imposed from above and enforced by the state
was a denial of both political liberty and Christian freedom.

Methodists denied the validity of this position. Rather, with Bishop
Frederick Bohn Fisher they held that prohibition followed temperance
as inevitably as the dawn follows the night, and took as their watchword
the battle cry first uttered at the 1888 General Conference of Northern
Methodism: The liquor traffic can never be legalized without sin. It
was such a gross evil, so destructive of all things pertaining to human
welfare, so deleterious to the coming kingdom of God, that it should be
brought under and remain under social control. What sophistry to brand
prohibition as sumptuary legislation or an invasion of personal liberty!
Could not the same indictment be made of civil-rights legislation or traffic regulations or minimum-wage laws or safety and sanitary codes?
Methodists believed man was freer and life sweeter when the state banned
liquor, just as when the state banned slavery and dueling and narcotics.
To paraphrase Reinhold Niebuhr's famous aphorism, man's capacity

for virtue makes prohibition possible; but man's inclination to license makes prohibition necessary.

Sincere in their convictions, with firmness in the right as God gave them to see the right, Methodists threw themselves into the crusade. All the great and terrible power of the organized church was brought to bear. Every Methodist was called to be a soldier. Every unit, every agency, every instrument, of the church was pressed into service. Alliance was made with other dry forces. The Anti-Saloon League of America was founded by a Methodist and largely officered by Methodists. Northern Methodists called it "our child and our messenger";[12] and Southern Methodists, "our approved agency for active, efficient co-operation with the members of other Churches and Temperance organizations in the fight against the common enemy." [13] A famous Northern minister remembered that when he was a boy, "it seemed that God, Buffalo Bill, and Frances Willard were the three most wonderful people on the earth," [14] and a Southern minister avowed that "the Woman's Christian Temperance Union means Frances E. Willard, and Frances E. Willard means the incarnation of twentieth century Methodism." [15]

As early as 1872, Methodists made clear their intention to cast their ballots in a manner designed to put the liquor traffic in the course of ultimate extinction, and after the adoption of the Eighteenth Amendment they declared: "The law must be administered by its friends. In our States—from constable to governor—and in the nation—from revenue agent to President—officials must be selected who believe in enforcement, not only because prohibition is the law, but because it ought to be the law." [16] To the accusation that this was meddling in politics, the Northern bishops replied: "We have bad politics because so few people insist upon good politics. The sinner goeth to the primary, and the righteous hold an indignation meeting." [17] And to the charge of lobbying, a Methodist editor replied:

The chief things we are accused of promoting at Washington are Prohibition and peace. Think of it! With the munitions lobby, the tariff lobby, the power

[12] *The Daily Christian Advocate*, the Methodist Episcopal Church, May 27, 1912, p. 666.

[13] *The Daily Christian Advocate*, the Methodist Episcopal Church, South, May 19, 1926, p. 104.

[14] Ernest Fremont Tittle, "Frances Willard," MS, sermon delivered October, 1, 1939.

[15] *The Daily Christian Advocate*, the Methodist Episcopal Church, South, May 17, 1898, p. 3.

[16] *Journal of the General Conference of the Methodist Episcopal Church, South*, 1926, p. 292.

[17] *Journal of the General Conference of the Methodist Episcopal Church*, 1924, p. 187.

lobby, the alien lobby, the oil lobby and others as odorous at work more under cover than in the open, with fifty dollars to the church's one, the only lobby which is denounced as an enemy of the republic is guilty of working openly for a sober nation and a warless world! And the accusers remain at liberty, as if they were mentally competent.[18]

The Failure of Prohibition

Protestantism and more especially Methodism won a great victory with the adoption of the Eighteenth Amendment in 1919. Thus far an attempt has been made to show that for Methodists national prohibition was the logical fruit of their perfectionist theology, their concern for their brother, their social passion which sought the approximation of the kingdom of God. The typical temperance crusader was not a bigot but an idealist who desired to liberate men from the bondage of drink. Methodists believed control by the state as appropriate here as in any area of social justice.

Yet, in slightly over a decade the national prohibition experiment was abandoned. Did repeal mark the triumph of the children of darkness over the children of light? Was prohibition doomed from the onset by an Aristotelian fatal flaw? Were the crusaders themselves partially responsible for the destruction of their own handiwork? Or did the experiment, noble in purpose, fail because of a combination of these and other reasons?

To begin with, we can dismiss without discussion such absurdities as Mencken's charge that the Eighteenth Amendment caused human suffering comparable to the Black Death or the Thirty Years' War, and Herbert Asbury's twin symbols of prohibition, the Tommy gun and the poisoned cup. Isn't it comforting to be informed that the Dry Decade was somehow unique in spawning gangsters, racketeers, triggermen, venal judges, corrupt police, crooked politicians, lawless citizens? Isn't it grand how these elements disappeared from American society with repeal?

On the other hand, the drys are not correct in the contention that a powerful wet lobby effected repeal against the true wishes of the American people. Ironically, this is reminiscent of the false charge that prohibition in the first instance was foisted upon the country while the "boys were in France." It is probably, though paradoxically, true that a bare majority of Americans were willing to accept prohibition in the beginning, but that a larger majority willed its death at the end. Why

[18] "The Chicago Tribune and the Churches," *Northwestern Christian Advocate,* February 7, 1929, p. 124.

should this be? What truths about the nature of American society, of Methodism, and of prohibition does this reveal?

In the first place, prior to World War I, Protestantism in general and Methodism in particular still could count upon its historic position as the accepted senior partner in the national culture. The Eighteenth Amendment was a stunning vindication of the conviction that what was good for evangelical Protestantism was good for the country. In prohibition the Protestant ethos and the American creed, Methodists believed, met in prideful identification. It was a reassuring sign that America was moving toward the Protestant vision of the perfect society and that the reins of power and hence control of direction still remained in Protestant hands. At that very moment, however, discerning Methodists felt the reins slipping. Historic processes were at work that in time—and it was really not very long—were to reduce evangelical Protestantism to the status of an estranged though vital partner in a pluralistic society.

Historically Methodism's strength and the heart of prohibitionist fervor had been in country and village. Yet the noble experiment was launched when the tides of population, power, and prestige were running heavily to the city. This is not to say that urban America was devoid of prohibition sentiment. Rather, it is to say that rural America was the vital center and that as the older, pastoral America suffered erosion, so did the chances of successful prohibition. As the dry cause was symbolized by the sturdy Yankee yeoman, erect in field or village green, unspotted from the urban world, the wet incubus was symbolized by the ignorant immigrant proletarian slouched in factory or saloon. If somehow the Alfred Emanuel Smiths could have been transmuted into William Jennings Bryans, then prohibition might have succeeded. As it was, the issue of drink exacerbated rural-urban, old-line Yankee-immigrant tensions. The legislative superintendent of the Anti-Saloon League warned in 1917 that the Eighteenth Amendment had to pass before 1920, because "when 1920 comes and reapportionment is here, forty new wet Congressmen will come from the great wet centers with their rapidly increasing population." [19] In this sense, prohibition was enacted at the last possible moment in American history. In another sense, it was enacted too late to receive the overwhelming popular support necessary to enforcement.

Prohibition thus illuminates rural-urban, "old" American versus "new" American tensions. Additionally, it contributed to Protestant-Catholic-Jew strains. To be sure, some Catholics and some Jews supported it. But only the Protestant churches as churches officially indorsed the Eighteenth

[19] Quoted in Carter, *Decline and Revival of the Social Gospel*, p. 37.

Amendment. It is important to make clear that Methodists did not dis-favor liquor because it was often the beverage of Catholic immigrants. Rather, the fact that Methodism was dry and Catholicism was not simply widened a breech already sufficiently serious because of more funda-mental differences.

There are other, less crucial explanations for the failure of prohibition. For instance, if the temperance passion grew largely out of Christian compassion for the victims of drink, it was also streaked by an ugly vein of pharisaism. Although wets minimized the compassion and maximized the pharisaism, nonetheless the flaw was there. The vocabulary of the movement was militaristic. The wet "monsters of iniquity" would be "crushed" by the dry "soldiers of righteousness." To put the nation under prohibition, affirmed a speaker before the 1916 Northern General Con-ference, would mean

a new national preparedness, compared to which "watchful waiting" is creep-ing paralysis, and great standing armies and great fleets of dreadnoughts and everything else are flimsy toys. It means, above all, a Pentecost of divine mobili-zation, in which Christian men of many tongues will speak as one voice, at the polls, and a flame of patriotic enthusiasm will leap from the head of a real "church militant," armed with breechloading opinions, and independent bal-lots—the white bayonets of peace and good will toward men—that will assert and guarantee the right of Christian "kultur" to "a place in the sun," and make her a victor instead of a victim, in elections—a mundane locomotive, instead of a heavenly windmill, in the actual redemption of the world." [20]

One prohibitionist, forgetting the example of his Redeemer, growled that he would prefer the association of a hog to that of a winebibber. Perhaps the example is extreme, yet when the 1912 Northern General Conference was informed that in Kansas second offenders of the dry laws were sent to the penitentiary, the delegates cried, "Hurrah!" and "Good!"

In this connection it is sad that a movement designed to make men nobler should have been burdened in 1917-18 with the argument that sober soldiers made the fiercest fighters, that only clear-eyed young men could sight their rifles with deadly accuracy.

As the prohibition arguments were sometimes loveless, so some of the movement's leaders appear (at least, to the historian at long range) un-lovely. A few perhaps forgot the words of George Santayana: "Neither prosperity nor empire nor heaven can be worth winning at the price of a virulent temper, bloody hands, an anguished spirit, and a vain hatred

[20] *The Daily Christian Advocate*, the Methodist Episcopal Church, May 10, 1916, p. 166.

of the rest of the world." [21] Although Southern Methodism's sturdiest prohibition champion, Bishop Cannon, faced many false and cruel slanders, it is not irrelevant that one of his own brethren could charge him with an infirmity: "The infirmity to which I allude," said the accuser before the 1934 General Conference, "and I am going to be specific, is a love of power." [22]

Akin to this flaw was the prohibitionist's tendency to view history as a conspiracy. Methodist literature teems with references to a sinister "liquor traffic" and powerful "liquor barons." In advancing this conspiratorial interpretation, Methodists made the crucial mistake of underestimating the strength of the wets. The illusion is not unique. Pacifists believed a warless world hinged on the elimination of "merchants of death." Progressives believed a poverty-free world hinged on busting trusts and controlling "robber barons." Missing from the assessment is the key fact that the liquor traffic (as the slave trade) and the "liquor barons" (as the slave traders) survived only because they fulfilled a need and performed a function made possible and profitable through the support of large elements of society.

In turn akin to the conspiratorial view was the utopian view of history. A report to the 1912 Northern General Conference stated hopefully:

> Methodism, the ancient and consistent foe of the iniquitous liquor traffic, is girding herself anew for the war. Enthused, united, inspired, invincible, she goes forth to do battle for her Lord. Nor will she order a halt until the last battle is fought, the last victory won, and the white flag of temperance be flung to the breeze from the last redoubt of this arch enemy of all that is right and pure and good.[23]

And when prohibition was adopted, Methodists were informed: "The victory is as decisive as it is glorious." [24] It is understandable that American Methodists should sniff final and total victory. After all, Northern Methodists in 1916 were assured that the British Empire would soon be bone-dry ("The applause was deafening and continued for a long time") .[25] After all, Southern Methodists were informed that Russia had prohibited the use of vodka, France the use of absinthe, and "Eng-

---

[21] From "On Fanaticism," reprinted in an undated pamphlet by *The New Republic*.
[22] *The Daily Christian Advocate*, the Methodist Episcopal Church, South, May 4, 1934, p. 68.
[23] *The Daily Christian Advocate*, the Methodist Episcopal Church, May 13, 1912, p. 290.
[24] *Ibid.*, May 17, 1920, p. 329.
[25] *Ibid.*, May 4, 1916, p. 49.

land has, in a way, established prohibition among her soldiers." [26] Because Methodists anticipated the foe's unconditional surrender, they were unprepared to fight a guerrilla war after the presumed final victory in 1919. There was a natural decline in temperance education. It seemed an anomaly to press temperance education upon a society which had outlawed liquor. To do so would be to proceed on the assumption that the law was being widely violated. Thus, in the 1920's Methodist expectations proved utopian.

Complacency was not the only unfortunate result of the adoption of the Eighteenth Amendment. Humanitarian concern for the drunkard as victim was replaced by indignation at the drinker as criminal. "The fact of being in authority," believed Professor Paul Carter, "and armed with the law did more . . . to divorce prohibitionism from its own humane, reformist, Populist-Progressive roots than any other single cause." [27] In the 1920's the expressions of hostility toward lawbreakers were frightening in their intensity. In fact, the Northern General Conference memorialized Congress to enact a law "to deport aliens upon the second conviction for violation of our prohibition and narcotic laws"; [28] and it was suggested, though not carried, that native-born citizens be disenfranchised after three liquor convictions.

The dry cause was not made less vulnerable when some Methodists, emboldened by their success in placing liquor under the ban of law, demanded legislation in other areas. Read a report to the 1924 Northern General Conference:

The prize-fight will be outlawed, the stage cleaned up, the moving picture films regulated, gambling under the ban of law. . . . A wave of Americanism which has receded will come back enthroning the Bible in the Public Schools and the American Sabbath on its American foundations again as it was before the German-American Alliance and the Brewers' Association trampled this institution of our fathers into the mire, and the Puritan principles about the cleanness of home life, the freedom of the ballot box, the little red school house teaching morality and respect for religion as well as the principles of education, will be pedestaled in triumph.[29]

Indeed, it was urged by at least some Methodists that there be placed under state-enforced prohibition everything from tobacco to terpsichore.

[26] "The War and Temperance," Nashville Christian Advocate, November 20, 1914, p. 4.
[27] Decline and Revival of the Social Gospel, p. 38.
[28] The Daily Christian Advocate, the Methodist Episcopal Church, May 10, 1924, p. 262.
[29] Ibid., May 9, 1924, p. 227.

Let the issue be clearly stated. It was right that Methodists be concerned with the question of how a Christian employs his leisure. It was proper that a Christian avoid brutalizing amusement. It was good that a Christian enjoy recreation that re-creates rather than debilitates. This subject was discussed in meetings of all branches of Methodism, sometimes providing "The Hottest Contest of the Session," [30] and was widely debated in the Methodist press. Though Methodism proscribed many amusements with greater precision and severity than other denominations, the Methodist Churches returned increasingly, as the century deepened, to Wesley's wise and broad standard: the indulgence in only such diversions as can be used in the name of the Lord Jesus. In setting high standards of conduct for its own members, Methodism was wise. In attempting to impose these standards on all Americans through state-enforced legislation, however, the church was unwise, for this gave color to the charge that the proscription of liquor was only the first step toward the total regimentation of American moral life. Methodists were thus tempted to use the arm of the state to suppress evils less fundamental and less clearly social than drink.

They were further tempted, as all crusaders, to justify the use of unworthy ends in their zeal to attain a noble goal. Though few Methodists could say with William E. ("Pussyfoot") Johnson, "I had to lie, bribe, and drink to put over prohibition in America," [31] perhaps not a few succumbed to the rationalization of tarnished methods. When "extremism was hardly a possibility on this subject," [32] then is it really surprising that extreme means were sometimes employed? It is unnecessary to comment on the dangerous pragmatism lurking in the advice of a 1908 Northern General Conference speaker: "Wisdom requires the adoption of a plan which will secure to that end [prohibition] the cooperation of every man who desires that thing, REGARDLESS OF WHAT HE THINKS ABOUT ANYTHING ELSE." [33]

It remains to mention the last, great flaw in the prohibition movement. Originally an integral and legitimate element in the social gospel, for some Methodists prohibition became in time the *only* component in social Christianity; it evolved from a worthy cause to The Cause. To borrow an allusion from the free-silver movement, prohibition was a cowbird nudging other reforms from the social-gospel nest. At Northern

[30] *Ibid.*, May 28, 1900, p. 354.

[31] Quoted in Dabney, *Dry Messiah*, p. 136.

[32] *The Daily Christian Advocate*, the Methodist Episcopal Church, South, May 9, 1902, p. 6.

[33] *The Daily Christian Advocate*, the Methodist Episcopal Church, May 13, 1908, p. 4.

Methodism's 1908 General Conference the portions of the Pastoral Address dealing with prohibition touched off a scene "which for enthusiasm and thrilling effect has seldom been exceeded in that body."

A tumultuous and long continued applause followed these words, and as it continued, the whole vast audience sprang to their feet and soon the people were waving their handkerchiefs till the great hall was an ocean beyond description. Scarcely had the audience at last subsided to their seats, when some one started "America," and again every one on the platform, men and women, everywhere in the hall were on their feet. Then followed "Our God is Marching On." The singing was a little less than rapturous. No one who was present will ever forget that scene.[34]

It would not have mattered if they had, for the scene was repeated at the next General Conference. In truth, such a response was commonplace among Methodists everywhere, in General Conference, Annual Conference, or congregational assembly. A bishop boasted:

So intense is the conviction of the Methodist preacher concerning the rum abomination, and so susceptible is he to an emotional appeal, that the dullest official speech-maker, failing to arouse interest in behalf of his cause, is sure to turn aside temporarily to the temperance question, and seldom fails to start a tempest of enthusiasm which carries him triumphantly across the barren spot in his discourse, and makes his effort a rhetorical success.[35]

In a puzzled mood a great Methodist preacher recalled that, though his ministry had extended over thirty years to one congregation and though his sermons were widely admired for their strength and social passion, only on one occasion had his people interrupted a sermon with applause: this in response to a reference to the evils of drink.

All this is not to denigrate the true worth of the prohibition passion. It is to observe in sadness that no other crusade—to end poverty, war, segregation—compelled such universal dedication from Methodists. Prohibition was a jealous mistress. It demanded total commitment; it tolerated no halfheartedness; it lured men away from other reforms; and it involved Methodists in dangerous games, most notably the election of 1928.

On April 7, 1933, beer was once again legally consumed in nineteen states and the District of Columbia. Prohibitionists faced their Appomattox. Weary, perplexed, and grieved, their spirits were yet unbroken. They would have understood the mood of the ragged veteran of the Army

---

[34] *Ibid.*, May 8, 1908, p. 2.
[35] *Ibid.*, May 11, 1916, p. 177.

WORTH M. TIPPY
Pastor
JOHN G. SCHAIBLY
Assistant Pastor

CHURCH OFFICE:
DAILY HOURS, 9:00 A. M.—5 P. M.
TELEPHONES, BELL, EAST 1002 J
CUYAHOGA, CENTRAL 2128 L

EPWORTH MEMORIAL
METHODIST EPISCOPAL CHURCH
PROSPECT AVENUE AND
EAST 55TH STREET . . .

MRS. M. M. McKENZIE
Office Secretary
MRS. EVA B. PALMER
Sunday-School Visitor
MARY AGNES GRIFFIN
Editorial Secretary
E. LOUISE WILLMOTT
Deaconess
C. W. SUTTON
Financial Secretary.

CLEVELAND November 27, 1907

Dear Sir and Brother :

Complete arrangements have now been made for the conference in Washington, on Tuesday and Wednesday, December third and fourth, to consider the organization of a Methodist Union for Social Service. A careful program has been planned, with ample provision for discussion. The sessions will be held in the Ebbitt House, where special rates have been secured.

The conference will open Tuesday morning at ten o'clock, and adjourn in time for the opening of the national convention of the City Evangelization Union, in Baltimore, Wednesday afternoon. It is hoped that the members of the conference will be presented to the President on Tuesday or Wednesday.

I am gratified to say that a sufficient number of influential ministers and laymen of the church have agreed to be present to assure the success of the conference, and also that the call has received the unqualified approval of all who have replied to the Secretary.

It is the hope of the committee that nothing will deter those who have consented to attend the conference ; that a few who could not give definite answers, will be able to come ; and that some, whose engagements necessitated a negative answer, may find it possible at the eleventh hour to get away.

Very truly yours,

Worth M. Tippy

November 11, 1907.

Mr. J. R. Joy,

New York, N. Y.

My Dear Jim:-

The enclosed circular will explain itself. The suggestion made has met with the heartiest response wherever it has been mentioned. I write this personal word only to say that in my judgment this movement may mean something large for the Methodist Church, and for the Kingdom of God. If it is in any way possible for you to adjust your plans so as to be present at this first meeting, I sincerely hope that you will do so. Special hotel rates have been granted. Will you kindly write Mr. Tippy as to the probability of your being with us?

Cordially yours,

Herbert Welch

---

1. The beginnings of the Methodist Federation for Social Service

(papers in The Methodist Publishing House Library, Nashville)

Methodist Publishing Through the Years

PICTURE LESSON PAPER

Lost!

One pair of bright eyes,
Two dimples so merry,
One clear, sunny brow,
One mouth like a cherry.

O! sad are we now,
For our darling Kitty
Has gone to Cross-land;
It is such a pity!

4. A page from *Picture Lesson Paper*, June, 1877

ACCOUNT OF THE HAPPY DEATH

OF

CAROLINE ANNE SMITH,

BY THE REV. ADAM CLARKE, LL. D.

" A young saint, an old devil," was a maxim of such unaccountable prevalence formerly, that

3. Happy deaths of Christian children were a favorite subject during these early years. This account, by a distinguished author, is from the *Sunday School and Youth's Library*, 1829.

THE CHILD'S MAGAZINE.

No. 7.   JANUARY, 1828.   Vol. 1.

THE FIRST SABBATH OF THE YEAR.

" A happy new year to you," said James Brown to his school fellow, Thomas Jones, as they met in their way to the Sunday school.

2. The solid success of Methodist publications over the years has been due, in large part, to their flexibility—to their ability to change as the ages changed, and to both lead and reflect the spirit of the times. *The Child's Magazine* was one of the earliest Methodist publications for children.

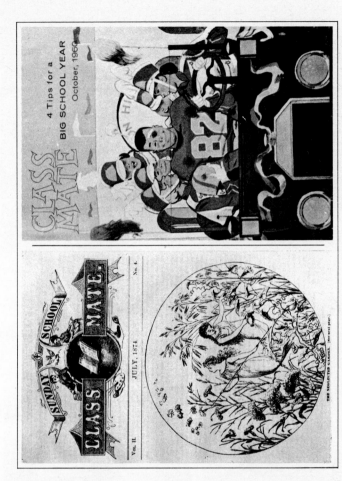

5. A page from *Pictures and Stories*, November 4, 1956

6. *Classmate* is one of the oldest Sunday school publications still in existence. In October, 1960, the format "whistled" to modern young people.

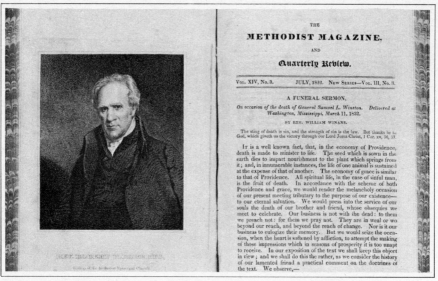

7. *The Methodist Magazine and Quarterly Review*—perhaps the most influential of all Methodist periodicals (1818-1932). The engraving is of Bishop Robert R. Roberts.

THE UTTERANCES OF NATURE.—The mind that has been attentive to the voice of nature, and the heart that has felt the power of her utterances, will respond to this beautiful passage from Whittier:

There is a religion in every thing around us, a calm and holy religion in the unbreathing things of nature, which man would do well to imitate. It is a meek and blessed influence, stealing, as it were, unawares upon the heart. It comes—it has no terror, no gloom in its approaches. It has not to rouse up the passions; it is untrammeled, unled by the creeds, and unshadowed by the superstitions of man. It is fresh from the hands of the Author, and glowing from the

WONDERS OF CHEMISTRY.—Science is full of wonders, but chemistry is the science of wonders. The following from Lyon Playfair will awake curiosity:

The horseshoe nails dropped in the streets during the daily traffic reappear in the form of swords and guns. The clippings of the traveling tinker are mixed with the parings of horses' hoofs from the smithy, or the cast-off woolen garments of the poorest inhabitants of a sister isle, and soon afterward, in the form of dyes of brightest blue, grace the dress of courtly dames. The main ingredient of the ink

© 1958 by Lovick Pierce

8. The *Ladies' Repository* in 1860 carried this type of material for families (the illustration is of "Benevolence"). Its descendant is *Together*, the family magazine for Methodists developed in 1956.

Two of Methodism's great ecumenical leaders
of the twentieth century: John R. Mott, a layman,
and Bishop G. Bromley Oxnam.

9. This picture of Mott (r.), with George K. A.
Bell, Bishop of Chichester (l.), was taken at the
meeting of the Central Committee of the World
Council of Churches, Toronto, 1950.

10. Bishop Oxnam (l.) and Geoffrey Fisher, Archbishop of Canter-
bury (r.), Evanston, 1954.

The Churches of Methodism

11. The seven ages of McKendree Church, Nashville, Tennessee (used by permission of Cullen T. Carter). The changing tastes in Methodist architecture can be traced for over a century in the buildings of this one church.

12. The Strawbridge Church, Sam's Creek, Maryland

(drawing by T. C. Ruckle, from Roberts, *Centenary Album*)

13. The interior of St. George's, Philadelphia, a beautiful example of colonial church architecture

14. St. Timothy's Methodist Church, Cedar Falls, Iowa

15. Dr. John F. Goucher, standing in the pulpit used by Robert Strawbridge, and Bishop Earl Cranston, seated, lead the opening worship service at the first meeting of the Joint Commission on Unification, Baltimore, 1916

(photograph from Lovely Lane Museum)

16. Methodist Unification. This photograph was taken at the last General Conference of the Methodist Episcopal Church, South. The Plan of Union had been ratified the day before, April 29, 1938, and the leaders of the three churches posed for this historic picture.

(photograph courtesy of Bishop James H. Straughn)

of Northern Virginia who grasped Lee's hand and said softly: "Goodbye, General. God bless you. We will go home, make three more crops, and try them again."

If the Civil War ultimately became a "lost cause" for Lee's veteran, throughout the remainder of the 1930's and up to and beyond unification, the Methodist Episcopal, Methodist Episcopal, South, and Methodist Protestant churches refused to admit that the prohibition fight was irretrievably lost; and they adhered to the standard of personal abstinence and state control.

2

The Challenge of Immigration

We have seen how the provisional failure of the crusade against spirituous liquor was, as Methodists believed, a checkmate to the cause of Christ. Additionally, the failure was symbolic of substantive changes in the nature of the American people. It is to a crucial aspect of this transformation that we now turn.

"My country in 1900 is something totally different from my own country of 1860," lamented Henry Adams. "I am wholly a stranger in it." [36] Adams' sense of estrangement from the land he loved was not a pose, for the America of William McKinley was a million light-years from the America of President John Adams and President John Quincy Adams and even President Lincoln, under whom Henry's father had served with the devotion and distinction expected from an Adams. Yet, if Henry Adams viewed the past in a bittersweet mood, he looked to the future with foreboding. "The child born in 1900," he predicted, "would . . . be born into a new world which would not be a unity but a multiple." [37] When Adams died in 1918, the unity of Christendom, symbolized for him in the Virgin Mary, was shattered, and the unity of America, symbolized for us in William McKinley, was eroded. Dean Inge has Adam (not Adams) remarking to Eve: "You know, my dear, we live in an age of transition." The perception that all generations endure the shock of change, however, should not obscure the further truth that the trauma was uncommonly severe for twentieth-century Americans.

[36] Worthington Chauncey Ford, ed., *The Letters of Henry Adams* (1892-1918) (Boston: Houghton, Mifflin, 1938), II, 279-80.
[37] *The Education of Henry Adams* (Boston: Houghton, Mifflin, 1927), p. 53.

In 1900 the Republican candidate for the presidency, of Scotch-Irish descent, born in the Methodist stronghold of Ohio, and of deep Methodist loyalties, defeated William Jennings Bryan, the very embodiment of midwestern, agrarian, old-stock, evangelical Protestantism, after Bryan had wrested Populist-Democratic leadership from a devout Methodist layman, General James B. Weaver. McKinley's running mate, though termed a "damn cowboy" in the circles of corporate power, was eminently satisfactory to many Methodists, for had not Theodore Roosevelt singled out Methodism as the greatest and most representative church in America? And he was to address the Northern General Conference in these warming words:

The Methodist Church plays a great part in many lands; and yet I think I can say that in none other has it played so great and peculiar a part as here in the United States. Its history is indissolubly interwoven with the history of our country for the six score years since the constitutional convention made us really a nation. Methodism in America entered on its period of rapid growth just about the time of Washington's first presidency. Its essential democracy, its fiery and restless energy of spirit, and the wide play that it gave to individual initiative, all tended to make it peculiarly congenial to a hardy and virile folk, democratic to the core, prizing individual independence above all earthly possessions, and engaged in the rough and stern work of conquering a continent.[38]

On September 6, 1901, William McKinley was felled by an assassin's bullet fired by a twenty-eight-year-old Polish-American with the "sinister" name of Czolgosz, probably an anarchist and certainly not a Methodist. Though the mortally wounded President pleaded, "Go easy with him, boys," [39] Czolgosz, the "poor misguided fellow" (to use his victim's words), was claimed by the electric chair. To many good citizens, McKinley's destruction foreshadowed that of all Anglo-Saxon, Protestant, pioneer Americans should the country continue to be flooded by "mongrel" worshipers of Bacchus or Baal or the Whore of Babylon—or Marx. This nightmare steeled good men to pagan acts of discrimination, exclusion, deportation, and violence. By mid-century the "new barbarians" prevailed. America, once the kingdom of the McKinleys and Bryans and Weavers, had given her most honored keys to John Fitzgerald Kennedy. "Protestant America is now as obsolete as the side-wheel showboat, the cigar-store Indian, or the Fourth of July oration," pronounced a Protes-

[38] *The Daily Christian Advocate*, the Methodist Episcopal Church, May 19, 1908, p. 5.
[39] Quoted in Walter Lord, *The Good Years* (New York: Harper & Brothers, 1960), p. 51.

tant spokesman at mid-century.[40] And at mid-century, also, a Roman Catholic historian felt free to observe:

Protestantism—especially American Protestantism—is now so doctrinally decayed as to be incapable of offering any serious opposition to the sharp sword of the Spirit, as soon as we can make up our minds to use it. Except for isolated "fundamentalists,"—and these are pretty thoroughly discredited and without intellectual leadership—Catholicism could cut through Protestantism as through so much butter.[41]

Yet if in one sense the nightmare became a reality—if the sons of Puritan New England and of frontier camp meetings did indeed see their commanding position in society evaporate—in a more crucial sense the reality was not quite nightmarish after all. Perhaps Henry Adams was wrong. Perhaps there were gains as well as losses in passing from a unitary to a pluralistic culture. Perhaps it was not unbearable for the William McKinleys to share power with the John Kennedys. Perhaps the values of a Bryan and an Abraham Ribicoff were not mutually exclusive. To be sure, Methodism endured an alienation from American society at mid-century that she had not known in the palmy days of McKinley. However, perhaps in this new tension with society Methodism could be truer to her best self and speak with greater revelance to a broken world than in that earlier age when Methodism and Americanism were considered identical. In truth, though in 1900 Methodists were quite pridefully aware of their conquest of a continent, they were innocent of the humbling awareness that they also had been seductively enveloped by a culture.

Historians of immigration make much of the "shock of alienation" experienced by the "uprooted" as they migrated from the womblike warmth and psychological security of their familiar European villages to the cold, strange New World. These insights are altogether valid, for the immigrant's ordeal was seldom physically easy and never emotionally trivial. The obverse side of the coin, however, has been turned by fewer historians. How does a man—or a church—accustomed to power and prestige, respond when strangers enter the land to dethrone him? How does a man—or a church—cherishing deeply felt values respond when strangers enter the land to destroy these values? How does a man—or a church —confident that his dreams for society accord with divine favor, respond when strangers enter the land carrying different and repugnant blueprints for society? A vital chapter in Methodism's history in the United

---

[40] Martin E. Marty, *The New Shape of American Religion* (New York: Harper & Brothers, 1958), p. 72.

[41] Quoted in Robert T. Handy, "The American Religious Depression, 1925-1935," *Church History*, March, 1960, p. 14.

States centers on the church's response to the ethnic and religious transformation of American society in the twentieth century.

Changing Immigration Patterns

Between the year William McKinley enlisted as a private in the 23rd Ohio Volunteer Infantry and his re-election to the presidency in 1900 (he was the last Civil War veteran to occupy the White House), fourteen million immigrants came to the United States. Between the last shot at Appomattox and Czolgosz' two shots, the annual number of entrants exceeded 400,000 in sixteen of the years. Until the last decade of the century, the majority of the uprooted stemmed from the traditional sources of the British Isles, Germany, and Scandinavia. Then "new" immigrants from Southern and Eastern Europe—Italians, Slavs, Magyars, Jews— formerly a trickle, became a torrent, accounting for over 50 per cent of the total.

In 1900 one third of the nation's population of 75,000,000 consisted of the foreign-born or the children of foreign-born. Of the 65,000,000 Americans whom the census classified as white, only 40,000,000 were the children of native-born parents. In the twelve largest cities, immigrants constituted over 40 per cent of the inhabitants. In the 547 cities of 8,000 or more, foreigners by birth or parentage comprised over two thirds of the total. For one year only, 1899, the federal immigration authorities compiled a record of the religious affiliation of immigrants. They were divided: Roman Catholics, 52.1 per cent; Protestants, 18.5 per cent; Jewish, 10.4 per cent; Greek Orthodox, 4 per cent; Brahmins and Buddhists, 0.9 per cent; miscellaneous, 13.9 per cent. If this was typical, little wonder that the Roman Catholic Church gained in membership 114.1 per cent from 1890 to 1916, for immigration accelerated rather than slackened in the opening years of the twentieth century. In the period prior to the outbreak of World War I, an average of 1,000,000 immigrants entered the United States annually. And now those coming from Italy, Poland, Austria, Russia, Greece, and the Balkans accounted for 72 per cent of the total. The immigrant impulse was temporarily blocked by the war. After silence fell on the western front, it burst anew with even greater force. From June, 1920, to June, 1921, more than 800,000 persons poured into the country, and consuls in Europe reported that millions more were planning to leave. Then, in one of the most momentous enactments in American history, Congress virtually closed the gates, and the Statue of Liberty lost all relevance save for returning tourists—and a handful of immigrants. (Probably the whole twenty-five year period after 1925 saw fewer immigrants to the United States than the single year 1907.)

These unadorned statistics provide a backdrop to our sketch of how Methodism came to a new understanding of a crucial aspect of the nature of American society, and, of not less importance, of the image that Methodists had of their own church. In 1900 the "new" immigrants, despite their number, were of minority status in the national consciousness. The senior partner in the American enterprise was still the old-stock Protestant. The enterprise was soon to be placed (as the minority groups believed) on a more democratic basis.

For a variety of reasons Methodism was ill prepared to minister to the uprooted. For one thing, by 1900 Methodism had become a church of the older immigration—English, Scottish and Scotch-Irish, German, Dutch, and Scandinavian—whereas increasingly the "new" immigrants came from Southern and Eastern Europe. To be sure, Methodism received limited reinforcements from Canada and the British Isles, but this fact did not alter the basic trend. For another thing, by 1900 Methodism's greatest strength was in country, village, and town, whereas the "new" immigrants centered in the largest cities, especially those near ports of debarkation. Then, too, by 1900 most Methodists were members of the middle and upper-middle classes. This is not to say that the church embraced only the very wealthy. On the contrary, hard-scrabble southern and western farmers remained an important element, as did hard-pressed white-collar salaried employees and the more skilled blue-collar workers. Yet, if not wealthy, most Methodists worked at respectable trades (including farming) and professions, whereas the "new" immigrants provided the muscle for the toughest, least skilled, and lowest paid labor. Lastly, Methodism was handicapped in reaching the immigrants because the majority of them were rooted in a religious tradition hostile to Protestantism. Thus, sociological and psychological barriers separated the church from the newcomers. Ethnic exclusiveness, physical isolation, and class pride combined with objective religious differences to segregate the immigrant.

Despite the formidable obstacles, Methodism made a mighty effort to break the barriers. This magnificent story of home missions, church extension, urban evangelism, and compassionate charity—and charity in the sense of self-sacrificial love rather than merely almsgiving—is told elsewhere. It is a thrilling tale and one Methodists may rightfully cherish.

Unhappily, however, it is a story ignored by most students of immigration and nativism. Frequently these scholars lay major responsibility for bigotry and discrimination at the door of the Protestant churches. Even the sympathetic observer Will Herberg believes the Protestant approach to the immigrant and his urban problems has been that of "morally sensitive middle-class people striving to do something for the 'underprivileged.' The spirit of *noblesse oblige* and Christian charity are curiously compounded in this concern, but there is little trace either of the evangelical fervor or of the movement from within the people themselves that won the continent for Christianity." [42]

In the next few pages let us see if the Methodist attitude toward the "new" immigrant was completely dominated by hate, fear, or, at best, condescension. The evidence to the contrary is voluminous, and only a few isolated, though not unrepresentative, examples of Methodist concern and compassion can be cited.

ORIENTALS

To begin with, many Methodists said with Oliver Wendell Holmes: "We are the Romans of the modern world, the great assimilating people." They read Israel Zangwill's drama *The Melting Pot* and recalled the ancient national vision within which America was creating the future by blending all races. The darkest shadow across the sunny face of this dream was cast by immigrants from the Orient. If most Americans and probably most Methodists believed the assimilation of Chinese and Japanese immigrants especially troublesome, nonetheless, after the Civil War, Methodists established missions to minister to these groups; and when mobs of San Francisco bravoes hunted their helpless prey, the Methodist Mission House offered sanctuary. Early in the twentieth century much of the Methodist press protested both mob violence and official discrimination. For example, when Japanese children were excluded from the San Francisco public schools, the Nashville *Christian Advocate* held "it would be better for all concerned if they were allowed to go to the American schools." [43] As to the Oriental-exclusion laws in force, this journal termed them "an anachronism and a shame." [44] Inasmuch as these views were held by a paper published in a section of the country allegedly devoted to the maintenance of Anglo-Saxon purity, it is not surprising to find the Methodist press in the North repeatedly flaying anti-Oriental discrimination.

This attitude was paralleled in conference action. For instance, prior to the end of the nineteenth century the California Conference voiced opposition to discriminatory restrictions on Chinese immigrants, and early in the new century the Southern General Conference resolved that the Chinese and Japanese be not treated by the authorities with "in-

[42] *Protestant, Catholic, Jew* (Garden City, N. Y.: Doubleday & Co., 1955), p. 135.
[43] "The Japanese in San Francisco," November 16, 1906, p. 5.
[44] "Extraterritoriality," July 12, 1906, p. 5.

justice or discourtesy." [45] Two years later the Northern bishops claimed "for the immigrants from Eastern Asia who are already here, and for those who lawfully come, the most just and equitable treatment. Especially do we insist upon protection for them from the mob spirit." [46] In 1920 the bishops again recognized that "the world is not a white man's world" and admonished Methodists to "think straight about races clear round the world. Talk of 'lesser breeds,' inferior castes, talk even of 'white man's burdens' is not for us today. We must not shut any door of hope in any face of any color." [47]

Festering prejudice against the Orientals reached a climax with the immigration act of 1924. Earlier action had blocked Chinese and effectively curbed Japanese immigration, but now Congress in its ineluctable wisdom effected total exclusion. In exchange for the dubious benefit of barring some 250 Japanese annually from entering the country, Congress gratuitously insulted a proud and sensitive people, seriously hindered Christian missions, strengthened the hand of anti-American militarists, and laid a plank in the long road to Pearl Harbor. Methodists recognized folly when they saw it. The 1924 Northern General Conference adopted a two-page resolution prepared by the superintendent of the Pacific Japanese Mission, criticizing the proposed exclusion act, and mailed copies to every congressman. "As Christians," read the resolution, "we cannot countenance racial prejudice and discrimination, but insist that when this great Nation speaks through its legislation, it must be in a manner which will commend itself to the thinking and conscience of the nations of the world regardless of color or previous condition." [48] The Episcopal Address of 1928 termed the bill an utter perversion of Christian and American standards, meriting unmeasured condemnation. The conference then adopted a resolution introduced by E. Stanley Jones urging all Christian citizens to unite in removing "such legislation that restricts immigration and the rights of citizenship on grounds of race and color," [49] and later the conference spoke to this point. Methodist missionaries and societies recorded their opposition. The long-range implications of exclusion were not ignored. Questioned one writer:

If we cannot learn to like and to live with the mere handful of Japanese, selected Japanese, who are now amongst us, what are we to do in the next few years when a thousand avenues of contact are most surely going to open up

[45] *The Daily Christian Advocate*, the Methodist Episcopal Church, South, May 7, 1906, p. 6.
[46] *The Daily Christian Advocate*, the Methodist Episcopal Church, May 8, 1908, p. 3.
[47] *Ibid.*, May 3, 1920, pp. 32-33.
[48] *Ibid.*, May 7, 1924, p. 149.
[49] *Ibid.*, May 8, 1928, p. 182.

between us and the other millions of them across the sea? And if we have such a desperate time granting freedom and equality of opportunity to the Japanese who are at this particular juncture the most educated, progressive and American-like of all the people of the East, what is to become of us when the millions of China and of India and Africa tomorrow and the day after struggle to their knees, then to their feet and finally stand facing us eye to eye claiming a place with us as our peers? [50]

Most of the various *Christian Advocates* concurred in this judgment, while the conservative *Arkansas Methodist* termed the law "unwise action" [51] and the liberal *Zion's Herald* characterized it as "about the worst piece of blundering at Washington in many a day." [52]

JEWS

Involving greater numbers and arousing scarcely less inflamed emotions were the Jewish immigrants, nearly two million of whom entered the United States in the thirty-five years prior to World War I—an exodus then paralleled only by the great dispersion following the destruction of Jerusalem. As we shall see, Protestants, including many Methodists, were not immune to the virus of anti-Semitism. Most scholars, however, have painted an excessively dark picture of the Protestant (and Methodist) attitude toward the Jew. Methodists already know what secular scholars might find illuminating: namely, that an examination of General Conference and Annual Conference records reveal numerous condemnations of anti-Semitism; that Methodist leaders in sermons, statements, and petitions expressed profound outrage at the sin; that Methodist agencies and boards confessed shame and guilt at the persecution of Jews by Christians; that Methodists often led in movements to root out the evil in the United States and temper the consequences of the terror in Europe; that Methodists and Jews worked together in common causes; that Methodist pulpits were open to rabbis; and that many Methodist men and women accorded to the Jew precisely what they hoped to be accorded by him—justice, respect, and, in truth, love.

It is to be expected that the publications of the Methodist Federation for Social Service would display these attitudes. It is to be anticipated that the entire Methodist press would cry out in horror at the persecutions in Nazi Germany. It is perhaps not surprising that Henry Ford's publication of the "Protocols of Zion" and other spurious anti-Semitic documents in the 1920's should be termed "humbuggery" by the *North-*

[50] Charles Wheeler Iglehart, "Christian America and Japanese Exclusion," New York *Christian Advocate,* July 3, 1924, p. 842.

[51] "Unwise Action," April 24, 1924, p. 1.

[52] "Japan Not 'Quieting Down,'" July 9, 1924, p. 867.

western Christian Advocate and an "abominable libel" by the New York *Christian Advocate;* and that the Nashville *Christian Advocate* rebuked Mr. Ford: "Our democracy cannot stand if our people misrepresent each other and are at war amongst themselves. This nation is made up of many nationalities and many types of people, and its continuance in peace and progress depends upon our mutual understandings, our coöperation, and our adherence to common ideals." [53] Rather, what might prove revealing to students of anti-Semitism who have not examined Methodist sources is to note that at the turn of the century the Methodist press vigorously condemned "brutal and cowardly" attacks upon Jews, urging that the offenders be dealt with "according to the strict letter of justice." [54] And the following editorial, dealing with pogroms in Russia, is not without insight:

It is intolerable. It is a monstrous wickedness. For our part the sympathy which we have hitherto cherished for the Czar of Russia is rapidly filtering away, leaving only a residuum of bitter contempt. We begin to understand the anarchists. Not many of them, we fancy, are Jews—much as the Jews are taxed with their excesses. But it surely would not be strange if they were. *Our only consolation is that America still offers a harbor of refuge for the persecuted. We hope it will continue to do so. Let them come on.* Here they will learn that Christianity means something higher and better than the picture of a saint to be hung over a balcony, so that "Christian" soldiers may pass on to the next house to vent their brutal lust and greed. The Jews do not always get all that they deserve of consideration and esteem in these United States, but they can at least count on common justice under the law and liberty to live and trade and worship as they will.[55]

Nativism

Though Orientals and Jews seemed to present the clearest and most present danger to the purity of American institutions and blood, the "mongrel" Italians, Slavs, and Magyars loomed only less menacing. If some Methodists trembled at the threat, many responded in confidence and compassion. For example, in 1906 the Southern bishops counseled:

To meet these coming thousands with the educative and redemptive agencies of the gospel is the urgent duty of the Christian Churches of these Southern States. When the Lord saw the multitudes who were as sheep without a shepherd,

[53] "Mr. Ford's Apology," July 29, 1927, p. 932.
[54] "Jew-Baiting in New York," Nashville *Christian Advocate,* August 14, 1902, p. 3.
[55] "An International Outrage," Nashville *Christian Advocate,* September 21, 1906, p. 4. Italics mine.

it is said that "he was moved with compassion." That same compassionate love for neglected peoples and the Christless multitudes must stir the energies of the Church today.[56]

To be sure, there is condescension here, but the point to be underscored (and one usually ignored by historians) is that the bishops spoke in love, not hate. In 1912 the New York *Christian Advocate* observed: "The doleful prognostications of alarmists, who twenty-five years ago began predicting the decay of the American republic in consequence of the enormous immigration which the United States was attempting to assimilate, have been seriously discredited by the facts which time has disclosed." Indeed, the editors continued, "the State is stronger today than when the swollen stream of immigration began first to attract the fearful gaze of our political analysts." Instead of indulging in "wild talk concerning the inferiority of the immigrant," Americans should "exercise that considerateness which alone can entitle us to be called a Christian nation." Ultimately, the editors believed, the product of immigration and assimilation will be an "American of such a sort as cannot be easily wasted by even the destructive agencies of our highly wrought modern life." [57]

A third example, from a period of intense nativism, is the report of the Social Service Committee adopted by the Rock River Annual Conference in 1921:

We look with growing disapproval upon any kind of so-called "Americanization" which fails to show due respect for the personality of the foreign-born, and refuses to recognize the contribution which the immigrant himself may make to the development of our national character and the enrichment of our national life.

In respect of Americanization, we believe that the best results will be obtained by meeting the foreign-born with justice and sympathy and brotherly kindness. In the nineteenth chapter of Leviticus it is written:

"If a stranger sojourn with thee in your land, ye shall not do him wrong. The stranger that sojourneth with you shall be unto you as the home-born among you, and thou shall love him as thyself; for ye were sojourners in the land of Egypt: I am Jehovah your Lord."

We believe that this famous passage contains a suggestion for better methods of Americanization than some of the rough and ready ones that are commonly employed.[58]

The compelling injunction found in Lev. 19:33-34 was obeyed by many Methodists. Unfortunately, others gave prior loyalty to the con-

[56] *The Daily Christian Advocate*, the Methodist Episcopal Church, South, May 4, 1906, p. 4.
[57] "The Lure of the Western World," November 14, 1912, pp. 1611-12.
[58] *Journal of the Rock River Annual Conference*, 1921, pp. 66-67.

viction that the United States belonged in some special sense to the Anglo-Saxon "race" and the Protestant faith. Nativism and its handmaiden, racism, luxuriated in the opening decades of the twentieth century, culminating in the tribal '20's with the revived Ku Klux Klan and the virtual sealing of immigration in the 1924 act. Fear that alien hordes would undermine American institutions, lower standards of living, pollute the once sturdy Anglo-Saxon stock, and contaminate a Protestant culture was shared by southern agrarians such as Tom Watson, New England Brahmins such as Henry Cabot Lodge, labor leaders such as Samuel Gompers, financiers such as Elihu Root, Republicans such as Theodore Roosevelt, Democrats such as William Jennings Bryan, pseudo scholars such as Madison Grant and Lothrop Stoddard, reformers such as Edward A. Ross and John R. Commons, and radicals such as Henry George and Eugene V. Debs.

John C. Kilgo, then president of Trinity College, laid bare the issue in a fraternal message to Northern Methodists:

The need of a great religious awakening in this nation is stressed by the moral condition of the immigrants that are pouring into this country. The voyage across the seas does not regenerate their ideals nor purify and ennoble their motives, while the atmosphere of freedom tends rather to intoxicate than to tame them. To close the ports of America against them would be a narrow exclusiveness, yet the monuments of Garfield and McKinley are perpetual warnings against some of the unpronounceable names that land at Castle Garden. There is a battle going on in the streets of every American city between heathenism and Christianity, and the issue is, whether this nation shall be a Christian nation or a pagan nation. American Methodism should not forget the property rights of God to this country, property rights which He has recorded on every page of its history. Unless the churches of America are desperately aggressive, pagan altars will rise in the shadows of Christian temples, and American morals will become a compound of Christian teachings and heathenish folly. This is a free land, but it is not the rendezvous of idolatry, paganism, and antiquated superstitions.[59]

Thus, within twentieth-century Methodism confidence and fear, compassion and pride, rested in uneasy symbiosis. These conflicting attitudes toward the "new" immigrants were brought to sharp focus with the passage of the Johnson-Reed Act of 1924. Under this law ultimately a total of only 150,000 European immigrants were to be permitted to enter the United States annually, with the quotas assigned according to a "national origins" principle which favored immigrants from Northwest-

[59] *The Daily Christian Advocate*, the Methodist Episcopal Church, May 12, 1904, p. 124.

ern Europe and discriminated against those from Southern and Eastern Europe. Now, it is absolutely clear from the record that Methodism overwhelmingly favored tighter immigration restriction. If this is in itself illiberalism, as many scholars insist, then Methodism must acknowledge its guilt. On the other hand, it is equally evident from the record that most Methodists opposed the discriminatory aspects of the 1924 law. The Methodist position, balancing exception against exception, was plainly stated by the 1924 Northern General Conference:

"We deplore as unpatriotic and un-Christian movements, policies and programs in many sections, that discriminate against and humiliate aliens, merely as aliens, or as aliens ineligible to naturalization, and that single out certain races and religious groups for discriminatory and unfriendly treatment." We urge a Federal law raising the standards for admission into the United States *applying them to all peoples alike,* and granting the privilege of citizenship to all persons thus admitted and lawfully residing in the United States who duly qualify, *regardless of their race, color, or nationality.*[60]

Perhaps it is further significant of Methodist compassion that the *Arkansas Methodist,* after editorially supporting stricter immigration standards, continued: "After saying that, we argue that the Turkish atrocities committed against the peaceful Armenians are such that we should provide asylum for the whole people." [61] And in the next decade almost all of Methodism championed the idea of providing asylum for the victims of Nazi terror.

The Ku Klux Klan

When the members of Congress enacted the discriminatory immigration measure of 1924, they embodied into law attitudes already finding outlet through unofficial and sometimes extralegal channels. Numerous "patriotic" societies were formed to preserve America as it had been in that golden age when men shared a common ancestry (Anglo-Saxon), a common memory (Jamestown and Plymouth Rock), a common faith (Protestantism), and a common dream (of an ordered, unified, Godly City on a Hill). This, at any rate, was the image held by millions of frightened, disturbed, angry old-stock Americans as cataclysmic changes in society took place about them. And it is this authentic concern for the fate of their country that explains why perhaps four or five million citizens gave their allegiance to the revived Ku Klux Klan in the 1920's.

[60] *Ibid.,* May 12, 1924, p. 276. Italics mine.
[61] "Let Us Fulfill Our Destiny," January 11, 1923, p. 1.

Yet the basic assumptions and methods of the Klan were un-American and unchristian, and it is humiliating to Methodists that scholars have assumed that Methodist laymen and clergy worked hand in glove with the hooded "patriots." The assumption is not without a certain validity, as the record and, indeed, the memories of men attest. However, before a final verdict of guilty is rendered, perhaps a few additional facts should be recalled.

In the first place, it seems apparent that if Methodism and the Klan had joined forces, the church press would have supported this alliance or at least remained judiciously silent. Such was not the case. The *Northwestern Christian Advocate* termed the Klan an abnormal and vicious organization. The Klan, according to the New York *Christian Advocate,* was neither Christian nor American. Ministers approached by the bed-sheeted knights with bribes of money should cry, "Thy money perish with thee." The fact is, the editors considered "The K.K.K. No Per Cent American." It was a "group which hides its very face from the light of day, and pursues its ends by the method of the mask, the black hand, and the poison pen." The Nashville *Christian Advocate* devoted less space to the Klan, yet several contributors denounced the group, and the editors said: "We sincerely trust that there may be found in the South only a few who have any sympathy whatever with the revived Ku-Klux organizations." [62] The North Carolina, Western, and Pacific *Christian Advocates* and *Zion's Herald* warned against the Klan; the *Wesleyan Christian Advocate* could not believe that "any considerable number of our people will identify secret methods, sectionalism, partisanism, and racial hatred with American democracy," and admonished its readers to resist the "Un-American and undemocratic order." Even the conservative *Arkansas Methodist,* while not always disapproving of the Klan's aims, condemned its methods as dangerous, saying: "Let us have none of it." A rather close investigation does not reveal a single endorsement of the Klan in Methodist journals.

Secondly, the Northern General Conference and the Social Service Commission of Southern Methodism condemned the masked and hooded society.

Thirdly, individual laymen and churchmen, including almost all the outstanding leaders of Methodism, publicly and forcefully took the measure of the Klan in unmeasured terms. In 1921 a Southern Methodist official called the Klan "dangerous," "vicious," "evil," a "leprous social disease" producing only "deceit, delusions, hopelessness, anarchy, and cruelty." Ernest Fremont Tittle, Ralph Sockman, Lynn Harold Hough,

[62] January 21, 1921, p. 69.

and other famous Methodist ministers repudiated the Klan and persuaded their Annual Conferences to adopt anti-Klan resolutions. And, of course, men such as Harry F. Ward were extremely energetic in combating it. The episcopacy was not silent. For instance, Bishops William Anderson, Luther Wilson, William F. McMurray, Francis J. McConnell, Edwin Mouzon, William P. Thirkield, and Edwin Hughes all fought the Klan. In some cases, such as that of Bishop McMurray, this meant an exchange of physical blows.

Though it took courage for a bishop or a metropolitan pastor to op- pose the Klan, the true heroes of the Klan war were unremembered, ob- scure rural and village parsons, for it was they who faced the greatest pressure and, in fact, physical danger. A Methodist parson in Carrsville, Kentucky, spoke for many when he wrote in a private letter to a friend in Texas: "I have been minister and teacher for more than 40 years, and have always opposed all such organizations whose slogan was 'to hate somebody.' I shall not approve such, nor their meddling in my church affairs, whether they want me to persecute Jews and Catholics, or whether they ask me to fight Swedes and Baptists." [63]

The Ku Klux Klan cast ominous shadows over the American country- side in the 1920's. In the end, its preachments of hatred and practices of terror were doomed because they conflicted with long-cherished ideals of decency and fair play held by the overwhelming majority of Americans, including even most Klansmen. But shadows just as dark, if not so length- ened, were also cast by a host of "patriotic" organizations during the 1930's, the largest, best financed, and best publicized being the Silver Shirt Legion of America. The founder of this profitable if pernicious organization was goateed, undersized, wizened William Dudley Pelley, who declared himself to be the son of a Methodist minister; and Protes- tant clergymen, including Methodists, were active as organizers and speakers.

Many Methodist leaders, conferences, and papers deplored these fas- cist-style societies. For instance, the Ohio Annual Conference declared: "Against all hate provoking, race insulting groups, be they Bund or Silver Shirt, Methodism hurls the titanic forces of its witness of the spirit. We have neither part nor parcel in any Christian Front that turns its back on the Christian faith in brotherhood and democracy." [64] Method- ists were further warned to "keep their shirts on" and not exchange them for ones of silver, for, as one Methodist editor observed: "Any

[63] Citations of sources dealing with the Klan and Methodism may be found in Robert Moats Miller, "A Note on the Relationship Between the Protestant Churches and the Revived Ku Klux Klan," *Journal of Southern History,* August, 1956, pp. 355-68.

[64] Quoted in *Social Questions Bulletin,* November, 1939, p. 4.

American who can't be patriotic until he has paid ten dollars to a gabby racketeer and put on a trick shirt couldn't save a wide place in the road from an invasion of domestic ducks." [65]

It is manifest that the majority of Methodists were too deeply responsive to the Christian ethic to be bamboozled into donning the garish attire of the Black Legion, Silver Shirts, or Klan. Unquestionably Methodists were upset by the transformations sweeping American society in the twentieth century. Undoubtedly they viewed with apprehension the seizure of power by Americans with strange names. And as, in seeming helplessness, they felt "their" America slipping away, inevitably jealousy and enmity commingled with apprehension. But it is of great significance that neither Methodism nor any other Protestant church long established in America sought to retain its commanding position through inquisitions, forced conversions, or privileged relationship with the state. Methodism sought to transform immigrant slums into safe and sanitary neighborhoods, not into concentration camps. Methodism sought to transform sweated immigrant workers into free men, not into slave laborers. Methodism sought to raise illiterate immigrants to the status of educated citizens, not reduce them to a servile caste. Methodism sought to introduce Christ Jesus, not the forced closing of competing churches. In sum, though Methodism in the first half of the twentieth century lost (relatively, at least) the commanding status it had enjoyed in American society in 1900, it might have been worse. Had Methodism, in co-operation with other powerful Protestant churches, maintained its position through the ruthless suppression of ethnic and religious minorities (as other churches in other lands have done), it would have profited little, for the price would have been Methodism's soul. Happily, Methodism did not.

The Election of 1928

Methodism's most dangerous and, it would seem, misguided commitment to damming the tides running against old-stock, Protestant domination came in the presidential election of 1928. The candidates were Herbert Hoover and Alfred Emanuel Smith—the latter of whom was a Catholic, a New Yorker from the Fulton Fish Market area though more recently from the governor's mansion in Albany, a wet, and the grandson of Irish immigrants.

[65] "Never Swap Shirts Too Far from a Laundry," *Northwestern Christian Advocate,* November 9, 1933, p. 1060.

Methodism, for the only time in the twentieth century, officially, openly, and unequivocally committed itself to the defeat of a presidential candidate. Both the Northern and the Southern General Conferences specifically served notice that they would fight any candidate whose record and
attitude were hostile to prohibition—and this meant Smith. Methodist
agencies actively entered the campaign. In mid-July, 1928, Bishop James
Cannon was elected chairman of the anti-Smith Democrats at a conference of drys from every southern state held at Asheville, North Carolina. A week later three other Southern Methodist bishops—Edwin D.
Mouzon, John M. Moore, and Horace M. Du Bose—joined Cannon in
issuing a signed statement affirming their intention to wage a militant
fight against Smith on the grounds of his prohibition policy. Although
Bishops Warren A. Candler and Collins Denny and eighty-three Southern Methodist laymen publicly decried the "dragging of our beloved
church into politics," the Cannon forces prevailed. An examination of
more than a dozen Methodist papers reveals that every one of them
editorially opposed Smith. According to Bishop Du Bose, out of 8,500
Southern Methodist preachers, only four supported Smith. Several
scholars credit Bishop Cannon as the man most responsible for enabling
Hoover to crack the "solid South," and numerous historians have singled
out the Methodist churches for a militancy in the campaign exceeding
that of any other Protestant denomination.

Methodists avowed that they entered the political arena because the
fate of the "noble experiment" hung in the balance. It is not necessary to
take a cynical view of this explanation. As we have seen, many Methodists sincerely believed the crusade to free America from the bondage of
liquor was the greatest moral issue facing the nation. It is hardly to be
expected, then, that men and women who had devoted a lifetime to fighting the liquor traffic, who saw in the Eighteenth Amendment the greatest
victory over evil in all history, would remain indifferent when that victory was jeopardized.

Though this explains in large measure Methodist political intervention
in the election of 1928, it does not justify such action. Rather, it simply
underscores a point made earlier: Methodist prohibitionists permitted
this single question to override all other issues and to justify their embracing imprudent tactics.

Moreover, the evidence is damaging that Methodists attacked Smith not
solely because he was a wet, but also because he was one of the "new"
Americans who were not considered really Americans at all, but strangers
in the land, loyal to alien popes and ideas. In 1928 most Methodists were
unable to bring themselves to vote for a Roman Catholic, an Irish boy off
the sidewalks of New York.

Though victory was claimed by the anti-Smith forces, the election of 1928 was the Indian summer of Anglo-Saxon, Protestant, town-and-country domination in the United States. Within five years prohibition was repealed, and within thirty-five years an Irish Catholic resided in the White House. Changes in the nature of American society had diminished the secular power of Methodism. Paradoxically, there are impressive signs that the spiritual power of Methodism is greater at mid-century than in 1900.

In the free and fluid society of America, it was not intolerably long, at least by historic, comparative standards, before the "beaten men of beaten races" emerged as fully equal citizens in a land where only recently their fathers had been strangers. What was unthinkable in 1900 became a possibility in 1928 and a reality in 1960—the election to the presidency of an Irish Catholic. To be sure, no Jew had quite attained that height, and ethnic tensions were not totally absent at mid-century. To be sure, also, Catholic-Protestant tensions prevailed, but mostly they now stemmed less from ignorant bigotry than from informed awareness of very fundamental differences of conviction and policy such as, for example, in the seeking of public aid for parochial schools.

3

Concern for the Problems of Negroes

There remained one minority group for whom the honor of the presidency remained in the unbearably distant future. Ironically, these citizens were not "new" immigrants, for at the earliest their ancestors had reached Virginia before the Pilgrims touched at Plymouth Rock and at the latest in 1808, when the African slave trade ended. Though at mid-century the White House remained closed to them, in a very real sense the gains in condition and status made by Negroes in the twentieth century relatively far exceeded those achieved by even the humblest European immigrants.

The development of independent Negro Methodist churches, the slavery fissure, the work of the Freedmen's Aid Society, the support given by Methodism to Negro schools and hospitals and churches, missions to the Negroes, the question of Negro bishops and of segregated Annual Conferences, the status of Negroes in Methodist schools and seminaries, the Negro issue in unification—these and other matters are treated elsewhere herein. And they are the vital issues, for if the challenge to "let the Church be the Church" is valid, then how Methodists accepted the Negro minority within their own fellowship is the truly relevant question. The next few pages are concerned with only the secondary matter—though one that illuminates the church's own soul—of how Methodists viewed the condition and status of the Negro in American society.

The Wave of Racism

"We do not despair because the clouds of race prejudice apparently lower more darkly than ever," confided the fraternal delegate from the Colored Methodist Episcopal Church to the 1900 Northern General Conference. "Nor are we discouraged because conditions seem to grow more desperate. God still lives." [66] Thus spoke the faith of the catacombs. At that moment in history the American Negro knew his darkest hour. The Populist '90's and the Progressive early 1900's witnessed ferocious extralegal violence; no Negro knew physical security in shop, street, or sharecropper shack. And the legal lines of segregation tightened.

For up and down the avenues and byways of Southern life appeared with increasing profusion the little signs: "Whites Only" or "Colored." Sometimes the law prescribed their dimensions in inches, and in one case the kind and color of paint. Many appeared without requirement by law—over entrances and exits, at theaters and boarding houses, toilets and water fountains, waiting rooms and ticket windows.[67]

It is one of the supreme ironies of American history that the Populist-Progressive era—an age which saw every other cancerous social growth undergo surgery—coincided with the crest of the wave of racism. In fact, many progressive reformers, including leaders of the social gospel, were either indifferent to the Negro's plight or actually hostile to his aspirations. Negro-white contacts were proscribed with increasing severity. In the opening decades of the twentieth century a caste system was imposed upon the Negro, steel-like in its rigidity—a system enforced by laws unknown in the 1870's and 1880's. Compounding the terror was the numbing awareness that no longer could the Negro lift his eyes to northern liberals for help. By 1900 not even the ashes of the old abolitionist fervor were warm, and "enlightened" Yankees now acquiesced tolerantly in

[66] *The Daily Christian Advocate*, the Methodist Episcopal Church, May 23, 1900, p. 300.
[67] C. Vann Woodward, *The Strange Career of Jim Crow* (Galaxy Book ed.; New York: Oxford University Press, 1957), pp. 82-83.

the South's solution to *her* peculiar problem. After all, in 1900 nearly nine tenths of the nine million Negroes in the United States lived in the South, and even the remaining tenth in the North knew discrimination. Moreover, the "new" immigrants provided the North with a "race" problem of its own.

The fraternal delegate from the Colored Methodist Episcopal Church to the 1900 General Conference concluded his speech with a little story:

> The captain of a passing vessel who had seen the signals of a disabled and laboring vessel in a terrible night storm shouted to the captain of the tossing ship: "Shall we lower the boats to take you off?" "No," replied the other, "but lay by us until the morning." So if you ask us what we wish you to do for us during this dark night of peril and prejudice, we reply: "Lay by us until the morning." [68]

The guest might have been making his plea not only for the Colored Methodist Episcopal Church but for all colored people in the land.

Yet the General Conference of 1900 gave reason for hope. The delegates adopted a resolution vigorously condemning mob violence, as did the bishops in their address. The report of the secretary of the Freedmen's Aid and Southern Education Society credited the Negro with having made amazing progress since Emancipation. And though the 280,000 colored members of the Methodist Episcopal Church were denied a bishop of "African descent," nonetheless Dr. J. W. E. Bowen did well in the balloting. "I am not afraid of the so-called color line," said one white delegate. "Indeed, I do not know what that color line is. When it comes to the matter of color we all have more or less of it. Some of us are black, some are red, some are yellow; and, for aught I know, there may be some here this morning who are a little bit blue." [69] A Negro delegate spoke stanchly:

> We wish to say what has been said for us and by us, that we are *loyal*. We are at home. We are not going anywhere. We will peaceably wait in our own Church until the Church, seeing and admitting our needs from every standpoint, they grant us what we need. If any church hopes to profit by the failure of this General Conference to elect a Bishop of African descent, let the hope be gone. We contend for a principle, and, if we die without the sight, we will report to God that we were faithful over a few things. We believe Methodism will study, reason, pray and work itself out of any condition for the glory of God. We will not

[68] *The Daily Christian Advocate,* the Methodist Episcopal Church, May 23, 1900, p. 301.
[69] *Ibid.,* May 16, 1900, p. 197.

frustrate her purpose by running, but will hold our ground world without end. Amen."[70]

Finally, the 1900 Conference at Chicago resolved:

That we highly appreciate the wisdom and fairness of the present method of entertaining the General Conference, and recommend that in future invitations from cities offering to entertain the General Conference, be accompanied by like guarantees of equal treatment to all delegates who may attend; and where there is a failure to send such guarantee with the invitation, the Committee on Entertainment of the General Conference be requested to ask for the same before concluding arrangements.[71]

Despite this assurance, the Negro delegates to the 1904 Northern General Conference meeting in Los Angeles "fell," as one of them said, "into the hands of the Philistines. Our reception will ever linger in our memories to remind us that even among angels there are—well—antipodal manifestations serving. . . to emphasize the existence of a prejudice which is as cruel as death, and which our immortal founder has declared to be the sum of all villanies." [72] The delegates then resolved "that this General Conference not only disapproves of this reprehensible treatment of its membership, but heartily and unqualifiedly condemn it as unwise, unjust, and unchristian." [73] The conference in numerous resolutions, reports, and speeches deplored the Negro's having been "most blunderingly and unjustly treated." The bishops, as to be anticipated, scored lynching (there were 104 instances the previous year). Much more significant is the gritty manner in which they continued:

Some would fain abridge and even overthrow the civil and political rights guaranteed to them [the Negroes] by the constitution. A few would subject them to a reign of intimidation and to practical peonage. More would make them mere "hewers of wood and drawers of water." . . . But the essential conditions of public welfare in a country like this require that men of every nationality, color, and language shall be free according to personal merit to rise in the ranks and above the ranks.

While, therefore, there is ample reason to rejoice in the great recent advance in manual training for both colored and white youth, there is also absolute need for higher and the highest intellectual opportunities to be open to both. The negro does not need to be, nay, can only be hurt by being coddled or patronized or made the childish recipient of privileges. Let him—let us also—steadily, reasonably, firmly and sturdily assert, seek to realize, and maintain his rights, and his privileges will take care of themselves.

[70] *Ibid.*, May 26, 1900, p. 339.
[71] *Ibid.*, May 8, 1900, p. 85.
[72] *Ibid.*, May 11, 1904, p. 99.
[73] *Ibid.*

Let him—let us also—steadily, reasonably, firmly and sturdily seek to realize and maintain his rights, including the right of suffrage on the same terms prescribed for other citizens, and his privileges will take care of themselves.[74]

The social passion of the 1908 General Conference is well known, and the famous Social Creed of Methodism, adopted by the conference, opened with the affirmation that the church stands for equal rights and complete justice for all men in all stations of life. Nor were the 1912 and 1916 General Conferences silent. For instance, in 1912 a resolution was introduced to make lynching a *federal* crime, and in 1916 the bishops recognized: "The white man's prejudice is the colored man's burden. It is not always a conspiracy of the passions. Neither is it an 'inherent baseness.' It is more an inheritance or result of environment." [75]

It is true that these attitudes seem somewhat limited, from the perspectives of mid-century, and inadequate to God's absolute law of love. It is further true that by World War I segregation was the general pattern within the Northern Annual Conferences, congregations, and schools, and that race remained until 1920 a bar to the episcopacy in the United States. Nevertheless, it seems evident that the Methodist Episcopal Church sought for the Negro a higher status in American society than almost anyone, including leading progressives, was willing to accord; and that within the church itself Negroes were elected or appointed to numerous important administrative posts and served on all the boards of the church.

Furthermore, concern for the Negro was not confined to the quadrennial General Conferences. For instance, in 1900 a writer in the New York *Christian Advocate* recognized that "the most stubborn problem before the Christian Church today is the mastery of race prejudice." [76] In that year also the Freedmen's Aid and Southern Education Society specifically condemned disenfranchisement laws such "as the 'grandfather clause' as partial, unjust, un-American, un-democratic, and oppressive." [77] And concern at every level within the church increased as the century deepened.

At the first General Conference of Southern Methodism in the twentieth century the fraternal delegate from the Colored Methodist Episcopal Church said: "We, as well-raised children, delight to look on the greatness of our parent." He asked only one boon: "And that is, wherever, whether in town or city, you are strong and we are striving to house our people, please give us attention, and remember it is your little black

---

[74] *Ibid.*, May 6, 1904, p. 38.

[75] *Ibid.*, May 3, 1916, p. 41.

[76] R. S. Lovinggood, "Reasons for a Bishop of African Descent in the Methodist Episcopal Church," April 5, 1900, p. 539.

[77] News item, New York *Christian Advocate*, November 22, 1900, p. 1900.

child out of doors and asks for help." [78] There was applause. The speech of the fraternal delegate from the African Methodist Episcopal Church was also warmly received. Observed the *Daily Advocate* commentator:

During the progress of the speech there was frequent and hearty applause, and at the end of it the most unbounded good humor. We wish Dr. Parks and his Church mighty well. Whatever good comes to them will be a blessing to us. May the God and Father of our Lord Jesus Christ pour out the richest gifts of His providence and His grace upon our sable brethren, make them strong workers for truth and righteousness, and give abundant success to all their efforts.[79]

Four quadrenniums later at the conclusion of an address by a Negro guest the conference stood and sang:

> Blest be the tie that binds
> Our hearts in Christian love.

And the bishops confessed that Southern Methodists must give greater aid to their colored brethren, to whom they were "bound by peculiar obligations of duty and honor." [80]

These occasions illustrate majority opinion of Methodists, Negro and white, in the South in the opening two decades of the twentieth century. On the one hand, the Negroes appeared humble, patient, and somehow childlike—"Uncle Toms," to use the contemptuous term of the younger, angry Negroes. The scorn is unmerited, for the servile attitude of the Negro leaders of Booker T. Washington's generation painfully reveals the season of violence in which they lived. On the other hand, white Methodists displayed an attitude of kindly paternalism. Negroes must be protected from mob violence. They should be encouraged to remain in the South, for colonization is a hopeless dream and migration to the North a cold, cruel experience. Aid to Negro schools and churches and hospitals should be freely given. Hearts must join in Christian love. But all this within the framework of a segregated society and a caste system destined to stand forever. The antipathy of race, said the Nashville *Christian Advocate,* "is so deep-seated and so ineradicable that the man, white or black, who looks forward to its elimination, be the progress of the negro race what it may, is simply a fool." [81]

[78] *The Daily Christian Advocate,* the Methodist Episcopal Church, South, May 22, 1902, p. 5.
[79] *Ibid.,* May 15, 1902, p. 1.
[80] *Ibid.,* May 3, 1918, p. 7.
[81] "A Problem Solved," July 5, 1906, p. 6.

To be sure, a few Southern Methodists spoke in hate ("We will keep the Negro in his place if we have to dig his grave" [82]) , and a few walked the last mile toward equality, but the sources mostly reveal acceptance of segregation, albeit segregation tempered with kindness and helpfulness.

To sum up the period 1900-1920, for the Negro it was a time of despair. Northern Methodists sought in many instances greater justice and greater equality and, at least for some, the end of segregation. The attitude of the Methodist Episcopal Church, South, might be stated in the words found on an old English tombstone: "She averaged well for the community."

Progress in Reform

The period 1920-39 was one of turbulence and ultimate advance. Immediately following the Armistice, race riots and lynchings swept the land. Then, as the '20's deepened, though the postwar riots passed, Judge Lynch and his deputies, the Ku Kluxers, continued to terrorize the black man. The depression smashed upon black and white in 1929, and racial strains were heightened by economic hardship. Paradoxically, common suffering also brought the races closer together, and by the end of the '30's the nation was on the edge of the major break-through in race relations that came in the 1940's and 1950's.

In the two decades following World War I the United States was shamed by 528 lynchings. Methodism was not silent. Every General Conference of the major branches of Methodism that united in 1939 spoke out. Northern Methodists indorsed federal antilynching legislation, and the Southern General Conference, while unprepared to go this far, nonetheless hit hard. "Lynching most frequently grows out of race prejudice," read a 1934 report. "Often it relates itself to property values or personal piques and is even resorted to as a blind for a white man's guilt." [83] The official organ of Southern Methodists, the Nashville *Christian Advocate,* lashed lynchers in scores of editorials, and by the 1930's indorsed federal action. Annual Conferences, local congregations, and individual ministers and laymen worked to free America from this shame, as did the Epworth League, the National Council of Methodist Youth, missionary groups, and, of course, the Methodist Federation for Social Service. Nor should it be forgotten that the Association of Southern

[82] The Rev. S. A. Steele quoted in J. D. Walsh, "Recent Aspects of the Negro Problem," New York *Christian Advocate,* July 2, 1908, p. 1105.
[83] *Journal of the General Conference of the Methodist Episcopal Church, South,* 1934, p. 330.

Women for the Prevention of Lynching and the Commission on Interracial Co-operation, two splendid groups of Southern Christians, were heavily indebted to Methodist leadership, especially that of the great Dr. Will W. Alexander.

Lest it be assumed that Methodists were too delicate to answer the excuse usually given to justify lynching, these words from the *Northwestern Christian Advocate* are quoted: "We confess it makes us sick when white men in the South speak so nobly of keeping their own women inviolate, while they have nothing to say against a social order in which Negro womanhood is so easily robbed of its chance at chastity." [84] And the editors of the Nashville *Christian Advocate* spoke with equal honesty: "I would like to request those who deal in such specious vaporing to send me a list of Negro rapists who were convicted by sufficient evidence, whom the courts turned loose." Furthermore, "Where will you draw the line? You propose that some crimes shall take the way of an orderly court procedure, while you turn over other crimes to be dealt with by criminals, the vagabonds and riff-raff, the most vicious and depraved elements of society, and expect that lawless and murderous group to cure crime!" As to the charge that antilynching agitation is Communist-inspired: "It is true beyond question that if the Negro is not dealt with legally and justly, it does prepare the soil for Communism. It is a weak refuge, however, to endeavor to hide our own responsibility for lawless violence behind any outside agitators." [85]

The Methodist record concerning lynching is honorable, but Methodists were not content to secure for their Negro brothers simply security from physical violence. In 1920 the Northern bishops declared:

Much of the talk today about race consciousness is an unconscious recrudescence of the spirit that Jesus came to destroy, and leads straight to new hostilities. It flows from the feeling of superiority. We have repudiated election as applied to individuals and largely retained it as applied to races. But our church must this day cry out in Christ's name that in Christ there is neither Jew nor Greek, barbarian, Scythian, bond or free; that no men and no races are at the mercy of their environment or their heredity.[86]

Additionally, a number of reports called for racial justice. The addresses of the Negro fraternal delegates were bolder in tone. And it was

[84] "The Lynching-Race Purity Plea," December 9, 1926, p. 1156.

[85] "Race Relations and a Reply to Criticism," February 9, 1934, p. 166. In the original context this passage is italicized.

[86] *The Daily Christian Advocate*, the Methodist Episcopal Church, May 3, 1920, p. 33.

this conference, after a quarter century of discussion, that finally elected Negro bishops for work of the church in the United States. When Bishops Thirkield and William McDowell escorted Bishop-elect Robert E. Jones to the platform, the conference rose en masse and burst into spontaneous applause. Then the Doxology and "Mine Eyes Have Seen the Glory of the Coming of the Lord" were sung.

Even as the delegates sang, the American scene was aflame with violence, as scores of lynchings and race riots seared the Negro in 1919 and 1920. Many of the fiercest riots occurred in border and northern cities. Much of the Methodist press placed the responsibility squarely on the whites, discerning only one hope: "If the race troubles in Washington and Chicago shall awaken the people to give the colored American a square deal the bloodshed will not have been entirely in vain." [87] Methodist leaders valiantly combatted the fury. For example, Bishop William Alfred Quayle assumed leadership of the forces of sanity in East St. Louis, scene of terror; and Ernest Fremont Tittle, speaking for Negro servicemen, frequent lynch victims, pleaded: "These men, so willing to fight for democracy, surely deserve all the blessings of it and an equal chance to share in the opportunities offered by it." [88]

Four years later the bishops again spoke on the race issue. The conference also adopted a resolution by E. Stanley Jones rejecting "as unchristian and untrue the idea that certain races are born to . . . inherent and fixed inferiority and subordination. We stand for the life of open opportunity for all." [89] The 1928 General Conference called for the Negro to be protected in his vote and that he be accorded equality of opportunity. Bishop Jones presided over a session, and the delegates adopted a resolution thanking him for his courtesy and skill.

Meanwhile, the Northern Methodist press carried literally thousands of editorials and articles on the race issue. *Zion's Herald* was perhaps the most outspoken, but the various *Christian Advocates* were almost as advanced. The tone of these items was not paternalistic. Inherently the white man was not superior to the black. The Negro merited not merely kindness, but justice and equality—and in many of the arguments, though not in all, equality that was not on a segregated basis. Annual Conferences also sought, as did the Michigan Conference in 1927, to help the Negro to be "physically free from peonage, mentally free from ignorance, politically free from disfranchisement and socially free from

[87] "What Makes Race Riots?" New York *Christian Advocate,* August 7, 1919, p. 994.
[88] Evanston *News-Index,* April 4, 1919, p. 1.
[89] *Journal of the General Conference of the Methodist Episcopal Church,* 1924, p. 295.

insult." [90] The Board of Bishops declared it to be their desire that no invitations to social functions be accepted unless they were sufficiently broad to include all members; the Federation for Social Service worked for the desegregation of every area of society; and ministers informed their congregations that a better test of a person's Christianity than having him recite the Apostles' Creed is to observe the way he pronounces the word "Negro."

The 1932 General Conference met in the teeth of the nation's severest depression, and its cruel consequences, coupled with the normal ravages of segregation, gave point to the fraternal inquiry of Bishop Randall Carter of the Colored Methodist Episcopal Church: Must the Negro "always be living on a knife's edge"? [91] The conference answered, No. In addition to the usual addresses, reports, and resolutions condemning racial injustice, the delegates resolved "that our Church shall operate all its Boards, Commissions, official groups, and institutions without discrimination against any person on account of either race or nation." [92] On the sixth day of the conference, Ernest Fremont Tittle, striding purposefully to the platform, handed a resolution to the secretary: "Whereas: 'There cannot be Greek and Jew, circumcision and uncircumcision; barbarian, Scythian, bondman, freeman, but Christ is all and in all'; therefore, Be it resolved" that the General Conference of the Methodist Episcopal Church meet only in cities where hotel services and facilities were unsegregated—the management agreeing to this stipulation in advance and in writing.[93] The conference snapped to attention, and on that Saturday morning even dozing delegates were alerted by loud cheers and half a hundred shouts of "Mr. Chairman!" In the ensuing debate Tittle spoke only briefly: "I believe that if no city under those conditions would be willing to entertain us, it would be better for us not to meet and that our refusal to meet would advance the Kingdom of God as much as our meeting under present conditions." [94] The resolution easily carried.

The next General Conference met in Columbus, Ohio, in 1936. It was unmarred by segregation, and the Negro delegates prepared a resolution commending Columbus for making good its promise. The bishops reviewed the church's attitude in the past two decades:

[90] Quoted in *Information Service*, October 22, 1927, p. 3.
[91] *The Daily Christian Advocate*, the Methodist Episcopal Church, May 14, 1932, p. 305.
[92] *Ibid.*, May 24, 1932, p. 594.
[93] *Ibid.*, May 9, 1932, p. 142.
[94] *Ibid.*

Concerning the whole question of race relations, we repeat with new emphasis the utterances of the last four Episcopal Addresses, and the resolutions of the last four General Conferences. We have nothing to rescind. We renew our protest against unfair discriminations everywhere; against political disfranchisement; against lynchings, and against all illegal punishments for alleged crimes; against unequal privileges in matters ecclesiastical or commercial; against all prejudiced attitudes and behaviors that contradict the spirit of Christ's Kingdom and break the unity of the household of God.[95]

Nevertheless, the Negro issue shadowed the conference, for this meeting was to vote on the Plan of Union, and the place of the Negro in unification created the most critical tensions. But this compelling debate and the ultimate compromise more properly belong to the story of unification, related in the following chapter.

Suffice it to say that in the '30's the Northern Methodist press, Annual Conferences, Epworth assemblies, Federation for Social Service, National Council of Methodist Youth, boards and agencies, ministers and laymen, fought the good fight to erase the color line in Methodism and in American society.

A Negro fraternal delegate to the 1922 Southern General Conference cried: "How long, O knightly America, how long; how long, O Southern Methodism, thou Zion of God, how long shall we be denied a freeman's place in the nation's civilization? And we have faith that that cry is not lifted in vain." [96] The faith was not misplaced. It is true that some Southern Methodists embraced without compunction extreme racist theories. It is true that some journals, such as the *Arkansas Methodist,* found little to condemn in existing caste patterns. It is further true that some leaders, including distinguished bishops, upheld the ideal of a segregated church in a segregated society. Yet as the years passed, Southern Methodists increasingly attempted to overcome pride in their own hearts and prejudice in their own church. There were many men and women of good hope who hoped for Methodism a colorblind church.

Some assumed leadership of such groups as the Commission on Interracial Co-operation and the Association of Southern Women for the Prevention of Lynching, believing the words of Professor William Sheldon of Emory to be true: "There are those who are willing to give their lives to darkest Africa, who are unwilling to give anything to darkest

[95] *Ibid.,* May 4, 1936, p. 70.
[96] *The Daily Christian Advocate,* the Methodist Episcopal Church, South, May 16, 1922, p. 96.

America or to show the slightest consideration for the African neighbor." [97] Some agreed with the Southern bishops, who in 1922 declared
that "such are the necessary relations between the two races in the South
that one cannot suffer without causing the other to suffer likewise." [98]
The bishops put it more bluntly in 1926:

Christianity is a failure unless it can bring the different races of the world into
right relations with one another and set them to living on the basis of brotherhood in the household of God. Men must be brothers, if there is to be any
brotherhood. God demands it. Thou shalt love thy neighbor as thyself. It is
not thou mayest be brotherly; *thou shalt.*[99]

Again and again the bishops held that Negroes "deserve and should have
equality before the law, social, civil, and industrial justice, equitable
educational, community and religious advantages, and a human chance
at the finer spiritual realities of American life." [100] Southern Methodists
agreed to "see to it that there are no legal barriers erected against any
man, individually, within our citizenship; that there be guaranteed
by law the equal protection to life, liberty, and property." [101]
The Nashville *Christian Advocate* was clearly one of the most liberal
denominational journals published in the South on the race question.
Not only did it demand justice for the Negro; it did so without undue
patronage and by pinpointing the inequities he suffered. "The unavoid-
able fact is," maintained the editors, "racial prejudice and racial enmity
are un-Christian—are now and ever will be." [102] And the following editorial sums up much Southern Methodist opinion in the 1930's:

How often do we hear, "The Negro is all right in his place." As to that matter, the white man is all right in his place, but he is too frequently out of place.
We are told that the Negro is inferior and will always remain so. Those who
reiterate this seem to doubt it, since they feel impelled to resort to artificial

[97] *The Daily Christian Advocate,* the Methodist Episcopal Church, May 8, 1924,
p. 189. Professor Sheldon was the fraternal delegate to the Northern Conference from
the Southern Church.
[98] *Journal of the General Conference of the Methodist Episcopal Church, South,*
1922, p. 356.
[99] *The Daily Christian Advocate,* the Methodist Episcopal Church, South, May 6,
1926, p. 7.
[100] *Ibid.,* April 27, 1934, p. 15.
[101] *Journal of the General Conference of the Methodist Episcopal Church, South,*
1934, p. 295.
[102] Reply to a letter to the editors, February 28, 1936, p. 287.

pressure to "keep him down." . . . The fact is any person of one race is only superior to a member of any other race as he is *superior*.[103]

4

The Labor Movement

If a comparison of William McKinley with John F. Kennedy and Booker T. Washington with Martin Luther King illuminates the swiftly changing nature of American society in the twentieth century, hardly less meaningful, though not necessarily in the same sense, is the contrast between Samuel Gompers and James Hoffa. At the time of McKinley's first inauguration, Gompers' American Federation of Labor possessed only 250,000 members, and this was a commanding proportion of total trade-union membership. Shortly after President Kennedy took office, Hoffa's teamsters numbered 1,700,000, and Mr. Hoffa received an annual salary of $75,000 plus emoluments.

During the thirty-month period following January, 1902, 180 union men were killed, 1,651 injured, and over 5,000 arrested in the industrial war. Labor faced mammoth corporate empires; tough captains of industry; a hostile Congress and state legislatures and courts; armies of scabs, spies, and hired thugs; and, above all, the almost unbroken enmity of middle-class white-collar and farming America and its allies—the schools, the press, indeed, the churches.

The decades slipped by. At mid-century the merger of the A.F. of L. and the C.I.O. brought 15,500,000 workers within a single organization. Altogether (excluding farm workers, the self-employed, and the professional people) more than one third of the labor force were now trade-union members. A great, almost sovereign, countervailing power now checked and balanced corporate power. Labor had made the deliberate and pragmatic decision to obtain "more and more" of the capitalist "pie." At mid-century few thoughtful Americans doubted the success of the effort, though some now doubted the justice of the labor movement and, perhaps, the wisdom of the support they had once given to it.

A sense of history helps. In the McKinley era the average working day in industry was in the neighborhood of 10 hours, 6 days a week: total, 60 hours a week or, to be precise, 59.1. In unorganized industries the

---

[103] "Race Prejudice," November 12, 1937, pp. 1444-45.

figure was higher, as high as 84 hours. At the time when the International Ladies' Garment Workers Union was established in 1900, the hours in this trade in New York were 70 a week. In the McKinley era the average annual earnings of workers in nonagricultural pursuits was something between $400 and $500 a year. For unskilled workers they were less— under $460 in the North, under $300 in the South. Women and children (in 1900 probably 1,700,000 children under sixteen were "gainfully employed," and the number was increasing) worked full days for literally pennies. In the McKinley era 1 out of every 137 trainmen was killed on the job. As late as 1913, 25,000 workers were killed at their toil, and another 700,000 were seriously injured. The Triangle Shirtwaist Factory fire in New York in 1911 alone took the lives of 148 trapped immigrant girls. An 1897 report read:

In the large stamping works and canning factories in a city like Chicago, not a day passes but some child is made a helpless cripple. These accidents occur after three o'clock in the afternoon. The child that has begun his work in the morning with a reasonable degree of vigor, after working under constant pressure for several hours, at about three o'clock becomes so wearied, beyond the point of recovery, that he can no longer direct the tired fingers and aching arms with any degree of accuracy. He thus becomes the prey of the great cutting knives, or of the jaws of the tin-stamping machine.[104]

In the McKinley era millions of workers were ground by poverty and brutalized by soulless toil, the emptiness of the ages in their faces and on their backs the burden of the world.

In assessing Methodism's relation to labor in the twentieth century it is wise, then, to recall the burdened figure of Gompers as well as the affluent image of Hoffa.

In his autobiography Bishop Francis J. McConnell tells a little story with, however, broad relevance to the entire question of Methodism's relationship to labor:

A score of ministers at a labor-union convention, meeting in Denver, asked the convention to send a score of labor-union men to meet the ministers at a luncheon "to talk things over." The twenty guests came with a belligerent woman to do their talking. This woman rose and announced that she would utter a searching challenge. She would close her eyes and then swing her hand around. She dared the minister at whom she was pointing when she opened her eyes to answer this question: "How many times in the last fifteen years have you

[104] Quoted in Frederick Lewis Allen, *The Big Change* (New York: Harper & Brothers, 1952), p. 56.

attended a meeting of laboring men or of the socially discontented?" When she opened her eyes, her finger was pointing to Harry Ward, and she asked her question. Ward replied, "Madam, I will answer your question if you will answer one from me. How many times have you been in church in the last fifteen years?"

She answered with a good deal of bravado, "I have attended church once in that time. That was at the funeral of a friend."

Ward answered, "I thought so. In that time, counting out my vacation period, I have attended an average of about three meetings a week of the nature you asked about."

The woman turned to the chairman and asked, "What shall I ask him next?"

He replied, "I'm blessed if I know." He didn't say blessed, but blessed was suggested by contrast.[105]

This story, it is true, underscores labor's sense of alienation from the church. Happily, it also illustrates the church's determination to heal this estrangement.

Almost all scholars agree that much of Protestantism in 1900 was cut off by its constituency from the harshest impact of industrialization. Professors Waldo Beach and John C. Bennett state:

During the latter part of the nineteenth century, Protestant ethics had fallen, for the most part, into the doldrums of a Victorian, pietistic, socially myopic, and cushioned-pew program for personal purity. The common ideal of the Christian life was to avoid the gross sins of the flesh, to follow the Benjamin Franklin virtues of thrift, honesty, and respectability, to love one's immediate neighbor in good deeds of charity, and thus to prepare oneself for the destination of heaven. The economic structures of life were either regarded as outside the province of ethics or else given a tacit sanction through the Puritan doctrine of vocation, which had been transformed into the "gospel of work" and thence into the "gospel of wealth." The notorious "rugged individualism" of capitalism was blessed as Christian if mitigated by active philanthropy. The Protestant church looked at questions of economic ethics through the eyes of the middle-class bourgeoisie. It passed by on the other side from the masses of immigrant labor, or else offered them other-worldly bromides for their spiritual and economic hungers.[106]

The Methodists' Distance from Labor

This critical assessment is not unrelated to Methodism's particular position. Because most Methodists lived in country, village, or town, they

---

[105] *By the Way* (New York and Nashville: Abingdon-Cokesbury Press, 1952), p. 211. Used by permission.

[106] "Christian Ethics," in Arnold S. Nash, ed., *Protestant Thought in the Twentieth Century* (New York: The Macmillan Company, 1951), p. 127. Used by permission.

were partially sheltered from the realities of industrialization. Because most Methodists were farmers or elite workers or owner-managerial entrepreneurs, their economic interests seemingly clashed with the urban and often foreign-born masses. Moreover, as we have seen, ethnic and religious differences heightened geographic and economic tensions. The boast of Dr. John C. Kilgo (later a bishop) in 1900 is applicable to Northern as well as Southern Methodism:

If Greece made poets and sculptors, and the Elizabethan age produced great literature, this last half of our century has developed a wealth-producing genius. This is not a thing to be hated, and is not a mark of degeneracy; for great business talent is rare enough to be esteemed. These men have brought harmony out of industrial chaos, and reduced confusion to trustworthy order. Methodism has had a large part in the production of this wealth, and justly shares in its holdings. The General Rules of Methodism restrain extravagant and reckless expenses, and demand energy in work. Such a system is no less economic than it is spiritual. So the outcome is a Church that a century ago assembled the poor and outcast under spreading oaks, today brings together bankers, merchants, manufacturers, Senators, and chief rulers in large temples. Methodism owns much of our bank, railroad, and factory stock, government bonds, real estate, and every other form of legitimate wealth. Our people have been workers and savers, and great wealth has come to them. Such men as Cupples, Scruggs, Duke, Pelzer, Cole, and Williams, show that Southern Methodism is no hindrance to material success on the largest scale. We are going into the twentieth century with immense resources—running banks, factories, railroads, ship lines, city property, and governments. For all this we are thankful.[107]

Contrariwise, James F. Rusling's plea in 1900 is applicable to Southern as well as Northern Methodism:

I think our ministers should preach more on the Christian duty of getting rich and keeping rich. Plenty of "texts" on this line, if sought for. Our churches, colleges, universities, hospitals, missionary cause, Epworth Leagues, etc., all require money and one of the crying needs of the Methodist church today is *more millionaires* and multi-millionaires. Of course, I mean *good* millionaires. But if we had more men like John D. Rockefeller and Andrew Carnegie, we should not have to pass "the tin cup" so often, and our Twentieth Century Thank Offering of twenty millions would come a great deal [easier]. And we *will* have them some day. Methodism tends to make men rich. And why drive them away when they have become a little rich?[108]

[107] "This Great Century," Nashville *Christian Advocate,* April 19, 1900, p. 10.
[108] *The Daily Christian Advocate,* the Methodist Episcopal Church, May 2, 1900, p. 12.

The middle-class nature of Methodism is rather conclusively demonstrated in the composition of the 1904 Northern General Conference:

Of laymen, there were 55 merchants, 39 lawyers, 34 educators, 27 physicians, 20 bankers, 15 manufacturers, 12 judges, 9 capitalists; 7 each of clerks, contractors, farmers and real estate agents; 6 insurance agents; 5 each of railroad officials, editors and mechanics; 3 stock and fruit growers, 2 business managers of church papers, 1 each of local preachers, State governors, architects, mining operators, students, revenue collectors, undertakers, nurserymen, and 32 miscellaneous and unknown.[109]

Methodism was handicapped in reaching the unskilled urban masses, not alone because of the make-up of its constituency, but also because of its theological stress upon individual regeneration. If only the laborers suppressed bitterness and hatred in their hearts and if only the capitalists were converted to righteousness, then class tensions would be dissolved in the acids of the love that is the law of life. Further, the wealthy were comforted to know that they had been elected by the Lord to manage his wealth. This doctrine of stewardship gave great encouragement to worthy charitable and philanthropic enterprises. In truth, the most distinguishing characteristic of the very wealthy in the United States, as distinct from their counterparts in Europe, is their often lively social conscience and deep sense of public responsibility, derived in large measure from religious imperatives. Nonetheless, this doctrine of stewardship also gave divine sanction to a grossly inequitable distribution of the nation's wealth, for as the Rockefellers and Carnegies discovered, after a man reaches a certain degree of affluence, it is devilishly difficult to give the money away as fast as it comes in. The poor were admonished to accept meekly the lowly station in life Providence had assigned to them. But no matter. There would be sweet rewards in heaven, and on the near side of eternity their interest would be protected and cared for, as George F. Baer opined in an oft-quoted statement, "not by the labor agitators, but by the Christian men to whom God in his infinite wisdom has given control of the property interests of the country."

Warren S. Stone, president of the Brotherhood of Locomotive Engineers, remarked in 1924: "You want to know what labor thinks of the church. I tell you, very frankly, that labor does not think very much of the church, because the church does not think much of labor." [110] This

---

[109] *Ibid.*, May 4, 1904, p. 5.
[110] Quoted in *Zion's Herald*, April 16, 1924, p. 493.

view is merely a variant of the old charge that religion is the opiate of the masses. It was expressed by the "Wobblies" (the Industrial Workers of the World) in their marching song:

> Long-haired preachers come out every night,
> Try to tell you what's wrong and what's right;
> But when asked 'bout something to eat
> They will answer with voices so sweet:

> *Chorus*

> You will eat, bye and bye,
> In that glorious land above the sky;
> Work and pray, live on hay,
> You'll get pie in the sky when you die.

And in the blunt comment of an old miner: "The preacher points your eyes to heaven, and then the boss picks your pocket." At the opening of the century even the conservative Samuel Gompers admitted: "My associates have come to look upon the church and the ministry as the apologists and defenders of the wrong committed against the interests of the people." [111]

In the following four decades the Methodist press carried a number of articles by workingmen and churchmen demonstrating the absence of religion among large groups of laborers: miners, textile operators, migratory laborers, meat-packing hands, lumberjacks, steel-mill employees—the great mass of the American labor force. Similar articles appeared widely in the secular press, in scholarly studies by sociologists and church historians, in the reports of the American Academy of Political and Social Science, and in such volumes as *Labor Speaks for Itself on Religion*, edited by Jerome Davis.

In 1908 a miner wrote a letter to the editor of the New York *Christian Advocate* dealing with "The Methodist Clergy and the Labor Unions":

During my *fourteen* years' work in the mines *only one minister ever visited the mine in which I worked.* For *eight* years I sat under the preaching of one minister. *He was never in my place of labor once.* Yet in a very just strike of four months he was the workingmen's stoutest opponent. His talk against the union simply showed his crass ignorance of the situation and we won. He

[111] Quoted in William Warren Sweet, *Methodism in American History* (rev. ed.; Nashville: Abingdon Press, 1953), p. 355.

missed his opportunity. Is it strange that we had more faith in the miners' leader than in the minister? [112]

Decades later a Methodist minister reached broader but equally gloomy conclusions in an extremely significant study entitled *The Methodist Church and Industrial Workers in the Southern Soft Coal Fields*.[113] The Methodist churches in the southern coal fields, the author discovered, were either owned outright or supported by the company. In fact, they were management churches, not those of the workers. The minister was virtually a company employee and, in the eyes of the miners, a company stooge. Sensitive ministers recognized their ambiguous position but were too financially vulnerable to protest. One miner summed it up: "I have to bow and scrape to the company all week, and by God, when I come to Sunday, I'll not have any damn boss telling me how to believe the Bible."

The long company shadow also darkened the Pennsylvania coal region, as the 1923 report of the superintendent of the Blairsville District to the Pittsburgh Annual Conference stated:

I have met with a strange but not uncommon opposition from certain great coal companies that to me is ominous. When attempting to secure title to certain plots of ground for building churches, we have found it impossible to do so. The deeds not only recite the dimensions of the lots, often covered by first mortgages, but proceed to dictate what shall be preached and what is prohibited upon the property, with the penalty of forfeiture in case of any transgression of the conditions. In other words, our preachers are to be muzzled. The tragedy of the situation is that communities are left without a church.[114]

Nor was the situation happier in the steel-mill districts of Pennsylvania, as the Interchurch World Movement reports disclosed.

In 1926, Passaic, New Jersey, was racked by a bitter, violent textile strike. The Methodist press and the Federation for Social Service displayed intense interest. Indeed, Miss Winifred L. Chappell of the Federation conducted the research for the *Christian Century's* issue devoted entirely to the strike. When, however, a resolution calling for a Congressional investigation resulted, the signatories revealed how absolutely the Protestant churches were cut off from the workers: Katolicky sokol, Slovak Catholic sokol, Slovak Evangelical Union of America, St. Vladimir Russian Orthodox Society, Marie S.S. dei miracoli Italian Catholic Church, Ascension

[112] January 23, 1908, p. 143; from W. W. McEwan, Windsor, Ohio.

[113] Arthur Edwin Shelton, unpublished Th.D. dissertation, Boston University School of Theology, 1950.

[114] Quoted in *Information Service*, March 8, 1924, p. 2.

Ukrainian Church. The *Christian Century* commented upon this resolution: "Here is the church, intervening at last in an industrial situation which has compelled the attention of the nation. But what church?" [115]

Farther south and several years later, Dr. Liston Pope conducted a study of the mill towns of North Carolina, and more especially those of Gaston County, entitled *Millhands and Preachers*. Dr. Pope found the churches dominated by management and the ministers working hand in glove with the mill owners, being either indifferent to the conditions of the workers or intimidated into silence. Consequently, even in the strongly Protestant South, the churches, including the Methodist churches, often found themselves distrusted, detested, or ignored by the masses.

In part, as we have suggested, the gulf between Methodism and the industrial worker stemmed from the fact that the former was bound by its frontier-agrarian experiences and was simply innocent of the brutal facts of modern life. This point is beautifully illustrated by the casual manner in which the editors of the *Arkansas Methodist* received the news that United States Steel sweated its men twelve hours a day. After all, the farmer worked at least a twelve-hour day and no fuss was made. And if the unhappy steelworkers did not like their condition, "they could go to the farm and have nice outdoor, healthful employment at about one-fourth the wages, but they do not want the long hours and quiet and exposure to weather that the farm affords." [116] Surely naïveté rather than malice prompted this editorial.

Innocence or ignorance accounted for only a part of Methodism's difficulty in gaining a *rapprochement* with labor. Anxiety was also a factor. The dilemma was evident—and cruel. If Methodism hoped for labor great power and this power was attained, and *if* labor was converted to righteousness, the kingdom of God would be advanced. But what was to be the church's position if labor followed the path of class hatred, practiced violence, and gained a power as corrupted as that of the corporations? That is to say, what if labor utilized methods and attained goals blurring Methodism's dream of a harmonious and righteous society?

It is not simply that the *Northwestern Christian Advocate* branded the Industrial Workers of the World as Iniquitous Wastrels of the World and wild Bolsheviki. After all, the Wobblies did preach a bloody brand of class warfare. Nor is it that the New York *Christian Advocate* in 1919 charged labor unions with becoming drunken on the wine of false economic teachings and giving aid and comfort to rebellious and seditious movements among the masses. After all, 1919 was a year of fierce class

[115] Quoted in Donald B. Meyer, *The Protestant Search for Political Realism, 1919-1941* (Berkeley and Los Angeles: University of California Press, 1960), p. 100.

[116] "The Twelve-Hour Day," September 20, 1923, p. 1.

violence. Rather, it is that this theme of anxiety and fear is found running throughout all the opening decades of the twentieth century.

"We are to face some grave industrial perils," warned the Northern fraternal delegate to the 1898 Southern General Conference. "Dark clouds already gather upon the horizon. There are mutterings of a coming storm. Organized capital is often organized greed. Organized labor is often organized tyranny. Both are Christless." [117] After reviewing the abuses of unregenerate capitalists, a report to the 1904 Northern General Conference continued:

The stricken toiler turns upon the oppressor. He organizes strikes, boycotts, calls off his banded union brothers from their respective employments. He shuts the doors of the factories and in the stress of want and despair often resorts to acts of violence in the destruction of property and life while the employer sets [sic] encased in indifference. The grasping monopolist and the walking delegate are representatives of these two opposing forces.[118]

At the same General Conference the bishops spoke in a vein compounded of anxiety over the present and hope for the future—a hope based on a power the church was never to possess in the first half of the twentieth century:

The Church must come in between these vast contending forces [capital and labor], holding aloft the banner of the cross to which both must bow, and offering to both the Sermon on the Mount as the perfect charter of the right and duties of both. Never, until the Church shall lay the Golden Rule upon the conscience of capitalists and of laborers, will the golden millennium of industrial peace be ushered in.[119]

Methodist Outreach to Labor

It is time to turn to the major point made by Bishop McConnell in his little story concerning Harry F. Ward and the Denver lady laborite. Thus far our concern has been with estrangement and alienation, and we have observed how Methodism regarded the industrial masses with insensitivity, anxiety, and hostility. Increasingly historians (and theologians) view relationships in terms of power and pride and seek motiva-

[117] *The Daily Christian Advocate,* the Methodist Episcopal Church, South, May 19, 1898, p. 6.
[118] *The Daily Christian Advocate,* the Methodist Episcopal Church, May 19, 1904, p. 221.
[119] *Ibid.,* May 6, 1904, p. 38.

tion in terms of guilt or fear. The older, moralistic and simplistic interpretations are insufficient to explain the ambiguities and complexities of
history. Ironically, however, sophisticated analysis may sometimes obscure rather than illuminate the "truth" in history. To be sure, Methodism's attitude toward labor was flawed by fear on the one hand and
naïve optimism on the other, but it is simply unhistorical to rule out entirely considerations of Christian love. In truth, love was the commanding theme. Quite simply, Methodist commitment to labor's fate is comprehensible only in terms of Methodist loyalty to the God revealed
in Christ Jesus; with Methodist faithfulness to the imperative implied
in the words "of how much more value is a man than a sheep!" (Matt.
12:12 RSV); with Methodist memories of Wesley and the Kingswood
colliers and Asbury and the lonely frontiersmen. Northern Methodism's
compassion for the disinherited workers exceeded in extent and intensity
that of any other major Protestant denomination. Southern Methodism's
compassion exceeded that of any other major church in the South. These
flat statements are susceptible of objective demonstration by a mountain
of evidence. Unhappily, here the record can merely be suggested.

Northern Methodist love for the workingman was not strikingly evident at the close of the nineteenth century. To be sure, in 1888 the bishops expressed the concern that laboring people were drifting from the
church. Here and there sympathetic articles dotted the Methodist press.
Mission houses were established and at least one labor church. But it
seems that Methodism responded less rapidly to the challenge of industrialization than other denominations.

However, at the 1900 General Conference, Frank Mason North
awakened the church to her responsibilities in speeches and reports; and
another spokesman pleaded: "In the name of a poor, tired humanity—
caught in the rush and never being able to halt for a moment—in the
name of the rights of man's highest life demanding a decent chance for
developing mind and heart, we must lift up our voices and cease not until
he shall have room and time for rest and worship, for joy and love." [120]
The bishops, after reviewing the charge that the churches were rich
men's clubs, continued:

There is enough of truth in these allegations to set us upon serious inquiry.
Our Lord chose to become incarnate among the poor. He made it a proof of
his divine mission that to the poor the gospel was preached. And Methodism
began its work in like manner. With it, as with the gospel at the beginning, not
many wise men after the flesh, not many mighty, not many noble were called.
It saved the miner, the mechanic, the fisherman, the farm laborer, and some

[120] *Ibid.*, May 21, 1900, p. 257.

also in better conditions; and thus it saved society. Is it now doing this work? Is it willing to do it? Will an educated ministry consent to keep in heart-touch with men ignorant, or only half-trained? Will it be content to live plainly, that it may reach the plain people, and be supported by them? Will our rich men forbear social extravagance and social distinctions in the Church, that the gospel may better do its office for all men? How many of our churches be builded and managed that in them at the same time the brother of low degree may rejoice in that he is exalted, and the rich in that he is made low? [121]

As the years passed, the number of sympathetic articles in the Methodist press picked up, as did the utterances of clergymen and statements of official agencies. Then in 1908 Methodist social passion burst into full expression. Nearly a third of the Episcopal Address of the Northern General Conference was devoted to social themes, including a warm section on labor. Additionally, the 1908 conference adopted the famous Social Creed of Methodism:

The Methodist Episcopal Church stands—
For equal rights and complete justice for all men in all stations of life.
For the principle of conciliation and arbitration in industrial dissensions.
For the protection of the worker from dangerous machinery, occupational diseases, injuries, and mortality.
For the abolition of child labor.
For such regulation of the conditions of labor for women as shall safeguard the physical and moral health of the community.
For the suppression of the "sweating system."
For the gradual and reasonable reduction of the hours of labor to the lowest practical point, with work for all; and for that degree of leisure for all which is the condition of the highest human life.
For a release for [sic] employment one day in seven.
For a living wage in every industry.
For the highest wage that each industry can afford, and for the most equitable division of the products of industry that can ultimately be devised.
For the recognition of the Golden Rule and the mind of Christ as the supreme law of society and the sure remedy for all social ills.[122]

From this position the church never retreated. Indeed, the Social Creed was the foundation on which the church proceeded to construct a wide-ranging social-justice program including the eight-hour day; accident, sickness, old age, and unemployment insurance; the right of labor to organize and bargain collectively; and the supremacy of the service over the profit motive.

[121] *Ibid.*, May 4, 1900, p. 42.
[122] *Discipline*, 1908, Appendix, ¶59.

It is to be anticipated that the church would oppose the exploitation of little children—and it did, demanding federal control. The 1912 statement of the bishops is not unique in its forcefulness:

The outstanding infamy of the present labor situation is the chaining of little children to the wheels of trade. Dragged from their beds half-asleep in the early morning, or denied the natural hours of sleep with the coming of night, tens of thousands of them are being physically dwarfed and mentally stupefied and their careers blighted in the bud of their being, amid the whirring machinery of mills, the black tunnels of coal mines, the noisome air of sweatshops, and the all-hour and all-weather demands of messenger service, for which they are often inadequately clad. Neither Milton's nor Goethe's devil could have devised a plot against humankind more demoniacal in torture or in destructive consequences than this outrage upon helpless childhood by commercial greed.[123]

The bishops spoke so vigorously on broader aspects of the labor question that it is difficult to select examples for citation. For instance, in 1919 in a Pastoral Letter entitled "The Church and Social Reconstruction" they called for many industrial reforms, including collective bargaining as an essential instrument in the attainment of industrial justice. In 1928 they demanded for labor a wage capable of not merely prolonging existence but of supporting life, for it does not suffice to pay the toiler today only so much as shall enable him to resume his toil tomorrow. A Pastoral Letter issued in 1930 thundered that "no man has a right to eat his bread in the sweat of other men's brows. . . . Further we cannot escape the conviction that there is something basically unjust in a system that allows an industry to absorb the surplus earnings of its employees in prosperous periods and to cast them aside for society to care for when their labors are no longer profitable." [124] In the teeth of the depression the bishops declared:

Industry has as a rule given labor a grudging, insufficient wage, keeping it down by child exploitation, by suppression of legitimate organizations, and by other expedients, while at the same time huge fortunes have been amassed for the favored owners of the resources of production. To-day the burden is without conscience shifted to the worker who, after giving his labor for miserable financial results, is turned off to starve or beg. Thus, the machine, which might have been used to lift the load of poverty from the backs of all the people, has been used selfishly for the benefit of the few.[125]

123 *The Daily Christian Advocate,* the Methodist Episcopal Church, May 4, 1912, pp. 99-100.
    124 Quoted in the New York *Christian Advocate,* December 11, 1930, p. 1527.
    125 *Journal of the General Conference of the Methodist Episcopal Church,* 1932, pp. 173-74.

General Conference resolutions and reports echoed, sometimes faintly, more often strongly, the convictions of the bishops on labor. Annual Conferences in hundreds of instances championed the legitimate interests of labor. The New York East Conference was possibly the most deeply committed to the labor cause, but, in all conscience, a careful examination of the Rock River Conference journals reveals a record almost as outspoken. To cite specific conferences, however, is invidious, for from the Atlantic to the Pacific labor found a friend in the Methodist Annual Conferences.

The Northern Methodist press, balancing exception against exception, moved from a position of coolness toward labor in the late nineteenth century to one of tempered sympathy in the early decades of the twentieth century to one of enthusiastic warmth by the late '20's and '30's. A few examples must suffice. A 1912 article in the New York *Christian Advocate* carried this insight:

We of the Eastern seaboard know coal in terms of shovel and range and furnace—and check stub. That is one end of the equation. At the other end is the anthracite field where one hundred and seventy thousand mine workers know coal as bread and drink, rent and clothes, physician, disease and death. To them it is a medium of exchange, legal tender. Coal feeds them, maims them, kills them, buries them. Coal means one thing, and a comparatively small thing, to you. To these toilers in perpetual night—Slavs, Lithuanians, Poles, Italians, Hungarians, besides our native population—the whole problem is eloquent with larger and more vital significance. So we ask soberly, Have we paid the entire cost of a ton of coal? [126]

The entire Northern Church press favored federal control of child labor. For example, in 1916 the New York *Christian Advocate* said the single, sinister argument against Congressional legislation is the "profit to be made from the product of children"; and two decades later the *Northwestern Christian Advocate* dismissed the argument against federal action as "condensed, sublimated, and high-grade hot-air." [128]

Years of support of labor's right to organize and bargain collectively caused the *Northwestern Christian Advocate* to inquire in 1934: "How does it happen that, while our church saw the need for this industrial principle a quarter century ago, so many people have just found out about it?" [129] Opposition to minimum-wage and maximum-hours legislation reminded the editors that "the pagan idea of the devil take the

[126] Charles D. Walworth, "The Cost of a Ton of Coal," October 31, 1912, p. 1547.
[127] "At Last a Federal Child Labor Law," August 31, 1916, p. 1144.
[128] "A Silly Scare About Child Labor," February 1, 1934, p. 99.
[129] "Collective Bargaining Is Old Stuff," October 25, 1934, p. 875.

hindmost is still openly defended—and by people classed for the purposes of the census, and otherwise, as 'Christian.' " [130] The entire Northern Church press supported federal social-security legislation, and when the great act of 1935 was finally passed, the editor of *Zion's Herald* was encouraged in the "faith that God is in His heaven and that the kingdom of God is coming on earth." [131]

Nor did the Northern Church press withdraw its support when labor was driven to the ultimate weapon of the strike. Not unrepresentative of hundreds of editorials is the statement of *Zion's Herald:*

> In screaming headlines the newspapers of New England on Tuesday of last week announced, "Lawrence Strike Is Broken." Yes, but just what was "broken"? Was it not men who were broken? Cold and hungry, hopeless and forsaken, these workers, striving against a cut in wages already inadequate for proper comfort and self-development, finally had to surrender to the will of the mine owners. Self-respect was broken; ambition was broken; desire for self-improvement was broken; the spirit of self-sacrifice for wife and family was broken. Broken! What a terrible thing it is to break a fellow man even in the interests of profits and dividends! [132]

Northern Methodism gave witness to its concern for the laboring man not only through Episcopal Addresses, reports and resolutions at the General Conference and Annual Conference levels, and in its journals, but also through the Methodist Federation for Social Service. From its origin in 1907 to unification in 1939, the Federation championed the eight-hour day, minimum-wage laws, social security, safer conditions of work, and the right of labor to organize and bargain collectively. The Federation stood like a rock against the attempts of management to erase the wartime gains of labor, branding the "open shop" campaign of the early '20's a declaration of war against trade unionism. Throughout the Progressive era and the "Golden Twenties" the Federation challenged the accepted thesis that the entire country was basking in prosperity. Time and time again the troubled state of American miners, textile hands, and factory workers was laid bare. Numerous conferences, national and local, were held with business and labor leaders to the end that greater economic justice might be secured. The Federation investigated every man-sized strike of the period, invariably reporting that the grievances of the workers were real. Management's use of spies, company police, injunctions, black lists, and "yellow dog" contracts was excoriated. The depression heightened the Federation's championship of labor,

---

[130] "He Shifts His Load to Others," December 2, 1937, p. 1107.
[131] "The Social Security Bill," April 24, 1935, p. 388.
[132] "Broken!" November 18, 1931, p. 1444.

and though its leaders hoped Roosevelt would push on to socialism, none-theless specific New Deal measures designed to aid labor were endorsed.

Methodist clergymen, including many leaders and some who were or were to become bishops, intervened on labor's behalf in industrial dis-putes or in other ways worked intimately with labor. Again, it would be invidious to cite examples, for these men were found in Boston and New York, Pittsburgh and Detroit, Chicago and Denver, Los Angeles and Seattle, and many other areas. Nor were labor "martyrs" such as Tom Mooney and the Centralia "Wobblies" without support from Methodist churchmen, who repeatedly worked for the release of these "victims of class injustice."

However, Methodist participation in the famous investigation of the 1919 steel strike by the Interchurch World Movement must be mentioned. After all, Fred B. Fisher (later a bishop) was director of the Movement's Industrial Relations Department and requested the study in the original instance. For his participation, the management of steel subjected Dr. Fisher to vilification and slander. A spy was planted in his office to ran-sack his files. It was charged that he was pro-German and that his name was really spelled with a "c." When this accusation failed, management accused him of being pro-Russian, and of having a "strong bent toward mysticism," though what mysticism had to do with Bolshevism was never explained.

After all, also, Bishop McConnell was made chairman of the Commis-sion of Inquiry, and he too came under intense pressure. Nonetheless, the report was completed and published (after approval by a committee in-cluding Bishop Cannon) and to this day remains the most significant in-vestigation of an industrial dispute by a religious group. Ultimately, Elbert H. Gary (incidentally, a Methodist layman), chairman of the United States Steel Corporation, succumbed to the public will created largely by the McConnell report, and the twelve-hour day in the steel in-dustry was abolished. S. Parkes Cadman later observed that Gary "made the biggest mistake of his life on the day he let Frank McConnell cool his heels for two hours in the anteroom." [133]

The concern of Southern Methodism with the condition and status of the industrial worker was much less intense than that of the Northern Church. This is understandable. The Southern bishops grasped the heart of the matter in their 1906 Episcopal Address:

Certain grave problems that have been prominent, and more or less perilous, in other sections of our country, have *only recently* become acute in the South.

[133] Quoted in *Northwestern Christian Advocate*, May 20, 1937, p. 467.

The problems of the city, of rapidly increasing wealth, of the employer and the employed, of factory districts, of congested foreign populations, and of the forsaken rural sections have been transferred to these parallels. We *have been* a rural and a pastoral people. But now conditions are rapidly changing. Foreigners from Southern Europe are coming by the thousands, factories are multiplying, village and country neighborhoods are breaking up, and people are drifting into town and city. A wise, constructive statesmanship suggests that we now prepare for the inevitable tomorrow.[134]

Though the statesmanship was tardy, Southern Methodism made the effort. The Social Creed of Methodism was readily adopted, with all its reforms. In 1922 the Episcopal Address, after noting several examples of the Christian spirit in industry, went on to say:

But a comparative few of these instances of the benevolent use of power and opportunity are not enough. What the industrial classes are asking is not charity, not toleration, but the recognition of their right to a righteous compensation as the basis of a safe and intelligent family life and of themselves and their engagements as a necessary and honorable part of the great business life of our nation. We believe this claim to be just and worthy of respect on the part of all Christian Churches.[135]

On other occasions the bishops spoke, sometimes pinpointing specific abuses in southern textile mills, as did the Committee on Temperance and Social Service. Moreover, in 1927 Bishop Cannon joined with forty-one Southern Church leaders in issuing an "Appeal to Industrial Leaders of the South," vigorously indicting textile-mill conditions. A storm of abuse was unleashed upon the heads of the churchmen, but Bishop Cannon, never one to be intimidated, eloquently defended the "Appeal" and refused to retreat an inch.

The Nashville *Christian Advocate* was, in its attitude toward labor, clearly one of the most liberal journals in the South, though its liberalism was less evident early in the century. In 1900 the editors held: "Labor has exactly the same right to organize that is claimed by capital." [136] Here and later they defended the justice of the striking coal miners. As early as 1902 the *Advocate* was convinced that "to keep a child in the close, linty air of the mill, and engaged in labor, however light, eight hours a day is a crime against childhood." [137] In time the editors were

[134] *The Daily Christian Advocate,* the Methodist Episcopal Church, South, May 4, 1906, p. 3. Italics mine.
[135] *Journal of the General Conference of the Methodist Episcopal Church, South,* 1922, p. 359.
[136] "A Great Strike," September 27, 1900, p. 2.
[137] "Child Labor in the South," September 4, 1902, p. 2.

to support federal control, a position well in advance of majority opinion in the South. In 1910 the exploitation of women in New York factories was termed a disgrace to civilization, and conditions in Pennsylvania steel mills were branded slavery. The editors believed in a living wage because of their belief "in Christ, who has inspired every agency in this world which has been used for the uplift of men or wages." [138] In the '20's they painted conditions in southern textile mills in the blackest hues, while in the '30's New Deal labor-reform legislation was enthusiastically received. A contributor asked:

Are there not wrongs to be righted? Are strikes and hunger and poverty and unemployment to be accepted as "acts of God," or can they be ameliorated, remedied, prevented? To answer these questions in the negative is absurd. Already humanity has gone far from the days when all manual labor was done by slaves, or even from those when little children and half-naked women crawled about in the depths of English coal mines. That we have not yet gone far enough is witnessed by the widespread unrest in reference to wages, hours, unemployment, and the like.[139]

Further, Southern Methodists in Annual Conference or in such unofficial groups as the Council on a Christian Social Order or as individuals sometimes addressed themselves to industrial questions or mediated industrial disputes.

From the perspectives of mid-century, Methodism's hopes for labor were both frustrated and fulfilled. On the one hand, the widely expressed hope that the goals of the church and of organized labor were identical, that both sought the brotherhood of all men, that both cherished the vision of a just society, that both tapped men's noblest motives, that both represented men's highest idealism—this hope soured in the age of James Hoffa. To borrow an allusion from Reinhold Niebuhr, when the poor are historically "blessed," they become successful. In that case they cease to be poor and become powerful. They become too powerful, in fact.

On the other hand, though the meek were no longer meek, the America they inherited at mid-century was less streaked with class injustice than it had been in 1900. Thus, in supporting labor Methodism was not successful in converting a "bread and butter" movement to righteousness, but at least Methodism had helped secure for working men and women (and children) a measure of social justice unknown in any earlier society.

[138] "Editorial Observations," June 26, 1914, p. 7.
[139] The Watchman, "Labor Disputes," July 19, 1935, p. 903.

5

The Social Gospel

Thus far we have attempted to review Methodism's involvement in crucial aspects of American society. Methodists pursued a society unstained by liquor, unstrained by ethnic or religious tension, unscarred by racial pride, and unmarred by class injustice. These were but elements in the greater totality—the vision of the kingdom of God, the dear truth, the marrow of the gospel, as Rauschenbusch believed. And it was Walter Rauschenbusch, a Baptist, the greatest social prophet America had yet produced, who predicted:

The Methodists are likely to play a very important part in the social awakening of the American churches. . . . They have rarely backed away from a fight when the issue was clearly drawn between Jehovah and Diabolus. . . . Their leaders are fully determined to form their battalions on this new line of battle, and when they march, the ground will shake.[140]

Though the prediction was ultimately and gloriously fulfilled, in 1900 it seemed that Diabolus had little to fear from Methodists—little to fear, that is, to the extent that he achieved the damnation of souls through social conditions. By the opening years of the twentieth century an articulate and growing band of Protestant ministers and laymen were working their way toward what became known as the social gospel. These prophets—Washington Gladden, Richard Ely, W. D. P. Bliss, George D. Herron, Graham Taylor, Charles Stelzle, Walter Rauschenbusch, and others—sought to make relevant the individualistic and pietistic Protestant ethic to the complexities and brutalities of modern, urban, industrial America. They rediscovered a social ethic, as old as the prophets of Israel and never entirely forgotten, capable of reckoning with the social sins of America's Steel Age. They scourged the new kings of capitalism who "beat my people to pieces, and grind the faces of the poor" (Isa. 3:15 KJV). They responded to the challenge of the new urban-industrial jungle as their fathers had to the wilderness of frontier America. And they recalled from the distant past the words of Amos: "Let judgment run down as waters, and righteousness as a mighty stream" (5:24 KJV).

The social gospel, moreover, resulted not only from external challenge but also from internal need, for by 1900 much (though by no means all) of Protestantism had embraced a theology that *demanded* implementa-

[140] Quoted in Sweet, *Methodism in American History*, pp. 359-60.

tion in social action. The immanence of God, a solidaristic view of society, the essential goodness if not perfectibility of man, the inevitability of evolutionary progress, the moral order of the universe, the modern application of the social teaching of a historical Jesus, and, above all, the approximation of the kingdom of God in history—these composed the liberal theological soil that nurtured the social gospel. By mid-century the weakness and inadequacy of this theology seemed apparent to H. Richard Niebuhr, who wrote that it preached that "a God without wrath brought men without sin into a kingdom without judgment through the ministrations of a Christ without a cross." [141] Nevertheless, it was just such a theology that generated a social passion placing under judgment vast reaches of American society. Almost every Protestant church was permeated by the passion, and ultimately, in 1908, its force transcended denominational barriers, for in that year the Federal Council of the Churches of Christ in America was formed. It is fitting that this then most important co-operative advance in the history of Protestantism in America should be the child of one of the most significant developments in American church history—the rise of the social gospel.

Yet, as has been said, Methodists were tardy in confronting the Diabolus that roamed the mines and mills, smoking factories and smoke-filled corporation offices, slums and tenements of late nineteenth-century America. The tides of social Christianity were already running swiftly before Methodism contributed its force. Wesley's followers were as far removed from the cutting edge of the urban-industrial frontier as they had been in the advance of the agrarian frontier in Asbury's age. This latter situation was not long to be. During the famous Christmas Conference in Baltimore in 1784, the assemblage asked the question: "What may we reasonably believe to be God's design in raising up the Preachers called Methodists?" and recorded as the answer: "To reform the continent, and to spread scriptural Holiness over the land." In the nineteenth century Methodists responded magnificently to the challenge. Early in the twentieth century their descendants set out to reform a continent vastly changed from that of 1784, but one no less desperately in need of reformation.

Methodists hearkened to the cry of the poverty-racked city masses. We must remain and save the people, admonished the Northern bishops in 1896. Frank Mason North (how appropriate that the hymn "Where Cross the Crowded Ways of Life" should have come from his pen!) early recognized that the problem of poverty "lies very close to the problem of

[141] *The Kingdom of God in America* (Harper Torchbook ed.; New York: Harper & Brothers, 1959) , p. 193.

sin" and that the great cities spawned a "crowding, brutalizing, crushing horror which makes one sneer at civilization and wonder if God has forgotten to be just." [142] Methodist concern received increasing expression in conference addresses, reports, and resolutions and in the church press. This concern was translated into action through church extension, home missions, and, not least of all, the deaconess movement. City missions, institutional churches, settlement houses, hospitals, asylums, orphanages, homes for the aged, co-ordinating social unions, were some of the instruments utilized. "Compared with the Methodists," wrote a leading scholar in regard to one aspect of this work, "the contributions of other American denominations were insignificant." [143] Twentieth-century Methodism took seriously North's charge to the 1900 Northern General Conference: "Not with the despair of pessimism, but with the courage of confidence in God, the church must go forward to the conquest of these citadels of power." [144]

As Methodism sought to reach the new urban masses, so the church strove to continue its ministry to older rural communities. The problem was grave. Once-flourishing rural circuits were bleeding to death as the population seeped away to town and city. Once-vital rural churches deteriorated and then, in hundreds of instances, were abandoned. Every General Conference of Methodism expressed an awareness of the problem in Episcopal Addresses, reports, and resolutions. The gravity of the situation was underscored in the Methodist press. Soon an impressive movement was under way to revitalize the country church through surveys, conferences, educational courses, financial assistance, home missionaries, interchurch co-operation, and the construction of new churches and the consolidation of others.

In contrast to the broken humanity in urban wastelands and blighted rural areas were the new industrial and financial barons in their tawdry brownstone mansions and costly sham châteaux. The post–Civil War generation of Americans sat down to a Great Barbecue, Gargantuan in its rough plenty; indeed, no less than the entire resources of a vast rich continent. If at the end of the century some citizens had not been invited to the feast and others had been put off with the giblets and bones, a few (with the sharpest elbows and longest reach) were unhealthily bloated. These few liked to think of themselves as the fittest who had survived through a process of natural selection, and, of course, they appropriated and perverted Darwin to prove their point. They also found

[142] Quoted in Aaron Ignatius Abell, *The Urban Impact on American Protestantism, 1865-1900* (Cambridge: Harvard University Press, 1943) , p. 169.

[143] *Ibid.*, p. 202.

[144] *The Daily Christian Advocate*, the Methodist Episcopal Church, May 8, 1900, p. 95.

comfort, ironically, in the theological doctrine of election. In truth, they survived because they *were* capable, tireless, predatory, single-minded, primitive souls, never given to whining, never restrained by petty scruple. Not all were wreckers and pirates, and almost all were practicing Protestants, but even the giants who built constructively and well demanded a price for their transformation of America into an industrial world power. The price was rather high: in 1910 the wealthiest 1 per cent of the population owned 47 per cent of the national wealth and received about 15 per cent of the national income. Impressive acts of generous stewardship blur the harshness of these figures, but when Woodrow Wilson reviewed the march of industrialization since the Civil War, he spoke for all socially sensitive Americans when he lamented the much fine gold that had been tarnished.

Methodists sought to redress the balance between poverty and power, as we have seen, by championing labor reforms and by succoring the workingman's tenement-housed families. They also chipped away at the power of the corporate wealthy, agreeing with Lord Acton's dictum that power corrupts and absolute power corrupts absolutely. Methodists were further guided by an older and more imperative injunction. Warned the Nashville *Christian Advocate* in 1902:

> The greed of gain is the death of the soul. There is not a single sin to which it does not lead. Coarse, vulgar, brutalizing, it crowds down and crushes out all the better human instincts. Our Lord's warning against it is so terrible that in every age timid preachers have sought to take the edge off of it by their comments. But there it is imbedded in the very heart of the gospel: "It is easier for a camel to go through the eye of a needle, than for a rich man to enter the kingdom of God." [145]

Surveying the conspicuous consumption of the new rich, the editors of the New York *Christian Advocate* were reminded of the nobility of France who before the great Revolution walked on a carpet of flowers, unconscious that it covered an abyss. Bear with an earnest warning, pleaded a speaker at the 1908 Northern General Conference.

> Remember the Priest and the Levite who passed by on the other side—possibly they were not so much heartless as busy men—men hurrying, perhaps, to a General Conference at Jericho, where a High Priest was to be elected and a ritual to be revised. . . . In the clamor and confusion of these things let us not dare forget that humanity lies plundered and bleeding by the highway. God forbid that we should pass on the other side. [146]

[145] "The Age of Gold," February 20, 1902, p. 1.
[146] *The Daily Christian Advocate,* Methodist Episcopal Church, May 9, 1908, p. 3.

Consequently, Methodists denounced with Theodore Roosevelt the "malefactors of great wealth" and with Woodrow Wilson dreamed for the American people a "New Freedom." For instance, they favored progressive taxation including the proposed income tax in order to persuade "those who have large properties . . . to do what their stations and fortunes require of them." [147] Concerning the corruption of wealth: "Probably few generations of men in the world's history have shown more examples, and more flagrant examples, of this than the Americans of this Twentieth Century. . . . Moreover, they outrage public sentiment, they scorn moral restraints, they defy God, drunk as they are with the sense of power which mere money gives. It is a pitiable sight." [148]

In 1904 the Northern bishops denounced the vast, conscienceless combinations of capital shamefully robbing the unsuspecting public, and Southern Methodists believed these combinations must be made responsive to the public will. "If corporations have no souls, it is all the worse for corporations." [149] And "if the States cannot handle these matters, then the Federal Congress should legislate." [150]

To be sure, an important element within Methodism protested "turning the pulpit into a soap box" (to use the phrase worn thin in the service of "old-time religion"). This element rejected the insight that individuals are saved within their social context rather than out of it. Ministers were warned to preach only "Christ—and Him crucified." To be sure, an important proportion of Methodism remained eminently orthodox in its economic and political thinking, continuing to be bound by the steel ring of nineteenth-century ideas. To be sure, only rarely did official Methodist bodies give precise approval to specific reform measures of the Progressive era.

On balance, however, it seems clear that Methodism gave support to Theodore Roosevelt's New Nationalism and Wilson's New Freedom. Trust busting and conservation; the Federal Trade Commission and the Federal Reserve Act; the Hepburn Act and the Clayton Act; the protection of children and working women and men; the attack on corruption, crime, vice, slums—these things and more represented the political implementation of the social gospel. This conclusion was spelled out explicitly in the Methodist press and by individual leaders; it is implicit in the spirit of Progressivism.

[147] "The Need of an Income Tax," Nashville *Christian Advocate,* January 16, 1902, p. 2.
[148] "Riches and Religion," Nashville *Christian Advocate,* April 8, 1910, pp. 3-4.
[149] "Corporations and the Law," Nashville *Christian Advocate,* May 31, 1906, p. 5.
[150] "Publicity as a Remedy for Trusts," Nashville *Christian Advocate,* September 25, 1902, p. 2.

Progressivism

Progressivism was not an uprising of the ignorant, immigrant masses, nor was it simply a continuation of the angry agrarian Populist movement of the 1890's. On the contrary, Progressivism was a middle-class movement arising in a period of relative prosperity and drawing support mostly from well-educated, economically secure, old-stock Protestants. Though many now lived in cities, most carried memories of a rural boyhood, and they viewed an urban culture with suspicion. Professor Hofstadter has suggested that these middle-class Americans were suffering a relative loss of status and power in society. Their hands had once clutched securely the upper rungs of the ladder of success and prestige, but now predatory robber barons of industry and finance had bulled to the top, scrambling past men and professions (such as the clergy) once the acknowledged leaders of America. The middle classes suffered a reduction less in income than in outlook, as Lincoln Steffens observed at the time. Doubtless Progressivism did spring in part from frustration, envy, guilt, and loss of status, just as Methodism, as we have seen, was scarred by these flaws as the old nineteenth-century order passed.

However, Progressivism was born of hope as well as fear, compassion as well as frustration, idealism as well as envy. Progressives believed in man's dignity and worth. If not inherently good, man was inherently malleable, and in a perfected environment man would no longer be robbed of the opportunity of becoming "therefore perfect." Complementing this hopeful view of human nature was an optimistic view of history, and Progressives were confident that society could be made, and was indeed becoming, sweeter and fairer. Progressives spoke in highly moral language. The entire movement was permeated with moral urgency. Unregenerate doers of evil would be toppled from the thrones of power in a great crusade led by an enlightened, righteous elite. With "Teddy," they sang "Onward, Christian Soldiers," and stood at Armageddon to do battle for the Lord.

These attributes of Progressivism were intimately associated with the spirit of the social gospel. "We believe," read a report to the 1908 Northern General Conference, "that in the teachings of the New Testament will be found the ultimate solution of all the problems of our social order. When the spirit of Christ shall pervade the hearts of individuals and when his law of love to God and man shall dominate human society, then the evils which vex our civilization will disappear." [151]

---

[151] *The Daily Christian Advocate,* the Methodist Episcopal Church, May 23, 1908, p. 8.

The New York *Christian Advocate* urged Methodists to place "Christ uppermost in the politics of our country," for "the kingdom of God is capable of realization. Every day . . . [it is] being approximated. The social movements of our time give evidence that its triumph is hastening. Whatever can be done by political action to accelerate the conquest of the world for Jesus Christ sanctifies the ballot and glorifies the citizen who casts it." [152]

On the one hand, it is a tribute to the liberal spirit of Methodism that its attitudes were so akin to those of Progressivism. On the other hand, this gives substance to the accusation that Methodism merely reflected the temper of the age; that once again the church identified itself with American culture. As the church had been unable to transcend the sectional tensions of the Civil War era or the conservative *Zeitgeist* of the Gilded Age, so the church found itself sharing the reform fervor, the buoyant optimism, the roseate hopes, of Progressive America. Some later historians were to lampoon the fatuous innocence of reformers unblooded by war, depression, or the shadow of nuclear destruction; and the social-gospel movement received similar harsh (perhaps "condescending" is the proper word) treatment at the hands of theologians and church historians. Yet the words of Robert M. La Follette might be repeated without apology by many social gospelites, as well as by many Progressives:

This closes the account of my services in Wisconsin—a time full of struggle, and yet a time that I like to look back upon. It has been a fight supremely worth making, and I want it to be judged, as it will be ultimately, by results actually attained. If it can be shown that Wisconsin is a happier and better state to live in, that its institutions are more democratic, that the opportunities of all its people are more equal, that social justice more nearly prevails, that human life is safer and sweeter—then I shall rest content in the feeling that the Progressive movement has been successful. [153]

The Federal Council of Churches

The successful penetration of American Protestantism by the social gospel is symbolized by the formation of the Federal Council of the Churches of Christ in America. After several years of deliberations, the organizational meeting of the Council was held in Philadelphia in December, 1908, the constitution of the new body having already been ap-

---

[152] "Politics and Religion," October 24, 1912, p. 1511.
[153] Quoted in Arthur S. Link, *American Epoch* (New York: Alfred A. Knopf, 1955), p. 91.

proved by twenty-eight denominations. From the outset the Council was an outstanding champion of social Christianity. At the first meeting the Council adopted an eighteen-page report on "The Church and Modern Industry," presented and largely prepared by Frank Mason North. It then proceeded to issue the famous Social Creed of the Churches, which, after modification in 1912, was to stand for twenty years as the most representative position of American Protestantism on social issues. This statement was taken almost verbatim from the Social Creed of Methodism, set forth earlier in the year at the Northern General Conference. The Methodist Episcopal, the Methodist Episcopal, South, the Methodist Protestant, and the three Negro Methodist Episcopal churches were among the original members of the Council and co-operated actively in all its endeavors. Moreover, Bishop Eugene R. Hendrix, of the Southern Church, was the Council's first president, and Frank Mason North and Bishop McConnell were later to be accorded this high honor; and Methodists served with distinction in important executive posts.

The Methodist Federation for Social Service

The successful penetration of Methodism by the social gospel is symbolized by the formation on December 3, 1907, in Washington, D.C., of the Methodist Federation for Social Service. More the creation than the creator of the emergent social passion within Methodism, the Federation took as its purposes to "deepen within the church the sense of social obligation and opportunity, to study social problems from the Christian point of view, and to promote social service in the spirit of Jesus Christ." [154] The founders of the Federation were North, Herbert Welch (later a bishop), Elbert R. Zaring, Worth M. Tippy, and Harry F. Ward. In time most of the Methodist prophets were associated with it. Ward was to remain the commanding figure until after unification. Although always maintaining an unofficial relationship to the Methodist Episcopal Church it was looked upon as the executive agency to rally the forces of the church in support of social thought and reform. Bishop McConnell, later president of the Federation, described its purpose in more homely terms: that of raising disturbing questions—ahead of time. The Federation's unofficial status gave it the freedom necessary to pursue unfettered a prophetic role; the respect and support received from the church provided

[154] *The Daily Christian Advocate,* the Methodist Episcopal Church, May 16, 1908, p. 8.

needed funds and prestige. The Methodist Federation for Social Service quickly became the most influential organization of its type within American Protestantism.

American Foreign Policy

The social gospel came of age and Progressivism flourished in the period bracketed by the Spanish-American War and the First World War. It would require a volume to sketch Methodism's position toward war and peace and diplomacy in these years. Only a few broad generalizations can be undertaken here. To begin with, and contrary to scholarly opinion, not all of Methodism was aflame with desire to fight Catholic Spain and thereby secure new fields for Protestant evangelization. Though firmly imbedded in all textbooks, this thesis simply does not jibe with the widespread sentiment expressed, for example, at the 1898 Southern General Conference:

We have met the smallest number of Southern Methodists who do not profoundly deprecate the present war with Spain. Only a few hot-headed enthusiasts, who fail to consider the possible consequences of armed hostilities show any disposition to rejoice over the fact that we are engaged in a struggle of force with another nation. The general feeling is that war ought never to be begun when it can be honorably avoided, and that even the most justifiable war carries with it unnumbered evils of the most appalling character. But this feeling is in no wise inconsistent with the most genuine patriotism. When the fighting begins every true American must sympathize with his country, and do whatever he can to contribute to its success. . . . We trust, however, that our people will take great care not to tolerate in themselves the growth of any malevolent or bitter passions towards our enemies. If we are christians, we must avoid everything that contradicts our professions.[155]

In the second place and again contrary to scholarly opinion, in the great debate over imperialism not all of Methodism favored the acquisition of a colonial empire and thereby presumably the extension of Protestant missions. Though accepted by all textbooks, this thesis does not agree with the widespread sentiment expressed, for example, by the Nashville *Christian Advocate:* "A question of prime importance that needs to be now considered by all Americans is whether a people who set up a despotism over others can long maintain their own freedom." [156]

Thirdly, Methodism displayed sanity, restraint, forbearance, and good

[155] *The Daily Christian Advocate,* the Methodist Episcopal Church, South, May 9, 1898, p. 5.
[156] "Our Vassal States Again," February 15, 1900, p. 2.

will when tensions mounted between the United States and Germany over the Caribbean, with China over the Boxer incident, with Russia and Japan over the Open Door, and with Mexico over the loss of American lives and property in the revolutions. This fact is of great significance because in all these cases war was a possibility and, in truth, a high possibility with Japan and a probability with Mexico. Yet, to repeat, Methodism cautioned against precipitate action, restrained the hand of jingoists, and contributed to preservation of peace.

6

World War I and the Aftermath

When in 1914 the Great War crashed upon Europe, Methodists, as all Americans, were stunned by disbelief, for the bright, confident opening years of the new century had seemed to carry the promise of permanent peace and unchecked progress. The months that followed were ones of compassion for the European victims; thankfulness that America had been spared; hope that the United States could remain neutral; and the conviction that "when these clouds of war shall have lifted and the last echoes of the carnage shall have died away the Prince of Peace will be found standing in the midst of a greater army than he has yet led and that his victorious march will not cease until real, lasting peace shall have been secured for the nations." [157]

But neutrality proved impossible. The war came to America. It has been customary to condemn preachers for presenting arms with the rest of the nation. It has been fashionable to quote the more extreme preachments of hate from pulpit, church press, and assembly—and these unchristian preachments *are* inexcusable. However, the Southern bishops stated a position increasingly shared by historians in retrospect:

But we feel entirely justified in saying that our own country, though it has been drawn into active participation in the conflict, is in no wise responsible for originating it. Neither our rulers nor our people wanted it. As a nation we were more than content to live at peace with all men. By no act of ours had we incurred the just hostility of the belligerent powers. It gives us the greatest satisfaction to affirm that our President went to the utmost possible limit to keep us out of the fray. If he is censurable for anything—and we do not think he is—it is for having been too forbearing. Not till it became entirely necessary for us

[157] "The War," Nashville *Christian Advocate*, August 28, 1914, p. 5.

to fight or else submit to the most violent and brutal outrages at the hands of the German Kaiser and those who are banded together with him for the tyrannical domination of the world did Mr. Wilson at last advise the Congress to draw the sword. In our judgment he was fully warranted in taking this extreme step, and we should be less than patriotic and courageous Americans if we failed to give him our cordial support in every way.[158]

In the post-1918 period many Methodists recalled with shame their wartime patriotic enthusiasm; they lamented the fact that there were so few Methodist pacifists. This is an unnecessarily harsh indictment. To be sure, an element of Methodism was engulfed in hatred of the "Hun." But Methodists may also remember happily the church's ministry to the boys in service, to their families at home, and to the victims of war in America and in Europe. The National War Council of Northern Methodism, the War-Work Commission of Southern Methodism, and the War-Work Commission of the Methodist Protestant Church all creditably attempted to meet the spiritual hunger and physical need of youngsters in American camps and French trenches, bored lads in transports, and pain-racked boys in hospitals. Approximately 325 Methodist chaplains served "with the colors," and at least 500 Methodist ministers were engaged in Y.M.C.A. work. Nor did the work cease when the war ended, for disbanded soldiers, returned Negro servicemen, European refugees, and American influenza victims were succored.

The "Golden Twenties"

The decade of the 1920's is extraordinarily difficult to assess. Characterized as an age of "normalcy," it was in fact one of profound change. Termed the "era of wonderful nonsense," few periods in American history have been so fraught with tension. Remembered as the "Golden Twenties," it was for many a time of economic hardship. Singled out as a decade of unique reaction, it also perpetuated a progressive spirit and provided a bridge between the reform eras of Theodore Roosevelt and Franklin D. Roosevelt. The "Lost Generation" was indeed lost, not so much in the sense that it was uniquely immoral, but rather in the sense that the Americans of the 1920's were made bewildered, uncertain, and fearful by problems whose solutions were as yet unknown. Compounding this insecurity was the nagging thought that the old nineteenth-century verities were no longer relevant to the new problems. The age, observed

[158] *The Daily Christian Advocate,* the Methodist Episcopal Church, South, May 3, 1918, p. 8.

the Northern bishops with William James, was "one big, blooming, buzzing confusion." [159]

In their insecurity, some Methodists, as we have seen, joined the Ku Klux Klan. Others compromised with cherished Protestant principles by importuning the state to enact anti-evolution laws designed to protect old theological strongholds from the assaults of modernism, though, happily, the record of official Methodism is pretty clean in this matter. Even the great prohibition passion became streaked with a harsh, repressive spirit. Repression, too, seemed to be some Methodists' answer to the revolution in morals, for the times were indeed out of joint when the word "neck" abruptly became a verb; and when an F. Scott Fitzgerald heroine could say: "I'm hipped on Freud and all that, but its rotten that every bit of *real* love in the world is ninety-nine percent passion and one little soupçon of jealousy."

The trouble, some Methodists maintained, all stemmed from the subversive agitation of outsiders and the insidious propaganda of the dreaded Bolsheviki. The solution, consequently, was to deport alien agitators and to crush Communist-inspired, un-American radicalism. And in the 1920's foreigners were deported, dissent was stifled, liberals (including those within Methodism) came under suspicion.

Complacency mingled with fear to check the liberal fervor and questioning spirit that had seemed triumphant in the Progressive era. Many middle-class Methodists felt that the central problems of civilization had been solved. The government was in sensible Republican hands, and an emotionally drained citizenry welcomed the "normalcy" promised by Harding and the coolness (not to say placidity) promised by Coolidge. The economy was in the sensible hands of businessmen, and soon all America would bask in golden prosperity. And because America was sensible, she would be in the world but not of it, and hence in splendid isolation escape the wars and revolutions beyond her shores.

The very success of the businessmen in seeming to provide for the material needs of the nation enhanced the temptation for the church to emulate business techniques. Since means cannot be divorced from ends, ultimately the church came to accept the standards of business. Thus, some churches adopted the vulgar promotion tactics of the business world: "Public Worship Increases Your Efficiency," "Business Success and Religion Go Together," "Be a Sport—Come to Church." Almost of necessity, large institutional churches acquired the atmosphere of a corporation. Increasingly ministers became salesmen with a wonderfully fine

[159] *The Daily Christian Advocate,* the Methodist Episcopal Church, May 3, 1920, p. 28.

"line" to sell their congregations. Finally, as Henry Sloane Coffin observed, ministers ceased to be shepherds and became ranchers, for it was assumed that only a large church was a "successful" church and that the righteousness that exalted a nation could be measured by the statistics of conversion.

The supreme irony is that in adopting the methods and goals of a business culture, in adapting to the tides of secularization, in permitting the domestication of the church, Protestantism, far from being strengthened, suffered further drain of its internal dynamics.

However, it is imperative to introduce a dissenting report on behalf of Protestantism in general and Methodism in particular. Subjectively, our memories remind us that there lived in the United States in the 1920's Christian men and women who gave prior loyalty neither to Henry Ford nor to Sigmund Freud, but to the Lord our God, who is a great King above all gods. Objectively, the sources accessible to historians suggest that not all of Methodism capitulated to the secularism of American culture.

It may disprove more than it proves to point out that membership in the Methodist Protestant, Methodist Episcopal, and Methodist Episcopal, South, churches increased 12.3 per cent between 1916 and 1926. And perhaps it is not meaningful that in this decade the value of all church property more than doubled, and that the amount spent for new church structures skyrocketed. This evidence, after all, may simply confirm the charge of materialism. Moreover, if statistics are employed, it could be shown that contributions to missionary work declined drastically in the late 1920's.

However, the magnificent Centenary Movement of the Methodist Episcopal Church and the Methodist Episcopal Church, South, is simply not comprehensible except in terms of the devotion and sacrificial spirit of millions of Methodist laymen and women. Launched to commemorate the beginning of Methodist missions among the Wyandott Indians by John Stewart, the illiterate Negro preacher, in 1819, the Centenary captured the imagination of the Christian world. And it captured the hearts and purses of American Methodists. Within a year, subscriptions of over $140,000,000 had been pledged for foreign and home missions. "I am bound to say this," reported Dr. Edgar Blake (later a bishop) to the 1920 Northern General Conference, "that in the light of the whole situation, the success of the Centenary financial campaign is the most remarkable and striking financial achievement in the history of America, if not in the history of the world." [160] Despite lost pledges, despite soured hopes,

[160] *Ibid.*, May 7, 1920, p. 117.

despite some failures, Elmer T. Clark reported to the 1926 Southern General Conference:

No other single enterprise ever attracted so much attention, secured the co-operation of so many persons, or achieved such remarkable results in so short a period. . . . It is well-known everywhere that without this great advance movement our missionary work would doubtless have collapsed during the arduous days immediately following the World War. . . . It has been a gracious privilege to work in such a cause and we have confidence that the time will never come when our people do not look back with gratitude and gratification to the Centenary period during which it made the greatest advances in all its history.[161]

It would indeed be sad if Methodists did not look back with "gratitude and gratification." So many criticisms have been made of the Centenary and other denominational and interdenominational missionary movements of the early twentieth century, so many damaging observations have been drawn between the high hopes and the limited attainments of these movements, that it is easy to overlook a final fact: Millions of Christians in modest—and often very modest—financial circumstances made very real sacrifices so that millions of forgotten and burdened human beings throughout the world might receive a measure of material and spiritual succor.

Moreover, it is simply not accurate to state that all of Methodism succumbed to the secularist temper of the '20's, bowed before the "bitch goddess Success," and entered an "Age of Babbittonian Captivity." Repeatedly Methodists gave witness to a faith transcending caste, class, and culture. The church is not compelled to follow where others lead, admonished the Northern bishops in 1920. One and only one is our Maser, even Christ, affirmed a Methodist minister in Detroit when the business community attempted to muzzle the pulpit. "A pious 'spirituality' which accepts the exclusion of its religion from the political and economic realm worships a God who does not really count in this world," stated Halford E. Luccock.[162] "If we confine Jesus to heaven and imprison His spirit within our churches, shall we express surprise if the common people crown Karl Marx in the streets?" warned another Methodist minister.[163] When the talented advertising executive Bruce Barton in two popular books depicted Christ and the church in terms of American business culture, the contributing editor of the New York *Christian Advocate*, speaking for much of Methodism, protested:

[161] *The Daily Christian Advocate,* the Methodist Episcopal Church, South, May 10, 1926, p. 39.
[162] Quoted in Carter, *Decline and Revival of the Social Gospel,* p. 68.
[163] Roy H. Beane, "A Plea for Human Rights," *Zion's Herald,* April 23, 1930, p. 522.

Isn't it lovely? Such a church resembles nothing so much as a sun parlor of a large country club, or the perfumed rose room of a large hotel. It is the church with the engine lifted entirely out of it. It shows a remarkable lack of penetration into the real issues of life in the world today, to imagine that such a little esthetic paradise can ever speak healingly to the world's need and tragedy. The widespread mood of disillusion in the world today can never be met by blowing on a penny whistle or a few moments of silence. The gospel which is to redeem the world must be a stout gospel. It must work through the lives of men and women who will go to the Cross in sacrificial warfare against the malignant powers of evil and exploitation.

A pink-tea church will never do that. The picture Mr. Barton paints is just exactly the kind of church that every reactionary and Grand Duke of special privilege would like to see. They would like to be sure that the church is to be chloroformed with beauty and soft music. They do not want any of the harsh words of Jesus against the lust of greed which spoils and mangles life. . . . A business-like prayer, "Prosper me today," is so much more uplifting. . . .

It is a very "pretty" religion and that is just what is the matter with it. The world is not saved by "pretty" religion. Jesus died on a Cross and men who have carried His spirit into the world are men who had a profound religion, based on the proclamation of great truths that went to the very center of life.[164]

The paganism of American society was a theme very widely expressed in Methodist pulpits, journals, General Conferences, and Annual Conferences. Nor were Methodists deterred from performing their prophetic task of critical judgment by the accusation that all those who found America short of perfection were in the "pay of Moscow." Reactionaries who attempted to muzzle dissent, affirmed a columnist for the Nashville Christian Advocate, were like Dogberry, "to be 'writ down an ass.' "[165] And in 1927 the Northwestern Christian Advocate dismissed the notion of Communist subversion with the observation that the proportion of Communists to the population of the United States was about the same as the proportion of bald bachelors to the entire membership of the House of Representatives.

Thus, many Methodists stood firm as waves of hysteria eroded civil liberties in the "Great Red Scare" of 1919-20. Thus, not all Methodists remained silent when two immigrant anarchists, Nicola Sacco and Bartolomeo Vanzetti, were sentenced to death for a crime which, in the opinion of many liberals, they had not committed. Thus, finally, in the 1920's Methodist sources reveal considerable interest in and sympathy for the socialist experiment being conducted in Soviet Russia.

Bruce Barton's conception of Christianity did not go unchallenged in

[164] Halford E. Luccock, "The Church Nobody Knows," October 20, 1927, p. 1263.
[165] The Watchman, "Americanism," December 2, 1927, p. 1509.

the 1920's, as we have seen, yet it remains significant that his blasphemous biography of Jesus topped the nonfiction book list for the two years 1925 and 1926. Barton's popularity is symbolic of the domestication of an element of Protestantism (and Methodism) in the Golden Twenties. The 1930's gave the promise that the church might break free from the fetters of American culture, for the righteousness and attractiveness of that culture no longer seemed self-evident in a decade of bread lines, Hoovervilles, hunger riots, Okies, and unutterable despair compounded by demoniac events in Manchuria, China, Italy, Russia, Germany, Ethiopia, Spain, Czechoslovakia, and finally Poland.

The Great Depression

Paradoxically, Protestantism's recovery of its inner vitality at the end of the decade waited upon serious material losses at the onset of the depression. Methodism, as all major Protestant denominations, was cruelly hurt by the breakdown of the economy. Memberships declined relatively and absolutely. The Methodist Episcopal, Methodist Episcopal, South, and Methodist Protestant churches had 15.4 per cent fewer members in 1936 than in 1926, many of the losses being picked up by the Pentecostal and Holiness sects. Budgets were slashed, bishops as well as preachers suffered severe salary cuts, and administrative workers were reluctantly dismissed. The heavy indebtedness assumed in the halcyon '20's was now unbearably oppressive. Churches were abandoned and benevolent and missionary enterprises set adrift or sadly curtailed. In contradiction to earlier periods of economic dislocation, an anticipated religious revival failed to materialize. A people shorn of their material wealth did not turn to God. Because Methodism shared in the anguish that struck America in the 1929 crash, its critique of American society sharpened.

After witnessing the toll exacted by a year of depression, the Northern bishops were convinced that "there is something fundamentally wrong with a social system that, in the midst of plenteous abundance, dooms untold numbers of our people to unbearable poverty and distress through no apparent fault of their own." [166] At the 1932 Northern General Conference the bishops warned that the kingdom of God could not be built upon the poverty of the many and the absurd and cruel wealth of the few. The conference then proceeded to call for the "replacement of our present policy of unplanned, competitive individualism by a planned

[166] Quoted in the New York *Christian Advocate,* December 11, 1930, p. 1527.

industrial economy." [167] "The present industrial order," said the conference, "is unchristian, unethical and anti-social because it is largely based on the profit-motive which is a direct appeal to selfishness." [168] Southern Methodists declared in 1938 that

it is not enough to support in charity those whom we have first crushed. . . . An economic system which produces the results which we see all about us is subject to the most serious investigation in the light of Christian ideals. One of our serious needs is to deal with our economic order in terms of the Christian standards before those who are desperate—deal with it in terms of desperation.[169]

Meanwhile, Annual Conferences throughout the nation toughened their critiques. For instance, in 1935 the New York East Conference declared:

The twenty-five months of strenuous effort under the New Deal to reform the system has only proved that it is beyond reform. The conviction grows, therefore, that capitalism must be discarded and a planned Christian economy established. . . . The tenderness with which the sacred cow of private profits has been protected, while suffering has been indescribably inhuman, indicts both the intelligence and character of our nation.[170]

Convictions not dissimilar appeared widely in other Annual Conferences and the Methodist press. "To allow a few men to amass enormous wealth through a monopoly of natural resources which rightfully belong to all the people," believed the Nashville *Christian Advocate,* "is a piece of public stupidity which will not be tolerated one hour after the stupidity of the people ceases." [171] The monopoly would not be broken by moralistic preaching. "It is a soft and senseless sentimentalism that would ignore the necessity of coercion. There are capitalists guilty of oppression and injustice toward the weaker members of society whom a gospel appeal would not reach in a thousand years." [172] *Zion's Herald* broke even more sharply with capitalism, for, as the editors believed, it had brought mankind to the very verge of destruction. As for President Roosevelt, "He is dillydallying with the profit-makers. He is riding two horses going in opposite directions. Big business is closing in upon him. He is playing

[167] *The Daily Christian Advocate,* the Methodist Episcopal Church, May 20, 1932, p. 445.

[168] *Ibid.,* May 24, 1932, p. 594.

[169] *The Daily Christian Advocate,* the Methodist Episcopal Church, South, May 5, 1938, p. 145.

[170] Quoted in the New York *Times,* May 14, 1935, p. 21.

[171] "A Private Monopoly," October 13, 1933, p. 1286.

[172] "Economic Inequality," October 20, 1933, p. 1318.

into the hands of Fascism. Why does he not swing clear for man?" [173]

Methodism's gadfly, the Federation for Social Service, under the continuing leadership of Harry F. Ward, tacked sharply to the left. Always critical of the abuses of capitalism, the Federation now attacked the system itself, embracing the socialist vision of a classless society. The intensity of Ward's blinding vision blurred his good judgment. Ultimately, the Federation lost much of the respect that socially conscious Methodists had once rightfully accorded it.

Throughout the nation groups of Methodist laymen, clergymen, educators, and youth expressed a growing disenchantment, though rarely—in fact, very, very rarely—did this rejection of capitalism lead to enchantment with the utopian illusions of Marxism. Further, Methodist churchmen joined a host of militant, crusading, interdenominational movements such as the National Religion and Labor Foundation, the Fellowship of Socialist Christians, the United Christian Council for Democracy, the Fellowship of Southern Churchmen, and the Fellowship of Reconciliation. All these groups were rooted in the Christian tradition. None of them was a Communist front. Nonetheless, without exception they held a socialist society most nearly accorded with the kingdom of God.

It is hardly surprising that Methodist churchmen should participate in these movements, in light of the fact that, according to Kirby Page's poll of 100,499 clergymen in 1934, 34 per cent of the Methodists who responded (including a host of leaders) named socialism as the most preferred system for America. No other denomination accorded socialism so high a percentage.

Nor is it surprising that disturbed Methodist laymen (and clergymen) should seek to check the spread of this radical spirit, and a number of organizations, such as the Conference of Methodist Laymen, were formed and warnings issued, such as the Rev. Rembert G. Smith's *Moscow Over Methodism*. Methodist prophets also came under heavy attack from outside forces. But oak-hearted Methodists remained unintimidated. Everywhere Methodist congregations, even and especially those of conservative persuasion such as in Ernest Fremont Tittle's great Evanston church, upheld the freedom of the pulpit.

The fact is, the overwhelming majority of Methodists in the desperate '30's retained a deep commitment to "both the democratic form and the democratic ideal," firm in their determination "to resist every form of dictatorship, whether it come from the left of communism or the right of

[173] "A Glorious Example," February 6, 1935, p. 123.

fascism." [174] Their devotion to democracy and to a just social order rested on yet a firmer truth: The church of the redeemed is the only great redeeming agency.

1939—The Eve of Unification

The year 1939 was one of fulfillment and peril for America and Methodism. Political democracy had been preserved, social justice extended, and capitalism purged and strengthened. Unification of the three great historic branches of American Methodism was both result and portent of renewed spiritual vitality in the church. But even as the sun broke through to bathe Americans in new hope, the dark night of total war descended upon Europe and Asia.

Methodism had thrown itself into the peace crusade with high hopes and noble zeal, and for a glorious moment it seemed in truth that war had been outlawed, not only in a legal sense, but in the hearts of men as well. The League of Nations, the World Court, the Pact of Paris, disarmament conferences, and the other attempts at international co-operation had all received fervent Methodist support. It would require a very large volume even to begin to sketch the intensity of the Methodist passion for peace or to relate the scope of the church's crusade to leash the dogs of war. It can, however, be flatly stated that Methodism was more deeply penetrated by pacifism than any other major denomination. In fact, toward war Methodism displayed a conviction indistinguishable from that of the historic peace churches with, however, one signal difference. Methodism sought peace for the world, not in selfish withdrawal from the world, not in sullen or prideful isolation, but rather in active fellowship with men of good hope in all lands. In 1939, however, men of good hope everywhere were tortured by what seemed to many to be an irreconcilable tension between the imperatives of love and justice.

[174] *Journal of the General Conference of the Methodist Episcopal Church*, 1936, p. 519.

chapter 32

THE STORY OF UNIFICATION

1874-1939

Fraternal Relations

Federation to Unification

The Uniting Conference

The First General Conference

Structure of the New Church

IN THE YEAR 1874 THERE OCCURRED AN event of signal importance for American Methodism. Three members of the Methodist Episcopal Church appeared at the General Conference of the Methodist Episcopal Church, South, meeting in Louisville, Kentucky. They came as the first fraternal delegates from the Northern Church to the Southern Church following the unfortunate bisection of the Methodist Episcopal Church in 1844.

During the nineteenth century the Methodist Episcopal Church in America had split into three great segments.[1] In 1830 the Methodist Protestants had left the larger body to become a separate church. The original church was again split in 1844, becoming the Methodist Episcopal Church and the Methodist Episcopal Church, South. Imbedded in the cause of each catastrophe had been more than prejudice or a superficial variance of opinion. There had been a profound difference of viewpoint, a difference that had made continuation as one body impossible. Eventual union came in 1939 as the result of the creation of a wholly new organization rather than by a simple return to a former status.

Men of intense convictions had caused the splits, and men of equally profound principles would finally hammer out the constitution of the new church which rose mightier and stronger than the one that had previously been shattered.

A great deal of bitterness had been engendered at the time of and following the splits, and a necessary first step toward

---

[1] Small splinter groups also withdrew from the Methodist Episcopal Church in America, but, since they were not involved in the creation of The Methodist Church in 1939, they are not included in this study.

407

union was the establishment of a warm, friendly relationship among the churches. The fraternal delegates from the Northern Church to the Southern Church in 1874 were eminently fitted for this mission. The layman of the commission was General Clinton B. Fisk; the two ministers, Albert S. Hunt and Charles H. Fowler. All were men of broad outlook and were highly respected. All were excellent speakers, and Fowler in particular was one of the outstanding orators of the day. Little wonder that the usually cold, factual record of the *Journal* which marked the proceedings of the General Conference waxed warm as it stated that the addresses of the fraternal messengers "were characterized by excellent taste, great ability, and warm, fraternal sentiments, which were well received by the Conference and the immense audience in attendance." [2] A Committee on Fraternal Relations with the Methodist Episcopal Church, commissioned by the Southern General Conference to draw up a reply, added that "their utterances warmed our hearts. Their touching allusions to the common heritage of Methodist history, to our oneness of doctrines, polity, and usage, and their calling to mind the great work in which we are both engaged for the extension of the kingdom of their Lord and ours, stirred within us precious memories." [3]

The reply also outlined the relationship between the two churches previous to 1874, and added a series of paragraphs replete with sentiments of brotherhood and fraternity. It pointed, however, to certain problems centering in property rights and to other "disturbing questions" between the two churches. The reply ended with two resolutions. One said that, "in order to remove all obstacles to formal fraternity between the two churches, our College of Bishops is authorized to appoint a commission, consisting of three ministers and two laymen, to meet a similar commission authorized by the General Conference of the Methodist Episcopal Church, and to adjust all existing difficulties." The other resolutions called for the appointment of a fraternal delegation of two ministers and one layman by the College of Bishops "to bear our Christian salutations" to the next Northern General Conference. [4]

This fraternal delegation to the 1876 General Conference of the Methodist Episcopal Church included Dr. Lovick Pierce, who twenty-eight years before had been rebuffed when he had come to the Northern General Conference as a fraternal delegate from the new Methodist Episcopal

---

[2] *Journal of the General Conference of the Methodist Episcopal Church, South,* 1874, p. 416.

[3] *Ibid.,* p. 541.

[4] *Ibid.,* pp. 547-48. For details of the work of this fraternal delegation at the General Conference of the Methodist Episcopal Church in 1876, see Chapter 25.

Church, South. Now past ninety years of age, he was unable to attend the conference in person, but he sent a letter that breathed the spirit of brotherhood, understanding, and affection. "We protest," he wrote, "against any longer use of the popular phrase 'two Methodisms,' as between us. There is but *one* Episcopal Methodism in the United States of America, and you and we together make up this one Methodism." [5]

The reaction to this letter and to the speeches of the other fraternal delegates, Dr. James A. Duncan and Chancellor Landon C. Garland, was most favorable. The General Conference of the Northern Church approved the idea of a joint commission to "settle disturbing questions" and appointed five men to meet with the representatives of the Southern Church.[6]

The work of this joint commission, which met at Cape May City, New Jersey, August 17-23, 1876, cannot be praised too highly. In its "Declaration and Basis of Fraternity" the commission acknowledged that "each of said churches is a legitimate branch of Episcopal Methodism in the United States, having a common origin in the Methodist Episcopal Church organized in 1784"; and it pointed out that both churches together "have constituted one Methodist family, though in distinct ecclesiastical connections." [7]

Three broad "Rules for the Adjustment of Adverse Claims to Church Property" were unanimously adopted, and on the basis of these rules the commissioners went to work to settle definite cases presented for judgment. By August 21 they had completed the disposition of eleven disputes.

In his book *The Methodists Are One People* Bishop Paul N. Garber writes: "The Cape May agreement placed both branches of Methodism on a common basis of historical and ecclesiastical legitimacy and created a feeling of equality which for the first time made possible true fraternity and co-operation." [8] Bishop John M. Moore refers to it as the "golden milestone at the head of the highway that leads to unity and union in American Methodism." [9]

Both commissions reported their work to their respective General Conferences, and both conferences accepted their action as final. A question

[5] *Journal of the General Conference of the Methodist Episcopal Church*, 1876, p. 418.
[6] For details of the meeting of this joint commission—the Cape May Conference—see Chapter 25.
[7] Quoted in James M. Buckley, *A History of Methodism in the United States* (New York: The Christian Literature Co., 1897), II, 234.
[8] (Nashville: Cokesbury Press, 1939), p. 79.
[9] *The Long Road to Methodist Union* (Nashville: The Methodist Publishing House, 1943), p. 66.

concerning the power of the joint commission was raised in the General Conference of the Methodist Episcopal Church in May, 1880, but was settled by a resolution amended by James M. Buckley to read: *"Resolved, that we regard the action of the Commission on Fraternity, appointed by the Bishops by the order of the last General Conference, as final."* [10]

From the Cape May meeting forward, fraternal delegates from the one body regularly visited the other General Conference. No definite steps, however, were taken toward organic union. None of the fraternal messengers brought any proposals for union. Their addresses were usually emotional and often challenging statements that emphasized the ties of brotherhood and the necessity of working together. Concerning the address of the Rev. J. C. Kilgo of the Southern Church, for example, the May 12, 1904, *Daily Christian Advocate* of the Northern Church says: "No such enthusiasm has been known during this conference as was manifested during the delivery and at the close of Dr. Kilgo's eloquent and glorious message." [11]

As a whole the addresses of the fraternal messengers, while not directly related to organic union, had a salutary effect upon the relations between the churches and were a help toward easing the tensions between the North and the South. They were limited in their effect in that the messengers were only two or three persons who appeared in the midst of busy sessions to bring a greeting, then departed. But shortly after 1880 two events occurred in world Methodism which gave strong and far-reaching impetus to the whole idea of organic union in the Methodist Church.

On September 7, 1881, the First Ecumenical Methodist Conference convened in London. Its object was to secure "a closer alliance, a warmer fraternity, and a fuller co-operation" among Methodist organizations throughout the world.[12] A second significant event occurred in 1884, when the Centennial Methodist Conference was held in Baltimore, Maryland, commemorating the hundredth anniversary of the formal organization of the Methodist Episcopal Church in America.[13]

The success of the First Ecumenical Conference guaranteed the continuance of this type of conference, and similar meetings were held every decade. Today they are held every five years. Bishop Garber in speaking of their influence says:

[10] *Journal of the General Conference of the Methodist Episcopal Church,* 1880, p. 160.

[11] P. 114.

[12] *Proceedings of the Oecumenical Methodist Conference* (London: Wesleyan Conference Office, 1881), p. xi.

[13] For details of the First Ecumenical Methodist Conference and the Centennial Methodist Conference, see Chapter 25.

When the sons of Wesley met in these conferences, they caught the inspiring vision of the unity of Methodism and returned home determined to achieve that end. In 1883, two years after the first Ecumenical Conference, the four Canadian Methodist groups united to form the Methodist Church in Canada. A united Australian Methodism became a reality in 1902. The Ecumenical Methodist Conference of 1901 influenced union of British Methodists, for between 1902 and 1907 the Methodist New Connexion, the Bible Christians, and the United Methodists Free Church joined to form the United Methodist Church. The union of Irish Methodism was accomplished by 1905. Each succeeding Ecumenical Methodist Conference brought closer fraternity and organic union among the followers of Wesley.[14]

The Centennial Methodist Conference held in Baltimore in 1884 had an even more profound effect on the two separate branches of episcopal Methodism. Both churches were specifically involved in the preparation of and the participation in a one-week series of meetings to stress their common origin, doctrine, polity, and inherent brotherhood.

Dr. Horace Du Bose, afterward a bishop of the Southern Church, writes of the Centennial Conference: "The great Conference closed with an old-fashioned love feast. Testimonies were given by men of ripe experience in the two greater Methodist Churches and also by an African and an Indian. The historic gathering ended in a glow of spirit which sent its influence down the years." The conference "was the first full pulse beat of American Methodism after the lamentable, but historically necessary, events of 1844." [15]

It must not be hastily assumed that the events thus far outlined were moving the two episcopal Methodisms rapidly toward organic union. It is true that a spirit of good will and fraternity was developing among some of the leaders of the churches and among some of the members; but this is a far cry from any general acceptance of the idea of organic union. This was purely an introductory period when the two churches were slowly coming to understand each other's feelings and viewpoints. The Cape May Conference had not mentioned union, and, while the Ecumenical Conference of 1881 and the Centennial of 1884 had a salutary effect, no actual steps toward union were taken during this period by the two churches. A long series of events, meetings, and conferences was to take place before The Methodist Church became a reality.

---

[14] *The Methodists Are One People*, pp. 82-83. Used by permission.
[15] *A History of Methodism* (Nashville: Lamar and Smith, 1916), p. 44.

1

The Period of Federation (1894-1916)

In 1888 the General Conference of the Northern Church had appointed a commission with a high-sounding title and an ineffective life. It was called the Commission on Interecclesiastical Relations, to " 'hold themselves ready to enter into brotherly conference with all or any Christian bodies seeking the restoration of the organic unity of the Church,' or the increase of Christian and Church fraternity." [16] It accomplished little or nothing.

Something more was needed. Such action occurred when in 1894 the Southern Church created a Commission on the Federation of Methodism. The commission included Bishop John C. Granbery, Bishop R. K. Hargrove, Bishop W. W. Duncan, the Rev. E. E. Hoss (later a bishop), the Rev. George G. N. MacDonell, the Rev. J. H. Dye, Judge Walter Clark, Major R. W. Jones, and Asa Holt, Esq.[17]

The Northern Church in 1896 responded by creating a similar commission composed of Bishops S. M. Merrill, W. X. Ninde, J. N. Fitzgerald; the Rev. R. J. Cooke (later a bishop), the Rev. John F. Goucher, the Rev. L. B. Wilson (later a bishop); Robert T. Miller, Esq., T. B. Sweet, and Thomas H. Murray, Esq. Bishop J. F. Hurst was substituted for Bishop Fitzgerald and the Rev. L. B. Wilson for Dr. John F. Goucher.[18]

It is obvious from its very name that this Commission on the Federation of Methodism was to work, not for organic union, but for a type of federation in which both churches, while still retaining their own identities, would coexist side by side. Whenever possible, actual overlapping would be eliminated, and a united thrust would be made whenever or in whatever way this was deemed practical. The fact that union was not the immediate goal of the commission may have been disappointing to some, but what the plan envisaged was indeed a long stride beyond the fraternal relations that then existed between the two churches.

What many failed to realize either at this juncture or for some time thereafter was that union could never come about by a return to the *status*

[16] *Journal of the General Conference of the Methodist Episcopal Church,* 1888, p. 427.

[17] *Journal of the General Conference of the Methodist Episcopal Church, South,* 1894, p. 268.

[18] *Journal of the General Conference of the Methodist Episcopal Church,* 1896, pp. 237 ff.

quo of 1844. Union could come about only by a reorganization of the two churches in light of the legislative theories and ideas that had been evolved during the discussions and struggle at the time of the bisection of the church. Neither church was yet fully prepared to make the necessary adjustments and sacrifices which such an organic union entailed. "Federation," therefore, became the watchword, and under this banner the two churches moved slowly toward the deeper relationship that finally came about in 1939.

The Joint Commission on Federation, including the commissioners from both churches, met in Foundry Methodist Church, Washington, D.C., Friday morning, January 7, 1898. After two days of deliberation the following resolution was adopted:

That we recommend to the General Conferences of our respective Churches to adopt measures for the joint administration of our publishing interests in China and Japan.

Respecting joint missionary work in foreign fields, the following was unanimously adopted:

Appreciating fully the Christian comity which prevails among our missions in foreign lands, and having given careful consideration to the principles and desirability of coöperative administration as a means for lessening the expenditure of funds in the prosecution of the work, we therefore, without attempting to formulate any plan for such coöperation, commend the subject to the consideration of the two General Conferences.

Other resolutions adopted were:

That we recommend the taking of prompt steps for the preparation of a common catechism, a common hymn book, and a common order of public worship, and that other branches of Methodism be invited to coöperate in this undertaking.

That we recommend the respective General Conferences to enact provisions to the effect that where either Church is doing the work expected of Methodism, the other Church shall not organize a society nor erect a church building until the bishops having jurisdiction in the case of the work shall be consulted and his approval obtained.

We recommend to our respective General Conferences the provision of a plan by which a traveling preacher of an Annual Conference in either Church may be received into an Annual Conference of the other Church, retaining his credentials, without the formality of having his orders recognized.

That we have observed with much interest the growth of the Epworth Leagues in our respective Churches, and rejoice in the spirit of fraternity manifested in their biennial International Conferences, and commend to the several governing bodies of the Churches interested the question as to whether official recognition of these meetings can be given, and whether authoritative regulations are required to increase or promote their efficiency." [19]

The report was eventually adopted by both General Conferences, although the Northern Church in 1900 wanted to amend item 4 to read: ". . . The building of new churches shall be left to the decision of the presiding elders and the preachers in charge, subject to the approval of the Bishop having jurisdiction." The original statement, however, by 1904 had been finally adopted by both churches, and the Commissions on Federation of the two churches were continued.

These negotiations took some time, since the General Conferences met only every four years. In the meantime, however, other definite steps toward the federation of the two Methodist Churches were being taken. The Board of Missions of the Methodist Episcopal Church transferred its work in Brazil to the Board of Missions of the Methodist Episcopal Church, South. By agreement, also, the island of Cuba as a mission field fell to the Methodist Episcopal Church, South, and the islands of Puerto Rico and the Philippines to the supervision of the Methodist Episcopal Church.[20] By 1904, furthermore, the Commission on Federation had through proper channels created a common hymnal, a common catechism, and a common order of worship to be used by both churches. Eventually the publishing houses of the two churches in China and Mexico were consolidated, a common united Methodism was established in Japan, and a joint control was established over certain educational institutions in America. The imprints of the publishing houses of both churches began to appear on books mutually acceptable.

However, overlapping on the other fields in America was not so easily settled. The war of "altar against altar" continued in spite of the best efforts of the Commission on Federation. Northern Methodists continued to evangelize in the South, especially among the Negroes. They evangelized also among the whites with the help of Northerners who had moved into the South but desired churches of their own denomination.

Both churches pushed west, often ministering in the same communities and, at times, across the street from each other. On both sides loyalty to

---

[19] *Journal of the General Conference of the Methodist Episcopal Church, South,* 1898, pp. 237-47.

[20] *A Record of All Agreements Concerning Fraternity and Federation Between the Methodist Episcopal Church and the Methodist Episcopal Church, South, and the Declaration in Favor of Unification Made by the General Conference of the Methodist Episcopal Church, South* (Nashville: Publishing House of the Methodist Episcopal Church, South, 1914), pp. 22-23.

the ecclesiastical body was kept uppermost, often strongly influenced by ecclesiastical administrators and ecclesiastical beneficence.

In 1906, therefore, the Joint Commission on Federation sought from the two General Conferences the creation of a Federal Council of Methodism. Its purpose was to heal the growing rift. Both churches were in hearty agreement, and the Federal Council was formed with the strongest possible support of both bodies. Far-seeing and judicially minded men were placed upon it, and they were given extensive powers. By 1910 the council was given "final power to hear and determine, without appeal from its decisions, all cases of conflict or misunderstanding between the two branches of Methodism." [21]

In favoring this action, moreover, the Southern Church made a decided concession, for it was giving up in some measure its claim to the exclusive occupancy of the southern territory.

The hope that by this measure "altar against altar" would cease was disappointed, however. Except for a few isolated cases no federated churches resulted, no territory was exchanged, and no overlapping was eliminated.

Bishop Earl Cranston of the Northern Church proclaimed the uselessness of the council and the weakness of federation when he said:

What appears is (1) that these churches cannot live side by side without ever recurring outbreaks of the denominational competitive consciousness; (2) that formal fraternity is but a first aid recourse, not a remedy; and (3) that even compulsory arbitration gives little promise of better results than festering of local sores to the point of incurability.[22]

Meanwhile, the Joint Commission on Federation that had called for the creation of the Federal Council had itself been steadily moving for almost six years toward organic union. In 1916 the Joint Commission on Federation ceased to exist, and a Joint Commission on Unification from the two churches held a remarkable series of meetings, concluding in 1920, when a plan of unification was completed.

From Federation to a Commission on Unification

To understand fully how this Joint Commission on Unification came into existence, it is necessary to trace what proved to be an exciting and

[21] *Ibid.*, p. 25.
[22] *A Working Conference on the Union of American Methodism, Northwestern University, Evanston, Illinois* (New York: The Methodist Book Concern, 1916) , p. 77.

at times dramatic series of events involving first the Methodist Episcopal Church and the reunited Methodist Protestant Church and later the Methodist Episcopal Church, South.

Bishop James H. Straughn writes that the whole action was triggered by a discussion growing out of the Social Union of the Baltimore Annual Conference, a lay organization in the Methodist Episcopal Church which customarily invited the laymen of the Methodist Protestant Church to its banquets. Dr. S. Parkes Cadman of radio fame was the speaker on the subject "Methodism on Both Sides of the Atlantic." The discussion raised the question among some of the laymen of each church as to why "we meet like this without division and yet must remain apart in our churches." As a result, the laymen informally called into conference President Thomas H. Lewis of Western Maryland College (Methodist Protestant) , and Dr. John F. Goucher, founder of the Woman's College in Baltimore (Methodist Episcopal) . It was generally agreed to initiate some move for union at the coming General Conference in Baltimore of the Methodist Episcopal Church.[23]

In keeping with this thinking, the Commission on Federation of the Methodist Episcopal Church brought to its General Conference of 1908 a proposal that an invitation for organic union be extended to the now reunited Methodist Protestant Church. The commission further suggested that a deputation of one bishop, one minister, and one layman convey the invitation to the General Conference of the Methodist Protestant Church then meeting in Pittsburgh.

The Northern General Conference enthusiastically indorsed this proposal and appointed Bishop Henry W. Warren, Dr. John F. Goucher, and Senator John P. Dolliver. On Monday, May 18, they reached the Methodist Protestant Conference and were accorded a warm reception. They presented their invitation, which was in the form of a resolution, and each member of the delegation gave a brief address. The delegation then returned to the General Conference of the Methodist Episcopal Church in Baltimore.

The Methodist Protestants voted to adopt a resolution responding heartily to this invitation, and declared themselves ready to "go as far and as rapidly in consummating a universal Methodism as the interests and integrity of our own denomination will permit." [24]

Beyond this they agreed that "a commission, consisting of nine mem-

[23] James H. Straughn, *Inside Methodist Union* (Nashville: The Methodist Publishing House, 1958) , pp. 59-60.

[24] *Journal of the General Conference of the Methodist Episcopal Church*, 1908, p. 380.

bers, be appointed by this Conference . . . to promote and complete so far as may be possible the reunion of Methodists in America." [25]

After their adjournment, a delegation consisting of Thomas H. Lewis, the Rev. A. L. Reynolds of Ohio, and Dr. J. W. Hering, a layman of Maryland, appeared at the General Conference of the Methodist Episcopal Church still in session in Baltimore. They brought with them the resolution of the Methodist Protestant Church and stated that the purpose of their commission was to meet with a like commission of the Methodist Episcopal Church, and of the Methodist Episcopal Church, South, and of other Methodist Churches in this country "to promote and complete as far as may be possible the reunion of Methodists in America." [26]

It was on this occasion that President Lewis gave an address of which Liston H. Pearce, editor of the *Daily Christian Advocate,* wrote: "Never during this session have there been such tremendous outbursts of enthusiasm and approval." [27] And in brackets at the end of the recorded address in the General Conference *Journal* the editor added: "At the end of this address the audience arose and waved their handkerchiefs amid great applause and singing." [28]

The outburst of enthusiasm was caused by the emotional climax to Lewis' plea for union between the Methodist Episcopal Church and the Methodist Episcopal Church, South. His own church had long since achieved union within itself. Now, when contemplating further union, they were faced with a painful dilemma: With which church, North or South, should they unite? Said Lewis: "Our Church is in the South as well as in the North. . . . And when we think of going back home the question will recur insistently and painfully, 'Which home?' . . . Do not force us to separate from each other in order that we may rejoin the family. We want to unite with a united home." [29]

The result of this moving appeal was the adoption by the General Conference of the Methodist Episcopal Church of a report of its Commission on Federation inviting the Evangelical Association, the United Brethren, and other branches of Methodism it might believe to be sympathetic to confer concerning federation or organic union.

Two years later Dr. Lewis attended the sessions of the General Conference of the Southern Church, making another strong appeal for Methodist union. Ten thousand copies of his address were ordered printed

[25] *Journal of the General Conference of the Methodist Protestant Church,* 1908, p. 39.
[26] *Ibid.*
[27] "Summary of Yesterday's Proceedings," *The Daily Christian Advocate,* May 27, 1908, p. 1.
[28] *Journal of the General Conference of the Methodist Episcopal Church,* 1908, p. 684.
[29] *Ibid.,* p. 683.

in "convenient form," and the enthusiasm of the conference was unbounded.[30]

The upshot of these dramatic events was a historic meeting between
the commissioners of the Joint Commission on Federation of the two
episcopal churches and the recently appointed Commission of Nine of
the Methodist Protestant Church. The meeting was held in Baltimore,
November 30–December 2, 1910. In many ways it was as significant for
the history of unification as the Cape May Conference in 1876. It proved
to be an equally brilliant beacon marking the channel toward organic
union.

The commissioners of the Methodist Episcopal Church submitted a
statement of some length outlining the actions and resolutions already
taken and describing also a meeting in Ocean Grove earlier in the year
between commissioners of the episcopal churches and Dr. Lewis,
chairman of the commission appointed by the Methodist Protestant Church. The paper concluded with an electrifying challenge and
invitation to union. "With this explanation of the reasons by which
we are moved," the commissioners said, "we hereby tender a brotherly
invitation to the Commissions of the respective Churches to consider
with us at this time the desirability and practicability of organic union." [31]

The commissioners of the Southern Church were not fully convinced
that they were charged by their church with the responsibility of conducting negotiations toward organic union, but since they had been directed
by their most recent General Conference "to further, as far as is consistent
and practicable, a closer relation between ourselves and the Methodist
Episcopal Church, the Methodist Protestant Church, and other Methodist bodies," they decided to look favorably on the suggestion and to
"inquire what closer relations might be possible." [32]

It was a significant and historic decision. After interminable meetings
seeking to ease the tensions between the two churches, and after innumerable meetings searching for ways of working more closely together, the
representatives of the churches at last came to grips with the possibility
of organic union. It is not surprising that in this meeting a lengthy discussion followed this decision.

At the end of the discussion a special Committee of Nine was appointed
equally representing the three branches of Methodism. Three members of
each commission composed this special committee. They were directed
to consider various aspects of the whole situation and

[30] *Journal of the General Conference of the Methodist Episcopal Church, South,*
1910, p. 233.
[31] *A Record of All Agreements,* pp. 25-27.
[32] *Ibid.,* pp. 27-28.

if found practicable, to bring to this Joint Commission a plan for submission to the General Conferences and people of the respective Churches, said plan to provide for such unification, through reorganization of the Methodist Episcopal Churches concerned, as shall insure unity of purpose, administration, evangelistic effort, and all other functions for which our Methodism has stood from the beginning.[33]

The members of the committee were: Bishop Earl Cranston, Dr. John F. Goucher, and Dr. R. T. Miller of the Northern Church; Dr. Thomas H. Lewis, Dr. M. L. Jennings, and Mr. S. R. Harris of the Methodist Protestant Church; and Bishop E. E. Hoss, Dr. Frank M. Thomas, and the Hon. M. L. Walton of the Southern Church.

The Committee of Nine met in Cincinnati on January 18, 1911. Bishop Walden took the place of Dr. Goucher, who was out of the country, and Judge W. G. M. Thomas served in place of Judge Walton, detained by court duties.

Five papers in all were presented for consideration to the committee. One came from a group of ministers and laymen of both episcopal churches around Chattanooga. It was a carefully studied proposal of eight points setting forth a basis for union. Many of its ideas were later incorporated into the committee's report.

A second proposal was submitted by the three men of the Southern Church; a third by the commissioners of the Northern Church; and an additional paper was presented by the members of the committee from the Methodist Protestant Church. Later in the session a supplemental paper from the Northern Church was submitted by Bishop Cranston.

After four days of deliberation the committee, on the basis of the five papers before them, adopted the following "suggestions" to be reported to the next meeting of the Joint Commission on Federation:

1. We suggest, as a plan of reorganization, the merging of the Methodist Episcopal Church, the Methodist Protestant Church, the Methodist Episcopal Church, South, into one Church, to be known as the Methodist Episcopal Church in America or the Methodist Church in America.

2. We suggest that this Church shall have throughout common Articles of Faith, common conditions of membership, a common hymnal, a common catechism, and a common ritual.

3. We suggest that the governing power of the reorganized Church shall be vested in one General Conference and three or four Quadrennial Conferences, both General and Quadrennial Conferences to exercise their powers under constitutional provisions and restrictions, the General Conference to have full

[33] *Ibid.*, p. 29.

legislative power over all matters distinctively connectional, and the Quadrennial Conferences to have full legislative power over distinctively local affairs.

4. We suggest that the General Conference shall consist of two houses, each house to be composed of equal numbers of ministerial and lay delegates. The delegates in the first house shall be apportioned equally among the Quadrennial Conferences and elected under equitable rules to be provided therefor. The ministerial delegates in the second house shall be elected by the ministerial members of the Annual Conferences, and the lay delegates by the laity within the Annual Conferences under equitable rules provided therefor. Each Annual Conference shall have at least one ministerial and one lay delegate. The larger Conferences shall each have one additional ministerial and one additional lay delegate for every_____ministerial members of the Conference, also an additional ministerial and lay delegate where there is an excess of two-thirds of the fixed rate of representation. All legislation of the General Conference shall require the concurrent action of the two houses.

5. We suggest that the Quadrennial Conferences shall name the bishops from their several jurisdictions, the same to be confirmed by the first house of the General Conference. We suggest that the Quadrennial Conferences shall be composed of an equal number of ministerial and lay delegates to be chosen by the several Annual Conferences within their several jurisdictions according to an equitable plan to be provided for.

6. We suggest that the Annual Conferences, whose boundaries shall be fixed by the Quadrennial Conferences, be composed of all traveling, supernumerary, and superannuated preachers within their prescribed boundaries, and that the principle of lay representation in the Annual Conferences be recognized.

7. We suggest that neither General Conference nor any of the Quadrennial Conferences be invested with final authority to interpret the constitutionality of its own actions.[34]

The Joint Commission of the three churches met for three days in Chattanooga, Tennessee, May 10, 1911, to consider this report. Bishop Charles W. Smith of the Northern Church served in place of Dr. Goucher.

The commission approved the report with an important addition to item 3: "We suggest that the colored membership of the Methodist Episcopal Church, the Methodist Protestant Church and such acquisitions of colored Methodists as may enter into agreement with them, may be constituted and recognized as one of the Quadrennial or Jurisdictional Conferences of the proposed organization." A final resolution was also adopted: "We emphasize the statement that the suggestions here outlined are only tentative, that in no sense are these suggestions a plan, but merely the result of an exploration in search of a basis of union. . . . Other questions not yet touched will need to be weighed, analyzed and carefully stated." [35]

[34] *Ibid.*, pp. 38-39.
[35] *Ibid.*, pp. 43-44.

The Chattanooga Report, as it came to be known, however tentative it may have appeared, was of tremendous importance for unification. Perhaps it is not too much to say that in the end it became the real basis upon which unification was accomplished. Like Cape May in 1876 and the Joint Commission meeting in Baltimore in 1910, Chattanooga was a light marking the channel and pointing the way toward unification.

During the long series of meetings following, when a plan of union was actually hammered out, the suggestions made at Chattanooga were again and again referred to for direction and light. Bishop Cranston, at the second meeting of the Joint Commission on Unification in 1917, summarized the attitude of the delegates: "From the day of the Chattanooga Agreement down to this hour these two Churches are committed to the project of unification, . . . [on] the principles set forth at Chattanooga, . . . and we cannot get away from that." [36] The importance of Chattanooga in the final achievement of union cannot be overemphasized.

The General Conferences of the Northern Church and the Methodist Protestant Church met in 1912. To these bodies was first submitted the Chattanooga Report. (The General Conference of the Southern Church would not meet until 1914.) The Methodist Protestant Church passed a resolution which stated in part that

the series of suggestions agreed upon by the Joint Commission . . . are presented for the consideration principally of the two Episcopal Methodisms, since the first great problem with them is to discover a form of General Conference organization under which they can live harmoniously together. With this phase of the problem the Methodist Protestant Church has little immediate concern, having itself no sectional question. . . . Your Commission does not deem it necessary, therefore, that this General Conference should express itself on the merits of these suggestions at this time.[37]

This resolution explains why, during the next twenty years when the Methodist Episcopal Churches were trying to come to basic agreements for union, the Methodist Protestant Church stood to one side and took no part. The Methodist Protestants felt that they had long ago come to agreement within themselves, and were now waiting for the episcopal churches to achieve a similar agreement before all three churches could move forward together toward final union.

The Northern Church said: "We heartily approve the action of our

[36] *Joint Commission on Unification of the Methodist Episcopal Church, South, and the Methodist Episcopal Church* (Nashville: Publishing House of the Methodist Episcopal Church, South; New York: The Methodist Book Concern, 1918), I, 253.

[37] *Journal of the General Conference of the Methodist Protestant Church*, 1912, p. 45.

Commission on Federation in proposing the consideration of the question of organic union to the commissioners in joint session at Baltimore, believing that the membership of the Methodist Episcopal Church would welcome a corporate reunion of the Methodisms of America." The conference then appointed a Commission on Federation with full power and authority to continue negotiations concerning the "commendable purposes of advancing organic union or closer federation." [38]

The Southern Church took more definite action when the Chattanooga Report was submitted to their General Conference of 1914, meeting in Oklahoma City. The committee who considered the report brought back a declaration referring to the Chattanooga Report as "tentative," but containing the "basic principles of a genuine unification of the Methodist bodies in the United States, . . . by the method of reorganization." The committee recommended, however, that "the colored membership of the various Methodist bodies be formed into an independent organization holding fraternal relations with the . . . united church." The General Conference adopted this declaration and provided a method for appointing a Commission on Unification should the Northern Church in 1916 "declare itself in favor of unification." It added further that the name preferred for the united church was "the Methodist Church in America." [39]

Following a supporting speech by Bishop Hoss, who was a member of the Commission on Federation and who had been requested to address the conference, the declaration was unanimously and enthusiastically adopted.

Unification by reorganization was the gist of the declaration, and it was the keystone of Bishop Hoss's speech. There could be no return to the *status quo;* rather there must be a going forward to a reorganized though not reconstructed church.

This entire action now became a challenge for the next General Conference of the Northern Church, meeting at Saratoga Springs, New York, in 1916. It declared itself "in favor of unification" and proposed several recommendations: (*a*) that the General Conference be "made the supreme legislative, executive, and judicial body of the Church"; (*b*) that the number of the Quadrennial Conferences be increased; (*c*) that the General Conference consist of a single house; and (*d*) that "the colored membership of the reorganized Church be constituted into one or more quadrennial or Jurisdictional Conferences." The conference made provision for a commission and then added: "So sincerely do we believe that the union of the two Episcopal Methodisms is the will of God, and so earnestly and devoutly do we desire that these two Churches may be one, that we hereby authorize and instruct the Commissioners of the Methodist Episcopal Church to conduct the negotiations in a generous and brotherly spirit." [40]

Out of these actions and resolutions came the Joint Commission on Unification which held its first meeting in 1916.

The uniting of the two churches into one living organism was proving a slow process, as a review of the main events from 1874 reveals. It is true that only two years passed from the establishment of fraternal relations in 1874 until the Cape May Conference in 1876. But between the Cape May Conference and the first meeting of the Joint Commission on Federation in 1898 twenty-two more years had passed. The Ecumenical Conference in London and the Centennial in Baltimore had occurred during these years and had a salutary effect on the slow movement toword union, but it was evident that a new church would not be built overnight.

The Joint Commission on Federation had continued its work for eighteen years, or from 1898 until 1916, when it gave way to the Joint Commission on Unification. During these years the Federal Council, formed to settle disputes between the churches, had been of little help. More was expected from the Joint Commission on Unification.

2

The Intensive Effort (1916-25)

Unification was at last under way. The two episcopal churches had moved into the center of a broad channel. The winds and waves of dissension and disappointment, however, rocked their boats dangerously as they sought the meaning of "union by reorganization." After one of the meetings held in Traverse City, Michigan, for example, Bishop Edwin D. Mouzon wrote to Bishop Earl Cranston in tones of intense discouragement.

Fortunately, Bishop Cranston and Dr. Goucher, with whom he discussed the letter, did not share this pessimism. And it is still more fortunate that the discouragement of the Southern bishop was only tem-

[40] *Journal of the General Conference of the Methodist Episcopal Church*, 1916, pp. 711-12.

porary. Later, when the whole possibility of unification was in doubt, he wrote to Bishop Cranston a letter full of optimism and hope.[41]

The Joint Commission on Unification accomplished its work over a period of three years, meeting in six different cities. In December, 1916, it met at Baltimore; in June, 1917, at Traverse City; in January, 1918, in Savannah; in April of the same year in St. Louis; in July, 1919, in Cleveland; and January 15-20, 1920, it completed its work at Louisville. As already noted, the Methodist Protestant Church took no part in these proceedings, feeling the Northern and Southern Churches must come to some agreement before unification of the three bodies would be possible.

Baltimore

The meeting in Baltimore accomplished several important things.

First, it gave the commissioners an opportunity of meeting one another, of exchanging preliminary ideas, and of developing a mutual respect without which further progress would have been impossible. In discussing the various committees through which they would work and the procedures they would follow the commissioners touched upon many of the problems of unification, and they had the opportunity to state and hear a great many viewpoints.

Second, the commissioners began to understand the meaning of the term "unification by reorganization." It was very soon obvious there could be no return to the *status quo* that had existed before 1844. Nor could there be unification unless each of the churches was ready to make concessions and accept new ideas. It became equally obvious, however, that the church was not to be reconstructed. "I am against revolution," said E. C. Reeves, a layman of the Southern Church. "[We are not here] to create a new Church with new doctrines, polities, or anything of the kind."[42]

A. J. Lamar, book agent of the Southern Church, said: "This is largely a question of machinery—[let us] see how has the Methodist Episcopal Church been working with the machinery which it has? How has the Methodist Episcopal Church, South, been working with the machinery it has used in this particular? If they differ, which piece of machinery commends itself to us as a better piece, no matter which church has it?"[43]

The final plan, though, would not be mere readjustment. "There are

[41] MS letters in the archives of the Historical Society of the Baltimore Annual Conference, Lovely Lane Museum.
[42] *Joint Commission on Unification,* I, 73
[43] *Ibid.,* p. 76.

two things in this discussion against which we need constantly to guard,"
said J. W. Van Cleve, a minister of the Northern Church. "One of them is
the danger of immediacy, of trying to find something that will meet the
present situation without considering fairly how it will work out in the
future. . . . The other danger is . . . of taking too narrow a view of the
things we are dealing with, of being too limited locally." [44]

Third, certain definite conclusions were reached on committees and
procedures, and these were embodied in an optimistic address to the
churches. "It was agreed," the address stated, "that the fundamental and
the vital issues between us were the following: First, the General Conference and its powers. Second, the Jurisdictional Conferences, their number and their powers. Third, the status of the colored membership of the
Methodist Episcopal Church in the reorganized church." These subjects
were referred to three committees with instructions to present a detailed
report at the next session of the Joint Commission.[45] A Committee on
General Reference was also appointed.

Traverse City

The Joint Commission on Unification met in Traverse City on June
27, 1917. It continued in session until July 3.

Three full reports were presented without debate by each of three
committees: the Committee on General and Jurisdictional Conferences,
the Committee on Judicial Council, and the Committee on the Status of
the Negro Membership. A minority report was presented from the last
committee. It was signed by Bishop Collins Denny and a layman, H. H.
White, both of the Southern Church. Among other things it said: "We
have no reason to suppose that the report of the majority of this Committee will be acceptable to any branch of negro Methodists in America,
and there are grave reasons to believe that it will be objectionable to all,
especially to the colored membership of the Methodist Episcopal
Church." [46]

The major discussion now centered in the report of the Committee on
Conferences, and particularly the power of the General Conference and
the Regional or Jurisdictional Conferences and their interrelation.

At the very beginning of the discussion the Southern commissioners
made it clear that three or four strong regional conferences were a necessary part of the plan. The Northern commissioners had asked whether
the South would agree that the episcopal area become the unit of the

[44] *Ibid.*, p. 107.
[45] *Ibid.*, p. 205.
[46] *Ibid.*, p. 231.

Regional Conference. This, in the eyes of the South, would have reduced the effectiveness and the power of the Regional Conference almost to that of an Annual Conference, and to this they were opposed. They concluded: "We . . . are compelled to regard the Regional Conference as a basic principle of a genuine unification of our Methodist bodies, and we cannot, in the light of the action of our General Conference, depart from this basic principle." [47]

The Southern Church felt that the way of securing minority rights in a united church was through the Regional Conference; in the General Conference they would always be in the minority. At one point Bishop Collins Denny of the Southern Church had this to say: "I do not know, but it comes perilously near putting our branch of the Church in the reorganized Church in the position of having a trifle less than one-third of the delegations to the General Conference. Is that the purpose? I simply raise the question." [48]

Obviously if all the legislative, promotional, and electoral powers were lodged in the General Conference alone, powerful majorities could and would be tempted to overrun and dominate the entire church. But if certain powers were lodged in smaller Regional Conferences, some of the rights of the minority could be protected. For this reason the South wanted strong Regional Conferences with power, for example, to elect bishops, with adequate legislative powers for administrative and promotional purposes, and with power under certain circumstances and conditions to arrest General Conference action.

The North feared that with Regional Conferences having power to elect bishops, and with severe limitations thereby being imposed on the General Conference, the church would become sectionalized. The bishops elected by the Jurisdictional or Regional Conferences, they feared, would not be bishops of the whole church but diocesan bishops. The Northern Church wanted to lodge as little power as possible in the Regional Conference, using it only as an expedient. Bishop Denny quickly saw the dangers inherent in this attitude and said, in part:

We are here to see that what is dear to us, the right of local self-government in this matter, is contended for. We do not want to control anybody else; but, as far as we are able to manage it, we do not propose that anybody else shall control us. . . . These Regional Conferences, shorn down to an electoral party, will become what electors are in presidential elections in very little time—that is, they will be nothing in the world but the hand of the voters. [49]

[47] Ibid., pp. 248-49.
[48] Ibid., p. 346.
[49] Ibid., p. 314.

In the report that was tentatively accepted before adjournment, the selection of bishops was placed in the Jurisdictional Conferences, and adequate powers were given these conferences to assure the protection of minority groups. The North conceded much at this point. It was clearly pointed out, however, by both groups that bishops were by no means to be thought of as diocesan, and to clarify this certain powers in relation to bishops were given to the General Conference. Among them were powers to define and fix the privileges and powers and duties of the episcopacy.

Before the meeting adjourned another matter came up and was presented in such a way that it may have caused the temporary discouragement of Bishop Mouzon. It had to do with the status of the Negro in the reorganized church. It was interjected by Dr. Irvine G. Penn, a Negro commissioner.

When you come down to the number of Regional Conferences we face the fact that you have left out of this arrangement 350,000 *bona fide* members of the Methodist Episcopal Church. [He was referring to the Negro members of the Northern Church.] Brethren, if you are going to postpone this matter of the status of the negro in the reorganized Church and not going to face it at this meeting and decide definitely upon it, you should postpone the number of Regional Conferences. The position I take at this time is the position of the Chattanooga Agreement, and the Chattanooga Agreement suggests that the negro is to have Regional Conferences with representation in the General Conference, and it is not fair until that question is settled to determine the number of Regional Conferences.[50]

The matter was postponed, but the problem was not thereby made easier.

The problem centered in the fact that the Southern Church had no Negro membership. The Negro Methodists of the South had either joined the Colored Methodist Episcopal Church, sponsored by the Southern Church but separate from it; linked themselves with other entirely different denominations, such as the African Methodist Episcopal Church; or joined the Northern Church, where they had, for the most part, their own churches and conferences, but where also they had full standing in the General Conference and thus in the legislative councils of the church. Many of the Southern brethren did not want the Negroes represented in any numbers in the General Conference. If they had a Regional Conference of their own, as Dr. Penn was suggesting, they would then be represented in the General Conference and also have power to elect bishops—

[50] *Ibid.*, p. 432.

bishops who might conceivably be called upon to preside over a predominantly white General Conference.

On the basis of the preliminary discussions, three solutions were being offered: a) They would be left out of the reorganized church—350,000 Negroes bereft of their membership and told to unite with some other colored body or Methodist denomination.

b) They would be an integral part of the reorganized church but not a part of its legislative branch, the General Conference. This suggestion was made by one of the most outstanding of the Northern commissioners, Dr. Edgar Blake, secretary of the Sunday School Board of the Northern church and later bishop, at a Social Union banquet in Boston, February 15, 1917. The reaction was immediate and widespread. While here and there the idea was given favorable consideration, for the most part it drew forth almost violent statements of denunciation, especially from Negro leaders. "We would not want the blessing of a church that would accept such an attitude, much less a church that would demand it."

c) They would be given "full virile rights, man for man and individual for individual, in the Church to which they belong." [51]

This matter was not decided at Traverse City. Nor was there a summary statement or address prepared for the churches as had been done at the conclusion of the Baltimore meeting. It was agreed, however, to print the stenographic reports of all the meetings, and this was a happy decision. These reports are one of the finest possible orientations to the inner meaning and history of Methodism in America.

On adjournment most of the commissioners seemed to be in a reasonably optimistic frame of mind. A few were discouraged. Bishop Mouzon summarized this feeling when he said: "Now, there is one serious difficulty before us, and that is the status of the colored membership in the reorganized Church. . . . I do not know what the solution of that question is going to be. God knows." [52]

Savannah

The longest series of meetings of the Joint Commission on Unification was held in Savannah early in 1918. They began January 23 and adjourned February 6.

From the time of the Savannah meeting almost every discussion on unification sooner or later centered in the question of the status of the

[51] Ibid., p. 446.
[52] Ibid., p. 447.

Negro in the new church. A. J. Lamar of the Southern Church wanted to begin the Savannah meeting with this question, completely overlooking the Committee on the Judicial Council, which was scheduled to report first. Said he: "We all know and we have known from the beginning that the crux of the situation is the Status of the Colored Membership in the Methodist Episcopal Church. We can arrange everything else, and yet when we come to that, if we can't arrange that, if we come to a deadlock on that, it renders null and void everything that we have done before." [53]

It was an ominous warning, suggesting the difficulties that lay ahead. The commission, however, felt it wiser to follow agreed-upon procedures, and for two days discussed the report on the Judicial Council. It was accepted without much change.

The members of the Judicial Council would be elected by the General Conference, but could not be members of the General Conference once they were elected to office. A layman and a minister from each Jurisdictional Conference would comprise its membership. It was given power to determine the constitutionality of acts of the General and Quadrennial Conferences, to determine questions of law and all other appeals coming from Annual, Judicial, and Quadrennial Conferences, and from the General Conference. The decision of the Judicial Council would be final; provided that if, on a constitutional question, a majority of the members of the General Conference disapproved a decision of the Judicial Council, the question involved would be sent to the Annual Conferences for final decision. [54]

This settled the question concerning the authority of the General Conference to pass on the constitutionality of its own acts. In 1844, when the General Conference took its action against Bishop Andrew, it decided itself that this action was in keeping with the constitution. The claims of the minority were thrust aside by the same majority which had taken the original action. There was no other authority to whom the bishop himself or the minority could appeal. When the Southern Church was organized, the College of Bishops had the right to arrest legislation in the General Conference which they thought was unconstitutional. This could be further voted on by the Annual Conferences. Still later (1934) a judicial council was set up. But in the Northern Church the General Conference had continued to be its own judicial council. Both churches were ready for the change proposed in this plan of a separately constituted judicial body with powers much like those of the Supreme Court.

The status of the Negro was not so easily settled. The majority and

[53] *Ibid.*, II, 24.
[54] *Ibid.*, p. 27.

minority reports originally presented at Traverse City promised to satisfy few of the commissioners. To complicate matters further, the Committee on the Status of the Negro of the Joint Commission, realizing that the original reports introduced at Traverse City would satisfy no one, had appointed a subcommittee which had hammered out a report that was now placed before the Joint Commission. This report contained two plans: one, a preferential plan that would place the Negro membership in an associate regional jurisdiction or conference such as would be given the church in foreign lands; two, an alternate plan which would place the Negro in an associate General Conference with power to elect its own bishops, with some representation in the General Conference of the unified church, and with a constitutional relation to it.[55]

Beyond this, some of the commissioners held to a third solution that would give the Negro membership a full Regional Conference or Jurisdiction exactly like that of their white brethren.[56]

The report occasioned a great deal of debate and gave the commissioners the opportunity of fully airing their viewpoints.

H. H. White from Alexandria, Louisiana, of the Southern Church, read a lengthy paper on what he felt the position of the South to be. He said in part:

The South and our grand division of the Methodist Church believe:

(a) That the color line must be drawn firmly and unflinchingly, in State, Church, and society, without any deviation whatever; and no matter what the virtues, abilities, or accomplishments of individuals may be, there must be absolute separation of social relations. . . .

The only way in which a union of the Northern and Southern churches can be brought about will be by the immediate or gradual elimination of the negro membership and in good faith attempt on the part of both Churches, North and South, to cause all negro Methodists to unite in one great body, which should be brought, in so far as may be, under the tutorship, and which would receive the encouragement of the white Church.[57]

On the other hand, other commissioners from the South felt more like a layman, R. E. Blackwell of Virginia, who said:

The negroes are in the M. E. Church, and they are just as much a part of the Church as any other members. . . . I should hate for them to feel that we had shoved them out. . . . On the other hand, if we accept the plan, what shall we

[55] *Ibid.*, pp. 100-103.
[56] *Ibid.*, p. 388.
[57] *Ibid.*, pp. 137-39.

have? The negroes would be in separate churches, separate District Conferences, separate Annual Conferences, and once in four years they would have a small representation in the General Conference. Is there anything very alarming in that? [58]

Henry Wade Rogers of New York stated the matter bluntly when he said: "Don't ask us to agree to a General Conference that shall have no colored man in it." [59] Dr. Robert E. Jones, editor of the *Southwestern Advocate* and himself a colored man, after an impassioned address, said: "We will agree to a largely reduced representation in the General Conference. . . . We will agree to our bishops having jurisdiction within our territory—that is, that by some process they will be limited to our people. . . . I think that is all." [60] Dr. Penn, also a Negro, pointed out that in the preferential plan of the committee's report, there is "one thing . . . for which I could never stand—viz., that the negro cannot vote on constitutional questions. Gentlemen, I will tell you straight, but in love, that if I can prevent it, my people are not to be disfranchised in the Methodist Episcopal Church or in the reunited Methodist Church." [61]

It was pointed out that labor unions had opened their doors to the Negroes.[62] One commissioner, Claudius B. Spencer of the Northern Church, added: "What will be our message in mission lands if we draw a color line here at home?" [63]

A. J. Lamar of the Southern Church said in discouragement: "I believe the best thing we as a Commission can do would be to report back to our General Conferences that on account chiefly of this thing, . . . we have been unable to harmonize these differences, and we therefore report back to you for your decision as to what further steps shall be taken toward unification." [64]

This suggestion, however, was unacceptable to everyone. The commissioners felt that some plan could be and would be found. Finally, in order to harmonize the various views and reports, a committee of eight was appointed to report back as soon as possible. The committee consisted of: John M. Moore, Edgar Blake, H. M. Du Bose, J. J. Wallace, H. N. Snyder, Alexander Simpson, Jr., R. S. Hyer, and George Warren Brown. By the next day the committee was ready with a unanimous report that was then placed before the commission.[65]

[58] *Ibid.*, p. 143.
[59] *Ibid.*, p. 162.
[60] *Ibid.*, pp. 174-75.
[61] *Ibid.*, p. 253.
[62] *Ibid.*, p. 173.
[63] *Ibid.*, p. 295.
[64] *Ibid.*, p. 189.
[65] *Ibid.*, pp. 436, 389, 437.

It was a lengthy report which, among other provisions, provided for five associate regional jurisdictions, one of which was the Afro-American. Each was to be represented in the General Conference by five ministerial and five lay delegates, who would have the right to speak on matters relating to and affecting the interests of the jurisdictions they represented but with no power to vote.[66]

The report was approved in principle by the separate commissions of each of the churches "as a basis for determining the status of the Negro within the reorganized church." [67]

The discussion of the report continued, however, for three days, and the commission finally adjourned without settling the matter, to meet at St. Louis on Wednesday, April 10.

St. Louis

Before beginning an analysis of the meetings at St. Louis it might be well to point to a confusing procedure in the work of the Joint Commission. This was its method of accepting a report "tentatively" or "in principle" and later reconsidering it for further revision. This meant every report could be called up for further revision, and nothing was finally settled until the very end of the meetings and when the final plan was offered to the church.

At St. Louis, therefore, the first four days were given to reviewing and revising what had already been done. The Report on Conferences was considered in this way, and a decision reached also as to the number of Regional or Jurisdictional Conferences. Dr. Goucher suggested eight. Dr. Penn favored four, three of which would have boundaries running north and south and the fourth made up of the colored membership. Dr. Spencer wanted nine: three northern, three southern, and three border jurisdictions. Others thought in still higher numbers. On a motion of Edgar Blake the number proposed was six, and this was finally adopted.

Other portions of the report, as with the report on the Judicial Council, were tentatively adopted with minor revisions.

The matter of the status of the Negro was again discussed. Dr. Penn desired to increase the number of Negroes in the General Conference to fifty. There was no agreement. Since the Southern General Conference was to meet soon, the whole matter was left open.

The Southern commissioners frankly reported to the General Conference of the Methodist Episcopal Church, South: "Your Commissioners

[66] *Ibid.,* pp. 439-40.
[67] *Ibid.,* pp. 461-62.

deeply regret that our negotiations with our brethren were not more fruitful in immediate results. At the same time we are sure that our labors were not in vain." [68]

The General Conference continued the commission after expressing appreciation for their faithful and earnest efforts. The next meeting of the Joint Commission was in Cleveland, July 7-10, 1919.

Cleveland

At the Cleveland meeting the entire time was given to the status of the Negro in the reorganized church. The Northern members were now largely of one mind—"that the colored membership of the Church shall be constituted and recognized as a Quadrennial or Regional Conference, with proportionate representation in the General Conference." The Southern members proposed that there be a Regional Conference for the colored people, Latin America, Europe, Eastern Asia, and Southern Asia, and that these

shall have representation in the General Conference in proportion to their membership in full standing; *provided,* that each of such Regional Conferences shall be entitled to at least five clerical and five lay delegates. *Provided, further,* that the number of delegates from any one of these Conferences shall not exceed five per cent of the entire membership of the General Conference. . . . Whenever the membership in full standing of any of these Regional Conferences shall exceed four hundred thousand, upon request of said Conference, the General Conference shall organize the membership of said Conference into an Associate General Conference with the powers proposed for such Associate General Conference in the report of the Committee of Conference at the Savannah meeting of the Joint Commission. [69]

No agreement was reached, and the whole matter of a constitution for unification, including the status of the Negro in the new church, was placed in the hands of a special Joint Committee of Reference of fourteen, including Bishop W. F. McDowell, Edgar Blake, David G. Downey, John J. Wallace, James R. Joy, Elmer L. Kidney, and A. W. Harris of the Northern Church; and Bishop James Cannon, Frank M. Thomas, W. J. Young, Paul H. Linn, Percy D. Maddin, R. S. Hyer, and H. H. White of the Southern Church.

This Joint Committee of Reference met at Richmond, Virginia, November 7, 1919. After several days of earnest effort and on the basis of

---

[68] *Journal of the General Conference of the Methodist Episcopal Church, South,* 1918, pp. 463-64.

[69] *Joint Commission on Unification,* III, 280-81.

the entire discussion of all points, they framed a proposed constitution. This was submitted to the Joint Commission at a meeting in Louisville, Kentucky, January 15-20. Despite six days of discussion, this final constitution was accepted, without much change, for transmission to the General Conferences.

This was the first constitution actually submitted to the two General Conferences for their consideration and decision. This constitution was never submitted to the Methodist Protestant Church for its consideration. Some of the members of the Joint Commission had wondered if definite overtures should not be made to the Methodist Protestants. Nothing, however, had been done, probably because the Methodist Protestant church had made it abundantly clear that they were purposely standing aloof until the two episcopal Methodisms had come to a working agreement between themselves. As late as 1924 the fraternal delegate to the Northern Church's General Conference from the Methodist Protestant Church reiterated this stand. He was the Rev. Charles D. Sinkinson, pastor of the Methodist Protestant Church, Atlantic City, New Jersey. He was a member of his church's committee on church union. He spoke warmly in favor of union, and spoke of meeting many of the members of the Joint Commission on Unification of the two episcopal churches. He explained, however, that his church was remaining aloof from the negotiations between the two episcopal Methodisms until their unification was accomplished.

The First Proposed Constitution

The main features of this first constitution submitted to the Methodist Episcopal Churches were as follows: The name of the church would be The Methodist Church. There were to be six white Jurisdictional or Regional Conferences established on a geographical basis and one for "the Annual Conferences, Mission Conferences, and Missions embracing the work among colored people in the United States." The number and boundaries of the Regional Conferences in foreign countries were to be determined by the General Conference.

The Regional Conference was to have full power over all distinctly regional affairs within its jurisdiction. Each was to elect the number of bishops allotted to it by the General Conference. The bishops were to be confirmed by the General Conference, and consecrated by the bishops, unless two thirds of the members of the General Conference, present and voting, objected to their confirmation. The powers, duties, and privileges of a colored or foreign regional bishop were to be limited to the Regional Jurisdiction by or for which he was elected.

The Negro was to be represented in the General Conference: "Not less than thirty nor more than forty-two delegates, ministerial and lay, in equal number, chosen in such manner as the General Conference may determine . . . ; provided, that the number of delegates from said Regional Jurisdiction shall not exceed five per cent of the total membership of the General Conference."

Beyond this, whenever in any colored or foreign Regional Conference the membership in full connection would exceed 400,000, upon request of that conference the General Conference was to organize that conference into an Associate General Conference. An Associate General Conference was to be represented in the General Conference by ten ministerial and ten lay delegates, who would have the right to speak and vote on all matters affecting the interests of their jurisdiction. The General Conference could be represented in any Associate General Conference by ten ministerial and ten lay delegates.

A Judicial Council composed of fifteen ministers and laymen would be nominated by the bishops and elected by the General Conference. They would serve for eight years and would be eligible for re-election. They were not eligible for membership in the General or Regional Conferences. With certain restrictions, their rulings were final.

It was recommended that the General Conference "make an equitable provision for the financial support of the Colored Methodist Episcopal Church by setting apart a designated amount or a fixed percentage of the total annual offerings of the reorganized church for the support of the work among colored people." This church existed in the South separate from the Southern Church but assisted by it.[70]

The plan was a noble attempt at a difficult task. It met immediate opposition in the North, where there was a strong feeling against the Regional Conference. It was said in the South, on the other hand, that the plan, if adopted, would cause 200,000 members (in the South) to leave their church.

Particularly distasteful to the Northern Church was what many felt to be the divisive effect of the Regional Conferences. Many thought these would break the church into segments instead of unifying it. Bishop William Quayle, writing in the *Christian Advocate,* coined the word "ensmall" the church, about this phase of the plan.

Others felt that the so-called "veto power" of the Regional Conference was a hurtful feature. This feature of the plan provided that whenever a majority of each of two regional delegations so requested, the vote

[70] *Ibid.,* pp. 561-67.

on any motion or resolution, including amendments to the constitution, in the General Conference should be taken by regional delegations, and it would require two thirds of the regional delegates, the members of each regional delegation voting as one body, to adopt the motion or resolution. This was considered by many to constitute a veto power. It was a most unpopular provision in the North.

Many of the Southern men and churches were basically opposed to union on any plan, and many others objected to the status of the Negro in the proposed constitution.

The General Conference of the Northern Church met first and referred the proposal to a special committee. This committee recommended that, since considerable numbers in each church were not entirely satisfied with the plan, a Joint General Convention with the Methodist Episcopal Church, South, be called. This would consider the plan submitted by the Joint Commission and any other plan or plans that might be proposed. They recommended the continuation of a Commission on Unification.

To this recommendation was attached this affirmation: "We reaffirm our deep conviction that the Methodist Episcopal Church and the Methodist Episcopal Church, South, should be reunited in one Church. And so earnestly do we desire a reunion that we declare ourselves ready to accept any equitable plan of union that shall be mutually satisfactory to the membership of both Churches." [71]

The entire series of recommendations was adopted by the General Conference.

The Southern Church at its meeting in 1922 said: "Knowing that there may be differences of opinion as to the details, we approve in principle the plan of unification by reorganization wrought out by the Joint Commission on Unification and submitted . . . to this General Conference." A commission of five bishops, ten traveling elders, and ten laymen was appointed to continue negotiations, following the basic principles already agreed upon by the Joint Commission, "or upon such other basis as our Commission may determine." In response to the proposal of the Northern Church for a Joint General Convention, they proposed instead a special session of the Southern General Conference "when a plan for unification is endorsed by a two-third vote of each Commission, and approved by the General Conference of the Methodist Episcopal Church." [72]

As the result of these actions the new Joint Commission met to begin work again.

[71] *Journal of the General Conference of the Methodist Episcopal Church*, 1920, pp. 701-4.

[72] *Journal of the General Conference of the Methodist Episcopal Church, South*, 1922, pp. 221-22.

The Second Proposed Constitution and Its Defeat

The new Joint Commission, composed largely of the members of the commissions who had been serving to this time, met in Cincinnati, January 18-19, 1923. Bishop McDowell was the chairman of the Northern commission and Bishop Mouzon of the Southern commission. The Northern commission had been instructed by their General Conference "to act with the Commission from the Methodist Episcopal Church, South, either in arranging for the Convention proposed . . . , or in perfecting the plans already before the two Churches, or in working out new plans of unification for submission to the Churches." [73] The Southern commission had authority to negotiate on such basis as they themselves determined.[74] The Joint Commission, therefore, proceeded to its work free of limitations and restrictions from either side. It was at liberty to consider whatever proposals might lead to an acceptable plan of union.

The two commissions held two joint meetings; the first, already referred to, at Cincinnati, January 18-19, 1923, and the second at Cleveland, July 24-25, 1923.

At the first meeting a statement of principles was approved which was committed to a Committee of Reference for further consideration and development. This Committee of Reference met in St. Louis, March 27-29, 1923, held six sessions, and adopted a report.

At the second meeting of the Joint Commission held at Cleveland this report was received and, after consideration, approved for presentation to the General Conference of each church.

The plan thus submitted was unique, in that while it established only one General Conference, it settled the racial question by having two Regional or Jurisdictional Conferences, one to be composed of the Annual Conferences of the Methodist Episcopal Church and the other to be composed of the Annual Conferences of the Methodist Episcopal Church, South. Each jurisdiction would possess full powers of the General Conference of each church except such powers as would be "vested in the General Conference" of the reorganized church. The bishops would be elected by the Jurisdictional Conferences, but they could not serve in any jurisdiction other than the one by which they had been elected, without the consent of the majority of the bishops of the jurisdiction involved. There would be a judicial council very much like that previously suggested

[73] *Journal of the General Conference of the Methodist Episcopal Church,* 1920, p. 703.

[74] *Journal of the General Conference of the Methodist Episcopal Church,* 1924, p. 1715.

by the Joint Commission. Other matters would be largely the same. No name was suggested.

This new plan was immediately adopted by the General Conference of the Northern Church in May, 1924, at Springfield, Massachusetts.

The South had previously voted to call a special session of their General Conference when a plan of unification was approved by a two-thirds vote of each commission and by the General Conference of the Methodist Episcopal Church. The College of Bishops, therefore, proceeded to call a special session, although some of the bishops felt that the action was illegal. They felt the General Conference had no right to instruct the bishops to issue the call.

The special General Conference of the Southern Church was held in July, 1924, and lasted three days. The opposition to the plan was led by A. J. Lamar, who claimed to be in favor of unification but not of this particular plan. His ideas were defeated by a resounding vote, and the conference voted in favor of the plan of unification, 298 to 74.

It would seem that, having passed the General Conference by such a large majority, the plan would face little opposition of any strength in the Southern Annual Conferences, where it now had to be passed by a three-fourths majority. However, the dissenters were by no means quieted. Bishop John M. Moore, who was as close to the situation as any man, writes: "The opposition gathered strength in some states. . . . 'Absorption of the South by the North,' 'Northern preachers will take our leading churches,' 'no protection of our property or our institutions,' 'no name,' 'no constitution,' 'modernism in the North' were made the rallying cries for inciting and developing discontent, distrust, and disaffection." [75]

The plan passed the Annual Conferences by a majority; but it failed of the necessary three fourths of all the votes cast and thus was defeated. The final count was 4,528 for and 4,108 against. For the moment, at least, unification was defeated.

3

Forces Making for Union

A wave of disappointment naturally swept over the churches after the failure of the North and the South to unite in 1925. Some people said,

[75] *The Long Road to Methodist Union,* p. 179.

"Union is dead." A greater number, however, felt that the march toward union had only been temporarily halted.

Halford E. Luccock, contributing editor of the New York *Christian Advocate,* wrote: "Unification has met in the South, by a small margin, mathematical defeat. It comes to an ecclesiastical halt. But the effort has been a moral and spiritual victory." [76]

John S. Chadwick, special correspondent to the New York *Advocate* from the Methodist Episcopal Church, South, analyzed the situation in his column "From Down South":

Just how long Unification will be delayed by this decisive vote of the Southern Church is a question concerning which there are wide differences of opinion. ... There are some ardent pros who insist that the question will not be an issue for a decade, some say for a generation; there are antis who say that union cannot be long delayed. . . . There are more pros than antis who believe that union will not be long delayed, and more antis than pros who hold to the "dead and buried" idea.[77]

Stronger opposition had come from the laymen than from the preachers, Dr. Chadwick contended. The states leading the fight against the plan were Virginia, West Virginia, South Carolina, Georgia, Alabama, and Mississippi. Five bishops, three of whom had been on the Joint Commission, had strongly opposed the plan: Candler, Denny, Ainsworth, Darlington, and Dickey. The nine remaining bishops, who were for the plan, had made an excellent showing in the voting in the conferences over which they presided, but they had only 40 per cent of the voting strength of the church in their conferences.

A peripheral result of the voting on unification was the renewed almost passionate insistence on the part of the Southern laymen for a larger share in the direction of the church's affairs. The 1926 General Conference swept through a move for a lay member of the Annual Conference for each pastoral charge. It was felt in some quarters that the preachers had tried to "put over something on [the laymen]." [78]

The youth of both churches, however, were aggressively in favor of unification. Nine hundred college students representing 175 institutions met December 29–January 1, 1926, in an Interdenominational Student Conference at Evanston, Illinois. Wrote Malcolm R. Eiselen, special correspondent to the *Christian Advocate:* "The most recurring note of the entire conference was this insistence upon a united Christian church, with

[76] New York *Christian Advocate,* December 3, 1925, p. 1487.
[77] *Ibid.,* December 24, 1925, p. 1595.
[78] *Ibid.*

a united program of spiritual and social guidance." As a first practical step, the body went on record as favoring "an immediate unification of the young people's societies of the various churches." [79]

More surprising was the action taken by the Methodist Young People's Convention which met in Memphis, Tennessee, December 31–January 3, 1926. The convention consisted of four thousand youth representatives of Methodist colleges, state educational institutions, and the church at large. Wrote special correspondent Emily J. Reid: "The declaration which swept the great convention with tumultuous applause was youth's call to the Christian Church in America to apply in its own domain its ideas of brotherhood, co-operation and service. To this end it went on record as favoring the continuation of efforts to secure the unification of all the forces of American Methodism on a satisfactory basis." [80]

Other reactions to the vote on unification were as extreme as the two opposing positions appearing in different magazine articles: one by a layman, David Rankin Barbee, writing in the *Southern Methodist*, Memphis, Tennessee: "The Southern Church has no intention of entering a church in which Negroes have social and ecclesiastical equality with the whites." The other, an editorial appearing in *The Central Methodist*, published at Louisville, Kentucky: "It is enough for us that we witness in this vote, both of our own people and of the Church, South, the lovely sunrise. . . . That sun can never go backward." [81]

In the face of these many opposing ideas the churches for the moment wisely decided to pause in their efforts.

The General Conference of the Southern Church declared in 1926 that there should be no agitation, discussion, or further negotiations concerning unification during the ensuing quadrennium. The Northern Church accepted this decision.

The idea of union was kept alive, however, by other actions on the part of both churches. The Southern Church appointed a Committee on Research and Investigation to make an extensive study of the question in its historic, economic, social, and legal aspects and report their findings to the next General Conference. The Northern Church, "to keep alive the vision of union," continued a Commission on Union for any further negotiations. Its bishops in 1928 said:

Accepting our full measure of responsibility for the disunion of these years, we believe that we speak not for ourselves alone, but for the world-wide Methodist Episcopal Church represented here when we declare our readiness to hasten

[79] *Ibid.*, January 7, 1926, p. 18.
[80] *Ibid.*, January 14, 1926, p. 49.
[81] *Ibid.*, December 31, 1925, pp. 1612-13.

the restoration of unity and union by the acceptance of any basis of agreement which may be reached by the accredited Commissioners of the two churches.[82]

General forces were at work, moreover, driving the two churches inevitably toward union. Some were inherent in the situation itself. Others were the result of the circumstances and events of the day. Among these unifying forces were: (*a*) the similarity of doctrinal standards among the churches; (*b*) the unnecessary overlapping of effort and churches; (*c*) the disappearance of ecclesiastical polity differences; (*d*) the growth of a better feeling between the churches, fostered by the birth of new generations, the helpful conduct of the Methodist Protestant Church, the emphasis upon education and a growing historical-mindedness, and travel; (*e*) the challenge of world problems which could not be met by a divided church; (*f*) the universal spirit in favor of union; (*g*) the men who were leading the churches and the battle for unification.

To turn now to the first force mentioned, all three branches of Methodism still retained the undergirding of the same Methodist fundamentals. There were no doctrinal differences among the churches which would have caused them to remain apart. They claimed a common origin in John Wesley, Francis Asbury, Thomas Coke, and other giants of early Methodism. This unity was expressly stated at Cape May and repeated innumerable times by fraternal delegates to the various General Conferences. After 1904, moreover, the Northern and Southern Churches not only recognized the common creed and theology which had always been acknowledged by both but were also using a common hymnal and a common order of worship. One could have attended churches in the northernmost sections of the country or the southernmost part of the nation and found a striking similarity in worship, preaching, and beliefs.

Second, it was evident that the existence of two denominations caused foolish and costly overlapping of effort. The two churches were often in a community where one would have done as well, or better. As late as 1924 the two churches were competing in twenty-four different states, and the Methodist Protestant Church in some places made a third competitor. The Rev. John C. Kilgo of the Southern Church, who in 1904 had made a tremendous effect by his speech as fraternal delegate to the Northern Church, expressed the popular impatience when he wrote:

Why should the southern branch of the Methodist church tax its membership to build and sustain churches in California and Oregon and other regions in

[82] *Journal of the General Conference of the Methodist Episcopal Church*, 1928, p. 202.

which the northern branch of Methodism is better established? Or why should
the northern branch of Methodism continue to expend money in Tennessee and
Texas and Florida . . . ? Such a policy is a reckless waste of money.[83]

Overlapping, furthermore, with its accompanying evils of "altar against
altar," caused a bitterness in communities that was harmful to the work
of the church. In 1891 Bishop E. E. Hoss of the Southern Church warned
that when any Methodist denomination goes into a small village in which
there is already a Methodist church of another denomination, and builds
a house and sends a pastor, it makes it absolutely unnecessary for the devil
to be personally present in that village.

A third factor aiding union was the gradual disappearance of polity
differences. An insistence on lay representation and an objection to the
power of the bishop had been among the important issues causing the
Methodist Protestant Church to organize. By the end of the nineteenth
century these were largely dead issues. In 1866 the Southern Church made
provision for equal representation of laymen and preachers in the General Conference and admitted laymen on a limited basis to the Annual
Conferences. By 1922 these rights had also been extended to women. By
1926 there was a lay member in the Annual Conference for each charge. In
1896 equal representation in the General Conference for laymen and
preachers was granted in the Northern Church, and lay rights were extended to women in 1900. Laymen were not admitted to the Annual Conference until 1932, but this was not a serious block to union.

On the other hand, the Methodist Protestant Church had discovered
there was little to fear and something to gain in an episcopal form of
government. They increasingly felt the need of a stronger executive administration than could be secured by electing a new president every four
years. In 1920 they made the presidency a full-time position; in 1930
one of their presidents, J. C. Broomfield, later Bishop Broomfield, said:
"Because of the way in which Episcopal Methodism is democratizing its
episcopacy, and because of the way in which our folks are autocratizing
the presidency, and the executive committee of its General Conference,
the question of the episcopacy is increasingly ceasing to be an issue with
us." [84]

A fourth fact that favored union was the better feeling and understanding growing up between the two churches. New generations were being
born who were not a part of the emotional upheavals which had caused
the separation of the churches. It was said that the cradle and the grave

[83] "A Plea for the Union of Methodism in America," *The South Atlantic Quarterly,*
July, 1906.
[84] Garber, *Methodists Are One People,* p. 98.

were the best friends to organic union. Not all persons caught in the web of separation held forever to their animosities or to their differences of opinion. Many thoughtful leaders were ready to forget the past, and urged that many of the things of the past be forever buried, so that the challenge of the future might be adequately met.

The spirit and conduct of the Methodist Protestant Church was, for the most part, helpful. As early as 1848, before the Methodist Protestant Church had split into two camps over the slavery question, it had made a gesture of fraternity to the Methodist Episcopal Church, meeting for its General Conference in Pittsburgh, Pennsylvania. The pulpits of two Methodist Protestant churches were opened for guest preachers from the Methodist Episcopal Church, "Bishop Waugh preaching in the Pittsburgh church and administered the Lord's Supper with its Discipline, and Bishop Morris next Sabbath preached in the Allegheny church. . . . In this act, however, the olive branch was tendered by the new to the old, and accepted by them, and Christian fraternity inaugurated between the two denominations." [85]

In 1872 and 1876 fraternal delegates had been sent to the Northern Church by both branches of the bisected Methodist Protestant Church. They were warmly received. However, a break occurred in 1880 between the reunited Methodist Protestant Church and the Methodist Episcopal Church. It is explained by E. J. Drinkhouse in rather extravagant language:

> Fraternal messengers were authorized to the Methodist Episcopal Church, South, and the Cumberland Presbyterian Church. It will be noticed that at this Conference no fraternal interchange occurred with the Methodist Episcopal Church, and it needs explanation historically. It having been found by that dominating Church that much of its General Conference time had been occupied in the reception of fraternal messengers during the era of such interchanges inaugurated by it; . . . it was officially announced that, with certain exceptions named by it, such interchanges in the future would be, if desired, by correspondence only. As the Methodist Protestant Church was one of the American Methodisms omitted, self-respect made it impossible for it to accept the poor boon of a recognition by correspondence.[86]

In 1884, as we have already seen, the Methodist Protestant Church sent fraternal delegates to the Centennial Conference of Methodism, held in Baltimore, where they gave inspiring addresses slanted toward the idea of union. However, the General Conference of the Methodist Protestant

---

[85] Edward J. Drinkhouse, *History of Methodist Reform . . . with Special Reference to the History of the Methodist Protestant Church* (Baltimore and Pittsburgh: Board of Publication of the Methodist Protestant Church, 1899), II, 357.

[86] *Ibid.*, p. 589.

Church rejected any thought of organic union in 1884, stating that "so long as the question of organic union is under the consideration of our General Conference, our Church will be in a continual confusion and a state of unrest." [87]

Nevertheless, in 1892 they sent a telegram to the General Conference of the Methodist Episcopal Church, in session at Omaha, Nebraska. It read: "Christian greetings General Conference Methodist Protestant Church in session Westminster, Md. Read one hundred and thirty-third Psalm." [88] The psalm begins: "Behold, how good and how pleasant it is for brethren to dwell together in unity!"

No reply was received. But in 1896 greetings were again ordered sent by the Methodist Protestants to the General Conference of the Methodist Episcopal Church, then in session in Cleveland, Ohio, for it had been discovered that a reply from that church "had failed of transmission." [89]

The most important communication between the churches, as we have seen, occurred in 1908, when the address of Thomas H. Lewis was received with enthusiastic acclaim.

Spasmodically the Methodist Protestant Church had sent fraternal delegates or greetings to the Methodist Episcopal Church, South. Some of the Methodist Protestant churches and conferences, as is told in another part of this history, had united with the Southern Church following the time when the Methodist Protestant Church had been split apart. They did not return when the two branches of the Methodist Protestant Church reunited in 1877, but they naturally held a warm feeling for their mother church.

Beyond this, and possibly more important than all else, was the conduct of the Methodist Protestant Church, as we shall see, after the defeat of a plan of union between the episcopal Methodisms in 1925. It was the Methodist Protestant men who took up the whole question of union again in 1930 and began the movement that ended in the Uniting Conference of 1939. No Methodist historian dare underestimate the contribution of the Methodist Protestants to the organic union of the three Methodisms in America.

Good feeling was also established as a result of a greater emphasis upon education. Universities such as Emory, with its Candler School of Theology; Vanderbilt; Duke; and Southern Methodist University, with Perkins School of Theology, were built. They drew faculty and students from all over the country. With academic objectivity they refused to be sectional-

[87] *Ibid.*, p. 640.
[88] *Journal of the General Conference of the Methodist Episcopal Church*, 1892, p. 608.
[89] Drinkhouse, *History of Methodist Reform*, II, 675.

ized. They refused to consider themselves as only a part of the total Methodist Church. Much of the leadership which later worked for union came from these schools.

Better feeling was also fostered by a sincere attempt to see the controversy from both sides. William Warren Sweet calls this a "growing historical mindedness," and he defines this attitude as the "willingness to consider all sides of all the historic issues which caused division." [90] The three denominations began gradually to accept the same interpretation of the past. All three became willing to concede the errors on the part of their own leadership and the value in some of the positions taken by the other churches. Methodists were becoming realistic rather than emotional about union. They were no longer as interested in maintaining past prejudices as they were in planning for future potentials.

Industry, travel, and cultural life in the country were also creating a better feeling between the two churches. Provincialism was on the way out. Travel had increased mightily. The automobile, the radio, the airplane, brought people closer together. Industrialists traveled everywhere and built business houses with no thought of sectionalism or past controversy. Thomas H. Lewis, onetime president of the Methodist Protestant Church, said: "Surely Christian men can do for love what the ungodly find it possible to do for mere gain." [91]

A fifth force working for union emerged following the First World War from the world problems with which the churches were concerned. A divided church could hardly speak with any commanding voice in favor of international unity. If churches with a common origin and similar doctrines, polity, and principles could not unite, how could nations with far different backgrounds, cultures, and racial conditions be expected to come together? The hope for a united world brought with it the necessity for a united church. Only a united church could witness effectively in a strife-torn world.

Many of the meetings of the Joint Commission on Unification were held during the First World War. Men were more and more impressed with the necessity of providing a united church for soldiers from both the North and the South who were fighting for a common cause. These men would necessarily have little sympathy with church divisions which kept them from worshiping together on their return home. Union on the field of battle was one factor in creating union at home.

Beyond this, conditions everywhere made the churches increasingly aware that they had no energy to expend in continuing the futile battle

[90] *Methodism in American History* (Nashville: Abingdon Press, 1953), p. 401.
[91] Garber, *Methodists Are One People*, p. 102.

between themselves when they needed every man and dollar and every bit of energy to destroy the materialism, the public and private immorality, and the secularism which were laying hold of the country and the world. More than ever they needed to band together against common enemies that were seeking to destroy Christ's Church. To continue a division of forces at a time like this was the height of folly, and this conviction was more and more impressing itself on the thinking of churchmen everywhere.

A sixth force working for unification was the fact that the spirit of union was in the air. In 1916 a Working Conference on the Union of American Methodism was held at Harris Hall, Northwestern University, Evanston, Illinois. It was sponsored by the John Richard Lindgren Foundation for the Promotion of International Peace and Christian Unity. Some of the best historians of the church were brought together to speak to specially chosen delegates about the whole matter of unification, both from the viewpoint of its problems and from the viewpoint of its possible solution. The entire series of lectures was published in book form.[92] All of Protestantism was interested in the subject.

Bishop Garber writes:

The pronounced trend toward organic union of Methodists everywhere aided the work of the commissioners. In 1930, with the permission of the mother churches, the Korean Annual Conferences of the Methodist Episcopal Church and of the Methodist Episcopal Church, South, respectively, united to form the Korean Methodist Church. In like manner, in 1930, the Methodist Church of Mexico came into existence through a merger of the Northern and the Southern Methodists in Mexico. In 1932 a united Methodism became a reality in England through the union of the Wesleyan Methodist Church, the Primitive Methodist Church, and the United Methodist Church.

The celebration in 1934 of the one hundred and fiftieth anniversary of the beginning of organized Methodism in America occurred while the commissioners were preparing [what proved to be the final] Plan of Union, and strengthened the opinion in favor of unification. In adopting the plan for the Sesquicentennial Celebration, the hope was expressed by the three churches that it might have, as a practical result, the union of American Methodism by at least the year 1944. In addition to celebrations in annual conferences and in local churches, a central celebration was held at Baltimore, October 10-14, 1934. Thursday, October 1, was designated as "One Day of Union," when the people present acted as if unification had already become a reality. Before the conference adjourned a report was adopted which stated: "We desire to say to the Methodists of our land that the time has fully come for us to move forward in one body.

---

[92] *A Working Conference on the Union of American Methodism.*

Only so shall we keep faith with our fathers, and only so can we keep faith with our children." [93]

A seventh and possibly the most powerful factor toward bringing about union was the caliber and the number of the leaders in the church who gave their lives in earnest dedication to the completion of this task. They honestly felt that a divided church was a sin against God, contrary to the spirit and wishes of Jesus Christ. Inspired by this conviction, they refused even in the darkest hours of discouragement to let union die. Many of those who first fostered union among the churches died before its accomplishment, but before their deaths they had passed on to others their own irresistible zeal and courage. Neither the cold indifference of some church leaders, nor the heated opposition of some preachers and laymen, nor the irritating delays caused by church machinery and politics, nor the realization of the hopelessness of their task could stop these men.

In January of 1925, when a vote for unification was slowly being lost in the Annual Conferences of the Methodist Episcopal Church, South, Bishop Mouzon wrote to Bishop Cranston:

We are having a rather hard time of it in the Methodist Episcopal Church, South, and I, in particular, am having my full share of criticism; but continually I ask myself this question: "Am I right in the sight of Jesus Christ," and I always get the same answer, namely, that His approval rests upon what I am doing. . . .

About the whole unification problem, I feel that though we might be unfortunate enough not to receive the three-fourths majority needed by the time the vote is taken, we shall have fully won our *cause* even though for the time being we may have lost the *vote*. Which is to say, we have already won before the intelligent and spiritual leadership of our church and that makes certain success in the long run. Do not think that I am discouraged. News from the conferences comes in every day that encourages me.[94]

A month later Dr. John M. Moore, later Bishop Moore, wrote to Bishop Cranston: "We will not stop. The unification of our two churches must be. The men who are vociferous today cannot speak the word for tomorrow. There is a higher voice that brings peace to troubled waters. So long as I live, I shall plead this cause." [95]

Dr. Goucher had once written to Bishop Mouzon: "The problem is vast, intricate, delicate." [96] It was imbedded not only in the ecclesiastical his-

[93] *Methodists Are One People*, pp. 123-24. Used by permission.
[94] MS letter of January 20, 1925, in the archives of the Historical Society of the Baltimore Annual Conference, Lovely Lane Museum.
[95] MS letter of March 2, 1925, Lovely Lane archives.
[96] MS letter of July 28, 1917, Lovely Lane archives.

tory of the churches and the times, but also in the political, economic, and cultural history of the country. It was a problem that required for its solution far more than a few pat answers or Christian platitudes.

The problem required, above all, men of character who would take the task of unification seriously. That there were such men is witnessed by what was accomplished through the years, and a few of these men should be especially mentioned. Chairman of the Northern commission had been Bishop Earl Cranston; chairman of the Southern commission, Bishop Warren A. Candler. Bishop Cranston, who was seventy-six years old and had been retired, had been a Union soldier, rising to the rank of a captain. A publishing agent before his election to the episcopacy, he was an able administrator and an inspiring leader and speaker. His service to unification lay not so much in his contributions to a definite plan but rather in his constant insistence that a satisfactory plan would finally be worked out. He wrote and lectured extensively for this cause.

Bishop Candler as a boy of seven had watched Sherman's army march by his widowed mother's home. He struggled for an education during the tragic days of Reconstruction. At seventeen he was a circuit rider, at twenty-three a presiding elder, at thirty-one a college president, and at forty-one a bishop. He was best known as a brilliant preacher and a rugged opponent of unification. His influence did more to defeat the plan in 1925 than any other single factor. He again opposed the plan in 1930-38, not because he objected to unification but rather because he felt there were inherent weaknesses in the plan suggested. He proved an impartial chairman, however, and while he held himself aloof from assisting in formulating any particular plan, his readiness to discuss the whole matter in a brotherly spirit was in itself an aid to unification.

Of the Northern commission, Bishop William Fraser McDowell was noted not so much for his creative ability as for a gift for summarizing what had been said and for formulating it in such a way as to secure action. He had an expansive spirit and an understanding mind. He had been chancellor of the University of Denver and corresponding secretary of the Board of Education of the Methodist Episcopal Church. As a preacher he knew no peer, and he was popular both in the North and in the South. He understood both sections of the country well, and his numerous contacts and warm spirit were a decided aid. During this crucial time he served on every commission that dealt with union.

Bishop John W. Hamilton, retired, had come from a plain background. He was, however, a sound scholar, a witty raconteur, an extraordinary preacher with a fine face and a dignified manner. His chief concern on the commission was to give a satisfactory status to the Negro in the new church. However, he was always considerate of the opinions of others, and this generosity made his strong stand for the Negro more acceptable.

The most creative minds of the Northern commission were Edgar Blake, elected to the episcopacy in 1920, and Bishop Frederick Deland Leete. Bishop Leete was a tall, slim man, while Blake was almost diminutive, with a mild manner that gave no suggestion of his brilliant intellect and strong will.

Bishop Leete knew both sections of the church, having held prominent pastorates in the North and having served as bishop of the Atlanta area. He also served on every commission that dealt with union at this time, and his service was effective in subcommittees as well as in the Joint Commission meetings. He had a clear idea of the problems that faced the commission, and he always stated his ideas clearly and with understanding.

Edgar Blake served indefatigably. He realized almost at once that union could never be achieved without the creation of the Jurisdictional or Regional Conference and a Judicial Council. He understood, moreover, that the number of jurisdictions was a matter of importance. Too few, which might result in great power for the jurisdictions created, would not be satisfactory to the North; too many, which would reduce their power proportionately, would hardly be acceptable to the South. His suggestion was for six white jurisdictions and one Negro, very nearly approximating the number today. His inventive genius made him an indispensable member of the Joint Commission.

Some other leaders of the North included Book Editor David G. Downey, who was slow to accept the jurisdictional idea; Dr. John F. Goucher, president of Goucher College (his was a brotherly spirit whose contribution lay in a conciliatory manner) ; and Robert E. Jones, editor of the *Southwestern Advocate*. Jones wanted a satisfactory status for the Negro in the new church, and conducted himself in a way to win both North and South to his viewpoint. He served on all commissions dealing with union in these years and was a most acceptable commissioner.

Among the laymen, a former vice-president of the United States, Charles W. Fairbanks, served for a time. His place was early taken by New York *Advocate* Editor James R. Joy, who was the only layman of the Northern Church who served on all commissions dealing with union during this era. Both Judge Wade Rogers of the Federal Circuit Court in New York and Alexander Simpson, a lawyer of Philadelphia and later Chief Justice of Pennsylvania, served with distinction. Other laymen also were helpful.

Bishop John M. Moore described the Southern members of the first Joint Commission on Unification in the following paragraphs:

Six members of the Southern Commission served on all the Commissions that dealt with union: Bishop Edwin D. Mouzon, Dr. H. N. Snyder, Dr. J. H. Reynolds, the Hon. P. D. Maddin, Judge H. H. White, and this author. Of the ten ministers of the Commission, six [actually five] were connectional officers: Dr. A. J. Lamar, Publishing Agent: T. N. Ivey, Editor of *The Nashville Christian Advocate*; H. M. Du Bose, Editor of *The Methodist Reveiw; E. B. Chappell, Editor of Sunday School Literature; and John M. Moore, Secretary of Home Missions. Two were college presidents: President A. F. Watkins of Millsaps College, and President C. M. Bishop of Southwestern University. Two were pastors: Dr. W. N. Ainsworth of Georgia and Dr. F. M. Thomas of Kentucky. Dr. W. J. Young was Professor in Emory School of Theology in 1918. John M. Moore, H. M. Du Bose, and W. N. Ainsworth were elected bishops in 1918.

Of the ten laymen, one was a banker, Mr. John R. Pepper, of Memphis. Four were college presidents: President H. N. Snyder of Wofford, President R. S. Hyer of Southern Methodist University, President R. E. Blackwell of Randolph-Macon, and President J. H. Reynolds of Hendrix. Five were lawyers: P. D. Maddin, H. H. White, Colonel E. C. Reeves, M. L. Walton, and T. D. Samford.[97]

The clearest thinkers and the most vigorous leaders of the Southern commissioners were Bishop Moore and Bishop Mouzon. Bishop Mouzon's greatest contribution to unification lay in the untiring zeal with which he espoused this cause and the courage with which he advocated the plans of unification. His seniority as a bishop finally brought him to the chairmanship of the Southern commission of the Joint Commission and thus made him one of the joint chairmen.

Bishop Moore had served as secretary of the Board of Missions of his church before his election to the episcopacy. He had a widespread personal relationship with ministers in the South, which, combined with his zeal for unification, made him an invaluable member of the Joint Commission. He knew the mind of the South as few men did. Both Bishop Moore and Bishop Mouzon were close friends of Bishop Cranston of the Northern Church. It was this warm friendship, typical of many such friendships reaching across the churches, which proved most salutary for unification.

Bishops Hoss, Denny, and Ainsworth all stood in opposition to the plan of union defeated in 1925, but this does not mean they were unalterably opposed to unification.

Bishop Hoss, like Bishop Candler, felt there were serious defects in this plan of union. He was in feeble health and died in 1919. While he lived, however, he proved an alert debater and a powerful advocate of the jurisdictional system and of strong constitutional checks upon the General Conference.

Bishop Ainsworth sincerely felt unification would cost the Southern

[97] *The Long Road to Methodist Union,* p. 130. Used by permission.

Church a large percentage of its membership. For this reason he was opposed to unification until the right time and the right plan for union should be linked. Bishop Leete tells how Bishop Ainsworth broke an impasse in the discussions on the Jurisdictional Conference with an exceedingly valuable suggestion. Various plans for jurisdictional areas were discussed, but none of them crossed the Mason-Dixon Line, and the Joint Commission felt this kind of union would be in name only. It was Bishop Ainsworth who suggested placing Kansas and Nebraska in the same jurisdiction. This idea was enthusiastically received, and it still prevails.[98]

Bishop Denny died in 1943 when nearly ninety years of age. He never lost the early impressions of his childhood, and this may account for his ceaseless opposition to unification. One of his most vivid recollections, he would say, was of his father marching away to war. His was a brilliant mind. For nineteen years before becoming a bishop he had been professor of mental and moral philosophy at Vanderbilt University. His brotherly spirit aided, in the end, the unification to which he was opposed. He refused to become a bishop in the new church.

Two strong exponents for unification on the Southern commission were Dr. A. J. Lamar, publishing agent, and T. N. Ivey, editor of the Nashville *Christian Advocate*. While Dr. Lamar opposed the plan in 1925, he was basically in favor of unification and worked constantly for its accomplishment. Dr. Ivey made valuable contributions to the work of the commission.

The men of both commissions were brilliant, thoughtful, serious-minded men who agreed nowhere more certainly than in their love for their respective churches and their loyalty to Jesus Christ.

One other man should also be mentioned—the man who would serve as chairman of the commission of the Northern Church when, in 1939, unification was finally accomplished. He is Bishop Edwin H. Hughes. Bishop Moore, who served as chairman of the Southern commission at that time, and President Straughn, who served as chairman of the Methodist Protestant commission, are noted elsewhere. Bishop Hughes was a witty, brilliant preacher, popular both in the North and in the South. He traveled the entire country and was a familiar figure to Methodist leaders of all three churches. He had the confidence of all three churches, and this was no small matter in the final accomplishment of union.

The Methodist Protestant Church, as we have already noted, took no part in the negotiations between the episcopal Methodisms that ended in the defeat of 1925. The life and influence of Dr. T. H. Lewis, however, should be mentioned. The meaning of his work for unification is

[98] Frederick D. Leete, *Methodist Bishops* (Nashville: Parthenon Press, 1948), p. 420.

summarized in the remark of J. L. Hillman of the Northern Church, who at the General Conference of the Methodist Episcopal Church in 1916 introduced the fraternal delegates of the Methodist Protestant Church to the General Conference by saying: "I think it is the feeling of our Church that if the Methodist Protestant Church had never done anything else than give to our country that man who, I think, . . . in the years to come, will be named as the chiefest among the apostles and prophets of Methodist Union—I refer to Dr. T. H. Lewis—it would have had ample reason for existence." [99]

4

The Period of Triumph

The period of triumph begins as Methodist Protestant leaders informally investigate the possibility of union once again. In his book *Inside Methodist Union* Bishop James H. Straughn quotes a valuable letter from Bishop Herbert Welch of the Northern Church outlining these preliminary steps toward the final victory for Methodist union:

The Methodist Episcopal General Conference of 1928 appointed a Commission on Interdenominational Relations. McDowell became general Chairman, Mead Chairman of a sub-committee on Relations with Other Methodist Churches, I Chairman for Relations with Other-than-Methodist Churches. . . .

About . . . December 1929, Drs. Hawley and Allen came to my office in Pittsburgh . . . to talk about the possibility of the Methodist Protestants as a body coming into the Methodist Episcopal Church. . . . I asked what specific provisions the Methodist Protestants would expect in any such plan. They mentioned two: (1) that Methodist Protestant preachers should receive, in the matter of appointments, the same consideration as the Methodist Episcopal; and (2) that years spent in the Methodist Protestant ministry should be credited for pension equally with the Methodist Episcopal. My answer naturally was that those provisions would appeal to all as perfectly fair and would undoubtedly be agreed to.

When I asked if the episcopacy offered no obstacle, they responded: "We have no objection to the episcopacy as it now exists." . . . I told the brethren that I would at once communicate to Bishop McDowell what they had said. . . .

Bishop McDowell agreed to come to Pittsburgh . . . , and a luncheon was

---

[99] *Journal of the General Conference of the Methodist Episcopal Church*, 1916, pp. 776-77.

arranged for January 20, 1930, at which he and I met Drs. Hawley, Allen and (I believe) Broomfield. . . . A little later, Bishop Mead . . . had [a] meeting with the interested brethren of the Methodist Protestant Church.

As a result of these consultations, a formal meeting was called between the Methodist Protestant Committee on Church Union (?) and the Commission on Interdenominational Relations of the Methodist Episcopal Church . . . in the William Penn Hotel on July 2, 1930. . . . After full discussion, it was agreed that [any proposal for union] called for a meeting with the Methodist Episcopal Church South before any action should be taken.

Accordingly, two informal conferences were later held at which Southern representatives were present: one at Chicago on Jan. 30, 1931 with Bishop McMurray; another during the Ecumenical Methodist Conference in Atlanta on Oct. 20, 1931, with Bishop J. M. Moore.

. . . And finally on Feb. 24, 1932, ten representatives of the three churches concerned met in Washington. . . . It was unanimously agreed that no further progress could be made until after the Methodist Episcopal South General Conference in the following May, which might probably widen the instructions to its Commission, [which could deal only with questions of comity].

As you know, the Southern Conference did take such action and negotiations proceeded on a new basis.[100]

Bishop Welch's letter is valuable, of course, because of its personal insights and for the picture of what was going on behind the scenes. Bishop Moore writes that the meeting at the William Penn Hotel in Pittsburgh was held July 1, 1930. Bishop Moore agrees with the general import of the Welch letter, however, stating that "the two Commissions decided to confine their work to mere discussions, without taking official action until such time as the Commission of the Church South could at least be present." [101]

These discussions were continued, as we know from the Welch letter, in Chicago on January 30, 1931. Bishop W. F. McMurry represented the Southern Church, but he made it clear that his commission had no authority to discuss union—only matters of comity and the exchange of conferences, churches, and property. The commissions of the Methodist Episcopal Church and the Methodist Protestant Church met again at an Ecumenical Conference in October, 1931, in Atlanta. Some of their number, according to Bishop Moore, had an informal meeting with him to secure his opinion as to the possibility of the Southern Church's joining the negotiations for unification.

The reasons for their inquiry were twofold: first, they wondered if it were wise to agitate the question so soon after the defeat of 1924. Second,

---

[100] Pp. 97-99.
[101] *The Long Road to Methodist Union*, p. 182.

they were concerned about the Southern reaction to the resolution of the 1928 Northern General Conference that it would hold its meetings only in those cities where the Negro delegates would be entertained on the same basis as the whites. Bishop Mouzon of the Southern Church in a newspaper interview had said that this resolution had postponed union indefinitely.

Bishop Moore, however, felt otherwise. In answer to the question whether the 1934 General Conference of the Southern Church would indorse new negotiations on union, he said: "Yes, the General Conference, in my opinion, will in all probability appoint a Commission on Methodist Union to begin renewed negotiations at once." [102]

As a result of this assurance the two commissions at their meeting in Pittsburgh, 1932, appointed a subcommittee which in turn invited the Comity Committee of the Southern Church to meet with them. This invitation was accepted as the Welch letter makes clear, and there was a meeting in Washington in February, 1932, between the Comity Committee of the Southern Church and the subcommittee of the commissions of the Methodist Protestant Church and the Methodist Episcopal Church. The outcome was the adoption of a paper recommending:

that we temporarily suspend all formal efforts of union now in progress between any of our Churches. . . .

That we unite . . . in recommending . . . to our General Conferences meeting in May, 1932 and 1934, the creation or continuation of Commissions authorized . . . to make and agree upon plans for the union of the three Churches here represented and others that may enter the negotiations upon invitation or with our approval.[103]

This paper went to all three General Conferences—to the Northern Church and the Methodist Protestant Church in 1932 and to the Methodist Episcopal Church, South, in 1934. Each church approved the principles of the paper, and each authorized a commission for union. In the Northern Church it was named the Commission on Interdenominational Relations of the Methodist Episcopal Church. In the Methodist Protestant Church it was known as the Commission on Union of the Methodist Protestant Church; and in the Southern Church it was called the Commission on Interdenominational Relations and Church Union of the Methodist Episcopal Church, South.

The three commissions held three meetings: in Chicago in August, 1934; in Louisville in March, 1935; and in Evanston in August, 1935.

[102] *Ibid.*, p. 183.
[103] *Journal of the General Conference of the Methodist Episcopal Church*, 1932, p. 1496.

At the first meeting an important step was taken in authorizing a sub-committee of fifteen, six from each of the two episcopal churches and three from the Methodist Protestant Church, to study the previous plans of union and all other proposals that might be presented from time to time, with a view to formulating a plan or plans for union.

This subcommittee on plans began work at once. It held four meetings during the following year. Its tentative report to the second commission meeting, in Louisville, 1935, settled two very important matters: (a) the principle of the Jurisdictional Conference was approved as a basis for the unification of the churches, and (b) the necessity of equal represen-tation of laymen and ministers in the Annual Conferences was estab-lished.

The subcommittee then continued work. Its final plan was adopted by the Joint Commission at the meeting held in Evanston in August.

The speed with which this plan was created was the result of the care-ful work of the various committees and commissions which had preceded this effort. The new Joint Commission had the benefit of all previous discussions and especially the "suggestions" adopted by the General Con-ferences of the Northern Church and the Southern Church in 1912 and 1914, already described in this chapter.

In brief, the new plan emphasized seven major ideas:

a) The name of the new church would be "The Methodist Church."

b) The church would have but one General Conference, which would be the highest legislative body of the church. This General Conference would be subject to five restrictive rules.

c) There were to be six Jurisdictional Conferences, five based on geo-graphical divisions, one to include the Negro Annual Conferences in America.

d) There was to be equal representation of ministers and laymen in the General, Jurisdictional, and Annual Conferences.

e) There was to be a Judicial Council related to the General Confer-ence and the Council of Bishops as the Supreme Court of the United States is related to Congress and the presidency.

f) The episcopacy was to be retained, and the delegates of the Meth-odist Protestant Church were authorized to elect two of their number to the office of bishop.

g) The Articles of Religion were to be those historically held in com-mon by the three uniting churches.

The plan passed the three General Conferences and the Annual Con-ferences by tremendous majorities. The Methodist Protestant Church was the first to ratify union. The General Conference, meeting in May, 1936, voted 142 "yes" and 39 "no"; the Annual Conferences, 20 "yes" and

5 "no." The vote by members in the Annual Conferences was 1,265 "yes" and 389 "no."

The Methodist Episcopal Church voted in 1936 also. In the General Conference the vote was 470 for and 83 against. In the Annual Conferences the vote by members was 17,239 "yes" and 1,862 "no."

The Methodist Episcopal Church, South, voted by Annual Conferences first, in order to hasten the decision, since its General Conference did not meet until 1938. In the Annual Conferences the vote was 7,650 "yes" and 1,247 "no." In the General Conference it stood 434 "yes" and 26 "no."

Some opposition had developed, and while not numerically large it was exceedingly vocal. Some persons in the Northern Church objected strongly to the Jurisdictional Conferences and the segregation of the Negroes at this level. Dr. Lewis O. Hartman, later bishop, said: "The separate jurisdiction for negroes represents, in my opinion, not only no progress, but a definite backward step in the field of race relations." Dr. E. F. Tittle, a delegate and pastor of First Methodist Church, Evanston, Illinois, said:

> The most intelligent, the most ethically sensitive [of our youth] are profoundly disturbed by what we are proposing now to do. . . . Some of them are calling attention to the fact that southeastern share-croppers, white and black, are form- ing a union in defense of human rights, a union which makes no profession of re- ligious faith, and they are asking, "Is it possible that an organization without any religious profession of faith can transcend a historic, irrational, un-Christian prejudice, whereas the Christian Church cannot do so?" [104]

David Jones, a Negro from North Carolina, said at the General Con- ference of the Northern Church: "Everyone knows the Plan is segregation, and segregation in the ugliest way, because it is couched in such pious terms." [105]

Bishop Francis J. McConnell of the Northern Church had written in a letter to *Zion's Herald:*

> The Plan at this point has nothing of daring or challenge. It simply recom- mends the solution . . . in a manner suggesting that the proponents are, as to this question, very devoted, very able, very well informed, very tired, and a trifle bored.

The proposed provisions do give the Negro more than he had had and made

---

[104] *The Daily Christian Advocate* for the General Conference of the Methodist Epis- copal Church, 1936, p. 87.
[105] *Ibid.*

it possible for him to take still more, if he will . . . speak up positively and aggressively on his own.[106]

The opponents of the plan, however, were unable to cope with the deep-seated desire for union, which at the moment was the most important consideration.

In the South opposition developed along legislative lines. The opposition soon realized that despite their best efforts the Plan of Union would be adopted both by a majority of the Annual Conferences and by the General Conference. They determined to destroy the possibility of union by challenging the legality of the whole procedure. The members of the commission were aware of this strategy. When the plan had been overwhelmingly adopted by the General Conference, therefore, Bishop Moore read a request from the College of Bishops to the Judicial Council that

the Judicial Council . . . determine the legality of the act of the General Conference of the Methodist Episcopal Church, South, on the 29th day of April, 1938, and of all actions of the members of the Annual Conferences of the Methodist Episcopal Church, South, in the ratification and adoption of the Plan of Union of the Methodist Episcopal Church, the Methodist Protestant Church, and the Methodist Episcopal Church, South.[107]

It was a wise request. The Judicial Council listened to lengthy arguments, deliberated for three days, and then handed down a decision which ended the matter. The Council stated that: (a) the actions of the members of the several Annual Conferences in approving the Plan of Union and authorizing its adoption, as reported to the General Conference, were and are legal; (b) the action of the General Conference in ratifying and adopting the Plan of Union was and is legal; (c) the union of the three churches has been legally authorized in accordance with the Plan of Union.[108]

The Plan of Union had been safely passed by all three churches.

The Uniting Conference

The Uniting Conference of the three churches was held in Kansas City, Missouri, April 26–May 10, 1939.

[106] March 4, 1936, p. 221.
[107] *Journal of the General Conference of the Methodist Episcopal Church, South,* 1938, p. 119.
[108] *Ibid.,* pp. 117-36.

The Episcopal Address was read by John M. Moore of the Southern Church. It was signed by the bishops of both the episcopal churches, with the exception of Bishop Collins Denny, who having opposed the Plan of Union, declined to become a bishop of The Methodist Church and refused to sign. It was also signed by the president of the General Conference of the Methodist Protestant Church, James H. Straughn.

The address was framed "with the dominant purpose of exalting the mission of a Conference unique in Methodist History." It boasted that "no more notable and responsible Christian body has ever assembled on this continent than this Uniting Conference." [109]

Optimistically, the bishops prophesied that "the fraternal spirit may be expected to have full sway in this Uniting Conference. On the larger matters we are already in agreement. Since we have never separated in faith, we will have no theological discussions. . . . This Methodism is no fabrication of ambitious, selfish ecclesiastics. It is rather the flowing together of great streams going out to the same seas." The concluding paragraphs were a call to allegiance: "No ruler takes a throne nor chief magistrate a scepter of government without a solemn oath to protect, preserve, and defend the constitution of the country. At this glorious inauguration in Methodism with uplifted hand we and you take such an oath of allegiance to our great Church." [110]

Varied fraternal greetings were read at the conference. There was a lengthy message from President Franklin D. Roosevelt, dated Warm Springs, Georgia, Easter Day, 1939. Said the President: "To a world distracted by malice, envy, and ill will, the Kansas City assembly is a harbinger of better things. . . . The Methodists have pointed the way to union. May God prosper the work and hasten the day when Christians of all confessions shall present a united front to combat the forces of strife that threaten our heritage of religion." [111]

Early in the conference the Methodist Protestant delegates met in executive session to elect two of their number to the episcopacy. They chose for this high honor James Henry Straughn and John Calvin Broomfield. Both men had had wide executive experience. Bishop Straughn was at the time of his election the president of the General Conference of the Methodist Protestant Church. He had been president of West Lafayette College, West Lafayette, Ohio, and had also served as assistant to Thomas H. Lewis. Bishop Straughn had served as president of the General Conference since 1936. Bishop Broomfield, a native of Scotland, had started his

[109] *Journal of the Uniting Conference*, pp. 148-49.
[110] *Ibid.*, pp. 148-64.
[111] *Ibid.*, pp. 200-201.

career as a deep-sea fisherman. Later he had come to America, where he had worked as a day laborer. During forty-one years of active ministry, he had served only three churches. Bishop Broomfield had served as president of the General Conference of the Methodist Protestant Church for eight years.

The Sunday following their election the two men were consecrated as bishops in the united church. They were consecrated, not ordained, to this office—an interpretation of the episcopacy that was continued by the first General Conference of The Methodist Church, held a year later. Thus it was confirmed by the highest legislative body of the united church that the episcopacy is not a higher order of the ministry but an office.

The expected steps for union moved along smoothly. The Declaration of Plan of Union was read by representatives of each of the participating churches in the order in which their churches had ratified the plan. James H. Straughn, as chairman of the Commission on Methodist Union of the Methodist Protestant Church, presented the declaration of that church; Bishop Edwin H. Hughes, chairman of the Commission on Interdenominational Relations of the Methodist Episcopal Church, then presented the declaration of that church; and finally Bishop John M. Moore, chairman of the Commission on Interdenominational Relations and Church Union of the Methodist Episcopal Church, South, presented the declaration of the Southern Church.

Dr. Harry E. Woolever, secretary of the Northern Church's commission in the Joint Commission, then presented the report of the Joint Commission on Methodist Union. Among other facts he listed the entire personnel of the Joint Commission. His report also stated that a carefully selected committee of over two hundred had prepared the Prospectus of the *Discipline* of The Methodist Church. This Prospectus had been placed in the hands of the delegates for preliminary study before their coming to the Uniting Conference and was now turned over to them for their further consideration and action. In short, the Uniting Conference was to erect the structure of the new church by hammering out a *Discipline*. The conference eventually not only wrote a *Discipline* but also set the date of the first General Conference of the new church for 1940. This first General Conference wrote another *Discipline*, but it introduced few changes of importance into the *Discipline* of 1939 written by the Uniting Conference. The Uniting Conference was to do its work so well that little change would be required.

To attempt a detailed analysis of the 1939 *Discipline* would be impossible at this point. Certain salient points, however, will be noted, as well as the general structure of the new church.

THE PATTERN OF CONFERENCES

All three churches had had as their highest legislative body the General Conference, which met once every four years. The powers granted and the restrictions laid upon the General Conference had followed substantially the same pattern. In its "Restrictive Rules on Legislative Assemblies," Article X, the Methodist Protestant Church had said: "No rule shall be passed to abolish an efficient itineracy," whereas the episcopal churches had said: "The General Conference shall not change nor alter any part or rule of our government so as to do away Episcopacy, nor destroy the plan of our General Superintendency." The Methodist Protestant Church had also stated: "No higher order of ministers shall be authorized than that of elder." The episcopal churches would probably have agreed with this statement, but it was not included in the restrictive rules laid upon the General Conference of The Methodist Church.

Another rule of the Methodist Protestant Church which was omitted by the new church stated: "No rule shall be passed infringing the liberty of speech, or of the press; but for every abuse of liberty the offender shall be dealt with as in other cases of indulging in sinful words and tempers." The Methodist Protestant Church had likewise had a rule which said: "No rule shall be passed which shall contravene any law of God." This also was omitted from the restrictive rules laid upon the General Conference! A prolonged statement in the restrictive rules of the Southern Church with reference to the number of delegates in the General Conference and a statement in the Northern Church about missionary bishops were likewise dropped. The Methodist Protestant Church constitution had listed eight restrictive rules, the two episcopal churches each six.

In The Methodist Church there are five restrictive rules. The first protects the Articles of Religion from any action by the General Conference, and forbids the General Conference to establish "any new standards or rules of doctrine contrary to our present existing and established standards of doctrine." The second protects the episcopacy, but it does not protect the church from the episcopacy; there is nothing in the present rules, as there had been in the Methodist Protestant Church, making it impossible for the General Conference to establish a higher order of the ministry than elder. (In years to come this may prove an important omission, especially if the bishops begin to assume a distinctive garb and insist on the exaltation of their office beyond what was characteristic of early Methodism. In recent years the wearing of purple on their *rabats* and their robes by some bishops and a special insigne on their gowns could be a drift in this direction, from which no restrictive rule adequately protects the church.) The third restrictive rule guarantees the right of a fair trial for accused members of the church or its ministers; the fourth protects the General Rules of the United Societies. The last forbids the appropriating by the General Conference of "the produce of the Publishing House, the Book Concern, or the Chartered Fund to any purpose other than for the benefit of the traveling, supernumerary, superannuated, and worn-out preachers, their wives, widows, and children." The powers of the General Conference were substantially what they had been in the three churches, with the notable exception of the power to elect bishops. The General Conference is the highest legislative body of the church.

The promotional conference for the new church, however, was to be the Jurisdictional Conference. There were to be six Jurisdictional Conferences, five based on geographical divisions and one gathering into itself all the Negro Annual Conferences, the Negro Mission Conferences and missions in the United States. All Jurisdictional Conferences were to have the same status and the same privileges of action. Among other powers was their prerogative to elect the bishops of the church. This meant that Negroes would elect bishops also—bishops who would presumably preside at some sessions of the General Conference. All the jurisdictions were to be represented on all the general boards of the church, and thus Negroes would sit on these boards on a basis of equality with their white brethren. Only on the local level and in the Jurisdictional Conference would any form of segregation be retained. Negroes would be largely in their own churches, in their own Annual Conferences, and would elect delegates to their own Jurisdictional Conference. A Negro church might conceivably be next door to a white church, but since both would be in their own Annual Conference and in their own Jurisdictional Conference, they might hardly be aware of each other's presence.

The jurisdictional system, as we have seen, had long been advocated for the new church. It had never, however, been placed in actual operation. It can benefit and at the same time endanger the future of The Methodist Church. It can benefit the church by providing powerful promotional agencies for the church's whole program. It can ensure a wise choice of bishops by making it possible for the electors to know more intimately the men who are elected to this high office. Beyond this, it can make certain that in every particular each phase of the church's life is given attention. What might be considered too small for the General Conference to deal with need not be overlooked by the jurisdictional program. Since all jurisdictions are given equal status in the church, it provides the Negro the opportunity of developing and contributing leadership. Without some such system he might be overshadowed, without much hope of rising above a certain level.

The system, however, is dangerous, since it segregates the Negro on the everyday levels of the church's life. If the jurisdictional system is sanctioned for this purpose, it endangers the fellowship of the church and defeats one great work of God's kingdom on earth, the creation of real brotherhood among men.

The Central and Mission Conferences constituted the structure of Methodism overseas and in the mission fields. They were given powers similar to those of the Jurisdictional Conferences. The new church followed without much change the provisions in the Northern Church, which were more nearly complete than those of the Southern Church.

All three churches had held in common that the Annual Conference was basic to the operation of the church. This is still true in The Methodist Church.

The Annual Conference was to be composed fundamentally of all the preachers in full connection with it and a lay member elected by each pastoral charge. As the basic body of the church it votes on all constitutional amendments. It elects representatives to the Jurisdictional and General Conferences of the church. It votes on the ordination of ministers and all matters relating to their character and conference relations, except that laymen may not vote on these particular items. It enrolls the churches and provides the only membership the minister has in The Methodist Church. All this, of course, is fundamental to the operation of the church.

A District Conference presided over by a district superintendent was optional at the will of the Annual Conference. Its membership and duties were outlined by the General Conference. It inquired into the general welfare of the churches of its district under the head of eleven specified items. Its most important function was the licensing of proper persons to preach.

The ruling body in the local church in each of the uniting churches had been the Quarterly Conference. It was presided over in the episcopal churches by the district superintendent and in the Methodist Protestant Church by the pastor, the president of the Annual Conference, or a specially chosen chairman. In The Methodist Church the Quarterly Conference is still the ruling body in the local church and is presided over by the district superintendent or an elder appointed by him.

By action of the Uniting Conference, the Quarterly Conference was to elect or arrange for the election of many of the important officers and personnel of the local church and also the church's lay member of the Annual Conference. It was to recommend to the District Conference persons for a license to preach or to elect such persons itself in the absence of the District Conference. It was to supervise and promote the financial interests of the charge, particularly the support of the ministry and missions. These and other duties made it vital to the life of the church.

The local-church administrative body in the Methodist Episcopal Church had sometimes been the Official Board, which met monthly; the board, however, could exist only at "the pleasure" of the Quarterly Conference which organized it. The administrative body in the Methodist Protestant Church had been the trustees and the stewards; while the Southern Church had the Church Conference, which met as often as necessary. All too often, however, in the actual work of the local church the administrative body had been the board of trustees, a small, tightly knit group which too often gave few, if any, public reports of its work.

In The Methodist Church it was mandatory that each church have an Official Board as its administrative body, although a Church Conference could also be established if the church so desired. The Official Board was to meet once a month and to have the broadest possible membership, representing all phases of church life and all its organizations. It was a long step in the direction of greater democracy in the local situation.

THE COUNCIL OF BISHOPS

The Council of Bishops as a constitutional body, holding an authority in itself outside the General Conference, was new to all three churches. The Methodist Protestant Church had no bishops. The Southern Church elected bishops in its General Conference and composed them into a College of Bishops whose duties were defined in the *Discipline:* "to hold semiannual meetings to survey and consider all the work of the church at large." The Northern Church likewise elected its bishops in the General Conference but made no provision for the Board of Bishops, which grew up out of custom. Neither the College of Bishops nor the Board of Bishops was a constitutional body.

In The Methodist Church the General Conference is authorized to define the powers, duties, and privileges of the bishops, but the bishops are directly responsible to the Jurisdictional Conferences which elect them. The bishops, moreover, hold their only official membership in The Methodist Church in the Council of Bishops. They are ineligible for membership anywhere else in the various conferences of The Methodist Church, although an Annual Conference may carry their names as honorary members. The General Conference has no authority over their membership other than that which applies to all ministers of the church. The Council of Bishops was to meet at least once a year and plan for the general oversight of the temporal and spiritual interests of the entire church.

It is difficult to see how the council has gained much besides status in becoming a constitutional body. The council was not assigned any important functions not already being fulfilled in the former College of Bishops and the former Board of Bishops. In fact, some functions were taken away. Until 1934 the College of Bishops in the Southern Church had served as a kind of judicial council for the church. This power was removed when that church created a Judicial Council separate from the College of Bishops. In the Northern Church, while the General Conference continued to act as its own judicial council, custom more and more gave this role to the Board of Bishops, which made rulings and decisions. Beyond this the bishops in both churches were accustomed to assigning the bishops to preside over the various Annual Conferences. This is now done only partly by the Council of Bishops, in an emergency. For the most part it is fulfilled by the bishops of each jurisdiction gathered in an informal body called the College of Bishops of that particular jurisdiction.

But status has been granted the Council of Bishops, and status can prove an important factor in enlarging the influence and power of an organization. Only time will tell whether the Council of Bishops will become a danger or an asset to the church. As a planning body the council can assume more and more authority until the agencies of the church become a mere echo of the council, and the conscience of the church grows callous as the church follows the dictates of her bishops rather than the voice of God.

There is nothing, furthermore, except its own custom, to prevent the Council of Bishops from electing a permanent, lifelong president and thus creating a form of archbishopric, and, by so doing, gradually establishing a powerful hierarchy in the church.

That these things have not come to pass as yet is evidence of the understanding the bishops have had of their role in the new church. That they can be brought to pass is obvious. That the Council of Bishops can provide valuable oversight and inspiration and by its plans challenge the interests of the church to the highest and the best, is what gives the Council of Bishops its opportunity for the soundest, broadest possible service to the church.

THE JUDICIAL COUNCIL

The members of the Judicial Council for the new church were elected by ballot at the Uniting Conference. They were: ministers of the Northern Church—Francis R. Baylor of the Baltimore Conference and Walter C. Buckner of the Southern California Conference; laymen of the Northern Church—Henry R. Van Deusen of the Wyoming Conference and

Vincent P. Clarke of the New England Conference; ministers of the Southern Church—J. Stewart French of the Holston Conference and W. G. Henry of the North Georgia Conference; laymen of the Southern Church—Martin E. Lawson of the Southwest Missouri Conference and M. A. Childers of the West Texas Conference. George R. Brown, a minister of the Methodist Protestant Church, was likewise elected to the council.

The concept of a judicial council was the contribution of the Southern Church. It was part of its *Discipline,* having been adopted in 1934, and, in principle, part of its organization since the bisection of the church in 1844. Never again would the Southern Methodists sit as a part of a General Conference which was the sole judge of the constitutionality of its own acts.

Both the Northern Church and the Methodist Protestant Church had come to accept the Judicial Council not so much by the persuasive arguments of the Southern commissioners, when the details for union were being hammered out, as by a real appreciation of the church's need for such a body. The Methodist Protestant Church had attempted to meet this need by a makeshift arrangement whereby when a majority of all Annual Conferences called for a judicial decision on any rule or act of the General Conference, each Annual Conference was to appoint at its next session two judicial delegates, one minister and one layman, who together would make up a kind of court. It was not a standing court, and it could be composed of members of the General Conference whose acts it was to judge.

The Methodist Episcopal Church did not have even this arrangement, although, as we have indicated, its Board of Bishops handed down rulings from time to time.

The Judicial Council, it was conceded by all, was a necessary feature of the new church.

THE BOARDS AND COMMISSIONS

As has been shown, a great deal of preliminary work had been done on the Prospectus for the new *Discipline* by a special committee of two hundred. The committee had succeeded in working out a great many practical compromises which smoothed the work of the Uniting Conference.

In the case of the Boards of Missions and Education, for example, excellent compromises had been worked out. For the Board of Missions and Church Extension, the question centered in whether there should be one mission board, as in the former Southern Church, or two or possibly three boards, as in the former Northern Church, with its foreign and home boards and its women's work totally unrelated to the other two boards.

It was agreed that there should be one board with power of "general oversight over the missionary and church extension program of The Methodist Church, with special reference to its development and expansion." This board was to determine policy and program, fields to be occupied, and the nature of the work to be undertaken. Under this single board, however, were to be three co-ordinate administrative divisions: Division of Foreign Missions, Division of Home Missions and Church Extension, and the Woman's Division of Christian Service, each to be largely autonomous. The Woman's Division of Christian Service, furthermore, was given authority "to regulate its own proceedings; to select fields of labor; to accept, train, commission and maintain workers; to sue and be sued; to buy and sell property; to secure and administer funds for the support of all work under its charge." [112]

The Board of Education of The Methodist Church also followed this general pattern. There was to be one board but three divisions. The Division of Educational Institutions was to deal with colleges, theological schools, Wesley Foundations, loans to students, and other related matters. The Division of the Local Church was to handle Christian education in the local church, while the Editorial Division was to provide curriculum materials.

Several other boards were also established by the conference. Among these was the Board of Hospitals and Homes of The Methodist Church. This board was charged with the "promotion and general advisory supervision of all hospitals or other organizations and institutions not affiliated with any other Board of the Church, for the care of the sick, homes for the aged and children, to preserve and promote the Christian character of these institutions and conserve their spiritual value as institutions of the Church." [113] This had been a separate board only in the Northern Church. It operated as a part of the Board of Missions in the Southern Church, and had no existence in the Methodist Protestant Church.

A Board of Pensions of The Methodist Church was also created, and here especially the greatest care was exercised to meet all the legal requirements involved in the merger. The Board of Pensions was to have the "administration of the support of Conference Claimants of The Methodist Church." Legally the new board would be the successor to three boards of the uniting churches: the Board of Pensions and Relief of the Methodist Episcopal Church, which was incorporated under the laws

[112] *Ibid.*, pp. 555-91.
[113] *Ibid.*, p. 550.

of the state of Illinois in that name; the Board of Finance of the Methodist Episcopal Church, South, which was incorporated under the laws of the state of Missouri in that name; and the Board of Managers of the General Fund for Superannuates of the Methodist Protestant Church, which was incorporated under the laws of the state of Maryland in that name. The choice for the location of the new board was placed in the hands of a special committee.

Another board created by the Uniting Conference was the Board of Lay Activities. This was new to the Northern and the Methodist Protestant Churches; its organization, purpose, and various officers were taken over from the Southern Church.

The Methodist Protestant Church had had a laymen's fellowship which was somewhat akin to the Board of Lay Activities. The Methodist Episcopal Church had had a section in its *Discipline* providing for a General Conference Laymen's Association and an Annual Conference "Brotherhood, Laymen's Association, Junior Laymen, or similar organization for the purpose of cultivating a more effective participation of men in the total activities of the Church." Neither of the churches, however, had had the highly developed arrangement for lay participation that characterized the Southern Church.

The purpose of the Board of Lay Activities in the new church was "to deepen the spiritual life of the laymen of the Church and to secure among laymen an increasing loyalty and interest with the ultimate end in view of an active working force in each local Church." Included in the plan for this board were the offices of conference lay leader, district lay leader, charge lay leader, and church lay leader.

A Board of Temperance was created "to make more effectual the efforts of The Methodist Church in creating a Christian public sentiment, and in crystallizing opposition to all public violations of the moral law." Its headquarters was to be in Washington, D. C. This board was from the organization of the Northern Church, since no such board existed in the other two churches. Both the Southern Church and the Methodist Protestant Church were strongly opposed to the liquor traffic, but neither had created a board of temperance.

A Board of Publication was established to direct and control the Methodist Publishing House. Until this organization could be put into effect, an interim Board of Publication was to consist of the members of the Book Committees of the Methodist Episcopal Church and the Methodist Episcopal Church, South, and the Board of Publication of the Methodist Protestant Church. The publishing agents and the editors of the three churches were to continue to perform their customary duties until the new board could be organized, new publishing agents elected, and decisions made as to future publications in the united church.

At least four commissions were part of the new arrangements. One of the most important of these was the General Commission on World Service and Finance, which had the following duties: "to secure full information regarding the general interests of the Church, in order that none may be neglected, jeopardized, or excluded, [and to] recommend to the General Conference . . . the total amount to be apportioned for all connectional interests." Provision was also made for emergency needs.[114] This agency was similar in structure to the World Service Commission of the Northern Church and the General Commission on Budget of the Southern Church. The boards and agencies in the Methodist Protestant Church had made their appeal directly to the General Conference.

The Commission on Evangelism in The Methodist Church was given a strong position. There was no such board or commission in the Methodist Protestant Church. It existed in the Northern Church, but its duties were not outlined in the *Discipline*. In the Southern Church it had been under the direction of the Board of Missions. Now it was to be a separate commission with headquarters of its own. The reason for its creation was stated as follows: "In order that this all-important subject may be lifted up and held in the place of central prominence throughout the Methodist communion, the Conference authorizes the creation of a Commission on Evangelism which shall devote itself to the promotion of evangelism in all its types and phases." The commission was charged with the responsibility of promoting evangelism among both ministers and laity.

A third commission, the General Conference Commission on World Peace, was taken from the Northern Church. A concern for world peace in the Southern Church had been emphasized through the Board of Lay Activities. In the Methodist Protestant Church there was no board or commission charged with this responsibility. Now the Uniting Conference created a Commission on World Peace with functions and activities described under paragraph 1464 of the *Discipline* of the Northern Church. The financial support was to be provided by the Commission on World Service and Finance.

All three of the uniting churches had had provisions for courses of study for ministers. This provision was continued as the Commission on Courses of Study within the Division of Educational Institutions of the Board of Education. Other, less important commissions were also established.

---

[114] *Ibid.*, pp. 526-29.

A Board of Trustees was to be incorporated under the name "The Board of Trustees of The Methodist Church." It was to be the successor to two existing boards: the Board of Trustees of the Methodist Episcopal Church, whose headquarters were at Cincinnati, and the Board of Trustees of the Methodist Episcopal Church, South, whose headquarters were in Nashville.

Until the personnel of the new boards and commissions could be elected and their organizations completed by the General and Jurisdictional Conferences of The Methodist Church, the work of existing boards and commissions was to be carried on much as it had been by the three churches. Special enabling acts were passed to this effect. It was agreed, in order to hasten this process of organization, that the first General Conference of The Methodist Church should be held in 1940. It subsequently convened in Atlantic City on April 24, 1940.

THE MINISTRY

The length of office of a district superintendent was quickly settled. In the Southern Church a district superintendent (called a presiding elder) had been able to serve only four out of any eight consecutive years; in the Northern Church six or, under special conditions, eight out of twelve. In The Methodist Church he could now serve six out of any nine consecutive years.

The Northern Church had had a kinder and more carefully regulated method for retiring its bishops than the Southern Church. This was conceded by the Southern Church long before union, and it was part of the discussions about the episcopacy in the Joint Commission on Federation after 1910. Until 1938 the Southern Church continued its system of retiring a bishop whenever the General Conference felt this to be necessary. This action was usually taken on the written recommendation of twenty traveling elders and after the bishop had had a chance to defend himself before the Committee on Episcopacy. The Northern Church, on the other hand, had an age limit beyond which a bishop could not serve. In The Methodist Church a bishop was retired whose seventieth birthday preceded the first day of the regular session of his Jurisdictional Conference, although the law also stated that "a Bishop, at any age and for any reason deemed sufficient by his Jurisdictional Conference, may be released by that body from the obligation to travel through the Connection at large, and from residential supervision." [115]

In keeping with the customs of all three churches no age was set for the

---

[115] *Discipline of The Methodist Church,* 1939, ¶ 404.

automatic retirement of a minister. The age for retirement, as we shall see, was set by the first General Conference in 1940.

With regard to the length of tenure in a pastorate, the Southern Church had ruled that a preacher could not be appointed to a church more than four consecutive years except by a majority vote of the presiding elders in the bishop's cabinet. No such restriction was now placed upon the appointment of a pastor in The Methodist Church. Thus, the broader attitude of the Northern Church and the Methodist Protestant Church with regard to the length of a pastorate prevailed.

The two episcopal churches brought into the new church their rule forbidding ministers to use tobacco. The Methodist Protestant Church had no such rule.

All three churches had fairly strict rules forbidding a minister to perform the marriage of divorced persons. The new church, however, followed the broader rule of the Northern Church. The Southern Church permitted the solemnization of the marriage of divorced persons only in the case of the innocent party whose divorce had been obtained "for the one scriptural cause." The Methodist Protestant Church stated that ministers should not celebrate the marriage of divorced persons who had violated their marriage vows. The new rule permitted remarriage for innocent parties when it was clearly established that the true cause for divorce was adultery or "other vicious conditions."

The Uniting Conference supported the position that "a member of the Church, who after private reproof . . . by the Pastor or Class Leader, persists in using, buying, or selling intoxicating liquors as a beverage, . . . shall be brought to trial." [116] This had been a part of the *Disciplines* of the Northern and Southern Churches. It had not appeared in the *Discipline* of the Methodist Protestant Church.

The Uniting Conference wrote into the *Discipline of The Methodist Church* the usual reasons for bringing a church member to trial. However, noticeably omitted were specific paragraphs found in the *Discipline* of the Northern Church on "Neglect of the Means of Grace," "Disagreement in Business—Arbitration," "Fraud and Dishonesty," and similar paragraphs found in the rules of the other two churches. Probably it was felt that the reasons for bringing a member to trial as set down in the new *Discipline* were broad enough to cover these ideas; but it is startling to observe that the only specific reason for bringing a person to trial is in the matter of intoxicating liquors.

The Uniting Conference failed by a close vote to grant full clergy rights

[116] *Journal of the Uniting Conference*, p. 474.

to women. It decided that women can be trained for the ministry and can be ordained but cannot become members of a conference.

THE SOCIAL CREED

Beyond these actions, impassioned speeches centered in the discussions of the Social Creed of The Methodist Church and more particularly whether The Methodist Church should give support to its conscientious objectors to war.

The Methodist Episcopal Church had adopted its first formal statement of a social creed at its General Conference in 1908, held in Baltimore. In December of that year the Federal Council of Churches, which had just been organized, adopted as its social ideals the essentials of the creed framed by the Methodist Episcopal Church. The Methodist Episcopal Church, South, adopted a social creed much like the two already in existence at its General Conference in 1914. The Methodist Protestant Church in 1916 literally adopted the creed of the Methodist Episcopal Church when its General Conference went on record as stating:

Because the Methodist Protestant Church is vitally and sympathetically interested in every social and philanthropic movement that makes for human welfare, and we have a league, offensive and defensive, with all who labor for the establishment of the Kingdom of God on earth, we heartily and in the spirit of fraternity concur in the comprehensive and unequivocal declaration promulgated by the General Conference of the Methodist Episcopal Church and adopted by the Federal Council of Churches.[117]

The emphases in the creeds of the three churches were changed from time to time, as well as their form. At the time of the Uniting Conference the social creed of the Southern Church was taken from that of the Federal Council of Churches—a succinct statement of sixteen brief paragraphs and a brief statement on "The Church and War." The Northern Church had no kindred brief statement embodying its social outlook. Its attitudes were set forth in a lengthy eleven-page dissertation on "Social and Economic Questions" and "War and Peace" in paragraphs 1463-64 of the 1936 *Discipline*. No social creed as such is to be found in the 1936 *Constitution and Discipline of the Methodist Protestant Church*.

At the Uniting Conference a social creed was presented by the Committee on Membership and Temporal Economy. It contained a Preamble, three sections on "The Religious Position," and twenty sections on the creed itself.

Section 7, dealing with the subject of social planning, caused some de-

[117] *Journal of the General Conference of the Methodist Protestant Church*, 1916, p. 138.

bate. J. B. Campbell of Northwest Indiana moved for its deletion. Said Mr. Campbell: "We have been experimenting along the lines of social planning for several years. Many of us do not think it has proved to be a successful experiment. I move its deletion." Obviously, the current political situation was influencing the thinking of the delegates. The chairman of the committee spoke only halfheartedly in favor of retaining the section. By a close vote it was deleted.[118]

On the matter of conscientious objectors, a layman, Governor Alfred M. Landon of Kansas, moved that section 16 of the Social Creed, which gave support to conscientious objectors, be referred to the Committee on Membership and Temporal Economy for "harmonization with the resolution already referred to that Committee calling for national action against the sale of munitions to Japan." The governor held that if both these resolutions were accepted, The Methodist Church would be "in the position of interfering in the delicate foreign relationships of this country and refusing to accept the responsibility for our interference." [119]

The governor's motion to refer caused the most heated debate of the entire conference. Said one delegate: "I think it should be deleted tonight. There is no use in referring it; we are judges enough. . . . I am going to be one that votes against it tonight." [120]

On the other hand, favoring support of conscientious objectors was Richard T. Baker of Upper Iowa: "Primitive Christians were conscientious objectors. The history books are available for any one who can read. . . . Each of them tells stories again and again of martyrs who were converted to Christianity, threw down their arms, served notice on the Roman authorities that they would not and could not fight and were summarily put to death. In their stand they not only had the sanction of the church; they had its sternest exhortation." [121]

After further speeches pro and con, the motion to refer was defeated, and the section remained as part of the Social Creed.

The entire creed, with the exception of section 7, previously mentioned, was adopted after a stirring speech by Lynn Harold Hough of Drew Theological Seminary.[122]

The historic position of the church in its "devotion to the Federal Government" was reaffirmed by the Uniting Conference on a motion by Harold Paul Sloan, editor of the *Christian Advocate,* and signed by fifteen men of the conference.

[118] *The Daily Christian Advocate,* May 11, 1939, p. 430.
[119] *Ibid.,* pp. 430-31.
[120] *Ibid.,* p. 432.
[121] *Ibid.,* pp. 432-33.
[122] *Ibid.,* p. 433.

THE RITUAL

On a motion by Robert G. McCutchan, former dean of the School of Music of DePauw University, *The Methodist Hymnal,* already adopted officially by the three churches, became the official hymnal for The Methodist Church. This official hymnal had come into being in 1935 as the result of the work of a joint commission of the three churches. The General Conference of the Methodist Episcopal Church of 1928 had appointed a Commission on the Revision of the Hymnal and Psalter. The General Conference of the Methodist Episcopal Church, South, of 1930 had appointed a similar commission, and the Methodist Protestant Church had accepted an invitation to participate in the preparation of the hymnal. Robert G. McCutchan served as editor. The new hymnal had subsequently been adopted by each of the churches.

A significant change was made when the hymn "Holy! Holy! Holy!" was placed first in the hymnal. It succeeded the Wesley hymn "O For a Thousand Tongues to Sing" of the hymnal of 1905, in which both the Northern and Southern Churches had united. The change suggested that a greater emphasis would be placed upon corporate worship than had formerly been the case in the three churches, and was the result of a growing trend toward a richer liturgical service.

The Ritual of the new church as passed by the Uniting Conference can best be studied by a comparison of the three *Disciplines* at the time of union.

The Order for the Administration of the Sacrament of the Lord's Supper in the new *Discipline* followed fairly closely the form of the Northern Church. It was a lengthier service than found in either the Southern Church or the Methodist Protestant Church. The latter included the Ten Commandments, which the Southern Church did not use, but on the whole possessed a fairly simple ritual.

The Order for the Administration of the Sacrament of Baptism also followed the ritual of the Northern Church. Added, however, was the Order for the Baptism of Youth. This was taken from the Southern Church, which had three separate orders—for infants, for youth, and for adults. The Northern Church and the Methodist Protestant Church included only children and adults.

The Order for Receiving Persons into the Church was a condensed form of the ritual of the Northern Church. An Order for the Reception of Probationers, which had been part of the Methodist Protestant Church, was dropped, but a special Order for Receiving Children and Youth into the Church was added. This latter was for a membership class of youth or children and stated specifically that the pastor shall have "instructed

them in the things necessary for them to know as to the Doctrines and
Rules of the church." It was taken largely from the *Discipline* of the
Southern Church.

The ritual for matrimony had been pretty much the same in all three
churches, although the Northern Church had had a slightly longer service, making provision for a relative who might give the bride away and
for several additional lines in the ring ceremony. The new *Discipline* followed this longer ritual.

The ritual for the Burial of the Dead was similar in all three churches
and required little change. The Order for the Burial of a Child, however,
was taken over from the Northern Church.

Other forms in the new Ritual included Consecration and Ordination: Consecration of a Deaconess, Ordination of Deacons, Ordination
of Elders, and Consecration of Bishops. Beyond this there were services
for a cornerstone laying and for the dedication of a church, an organ, a
parish house, a hospital, an educational building, and a home.

These all had been in the *Discipline* of the Northern Church. The
Southern Church had included the cornerstone laying, the dedication
of a church, the ordination of deacons and elders, and the consecration of
a bishop. The Methodist Protestant Church had had only forms for the
ordination of elders and the setting apart of deaconesses, the laying of
a cornerstone, and the dedication of a church.

The trend in The Methodist Church was obviously toward more form
and a richer liturgical service.

SPECIAL COMMITTEES AND ACTIONS

The Uniting Conference requested that a special committee be appointed by the Council of Bishops "of two representatives from each
Jurisdiction to consider the matter of the location of Boards and Commissions authorized by the Uniting Conference and make report to the
General Conference of 1940." [123]

A Co-ordinating Committee of Nine was also called for. The committee
was instructed "to present to the next General Conference of The Methodist Church a definite plan for official organ or organs for The Methodist Church." All official papers of the three uniting churches were to
be published until the General Conference should order otherwise.[124]

Organizational meetings were held at the Uniting Conference for the
Jurisdictional Conferences of The Methodist Church, and provision was
made for their future meetings. There were six Jurisdictional Conferences

[123] *Journal of the Uniting Conference*, p. 365.
[124] *Ibid.*, pp. 636-37.

in all. The five geographical Jurisdictions were the Northeastern, the Southeastern, the North Central, the South Central, and the Western. The Central Jurisdiction included all Negro Annual Conferences. All the Jurisdictional Conferences were to have the same status and the same privileges of action.

Jurisdictional Conference delegates met, set the boundaries of the Annual Conferences within their own jurisdiction, and attended to other necessary organizational details.

A recommendation was forwarded to the first General Conference, 1940, to accept the invitation of the Provisional Committee of the World Council of Churches to join this body. Under the Plan of Union and on a resolution presented by Edmund D. Soper, president of Ohio Wesleyan University, membership in the Ecumenical Methodist Council, Western Section, was continued.

The Uniting Conference adjourned after an emotion-packed public service which twelve thousand persons attended. It was presided over by the three co-chairmen of the Joint Commission of Interdenominational Relations and Church Union—Bishop John M. Moore of the former Southern Church, Bishop Edwin Holt Hughes of the former Northern Church, and Bishop James H. Straughn of the former Methodist Protestant Church. So thoroughly had the task of the Uniting Conference been completed that the General Conference meeting the following year found little of importance requiring amendment or change.

Bishop Straughn describes the drama of the closing of the worship hour:

Bishop Moore: . . . "If you will adopt this Declaration of Union as a whole, you will stand and lift your right hand. The Bishops will do likewise."

The entire assemblage of Bishops and delegates arose, right hands uplifted. There was prolonged applause and the Bishops and delegates were seated.

Bishop Moore: "If you oppose the adoption of this Declaration, will you stand and lift your right hand. . . . No one stands."

The entire Conference arose and there was prolonged applause. [The voting was completed, and union became effective at 8:50 P.M., May 10, 1939.]

Bishop Moore: "The Declaration of Union has been adopted! The Methodist Church is! Long live The Methodist Church!"

. . . It was over; it was done! The Methodists are one people! The Uniting Conference was and still is the prophetic testimony of the unity and the solidarity of the Methodist Church. It was an unforgettable experience. . . . Dissent was a sacrilege. It was a bath of love.

The union of time is the union of eternity! [125]

[125] Straughn, *Inside Methodist Union*, p. 124.

One grace obviously lacking was an appropriate humility in the face of the future problems of the church. Too many people would have agreed with Bishop Straughn's implication that the new organization was in fact the Church Triumphant.

5

The First General Conference, 1940

The first General Conference of The Methodist Church was held April 24–May 7, 1940, at Atlantic City, New Jersey. Two committees created for specific tasks by the Uniting Conference reported. The first was the Committee on Location of Boards and Commissions. The report stated that, like the Uniting Conference, the committee sought to apply the principles of genuine unity in locating the boards and agencies. Full consideration had been given to all the legal requirements involved, and, to be sure that no legal requirements were overlooked, the General Conference was asked to create a committee for this specific purpose.

In Chicago were located the Board of Pensions, the Board of Lay Activities, the Commission on World Service and Finance, and the Commission on World Peace.

In Columbus, Ohio, was placed the Board of Hospitals and Homes.

In Cincinnati, Ohio, the Board of Trustees of The Methodist Church was located.

In Nashville, Tennessee, were situated the Board of Education, the Commission on Evangelism, and the Commission on the Courses of Study.

In New York was located the Board of Missions and Church Extension and all the divisions thereof.

The Board of Publications, for many reasons, could not be located in one city. It was authorized to continue the printing and manufacturing business of the church at New York, Cincinnati, Chicago, Nashville, Pittsburgh, and Baltimore, and later to combine these into a smaller number of units as the board might determine for the good of the whole church. One of the principal plants, however, was to be continued within the territory served from the Publishing House located at Nashville.

As was to be expected, considerable debate was occasioned by the report, and several amendments were offered. The report was finally referred to the Committee on Temporal Economy, and then, when it was reported back to the General Conference without change, it was again fully discussed. It was finally passed, much in its original form.

The Co-ordinating Committee created by the Uniting Conference also reported. It had been instructed to plan the official organ for The Methodist Church. A majority and a minority report were presented to the General Conference. Both reports were referred to the Committee on Publication, which accepted the majority report and recommended its adoption by the General Conference.

This report called for a weekly religious paper to be called the *Christian Advocate*. The Board of Publication was to issue such editions of the *Christian Advocate* as it deemed advisable. The editor and associate editors were to be elected quadrennially by the Board of Publication. Provisions were also made for a *Central Christian Advocate* for the Central Jurisdiction. This editor was also to be elected by the Board of Publication, but he was to be chosen from the Central Jurisdiction, and thus he was to be a Negro.

Other items of the report were of an administrative nature.

The minority report had sought to establish the definite number of the editions of the *Christian Advocate* to be published and the place of their publication. The report of the General Conference Committee on Publication was adopted, and the minority report was lost.

Other changes were written into the 1940 *Discipline*. Becoming effective in 1944, the automatic retirement of a pastor was to occur at the conference immediately following his seventy-second birthday. He was permitted, however, to request retirement as early as sixty-five years of age. Objection was raised to this change on the ground that it invaded the right of the Annual Conference to decide this matter. The objection was not sustained.

In the matter of appointments the 1940 *Discipline* added the provision that the district superintendent shall consult with the pastors when possible before the final announcement of appointments. A move to force the district superintendent to consult also with the Pastoral Relations Committees involved was voted down.

It was decided that the consecration of a bishop should be at the session of the Jurisdictional or Central Conference at which he is elected.

The Ritual of the new church was left largely unchanged except that under "Reception of Members" there was added "An Order For Receiving Persons as Preparatory Members."

The 1939 Uniting Conference and the 1940 General Conference of the new church had together set up the structure of The Methodist Church, but most of the work had been accomplished in 1939. The Methodist Church was now a reality.

Unification was not a return; it was a progress. Each church accepted new ideas and contributed new principles in the reorganized church.

Briefly, the Methodist Protestant Church accepted the episcopacy, and it surrendered the right of appeal by a minister in his appointment. In the words of Bishop Straughn, it also accepted " 'bulk' control over all its affairs." [126] Together with the Methodist Episcopal Church, it accepted the Judicial Council and the Jurisdictional Conference. It contributed, among other things, a new spirit of independence on the part of conferences, churches, and men, and gave a new incentive to the maintenance of personal rights which all too often are lost in a great governing machine.

Beyond this, it became part of a more effective itinerancy; it shared in a greater vision of world service, and it joined a broader fellowship. It gained educational contacts with the schools of every variety in every section of the country. It now began, also, to serve a greater variety of benevolent institutions.

The Methodist Episcopal Church, South, accepted Negroes in the new church, although it would have preferred seeing them transferred to the Colored Methodist Episcopal Church or a similar organization. It also accepted Negro representation in the General Conference and virtual integration of the races at the top legislative levels of the church. Together with the Methodist Episcopal Church, it accepted equal lay and ministerial representation in the Annual, Jurisdictional, and General Conferences.

All this was symbolized in some measure by the name of the new church, The Methodist Church. It was adopted only after long and trying debate, and it symbolized each church's surrendering, in reality, some measure of its own heritage. In the name, the Methodist Protestant Church gave up the word "Protestant," the Southern Church relinquished "South," and the Northern Church surrendered "Episcopal." All united in the one name which down through history has most perfectly described the sons of John Wesley, The Methodist Church.

---

[126] *Ibid.*, p. 129.

chapter 33

UNITED
METHODISM

1940-60

Adjustments in Structure

Expansion

Social Outreach

Changing Practices

The Ecumenical Movement

**Other Branches of
Methodism**

THE DEBUT OF THE METHODIST CHURCH, the culmination of efforts of leaders of the three constituent parts over many years, was a dramatic and newsworthy event. Even in the midst of their rejoicing, the churchmen who had brought their denominations into the new relationship recognized that this was only the beginning of many as yet unforeseeable developments. They could only guess how the task of achieving actual unification would be complicated by the political, social, and economic events of the period ahead.

United Methodism was not allowed a period of quiescence, a span of years in which the church could at leisure settle down to get its affairs shipshape. Continuously through the first two decades of its history crisis and change were taking place in the society within which the church sought to carry forward its work. In 1939 the nation was still in a depression, in spite of the efforts of the New Deal administration, with almost ten million men and women—one sixth of the total labor force—looking for work. That very year the war broke in Europe, and before long this nation also was embroiled. "Normalcy" never did return.

In the wake of the war came problems of demobilization, vast shiftings of civilian population, rising delinquency rates, inflation, and labor unrest. Soon tension with the Communist states began to overshadow other problems, and by 1950 the Korean conflict, which eventually involved almost six million American military personnel, shattered the hope for a period of peace. While the Korean War and the later agony of France in Vietnam were tem-

479

porarily ended by uneasy truces, international discord arose over Berlin, Indonesia, Algeria, the Near East, the Congo, and Cuba.

Nor was there a feeling of security and contentment at home. Many forces kept American society in a psychological and often a spiritual turmoil: fear of the Communists, with associated inquisitorial tactics such as those of Senator Joseph McCarthy and the House Un-American Activities Committee; a determination on the part of Negroes to bring an end to all types of segregation; the widespread demand for better housing; extensive metropolitan planning with large-scale slum clearance and urban renewal projects; labor unrest, as evidenced by the lengthy steel strike of 1959; and mounting unemployment at the end of the decade. At the same time living standards were rising, and the government was touching the life of every citizen at more points. There was a "democratization of welfare" and a "diffusion of affluence."

Inevitably The Methodist Church was affected by these stresses, just as were other churches. All were faced with the necessity of reconciling their loyalty to the nation with their loyalty to the gospel, of ministering to those whose morale or relationships were strained by the war, and at the same time of keeping the organizational processes moving efficiently so that the churches would grow and serve an ever larger population. For the Methodists there was the additional task of attempting to weld into one encompassing framework men and women from all parts of the nation with different, even though related, cultural and religious traditions, with varying ideas as to church structure, benevolence program, and the work of laymen. Each sectional group had an understandable and nostalgic attachment to its accustomed patterns. Boldness, vitality, courage, and a willingness to run a few risks were indeed essential for the launching of this great experiment.

1

Problems of Adjustment

The leaders in the movement for unification and those who had responsibility for the united church had one central purpose—to make that union effective. The final consummation of the union was celebrated with a strong evangelistic fervor—almost a "bath of love," as Bishop James H. Straughn, a leader of the former Methodist Protestant Church, expressed it.

These men were fully aware of the differences in practice which had grown up in the hundred years of separation and, being sensible men, knew that there would be reluctance on the part of rank-and-file members to accept changes in church organization and terminology. The devoted secretary of a Northern bishop, who was fully in favor of union, remarked that she hated to lose the good old word "Episcopal" from the name. It was bound to take time for the thousands of local congregations to become accustomed to the Woman's Society of Christian Service instead of the Ladies Aid and the Missionary Societies. And the ritual of the Holy Communion did not sound quite right when the words "Holy Spirit" were used instead of "Holy Ghost," or the Apostles' Creed when "again" was dropped from the phrase "rose again from the dead."

Especially in communities where congregations of both the Northern and Southern Churches had existed and were called on to unite did the members have to exercise Christian forbearance. In a Missouri town where both had small churches, one pastor was appointed to both in 1940 with the purpose of bringing them together. All tacitly acknowledged the folly of maintaining two separate organizations, and since the Southern Church had the larger membership and the better building, it was agreed at the end of the first year that that should be the home for the united congregation. However, as something of a compensatory gesture, the Northern congregation was permitted to bring its organ and install it in the Southern building, even though members of the latter considered it an inferior instrument.

Yet in spite of the defensiveness and at times resentment of many persons, ministers and lay people, there was a general resolve to achieve a full unity of the church, not simply through adoption of a uniform structure and ritual but through understanding and sharing. While there have been occasional expressions of regret that the three branches did unite, this is an attitude which has never been publicly voiced by the leaders of Methodism.

The Jurisdictional System

A major change for all three branches of Methodism was the introduction of the jurisdictional system, and it was in connection with this that some of the major adjustment problems of the new organization arose.

As things developed, the jurisdictional structure undoubtedly served as a safeguard for regional interests, especially in the South. On the other hand, it tended to give support to sectional or regional divisions within the denomination. An illustration of this was the assumption of many

that the theological seminaries had a unique relationship to the jurisdiction in which they happened to be located rather than to the whole
church—in spite of the fact that they received considerable help through
the benevolence giving of the denomination and that they preferred to
feel that they were servants of the whole church.

A concomitant of the jurisdictional system was that since bishops were
elected and assigned to their episcopal areas by the Jurisdictional Conferences, they became, in spite of the efforts of the Council of Bishops,
identified more and more with their respective jurisdictions. With only
one exception—the election of Gerald Kennedy to the episcopacy by the
Western Jurisdiction in 1948, while he was a pastor in the South Central
Jurisdiction—each jurisdiction elected to episcopacy men from within
its own membership. This ran counter to the American Methodist tradition that episcopal leaders were bishops of the whole church. In both
branches of the church prior to unification a bishop, elected by a General
Conference, might be assigned to any area throughout the communion.
After unification no bishop was assigned to an area outside the jurisdiction
which elected him.

Beginning in 1940 all sections of the church fulfilled at least the
minimum requirements of the jurisdictional system as set forth in the
constitution. Each Jurisdictional Conference met quadrennially following the General Conference, to elect and consecrate its new bishops and
make assignments to episcopal areas. It also elected jurisdictional representatives to serve on the various boards and agencies of the church, a
secretary, and a treasurer. After the quadrennial meeting, with its various
elections and reports, most jurisdictions had little business to conduct for
the next four years.

The Southeastern Jurisdiction, and to somewhat less degree the South
Central, as their members said, really made the jurisdictional system
work. The former, for example, established its headquarters at Atlanta,
Georgia. In addition to the quadrennial meeting it conducted a program
touching most aspects of the church's life. This work went forward under
the direction of a Jurisdictional Council which in 1956-60 had a membership of 103 and met at least yearly. Its staff consisted of two executive
secretaries—one in charge of the Committees on Education, Evangelism,
and Christian Social Emphasis, and also serving as director of the Lake
Junaluska Assembly; the other assigned to serve with the Committees on
Missions, Town and Country Work, Lay Activities, and Radio and
Television, and the Schools for Supply Pastors and Town and Country
Ministers. These committees, the jurisdictional counterpart of the General Conference boards, established goals and programs and promoted them
in the Annual Conferences, districts, and local churches. The jurisdiction,

which was a legal entity, owned outright the Lake Junaluska Assembly Grounds and Emory University, although the latter had its own separate financing. For its varied activities the Jurisdictional Council had an annual budget during the 1956-60 quadrennium of $158,000. It set up a jurisdiction-wide convocation each quadrennium to educate its constituency and advance the work of the church.

The other jurisdictions from the beginning showed less enthusiasm. They met once in four years as required, but not without some grumbling. The task of electing and consecrating bishops seemed to many to be the chief, if not the sole, reason for their coming together. These jurisdictions had no full-time executive secretaries, although a modest honorarium was paid to one or two officers for services rendered in connection with the quadrennial meeting. Some jurisdictional boards existed on paper; in 1960 the one active board in the Northeastern Jurisdiction was their Board of Lay Activities.

While there were few enthusiasts for the jurisdictional system in the North or West, some felt that a middle road between the neglect of the system in the North and the extensive use of it in the South would be beneficial to the church as a whole. In contrast to the strong support for the jurisdictional system in the South was the equally vigorous opposition voiced by a number of prominent leaders in the North. Bishop G. Bromley Oxnam, in an address to the Northeastern Jurisdictional Conference, June 13, 1956, asserted that the jurisdictional system was essentially provincial and restrictive in its effect, not only in the lower ranks of the church but also in the episcopacy:

For instance, there is danger present in the periodic meetings of the Colleges of Bishops of the Jurisdictions. Without intending to do so, these meetings of the Colleges of Bishops have the tendency to become caucuses in which the mind of a region is made up before the Council of Bishops meets, which means that decision is reached before the case of the whole church is heard. These meetings are close to the pressures of the local scene. There is the danger of responding too quickly to sectional prejudice. . . . Men who think in diocesan terms seldom think in world terms.[1]

A similar view was expressed by Bishop James C. Baker, writing in the summer of 1960:

[The jurisdictional system] carries danger of splitting the church apart and, therefore, there should be radical readjustments of it. In the North there have been few developments of organizations within the jurisdictions, and we have

[1] *Journal of the Fifth Northeastern Jurisdictional Conference of The Methodist Church,* 1956, pp. 258, 263.

before us the illustration of over-organization in the Southeastern Jurisdiction. If their plan should be followed generally, I think it would be a very grave disservice to Methodism.[2]

Southern churchmen were troubled at the criticism of the jurisdictional system by others in the church. They felt that their northern and western brethren made little effort to discover the real values inherent in it, and feared that there might eventually be an effort to eliminate this part of the church structure. These differences were definitely brought into the open in the quadrennium 1956-60, during which the dissatisfaction of many segments of the church over the existence of the Central Jurisdiction, based as it was on race, became more vocal. The General Conference of 1956 established a Commission to Study and Recommend Action Concerning the Jurisdictional System. This commission of seventy, made up of outstanding ministerial and lay leaders from all parts of the church, conducted a series of hearings in every jurisdiction to get the opinions of local Methodists as to the desirability of this feature of the church's structure. All who cared to testify were given opportunity to do so. Many of the witnesses directed their comments to the racial aspect of the Central Jurisdiction rather than to the jurisdictional system itself. After sharp disagreement and vigorous debate within the commission, a report was prepared which all signed (although with reservations at various points) and which was adopted practically unchanged, but after much argument, by the General Conference of 1960.

In essence the report reaffirmed the validity of the jurisdictional system—which, after all, was part of the constitution and could not be easily altered—and restated the right of each jurisdiction "under the present Discipline [to adopt its] own policies as to promotion and administration by jurisdictional organization as each Jurisdiction may determine." [3] In an effort to strengthen the feeling of connectionalism in the whole church, it proposed a constitutional amendment which would change the time of the quadrennial jurisdictional meetings from after the General Conference to the same time and place as the General Conference. However, because of southern pressure it carried an elastic provision that if the jurisdiction so desired, it could meet at some other place but within sixty days prior to the General Conference. The amendment also provided a method by which bishops could be transferred from one jurisdiction to another, and stipulated that newly elected bishops be consecrated at the General Conference. The intent was to demonstrate

---

[2] In a personal letter to the author.
[3] The Commission to Study and Recommend Action Concerning the Jurisdictional System, "Report to the 1960 General Conference of The Methodist Church," p. 13.

that bishops were officers of the entire church and not simply of a jurisdiction. The proposed amendment also raised the maximum General Conference membership from 900 to 1,400, including all members of the Jurisdictional Conferences as members of the General Conference.

This legislation was designed to conserve the jurisdictional system, but at the same time to discourage the development of five or six separate regional churches within the United States. It was viewed as a compromise between those who desired a considerable measure of regional self-regulation and the proponents of a strong and united church. However, it was defeated by a narrow margin when it was submitted to the Annual Conferences.

The Central Jurisdiction

One of the regional groups which was set up in the unification of the three American Methodist Churches was the Central Jurisdiction. This jurisdiction was unique in that it was organized on a racial rather than a geographical basis, in contrast to the other five jurisdictions of the united church. It was composed of the "Negro Annual Conferences, the Negro Mission Conferences and Missions in the United States of America."

The Central Jurisdiction is a symbol of the past and present history of the Negro in Methodism during the nearly two centuries of its existence in America; but more, it is a practical demonstration of the efforts of a great ecclesiastical organization, under most difficult social and political conditions, to include in its membership the most diverse racial groups. That the techniques followed and the results achieved have not always been ideal; and further that the Central Jurisdiction itself, as measured against the ideal of genuine Christian brotherhood, leaves much to be desired, are good examples of John Wesley's idea of the need of going on to perfection.

To appraise properly the Central Jurisdiction, therefore, one cannot begin with the setting up of that structural arrangement in the reorganized church in 1939, but must start at the very beginning of the Methodist movement in America and trace the Negro's connection with it to the present time. Such a study is intriguing and proves conclusively that whatever the institutional relationship may have been—or may happen to be at any particular moment—in the history of both the Methodist movement and the Negro, the two belong together.

The Methodists, because of their own relatively low social status, could not draw the same type of caste and class distinctions as did the older and more exclusive churches of New England and the Middle Atlantic Coast. Nevertheless, they began early to make distinctions where Negroes, whether free or slave, were concerned. Three months after Joseph Pilmoor arrived in America he wrote, "After preaching, I met the Negroes apart, and found many of them very happy." [4] This tendency is also in evidence early in Asbury's experience in America. In his *Journal,* December 8, 1772, Asbury writes, "In the evening the Negroes were collected, and I spoke to them in exhortation."

While the membership of John Street Church was interracial from the first, in the lists of membership published in 1787 whites and Negroes were listed separately. These lists give the names of 228 whites and 36 Negroes. St. George's Church in Philadelphia had also begun to list the two racial groups separately; in 1788 there were 270 white and 17 Negro members.

In addition to the separate seating arrangements provided for the Negro members of the congregation, discrimination was shown in other ways. Pilmoor's Journal entry for August 9, 1772, tells of a service where the church was not large enough to accommodate all who desired to attend: "As the ground was wet, they persuaded me to try to preach within and appointed men to stand at the doors to keep all the Negroes out till the white persons were got in, but the house would not near hold them."

In the light of these conditions it is not surprising that there should have developed a feeling of unrest, especially among free Negroes in the northern section of the country, and a desire to have more freedom of expression. This was primarily responsible for the rise of the independent Negro Methodist denominations.

THE NEGRO IN METHODISM, 1844-1939

One of the by-products of the division in 1844 was the development of a renewed and, in reality, more passionate interest on the part of the Southern Church in the evangelization of the slaves. William Capers, later a bishop, was one of the most zealous workers in this cause. "He developed a type of organization for serving the slaves which swept over the entire South." In 1847, the Southern Church reported 124,961 Negro members; in 1848, 127,241; in 1853, 146,949; in 1860, 171,857.[5]

The division did not have the same effect in the North, at least not immediately. Despite their espousal of the freedom of the slaves, local

---

[4] MS Journal at the Historical Center Library, Old St. George's, Philadelphia, transcribed by Cornelius Hudson. Entry for January 27, 1771.

[5] Willis J. Weatherford, *American Churches and the Negro* (Boston: The Christopher Publishing House, 1957), p. 108.

attitudes against the admission of Negroes into the churches changed slowly; and in a number of cases Negroes were encouraged to set up their own local congregations or to join the independent Negro denominations. The total enrollment of Negroes in the Methodist Episcopal Church in 1850—the last year of keeping separate lists of white and Negro members in the Annual Conferences of that church—was 26,309. The Civil War years, however, brought a greatly increased interest in the development of work among Negroes by the Northern Church.

One of the most constructive steps taken by the Methodist Episcopal Church following the Civil War was the setting up of schools for training leaders among the freedmen, both for the ordinary responsibilities of newly attained citizenship in a democratic country and for special leadership in the work of the church. The program for this type of work was first begun on an interdenominational basis, but very early there developed a tendency on the part of the churches to set up their own denominational boards. In line with this trend a group of Methodist leaders, ministers and laymen, met in Cincinnati on August 7-8, 1866, to determine a program for the Methodist Episcopal Church. The meeting resulted in the organization of the Freedmen's Aid Society, with the objective of working toward "the relief and education of the Freedmen and people of color in general, to co-operate with the Missionary and Church Extension Societies of the Methodist Episcopal Church." [6]

To summarize briefly the record of the episcopal Methodisms in their work with Negroes from 1844 to the unification of the churches in 1939:

The Methodist Episcopal Church, South, carried forward a vigorous program of evangelism among the slaves from 1844 to the Civil War years, with the result that a large number of Negroes were members of that church at the beginning of the Civil War. At the close of the war, however, and with the emancipation of the slaves, the logic of the situation made it seem the part of wisdom to set up the Negro membership as an independent church, having fraternal relations with the mother church and receiving financial aid from the benevolences of that church.

In the Methodist Episcopal Church the situation was more equivocal. This was especially true prior to the Civil War. While holding officially to the traditional position of John Wesley that peoples of every race, class, and nationality were welcome in Methodism, there was little effort made to win Negroes to the membership of the church. Following the emancipation of the slaves, however, the leaders of the church as well as the membership in general seemed to feel a moral obligation to help prepare the freedmen both for citizenship in the nation and in the

[6] *Official Report of the Organization Convention of the Freedmen's Aid Society,* p. 10.

kingdom of God. With this in mind, the Methodist Episcopal Church launched a vigorous program, both evangelistic and educational. By 1916, when unification began seriously to be considered, the Northern Church had a Negro membership of approximately 300,000.

NEGRO MEMBERSHIP AN ISSUE IN UNIFICATION

One of the major problems in the negotiations on Methodist unification from 1916 until 1939, when the Plan of Union was adopted, was the status of the Negro membership in the united church. Three groups were primarily concerned in this issue: the Methodist Episcopal Church, South, the white membership of the Methodist Episcopal Church, and the Negro membership of the Methodist Episcopal Church.

For the Southern Church, with its history and social background since 1844, the logical solution of the status of the Negro seemed to be the setting up of this group into an independent church, either alone or with other Negro church groups, with no organic relation to the white section of the church.

In the case of the Methodist Episcopal Church, whatever might have been the individual preferences of many of its members and local church congregations, there was the long tradition of the church in welcoming, theoretically at least, all groups into the fellowship of the church, irrespective of race, class, or national origin. Further, there was fresh in the memories of all concerned the very vigorous evangelistic and educational program the church had carried forward among the freedmen since the close of the Civil War, and there were thousands of loyal Methodists who were still committed to that program. Finally, there was the legal fact that the Negroes were as definitely a part of the church as was any other group in it, and could not be eliminated from its membership except by their own choice.

The Negro membership, although a minority group both in numbers and influence, was nevertheless conscious of its rights and prerogatives in the church of its choice and was not disposed to relinquish those rights. More important to them than rights and prerogatives, however, was their instinctive conviction that the Methodist fellowship represented a communion that was seriously seeking to achieve in that fellowship the answer to the prayer of our Lord "that they all may be one." They believed that their membership in such a communion would help to witness to the possibilities of that achievement.

It was these varying views which, over the period of nearly a quarter of a century, had to be resolved before the Plan of Union satisfactory to a majority of Methodists could be agreed upon. This meant compromise on all sides. For the Southern section of the new church, it meant giving up the insistence on a separate and independent church for the Negro group and accepting an arrangement which would leave them as full-fledged members of the church. For the Methodist Episcopal Church it meant giving up the concept of a strongly centralized General Conference for a regionally structured church, with the Negro membership constituting a separate regional group. For the Negro membership it meant accepting an arrangement by which their Annual Conferences would be set up as one of the regional groups, or jurisdictions, to be known as the Central Jurisdiction and to be racial rather than geographical.

While the Central Jurisdiction posed the problem of a separate racial structure, it did have manifest advantages, such as proportionate representation on all boards of the church and membership in its highest councils. Its members were eligible to hold the highest administrative posts in the church, without discrimination as to salaries and other items of expense.

THE WORK OF THE CENTRAL JURISDICTION

The Central Jurisdiction has been a functioning unit in the church since union in 1939. Both its friends and its foes have a right to inquire as to its effectiveness as a jurisdiction. The measuring scale should be based on the rights and powers granted to the several Jurisdictional Conferences under the constitution. These rights have to do with the number of delegates to the Jurisdictional Conference, the manner of their election, the time and place of meeting, and the powers and duties of the jurisdictions.

It is by its discharge of the powers and duties that the effectiveness of the jurisdiction is to be judged. The first and main responsibility, as borne out in the actual experience of all the jurisdictions, is "to elect bishops and to co-operate in carrying out such plans for their support as may be determined by the General Conference." A second very important responsibility is "to promote the evangelistic, educational, missionary, and benevolent interests of the church, and to provide for interests and institutions within their boundaries." Because of the immense geographical territory involved in the boundaries of the Central Jurisdiction, it has been deemed more practicable to develop its boards and other organizational structure on area and conference lines rather than on jurisdictional lines.

As measured by the first criterion—the election of bishops for the jurisdiction, and to that extent for the whole church—the Central Jurisdiction has been an unquestionable success. In the twenty years since 1940, it has elected twelve men to the episcopacy to serve the church in the

Central Jurisdiction and in Liberia, West Africa, which since 1944 has been designated by the church as the administrative responsibility of the Central Jurisdiction. These leaders, with their associates in the various echelons of the ministry and with the magnificent co-operation of the laymen of the jurisdiction, have done their work in the best traditions of The Methodist Church.

The second responsibility—that of promoting the institutions and benevolent interests of the church—can be traced by the following statistical survey.

On the basis of a study made for the 1960 General Conference the Central Jurisdiction showed a total membership of 308,577 in 1940; 346,945 in 1950; 361,388 in 1957—a gain of 17.1 per cent for the period 1940-57, as over against a gain of 30.4 per cent for the whole church.[7]

In church school membership, the totals in the Central Jurisdiction were 172,310 in 1940; 188,571 in 1957—a gain of 9.4 per cent for the period as against 30.2 per cent for the whole church. Only the Northeastern Jurisdiction had a smaller gain, 6.6 per cent. The largest gain in this field was in the Western Jurisdiction, 66.0 per cent.[8]

In the membership of the Woman's Society, the Central Jurisdiction reported a gain of 38.2 per cent from 1944 to 1957, as against 54 per cent for the whole church. Here the Southeastern Jurisdiction reported the largest gain, 263.2 per cent, and the North Central the smallest, 17 per cent.[9]

In World Service and General Benevolences, the Central Jurisdiction is credited as follows: $100,299 in 1940; $276,799 in 1950; $482,311 in 1957. This represents 2.2 per cent of the total amount paid by the whole church. The next lowest percentage paid by any jurisdiction that year was 10 per cent by the Western, which is understandable since it is the next smallest in size to the Central. The highest for the year was 24.4 per cent by the North Central Jurisdiction. The Central Jurisdiction increased its per capita giving from $0.58 in 1940 to $2.74 in 1957, while that of the whole church was $6.77.[10]

The Central Jurisdiction does not suffer disproportionately in comparison with the rest of the church in the matter of the support of the benevolence program, especially when the difference in economic status of the majority of its membership is taken into account.

In keeping with the time-honored tradition of American Methodism the basic administrative unit in the church is the Annual Conference.

[7] Frederick A. Shippey, "The Methodist Church Since Unification," p. 51.
[8] *Ibid.*, p. 59.
[9] *Ibid.*, p. 65.
[10] *Ibid.*, pp. 72, 75.

There were nineteen Annual Conferences in the Negro membership at the time of unification and a total membership of just over 300,000. In 1960 the Annual Conferences numbered seventeen, due to mergers of smaller conferences, with a total membership, according to the 1960 General Minutes, of 367,340. There are five areas in the United States and one in Liberia for which the Central Jurisdiction, by action of the General Conference, has provided episcopal leadership since 1944.

For years there has been anxiety, and even criticism in some quarters of the church, over the relatively low rate of increase in the membership of the Central Jurisdiction as compared to the average in the whole church. In the figures referred to above, the rate of increase in the Central Jurisdiction was 17.1 per cent as over against 30.4 per cent for the church at large. Contemporary population shifts have materially affected these membership figures. A large number of members of the Central Jurisdiction have migrated from the South into other sections of the country, where they have been lost to the Central Jurisdiction. Another important factor here was the legislation in 1952 which enabled local churches of the Central Jurisdiction to transfer to the jurisdiction in which they were geographically located. Amendment IX to the constitution further defined and simplified this process, and many large Negro congregations have so transferred. While such persons cannot technically be listed as members of the Central Jurisdiction, their places of origin should not be forgotten in evaluating the evangelistic efficiency of the Central Jurisdiction.

In the matter of ministerial leadership, the 1960 General Minutes show a total of 1,554 ministerial members of Annual Conferences, including those on trial and the retired members. In addition, there were 535 approved supply pastors. Of a total of 1,650 pastoral charges, 1,056 were filled by episcopal appointment of full members of conferences and the rest by supply pastors. In charge of the six areas, and serving as their resident bishops, are the bishops elected by the Jurisdictional Conference for the five areas in the United States and the Monrovia Area, Liberia. In 1960 the effective bishops and their assignments for the quadrennium were: Marquis L. Harris, Atlantic Coast Area; Edgar A. Love, Baltimore Area; Charles F. Golden, Nashville-Birmingham Area; Noah W. Moore, Jr., New Orleans Area; Matthew W. Clair, Jr., St. Louis Area; Prince A. Taylor, Jr., Monrovia Area. Others who served as bishops of the Central Jurisdiction until their death or retirement were Alexander P. Shaw, Edward W. Kelly, Willis J. King, John W. E. Bowen, Robert E. Jones, W. A. C. Hughes, Lorenzo H. King, and Robert N. Brooks.

Two members of the Central Jurisdiction have served on the Judicial

Council of The Methodist Church. J. Ernest Wilkins served from 1948 through 1959 and was for one quadrennium president of the council. Theodore M. Berry was elected in 1960.

COLLEGES AND UNIVERSITIES SERVING THE JURISDICTION

Reference has been made to the setting up of schools in the South, following the Civil War, for the training of leaders for the church and the nation. While a number of these institutions have been discontinued or merged with others, thirteen of them were still in operation in 1960. Along with similar institutions sponsored by other denominations these schools render valuable service to the members of the Central Jurisdiction. These schools are listed here in the areas where they are located:

Atlantic Coast Area: Bethune-Cookman College, Daytona Beach, Florida; Claflin College, Orangeburg, South Carolina; Clark College, Atlanta, Georgia; Gammon Theological Seminary (now merged with other seminaries in the Interdenominational Theological Center), Atlanta, Georgia; Paine College, Augusta, Georgia (sponsored by The Methodist Church and the Christian Methodist Church).

Baltimore Area: Bennett College, Greensboro, North Carolina.

Nashville-Birmingham Area: Rust College, Holly Springs, Mississippi; Meharry Medical College, Nashville, Tennessee; Morristown Industrial College, Morristown, Tennessee.

New Orleans Area: Dillard University, New Orleans, Louisiana; Huston-Tillotson College, Austin, Texas; Wiley College, Marshall, Texas.

St. Louis Area: Philander Smith College, Little Rock, Arkansas.

The majority of these institutions are in the typical liberal arts tradition, and all except one are fully accredited by their regional accrediting agencies. Three of them are unique, either in their history or type of service, or both, and so deserve special mention: Gammon Theological Seminary, Meharry Medical College, and Bennett College.

Gammon Theological Seminary was founded in 1883 through the cooperative efforts of Bishop Henry W. Warren and the Reverend Elijah Gammon, of Batavia, Illinois. Bishop Warren, an older brother of William F. Warren, one of the founders of Boston University, and himself later a co-founder of the Iliff School of Theology, discovered Mr. Gammon, who, after retiring from the ministry because of ill health, became a wealthy businessman. Gammon set up the school first as a department of Clark University (now Clark College). At his death he left a substantial endowment for its maintenance.

During the course of its history Gammon has made a distinct contribution to the ministerial training of Negroes in the various churches, North and South, serving members of the Negro race. Some twelve hundred persons have graduated from the institution. Among the alumni are twenty college presidents; thirty-nine college professors; twenty-four church board field representatives; fifty-four chaplains in the United States Army; ten editors of church periodicals; fifteen bishops, nine in The Methodist Church and six in other denominations.

Gammon came to another significant period in the history of the long years of its splendid service to the church and the race when it completed a merger with three other institutions working in the field of theological training to form the Interdenominational Theological Center in Atlanta. The constituent schools in this institution are Gammon Theological Seminary (Methodist) ; Morehouse College School of Religion (Baptist) ; Turner School of Theology (African Methodist Episcopal) ; and Phillips School of Theology (Christian Methodist Episcopal) . In this new setting Gammon gives promise of making a much more significant contribution to the training of the ministry than was possible in previous years. The Methodist Church continues financial support to the institution, and it receives in addition a very considerable amount of capital and endowment funds from the two Rockefeller Foundations, which made possible the merged institution.

Meharry Medical College is the second of these professional schools which deserve special mention. Meharry was one of the institutions established after the Civil War for the training of physicians, dentists, and related workers in the field of medicine, for service among the freedmen. The institution has had a long and distinguished record in this field, and is one of two fully accredited medical schools in the nation devoted primarily to the training of Negroes.

Bennett College, in Greensboro, North Carolina, was first established as a coeducational college and operated as such until 1926. In that year it was reorganized as a women's college, under the joint sponsorship of the Board of Education of the Methodist Episcopal Church and the Woman's Division of the Board of Missions. From 1926 until his death in 1955 Dr. David D. Jones served as the very capable president.

In addition to the work done under the auspices of the Division of Educational Institutions, which supervises the program of the liberal arts colleges and professional schools, the program of the Division of the Local Church of the Board of Education has received more intelligent study and has become more effective in the local churches of the Central Jurisdiction. An increasing number of Annual Conferences have begun to employ full-time executive secretaries and have made provision for more adequate budgets for Christian education in the work of these conferences.

Several of the Annual Conferences maintain such institutions as homes for the aged, friendship homes, community centers, orphanages, and (in co-operation with the Woman's Division of Christian Service) Bethlehem Houses, which minister to the life of the community. A unique institution in the jurisdiction is the Gulfside Assembly, located at Waveland, Mississippi. It was established under the leadership of Bishop Robert E. Jones, in 1923, and has rendered a notable service to the members of the Central Jurisdiction. It had, in 1960, the sponsorship of the Nashville-Birmingham and the New Orleans Areas.

THE CENTRAL CHRISTIAN ADVOCATE

One of the most influential agencies in the promotion of the program of the Central Jurisdiction has been the *Central Christian Advocate*. This journal was published for many years prior to unification under the name the *Southwestern Christian Advocate*. At the time of union the name was changed to *Central Christian Advocate,* and the paper continued its fine tradition of service. It is one of the regular publications of the Methodist Publishing House.

THE FUTURE OF THE CENTRAL JURISDICTION

It is merely stating a well-known fact to say that the Central Jurisdiction, as a final structural arrangement for the Negro membership in the church, was not favorably voted upon by the majority of the members of the Negro Annual Conferences. The record will show that a majority of the members of these conferences voted against the plan. Many who supported it did so as their part of the compromise which made unification possible, but regarded it as an interim plan of union, necessary in a growing together of relatively unacquainted groups, which would be changed in the course of the years.

In light of the continuing discussion in the church since unification on the question of the Central Jurisdiction, it is evident that an increasing number of people have been troubled as to the symbolic significance of this type of structure in a church which boasts of the inclusiveness of all peoples, irrespective of race or nationality. There is a growing conviction that in a multiracial fellowship like The Methodist Church, a way must be found to eliminate all barriers based exclusively on racial and color distinctions.

A genuine beginning in this direction was made at the General Conference of 1956 by the adoption of what is known as Amendment IX. This amendment, entitled "Abolition of the Central Jurisdiction," reads:

The Central Jurisdiction shall be abolished when all of the Annual Conferences now comprising it have been transferred to other jurisdictions in accordance with the voluntary procedure of Article V of this section. Each remaining bishop of the Central Jurisdiction shall thereupon be transferred to the jurisdiction to which the majority of the membership of his area have been transferred, and the Central Jurisdiction shall then be dissolved.

The 1960 General Conference made a further step toward the implementation of this action, which had already received a majority vote of the Annual Conferences, by setting up a Commission on Interjurisdictional Relations, to which was entrusted the continuing program of The Methodist Church "to abolish the Central Jurisdiction, promote interracial brotherhood through Christian love, and achieve a more inclusive church." [11]

It is clear that The Methodist Church definitely committed itself to the abolition of the Central Jurisdiction, which to many of its members seemed symbolic of a type of racial exclusiveness which the Christian church must continue to seek to eliminate from every phase of its institutional life. More significant still was the new approach to the problem suggested in the 1960 Episcopal Address. After stating some of the problems involved in the racial situation, both in the world and in the church, the bishops said, in part:

At the same time we are apt to forget, in the midst of our concern for a more adequate solution of the race problem in our Church, that the reality that creates this problem is actually one of our most important assets in it. We already *are* an inclusive church. We intend to remain one. We have come to the time when we must confidently declare to ourselves and to the world that the interracial character of The Methodist Church is one of our greatest sources of strength and opportunity. It may—and it does!—create problems, but in itself it is a great blessing for which we thank God, and an advantage which we must develop to its fullest in this new age.[12]

This should be our supreme objective, whatever the type of structural organization. We are already an inclusive church and must remain one. Such a church will be greatly needed in the years ahead if the world is to be won to Christ.

---

[11] *Discipline*, 1960, ¶ 2013.1.
[12] *Daily Christian Advocate*, April 28, 1960, p. 43.

Regional Distribution of the General Boards and General Church Meetings

Another sensitive point for merging institutions is, for each, the maintenance of prestige and power in its familiar headquarters. Fortunately the Methodist bodies, unlike many denominations, had no single headquarters. Before unification most of the boards of the Methodist Episcopal Church, South, were in Nashville, but the Board of Finance was in St. Louis and the Board of Church Extension in Louisville. The major agencies of the Methodist Episcopal Church were in Chicago, New York, Philadelphia, Washington, and Columbus. The Methodist Protestant Church accepted, by usage rather than by official designation, both Baltimore and Pittsburgh as denominational headquarters.

Twenty years after unification the picture had changed in a few respects. Offices in Columbus, Louisville, and St. Louis had been closed, except for certain legal and fiscal purposes. Several consolidations of agencies occurred, and a number of new boards and commissions were established. In 1960 the distribution of agency headquarters was as follows: In Chicago were the Council on World Service and Finance, the Board of Hospitals and Homes, the Board of Lay Activities, the Board of Pensions, and the Commission on Promotion and Cultivation.

In Nashville was the Board of Education, which had in 1952 absorbed the Commission on Ministerial Training (originally Courses of Study) and had added other important functions. Associated with it were the Interboard Commission on Missionary Education, the National Conference of the Methodist Youth Fellowship, and the Interboard Committee on Christian Vocations. The administrative leadership of the Board of Publication was concentrated there. These two boards and the Board of Evangelism, also with headquarters in Nashville, each built an attractive, efficient headquarters building, at costs of from $1 million to $2.5 million. The Television, Radio, and Film Commission also had its main office in Nashville.

In New York were the Division of World Missions, the Woman's Division of Christian Service, and the Joint Section of Education and Cultivation, all part of the Board of Missions. The Methodist Committee for Overseas Relief, formed in 1944, was housed with the Division of World Missions. The Commission on Public Relations and Methodist Information maintained its headquarters in New York, with branch offices in Chicago, Nashville, and Washington. The American Bible Society, recognized as one of the general missionary agencies of The Methodist Church, and the National Council of Churches, in which

Methodism had strong representation, were also in New York. During 1960 most of the New York Methodist agencies moved into the new Interchurch Center, which the National Council of Churches, with the co-operation of various denominations, had erected on Riverside Drive.

The Division of National Missions (formerly Home Missions and Church Extension) moved to Philadelphia in 1956 to occupy a building that it had owned for many years.

Washington increasingly became one of the headquarter cities for Methodism. The Board of Temperance, which owned property near the national Capitol, continued there after unification. In 1960 the General Conference united this board, the Board of World Peace, and the Board of Social and Economic Relations (both of which had centered their work in Chicago) to form the Board of Christian Social Concerns, and designated Washington as its headquarters. A new and much larger site was procured near the American University campus. Also in Washington were the Commission on Chaplains and the Commission on Camp Activities.

Each shift of the headquarters of a board and the erection of each new building were accompanied by lively discussion and sometimes sharp criticism, as northerners felt that too much of the church's administrative power was being tied irrevocably to Nashville, while westerners complained that the church did not give sufficient recognition to the growing power and importance of the great areas beyond the Mississippi River. However, there was an effort over the years to maintain something of a balance in the distribution of the agencies and in appointments to the staffs. Each location or relocation was approved by the General Conference; after 1952 the prior approval—or at least acquiescence—of the Co-ordinating Council was required.

Rivalry also existed among cities to entertain the General Conference and other large Methodist gatherings. The Uniting Conference of 1939 was held in Kansas City, the 1940 General Conference in Atlantic City, and the 1944 General Conference again in Kansas City. At that time there was some discrimination against Negro delegates by local restaurants. As a result, the conference adopted a resolution recommending "that committees arranging for general meetings of the church locate such meetings only in places where adequate and suitable entertainment can be provided for all delegates and representatives of the church." [13] Perhaps because of this action no General Conference from that time through 1960 was held in either the Southeastern or South Central Jurisdiction. Many southern churchmen felt that this was unfair to the

[13] *Discipline,* 1944, ¶ 2024.

southern jurisdictions, and in 1960 the General Conference adopted a recommendation of the Commission to Study the Jurisdictional System that "the meeting place of the General Conference be rotated among the jurisdictions, provided satisfactory arrangements can be made for entertainment, with special reference to the requirement for equality of accommodations for all races, without discrimination or segregation." [14] No one proposed that the protective stipulation be waived.

Conserving Historic Values and Co-ordinating Programs

Each of the three uniting churches had its own points of special strength. Both in planning for unification and in the years following, there was effort to conserve these distinctive values. One of them was the conviction, held most strongly by the Methodist Protestants, that laymen have at least as much responsibility for the conduct of the church as have the clergy. In part in deference to their insistence laymen were given more effective representation in Annual Conferences than they had had in either of the two larger denominations, one lay member being elected from each pastoral charge as a delegate, with full voting powers except on ministerial qualifications. In 1958 the position was further strengthened by the adoption of Constitutional Amendment X, which specified that "each pastoral charge served by more than one minister in full connection shall be entitled to two lay members" in the Annual Conference.

Each of the merging churches had its own pension system for ministers. That of the Methodist Episcopal Church was the most adequate. The problem of evolving a uniform system throughout the whole church was a nettling one. The size of reserves and the pension rates varied widely among the three churches and even among their Annual Conferences. Nevertheless the process was courageously begun. Adjustments were made and reserve funds developed. A standard clearinghouse was created in the Chicago office. It was arranged that the years of pension credit which a minister earned in each of the Annual Conferences he served were to be paid for by those conferences through the clearinghouse. No longer did the retired minister receive a monthly check from each conference for his years of annuity credit; one check, issued by the central office, covered his entire monthly pension.

The consolidation of the work of the several mission boards proved to be particularly advantageous. The co-ordination of programs saved

---

[14] *Discipline*, 1960, ¶ 505.

money and administrative time and permitted an expansion of the services rendered. In the Division of World Missions, within the Board of Missions, the process was rather simple, as matters of great importance could be decided around a table in New York City, far removed from the local pressures of the mission fields. The problem was more complicated in what came to be called the Division of National Missions. The predecessor boards had been in more or less open competition throughout the West and Southwest as well as in the border states. They had in some places financed rival programs in small towns and hamlets, in part in response to the appeals of overzealous denominational partisans. Such local tensions were not quickly resolved with the consummation of church union on the national level. Because of legal limitations the corporations which frequently held mortgages on competing churches in such towns could not be easily brought together. As Earl R. Brown, general executive secretary from 1944 to 1956, remarked: "Sectional differences confronted us at every turn. It took thirteen long patient years to consolidate the church-extension interests of the former denominations. But it was done with a minimum of irritation." [15]

The Northern and Southern Churches had followed somewhat different practices in handling benevolence funds. In the Northern Church there had been a more centralized pattern of fund collection and distribution. Most funds for home-mission projects were raised on an apportionment basis across the nation and paid to the Board of Home Missions, which in turn distributed the money. While the Southern Church had a somewhat similar arrangement, a much larger proportion of the money raised in an Annual Conference was distributed directly by its treasurer to the various mission projects within its bounds. Because of these differing traditions, the northern and western conferences on the average, after unification, paid proportionately more to the Council on World Service and Finance than did the southern conferences, while the latter gave a greater part of their benevolence dollar directly to their own local projects. This created some feelings of reproach and defensiveness. Neither method of distributing funds was intrinsically wrong. They simply involved different emphases. This fact was recognized and, quadrennium by quadrennium, the Council on World Service and Finance sought to adjust apportionments to the Annual Conferences to achieve a greater uniformity without working undue hardship on any section of the church.

[15] From a personal letter to the author.

The Progress of Unification in Twenty Years

In 1960 American Methodists were more nearly one people than at any time in the last one hundred years. Three denominations had now become one, united under one constitution, with one system of government and one array of boards. The membership of almost ten million was a source of pride, and permitted Methodist leaders to speak to the nation with an effectiveness not previously possible. Many of the fears brought to unification had been laid to rest, compromises had been achieved, and people from different parts of the nation found that there was stimulus and satisfaction in working together.

However, it was obvious at the General Conference of 1960 that the union was not yet socially and psychologically complete. If it had been, there would have been less need for reassurance, frequently given, that we are now one and shall never separate again. Sectional differences were much in evidence, especially in connection with the jurisdictional system and the place of the Negro congregation in Methodism. Even the cordial references to "our brethren from the South" or "from the North" indicated a deference which was based on a recognition of differences. After twenty years, Methodists were like people in a congregation which had recently received members of other races, who in their very politeness caused the newcomers to realize that they were not yet fully accepted as "part of the family." True union could come only slowly, through living together long enough to learn to trust one another and to forget the compromises that were made in order to achieve the union.

As a matter of fact, unification affected the leaders and those involved in the overhead organizational structure far more deeply than it did the rank-and-file laymen and ministers. Congregations in border areas or where there were a number of Methodist Protestant churches were more aware of church union, feeling both the tensions involved in readjustment and the advantages which were derived from it, than were most of the congregations in either the North or the South. The latter groups still thought and acted much as they did before unification. Union inevitably was most complete for the Methodist Protestant churches, for they lost more of their distinctive identity than did either of the larger groups.

Any uniting of massive organizations necessarily focuses attention on structure and compromise. The new institution must be based on principles which can meet the widest acceptance, and consequently tends to be conserving and conservative and to play down the experimental and the prophetic. The attention of Methodism, in spite of its commendable increase in benevolence giving and its watchword, "Advance for Christ," tended to be concentrated on its own organization and its own expansion. The hope was that as the union became more secure, perhaps The Methodist Church would become more bold for Christ and more forgetful of its sectional differences and its own machinery.

Methodist union was no mere marriage of convenience, nor was it a romantic love affair. Rather it was a carefully planned, long negotiated joining of forces by three churches with a common background which had, ever since their separation, felt rather uncomfortable about their divided and sometimes competing witness in a non-Christian world.

In spite of undoubted disadvantages associated with unification the church grew in size and in confidence. Its witness in other countries was strengthened, and much unbecoming competition in American towns and villages disappeared. Financial and personnel resources were more efficiently employed, and after two decades the united church was in a position to move forward with strength and with a more affirmative Christian witness.

2

An Expanding Church, 1940-60

With unification The Methodist Church became the largest Protestant denomination in America. Since that time it has registered steady if not spectacular expansion in almost every phase of its life. In the century following the separation of the Northern and Southern branches of the church, great changes had occurred in the nation: the opening of the West, the War Between the States, the rise of industrialism, the phenomenal growth of cities, the decline in the farm population and the relative importance of agriculture, the rise in the power and security of organized labor, World War I which thrust America toward the center of the international scene, and the depression decade which ushered in a new concept of economics and politics. By the time of the Uniting Conference the stage was being set for World War II. Hitler entered Prague on May 15, 1939, five days after the adjournment of the conference. Within four months the war broke.

America was indeed a different land than in 1844. In 1940 the population was 131,669,275. A century earlier it was only 17,069,453. This growth of 770 per cent was accompanied by profound modifications in the American way of life and the structure of American institutions. But change did not stop in 1940. The population in the next twenty years grew by more than forty-six million individuals. In 1940 there were slightly over thirty-two million families in the nation; by 1960 there were forty-five million, an increase of more than one third. The birth rate, which climbed slowly from 1935 to 1945, shot up after the war and remained high. Large families again became the fashion.

In order to win the war the nation initiated a program of population displacement such as had never been witnessed by America before. Not only were millions of service men and women taken from their homes, placed in training camps perhaps a thousand miles away, and then shipped to all quarters of the globe, but other millions of civilians and their families were also stimulated to pull up their roots and journey to a new location, persuaded perhaps by the promise of high wages in a defense industry, an intense feeling of patriotism, or the sheer promise of adventure.

An illustration of the problems resulting from such redistribution of people was to be seen in the burgeoning of defense-plant communities. The government established scores of these plants, many of them in the open country far removed from a metropolitan center. The people in near-by villages and towns were first delighted at the sudden prosperity and the sharp rise in real estate values, and then dismayed by the strains put on all of their municipal facilities. The public school enrollment quadrupled, the churches were filled with strange faces, and even the village jails proved inadequate to the new demands. Through its churches in or near some of these communities Methodism sought to minister by placing a full-time pastor in what had been one point on a three-point circuit. In other instances the Federal Council of Churches was able to secure land and sponsor a program for all Protestants. Sometimes the church building was merely a large shed or a Quonset hut, to be deserted or demolished when the settlement lost its function and disappeared. Often the service was missionary in type, when the heterogeneity and rapid turnover of the population made it impossible to achieve an organized local church.

After the war the movement of population exceeded anything previously known in American society. Year after year the census reported that in the preceding twelve months, one fifth of the population changed its place of residence. This mobility, plus population growth, plus the massing of people around the metropolitan cities, presented a challenge to united Methodism to organize congregations in the new communities and to minister to an increasingly rootless population.

Growth in Membership

The Annual Conferences reported in the first year after unification 7,360,187 members, and in addition 672,011 who were listed as non-resident. After 1952, by action of the General Conference, the non-resident members were no longer recorded separately. The 1960 General Minutes recorded a total of 9,910,741 members. This increase of approximately one fifth in twenty years seemed impressive at first glance, but not particularly so when viewed against the phenomenal rise in the total population; in fact, statistically Methodism did not quite keep pace with the national growth. Between 1950 and 1960 the increase in population and in Methodist membership were respectively: for the northeastern states, 13.1 per cent and 5.3 per cent; for the southeastern, 17.1 per cent and 11.0 per cent; for the north central, 17.3 per cent and 7.9 per cent; for the south central, 15.2 per cent and 14.1 per cent; and for the western, 39.3 per cent and 33.1 per cent.[16] In only the southwestern and western sections of the country did Methodism come even near keeping up with the population growth. In explanation or defense it was said that church records were better kept at the end than at the beginning of this period.

The General Conference of 1944 gave a new definition to the term "preparatory membership." Prior to that time a child who had been baptized was generally not included on the preparatory membership roll until he reaffirmed the baptismal vows taken for him by his parents and indicated his desire to prepare for full church membership. In 1941 only 151,554 persons were reported as "preparatory members now on roll." These were presumably children enrolled that year in membership training classes. The legislation of 1944 provided that all baptized children associated with a particular Methodist church were to be listed on the preparatory membership roll until they were received into full membership. This put the membership of baptized children in The Methodist Church on the same basis as in the Lutheran, Episcopal, and Roman Catholic churches. In 1960 there were 1,609,930 on this preparatory membership roll. In the late 1950's almost 400,000 persons were received on profession of faith annually into full membership, most of them from the preparatory roll.

The growing mobility of the American population was reflected in the gradual increase in the number of members removed or received by transfer from other congregations. In 1960 local churches received by transfer about 400,000 persons from other Methodist and non-Methodist

---

[16] Data compiled by George H. Jones of the Board of Evangelism.

churches, some 100,000 of them from the latter. More than balancing this figure, some 350,000 were removed by transfer and an additional 200,000 names were removed by Quarterly Conference action, meaning that the persons had been lost track of or were no longer interested in the local fellowship. As ministers in some city parishes noted, it was necessary to win to the church many persons every year in order to hold the membership at the same numerical level.

Much of the recruitment during this period must be credited to the work of laymen. In 1952 for the first time a Commission on Membership and Evangelism was constituted in each local church to assist the pastor in reaching new members. Where this commission worked seriously, substantial growth was generally registered.

Another tangible measure of the expansion of a denomination is the increase in the number of its pastoral charges. At the time of union there were about twenty-one thousand of these. By 1960 over three thousand had been added. To be sure, the actual number of preaching places declined, through the merging of many of the smaller congregations, so that the average membership per church rose from 174 in 1940 to 252 in 1960.

These two changes tell much about the development of the denomination in the intervening twenty years. The shrinkage in farm population, the consolidation of rural schools, greater ease of transportation, and the shortage of trained ministers encouraged the merging of small churches, especially if they were located within two or three miles of each other. Churches with fewer than a hundred members became less common, in cities as well as in rural areas, until in 1958 there were only 2,516 of them. While large circuits, some with as many as ten to fourteen preaching places, still existed in the North as well as in the South, the latter section of the country had proportionately more because of its dominantly rural character.

New Methodist congregations were being organized every year. According to a study made by the Department of Research and Survey, 1,053 were founded between January, 1950, and July, 1958.[17] The Southeastern Jurisdiction reported the largest accession—377—followed by the South Central with 319. For the other jurisdictions the figures were: Western, 155; North Central, 113; Northeastern, 52; and Central, 37. The establishment of these new congregations did not in all cases reflect a comparable expansion of membership. For example, 56 per cent of the persons composing them transferred from other Methodist churches,

[17] Roy A. Sturm and Robert L. Wilson, "Methodism's New Churches, 1950-1958" (multilith report; Philadelphia: Department of Research and Survey, Board of Missions of The Methodist Church, 1960).

13 per cent came from other denominations, and the rest on profession of faith or restoration to active rolls. While the mobility rate of Methodist members was not as high as that of the general population, 15 per cent of those who had joined these churches had, by the time the study was made, already transferred out, 87 per cent of them going to another Methodist church.

These new congregations, most of them suburban, were flourishing. A more detailed study of 221 of them which had been in existence for at least four years revealed that while they had an average membership of 95 at the time of their first annual report, four years later that figure had risen to 285. Their church schools grew almost as rapidly.

Since in every year some churches are closed or merged, there must be a relatively high birth rate of new congregations if the denomination is to thrive. In spite of the establishment of more than a thousand congregations in eight and a half years, Methodism did not meet the opportunities created by the growing population. It fell behind especially in the extensive new suburban developments. Occasionally a strong church at the center of a city resisted the establishment of new congregations on the developing fringe until it was almost too late to start a church there. This dog-in-the-manger attitude fortunately seemed to be on the wane in the 1950's.

Church Building and Benevolence Giving

Because of shortage of construction materials, Methodism could do little building during the war years. The obsolescence of older structures, the growth of many congregations, and the movement of population resulted in pressure for more and yet more building of new plants. The story can be simply told in terms of dollars expended by local churches for construction. In 1941, $21 million was paid on indebtedness and for new buildings and improvements. By 1950 the figure was $82 million. In 1960 it had snowballed to $180 million—about a third of all funds raised by local churches. Judged by property values as well as other criteria Methodism was certainly "big business." In fact, by 1960 the value of local church and parsonage property had reached over $3 billion—double what it was in 1952 and more than four times the 1940 figure. Even though the dollar had declined in value, this was an imposing total, and the debt on this property was less than 10 per cent.[18]

[18] The statistics on The Methodist Church given here—unless otherwise noted —have been gathered from the Quadrennial Reports of the several boards and from information supplied to the author by the staffs of the boards.

Not only did the church increase in membership and house itself more adequately; it also greatly expanded its benevolence giving. In the fiscal year ending with May, 1960, the total benevolence giving of the church, including payments by the Woman's Division of Christian Service, exceeded $80 million. This was a per capita increase of 136 per cent; even so, it meant an average payment of only $8.16 per member for church benevolences.

In 1940 The Methodist Church supported most of its benevolence enterprises through apportionments paid to the General Commission on World Service and Finance, which dispensed the funds to the general boards of the church to be used in accordance with the pattern approved by the General Conference. Not including the giving of the Woman's Societies—whose funds were handled through their own organization—about $4 million of the $8 million given for all benevolence purposes was channeled to World Service on apportionment (i.e., on an equitable basis of "assessment," a word which was carefully avoided). In 1960 giving to World Service agencies on apportionment totaled $12 million out of the $80 million given for benevolences—a much smaller proportion. The giving to World Service on apportionment increased between 1959 and 1960 by less than $10,000, while giving to Annual Conference benevolences increased by over $900,000. This change in the giving pattern reflected the desire of persons and churches to contribute more directly to specific causes with which they had a fairly immediate connection, rather than to general benevolence funds. They preferred to support church extension enterprises which they knew about, or institutions within their own Annual Conferences, or—through Advance Specials—some particular missionary undertaking in home or foreign field.

An important result of this changing pattern was that the boards and agencies of the church received during the two decades a steadily diminishing proportion of the benevolence giving of Methodists, for the maintenance of their own organization and for the support of the less dramatic and less vocal institutions which were dependent on them. The beneficiaries of this trend were the various causes which, with the approval of the General Advance Committee or the Annual Conference, could make a direct appeal to the churches. The amount of money raised for these enterprises increased ten times as fast—taking changes in purchasing power into account—as did the funds paid to World Service on apportionment. The most rapid increase in giving was for the specific projects designated as "Advance Specials." These contributions accounted for more than half of all benevolence giving in the church. Especially in our modern world, with its anonymity and facelessness, the appeal made by a particular boys' school or by the need for a new church in a suburb of one's own city was understandably greater than a request to make a payment "on apportionment" to World Service, which is the Methodist equivalent of the United Fund or Community Chest.

During its first two decades The Methodist Church was indeed an expanding organization—in membership, in number of churches, and in financial strength. However, even with the stimulus of unification, the elaborate organizational structure, and the devoted and vigorous service of its professional workers, the church did not quite keep pace with the growth of population, so that relatively its membership showed a small decline. And this occurred at a time when some Protestant denominations, and also the Roman Catholics, reported a growth rate well above that of the nation.

3

Developments in Structure and Function

A central concern of united Methodism through its first two decades was to remove the misunderstandings and suspicion which are a natural accompaniment of any merger and to develop a well co-ordinated, smoothly functioning organization. While the goal of a unified spirit had not been fully attained by 1960, marked progress was made toward it. Quadrennium by quadrennium alterations were proposed in the organizational structure of the church, with the hope of increasing the effectiveness of its witness in the many spheres of its influence.

The General Conference of 1940 was occupied in getting the united church under way and its boards established and located. Obviously, as is evidenced by the *Discipline* of that year, it did a patchwork job in the effort to tie together the legislation of the three predecessor churches. However, human institutions have a way of muddling ahead and performing their functions, working out details and clarifying relationships as they go.

By 1944 the boards of the church had completed their "shakedown cruise" and were operating with increasing smoothness and harmony. In the lower echelons, however, there was a feeling that Methodism had more machinery than it needed. Comments were heard about "needless waste," "growing bureaucracy," and "too many printed materials." By the General Conference of 1948 the demands for simplification and co-ordination began to crystallize.

A flood of memorials came from individuals, groups, and Annual Conferences, asking that the agencies of the church be made more efficient, that overlapping be eliminated, and that the quantity of promotional materials be reduced. At an early session of the conference, a special committee was appointed to study the memorials and make recommendations. It reported back, in part: "We believe that the lack of co-ordination and effectiveness of our present plan of promotion stems from certain duplications and overlapping of the programs of our general boards, commissions, and service agencies." It recommended the establishment of a commission "to make an impartial and objective study of all general boards, commissions, and service agencies of The Methodist Church, . . . their administrative and promotional programs, including publishing, investment policies, relationships of departments and divisions of each board . . . and their relationship to other boards." [19] The proposal was accepted, a budget of $240,000 for the quadrennium was voted, and a management consulting firm employed to undertake the analysis.

The resulting church survey, which covered every agency in the widespread Methodist organization, was, as one member of the commission stated, "exhaustive and exhausting." The report of the commission to the General Conference of 1952 brought 104 specific recommendations for consideration. After a dramatic two-day presentation and debate, the report was largely rejected, although certain important ideas and proposals were salvaged from it. There were several reasons for this debacle: It was charged that the survey agency itself was not aware of, and therefore could not take into proper consideration, the various centers of power and the delicate balance among them in The Methodist Church. The questionnaire it designed called forth a relatively poor response. Many important leaders of the church were not consulted. Some staff executives of boards and agencies felt that they were "treated like children" and had little opportunity to make suggestions concerning proposals which would affect their own future. The commission was unrealistic in attempting to make a large number of fundamental changes in the board structure of the church. Strong resistance might have been anticipated.

Yet the Church Survey Report was not without its tangible results. The establishment of the Co-ordinating Council was probably the most important of these. This body was given no program responsibility; instead it was assigned the task of reviewing, on request, overlapping in activity or lack of co-operation among or within general agencies, and of co-ordinating other aspects of the church's work.

[19] *Daily Christian Advocate*, May 7, 1948, p. 291.

The Council on World Service and Finance (formerly Commission) emerged as a stronger and better integrated agency, with more clearly defined responsibilities.

A third result was the creation of a Commission on Promotion and Cultivation. The Church Survey Commission had recommended this as part of a larger design—the establishment of a Department of Cultivation and Publication. Within this there would be a Board of Cultivation, in charge of promotional literature, films, radio, television, and Methodist information and public relations; a Board of Publications, responsible for church school literature, periodicals, and book editing and publishing; and a delimited Methodist Publishing House, to look after the business aspects of publishing, printing, and distributing. This plan was not adopted. The new Commission on Promotion and Cultivation superseded a committee which had been appointed in 1948 to implement the emphasis of the quadrennium, "The Advance for Christ and His Church." The 1952 legislation established the commission as a permanent agency and instructed that its general secretary should "co-ordinate and promote on a church-wide basis the program of world service, Advance Specials, Week of Dedication offerings, and all other general financial causes except as otherwise directed by the General Conference." [20] The commission was to review at least annually the plans of the general boards and agencies for the production and distribution of all free literature and promotional periodicals. It was instructed to publish a free program journal for pastors, which was subsequently given the title *The Methodist Story*. This was a broad mandate to carry forward a program of interpretation and promotion, to support the other benevolence agencies of the church.

A few other recommendations of the Church Survey Commission, regarded as incidental at the time, have had continuing influence. It urged that the number of members on the several boards be decreased. While the specific recommendations were not followed by the General Conference, a general pattern for reducing the size of boards was accepted, in spite of the opposition of the larger boards. It was instrumental in limiting the number of general board memberships of any bishop to three. (The proposal of the commission was two.) The General Conference also supported the recommendation that no layman or minister other than a bishop should be a member of more than one general board at any one time. It was at this session, though not at the direct suggestion of the report, that tenure on any board, commission, or council—except the Council of Bishops and the Judicial Council—was limited to twelve consecutive years.

[20] *Discipline,* 1952, ¶ 752.

All organizations resist change, especially if it comes in large doses. The work of the Church Survey Commission was not in vain. In countless indirect and subtle ways it continued to affect the life of the church. Yet it must be admitted that the grand plan, which had cost so much in money and time, was not accepted. Perhaps that is why many would agree with the senior bishop of the church, Herbert Welch, when he wrote in 1960, "The Church Survey had, as I see it, little of practical value."

Interpretation of the Constitution

Fundamental to the union of the three denominations was the development of a written constitution to which each church could subscribe. This constitution was designed to establish the basic components of the new church—the episcopacy, the General Conference, and so forth—and to indicate their duties and limitations. But, like other constitutions, it was also designed to protect rights—the rights of members, of Annual Conferences, and of regional groupings. A Judicial Council, with powers similar to those of the United States Supreme Court, was constituted to protect against ill-considered or prejudicial actions which might be taken by a legislative body or by an administrative officer. It had a power and a responsibility that are found in few, if any other, denominational councils.

As time passed, increasing use was made of the Judicial Council. During the first quadrennium—April, 1940, to December, 1943—only 16 cases came before it. The number rose steadily until in the period from April, 1956, to October, 1959, it handled 42. Through the General Conference of 1960 it had rendered decisions in 175 cases. Without doubt the quiet adjudication and definitive findings by the Judicial Council on issues sometimes hotly disputed saved The Methodist Church from many internal conflicts. Never once was a decision by the Judicial Council challenged. It had the respect of all segments of the denomination, and its verdicts were accepted without debate.

Through 1960 ten amendments to the constitution were adopted.[21] Most of these related to representation in the Annual, Central, Jurisdictional, or General Conferences. The one which caused most debate was Amendment IX, which was ratified in the Annual Conferences by a vote of thirteen to one and became effective in 1958. This amendment

---

[21] These are numbered as Amendments I to IV and VI to XI. The proposition named Amendment V was not ratified within the time limit; it was resubmitted in 1952 and ratified as Amendment VI.

provided a method by which churches and Annual Conferences within the Central Jurisdiction might transfer to a regional Annual Conference or jurisdiction if all the conferences involved approved. Eight churches but no Annual Conferences had taken advantage of the provision by the time of the General Conference of 1960.

Throughout the debate over the jurisdictional system and the position of Negro congregations within The Methodist Church, the constitution has been—to the distress of some and the satisfaction of others—a stabilizing influence, forestalling any sudden action. It has restrained the General Conference, even if it were so minded, from changing at any one session the basic structure of The Methodist Church.

The Episcopacy and District Superintendency

A closely co-ordinated administrative structure and a feeling of connectionalism were characteristic of Methodism from its early history. In this it stood in contrast to the opener, congregational-type denominations such as the Baptist and Presbyterian. After 1940 a number of factors joined to strengthen this characteristic. Church union created a denomination of great size, composed of diverse elements which needed to be welded together. Educational programs and financial objectives had to be formulated for a denomination with forty thousand local churches. At the same time people were becoming more mobile, money more plentiful, and the challenge of the secular culture more impelling. Under the pressure to get the united church functioning effectively and quickly, the logical procedure seemed to be to expand the organizational structure, and this was done sometimes with more enthusiasm than discretion. Commissions were appointed, responsibilities assigned to various offices, staff personnel and budgets enlarged.

From the beginnings of Methodism in America the episcopacy, or general superintendency, has been a cornerstone firmly established. Around it Methodist life and organization have revolved since 1784. As union was being considered in the twentieth century there was no question even from the Methodist Protestants as to the continuance of the episcopacy in the new church. The office was carefully set forth in the new constitution, which conserved the "plan, powers, privileges, and duties" of the episcopacy existing in both of the larger uniting churches. The only change was in the manner of election and consecration, which was to be by the Jurisdictional Conference instead of the General Conference. This revision, small as it may seem, did have significant results. The attachment of the bishops to the jurisdiction rather than to the

General Conference tended to make the episcopacy more regional in both interests and loyalty, even though many denied that this was necessarily so. Perhaps the clearest illustration of this came in 1954. At that time the Council of Bishops adopted a statement commending the Supreme Court of the United States for its school desegregation decision and urging compliance by all citizens. However, the bishops of the Southeastern Jurisdiction abstained from voting to support this resolution and later let it be known that they were not in harmony with it.

According to the constitution all of the bishops, whether from Jurisdictional or Central Conferences, were members of the Council of Bishops. This body, which met semiannually, had the responsibility to plan for the general oversight and promotion of the temporal and spiritual interests of the entire church. It is not easy to document the extent of leadership which the council exercised in the two decades after 1940. Nevertheless, the pronouncements issued by it—the quadrennial Episcopal Address to the General Conference and the briefer statements released annually or semiannually—set before the church emphases and points of view which the council believed to have more than ordinary importance. These opinions had a profound influence on legislative enactments of the General Conferences, the policies of the church press, the work of the church boards, and the preaching of Methodist ministers. Members of the council never publicly discussed the differences in outlook and the tensions which occasionally existed within it.

The quadrennial Episcopal Address was intended to represent the viewpoint of the entire Council of Bishops. The bishop chosen to write and deliver it generally found it a weighty responsibility because of the diversity of views on some points. The usual procedure was to outline the message, seek counsel from many people on the topics to be discussed, and then present a preliminary draft to his colleagues. On controversial issues—and there were such in each quadrennium—sharp debate would occur, and the writer would revise the document until by the time of the General Conference it would carry the support as well as the signatures of all of his colleagues.

During the 1950's there was increasing awareness of the hazard of regionalism or, as some said, provincialism, in the leadership of the church. Two plans, quite different in nature, were proposed for broadening the contacts between the bishops and the whole church and for giving them more of a world perspective. One type of opportunity, conceived by Bishop G. Bromley Oxnam, was provided through the Board of Missions and the Commission on Promotion and Cultivation. They arranged episcopal visitations, often of two or three months' duration, to various mission fields, the expectation being that each bishop would make two such trips during each quadrennium. In the course of a decade most bishops thus traveled to every continent and became acquainted with the church in many cultures. To be sure, these extensive travels of the bishops outside the country brought considerable criticism from ministers and laymen who felt that the bishop should remain in and administer his own area. The second device for stretching episcopal horizons was to bring recognized authorities in world and national affairs before the semiannual meetings of the Council of Bishops to speak on matters of world import, frequently without direct reference to religious implications. The give-and-take in these semiannual meetings, in which administrative goals and problems for the next year or quadrennium were discussed, was also an integrating experience.

The Commission to Study the Jurisdictional System urged in 1960 an additional method for making the bishops once again seem to be bishops of the total church. This was part of its proposed constitutional amendment, which would facilitate the transfer of bishops from one jurisdiction to another and also provide for their consecration at the General Conference. This effort failed with the rejection of Amendment XII.

While the description of the episcopal office did not change in the twenty years, and in fact was essentially the same as a century earlier, the emphasis of the bishops' work was shifting. Whereas formerly they were expected to be first of all outstanding preachers, evangelistic or prophetic, more and more the bishops were judged by their administrative skills—although this was not necessarily the basis on which they were elected. A major portion of their time came to be consumed in attendance at meetings of general boards, interagency committees, institutional boards within their own area, and the executive and financial committees of these agencies. In a large proportion of such meetings the bishop was the presiding officer and was looked to for leadership. In addition, he had his own area to administer, cabinet meetings to preside over, appointments to make, sermons to deliver, and buildings to dedicate.

Few ministers or laymen in an Annual Conference could realize how crowded was the datebook of their bishop, for they tended to see him in only one of his many administrative roles. As the church grew larger and its board structure more complex, the bishops became increasingly administratively involved. Scarcely any program throughout the church could be effective without episcopal backing.

The office of bishop has been recognized as the highest position in The Methodist Church, and ministers have felt that no greater honor could be accorded them than election to it. However, the once unparalleled authority of the bishop was within the two decades subtly and indirectly challenged by other centers of power. The bishops themselves

were becoming aware of this. Prior to church union the right of the
bishop to appoint a preacher to a pastoral charge was almost unrestricted.
In the North he was expected to consult with the superintendent of the
district in which the charge was located, and in the South he was required to "announce openly to the cabinet his appointments" before the
official declaration of his assignments. This latter provision appeared in
the 1939 *Discipline*. In 1940 the General Conference stipulated that
"before the final announcement of appointments is made the District
Superintendents shall consult with the Pastors when such consultation
is possible." [22] In 1953 an Annual Conference by vote requested the
Judicial Council to interpret the meaning of the word "consult." The
decision makes explicit the restriction on the power of appointment and
the involvement of the district superintendent in the making of the
appointment:

It is therefore the decision of the Judicial Council that while the final
authority in appointing preachers to their charges rests upon the presiding
Bishop, it does not relieve the District Superintendent of the responsibility of
consulting with the preacher in order to ascertain whether there are any reasons
why the appointment should not be made. Therefore, the final reading of the
appointment of preachers to their charges must be preceded by consultation of
the District Superintendent with the preacher. [23]

It had generally been assumed that the bishop determined the program within his own area. Increasingly in the new church the development of quadrennial emphases set a pattern which each bishop was
under obligation to follow. Toward the end of the 1950's several of the
bishops complained more or less openly that the responsibility for setting
the goals in church work was moving from the bishops to the large co-
ordinating bodies of the church—the Council of Secretaries and the Co-
ordinating Council.

A fascinating aspect of the office of bishop was that, apart from the
relatively few regulatory paragraphs in the *Discipline*, there had never
been a codification of their responsibilities. For example, it was widely
recognized that there were unwritten procedural rules involved in transferring a pastor from one area to another, yet even the bishops were not
in full agreement as to what these were. A number of churchmen, including a few of the bishops, thought that the office might benefit from
a thorough and objective study.

The next level of authority, subordinate to the episcopacy, was that of

[22] *Discipline*, 1940, ¶ 332.1.
[23] Judicial Council Decision No. 101, 1954 *General Minutes*, pp. 633-34.

the district superintendency. In contrast to the bishops, who were organized into the Council of Bishops, the superintendents have never operated as an authority group, except perhaps as they acted in a cabinet under a bishop. The superintendent derived authority directly from the bishop who appointed him. The position of bishop carried greater prestige, but his contact with local churches was more tenuous and much less frequent than that of the superintendent. Actually, the superintendent has served as the vital link in what Methodists call their connectional system.

Between 1940 and 1960 there was a steady enlargement of the duties assigned to the district superintendent. In the main, general boards as well as bishops regarded him as their contact man and expected him to push the official or connectional program. Like the bishop, and like many executives in secular society, the district superintendent found himself increasingly engulfed in administrative detail. While some men enjoyed this, others did not fit the role temperamentally, and many returned to the pastorate before they had served the maximum term of six years in the office. A recent study in which two thirds of the superintendents participated showed that the average superintendent was a member of the governing board of sixteen or more agencies, while a fourth of them were members of as many as twenty-two boards.[24] On most of these the superintendent was expected to carry considerable responsibility. Yet this was only one aspect of his administrative load. He was concerned with the program and progress of every church in his district and supervised the work of the pastors. In some cases, notably in the Central Jurisdiction, the average number of pastoral charges per district was less than twenty-five, but in the North Central Jurisdiction the average was fifty-six. While nearly all superintendents recognized the importance of their work, and most of them found it rewarding, a significant number of them seemed baffled by the variety and extent of their specific, time-consuming obligations. Keeping the organization functioning made it difficult for them to serve in the historic role of being a pastor to pastors and to devote time to long-range planning and church extension, so essential for the growth of the church in a mobile society.

Toward the end of the 1950's more attention was being given by the bishops and by the Commission on Promotion and Cultivation to instructing the novitiates in the superintendency in various aspects of their work. Yet half of the superintendents felt that they had received little

[24] Murray H. Leiffer, *Role of the District Superintendent in The Methodist Church* (Nashville: Parthenon Press, 1960), pp. 113-15.

aid from their bishop and that they were not well prepared for the office when they were placed in it. In the complicated organizational network of The Methodist Church the "D.S." was becoming more than ever the key man, as more than one of the bishops remarked. He was the chief coordinator, promoter, and trouble shooter, just above the charge level.

The General Boards and the Council of Secretaries

Prior to unification each of the three branches of Methodism had its own board structure. In the united church these boards—and especially their principal executive officers, who together constituted a Council of Secretaries—achieved an even greater prestige and authority. Stimulated by the size of the church, the possibility of greater financial support, and the opportunities for extending their work, the staffs of many of the boards recommended expansions of their fields of work and additional personnel. Generally the boards approved these proposals.

With the addition of boards, commissions, and departments, each eager to justify its existence, program planning and concern for promoting the work of the denomination tended to move from the local church, district, and Annual Conference to the national offices. For the average church member a great gulf existed between these extremes, and requests, plans, and programs seemed to descend from a mysterious, nebulous headquarters.

This complex organizational machinery was perhaps needed, if a great church was to function smoothly and influence the world, but it could have effective power behind it only if a substantial part of the Methodist membership felt that the work of the boards was their business too. The task of interpretation was not easy and was achieved only in small measure. This was illustrated in two church-wide studies. One, of the Board of Temperance, made it plain that even district lay leaders and a large number of the pastors were unacquainted with the four-fold purpose of that board and unaware of the disciplinary provision of the church on abstinence.[25] In another study, carried on by the Boston University School of Theology, less than fifty per cent of the sample of five thousand church members indicated that they looked to general church boards or publications for "some" or "much" guidance and leadership in areas of social responsibility.[26]

[25] Lay Leaders and Ministers Look at the General Board of Temperance of The Methodist Church (Evanston: Bureau of Social and Religious Research, 1958), pp. 92-93.
[26] S. Paul Schilling, Methodism and Society in Theological Perspective (Nashville: Abingdon Press, 1960), p. 299.

Each board had an elected or appointed membership, made up of one or more bishops elected by the Council of Bishops and ministers and laymen generally elected by the Jurisdictional Conferences. The board was required to meet at least once a year and had an executive committee which met at more frequent intervals. The primary functions of a board were to lay down general policies, to employ the executive secretary and perhaps other staff members, to establish the budget, and to receive reports of the work done.

In its careful study of the general agencies of the denomination, the Church Survey Commission in 1952 enumerated certain "major weaknesses . . . with respect to membership." Board committees were too large and met too often, considering matters that could be handled by staff and thus wasting travel expense money. Members generally neglected to report back to their constituency on board meetings. Sessions tended to be devoted to items pertaining to the particular agency, with too little attention to their relation to the total program of the church. A criticism frequently voiced by staff members as well as others was that most board members attended the meetings but did not speak up.

The primary reason for the existence of boards seemed logically to be to serve the local church. Yet laymen as a rule were scarcely aware of them. As the denomination grew in size, the task of maintaining liaison between the general boards and the local church became more difficult and at the same time more essential, both for the sake of the local church, which needed to feel that it had a vital relationship to the total church structure, and of the staff itself, which should be reflecting in its program the interests and requirements of its basic constituency.

Taken together, the general boards of the church constituted one of the most important centers of administrative authority and of program designing. Naturally they sought to maintain a close contact with the bishops and superintendents in each section of the church, so that their work could be effectively implemented and also so that their financial support would be secure.

In order to co-ordinate the promotional efforts of the various World Service agencies, a Council of Secretaries, consisting of the chief executives of each of the general boards and agencies, was established in 1940. It was enjoined to harmonize educational and promotional work and to eliminate duplication and competition. More detailed instruction concerning promotion and correlation was given by the General Conferences of 1944 and 1948. The secretaries were to co-operate with the bishops, district superintendents, pastors, and other church officers in keeping the total membership aware of the entire benevolence and educational work.

When in 1952 the Commission on Promotion and Cultivation was created, it took over the promotional responsibilities previously assigned to the Council of Secretaries, but the council continued under a mandate which specified its membership and simply stated that it should "meet periodically to consider matters of common interest and co-operation among the several boards and agencies . . . [and] report annually to the Council of Bishops and to the Council on World Service and Finance." [27] The General Conference of 1956 hopefully stated that the Council of Secretaries should "consider existing and emerging conditions and needs where the co-operative services of two or more agencies are needed, and devise ways and means of meeting those needs." [28] So it was that the council became one of the permanent administrative and planning agencies working with the Council of Bishops and the Co-ordinating Council to develop long-range objectives and programs for the total church.

Development of Quadrennial Emphases

The war, so far as the United States was concerned, was less than a year old when in August, 1942, the Council of Bishops convened the members of the Commission on World Service and Finance, the executive committee of the Woman's Division of Christian Service, and the Council of Secretaries, to ponder the world situation and Methodism's part in it. Out of days of discussion came a program called the "Crusade for Christ," which was presented to the 1944 General Conference. The report began with the sentence, "Christianity is never more creative than in an era of crisis," and it included five interlocking sections, one of which read in part, "The tragic and appalling world situation faced by the followers of Jesus Christ at this hour needs no amplification to the members of this General Conference. Never before has so much sorrow, desolation, and utter destruction come to so many peoples. The world awaits the healing touch of Christ upon its misery and desolation." [29]

The first of the five aspects of the crusade was "the crusade for a new world order," calling for critical study by church members of the international plight and the need for establishing world law and order. The second involved a proposal to raise $25 million to be used to alleviate the suffering of war victims and to extend the work of the church in foreign lands and at home. The last three were a call for a spiritual renaissance

[27] *Discipline*, 1952, ¶ 1598.
[28] *Discipline*, 1956, ¶ 1595.
[29] *Daily Christian Advocate*, May 2, 1944, p. 25.

within the church, a challenge to more serious stewardship, and a plea for increased attention to the church school.

With detailed planning and with zeal this program was initiated. The financial goal was surpassed, and the church as a whole experienced a sense of dynamic achievement. So effective was the crusade, which had been designed as a campaign of fourteen months' duration, that toward the end of the quadrennium a new program called "The Advance for Christ and His Church" was devised and presented to the 1948 General Conference. This too was enthusiastically adopted, and an Advance Committee authorized. By 1952 the idea of a quadrennial emphasis had been so generally accepted that provision for its continuance was written into the law of the church. The newly created Commission on Promotion and Cultivation took over the promotional work of the Advance Committee and of the Council of Secretaries. The General Conference placed on the new Co-ordinating Council the obligation in consultation with the Council of Bishops and the Council of Secretaries to "formulate and present to the General Conference . . . plans for a unified, ongoing program for the church, including long-range objectives." [30] While the responsibility for long-range planning was assigned to various councils working co-operatively, it was common knowledge that the basic suggestions generally came from the Council of Bishops which, as one of them remarked, "has to carry much of the program anyway."

With the passage of the quadrennia, the emphases became more extensive, until in 1960 they were about as diverse and far-reaching as the total program of the church. The ones proposed at that time included evangelistic outreach by personal witness; establishment of new church schools; claiming the inner city for Christ; meeting the challenge of small churches; recruiting youth and adults for Christian vocations; proclaiming the Lord Jesus Christ to university and college students; serving him through Christian social relations in the family, in public and private morality, through Christian brotherhood, by working for world peace, and in industrial life; intensifying missionary obedience; and, last but not least, faithful stewardship. Practically every agency had a stake in the endeavor. While the program was adopted by the 1960 General Conference without important dissent, and while no delegate contested the significance of any item which was included, there was a widespread feeling among members of the conference that all of the aims of the church were included. To emphasize them all was, as one man said, like playing a Beethoven symphony fortissimo throughout.

However, in spite of the proliferation of emphases and the feeling that the idea of a quadrennial emphasis was being overworked, no one

[30] *Discipline*, 1952, ¶ 1115.

could doubt that the great "forward" movements of preceding quadrennia brought direction and stimulation for the life of the church. That they also brought in increasing benevolence funds was abundantly clear. General benevolence apportionments were set at a higher level, but far more significant in terms of financial undergirding was the response to the plan for Advance Specials, which permitted a local church to select a particular project to which it would give money over and above its apportionment. In its first year of operation—1948-49—this device yielded about $2 million through these special gifts and the Week of Dedication offerings. Ten years later it produced about $13 million, $5 million of which was kept for special causes within the Annual Conferences.

Under the Commission on Promotion and Cultivation a unified plan of benevolence promotion was developed which set before the entire church the composite picture of its many benevolence agencies. The commission was as much concerned to educate the membership as to raise money to support the work, on the reasonable theory that financial objectives cannot be attained unless Christians see the full implication of their faith in action.

An important educational medium created by the commission was the quadrennial District Superintendents' Conference. To it were invited all district superintendents throughout the United States for a four-day convocation in the autumn following the General Conference. At that time the benevolence program which was to be stressed in the coming four years was presented in detail. Members of the Council of Bishops, secretaries of World Service agencies, and others spoke, and samples of the informational materials, literature, and visual aids were supplied. These meetings were without question excellent promotional opportunities and resulted in more effective co-operation on the part of superintendents in furthering the benevolence program in the churches of their districts.

The Co-ordinating Council

The establishment of the Co-ordinating Council in 1952, at the urgence of the Church Survey Commission, demonstrated the profound concern of the General Conference for more efficient functioning of the total organization of the church. This council was not designed to promote any benevolence program; it had no employed staff and prepared no educational literature. However, it was assigned a broad administrative task: to "study the general organizational structure of The Methodist Church and recommend to the General Conference such changes as it considers essential to maintain effective and economical operation." [31] If requested by a general board or an Annual Conference, it was required to review questions of overlapping in activity or lack of co-operation among general agencies and to suggest means of resolving these. It was to recommend to the General Conference, after conferring with the Council of Bishops and the Council on World Service and Finance, the number and timing of all special days to be observed on a church-wide basis. In consultation with the Council of Bishops and the Council of Secretaries, it had the task of formulating and presenting to the General Conference plans for a unified program for the church, including long-range objectives.

The council was also asked to consider the plans of any general agency which proposed to acquire real estate or erect a building and, judging in terms of the best interests of the church, to approve or disapprove the project. A disapproval would delay action until the matter could be reviewed by the next General Conference. This review procedure was established in order that the total church should have some control over the expenditure of large sums for real estate and buildings by its agencies, since such expenditures almost automatically determined the permanent location of such boards and agencies.

The council displayed restraint in exercising the broad powers which had been assigned to it and reluctance to initiate any studies of the structure of the church. However, in 1956 it did recommend that there be no increase in the size of membership on the various boards. Such was the prestige of the council that although several boards wished enlargement, the General Conference supported the council's recommendation. That conference also instructed the council, in co-operation with the Boards of Temperance, World Peace, and Social and Economic Relations, to present a plan for uniting those three agencies at the next General Conference. The council, working on this difficult assignment, which involved problems of organization and location as well as of personnel and traditional vested interests, prepared a detailed legislative proposal for a new and inclusive Board of Christian Social Concerns, which was accepted by the General Conference of 1960 in spite of strong opposition at particular points by some members in each of the uniting boards.

The creation of the Co-ordinating Council and the Commission on Promotion and Cultivation in 1952 roused criticism in a number of quarters on the ground that it increased the complexity of the church structure. On the other hand, a fairly clear division of responsibilities seemed to be emerging among the several administrative authorities.

[31] *Ibid.,* ¶ 1115.2.

Long-term, church-wide program planning continued to rest definitely with the Council of Bishops, the Council of Secretaries, and the Co-ordinating Council.[32] The secretaries with their staffs, under the direction of the general boards, carried the responsibility for detailed development of the church-wide programs. The general promotion of the unified program was the province of the Commission on Promotion and Cultivation. The Co-ordinating Council theoretically at least looked over the work of all the general boards and agencies and was prepared to untangle snarls if any should develop.

The General Conference stood in the background as the chief legislative body of the church. It received reports and, acting on recommendations, established new organizations and approved the quadrennial programs. But throughout the twenty years an interesting change was taking place. The General Conference seemed to be increasingly a body which authorized, sometimes with alterations, programs and plans developed by the established boards and councils and by special quadrennial commissions. This was particularly noticeable in the General Conference of 1960 where, although there was often lengthy debate, all the recommendations of the Co-ordinating Council, the Council on World Service and Finance, the Commission on Promotion and Cultivation, and the Commission to Study the Jurisdictional System were approved almost without change. Consequently there was concern in some quarters that the enlargement of the General Conference to fourteen hundred members, as proposed in the defeated constitutional Amendment XII of 1960, would increase the tendency of the General Conference to be simply a ratifying body.

The Ministry

Minimum standards for acceptance into the Methodist ministry had varied from one Annual Conference to another within the uniting denominations. In general, southern conferences had been somewhat more lenient in accepting into membership men with a high school education or perhaps one year of college. Especially in the rural areas—in both North and South—lay people and superintendents were inclined to feel that a conviction of a "call to preach" and a strong evangelistic fervor were the important qualifications for the ministry, and that to prevent a man who possessed them from entering into conference membership

[32] The distribution of authority among these councils for this task was not clear. The legislation seemed to place the primary responsibility on the Co-ordinating Council.

might be a direct flouting of God's will. To be sure, the traditional Methodist determination that the minister should continue to read and study survived in all three branches of the church, and certain requirements as to a course of study and examinations on reading were enforced with varying degrees of strictness.

After unification there was pressure from various sources to work toward uniform minimum standards on a level somewhat higher than had been maintained in certain areas. In 1940 there was no statement in the *Discipline* as to the minimum education required for admission to a conference on trial. The newly created Commission on Courses of Study for Ministers—renamed Commission on Ministerial Training in 1944—gave thoughtful attention to the motley provisions and prepared legislation to present to the 1944 General Conference, making the equivalent of graduation with a Bachelor of Arts degree from an approved college a prerequisite for admission on trial to an Annual Conference. To render this acceptable, it was necessary to include two provisos, permitting conferences by a three-fourths vote, and "under special conditions," to accept candidates with somewhat less academic preparation. However, the point had been made, and the General Conference was on record as favoring a formally educated ministry. It even voted for the statement: "It is expected of all candidates for the ministry that they shall complete a four-year college course of study leading to a Bachelor of Arts degree or its equivalent, and complete a course leading to the Bachelor of Divinity, or an equivalent degree, in one of our schools of theology." [33]

The Commission on Ministerial Training initiated a program offering educational opportunities for men who lacked academic background, and these were encouraged to enroll and work steadily to prepare themselves for professional advancement. Included were short courses during the summer in theological seminaries, one-week pastors' schools, and correspondence courses. The supply pastors, specifically those who were interested in a full-time career in the ministry but could not qualify for conference membership, became something of a cause during the 1940's among those disapproving higher educational requirements. There was some indignation over the limitations imposed on unordained local preachers in their administering the sacraments of baptism and Communion and performing the marriage ceremony. Strong effort was exerted for a time to secure for the supply pastors the right to vote in Annual Conferences. As the general prosperity of the country increased, however, and with shortage of ministers and rising salaries, supply

[33] *Discipline,* 1944, ¶ 322-23.

pastors found it easier to get the schooling necessary for admission. Further, educational attainment rose rapidly in the general population, especially after World War II, and the importance of a well-educated ministry became clearer.

The commission also received an assignment at the time of unification to study the whole problem of ministerial supply—rates of retirement, present and future adequacy of new recruits, most effective methods of enlisting ministerial candidates, and so forth. A report presented to the General Conference of 1944 [34] showed that in spite of a net gain in membership of almost three million, The Methodist Church in 1943 had approximately four thousand fewer effective ministers than did the three predecessor churches combined in 1910. When it was stated that within ten years approximately one third of all effective ministers then in service would be dead or retired, the entire conference gasped in shocked surprise. The seriousness of the situation was pointed up by the fact that according to the United States Census of 1940, half of all clergymen were older than 45.8 years. The median age for active Methodist ministers in 1943 was even higher, 49.0 years. In comparison, the median age for physicians, who must spend more years in professional training, was 44.1 years, and for lawyers and judges, 42.0. Only one small group of professional men, the veterinarians, had a higher median age—50.1 years—than the clergymen.

Evidently the church had not been devoting enough attention to ministerial recruitment and training. Impressed by the report and by an impassioned plea from Mrs. J. D. Bragg, president of the Woman's Division of Christian Service, the conference requested that the study be continued and urged that an adequate program of recruitment and training be developed. After that date an important act of each General Conference was the reception of a report on ministerial recruitment and theological seminaries.

In 1948 more liberal financial support for theological education through the benevolence program of the denomination was ordered. The same General Conference also established an Interboard Committee on Christian Vocations, to co-operate in developing "effective methods of selective recruiting for the ministry."

In 1952, partly as a result of the Church Survey, the Section of Ministerial Education—later a department—was established within the Division of Educational Institutions. Included in its responsibilities was supervision of the Conference Course of Study, pastors' schools, and correspondence courses. Another and rather delicate task was that of

[34] Murray Leiffer, "A Study of Retirement and Recruitment in the Methodist Ministry" (Chicago: The Methodist Publishing House, 1944).

increasing co-operation among the Methodist seminaries and strengthening their relation to the department and to the Board of Education. The department was aided in this by the new flow of funds coming through it to the seminaries from the World Service treasury. Certain scholarships and fellowships were established, to be awarded yearly by the department to students nominated by the seminaries.

In 1956 two new theological seminaries were authorized, bringing the total to twelve. One of these, the National Methodist Theological Seminary in Kansas City (renamed the Saint Paul School of Theology in 1961), opened its doors in 1959, and the other, the Methodist Theological School in Ohio, in 1960. Enrollment in Methodist seminaries increased steadily for more than a decade, although at the end of the 1950's it was leveling off. In the autumn of 1960 it was 3,210, twice the number in 1941-42. Yet in spite of the fact that there had been a steady upward trend in the number of persons graduating with the ministerial Bachelor of Divinity degree—in 1960, 601 from Methodist theological schools plus about 250 Methodists from non-Methodist schools—the needs of the church were far from met. The minimum number required annually to replace those retiring, dying, or leaving the ministry for other reasons was estimated to be twelve hundred. The sad fact appeared to be that considering its increased size, the church was doing only slightly better in recruiting in the latter part of the 1950's than twenty years earlier. However, the median age of ministers was slowly dropping, particularly in those Annual Conferences which had developed a vigorous program of recruitment.

A colorful and dramatic phase of ministerial history after unification was the campaign to secure clergy rights for women. Ordination for women had been possible for many years, and there were regularly to be found a few women pastors serving as accepted supplies in small or isolated charges which otherwise might not have had a minister. The fact that conference membership was closed to them because of their sex was a source of irritation to many church women, and the radicals among them had attempted to arouse support for equal rights but with very little success. After unification the effort was renewed with vigor. At the General Conferences of 1944, 1948, and 1952 memorials flowed in, requesting the opening of Annual Conference membership to women. In 1948 a secretary of status of women had been added to the officer list of the Annual Conference Woman's Society, and in 1952 the flood of memorials on this subject from local-church Woman's Societies was impressive. At each conference, however, the Committee on Ministry voted nonconcurrence, and the conference accepted its judgment, even though a minority report was presented and spiritedly debated.

By 1956 the battle was won, and a floor debate was hardly necessary. A sentence was ordered to be placed in the *Discipline* reading, "Women are included in all provisions of the Discipline referring to the ministry." [35] Everyone—or almost everyone—felt better, having become convinced that there would be no rush of women to apply for admission, and this proved indeed to be true.

The Local Church

The structure of the pastoral charge was not altered basically after unification, but in the first two decades it experienced a few interesting changes. Certainly it came to occupy a position of greater prominence in the law book of the church, the *Discipline*. In the first two *Disciplines* after unification, 1939 and 1940, legislation concerning the local church was placed at the very end of Part IV, which dealt with all conferences— General, Jurisdictional, Central, Annual, and so forth. Other data on local church organization, such as the conduct of its educational program, the administering of its property, and the work of many of its committees, were scattered in various sections. It was as though the *Discipline* had been designed primarily for use of the administrative officers of the entire church and the board secretaries. In 1944 this was changed, and a section dealing with the local church, bringing all relevant materials together, was given a conspicuous location immediately following the constitution.

Each general board or agency sought to have a matching committee in every local church, on the theory that its cause would be sure to receive attention. In 1944 it was specified that every pastoral charge was to have a Board of Missions and Church Extension, a Board of Education, a Committee on Hospitals and Homes, and, if desired, Committees on Evangelism, Temperance, and World Peace. All of these were in addition to the required Quarterly Conference and official board, with their various committees. While this elaborate organization was feasible in large churches, the smaller ones felt that they were heavily burdened and insisted that there was not enough leadership available to man all the committees. As a bishop remarked, the legislation had "much the appearance of being an attempt to put the armor of Saul on little David."

Many memorials were sent to the General Conference of 1948 requesting simplification of the structure of the local church. A result was the appointment of a Commission on the Study of the Local Church. The report which it brought to the General Conference of 1952 was adopted with few changes. The governing body of each charge, the Quarterly

---

[35] *Discipline*, 1956, ¶ 303.

Conference, was required to establish four commissions: Membership and Evangelism, Education, Missions, and Finance. Provision was also made for two optional commissions: Worship, and Social and Recreational Activities. In 1956 the latter was dropped, perhaps because it had no sponsoring general board, and an optional commission on Christian Social Relations was substituted. The work of these commissions was outlined in some detail, and each of them was linked directly or indirectly with a general board of the church. In addition, there were many committees reporting either directly to the Quarterly Conference, which met at least two times a year in every charge, or the official board, which in most places met monthly. The study commission evidently did not feel free to carry its work far enough to suggest the elimination of all overlapping, as between the official board and the Quarterly Conference, with their sometimes duplicating committees and reports.

A further change occurred in 1960, in conjunction with the creation of a general Board of Christian Social Concerns to replace the former Boards of Temperance, World Peace, and Social and Economic Relations. A fifth required commission, on Christian Social Concerns, was added to the basic structure of each local church, moving this aspect of Christian interest out of the optional category.

The average local church since unification was kept more aware of its denominational ties, in part because of the activities of its own commissions and the relation of these groups to the general boards, and in part because of the efforts of district superintendents, who visited every charge at least once a year bringing the total denominational program to the leaders of the congregation. The fact that the number of small churches decreased and the average size rose considerably within the two decades also permitted stronger lay leadership and fuller organization.

The Educational Program

Over the years after unification the Board of Education brought onto its staff an increasing number of trained men and women to reorganize all aspects of the Christian educational program. It began at once in 1939 to review the study courses for children and adults and to revise and rewrite texts and magazines. Beginning with 1947, the Curriculum Committee worked to develop what might be called "policy papers"—theological and educational statements to guide those writing church school literature.

The Commission on Education of the local church was instructed by the *Discipline* to "see that the literature used is appropriate for each class and group, and that it is selected from the literature approved by the Curriculum Committee of the General Board of Education." [36] Audio-visual materials were also to be in harmony with standards set by the general board. This pressure for the use of good, approved materials met with increasing response as the two decades passed. It was abetted by the fact that the district superintendent asked at the Quarterly Conference of every charge whether Methodist church school literature was used.

The high birth rate after World War II greatly crowded many church schools, especially in the children's departments. The very pressure of numbers forced church school leaders to improve facilities and look for better educational methods. This gave extra impetus to the Board of Education in its efforts to improve the training of church school teachers. The board had been given a general mandate at the time of unification to "provide programs for the training of pastors, teachers, officials, and others in the work of the local church, and promote these programs through various types of training schools, correspondence work, . . . educational conferences, councils, assemblies, and other meetings." [37]

Leadership training classes for Sunday school teachers who wished to become more proficient were a time-honored institution in Methodism. After unification the new Board of Education took hold at this point and gave concentrated attention to the promotion of Christian workers' schools in all areas, with the goal of having one within reach of every local church. Attendance gradually rose, with 161,000 reported in 1959.

A development after 1950 was the initiation of laboratory schools, where teachers learned through participation in actual teaching situations under skilled leadership. During 1959, 248 such schools were held in various parts of the United States. This project, originally started for the teachers of children, was later expanded to include workers with youth and adults. The church school extension program, inaugurated to meet the needs for religious education in defense-plant communities and other areas of rapid change, was continued after the war as a service to rural and small churches.

The training of very young children under Christian auspices was a matter of concern to the Division of the Local Church, as well as to many pastors and parents. A few churches carried on a program of religious education for kindergarten and first- or second-grade children in connection with weekday schools conducted by the church. This type of service was offered in some of the privileged suburban churches, where parents

---

[36] *Discipline*, 1952, ¶ 225.3.
[37] *Discipline*, 1940, ¶ 1123.

were anxious to have their children associate with others of their own age under Christian supervision. More numerous were the through-the-week nursery schools and kindergartens set up by local churches and church-sponsored settlement houses to help care for children of working mothers. The movement of married women into factory and office employment during the war created a need which the churches could meet in only a small part. The high standards for day nurseries set by state and local laws made such projects expensive to operate, and not many churches could afford them.

Unification brought an important innovation in youth work in The Methodist Church. The activities and programs for youth which had been promoted by a number of boards were gradually co-ordinated. The Methodist Youth Fellowship, incorporating all aspects of youth work except that with college students, was constituted in 1944, and every local church was expected to have such an organization to include all persons between twelve and twenty-three years of age. In 1960 the maximum youth age was dropped to twenty-one, in recognition of the earlier maturing and the high mobility of young people and the frequency of youthful marriage. In churches of sufficient size three subdivisions were advised—each with its own Sunday school classes, evening meetings, and other projects—for children of junior-high-school age, for senior-high-school youth, and for post-high-school and older youth groups.

In this area of church work, as in public education, there was much experimentation and an effort to keep the program "person centered." The youth must be understood first and the materials adapted to his capacities. Accordingly, the youth departments of the Editorial Division and the Division of the Local Church furnished quantities of materials designed to stimulate young people and their counselors to develop their own programs and projects. The "ready prepared" lessons of an earlier period were no longer in favor, and the staid *Classmate* was transformed into a paper which spoke the high-school students' language. Its color, art, and contents whistled to the youth of the 1960's.

In the area of work with youth the Board of Education of the newly united church inherited a rather difficult problem from its predecessors in the North. In 1934 young people in the Northern Church had organized a National Council of Methodist Youth. This was autonomous, and its only relation with the Board of Education was through the counseling of some of the board staff members. Two of these were later dismissed, perhaps because they were considered economic and social radicals. As a result, the youth who had followed their leading became cool toward the organized boards of The Methodist Church. The Methodist Episcopal Church, South, had established a Commission on Youth Crusade, which was continued in 1939 by the united church but not by the 1940 General Conference. No mention was made of either of these youth groups in the 1940 *Discipline*.

After unification, and in consultation with members of various interested boards, Methodist young people organized the National Conference of Methodist Youth, which proved to be a stimulating and effective force in the life of the church. Joseph W. Bell, who was active as a youth in the National Council and later became a staff member of the Board of Education, wrote: "There was even considerable suspicion by the new National Conference of Methodist Youth, following unification, of some of the major boards and agencies of the church and an attempt on the part of the National Conference to be an entity unto itself. It attempted to speak on various issues and to stimulate action in various areas. Much of this was very worthwhile effort." [38]

A special nation-wide youth conference under the sponsorship of the Board of Education was held over the year-end 1947-48, known as the Methodist Youth Conference. This was planned as youth's part in climaxing the Crusade for Christ, and brought together about eleven thousand Methodist youth and representative adults. At this dramatic assembly the new program of the Board of Missions providing three-year terms of service in various mission fields for youth was announced. Through sympathetic and patient work by the Board of Education, the suspicions of the National Conference of Methodist Youth were gradually removed, and many of its leaders became active in the program of the board. In 1952 there was a complete *rapprochement* and it became, by action of the General Conference, officially a part of Methodist structure under the sponsorship of the Division of the Local Church and the Division of Educational Institutions.

At first the National Conference of Methodist Youth had included college students among its members, but this group found its own special interests occupying more of its attention. After several years of consideration it was agreed to form two organizations—one for the Methodist Youth Fellowship and one for the Methodist Student Movement, which was limited to college students—and to dissolve the National Conference of Methodist Youth. This was accomplished at the General Conference of 1960.

The growing interest in wholesome family relationships and family counseling was reflected in the educational program of Methodism. In 1945 the Department of the Christian Family of the Division of the Local Church was organized. Beginning with 1948, each local church

---

[38] Quoted from a personal letter to the author.

was asked to observe National Family Week early in May. The first Sunday of the month was designated as Childhood Sunday. A magazine, *The Christian Home,* was published and leaflets and audio-visual materials prepared.

Since the early days of the camp meetings Methodists have appreciatively linked outdoor experiences with religious instruction and inspiration, so it was not surprising that a camp program came into full swing in the 1950's. By 1960, 222 church campsites were in use, valued at $16 million. Most of them were owned by Annual Conferences; forty-six had been acquired between 1956 and 1960. There was a rapid rise in attendance by all age groups, and family camps for parents and children became particularly popular. Demand for camping and week-end planning conferences and retreats expanded beyond the summer months, and in response facilities were in many instances winterized and placed on a year-round basis.

Adult educational work was traditionally stronger in the Methodist Episcopal Church, South, where the adult department of a church school often had as large an enrollment as the children's department. Two trends in adult education were noticeable during the 1950's. The first was a growing interest on the part of middle-aged and older persons in Bible study and the theological foundations of the Christian faith. A second trend, especially in the larger urban churches, was the increasing awareness of the needs of older persons. The rising number of those past sixty-five years of age and their concentration in older sections of the city created a new opportunity for a specialized ministry on the part of local churches. "Golden Age," "Borrowed Time," and "Sunset" clubs, welcoming nonchurch as well as church people, met a warm response from retired persons, who enjoyed the constructive activity and fellowship.

The interest of church leaders in audio-visual facilities and techniques was greatly stimulated by the development and widespread popularity of television. In 1948 in the United States there were only 200,000 television sets; by 1959 there were 48,500,000. This tremendous new influence on the thinking of people could not be ignored by the church. A commission to co-ordinate audio-visual services was authorized in 1948. By 1952 it was made an independent agency: the Radio and Film Commission. Four years later the title was changed to Television, Radio, and Film Commission—"Trafco," as it came to be called. A staff of competent professional people, working closely with the other boards and agencies of the church, produced an increasing flow of motion pictures and filmstrips for use on television and for distribution to churches.

In the three years from 1956 to 1959 there was an impressive output of thirty-four sound filmstrips and motion pictures for church use, five thirty-minute radio devotional programs for the armed services, six hundred TV spot announcements, and twenty-six "talk-back" films. The talk-back programs constituted a genuine innovation in television procedure. Each of them consisted of a twelve- to fifteen-minute dramatic film dealing with a real-life problem, followed by a discussion of the issues presented in the film by a panel of local ministers and laymen. The total program was kept within a thirty-minute compass and was telecast in its entirety. The intent was to stimulate groups meeting in homes and churches to continue the discussion at the end and seek the Christian answer to a difficult question.

It was in the summer of 1956 that the National Fellowship of Methodist Musicians was organized, with 110 charter members. The Board of Education, which had for the preceding quadrennium been responsible for formulating standards for directors of music in local churches, gave its blessing and moral support in the hope that the new society would improve the caliber of music in the local church. Within four years the new organization had grown to fifteen times its original size, with members in every state as well as several foreign lands. A department of Ministry of Music was created within the Division of the Local Church, with a full-time director to co-ordinate this work. The Editorial Division developed a new magazine, *Music Ministry*, for use by choirs and church musicians.

In its effort to improve standards of training and performance for directors of Christian education and directors of music, the Board of Education devised a system of certification based on professional training in the chosen field, demonstration of ability to do satisfactory work, and evidence of Christian character and concern. The board maintained rosters of persons who met these requirements and assisted local churches in obtaining properly prepared personnel. Unfortunately the number of qualified people was generally short of the demand.

Increasing Lay Leadership

The Protestant principle of the priesthood of all believers received strong support when Methodism was united. This was one of the most important contributions of the Methodist Protestant Church, which from its founding insisted on the rights of laymen in all aspects of church work. In the preceding decades the two larger denominations had begun to give more attention to this subject. The Southern Church had established a general Board of Lay Activities, with auxiliary boards in Annual Conferences, and had elected lay leaders in every district. The Men's

Brotherhood movement had grown in the Northern Church, where responsibility for promoting men's work had been placed with the Board of Education. In all three branches of Methodism women's organizations had long been among the most active groups in the local church. Yet except in the Methodist Protestant Church, laymen had exerted little influence in the higher echelons of the denomination.

After 1939 the part played by laymen in the life of the general church was gradually augmented. For example, lay delegates elected by the Quarterly Conference of each charge became full members in the Annual Conference, a status which they did not have in the former Methodist Episcopal Church. They were given equal rights with ministerial members, except that they could not vote on matters dealing with ministerial qualifications and relations. Practically all Annual Conference and General Conference committees and commissions were, after unification, composed of an equal number of laymen and ministers. This gave the laity a larger voice in the business of the conferences, and they began to participate somewhat more actively in discussions on the conference floor. However, even two decades after unification, the ministerial members did most of the talking.

In the new church laymen were also represented on approximately an equal basis on the general boards; in some cases, counting ex officio delegates from women's and youth organizations, they actually outnumbered the ministers. They were increasingly elected to staff positions formerly held by ministers, such as treasurer, editor, or public relations officer. Lay people were in 1960 the executive heads of five major agencies of the church: the Boards of Evangelism and Lay Activities, the Methodist Publishing House, the Woman's Division of Christian Service, and the Division of National Missions. Two of the three associate general secretaries in the Board of Christian Social Concerns were also laymen.

A general Board of Lay Activities was created by the united church "to deepen the spiritual life of the laymen of the church." The mandate to the board presumably included women as well as men, but in point of fact very few church lay leaders and even fewer on the district and conference level were women. The program of the Board of Lay Activities was frankly directed to men. Through the Annual Conference and district Boards of Lay Activities it sought to organize Methodist Men clubs in local churches, which corresponded to a certain extent with the Woman's Societies of Christian Service. The practice of chartering such Methodist Men clubs was initiated in 1942. By 1952 there were 4,800 and by 1960, 13,500 chartered clubs. These were the major channel through which the board reached the men of the church, supplemented by its literature—notably the magazine *The Methodist Layman*—and various audio-visual materials.

Much less control by the general board was exerted over Methodist Men clubs than by the Woman's Division over Woman's Societies. Many of the former were primarily social in nature, although in 1959 over half of the clubs within the Northeastern, South Central, and Western Jurisdictions reported that they were active in conducting every-member canvasses in their own churches as part of the emphasis on stewardship. About a fourth of them conducted projects for youth, and a fourth various evangelistic endeavors.

The general board, which employed a staff in 1960 of seven men, five of them laymen, had two departments: Stewardship and Finance, and Methodist Men. Its annual budget during the quadrennium 1956-60 was over half a million dollars, about one third of which came from World Service funds. In co-operation with other boards—Evangelism, Education, and Missions—it conducted district schools of stewardship. It also promoted, and through its conference boards helped to organize, simultaneous every-member canvasses in groups of churches. Its 1960 report to the General Conference claimed: "We have had sufficient experience in a large enough number of churches now to state with assurance that if a church will follow our program it will have from a minimum of 20% to 100% or more increase in giving to the program of the church the very first year it is used . . . [and] a deepening of the spiritual life of the church as a result of this program." [39]

National Conferences of Methodist Men were held in 1954 and 1957, with a registration of almost four thousand on the latter occasion. Lay speaking also received attention increasingly as the years passed. The purpose was to train and encourage laymen to conduct services and prayer meetings if asked by the pastor, and especially to provide preaching services where no pastor was available. All Methodist churches were requested to observe Laymen's Day each October, when the worship services were in many instances conducted by laymen.

Yet in spite of all the work of the board and of thousands of loyal lay leaders, only a small minority of the adult male members participated in the organized men's work in a local church. Among those churches with Methodist Men clubs, the average reported membership of the clubs ranged from twenty-five in the Central Jurisdiction to fifty-five in the South Central in 1959. Of course, it must be kept in mind that not much more than 40 per cent of the total Methodist membership consisted of men and boys.

As many a Methodist pastor would testify, the most active organiza-

---

[39] *Quadrennial Reports, General Conference, 1960,* p. 469.

tion within the local church was the Woman's Society of Christian Service. Practically every church had one. The total dues-paying membership in 1960 was more than 1,800,000, including 130,000 members of Wesleyan Service Guilds, an organization for employed women which met in the evening.

The Woman's Society, created in 1940, represented a complete realignment of the church work and interests of women, which had been divided among Ladies Aid Societies and a variety of missionary societies and boards in the uniting denominations. It was a closely knit organization, with supervising officers at each conference level, beginning with the Woman's Division of Christian Service in the Board of Missions and reaching to the local church society. A complete pattern of organization for a local society was given in the *Discipline,* calling for a set of officers and secretaries matching the structure of the Woman's Division. Through its literature department the division made available detailed descriptions of officers' duties, program suggestions, and large quantities of supplementary materials; and each local secretary was expected to send in quarterly reports covering her work to the corresponding secretary on the next higher level—the district—who in turn sent her report to the next. With this close organization and communication from top to bottom levels, the women of the church were without question the best-informed segment of the denomination's membership. While obviously not all women participated actively in the program designed for them, the fact that more than one in three of the women members of the church was a pledging member of the Woman's Society demonstrated the effectiveness of the organization.

The success of the program for women in missionary education and churchmanship is illustrated by the fact that in the year 1959-60 local church societies sent to the Woman's Division for its program about $10 million. In addition other sums were raised for local projects, such as a payment toward the general budget of the local church, redecoration of the parsonage, or a contribution for the local hospital.

An interesting illustration of the growing influence of laymen in the life of the church came during the General Conference of 1952, in connection with the struggle over the Church Survey Report. A General Conference committee of six was appointed, three representing each side in the controversy, to evolve a compromise plan by which as much value as possible might be salvaged from the report. Five of these six persons were laymen, chosen because of their ability and recognized position in the church. This same committee was later asked to iron out conflicts which arose in connection with the report of the Quadrennial Committee, which made recommendations concerning the emphases and program of the church. In these and other ways, the leadership skills of lay men and women were increasingly utilized throughout the church, to the great advantage of the denomination.

Publishing Interests

With Methodism's characteristic emphasis on the printed word and the heritage of a strong publishing interest in each of the three uniting churches, it is no wonder that under the stimulus of unification the publishing activity of the church burgeoned. Sales grew fivefold, to almost $26 million, during the two decades, and net income increased over $1 million by 1959-60. The capital assets in that year stood at $21 million. From its inception this publishing business had a broad mandate: to disseminate religious knowledge and to promote Christian education. Any profits beyond those needed for the development of the business were, by church law, to be appropriated to supplement the pensions of retired ministers. This annual contribution rose steadily until in 1955-56 it reached $600,000.

An early task of the Publishing House, in co-operation with the Editorial Division of the Board of Education, was the improvement and co-ordination of church school publications. Instead of the fifty-five periodicals used by the uniting churches, a series of twenty-four were published in 1942. Church school periodicals published in the first three months of 1960 totaled almost six million copies.

Abingdon Press (originally after unification Abingdon-Cokesbury) was the book publishing division of the Publishing House. It became one of the major book publishers of the nation, issuing by 1960 about a hundred new titles each year in addition to publishing the *Discipline, Hymnal,* and *Book of Worship* of the church. Two and a half million volumes were printed in 1959-60. Most of them had a direct bearing on the church and religious life: Bible study, sermons, church history, theology, books of inspiration and meditation. Considerable attention was given to children's books.

A notable publishing achievement was the editing and printing of the twelve-volume *Interpreter's Bible.* Only a firm with large resources could have run the risk of producing a work which cost around $2 million. The first volume appeared in 1951 and the last in 1957. The venture was cordially received by the entire Protestant community, and by 1960 more than a million volumes had been sold. No sooner had this undertaking been completed than an editorial board was appointed to prepare the *Interpreters' Dictionary of the Bible,* and over three hundred scholars began work on this four-volume set. Abingdon also brought out a line of paperbacks under the imprint Apex Books, reprints of popular works on religion and the Christian life.

Upon unification the *Christian Advocate* became the official paper of The Methodist Church, combining seven predecessors. The *Central Christian Advocate* was a companion publication for members of the Central Jurisdiction. After years of debate over ways of increasing the circulation of the *Advocate,* a proposal was brought to the General Conference of 1956 to launch a new magazine for the Christian family, designed in a popular style to compete with the "slick-paper" magazines. The new periodical, called *Together,* was given strong episcopal support, and many a church undertook to subscribe for every family on its rolls. Circulation by 1960 was an impressive million copies. The *Christian Advocate* then became a magazine for pastors and other church leaders. The *Central Christian Advocate* was continued to serve its special constituency. The scholarly *Religion in Life* was published quarterly with the aid of a substantial subsidy.

Back of the vast publication enterprise was much shrewd business know-how. The six printing and manufacturing plants which were in operation at the time of unification were over a period of years consolidated into two plants, one in Cincinnati and one in Nashville. The organizational structure was likewise streamlined. Instead of two publishing agents, one a minister and one a layman, the General Conference of 1952, on request of the Board of Publication, approved a single administrative head who was designated the president and publisher. The subordinate organization for administration consisted of two associate publishers, an executive vice-president, and five vice-presidents—all of whom were appointed by the president and confirmed by the board. The editors were elected quadrennially by the Board of Publication to serve the following special areas of publication: the *Central Christian Advocate,* the *Christian Advocate, Together,* books, and *Religion in Life.*

Nashville became the headquarters for practically all the work of the board except certain editorial functions connected with *Together* and the *Christian Advocate.* In 1957 the board erected a modern office building and printing plant in that city at a cost of $2.5 million. By 1960, 2,221 employees were on its payroll.

With the aid of a management consulting firm the Publishing House in 1959 projected the requirements of the church, insofar as publishing facilities were concerned, for the next fifteen years. As a result, six regional service centers for books and church school periodicals were established. Associated with each of these were two or three retail bookstores, with more retail outlets anticipated. The old Methodist name of Cokesbury was applied to the retail sales divisions and the bookstore outlets.

The unification of Methodism served as both catalyst and stimulant in the reorganization and development of the boards and agencies of The Methodist Church. The availability of increased resources and the opportunity to tackle old problems in a new way, to broaden the program and extend the outreach of the church, resulted in two decades of discussion, compromise, and building. The Methodist Church of 1960 was clearly the lineal descendant of the unification that took place two decades earlier. But its structure was more complicated, its personnel greatly enlarged, and its whole approach—whether in work on the mission field or in revamping the Publishing House—more sophisticated, fully alert to events in the secular world. Whether this same organizational vitality would be continued in the next decade, and whether it would be reflected in augmented spiritual leadership, was a matter of conjecture.

4

Outreach in a Changing World

The tradition of social concern, characteristic throughout Methodist history, was so deeply embedded in the uniting churches that it was bound to call for thought and action even though major attention had to be directed to making necessary adjustments in the new church, perfecting its structure and increasing its internal cohesiveness.

This concern for the world beyond itself was clearly shown in the developing missionary program of the new church. It was also reflected in a growing support for Methodist institutions which had a community outreach—its schools and colleges, hospitals and homes, and the chaplaincy. Finally, The Methodist Church could not be indifferent to the many crucial social issues of the mid-twentieth century, even though its members usually did not speak with one voice.

The Changing Missionary Picture

The nature of missionary work in other lands, as well as at home, underwent considerable modification in the two decades following 1940, due to changes in the world situation and in the church itself. The rapid rise of the spirit of nationalism in Asia and Africa, the ending of western colonialism in many sectors, the extension of Communism to China, and the appearance of Communist colonialism—these and other closely related factors vastly altered the world picture and inevitably affected missionary activity. Some countries, notably mainland China, were closed to American missionaries; others, such as India, Angola, and Indonesia, sharply restricted their entrance. Rising nationalism was tied with the demise of the myth of white superiority and with an increasing resentment of colored peoples against the domination of the white race. The evolution of socialistic political and economic systems in most of the emerging states tended to heighten the tension with so-called capitalistic nations and missionaries who came from them. There also was an astounding expansion of population in these newer countries, resulting in part from the lowered death rate and the various types of assistance from such sources as the World Health Organization, the Food and Agriculture Organization, and the Point Four program of the United States.

A revitalization of the non-Christian faiths of the Orient was a natural result of the people's unwonted pride in their own cultural heritage. The once passive attitude of Oriental religious leaders was replaced by a lively interest in gaining converts. This new dynamism, especially noteworthy in Islam and Buddhism, forced Christian missionaries to realize that they could no longer win adherents simply by good works and a program of social service. The missionary had to be able to defend his own theological beliefs in an atmosphere which had ceased to be gratefully tolerant and had become probing, critical, and frequently antagonistic.

The disorganization of missionary work occasioned by World War II and the insistence on cultural integrity within erstwhile "missionary lands" convinced most missionaries and board executives of the need to develop indigenous leadership at every level of the Christian enterprise. One criterion of missionary success came to be the encouragement of local leaders who would be competent to administer the schools and all other activities of the church in their own lands. Increasingly responsibility for the work in India, Southeast Asia, the Philippines, Japan, Latin America, and Africa was turned over to indigenous leadership. In Brazil, Korea, and Mexico the Methodist Church became autonomous though affiliated with the American church. While Christian workers from the United States continued to be assigned to these lands, they were generally there at the request of, and often under the direction of, indigenous church executives. This added a new dimension to the problem of missionary selection. As Eugene L. Smith, general secretary of the Division of World Missions, pointed out: "Missionaries live under highly developed paternalism of boards, while the churches they serve are sensitive and resentful to paternalism on the part of missionaries. The tendency of the paternalism in board relationships [is] to attract some candidates who are temperamentally incapable of mutuality in human relationships." He pointed out that a "question of great importance and complexity is whether in the future mission boards are to be the administrators or donors of gifts." [40] More and more the function of the missionary was to give aid to Christians on an interchurch basis rather than to bear testimony to non-Christians. Indigenous workers were considered more capable of extending the Christian enterprise than were those coming in from outside the country.

The uniting of the three branches of Methodism was most opportune from the standpoint of effectiveness in the missionary endeavor, which became progressively more difficult under world conditions of the 1940's and 50's. One advantage was that it was no longer necessary to distinguish in an Oriental country between the personnel and organizations of the Methodist Episcopal Church, South, and those of the Northern Church. Perhaps it was significant that in 1952 the Division of Foreign Missions was changed to Division of World Missions by the General Conference, a tardy recognition of the fact that there are no "foreigners" in the church of Christ.

Important for the support of missions was the establishment in 1948 of the Advance for Christ, a program to educate Methodists concerning the needs of the world and to stimulate giving to the benevolence agencies of the church. Under this program Advance Specials were provided for; local churches, districts, and Annual Conferences were encouraged to raise funds beyond their regular apportionment for a particular work on the approved project list. This might be the Union Theological Seminary in Manila, the building of a church in the Congo, or the support of a missionary in Sarawak. The Advance Special program encouraged more personal contact between the missionary on the field and the church people at home. It also proved an excellent means of raising supplemental funds. In 1959-60 receipts from this source by the Division of World Missions—approximately $6 million—constituted more than half its total income.

At the close of 1959 there were 1,108 missionaries of the Division of World Missions and 447 from the Woman's Division of Christian Service

[40] "Changing Patterns in the Christian World Mission," a paper presented at a consultation of Methodist theologians at Glen Lake, Michigan, June 27-30, 1957 (unpublished).

engaged in various aspects of the Christian enterprise outside the United States and its territories. In 1940 the comparable figures were 545 and 655. The biggest increase for the Division of World Missions came in the 1950's. These figures do not reflect the scope of the missionary recruitment program, because there was constant need to replace those who changed to other branches of religious work or who retired. More than a few women who began work for the Woman's Division married other missionaries and transferred to the Division of World Missions.

The missionary work conducted by the Woman's Division of Christian Service, one of the integral parts of the Board of Missions, was extended after unification. In 1960 the division maintained major programs—with more than five missionaries in each field—in the Congo, Liberia, Mozambique, Algeria, Southern Rhodesia; India, Pakistan, Burma, Malaya, the Philippines, Sarawak; Japan, Korea; Argentina, Bolivia, Brazil, Cuba, Mexico, Peru. Their work was chiefly with women and children—in evangelism, in the conduct of schools and hostels, and the operation of hospitals. In 1958 an ordained missionary of the Woman's Division, Miss Gusta A. Robinett, was made a district superintendent in the Sumatra Annual Conference, the first woman to hold this position in The Methodist Church.

Methodism's dual approach to missionary work—that is, by the Division of World Missions and the Woman's Division of Christian Service—can be understood only in the light of the role of women in American society and in The Methodist Church. The only way in which they could have an effective voice in setting missionary policies and programs in any of the uniting churches was through establishing their own missionary agencies parallel to those of the general churches. Even in the united church it is doubtful whether they would have had much administrative leadership if they had not continued to control the raising and spending of their own funds. Developments in the postunification period seemed to promise a continuation of this separation for years to come. At some times and places, especially on the mission field, there was rather serious misunderstanding and tension, in spite of the fact that organizationally there were many co-ordinating committees and that always presumably the intent was to be mutually helpful.

The United States itself has been considered a mission field by the church from the time of Francis Asbury. Each of the uniting churches had agencies which were brought together to form the Division of Home Missions and Church Extension—renamed the Division of National Missions in 1952—under the Board of Missions of the new church. Like the Division of World Missions and the Woman's Division of Christian Service, it operated essentially as a separate board, with its own execu-

tives, budget, program development, and channels to the Annual Conferences and local churches. The heads of all three divisions had equal
standing. Policy decisions and other plans formulated by the divisions
were reviewed at the annual meetings of the total board, but were rarely
challenged.

The Division of National Missions was hard pressed to keep up with
the opportunities for service which opened before it. Over the years its
work expanded and its staff was enlarged. Within the Section of Home
Missions the Department of Town and Country Work continued its
interest in the small church, the rural community, and towns and cities
of under ten thousand population. The heavy flow of people to cities
placed additional responsibilities on the Department of City Work. Not
only did new and different problems develop in the inner city, with
changes in nationality and racial composition and with extensive renewal programs, but the growing suburban population required special
attention and planning. At this point the two departments had an overlapping concern, especially in light of the fact that the unincorporated
places within the metropolitan areas were experiencing the most rapid
growth. Under departmental definitions these were rural people, but in
terms of cultural orientation they were among the most urbanized in
America. This conflict of interest was not resolved in either board structure or program.

The well-known Goodwill Industries was a third department in the
Section of Home Missions. It was an outgrowth of the program at Morgan Memorial Church in Boston, which gave work to and helped in the
rehabilitation of the physically handicapped. By 1960 this department
had aided in establishing Goodwill Industries in 141 cities, 17 of them
outside the United States. Many of these were considered Methodist institutions, but others preferred a nondenominational status with only
a marginal tie to the parent organization, from which they derived their
name and the basic idea of employing and rehabilitating handicapped
workers. In 1958 twenty million hours of employment were provided by
the Goodwill Industries for such people. The Department of Negro
Work was dropped after a decade of service, since Negroes no longer
wished to be designated as a group requiring a special ministry. The
other departments of the division included in their programs work with
Negro, Indian, and other minority groups.

While some research and survey work had been carried on within
various departments, it was not until 1948 that a Department of Research
and Survey was established under the Section of Home Missions. Year
by year the demand grew for its help in analyzing trends and in counseling concerning church planning and placement. As several of the

church boards began to develop research programs of their own, need for co-ordination was recognized. To deal with this emerging problem of overlap, the General Conference of 1960 requested the Co-ordinating Council to name one of its members who, with the director of the Department of Research and Survey of the Board of Missions and the director of the Department of Research and Statistics of the Council on World Service and Finance, should name and convoke an Interagency Committee on Research. This interagency committee brought together research personnel from various boards of the church and the seminaries to set up standards for conducting research, to review and evaluate research programs, and to minimize duplication.

The Section of Church Extension was a second major part of the Division of National Missions. Like its predecessor agencies it had primary responsibility to give counsel and financial aid in building new edifices for worship, education, and also parsonage use. It performed three main services. It granted donations and made loans to churches undertaking a building program. During the 1950's approximately $4 million annually was allotted to local congregations, about two thirds of it in the form of loans. Donations during the quadrennium 1956-60 exceeded $5 million, while loans exceeded $11 million—more than all the capital funds available for lending to churches in 1940.

The second service was giving architectural advice. With each year more congregations took advantage of this help. In 1959, 686 churches submitted building plans for criticism and approval.

The third, and by 1960 the most important, aspect of the work of the section was assisting local churches in fund raising. Members of the staff, on request, worked with the pastor and lay leaders to prepare a plan for an intensive financial and spiritual "crusade" to raise money for a building program. From 1956 to 1960, 1,356 such crusades brought in a total of almost $100 million.

Under its Department of Work in Home Fields, the Woman's Division also carried forward numerous home mission projects. These included the maintenance of a number of schools, most of them in rural areas, for persons who might otherwise lack educational opportunities. In 1960 it was responsible for ten elementary and senior high schools and three junior colleges. It gave partial support to eight senior colleges, most of them in the southern states or in the Caribbean. The division also maintained Christian education workers in rural areas and operated a number of social settlements in urban areas of underprivilege. It supported several homes for children and four residences for retired deaconesses and missionaries. Staff personnel for these agencies were almost entirely women, a considerable number of them deaconesses. This division, like the Division of National Missions, was faced with difficulty in securing a sufficient number of trained and consecrated leaders for its varied projects and in keeping accreditation for its educational institutions.

Higher Education

Throughout the history of their church Methodists have been concerned for education. Wherever they went they established colleges as well as churches. This urge did not diminish after unification, although its expression underwent considerable change because of educational developments in the nation. Because of financial problems, a few church secondary schools and colleges were forced to close their doors, but the large majority were strengthened in faculty and endowment. Physical plants were improved and enrollments climbed.

Prior to the Second World War a college education was the expected thing for young people from upper-income homes and a relatively small number of exceptionally competent or ambitious young people who could obtain scholarship help or earn their own expenses. But by 1945 the public attitude toward higher education was changing significantly. The GI Bill entitled young men and women who had performed military service in the war to as much as four years of college or graduate training with tuition paid and allowances provided, including extra stipend if a man were married. Millions took advantage of this opportunity and swelled the enrollments of colleges and universities until these were operating at more than maximum capacity.

In the next fifteen years state, municipal, and federal tax-supported colleges and universities expended billions of dollars for buildings. Whole new campuses were constructed and faculties greatly enlarged. By 1960 a college education was coming to be considered the right of every young person who had the intellectual ability to meet the standards. By the autumn of 1960, 38.4 per cent of the eighteen- and nineteen-year-olds were enrolled in a high school or college, compared with 29.4 per cent only ten years earlier and 28.9 per cent in 1940. Approximately one fifth of those who were twenty and twenty-one years of age were attending school. This was almost 30 per cent of the young men; there were far fewer young women, since many dropped out when they married.[41]

A school without accreditation had increasing difficulty in securing students, but accreditation meant the maintenance of high standards:

[41] Bureau of the Census, *Current Population Reports,* Series P-20, No. 107, January 16, 1961.

a good library, excellent science halls and laboratories, competent faculty. In their search for funds for these purposes, a few of the educational institutions founded by The Methodist Church wished to escape the denominational tie. An example of this was the University of Southern California. In 1928 the Annual Conference which had controlled it granted permission for a change in the charter to make the board of trustees self-perpetuating. In 1952 the university exercised this privilege and broke away from the conference, removing all reference to The Methodist Church from its charter, in order, it was stated, to gain support from Los Angeles for its medical school.

In spite of such losses, the educational outreach of The Methodist Church was impressive. In 1960 eight universities, twelve graduate schools of theology, seventy-seven senior colleges, and twenty-one junior colleges had Methodist ties, although in a few cases the relationship was rather tenuous. Of these, only two senior and two junior colleges were unaccredited, compared with thirty-four unaccredited Methodist colleges in 1940 and twenty in 1950.

This interest in higher education was demonstrated by the General Conference of 1956 when it created a special quadrennial Commission on Christian Higher Education—with correlated commissions in every Annual Conference—and besought greater concern for this subject as part of the quadrennial emphasis of 1956-60. A larger proportion of the benevolence dollar was appropriated for higher education than ever before, and Annual Conferences were urged to raise more money for the higher educational institutions of the church within their areas. A distinctive departure from precedent occurred when the conference voted to give a total of $1 million during the quadrennium toward the establishment of a School of International Service in American University, located in Washington, D.C.

Concern for the spiritual development of the mounting number of Methodist students in colleges and universities caused the Division of Educational Institutions of the Board of Education to give more attention to a program for the campus. An evidence of this was the creation in 1956 of a Department of College and University Religious Life. At unification the entire church had adopted the pattern of establishing Wesley Foundations at state and non-Methodist colleges and universities for the purpose of ministering to the religious needs of Methodist students—a pattern developed by James C. Baker at the University of Illinois prior to his election to the episcopacy in 1928. A program for "accrediting" Wesley Foundations was initiated in 1952 and by 1960, 181 were qualified. The department also maintained contact with 120 Methodist and 335 other units of the student Christian enterprise of which the Methodist Student Movement was a part. It was estimated in 1960 that approximately 16 per cent of the 3.5 million college and university students—not including junior colleges—were "Methodist preference."

A definite philosophy of student work had been developed over many years. It assumed that the department's function was to reach the future leaders of the nation, to stimulate their thinking and help them discover for themselves the meaning of the Christian faith for all phases of life. There was considerable experimentation in program, including social and recreational activities, seminars, retreats, and social service or action projects. Especially in the latter part of the 1950's healthy theological disputations and witnessing on the campus became an approved pattern. A survey made in 1960 showed that an overwhelming majority of the student organizations had Bible study programs. There was a concurrent awakening of interest in the subject of Methodism and the Wesleyan revival and greater use of the Wesley Orders of Common Prayer. The earlier stress on social and recreational activities and on the importance of numbers seemed to be in at least temporary eclipse.

Outreach in Social Services

The Methodist Church and its predecessors evolved over many decades an amazing array of institutions to minister to the needs of people. These ranged from seven-day-a-week churches and social settlements in the cities, with their programs for boys and girls as well as adults, to hospitals and homes for the ill and the elderly. Most of the agencies of The Methodist Church were involved in some form of social service ministry.

There were seventy-six Methodist hospitals in 1960, located in twenty-nine states. Only eight had been established after 1940. Eighty-five hospitals were founded by other Protestant denominations in the decade from 1950 to 1960, but only two by Methodists. The executive secretary of the Board of Hospitals and Homes pointed out that in the same period 105 hospitals, with a total of more than 26,000 beds, were built by the Roman Catholic Church. While the board favored accepting government subsidies in establishing and operating hospitals, many Methodists were reluctant to have church agencies accept such grants from public funds.

More progress after 1940 was made in the development of homes for the elderly. Of the ninety-six operating in 1960, only thirty-seven had been established prior to church union, and many of these had increased their capacity substantially after that date. The interest in building these homes was a logical result of the growing percentage of the population sixty-five years of age or older. The changing family pattern and the old-age insurance program stimulated and also made possible this program by which persons after retirement could maintain their independence with full security. It was estimated that in 1960, 1,250,000 members of The Methodist Church were sixty-five or over, but as of that date Methodist homes for the elderly could accommodate only 8,732, not counting the eight homes for retired ministers which had a capacity of 656.

Forty-four Methodist homes were maintained for children, with a capacity of almost four thousand. Only one of these was opened after 1940. Evidently there was a decreasing need for most types of children's homes. The long waiting lists of couples eager to adopt babies seemed to indicate that the usefulness of the old-style orphanage was disappearing. However, homes for troubled children and for boys and girls from broken families were in short supply. Some Methodist homes for children were being adapted to meet this growing need.

A total of 236 Methodist hospitals and homes—most of them sponsored and financed by an Annual Conference or a private corporation subordinate to it—were affiliated with the Board of Hospitals and Homes at the beginning of 1960. Generally these agencies operated under their own boards of trustees, but relied on the general board as consultant and aid in securing certain classes of personnel for their staffs. The assets of these institutions totaled almost half a billion dollars and their operating costs for the year 1960 were about $184 million.

Mention should also be made of the residences for business women, located in a few of the major cities, and of the two homes for unmarried mothers, one in Louisiana and one in Texas. The ministry of The Methodist Church to those who were ill or lonely or in need of special help reached from one side of the nation to the other.

Concern for Social Issues

Methodists have never been afraid of taking stands on controversial issues when they believed that Christian moral principles were involved. John Wesley's opposition to the slave trade and to smuggling was an early instance of this. Another was Bishop Francis J. McConnell's campaign in 1919 to convince the public that the twelve-hour day in the steel industry was morally wrong, and therefore management had to find a more humane program for scheduling its work. As he remarked on another occasion, "To be a Methodist is to put things strongly."

The Social Creed of the Methodist Episcopal Church stated clearly and simply the principles which it believed should govern the relations between employers and employees as well as other groups in society.

This Social Creed, expanded to cover many phases of human relationships, was adopted by the Uniting Conference. It underwent further revision as fresh insights were gained into old problems and as new issues confronted society. The depth and insistence of Methodist concern was demonstrated in the organization of agencies—the Board of Temperance and the Commission on World Peace—to promote Christian attitudes in social relations and also by the excellent programs in this area carried forward by the Board of Education and the Woman's Division of Christian Service, which co-operated closely with the "social action" agencies.

TEMPERANCE

No denomination in the United States was historically more forthright in its approach to the liquor traffic than Methodism. There was full agreement among the uniting churches that a Board of Temperance should be included as one of the agencies in the new denomination. It continued to exert an effective influence in the next two decades, as approach and strategy were revised to meet altered conditions.

During the 1940's drinking patterns changed considerably in the United States. The consumption of beverage alcohol rose on a per capita basis and the number of drinkers increased. The practice of serving liquor in homes and at public functions became commonplace. Among some social classes it became the expected thing. Drinking on college campuses was at first a problem for the school administration and then often reluctantly tolerated. Many a pastor admitted with chagrin that some of his respected church members had cocktail bars in their homes.

Faced with this situation, the Board of Temperance revamped and broadened its program. The four major emphases around which its work was organized after 1952 were: (1) Education. Between 1956 and 1960 the staff conducted twenty regional briefing conferences for Annual Conference and district leaders, and eight nation-wide week-long schools of alcohol studies for youth and adults. It shared in interboard training programs for local church leaders; furnished speakers for hundreds of meetings; held consultations in every Annual Conference; developed films and displays to educate youth and adults, Methodists and non-Methodists, on temperance problems. Staff members visited colleges and seminaries to lecture and hold seminars.

(2) Commitment. A logical outcome of temperance education is commitment, and local churches were invited to participate in an annual Commitment Day. The emphasis, which in 1956 and earlier had been on abstinence from alcohol, was broadened to deal with other social evils such as pornography, gambling, and narcotics. A commitment card was provided on which Methodists could indicate their determination to op-

pose these evils. Perhaps reflecting the temper of the period, there was more reaction on the part of some pastors and lay leaders against this emphasis than any of the others.

(3) Rehabilitation. As the number of alcoholics rose in the nation, the board decided it had a moral obligation to study the methods of rehabilitation and to offer guidance to pastors and other interested workers. It developed leaflets giving counsel concerning alcoholism and assisting families to understand the problems of an alcoholic member.

(4) Legislation and Community Action. While the board dropped the use of the word "prohibition," it continued its efforts to defeat the liquor interests in local option campaigns and the opening of new stores. It supported legislation to provide clinics to aid alcoholics and to stop the serving of liquor on airplanes.

In the latter part of the decade the board turned its attention in greater measure to fighting the use of narcotics, the distribution of salacious literature, and the public complacency concerning gambling.

After unification any person entering the Methodist ministry was required to indicate his willingness to abstain "from all indulgences, including tobacco, which may injure his influence." Scores of memorials urged the dropping of this requirement at every General Conference from unification through 1960. While it was evident that Methodists were divided in their opinion on the matter, the rule continued in effect.

There was also considerable opposition to the requirement, instituted in 1952, that "only morally disciplined persons . . . with special reference to total abstinence from alcoholic beverages" should be elected to membership on the official board of a church. But once the rule was accepted, the opposition was not strong enough to dislodge it.

PEACE AND WORLD ORDER

The conviction which was widely held throughout America following World War I, that all war was evil, was shared by the Methodists of the combining churches. War was morally wrong, and its preachers were expected to say so. One of the duties of a preacher, as listed in the 1938 *Discipline* of the Methodist Episcopal Church, South, was "to preach at least once each year on world peace, the evils of war, and the evils attendant upon compulsory military training in schools and colleges."

A Commission on World Peace, continued in the uniting church according to the pattern existing in the Methodist Episcopal Church, soon was involved in the swirling forces of World War II. The efforts of the government to gain the full support of its citizens for its program of defense, and the traditional teaching of the church that the Christian should obey the laws of the state, caused conflict of conscience in light of the equally deep concern of the Christian for world peace.

In 1940, when the war had already begun in Europe, and after much debate, the General Conference adopted a Statement on Peace and War which read in part: "The Methodist Church, although making no attempt to bind the consciences of its individual members, will not officially endorse, support, or participate in war." It further stated that "those of our members who, as conscientious objectors, seek exemption from military training . . . or from military service . . . have the authority and support of their Church." [42] Only a minority of Methodist young men claimed exemption as conscientious objectors in the days of conscription which followed, but the church through its commission gave them moral support.

The conviction that absolute loyalty belongs to God alone, and that the universal Body of Christ transcends all divisions of race, nation, and class, resulted in the addition of a statement in the Social Creed concerning the church and war in the year 1944, at the height of the conflict: "We stand for these propositions: Christianity cannot be nationalistic; it must be universal in its outlook and appeal." [43] The leaders of the church were urged, on theological grounds, to work for the establishment of an international organization and the limitation of national sovereignty. The lengthy resolution on conditions of peace which was adopted at the same session dealt with such far-ranging subjects as the treatment of enemy nations, colonial administration, and the legitimate aspirations of dependent peoples. All churchmen were urged to study the bases for a just and durable peace.[44]

But the General Conference was not all of one mind, and these resolutions carried only after heated discussion and with a large minority opposition. A prior attempt to adopt a stronger statement against war, in which there was brilliant debate between Ernest Fremont Tittle and Lynn Harold Hough, was defeated by a small margin.

In 1952 the Commission on World Peace was given additional status and support and renamed the Board of World Peace. Its functions continued to be much the same: to educate the Methodist constituency concerning the conditions for peace and to organize effective action for its advancement through the church. In line with the resolutions adopted by succeeding General Conferences, it opposed compulsory military training and supported youth who took a conscientious objector's position.

[42] *Discipline*, 1940, ¶ 1716.
[43] *Discipline*, 1944, ¶ 2010.15.
[44] *Ibid.*, ¶ 2015.

Whether in periods of war or of quasi-peace the commission—later the board—sought to bring a critical Christian judgment to bear on the conflicts which developed between nations, to replace propaganda with reliable information, prejudices with good will.

ECONOMIC ISSUES

In looking back to the opening of the twentieth century, it is interesting to observe that the ethical concern of the church was directed almost entirely to economic issues. Consequently when the first Social Creed was adopted in 1908, it dealt principally with such issues as hours of work, employment of women, child labor, one day's rest in seven, and the right of collective bargaining.

The conviction of many Methodist leaders that Christian doctrine carried important implications for the work life of society did not diminish with the passage of the years. Perhaps it was because of the existence of the Methodist Federation for Social Service—an unofficial organization dating from 1907—which sought "to deepen in the church the sense of social obligation . . . and to promote social action in the spirit of Jesus" that no official agency was created by the church to deal with economic issues. However, especially during the years immediately following World War II, when Senator Joseph McCarthy and the Un-American Activities Committee of the House of Representatives were most zealously seeking out "subversives," this organization came under sharp attack. It had from the start been avowedly liberal and "left of center" in its economic and social theories, but it was then accused of being radical and Communist-tinged, and was even included in the proscribed list of the House Un-American Activities Committee. Furthering the attack on it was another unofficial organization, the Methodist Circuit Riders, a group of determined, conservative laymen centered chiefly in the South. The relation of the Federation to The Methodist Church was discussed at length at two General Conferences, and finally in 1952 it was asked to remove the word "Methodist" from its name. Although its officers consistently denied the charges against it—and these were not substantiated—the organization, which was never large, gradually lost support.

This controversy led to the proposal, recommended by the Church Survey and adopted by the General Conference of 1952, that an official Board of Social and Economic Relations be established. This would have a broad membership, elected by the jurisdictions, representing various economic and social views. It would speak on behalf of the church —although, according to the *Discipline* no person, paper, or organization had the authority to speak officially for The Methodist Church except the General Conference—and carry on a program of education and social action.

This new board was, for its members as well as in its wider contacts, a debating and educational organization, concerned with three important fields: economic life, race relations, and civic and social welfare. A basic feature of its work was the assembling and distributing of reliable information on controversial issues. To this end the writing of a number of books, some of them based on group research and discussion, was sponsored, and the arguments on various sides of issues were frankly stated. Equally important were the regional and national conferences organized by the board. In the 1956-60 quadrennium, many Industrial Relations Seminars were held, dealing with such topics as "The Responsibility of the Church in Industrial Life," "An Effective Ministry in the Industrial Parish," and "Agricultural Economics." The effort was to bring together clergy and laity, leaders of management and of labor, the consumer and producer, to acquaint them with the viewpoints of others and together to hew out a Christian way of coping with tough economic problems.

In 1958 the board, in co-operation with six other general agencies of the church, set up a National Industrial Relations Conference on "The Church in a Working World." A highlight of the conference was the celebration of the fiftieth anniversary of the Social Creed. The board also conducted numerous conferences on race relations and on issues involving the church and the state. Certainly no Methodist could accuse the board of avoiding controversial matters. Inevitably in many cases there was criticism from some quarters of its findings and recommendations.

RACE RELATIONS

Few Methodist leaders would admit that in either organization or functioning The Methodist Church showed prejudice or discrimination on the basis of race. Even the effort to eliminate the Central Jurisdiction and to incorporate its churches and members into the geographic jurisdictions was opposed by some Negroes as well as some whites, by certain white northern proponents of racial justice as well as by many southern conservatives. Nevertheless, to those who did not feel the necessity of defending the church against criticism, it seemed clear that Negro Methodists were not wanted in most white Methodist congregations, and also that large numbers of Negro leaders and rank-and-file members were unwilling to give up the advantages secured to them through their separate jurisdiction. These included a guarantee of at least equal and in some cases a disproportionately large number of board memberships and other leadership posts in the church.

The church in the 1950's was bound to be affected by the racial tensions in secular society. In 1954 the United States Supreme Court unanimously declared that "separate but equal" public schools deprived Negro children of certain rights, and therefore desegregation of public schools must proceed with all deliberate speed. This was a landmark in the continuing debate on the role of the Negro in American society. The steady pressure of Negroes for complete economic and social equality continued with such movements as the Montgomery bus strike in 1955-56 and the "sit-in" demonstrations which began in 1959.

Increasingly through the decade some white congregations in the North and also a few in the South, under the leadership of their ministers, welcomed persons of other racial groups into their fellowship. There were, however, instances in the South where a minister who expressed sympathy with the aspirations of the Negro for equal educational and economic opportunities was faced with the bitter opposition of his parishioners, eventuating in his removal to another charge.

In this critical situation the Board of Social and Economic Relations sought to interpret the issues and to find Christian solutions. Between 1956 and 1959 it conducted nineteen interracial leadership conferences. These were held in both North and South, always in co-operation with the resident bishop or bishops, the Central Jurisdiction as well as the regional jurisdictions being represented by ministerial and lay leaders. The debate was hot in many of these gatherings, but the frank discussion led ordinarily to improved understanding within the denomination. In addition, an International Human Relations Conference was sponsored in Dallas in 1959. It discussed three questions: What is our Christian witness on race? What is the nature of the present racial crisis? What can Methodists do?

Inevitably at the General Conference of 1960 this touchy subject of race relations was argued, in many different contexts, both on the floor of the conference and in the corridors between sessions. There seemed no longer any question but that ultimately the Central Jurisdiction would be dissolved. Yet few would hazard a guess as to when this would occur.

One of the most trenchant debates took place at the final session of the conference, when ordinarily debate was strictly limited so that business could be pushed through with dispatch. It was over a resolution which, among other things, expressed regret "that many citizens . . . are denied basic human rights" and commended students participating in sit-in demonstrations "for the dignified, non-violent manner in which they have conducted themselves." The vote on the resolution, which was adopted, seemed to numerous observers to be largely along regional lines among the whites. The Negroes and overseas delegates supported it strongly. It was clear by the whole conduct of the General Conference of 1960 that the issue of complete desegregation at all levels of church organization would be steadily pressed for, but probably would be a long time in coming.

ISSUES OF CHURCH AND STATE AND CIVIL LIBERTIES

United Methodism, like its predecessor denominations, constantly avowed its loyalty to the government. In fact, one of the Articles of Religion declares: "It is the duty of all Christians . . . to observe and obey the laws and commands of the governing or supreme authority of the country . . . and to use all laudable means to encourage and enjoin obedience to the powers that be." In one form or another and at greater length, the same idea was expressed through the decades in the Methodist Social Creed, which stated: "The Methodist Church, true to the principles of the New Testament, teaches respect for properly constituted civil authority. It holds that government rests upon the support of its conscientious citizenship." [45] At the same time the church, through statements issued by the bishops and resolutions passed by the General Conferences, insisted that primary loyalty belonged to God.

At the height of the loyalty oath controversy, the 1956 General Conference adopted a resolution which read in part:

We protest legislation requiring the loyalty oath of any church to any state or nation. The Church must be in the world but not of it. She belongs to no class, nation, or race. She belongs to Christ. The Church cannot serve two masters. She can obey but one, Jesus Christ. . . . Freedom is secure and justice is maintained only as the Church lives and works among men, not as a creature subservient to the state, but as a free, unintimidated voice, speaking for Almighty God. [46]

The Methodist Church has also, with equal firmness, emphasized that no church should receive special recognition from the state and that there should be complete religious freedom for all persons. The General Conference of 1956 asked the Co-ordinating Council to make a study of the organization known as Protestants and Other Americans United for Separation of Church and State (POAU). This was a nondenominational watch-dog organization designed to prevent any breaching of the

[45] *Discipline*, 1940, ¶ 1712.16. Later editions carried slight revisions.
[46] *Discipline*, 1956, ¶ 2025.

wall of separation between church and state. It assisted in the conduct of lawsuits to keep any particular communion from exercising undue influence or seeking special privileges in the public schools. Bishop G. Bromley Oxnam was one of the founders and in 1960 was a vice-president of POAU. In its report to the 1960 General Conference, the Co-ordinating Council declared, "Study of public records and press reports reveals a rising and truculent pressure for state support of church agencies." It recommended that the General Conference commend the efforts of this organization and give encouragement to Annual Conferences, if they saw fit, to furnish moral and financial support to it. The conference adopted the report.

In 1952, 1956, and again in 1960 the General Conference declared, "We are unalterably opposed to the diversion of tax funds to the support of private and sectarian schools. In a short time this scattering process can destroy our American public school system and weaken the foundations of national unity." [47] At the same time it urged that religion had a rightful place in the public school program and that moral truths and spiritual values could be taught without violating the principle of separation of church and state. The 1960 Episcopal Address sounded the same note:

> The Methodist Church has long been a firm advocate of free public education as vital to the welfare of the American people. . . . There are always those who would like to control public education for the purposes of their special propaganda. . . . We appeal, therefore, to our Methodist people to give all possible aid and encouragement to our public educators. . . . We have never looked with favor upon parochial schools, designed primarily to serve denominational interests and to foster institutional control of the educational process.[48]

The Board of Social and Economic Relations between 1956 and 1960 undertook a series of consultations in co-operation with the New York East Annual Conference on the subject of church and state. The reports on these conversations presented the various issues in this field, including efforts to establish formal diplomatic relations with the Vatican, with documentation and analysis. The 1960 annual report of the board forecast that it would give more attention to the subject of state-church relations in the future than in the past.

The years following World War II witnessed a characteristic postwar resurgence of flamboyant patriotism and agitation for the suppression of individuals or groups who were suspected of being unpatriotic or not sufficiently patriotic. In the process civil liberties were frequently in-

---

[47] *Discipline,* 1960, ¶ 2028.
[48] *Daily Christian Advocate,* April 28, 1960, p. 44.

fringed, and numerous court actions had to be taken to protect the right of citizens to dissent. Naturally in so large an organization as The Methodist Church, there were both members of the chauvinistic agencies and persons who felt that some actions of these agencies constituted a threat to civil liberties.

The most notorious case involving Methodists was the accusation by a member of the House of Representatives that G. Bromley Oxnam, the resident bishop in Washington, D. C., was a member of subversive organizations and was "soft" on Communism. Bishop Oxnam demanded a hearing before the House Un-American Activities Committee to clear the record. In this he had the unanimous support of the Council of Bishops and the legal assistance of Charles C. Parlin, one of Methodism's leading laymen. The hearing itself, a fatiguing session lasting from two o'clock until midnight, July 21, 1953, was televised across the nation. There was no formal withdrawal of charges made by the chairman of the committee. Nevertheless, the thinness of the evidence and the unfairness of the inquisitorial techniques used resulted in broad public support for the bishop. In fact, this "trial" at least temporarily diminished public respect for the committee. The brilliant defense of the rights of the individual citizen to security from unsubstantiated accusations and star-chamber trials was subsequently set forth in Bishop Oxnam's book *I Protest*. While doubtless many Methodists were deeply disturbed by the charges and the subsequent hearing, the church as a whole maintained full confidence in Bishop Oxnam and found satisfaction in his courageous stand.

CO-ORDINATION OF THE SOCIAL ACTION AGENCIES

A conviction that the three social action boards of the church should develop a unified program grew stronger during the 1952-56 quadrennium. According to the 1952 *Discipline,* a Committee on Temperance and also a Committee on World Peace might be authorized by the official board, and a Committee on Social and Economic Relations by the Quarterly Conference of the local charge. Only the larger churches had enough members to develop three vital committees dealing respectively with temperance, world peace, and social and economic relations. Further, churches in which there was a deep interest in temperance might have a strong committee concerned with that issue but completely neglect the profoundly important subjects of world peace and race relations. Many local churches established a Committee on Christian Social Relations to cover all three of these interests, as did some Annual Conferences.

The General Conference of 1956 instructed the Co-ordinating Council to conduct studies in co-operation with these three boards, looking forward to the development of some plan for uniting them in 1960. After much discussion and some compromises, the Co-ordinating Council prepared legislation for the creation of an inclusive Board of Christian Social Concerns. This plan, with only slight alterations, was adopted by the General Conference. The legislation made the new board one of the three largest in the church, with representation based on the number of members in each jurisdiction and with no jurisdiction represented by fewer than three ministers and three laymen. There were to be nine members-at-large, selected on the basis of their specialized skills and knowledge.

A jurisdictional board (optional) and an Annual Conference board (mandatory) were provided for, and each Quarterly Conference was instructed to constitute a Commission on Christian Social Concerns, on a par with the four commissions which had previously been required for each charge. By these actions the General Conference indicated its desire to have strong, effective co-ordination of the many social concerns of the church and to have all of them brought to the attention of every congregation.

The Chaplaincy

In 1941, even before the United States was involved in World War II, the Council of Bishops realized that the critical conditions facing the world would be associated with growing military forces and a corresponding demand for chaplains in the armed services. It created the Methodist Emergency Committee to explore the needs, and in 1942 established the Commission on Chaplains as a separate agency. By then the need for literally hundreds of Methodist chaplains was more than apparent; it had become critical and was given top priority by the bishops. The commission, operating under the Council of Bishops, developed standards and proceeded to recruit candidates until by 1944 there were more than 1,300 Methodist ministers serving as chaplains in the armed forces. They constituted the largest single Protestant group.

In 1944 Methodist chaplains reported 4,232 baptisms and 9,730 professions of faith. But this was a measure of only one aspect of their varied ministry, which included the conduct of Protestant—not denominational—worship services, counseling with men and women, burying the dead, visiting those who were hospitalized, keeping in touch with families, and, with the help of assistants, making provision for recreational and social life of enlisted and officer personnel.

This was the most widespread war in history, and more American troops were involved than ever before, many of them youth who had previously been taught that war was wrong. The chaplains, like their men, were separated from their families for long periods of time and by thousands of miles. The result was that the emotional, religious, and military demands on the chaplains were difficult almost beyond description. Bishop Adna W. Leonard, chairman of the commission, was invited in 1943 at the request of President Roosevelt to visit American troops and confer with chaplains. On the flight from England to Iceland the plane crashed and he was killed.

The drastic reduction of the armed forces following the conclusion of the war was accompanied by a mustering out of chaplains. The need rose again with the Korean War and remained high because of the peacetime draft. While the General Conference of 1944 gave hearty approval to the work of the commission, it remained a creature of the Council of Bishops until the General Conference of 1948 established it as one of the permanent agencies of the church.

Especially in the quadrennium 1956-60 plans were evolved to improve the quality of persons receiving the endorsement of the commission, without which no Methodist minister could become a chaplain. Of the 566 applicants during the quadrennium, 420 were approved, and of these 392 were actually commissioned and appointed as chaplains by one of the armed services. A dramatic new aspect of the work during this period was the assignment of chaplains to work with isolated units at radar sites. One Methodist was stationed at isolated Goose Bay Air Base in Labrador, where he became a new type of circuit rider, visiting the radar sites along the rugged coast by air, boat, or dog-sled. Another served for a time at the Thule Air Base, less than a thousand miles from the North Pole. He with other Protestant chaplains in that far outpost ministered to a community of six thousand men. Methodist chaplains had tours of duty in the Antarctic, and carried the ministry of the church to little-known and lonely places on every continent.

Following World War II there was increasing demand for ministers to serve as chaplains in hospitals of the Veterans Administration, in prisons, reformatories, mental institutions, and general hospitals. In response, theological seminaries began to offer courses in this field, and the Council for Clinical Training, an interdenominational agency, provided opportunities for learning through what was essentially an internship in hospitals of different types. The Commission on Chaplains, whose authority was extended in 1956 to recruit and endorse chaplains for work "in industry; and in state and local public and private institutions, other than those of The Methodist Church," worked co-operatively with the council. Supervision of chaplains in Methodist agencies was under the control of the Board of Hospitals and Homes.

Responsibility for the chaplaincy in industry fell to the Commission on Chaplains. In 1957, in co-operation with the Board of Social and Economic Relations, it held in Washington a conference on "Methodism's Ministry to Industry." That pioneering conference explored the various possible types of industrial chaplaincy. Methodism had by 1960 developed no formal method of recruiting or endorsing men for the industrial chaplaincy. There were, in fact, few Methodist ministers in this type of work. The opposition on the part of many labor groups and others to the employment of full-time industrial chaplains seemed to indicate that this might not constitute a growing vocation. However, the need for the church and its ministers to become more aware of industrial workers and to draw them into the full fellowship of the church could not be denied.

5

Changing Worship Patterns and Practices

Every human organization has two aspects: first and most important, its central idea or purpose; second, to protect and advance this idea, institutional structure and machinery. The latter is necessary, but logically it must always remain secondary. Yet, such is the human tendency to become absorbed in the tangible and manageable details of conducting an organization, the living purpose for which it has come into being is liable to be overshadowed.

The Methodist Church, understandably, was forced after unification to give much attention to structural details. The General Conferences, as well as most Annual Conferences, seemed to devote the major part of their time to discussion of procedures by which the tremendous network of responsibilities characterizing a church of over nine million members could be carried forward. While the underlying purpose of the activities of church boards and agencies was always avowedly to educate and to deepen the spiritual life of the membership, and to strengthen the witness of the church on behalf of the Christian gospel, an uninvolved observer might have got the impression that keeping the organization operating smoothly almost became an end in itself.

Did Methodists grow in the understanding of their faith, and did they improve in the living of it? One would be bold indeed to make specific judgments regarding the spiritual life of persons or of institutions. By its very nature this is subtle and pervasive, never explicit and definitive. It is safer to cite statistics on membership, attendance, and financial contributions.

Much was said in the latter 1950's about a return to religion in the United States. And it was true that the statistics of church membership indicated that, year by year, a progressively larger proportion of the population was included on the church rolls. Yet across the nation there did not seem to be a great upsurge in church attendance or a noticeable spiritualizing of the goals of human endeavor. Bishop Gerald Kennedy wrote:

So far as the spiritual life of the church is concerned it is not what it ought to be and I doubt if it ever has been. I believe with all my heart that The Methodist Church is more alive to the relevant issues of the day than any other denomination. The problem seems to me to be one of relevancy. So much of our so-called spiritual revival is nothing more than retreat or withdrawal to an ivory tower. I think our main problem is to find spiritual rebirth in the midst of action.[49]

There were straws in the wind which, while they might not reveal all the cross currents in the life of the church, did witness to the fact that creative religious thinking was going on, not only in the minds of professional religious leaders but also among rank-and-file church members. Changes in the use of liturgy and in church architecture obviously are not an adequate measure of the spiritual vitality of a people, but they merit attention. Of greater significance is the renewed interest in Bible study and participation in the worship service.

New Ideas in Church Architecture

The creative and fresh approaches to church architecture were a sign of an awakening interest in religion and the outward forms of its expression. New construction materials as well as new ideas were boldly employed in the erection of many sanctuaries and educational buildings.

[49] In a personal letter to the author.

While some Methodist congregations were rediscovering the beauties of traditional Gothic architecture, others joined in frank experimentation as to placement of the communion table, the pulpit, and the lectern, the disposition of the choir, and the pattern of seating in the sanctuary. As a result Methodist churches, which had often looked like assembly halls, began to have a more distinctive appearance and to suggest their function as places of worship.

It was becoming more common for churches to ask that their plans be reviewed by the Department of Architecture of the Board of Missions. Equally important, all building committees of local churches were enjoined by the *Discipline* to "submit to the District Board of Church Location and Building, for its consideration and approval, a statement of the need for the proposed facilities, and the sketches, estimates, and plans." [50] This prevented some of the more serious mistakes in site selection, financing, and designing of facilities.

More emphasis was placed on space, so that the church might have an appropriate setting. Especially in newer suburban areas congregations sought to acquire at least three to five acres, and in many instances ten or more, for their church buildings and grounds. Parking lots had become as much of a necessity as seats in the sanctuary. People moving to the suburbs to enjoy the luxury of open space did not want their church constricted to two or three lots on the main street. With the prospect of larger memberships and with swelling numbers of children, especially in suburban areas, new congregations were no longer satisfied with a church plant consisting of a sanctuary plus a basement plus a parsonage. Educational buildings and social halls, where adults as well as children could come together for church gatherings, became the rule rather than the exception.

Still one other marked change occurred during this period. As building costs rose sharply, the conventional Sunday morning service, with church school preceding or following it, gave way to multiple services. Some churches held as many as three worship services on a Sunday morning, with co-ordinated church school sessions. This made it possible to use the expensive buildings to better advantage, and also provided an opportunity to reach those who preferred an earlier or a later hour.

Increasing Use of Liturgy

Admittedly, participating in ceremony and ritual may for some people be a substitute for full yielding of the self to God or for embodying their

---

[50] *Discipline*, 1960, ¶ 180.5.

beliefs in conduct. Nevertheless, the use of liturgy and Christian symbols and the participation in dignified public worship have been important aids to devotion on the part of millions of Christians. Early Methodism (but never John Wesley) had been rather suspicious of the "embellishment" of worship services. In the twenty years after unification there was a growing appreciation of the traditional orders of worship, prayers, and rituals.

The desire to have a Methodist book of worship was an expression of this interest. The General Conference of 1944 received a report from the Commission on Rituals and Orders of Worship which was essentially a preliminary edition of a book of worship. After trial use and some revision, the *Methodist Book of Worship* was published as a companion to the *Methodist Hymnal* in 1945. It contained orders of worship for morning and evening services, including an order adapted from the Sunday Service of John Wesley; prayers for use on various occasions; affirmations of faith; orders of worship for special days in the Christian Year; prayers for the sick; and aids to personal and family devotions. It also contained the ritual for the holy rites and offices of the church, plus several new dedicatory services—for a church-school building, a hospital, an organ. The use of the *Book of Worship* was slowly broadened. As might be expected, it was accepted more fully by younger ministers and by the congregations which they led. The General Conference of 1956 ordered a revision of the *Book of Worship*, and a proposed revision was authorized in 1960 for use in the following quadrennium.

The Christian Year, with its many teaching and worship implications, was largely overlooked in the seminaries prior to 1940, and was practically unheard of in the average local church. By 1960 seminary students were well aware of the sequence, and more and more churches were celebrating Advent and observing Pentecost, appreciating the ties with historic Christianity. A few Methodist churches in the 1950's began to use communion table cloths and other hangings of appropriate color for the various seasons of the Christian Year, as established by the historic practice of the Anglican and Roman Catholic Churches. A much larger number in different sections of the country placed candles on the communion table, lit in a few instances by choir boys before the Sunday service began. A processional hymn, sung as the choir and minister—often robed in a pulpit gown—advanced to their places, was a part of the service in far more churches in 1960 than in 1940.

Renewed Interest in the Bible

Perhaps it was due to the lowered attendance or to a shift away from a Bible-centered curriculum in the church school in the 1920's and 1930's, or perhaps it was due to a change in preaching emphasis of the pastors of that period, that there seemed to be a dearth of knowledge of biblical and church history on the part of Methodist adults in the 1940's and '50's. Many of them did not know how to look up a text in the Bible and were unacquainted with its contents, except for the best-known parables and characters.

Not only was the average Methodist layman rather hazy about the specific content of the Bible and basic Christian beliefs, but he had difficulty relating them to the issues which he faced in his daily life. S. Paul Schilling reported on the beliefs of Methodists in 1959 as part of a study sponsored by the Board of Social and Economic Relations. More than five thousand responses to a questionnaire filled out by Methodist laymen—assumed to be representative—were examined, and a number of conclusions were reached. Two of them were:

The respondents hold that religious beliefs strongly influence conduct, though often no consistent connection is discernible between the theological convictions and the ethical and social positions which they themselves affirm. . . .

These Methodists believe that the church has real responsibility for social change, but they are doubtful and divided as to how this responsibility is to be exercised, and they do not relate it clearly to Biblical or theological foundations.[51]

The pendulum, which had been swinging away from emphasis on the Bible, finally spent its force and began to move in the opposite direction, as pendulums have a way of doing. This was first noticed in the seminaries and the ministry. Seminaries in 1960 were generally requiring their students to take more courses in the Bible and there was larger enrollment in courses in the biblical languages. Nor was this simply a quantitative change; seminary faculties had an increased appreciation of the relevance of the Bible for theology. This was a logical accompaniment of the rise of neo-orthodoxy—first among European theologians and then American, subsequently among rank-and-file seminary teachers of Bible and theology, and finally among pastors.

Possibly it was a reflection of the renewed interest in biblical and doctrinal preaching which led in many churches to an awakened desire on

[51] Schilling, *Methodism and Society in Theological Perspective*, p. 168.

the part of lay men and women to study the foundations of their faith. Pastors by 1960 were again teaching adult classes in church history and the Bible. Research studies in churches of different types showed that in many places there was an interest on the part of at least a small minority of laymen in biblical and theological instruction as well as in "social concern" courses.

Deepening the Meaning of Church Membership

Beginning with 1952 every Methodist church had a Commission on Membership and Evangelism, which was more or less active depending on the ministerial leadership and the lay concern. In some churches the commission conducted, with the help of other members, a house-to-house family canvass in the immediate vicinity once a year, and over a wider area about every two or three years. Alert commissions sought out the newcomers to the community, inviting them to attend church and to bring their children to the church school. Participation in evangelism of various types was greater in 1960 than in 1940.

In every region pastors were giving more attention to preparing the youth of the church school for the full responsibilities of membership. The pastor in some churches took charge of the class of twelve-year-olds each year for a three-month period, making it a membership-training class. Other pastors requested the youth seeking admission to the church, and also adults transferring from Methodist and non-Methodist churches, to attend a series of three or four instruction sessions where the meaning of the Christian faith and the significance of church membership were discussed. Joining The Methodist Church in most communities was no longer taken as casually as in 1940.

Devotional literature, such as the *Upper Room,* had greatly increased circulation in the decades following unification. People were encouraged to use these booklets, which contained scriptural readings and a short message for each day. The Department of Spiritual Life of the Woman's Division of Christian Service furnished suggestions and resources and urged each local church society to develop a group who would meet together periodically for Bible study, prayer, and meditation. In some churches prayer cells for both men and women were formed.

To be sure, only a small proportion of any membership was touched by these more concentrated efforts to develop the spiritual life. Nevertheless, the concern for the personal experience of religion, so prominent in the days of Wesley and expressed in the class meeting, was becoming more prevalent than it had been in many a decade. While some socially minded members were troubled lest Methodists lose their social passion, others were sure that personal religious experience was the taproot out of which genuine Christian social motivation must spring.

In the Episcopal Address read by Bishop William C. Martin at the 1960 General Conference, the bishops warned:

> Yet no church can live off the glories of its past or repeat its triumphs merely by repeating its tactics. . . . We are a big church and we can all too easily lapse into the complacency that goes with size and organizational efficiency. We can almost insensibly drift into a pattern of dependence on proper form or ritual, technique and program. In a word, we can become the same sort of church as that which Wesley and his preachers set out to reform and revive more than two centuries ago.[52]

In the great movement that was Methodism there was room for many different emphases and points of view. With all the ranks of leadership in this denomination there was no real hierarchy, no final human authority who could speak ex cathedra for the denomination. Perhaps the most general characteristic of Methodism was that, with the freedom from doctrinal bonds and exact rules of conduct, its adherents were perpetually and critically examining themselves, their motives, and accomplishments. The gadflies were ever about, along with the ritualists, the priests, and the bureaucrats. And Methodism seldom permitted itself to run contentedly in a groove. Though it might not attain to perfection, its conscience and its warmth of heart kept it ever striving for this goal, both as individuals and as an institution.

6

Methodism and the Ecumenical Movement

Rising to address the Ecumenical Methodist Conference at Oxford, 1951, was Dr. Charles W. Ranson, secretary of the International Missionary Council. "What is Methodism's chief contribution to the Ecumenical Movement?" he asked. And his simple answer was "Dr. John R. Mott." Not a special doctrinal emphasis, nor a form of ministry, nor strength of numbers—but one great man. In the audience sat that man, to whom more credit is due for the twentieth-century ecumenical refor-

[52] *Daily Christian Advocate,* April 28, 1960, p. 35.

mation of the church than any other. One of his biographers did not ex-
aggerate when he wrote, "No religious leader in all history has equaled
the geographic scope and time-span of Mott's service." [53]

The achievements of this Methodist layman seem legendary. From
1891, when he first visited Europe in the interests of the movement of
Christian students, to his death in 1955 just before his ninetieth year,
he played a leading role in almost every organization or project connected with the world-wide mission and unity of the non-Roman
churches. He never ceased being a responsible member of The Methodist
Church, nor did he relax his efforts to draw other Methodists into the
Ecumenical Movement. Just after unification he wrote, "If there be among
Methodist leaders any who in this day question whether the Church
should throw itself with abandon into this ecumenical movement . . .
let them heed the words of Christ, . . . 'It is more blessed to give than
to receive.' " [54]

A dramatic witness to this man's accomplishments was made at a
solemn memorial service shortly after his death. It was in the ancient
cathedral of Saint Pierre in Geneva. Four men spoke in praise of the
famous man. They were the general secretaries of four ecumenical organizations: the World's Student Christian Federation, the International
Missionary Council, the World Alliance of the Y.M.C.A., and the World
Council of Churches. The one man most responsible for the forming of
each of these was the Methodist John R. Mott.

In 1946 the Nobel Peace Prize had been awarded to Mott. In responding to the citation, he uttered words which succinctly characterize his
amazing career: "My life might be summed up as an earnest and undis-
courageable effort to weave together all nations, all races, and all religious
communions in friendliness, in fellowship, and in co-operation." [55]
Without Mott's work, quite simply, it is hard to say whether there would
have been an Ecumenical Movement at all.

The International Missionary Council

Among the varied ecumenical interests of Dr. Mott, the most significant in his view was the co-operation of Christians in faithful and effective mission throughout the world. He was not naïve when he called

[53] Galen M. Fisher, *John R. Mott, Architect of Co-operation and Unity* (New York:
Association Press, 1952) , p. 1.

[54] John R. Mott, *Methodists United for Action* (Nashville: Board of Missions of
The Methodist Church, 1939) , p. 115.

[55] Fisher, *John R. Mott*, p. 2.

hundreds of students to "the evangelization of the world in this generation," for he knew that it was humanly possible to bring the gospel to people of every nation. In 1910 he had presided over the World Missionary Conference at Edinburgh. This unique event in church history was the fountainhead of the Ecumenical Movement. And one of its organizational consequences was the International Missionary Council, which gathered together many mission boards and societies with national Christian councils of numerous countries.

During the years of the Council's existence, The Methodist Church's missionary leaders gave notable service in its conferences and co-ordinating work. So prominent were the efforts of Bishop James C. Baker that in 1942, when Mott felt obliged to resign as chairman, he personally designated Baker as his successor in this position of honor and responsibility. Ralph E. Diffendorfer and his successor as general secretary of the Division of World Missions, Eugene L. Smith, were key men in missionary study and planning of conferences. In 1949 Dr. Glora Wysner became the first woman staff member. In 1952 was published the definitive history of the International Missionary Council, *Ecumenical Foundations,* by a Methodist scholar, Dr. W. Richey Hogg.

Also in 1952 the important assembly met at Willingen, Germany, to study the missionary obligation of the church in the light of both theology and the critical state of man's society. Bishop S. U. Barbieri of Argentina was the chaplain, and three of the staff of the Board of Missions —Eugene Smith, James K. Mathews, and M. O. Williams—were active participants. In 1958, after Ranson had stepped down as general secretary, it was formally agreed to invite Mathews to succeed him. But when Mathews declined, the post was offered to and accepted by Bishop J. E. L. Newbigin of the Church of South India.

The mention of these individual leaders of the missionary movement is merely an indication of the diffuse ways in which The Methodist Church both gave and received in the International Missionary Council. After World War II some radical changes in the churches' missionary outreach and strategy were wrought. Methodists pointed the way for other churches with their short-term service projects for young people going to Asian, African, and South American lands. They kept pace with the process of devolution of authority and responsibility into the hands of indigenous churches. They joined in numerous co-operative ventures with other denominations, and generally supported unitive efforts among divided churches. In 1960, upon Methodist initiative, a common training program for American missionary candidates of eight denominations was begun, with its center at Stony Point, New York.

Toward Formation of the World Council of Churches

Even as final plans were being made for the Methodist union of 1939, another kind of union with the widest ramifications was being advanced. This was the merging of the Faith and Order Movement with the Life and Work Movement to form the World Council of Churches. Both great streams of the Ecumenical Movement had met in the summer of 1937 in conferences respectively at Edinburgh and Oxford, and both had voted in favor of forming the new council. A joint committee of fourteen distinguished churchmen was appointed to make further plans. Dr. Mott was the one American Methodist who belonged to this committee, which met at Utrecht in 1938. There it was planned to hold the inaugural assembly in 1941. But the great and terrible war crushed this plan as it did the plans, hopes, and lives of so many persons and nations. The council could not be formally constituted until 1948.

It would scarcely be accurate to maintain that American Methodists other than Mott played decisive roles in either the Life and Work or the Faith and Order conferences before 1948. One might explain a certain detachment from the Faith and Order Movement in view of the fact that its time of origin and its conferences at Lausanne, 1927, and Edinburgh, 1937, coincided with that period of Methodist history when doctrinal and theological questions were most minimized. And Faith and Order has always been concerned mainly with theology. But this explanation is dubious in view of the fact that Methodist participation in the Life and Work Movement, with its preoccupation with social and ethical issues, was also modest. More plausible, but still a conjecture, is the explanation that Methodists did not feel affinity with the churches of Europe or even with the ancestral Church of England and these were the churches most active in both movements. A further proposal is that the strong sentiments for world peace, which prevailed among Methodists during the 1920's and '30's found more expression in isolationist convictions than in efforts to build up international ties.

Yet it should be noted that Bishops James Cannon, Jr., and John L. Nuelsen and Dr. Lynn Harold Hough, dean of Drew Theological Seminary, had participated in annual meetings of the Universal Christian Council for Life and Work prior to 1937. While Dr. Mott was the only Methodist among the nineteen officers of the Oxford Conference, the participating delegates included Bishops Baker, Cannon, Paul B. Kern, James A. Hamlett, and Raymond J. Wade, as well as future bishops Ivan Lee Holt and J. H. Straughn.

At the World Conference on Faith and Order at Edinburgh the most articulate Methodist participant was Bishop Francis J. McConnell, who had carried his church's interests in such circles for more than a decade. A number of the Oxford delegates went also to Edinburgh that summer, and were joined by Bishops C. W. Flint, S. L. Greene, John M. Moore, G. Bromley Oxnam, and such Methodist educators as Albert C. Knudson, Harris Franklin Rall, and Edmund D. Soper. Although these events slightly antedated Methodist union, they are worth noting as antecedents to the developments in the Ecumenical Movement which followed the war.

Despite the great martial conflict it was possible to continue the Faith and Order studies in Great Britain and the United States. In 1940 an American Theological Committee was established to study the question of the nature of the church. At this time Clarence T. Craig, later to become dean of Drew Theological Seminary, entered the arena of ecumenical studies, soon taking the lead in the American committee. Dr. Rall was also a major contributor to this study. A study commission on intercommunion problems was also launched, with Dean Hough as the principal Methodist member. These and related studies became the grist for the mill of the Faith and Order Conference at Lund, Sweden, in 1952.

Less than a year after the German surrender, the provisional committee of the World Council of Churches convened in Geneva to pick up the scattered strands of the movement. Actually the ties had been maintained amazingly well despite the international chaos. Plans for the Amsterdam assembly of 1948 were made rapidly, with the assurance that numerous churches would be members of the council. Indeed, all Methodist churches in the world voted affirmatively on the invitation to join.

The leadership of American Methodists at this time was still a small element. In the provisional committee of thirty-five members only Dr. Mott and Bishop Oxnam represented American Methodism as a whole; and only Mott was present at Geneva. But it should be noted that Bishop Paul N. Garber, then stationed in Geneva, was working effectively with the urgent program of reconstruction and interchurch aid in devastated Europe.

During these formative '40's an intensifying support for the World Council among American churches was being built up through the council's New York office. Much of the credit for this growing support was due a Methodist laywoman, Miss Eleanor Kent Browne. In 1960 she continued to manage countless details in relation to the council and the churches.

In the summer of 1946 was constituted the Commission of the Churches on International Affairs, under the joint sponsorship of the World Council and the International Missionary Council. One of the original members was Bishop Oxnam, who mediated the strong concern of the Methodists for world peace to the commission, which in turn provided greater effectiveness in dealing with various governments and the United Nations than The Methodist Church by itself could realize.

When several hundred Methodists from all the earth gathered in Springfield, Massachusetts, in September of 1947 for the Seventh Ecumenical Methodist Conference, they heard a series of addresses which heartily supported the church unity movement and the World Council of Churches. The conference message declared, "Methodism should be one of the strongest pillars in this co-operative movement. We will give ourselves to the tasks of the World Council." [56] The same note was reiterated in the Episcopal Address to the General Conference at Boston in April, 1948. Indeed, the address was an aggressive summons to Methodists to take part not only in the World Council and co-operative endeavors but also in all valid movements toward church union. Following the line of Bishop Oxnam's stirring address to the conference at Springfield the year before, the bishops now asserted that steps should be taken toward union with other Protestant bodies, and that the distant vision of union with Eastern Orthodox churches should not be lost.

The World Council at Work

Though its citizens were just over three years away from the horrors of Nazi occupation, the city of Amsterdam affected a gay mood in August, 1948. Most of the people were excited over the coronation of Juliana as queen. But serious Christians knew that they were the hosts to a conference unprecedented in the history of the church. The World Council of Churches was formally voted into existence, as the delegates spontaneously adopted a terse declaration embedded in the conference message: "We intend to stay together." Who intended this? One hundred forty-seven churches from forty-four countries. Among these were The Methodist Church, the A.M.E. Church, the A.M.E. Zion Church, and the C.M.E. Church. Their delegates and consultants numbered nearly fifty of the more than seven hundred official participants.[57]

[56] *Proceedings of the Seventh Ecumenical Methodist Conference* (Nashville: The Methodist Publishing House, 1948), p. 302.

[57] For names of Methodists present see *The First Assembly of the World Council of Churches* (New York: Harper & Brothers, 1949), pp. 223-67.

It was at Amsterdam that American Methodists began to appear in strength among their fellow Christians of the Ecumenical Movement. Yet even here their role was a comparatively modest one. The second assembly at Evanston, 1954, first marked the degree of participation which was commensurate with their numerical membership.

At Amsterdam the names of Mott and Oxnam once again headed the list of Methodists. It had been agreed in 1946 that Mott would be one of five presidents of the new council. But now the presidium was enlarged to six; Mott was given the special position as honorary president, and Oxnam named one of the six.

Although much of the discussion in the four study sections of the assembly had to do with theological questions, there were only two professional theologians representing American Methodism. Dr. Craig distinguished himself in the section on "The Universal Church in God's Design" and Dr. Georgia Harkness in the one on "The Church's Witness to God's Design." Bishop Hamlett of the C.M.E. Church was an officer of the section on church and society.

One assembly worship was led by Bishop Holt; and Dr. Ralph W. Sockman was one of the preachers, along with Bishop Otto Dibelius and Pastor Pierre Maury, at the great closing service.

The main task of this assembly, of course, was to complete the organizing of the new council. In the matter of finance the guiding hand was that of Bishop Oxnam, and the largest contributions began and continue to come from The Methodist Church. The first central committee included among its ninety members the following Methodists from America: Bishops Baker and Holt, Dr. Sockman, and J. E. Moreland, president of Randolph-Macon College.

It is easy to garner from the records the names of Methodists who took part in this assembly. It is less easy to determine how much real feeling of support there was among Methodists generally for the World Council, or how influential the council's growing program became in the Methodist churches. But every pastor was supplied with copies of the study books prepared for Amsterdam, thus introducing him not only to the fact of the council's existence but also to the substance of its concerns for church and world.

Whatever may have been the domestic reaction to Amsterdam, its effect upon the churches' mission was immediate and clear. In 1949 there took place at Bangkok the Eastern Asia Christian Conference, under the auspices of the World Council and the International Missionary Council. This sought to give practical expression to the new ecumenical understanding of mission in that broadly diverse and densely populated portion of the earth. A similar conference met in Indonesia in 1957; and the body was constituted as a permanent council at Kuala Lumpur, Malaya, in 1959. Over the years numerous Methodist leaders from India, Malaya, the Philippines, Japan, Korea, and the Board of Missions assumed important responsibilities in this significant step forward in Christian missions.

Within the World Council the Commission on Faith and Order continued the intensive theological study with respect to the deepest issues affecting the division and unity of the church. The next ecumenical milestone after Amsterdam was the Third World Conference on Faith and Order held in 1952 at Lund, Sweden. The contribution of Methodist theologians was more evident here than in any previous ecumenical undertaking. It was largely upon the suggestion of Albert C. Outler, professor of theology at Perkins School of Theology, that a new study was begun on the meaning of tradition for church unity. Walter G. Muelder, dean of Boston University School of Theology, was the leading thinker on the perplexing problem of the role of nontheological factors in the unity and division of churches. Dean Craig, who had done much to prepare for the conference, was prevented by illness from attending. When the new membership list of the commission was drawn up, Craig was made vice-chairman, Dr. Outler and Bishops H. B. Amstutz, S. U. Barbieri, Holt, and A. J. Allan of the A.M.E. Church were made members. The executive secretary elected at Lund was Dr. J. Robert Nelson, who served in the Geneva headquarters.

Two years later it was the privilege of The Methodist Church in a special way to play host to the second assembly of the World Council. This was hailed as the greatest religious event likely to take place in the United States in the twentieth century. It was held on the campus of Northwestern University, whose dean emeritus, J. A. James, thus realized a dream he had held since he was a delegate to Lausanne, 1927, of holding an ecumenical conference there. Most of the assembly's worship services were in the First Methodist Church of Evanston, of which Dr. Harold A. Bosley, was pastor. A liturgical high point was the service of Holy Communion conducted by Bishop Holt and others.

Leading their sections of the serious study at the assembly were Bishop Richard C. Raines on evangelism and Dr. Nelson on faith and order. Dr. Moreland headed the strategic nominations committee and Bishop William C. Martin the general policy committee. Other Methodist delegates, visitors, and consultants were too numerous to mention by name.[58]

Toward the end of the assembly the new officers and committee mem-

[58] See *The Evanston Report* (New York: Harper & Brothers, 1955), pp. 264-98.

bers were elected. Dr. Mott, who had attended most of the plenary sessions with punctuality and dignity, was acclaimed still as honorary president. But within a few months his magnificent life on earth came to an end. The Methodist member of the presidium was Bishop Barbieri, who also represented the Protestant Christians of Latin America. Designated to serve for seven years on the important central committee were Mrs. Frank Brooks, Charles C. Parlin, and Bishops Martin and Oxnam, and Bishop D. Ward Nichols of the A.M.E. church.

When the closing service in the First Methodist Church, with Bishop Berggrav of Norway as preacher, brought the assembly to its end on August 31, it was evident that something of tremendous importance had happened in American church life. Many thousands of Christians, including a large number of interested pastors, teachers, and local council executives, had come to witness the event. Hundreds of journalists had written millions of words for papers everywhere. Church journals were preoccupied with the messages and personalities of the assembly. Very soon the churches began to study and appropriate the messages on Christ the Hope of the World, church unity, evangelism, intergroup relations, laity, international affairs, and social responsibility of the churches. In short, the Ecumenical Movement had "arrived" at Evanston and was no longer to be regarded as something novel, foreign, and strange. Henceforth it would be difficult to consider any aspect of denominational program planning without taking into account its ecumenical implications.

The assembly also had the effect of discrediting the common notion that American churches were not interested in theological issues. The threatened breach between Continental and American theology did not occur at Evanston. And that very summer plans were initiated for the first conference to be held in America on the various questions of faith and order as these affect church unity. This was the North American Conference on Faith and Order, which took as its theme "The Nature of the Unity We Seek." It was held at Oberlin College in the summer of 1957. Preparatory studies were carried on for a two-year period by hundreds of theologians, pastors, and laymen, including many Methodists. They dealt with all those perplexing issues of Christology, ecclesiology, sacraments, ministry, and worship, as well as sociological and racial factors, which cause and perpetuate divisions among churches.

The fifty-six Methodist delegates to Oberlin were gratified to find themselves well represented in the conference program.[59] Of the seven major addresses, three were presented by Dr. Outler, Dean Muelder, and

[59] For names, see Paul S. Minear, ed., *The Nature of the Unity We Seek* (St. Louis: Bethany Press, 1958), pp. 289-93.

Dr. Nelson. Among the officers of study sections were Dr. Harkness, Dr. Merrimon Cuninggim, dean of Perkins School of Theology, and Bishop F. Gerald Ensley.

One of the significant actions later taken by Methodist delegates was to recommend the formation of a Methodist Commission on Ecumenical Consultation. With the rapidly growing volume of reports on studies and current affairs arising in the Ecumenical Movement, there was urgent need for such a body, which would enable The Methodist Church to deal more responsibly with these matters. This commission was formally authorized by the General Conference of 1960.

The task of the new commission was twofold. First, it was to formulate responses to the reports and findings of ecumenical conferences, and to appropriate these where feasible for Methodist life and thought. The second aspect of the task was to make a positive Methodist contribution to the ecumenical quest for a right understanding of God's will for the church in the world. Since 1954 the number of Methodists taking part in ecumenical study commissions and writing books and articles of relevance was growing significantly.

An important but easily overlooked development took place in the theological seminaries. Several Methodist schools instituted courses in the field of ecumenics, providing studies for pastors and also preparing men for specialized ministry of an interdenominational character. For example, Dean Muelder spent a semester teaching at the Ecumenical Institute in Switzerland; soon thereafter he brought the eminent Swedish Lutheran scholar, Dr. Nils Ehrenstrom, from the World Council's study department to a new chair in ecumenics at Boston. The tendency of Methodist seminaries to engage professors of other denominations was a further sign of this important effect of the Ecumenical Movement upon theological education, and hence upon the ministry and thought of the church.

The National Council of Churches

Despite the divisions of American Protestant churches during more than three centuries, there have been persistent efforts to pull the separated bodies of Christianity into co-operative programs and more visible unity in federations and unions. Eight years after the twentieth century began, the Federal Council of the Churches of Christ in America was constituted. During the following decades it made an inestimable contribution to the churches of the land, especially with respect to social witness and service; and it also prepared the way for more intensive unitive efforts yet to come. Methodist leaders from the outset were actively engaged in the life of the Federal Council, and gave to it much of the impetus for social reform. Bishops McConnell, Holt, and Oxnam served as presidents of the council; usually there were more than one hundred Methodist delegates at a time. The number of bishops belonging to the council rose as high as thirty. As a rule Methodists contributed more than twice as much to the budget as any other member communion.

Co-operative efforts were by no means confined to the Federal Council, however. A large number of interdenominational organizations with special interests and goals sprang up in the early years of the ecumenical era. Among these were the following: Foreign Missions Conference of North America; Home Missions Council of North America; International Council of Religious Education; Missionary Education Movement of the United States and Canada; National Protestant Council on Higher Education; United Council of Church Women; United Stewardship Council.

The boards and agencies of the three branches of Methodism were intricately involved in the work of these and still other agencies. Confusion was inevitable, as was inefficiency and costly waste of the churches' resources. Even as Methodist unification was being effected in the late 1930's, church leaders were discussing the need to bring these various organizations into a more orderly and unified expression. In 1940 there was established a joint committee, representing the Federal Council and the other agencies, to explore the possibilities of unifying these organizations. Perhaps impelled by the sense of urgency during the war years, when churches felt strong responsibility for their common tasks, the leaders of these eight separate councils came rather quickly to agreement on merger. They were joined by Church World Service, which after the war was rising to the height of its opportunity, the Protestant Radio Commission, the Protestant Film Commission, and the Interseminary Committee. A constitution for the proposed National Council of Churches of Christ in the United States of America had been set forth in 1944. By January, 1950, all the member churches and appropriate agencies had voted in favor of it.

The American equivalent of "Amsterdam, 1948" was "Cleveland, 1950." On November 29 of that year, in a service of solemn liturgical dignity, the National Council became a reality.[60] Henceforth the co-

---

[60] For a full account, see *Christian Faith in Action* (New York: National Council of the Churches of Christ in the United States, 1951).

operating churches would regard this as their comprehensive instrument for united work and witness in America.

During the following days at Cleveland, Methodists led in worship or spoke from the rostrum on main concerns of the new council. The Negro Methodist churches were represented by Bishops Hamlett, J. A. Gregg, D. Ward Nichols, and W. J. Walls.

As the new council was organized, a number of Methodists were designated as officers and staff. Arthur S. Flemming, then president of Ohio Wesleyan University, became the first chairman of the Division of Christian Life and Work. Mrs. Abbie Clement Jackson of the A.M.E. Zion Church was elected a vice-president of the council. Dr. Gerald E. Knoff was appointed general director of the Commission on General Christian Education, and Dr. John O. Gross of the Board of Education was elected chairman of the Commission on Higher Education. Dr. C. P. Hargraves, long active in Methodist missionary and educational work, became chairman of the Joint Commission on Missionary Education. And Dr. A. Dudley Ward, later secretary of the Board of Social and Economic Relations, was appointed director of studies on the Church and Economic Life. Although still others held lesser positions, it is clear that in proportion to the numerical strength of the Methodists, relatively few of them were named to the very large corps of executive staff. An explanation often suggested for the comparatively small number of Methodists in full-time offices of the Ecumenical Movement is the fact that ministers are tied rather closely to their Annual Conferences and thus not so free for detached service as are those under a different polity.

The rise of the National Council both opened new opportunities and posed new threats to the churches, because almost every specialized interest which found organizational expression in the structure of a single denomination now had its counterpart in the council: home and world missions, evangelism, church-school education and higher education, economic and social issues, international affairs, worship, broadcasting and films, and others. This did not mean that member churches of the council forfeited their responsibility in these areas. On the contrary, they were enabled to carry out their purposes more effectively than in denominational isolation. On the other hand, the very existence and functions of the ecumenical agencies, even though they had no authority or prerogative except that granted by the churches, raised the question over each denominational commission or board of how its particular exclusively denominational work could be justified.

The effect of the National Council's total work can be calculated to a degree by the dimensions of its staff and committee membership. In his address to the assembly at Boston in 1954, closing his term as president of the council, Bishop W. C. Martin noted that there were nearly 700 full-time workers and no less than 5,775 church members serving voluntarily as officers and members of committees. If one adds to this number the hundreds of other Christians who took part in the various conferences held under the council's auspices, and the thousands regularly involved in the work of the nearly one thousand state and local councils of churches in the United States, he has a mental grasp of the extent to which the concerns of ecumenical Christianity were carried into the congregations of the member communions. In spite of these impressive statistics, by 1960 Christian laymen and pastors had scarcely begun to avail themselves of the potentialities for united witness and service in local communities and wider areas of society.

Christian Students in Ecumenical Advance

Church leaders who never participated in the Methodist Student Movement or its counterparts cannot quite appreciate the disproportionate influence which students have had within the Ecumenical Movement. Yet, since the days when Mott was himself a college student, there has been accumulating evidence of their indispensability and wide effect.

Since 1895 the World's Student Christian Federation had brought thousands of young Christians out of the isolation of their homes and local churches and denominations into conferences for study and discussion of essential issues. Naturally a large but indeterminate number of these were American Methodists. Of comparable importance, and even older than the Federation, were the Student Volunteer Movement, for missions; the Interseminary Movement of theological students; and the student organizations of the Y.M.C.A. and the Y.W.C.A. These in addition to the various denominational student movements constituted a kind of ecumenical movement on the college campuses across the nation. In 1944 an agreement was reached which brought fourteen student movements into the United Student Christian Council. And a still more comprehensive merger in 1959 was effected when the National Student Christian Federation was formed. This body became a related agency of the National Council of Churches. Dr. Hiel D. Bollinger of the Board of Education and Professor John W. Deschner were the Methodists who gave most notable leadership in these developments.

The World Parish of Methodism

The word "ecumenical" is as ancient as the Christian Church itself, but in the vocabularies of most Protestant denominations it had become obsolete or simply had been forgotten until about 1925. However, Methodists had preserved the word as a designation of their loosely organized world-wide movement. The First Ecumenical Methodist Conference was held at the famous City Road Chapel in London in 1881. Every decade thereafter through 1931 conferences met. The time schedule was changed due to the war, so that the seventh conference was held in 1947, the eighth in 1951, and thereafter every five years.[61]

It was not until the 1947 conference that serious efforts were made to establish a permanent structure for the Ecumenical Methodist Council. By 1951 there were appointed standing committees on finance, evangelism, faith and order, exchange of preachers, women's work, youth, and education. At this meeting also it was agreed to change the name to the World Methodist Council, since the word "ecumenical" had acquired connotations which made it inappropriate as a designation for a council of Methodists only.

It is significant that the building up of the council after 1951 was achieved mainly by persons who were also active in the Ecumenical Movement at large. Particular mention must be made of Bishop Holt, who had labored untiringly for the council; Dr. Elmer T. Clark, who did much to establish a headquarters building at Lake Junaluska, North Carolina; and two laymen, Charles C. Parlin and Edwin L. Jones.

The council recorded a number of real accomplishments. It strengthened the ties between the large Methodist churches of Britain and America, as well as the bonds between these and the many small bodies of Methodists throughout the world. It provided occasions for studying the distinctive tradition of Methodism in the light of wider historical and theological study. Since conferences of the World Council of Churches were of limited size, the World Methodist Council enabled larger numbers of Methodists to experience worship and discussion in an international context. Finally, the presence at its conferences of many delegates from Methodist churches engaged in church-union negotiations in their own countries dramatized the extensiveness of the church unity movement and raised basic issues about the relation and tension of denominationalism and ecumenism.

Most of the other denominational families established world councils,

[61] For a brief summary of the conferences, see Ivan Lee Holt and Elmer T. Clark, *The World Methodist Movement* (Nashville: The Upper Room, 1956), pp. 89-120.

alliances, or federations analogous to the Methodists. Each had to face the choice of two alternatives: either to encourage the solidifying of world-wide ecclesiastical structure for its own churches, or else to assist its churches in establishing closer unity with other Christians in their own localities and regions. These actions are at variance with each other, and the implications of one or the other for the unity and the mission of the church are obvious.

Christian Unity or Church Unity?

In the Ecumenical Movement at large it is understood that the three purposes of unity, mission, and renewal must be sought simultaneously. Any one of these without the other two cannot be held to represent the full meaning of the movement. Nevertheless it is the question of unity which usually comes first to mind when the Ecumenical Movement is mentioned. But "unity" itself is ambiguous unless modified by such adjectives as "Christian" or "church" or "organic."

Christian unity is usually accepted as the name for that sense of oneness in faith in Jesus Christ which prompts Christians, in spite of their historic denominational divisions, to express their mutual affection and common purpose in conferences and co-operative work. It has been shown that American Methodists have not remained apart from the various councils which exist to promote this dimension of unity. And there are many Christians who believe that the co-operative labors of the churches are an adequate expression of the church's unity.

Church unity is a stronger concept, referring to the formal relationships into which divided church bodies enter when they agree upon terms of mutual recognition and intercommunion, or when they go further to full communion or merge into one united church. The several councils of the Ecumenical Movement have made it abundantly clear that they have neither warrant nor ability to bring about the union of separate churches. This is the prerogative of the churches themselves. And very few churches in America have been unaffected by recent unions or efforts to negotiate them.

The union of three Methodist bodies in 1939 was a triumph of charity and persistence in astute negotiation. Although no major issue of a doctrinal or liturgical sort had to be overcome, there were other difficult factors which made unification a real achievement. And it is interesting to note how the contagious spirit of church unity prompted many Methodist leaders to keep speaking of the need for wider union. Writing in 1939, Dr. Mott posed the question: "Why should not our new Church here in the United States, in the years that lie ahead, take the initiative in bringing about organic union with other communions?" [62] And Bishop Oxnam, speaking in 1947, declared a kind of credo on the need and possibility of church union: "I believe union must be established. I believe that the union of the larger Protestant churches could be consummated within a decade. I believe our laity and our clergy desire union. I believe our Lord is calling upon us to unite." [63]

Despite these unqualified proddings by Methodism's two foremost spokesmen in the Ecumenical Movement, twenty years after Methodist union no agreement had been reached with any other denomination. But efforts were made—and are still alive.

Only in Japan have Methodists of American connection entered a united church, the *Kyodan*. This was formed under coercion of the Japanese government in 1941, and was continued after the war. In 1960 the large Methodist Church of Southern Asia was moving toward union in the proposed Church of North India, along with Anglicans, Presbyterians, Congregationalists, British Methodists, Brethren, Disciples, and Baptists.

The affinity between Methodists and the predecessors of the Evangelical United Brethren goes back to the late eighteenth century, and through the decades there have been unusually cordial relations. Since 1956 there have been deliberate negotiations concerning the merger of this body with The Methodist Church. The probability of consummating that union remains very hopeful.

Meanwhile the Methodist Commission on Church Union began in 1950 to hold conversations with the Commission on Approaches to Unity of the Protestant Episcopal Church. The attempt to find a basis for establishing intercommunion between the two churches is still being pressed.

A more ambitious plan for comprehensive union was initiated in 1946 by the Congregational-Christian General Council. It drew representatives of nine denominations into conference, and Bishop Holt was elected president of the group. The "Greenwich Plan" (named for the meeting place in Connecticut) called for a merger of these bodies according to a pattern allowing maximum retention of existing polity and practice of each church. Despite the notable work done and the interest aroused for this plan, it has not succeeded in gaining the official endorsement of the communions concerned.

Thus, in 1960 the Methodists of America continued to be challenged by the ecumenical revolution of the twentieth century—both to find

[62] *Methodists United for Action*, p. 124.
[63] *Proceedings of the Seventh Ecumenical Methodist Conference*, p. 114.

motivation and method for increasing participation within the various councils of churches, and to turn resolutions concerning visible church unity into reality, for the sake of the life and mission of Christ's whole church on earth.

7

Other Branches of Methodism, 1960

All too often writers and orators of the major Methodist body make sweeping references to "America's ten million Methodist members." This mistaking of the part for the whole, of The Methodist Church for the Methodist churches, is not only a provincialism. It sells American Methodism short by 20 per cent. By omission, such phrases deny about two and one half million followers of the Wesleys their equal right to the name "Methodist."

Presumptuous as it may sound, reference to the nation's ten million Methodists is made because of thoughtlessness or lack of information. Many persons are so absorbed in The Methodist Church that they are simply unaware that combined membership figures of the twenty-one different branches of the Methodist family in the United States totaled just under twelve and a half million in 1960.[64]

The Three Major Negro Bodies

Every fifth Methodist in the United States in 1960 belonged to one or another of the three major independent Negro bodies: the African Methodist Episcopal Church, the African Methodist Episcopal Zion Church, or the Christian Methodist Episcopal Church. These three churches together reported in 1960 a total of 11,437 congregations with a combined membership of 2,338,468.[65]

The three denominations, in doctrine and form of worship, are al-

[64] This figure is taken from the membership statistics of the Methodist bodies given in *Yearbook of American Churches, 1961*, ed. Benson Y. Landis (New York: National Council of the Churches of Christ in the U.S.A., 1960), except for The Methodist Church. Its membership of 9,910,741 comes from the 1960 *General Minutes*.

[65] *Yearbook of American Churches, 1961*. Current statistics, unless otherwise noted, are from this same source.

most indistinguishable. All have the same type of General Conference, Annual Conference, and district organization. Their bishops are elected for life. Their ministers belong to the same kind of itinerancy. The word "discipline" has the same meaning for all. Each denomination holds active membership in the National Council of Churches and in the World Council of Churches. All three are interested participants in the World Methodist Council.

In the past occasional encouraging talk of union has been followed by retreats from the idea. Around 1916 a merger of the three bodies seemed a distinct possibility for a time. As recently as 1961 the Board of Bishops of the A.M.E. Zion Church declared that this church "stands ready to enter union under the leadership of Godly men, . . . who would fulfill the prayer of Jesus 'that all may be one.' " [66] All three bodies have set up commissions on union. A frequently expressed opinion has been that a first step toward complete Methodist union is for these three bodies to get together, then to engage in conversations with The Methodist Church.

THE AFRICAN METHODIST EPISCOPAL CHURCH

No census of the African Methodist Episcopal Church seems to have been taken between 1951 and 1960. Figures repeated each year of this decade showed 5,878 churches with 1,166,301 members. Sunday schools numbered 6,472, with a total enrollment of 363,432.

The church has financed its overhead and benevolent program through "dollar money." For many years every local church was under the obligation to raise one dollar every year for each member. By 1956, however, the requirements had reached four dollars a year. In 1961 every class leader was expected to collect half of this amount semiannually.

The Bishops' Council of this denomination is composed of the general superintendents in charge of thirteen episcopal districts in the United States and of five others overseas. It exercises authority over the church between sessions of the quadrennial General Conference. A general board supervises financial matters. One layman and one minister from each of the eighteen episcopal districts and five members at large make up this board. The Judicial Council of this church is composed of three bishops, three elders, and three laymen.

Administrative boards for such causes as missions, Sunday schools, church extension, education, Christian education, evangelism, pensions, research and history, and religious literature are well organized and manned. Five of these boards are in Nashville, Tennessee. The others

<hr>

[66] "Message of the Board of Bishops, 1961," *Missionary Seer*, February, 1961, p. 4.

are scattered between New York, Washington, D.C., Philadelphia, and Columbia, South Carolina. A Woman's Missionary Society has headquarters in Washington, D.C.

In the past four decades this denomination has been torn with considerable dissension. In the late 1920's discontent was registered in various parts of the church by persons who felt that long tenure in their districts had produced some dictator complexes among the bishops. Relief was sought by the strategic introduction into the 1928 General Conference of a resolution that, when passed by a secret ballot, changed the assignments of all bishops who had served an episcopal district for two or more quadrennia. This apparently did not entirely solve the problem, since the General Conference of 1932 tried several bishops, finding two of them guilty and suspending two others.

Litigation in Tennessee courts lasting from 1936 to 1949 finally brought damages to the church of a hundred thousand dollars and interest from a layman who had long edited church periodicals and curriculum materials in Nashville. He refused to surrender his position, the building, or the equipment when a successor was elected by the General Conference.

In 1947 a dispute involving the expulsion of another bishop reached a federal district court in Pennsylvania. The judge upheld the procedures by which the church had called a special session of the General Conference for the trial of a bishop and the assignment of another bishop to succeed him. Again in the late '50's extended litigation resulted in the expulsion of still another bishop.

Accredited institutions of higher learning conducted by the African Methodist Episcopal Church are Allen University, Columbia, South Carolina; Morris Brown College, Atlanta, Georgia; Payne Theological Seminary at Wilberforce University, Wilberforce, Ohio; and Jackson Theological Seminary at Shorter College, North Little Rock, Arkansas. In the list of other institutions are Daniel Payne College, Birmingham, Alabama; Edward Waters College, Jacksonville, Florida; Paul Quinn College, Waco, Texas; Kittrell College, Kittrell, North Carolina; and Monrovia College, Monrovia, Liberia.

The denomination's general periodical is the *Christian Recorder*. The *Southwestern Christian Recorder* is also published in Nashville. *Voice of Missions*, a monthly, is produced by the Board of Missions in New York. This, with the *Woman's Missionary Recorder,* promotes the world interests of the church. A quarterly, the *A.M.E. Review,* is published in Philadelphia. Curriculum materials and general religious literature come from Nashville.

584   HISTORY OF AMERICAN METHODISM

THE AFRICAN METHODIST EPISCOPAL ZION CHURCH

Second in size among the three large Negro bodies is the African Methodist Episcopal Zion Church. "Zion," a name derived from the first church home in New York, has remained a shibboleth and an identification for the denomination, just as the name of the original "Bethel" Church is still used in reference to the A.M.E. Church.

Twelve bishops administer the episcopal districts, of which two are entirely overseas and two involve both foreign and domestic responsibilities. Of fifty-two Annual Conferences, seven are overseas. The twelve general officers of the church include a general secretary-auditor, a financial secretary, and the usual administrative secretaries for such interests as home missions, foreign missions, Christian education, church extension, evangelism, and publishing.

The weekly *Star of Zion,* published on the church's own presses in Charlotte, North Carolina, is the general organ. Promoting world evangelism is the *Missionary Seer,* a monthly. Other official publications are the *Quarterly Review, Church School Herald,* and curriculum periodicals.

In 1954 a denominational office of public relations was set up in New York with part-time direction. The bureau moved to Washington, D.C., in 1960 with a full-time director.

The top educational institution of this church is the fully accredited Livingstone College, in Salisbury, North Carolina, with which Hood Theological Seminary is affiliated. In 1898 James E. K. Aggrey was brought from the Gold Coast to this institution by Bishop John B. Small. After training here and in other schools, and then teaching in this college, he returned as an educator and philosopher to make his contribution to the intellectual and religious life of his emerging country (known as Ghana since 1957). The denomination supports five other educational institutions of junior college and preparatory rank.

Each episcopal district has a summer assembly center where refresher courses for ministers, educational institutes, and evangelistic programs are carried on.

Four bishops who have missionary assignments supervise the overseas program of the church. The first mission opened in Liberia in 1876, followed by Ghana in 1896. The program in Nigeria followed a request in 1930 of established churches seeking to affiliate with "Zion." Missions in British Guiana, South America, date from 1911. Reactivation in 1958 of work begun in 1877 which had languished resulted in the Bahama Island Conference. Administration of the missionary program is from the Interchurch Center in New York.

Members of the 242 overseas churches numbered 27,245 in 1960.[67] Financial support of the year's foreign program of $46,790 came from two sources: the Woman's Home and Foreign Missionary Society and the general church, the women furnishing the larger share.[68]

Figures published in the September, 1960, *Missionary Seer* (p. 6) showed the denomination to have 3,000 churches with 780,000 members. There were 2,400 pastors with charges.

As would be expected, and as is true of all the major branches of Methodism, the A.M.E. Zion Church leaders are deeply concerned in the struggle to end housing discrimination, to obtain full voting rights in practice as well as in theory, and to see completed the desegregation of schools and public facilities of all kinds. In 1961 the bishops pointed out that present "shameful, inhuman, and unChristian acts . . . reflect gruesomely on Christianity before the world of competing religions and atheistic Communism." They further asserted that "our church wants it known from the 'housetop' that we hold no bitterness and we preach no violence, but we are determined with the help of Almighty God to have our people enjoy full freedom as guaranteed by the Constitution." [69]

THE CHRISTIAN METHODIST EPISCOPAL CHURCH

Youngest and smallest of the three major Negro Methodist bodies, the Christian Methodist Episcopal Church was founded in 1870 as the Colored Methodist Episcopal Church. The name was changed when the 1954 General Conference ordered it by a large vote.

Differing from the A.M.E. and the A.M.E. Zion, the C.M.E. General Conference elects bishops without open campaigns, announcements, circulars, and appeals. The College of Bishops is in charge of the denomination's nine episcopal districts and thirty-seven Annual Conferences. A bishop presides over each of the administrative boards, which are kingdom extension, Christian education, publishing, claimants, finance, evangelism, and lay activities.

In 1951 the church reported 2,469 churches with 392,167 members, and 1,820 pastors with charges.

From the time of its first General Conference in 1870, a primary objective of the newly independent church has been the establishment of institutions of higher education. Lane College in Jackson, Tennessee, was founded in 1882, taking its name from C.M.E. Bishop Isaac Lane, who spent sixty-four years in the episcopacy, forty-one of these in effective re-

[67] *Quadrennial Report of the A.M.E. Zion Church, 1960,* p. 31.
[68] "What Is the Department of Foreign Missions of the A.M.E. Zion Church?" (leaflet published by the Department of Foreign Missions, New York, 1960.)
[69] "Message of the Board of Bishops," p. 11.

lation, and who died in his 104th year. In the same year was founded Paine College in Augusta, Georgia. Through the years it was aided by the Southern Church. Other colleges include Miles College, Birmingham, Alabama; Mississippi Industrial, Holly Springs, Mississippi; and Texas College, Tyler, Texas.

The Christian Index, a weekly started in 1868 for Negro members of the Methodist Episcopal Church, South, is still the official magazine, published in Jackson, Tennessee. The bimonthly *Eastern Index* comes from Indianapolis.

The kindly feelings cherished in 1870 between the Southern Church and its offspring, the C.M.E. Church, have continued. At the time of Methodist union in 1939 a recommendation was made that "the financial support of the Colored Methodist Episcopal Church be continued by those jurisdictional divisions with which said Church is historically related." [70]

In its 1960 *Discipline* (par. 250.3) The Methodist Church specified that "due recognition shall be given to the historic responsibility of the former Methodist Episcopal Church, South, for aid to the Christian Methodist Episcopal Church."

The Primitive Methodist Church

Immigrant missionaries brought this denomination to America in 1829. They had belonged to an English offshoot of Wesleyan Methodism known as the Primitive Methodist Church. Not all present-day members are happy about the name. They feel it has hindered their expansion, and a change is being considered.

For a number of years after the first conference in 1832, preachers came by appointment from the mother group in England. New England churches, once in an Eastern Conference, came into the Pennsylvania Conference in 1948. Similarly a Western Conference, chartered in 1860, became the western district of the Pennsylvania Conference in 1926. The Pennsylvania Conference itself was organized in 1872 and is now the only conference of the church.[71]

Seventy-five ordained clergymen administered the ninety churches composing the denomination in 1960. Each church maintained a Sunday school. The denomination now follows a unique system of pastoral appointments. Local churches may invite ministers, making a first, a second,

---

[70] *Discipline,* 1940, p. 36.

[71] This information comes from the Rev. Wesley Boyd, editor of the *Primitive Methodist Journal,* in a personal letter to the author July 3, 1961.

and a third choice. A conference stationing committee appoints pastors to those churches not expressing preferences or whose invitations are not accepted, after ratifying ministerial acceptances. About half of the churches prefer to leave assignment of pastors to this committee.

Quadrennial General Conferences have been held in September, but beginning in 1962 they will meet in May following the Annual Conference session. General church officers are a president, vice-president, secretary, and treasurer. The denomination maintains a summer conference grounds in the Poconos near Gouldsboro, Pennsylvania. The monthly *Primitive Methodist Journal* is published in Shenandoah, Pennsylvania.

The church is affiliated with the National Association of Evangelicals, and emphasizes such Wesleyan doctrines as redemption, repentance, justification, and sanctification. As in larger Methodist branches, Christian perfection is the creed but is rarely mentioned.

Missionary work has centered in Guatemala, where 22 churches with a membership of 1,253 are in operation. A daily radio program has proved fruitful. Ten persons serve this mission; nine other missionaries work under other boards but are supported by this church.[72]

After the churches had unanimously voted to unite with the Methodist Protestant Church, the 1938 General Conference turned down the proposal by but thirteen votes. Had this merger carried, the Primitive Methodist Church would have been part of Methodist reunion in 1939. Meanwhile, in 1960 union with the Evangelical Congregation Church (a body with Methodistic government and theology) was being explored.

The Wesleyan Methodist Church

The Wesleyan Methodist Church of America celebrated its centennial in 1943, recalling the withdrawal of the fathers from the Methodist Episcopal Church because it was soft on slavery and hard on abolitionists. The secessionists, led by the Rev. Orange Scott in 1843, organized a church "free from episcopacy and slavery." [73] After some debate, the name chosen was the Wesleyan Methodist Connection of America. In 1891 the word "church" in parentheses was inserted following the word "connection," to clarify this frequently misunderstood term. In 1947 the "Wesleyan Methodist Church of America" was made official. It is the only body to continue this historic name.

[72] *Primitive Methodist Journal*, May, 1961.
[73] Ira Ford McLeister, *History of the Wesleyan Methodist Church of America*, rev. by Roy Stephen Nicholson (Marion, Ind.: Wesleyan Methodist Publishing Association, 1959) , p. 31.

Through the years the Wesleyan Methodists have adhered with fidelity to the doctrines of John Wesley, zealously maintaining the Articles of Religion. Indeed, the 1951 General Conference strengthened the Article on the Sufficiency and Full Authority of the Holy Scriptures, reasoning that "an effective doctrine of holiness, upon which particular stress is placed, cannot be maintained upon . . . a relaxed view of Biblical inerrancy." [74]

The Wesleyan Methodist Church claims to be the first (1848) denomination in America to adopt an Article on entire sanctification. They also hold to Christ's second coming, "in like manner as He went away." Evolution is repudiated in favor of the belief that man came upon the earth "by the immediate creative act of God." [75]

Candidates for the ministry attend only such seminaries as are in unity with them in doctrinal matters. Conformity to Wesley's General Rules, which carry the force of constitutional law, is a condition of membership. Membership in secret societies and the use of intoxicants and tobacco is prohibited. Divorce forfeits membership for any but the innocent party in a decree granted for adultery. In 1955 came official warnings against "the perilous trend toward immodesty in dress . . . [and] apparel which does not . . . properly clothe the person." [76]

In 1947 a plan creating a full-time executive president was adopted. Since 1959 three general superintendents have replaced the one president. The Board of Administration (formerly the Book Committee) exercises basic control of every incorporated Wesleyan Methodist society and institution. Other general offices created during the twentieth century, when former fears of bureaucracy had sufficiently abated, were Sunday school secretary, foreign missions secretary, secretariat for church extension and evangelism, and general secretary of Wesleyan youth.

Following a 1957 fire which destroyed the long-held Syracuse headquarters, offices and publishing house moved to Marion, Indiana. Here are published the *Wesleyan Methodist, Wesleyan Missionary,* and *Wesleyan Youth,* as well as curriculum materials. Four colleges are so close a part of Wesleyan organization that their supporting constituencies compose the four areas into which the twenty-eight Annual Conferences are divided.

In 1960 the church supported missionary work in fourteen countries. There were 112 missionaries in the field and 340 national workers. The year's program cost $320,000. Home missionaries serve American Indians,

[74] *General Conference Minutes of the Wesleyan Methodist Church,* 1959, p. 248.
[75] *The Wesleyan Methodist Church of America—Interesting Facts for Interested Friends* (an official pamphlet published by the Wesleyan Methodist Publishing Association, 1958), p. 7.
[76] McLeister, *History of the Wesleyan Methodist Church,* p. 489.

border Mexicans, and mountaineers. In New York and Israel, missions to the Jews are conducted.

The 1955 General Conference turned down a proposal to unite with the Free Methodists by a vote of sixty-two for, ninety-six against. The chief obstacle was fear of the Free Methodists' mild form of episcopacy. A joint plan of union in 1955, approved by the Pilgrim Holiness Church in 1958, lost in the 1959 Wesleyan General Conference by a fraction in attaining the required two-thirds majority.

The reluctance of the denomination to participate in the National and World Councils is, according to leaders, not a desire for disunity.[77] It is rather a fear that to go along with movements tending toward a world church might involve a sacrifice of principles. In line with this fear, the Wesleyans withdrew from the International Council of Religious Education in 1951.

The editor of the *Wesleyan Methodist,* in a report to the 1959 General Conference, said that his paper "has pled for moderation in the question of desegregation [and] lamented the extreme positions taken by persons on both sides of this question." [78]

Wesleyan Methodists were in second place in 1960 for per capita giving among denominations reporting to the Department of Stewardship of the National Council of Churches, contributing $228.13 per member for all purposes. Benevolence contributions of $46.54 per member put this group in fifth place.[79] Sixty per cent of members are enrolled tithers.[80]

In 1960 the Wesleyan Methodist Church reported 35,581 members in 1,077 churches.[81] To these "full" members might be added 3,756 associate and 4,124 junior members. Overseas there were 106 organized and 80 unorganized churches with 8,027 full members and 2,008 associate members.[82] Total giving in 1959-60 for all purposes was $8,018,027, of which $664,312 was for benevolence.

The Free Methodist Church

While many of the reasons underlying the establishment of the Free Methodist Church in 1860 parallel those which caused the Wesleyan defection in 1843, there was one marked difference: the Free Methodist

[77] *Ibid.,* p. 478.

[78] *General Conference Minutes of the Wesleyan Methodist Church,* 1959, p. 61.

[79] *Statistics of Church Finances* (New York: Department of Stewardship, National Council of Churches, 1960) , p. 4.

[80] *The Wesleyan Methodist Church of America,* p. 33.

[81] The *Wesleyan Methodist,* January 25, 1961, p. 9.

[82] *Ibid.,* February 8, 1961, p. 8.

Church was organized by ministers expelled from their conferences and by laymen who had been "read out" of their churches. Founders of the Wesleyan Church had withdrawn from the Methodist Episcopal Church voluntarily.

In 1910 the Genesee Conference made it evident that the expulsion fifty years earlier of the Rev. Benjamin Titus Roberts and his sympathizers was unwarranted, and returned the credentials they had cancelled. "Looked at half a century later it seems unjust and therefore exceedingly unwise," Dr. Ray Allen said in making the restoration. "Those expelled brethren were among the best men the Conference contained." [83]

These reformers condemned pew renting and pew sales, deplored neglect of the doctrine of entire sanctification, criticized merchandising methods in church finance, opposed oath-bound secret societies, fought the use of liquor and tobacco, and preached abolition. The same doctrinal emphases have been carried on in the twentieth century. "With those loose religious beliefs associated with the words 'liberal,' 'evolution,' 'modernist,' the Free Methodist Church has no fellowship," a spokesman wrote. "We believe that evolution is not only contrary to the teachings of the Scriptures, but stands absolutely unsupported by a single proven fact of science." [84]

The only reversal from the stand of the founders has been the repeal of the prohibition of choirs and instrumental music. Local option on this matter was granted in 1943 by the close vote of eighty-eight to eighty-four. In 1955 the anti-choir restriction was deleted. Collaboration with the Wesleyan Methodists in publication of a hymnal occurred first in 1910, then 1951.

The name given the new society at its organization was accepted with enthusiasm. The Free Methodist Church meant *free* seats, *free*dom from ecclesiastical domination, *free*dom from sin, and *free*dom in worship. During its history the Free Methodist Church has been selective in its membership, taking "too many unpopular positions to be accused of making size the main quest." [85] By 1903 the church numbered 30,149. At its 1960 centennial its 1,340 churches enrolled 45,036 full members sixteen years or older, 3,782 under sixteen, and 7,959 preparatory members—a total of 56,777. There were 2,119 ministers. Overseas members numbered 39,523, and preachers in conference relation were 1,911. The

[83] Leslie Ray Marston, *A Living Witness* (Winona Lake, Ind.: Light and Life Press, 1960) , p. 247.

[84] Carl L. Howland, *The Story of Our Church* (Winona Lake, Ind.: Free Methodist Publishing House, 1940) , p. 75.

[85] *Ibid.*, p. 113.

centennial grand total membership in all categories and all countries was 98,211.[86]

The Free Methodist Church has frequently been among the leading Protestant bodies in per capita giving. In the tabulation for the calendar year 1959, it stood at the top of the list in giving for all purposes, with an annual gift per member of $269.71. It was also first in per capita benevolent giving, the figure being $156.07.[87]

At the end of the denomination's first century 200 missionaries were serving 22 fields. An appropriation of $818,000 provided the services of 1,400 national pastors, evangelists, and teachers, the operation of 14 Bible schools for workers, 210 day schools, and 18 hospitals and dispensaries.[88]

The four bishops of the Free Methodist Church, unlike those of the parent organization, are elected for four-year terms, with re-election permissible. They chair the four commissions on administration, missions, education, and evangelism. A board of administration and general secretaries carry out the programs. The denomination takes particular satisfaction in its Sunday schools, the number of which (1,374 in 1960) surpasses its churches. Average attendance is unusually high, 96,677 out of 145,590.[89]

Four four-year colleges have been developed, and five junior colleges. An affiliation with Asbury Theological Seminary, Wilmore, Kentucky (independent conservative), was replaced in 1947 by the John Wesley Seminary Foundation, which provides scholarships and guidance for qualified students.

The *Free Methodist* with its circulation of 30,000 reaches nearly every home of the 56,777 members in English-speaking countries. Other periodicals in 1960 were *Missionary Tidings* (for women), *The Sunday School Journal,* and *Youth in Action.* Since 1943 the church has used radio successfully in a weekly "Light and Life Hour."

Zealous to perpetuate sound doctrine, Free Methodists have found it difficult to be ecumenical without compromising their denominational distinctiveness. In 1959, however, a merger with the small Holiness Movement Church of Canada brought several hundred members, and with them an Egyptian national church of 5,000 members.

By affiliating with the National Holiness Association, the National Association of Evangelicals, and the quinquennial World Methodist Con-

---

[86] *Centenary Yearbook of the Free Methodist Church, 1960* (Winona Lake: Free Methodist Publishing House), pp. 444-45, 442.

[87] *Statistics of Church Finances, 1960,* p. 4.

[88] Marston, *A Living Witness,* p. 466.

[89] *Centenary Yearbook,* p. 443.

ference, the denomination steers a course, as Bishop Leslie R. Marston puts it, "between secular bigotry and ecumenical indifference." [90]

Spokesmen for the church explain the absence of the Free Methodist Church from the list of members of the National and World Councils on two grounds: the liberal position held by a large proportion of the leaders and the inadequate doctrinal requirements. "But the church does not withhold fellowship from those who belong to the Council merely on the basis of their affiliation." [91] To make it clear that Free Methodists hold no animosity toward those who do not see doctrinal matters their way, they demonstrate ready willingness to co-operate strongly in matters of moral reform and civic improvement.

The Southern Methodist Church

Two small Methodist bodies, the Southern Methodist Church and the Evangelical Methodist Church, are relatively young. In January, 1939, a "Laymen's Organization for the Preservation of the Methodist Episcopal Church, South," established the Southern Methodist Church as a haven for those who shrank from contagion with the "alarming infidelity and apostasy found in the M.E. Church, North." [92] However, this new denomination, on the theory that the few rural churches declining to participate in Methodist reunion in 1939 now constitute the continuing body of the former Methodist Episcopal Church, South, prefers "to reckon its inception . . . from the year 1845 when the division came in the Methodist Episcopal Church." [93] The courts have disagreed with this claim, granting The Methodist Church all properties and full control of the name Methodist Episcopal Church, South.

The Southern Methodist Church dispensed with bishops and district superintendents. In order "to perpetuate the faith of John Wesley," [94] a South Carolina Conference was formed of about ten circuits and station churches. The Mid-south and the South-west Annual Conferences merged in 1961. The denomination reported 31 pastoral charges, 48 churches, and an inclusive membership of 4,608 for 1960.

Sessions of the General Conference have occurred at irregular inter-

[90] *The Spirit and Emphasis of Free Methodism* (an official leaflet published by the Free Methodist Publishing House, n.d.), p. 3.

[91] Marston, *A Living Witness*, p. 563.

[92] Lynn Corbett, *What, Why, How?—History, Organization, and Doctrinal Belief of the Southern Methodist Church* (Greenville, S. C.: Foundry Press, 1956), p. 3.

[93] The Rev. Wallace R. Terry, Jr., president of Southern Methodist College, in a personal letter to the author, March 24, 1961.

[94] Corbett, *What, Why, How?* p. 3.

vals, the sixth meeting in 1958. Laymen and clergy have equal voting power. A president and secretary are elected. A pastoral placement system allows congregations to call their own ministers. Churches and parsonages are owned and controlled by local members.

The church announces with some pride its doctrine of racial exclusiveness. Between "Of Satan, Angels, and Demons" and "Of the Clergy" is this Article of Religion: "Of Segregation: The Southern Methodist Church is a segregated church. We believe that integration . . . is not the answer to current social problems." [95]

The president of the Southern Methodist Church, reporting to the General Conference his attendance at the American Council of Churches convention, stated that he had been "especially blessed by the message delivered . . . by Dr. Carl McIntire." He also explained that "the purpose of the A.C.C. is to oppose the National Council of the Churches of Christ in the U.S.A." [96]

Southern Methodist College was opened in Aiken, South Carolina, in 1956. Primarily a junior college, the institution offers a five-year course leading to a Bachelor of Theology degree. Courses listed in the 1960-61 bulletin include ecclesiology, Christology and pneumatology, anthropology, hamartiology and soteriology, eschatology, and hermeneutics. In spite of this mature nutriment for ministerial candidates, Mrs. A. C. Aston, a delegate, rose in the 1958 General Conference to declare her opposition "to the method of obtaining preachers for the Southern Methodist Church by ordaining school boys." [97]

The Evangelical Methodist Church

Two familiar grievances brought the Evangelical Methodist Church into being May 9, 1946, at Memphis, Tennessee. Five or six preachers and congregations could not endure what they regarded as arbitrary and autocratic supervision, and they were worried about modernism in The Methodist Church. They sought to create a denominational environment where their revivalistic zeal could be exercised without restraint.

Within two years the church listed 40 ministers and 60 churches, and by 1960, 99 churches with 5,779 members and 100 Sunday schools with an enrollment of 9,493 were reported. Meanwhile, a mission in Mexico was launched and another in Colombia was acquired.

[95] *Ibid.*, p. 16.
[96] *Minutes of the General Conference of the Southern Methodist Church* (Memphis, 1958) , pp. 10-11.
[97] *Ibid.*, p. 16.

Leaders of the secession describe the denomination as "fundamental in doctrine, evangelistic in program, congregational in government." [98]

In 1958 attempts to merge the Evangelical Methodist Church and the Southern Methodist Church failed because the Evangelicals would not accept the requirement that the name of the new church be "The Southern Methodist Church."

The Evangelical Methodist is published in Street, Maryland, and *The Voice of Methodism* in Wilmore, Kentucky. The church has three conferences, with a general superintendent over each. It operates along congregational lines.

Smaller Methodist Bodies

The type of organization of four small Methodist bodies makes the name "congregational" descriptive. The Congregational Methodist Church is the result of the 1852 withdrawal of Georgia members from the Methodist Episcopal Church, South, because of a distaste for the episcopacy and the itinerancy. The present church is the survivor, after two thirds of the members left in 1887 to become Congregationalists. The 223 churches in 1957 had a membership of 14,274, all church officers residing in Texas.

The Congregational Methodist Church of the U.S.A., organized in 1852, reported 100 churches in 1954 with 7,500 members. Incorporated in Anniston, Alabama, in 1937, the church has a monthly, *The Watchman*, distributed from Decatur, Mississippi.

The New Congregational Methodist Church, which grew out of an 1881 conflict over the consolidation of several rural churches in Georgia and Florida, has added footwashing to the usual Methodist rites. Eleven churches enrolled 518 members in 1958, six clergymen having charges.

The Reformed New Congregational Methodist Church has adopted the discipline of Wesleyan and Free Methodists regarding lodges, dress, and amusements. Founded by a Congregational Methodist evangelist in 1916, this group reported 8 churches with 329 members in 1936.[99]

An offshoot of Congregational Methodism is the Cumberland Methodist Church. With its four churches and sixty members it is the smallest denomination in the Methodist family. It was organized in Tennessee in 1950.

[98] Statement by the Rev. W. W. Breckbill of Altoona, Pennsylvania—one of the cofounders—in a personal conversation with the author, June 24, 1961.

[99] Frank S. Mead, *Handbook of Denominations in the United States* (2nd rev. ed.; Nashville: Abingdon Press, 1961), p. 162.

The Holiness Methodist Church is the name of at least two Methodist bodies. The Constitution Northwestern Holiness Association, organized in North Dakota in 1909, took the Methodist name in 1920. It reported 30 churches and a membership of 1,000, administered from Minneapolis.

A smaller North Carolina Holiness Group with 7 churches, 5 ministers, and 360 members, has changed its official title to the Lumber River Annual Conference of the Holiness Methodist Church. It was founded in 1900.

The Holiness Methodists cited by Dr. Elmer T. Clark [100] are a North Carolina offshoot of the Wesleyan Methodist Church. This body was organized in 1913, and reported 4 churches and 600 members in 1913.

The Fundamental Methodist Church, Inc., with headquarters in Springfield, Missouri, is an antimodernism secession from The Methodist Church. Fifteen churches list 696 members.

Several small groups have withdrawn from the three major Negro bodies. The Independent A.M.E. Church was organized by elders of Jacksonville, Florida, following disputes with their presiding elders. In 1940, 12 churches had 1,000 members. This body is unique in ordaining deacons at the Annual Conference and elders and bishops at the General Conference.

The Reformed Methodist Union Episcopal Church split from the A.M.E. Church in 1885 over disputed elections of delegates to the General Conference. In 1896 it reversed earlier practices and adopted an episcopal and connectional polity. It reported 33 churches with 11,000 members in 1954.

The Reformed Zion Union Apostolic Church, which broke from the A.M.E. Zion Church in Virginia in 1869, reported 2 episcopal districts, 52 churches, and 12,000 members in 1956.

The Union American Methodist Episcopal Church had 256 churches in 1957 with 27,560 members and 3 bishops. The name was taken in 1850 after a division of the original Union Church of Africans, founded in 1813 by the Rev. Peter Spencer.

The African Union First Colored Methodist Protestant Church, Inc., resulted from an 1866 union of the African Union Church and the First Colored Methodist Protestant Church. The official name formerly included the words "of America or Elsewhere." Its 33 churches in 1953 had 5,000 members. Home missions are carried on by a woman's group called the Grand Body.

[100] Elmer T. Clark, *The Small Sects in America* (Nashville: Abingdon Press, 1949), p. 65.

chapter 34

METHODISM'S CONTRIBUTION TO AMERICA

American Culture

The Frontier

The Civil War

Free Grace and
 Free Will

The Revival

J UST OVER A CENTURY AGO, A GERMAN immigrant who had become a professor of theology in the United States took upon himself the assignment of explaining the mystery of the New World to the citizens of the Old World. Philip Schaff (or Schaf, as he still wrote it sometimes) had come from a German-Swiss home through German universities to a theological professorship in Mercersburg, Pennsylvania.[1] His German lectures on America were delivered in Berlin on March 20 and 30, 1854, and were published in an English translation in 1855. They have been called by their recent editor "the preëminent accounting to the home country by an immigrant of the early nineteenth century as to what translation to the New World means."[2] As such, the book is of great importance to anyone interested in isolating and identifying the genius of American history. But because Schaff was a historian of the entire church, who looked at the American spirit from the perspective of the centuries of Christian tradition, his assessment is of particular value to the student of America's religious development.

In recent decades interpreters of American thought and culture have continually drawn upon Alexis de Tocqueville's *Democracy in America* and upon such works as Michel-Guillaume

[1] Cf. James Hastings Nichols, *Romanticism in American Theology: Nevin and Schaff at Mercersburg* (Chicago: University of Chicago Press, 1961), pp. 230-32, on the background of Schaff's lectures on America.

[2] Perry Miller, "Editor's Introduction" to Philip Schaff, *America: A Sketch of Its Political, Social, and Religious Character* (Cambridge, Mass.: The Belknap Press of Harvard University, 1961), p. xxvii.

596

Jean de Crèvecoeur's *Letters from an American Farmer* for insights into the uniqueness of America. Neither of these perceptive Frenchmen, for all their astute observation of the religious life of America, saw the realities of church life and thought in the United States as clearly as did Schaff. Because Schaff's survey of the American churches included a brief but careful explanation of Methodism, this chapter of the present *History of American Methodism,* written by a historian of Christian thought who has many theological and historical affinities with Philip Schaff, will draw upon his description of the Methodists, relating the judgments he formulated a century ago to the problem of the contribution of Methodism to American thought and culture.

1

Methodism and American Culture

The Most American of Churches

It is generally believed that the three major religious groups owing their origins to American soil are the Church of Christ, Scientist, the Disciples of Christ, and the Church of Jesus Christ of Latter-day Saints. But only in a technical sense may The Methodist Church be excluded from such a list. As Schaff correctly pointed out, "Methodism . . . may almost as well be called an American product, as an English. . . . In fact Methodism established itself independently in America, even before it did in England." [3] The history of American Methodism actually spans the history of the republic. Despite the difficulties encountered in the years of the American Revolution, the church soon lost the stigma of Toryism and became so closely identified with the new nation that it was, and still is, thought of as the most American of churches, embodying many of the characteristics associated by both natives and foreigners with the typical American.

One interesting index to the importance of Methodism for the development of American thought and culture can be found in the realm of language. The coming-of-age of America in one field after another has been reflected by the creation of original words and phrases or by the adaptation of traditional ones to new usage. Sometimes these original

[3] *America,* p. 136.

American coinages find their way not only into British speech, much to the consternation of purists, but even into the languages of the European Continent. The most obvious instance is probably "jazz." But students of American English have also made clear that "in several areas of speech the English make daily use of terms that have never penetrated to the United States—for example, in that of ecclesiastical activity." [4] On the other hand, the special development of Protestantism in the United States has likewise been reflected in our language. Thus the word "church" as a verb has traditionally referred to the ritual in *The Book of Common Prayer* by which a woman, after childbirth, gave public thanks to God for the birth of her child; in the United States, however, "to church" has come to mean "to subject to church discipline." In earlier English speech "to pledge" meant to drink a toast, as in Ben Jonson's line, "And I will pledge with mine"; because of the drive for temperance, led by Methodist preachers and bishops, "to pledge" or "to take the pledge" eventually meant—particularly, though not, of course, exclusively, in the United States—to abstain from all toasts. Numerous other technical terms of American religion remain as a legacy from the days of the Methodist revivals on the frontier. The "jerks" were a phenomenon of the revival; the *Oxford English Dictionary* cites one of the earliest instances of the term in the history of the language: "These Methodis' sets people crazy with the jerks, I've hearn tell." Largely because of the revival, "commitment" and "decision" have become the standard terms in American English for the establishment of the relation of faith between God and man, and "to get religion" seems to have been derived from the same historical source.

These philological data suggest the intimate connection between the people called Methodists and the American way. Even Americans who are devoted to no religion except the democratic faith are obliged to speak about this in a Wesleyan vocabulary. The language and thought of those who are "Protestant but not Christian" [5] is conditioned by this stream of American Christianity. Methodism was not alone in the development of frontier religion and of its vocabulary, of course, but it, more than any other church, caught up the spirit of the revival. One leading historian of the revival, who reads it primarily within the context of American history rather than of church history, has observed: "A

---

[4] H. L. Mencken, *The American Language, Supplement One* (New York: Alfred A. Knopf, 1956), p. 500.

[5] In a paper delivered to a seminar of the American Association of Colleges of Teacher Education, October 4-8, 1961, I used this phrase as a title for an essay on the cultural religion of the United States, described by recent critics as actually Protestantism-minus-Christianity.

doctrine which allowed an individual some say in his (or her) eternal destiny harmonized better with democratic theory, and Methodism was thus several steps ahead in the race for converts in the new and professedly equalitarian America." [6] As the next section of this chapter will point out, Methodism succeeded so well in shaping the typically American understanding of religion that the Americanization of other churches, notably of those churches whose origins lay on the European Continent, entailed the adoption of Methodist practices and "new measures." The religious distribution of the Senate and the House of Representatives since the Civil War has frequently indicated that Methodism is not only the largest of the Protestant bodies, but also the most representatively American—or, perhaps, that Methodism, equally with Puritanism, constitutes the main stream of America's religious history.

The Free Church as the American Establishment

From what has been said thus far it appears that the contribution of Methodism to the development of American thought and culture has been far more decisive than the conventional mythology about the Pilgrim Fathers would lead one to suppose. It is, of course, true that the "deepest roots" of "the ecclesiastical life of North America" lie in "the emigration of the Puritan 'Pilgrim Fathers.' " [7] But one need only examine the history and the present state of the colonial church bodies in the United States to discern that they have acquired many of the characteristics of the Methodism against which they once reacted so violently.[8] Schaff observed this process at work in the churches which he and his hearers understood best, the Reformed and the Lutheran bodies that stood in the German tradition. "In America," he wrote, Methodism "has had, perhaps, of all sections of the church, next to Puritanism, the greatest influence on the general religious life." [9] Therefore he interpreted the "American Lutheranism" being advocated by Samuel Simon Schmucker and his followers as "an amalgamation of Lutheranism with American Puritanic and Methodistic elements." [10] So "Meth-

[6] Bernard A. Weisberger, *They Gathered at the River: The Story of the Great Revivalists and Their Impact upon Religion in America* (Boston: Little, Brown, and Company, 1958), p. 43.

[7] Schaff, *America,* p. 89.

[8] Cf. Carl Bridenbaugh, *Mitre and Sceptre. Transatlantic Faiths, Ideas, Personalities, and Politics 1689-1775* (New York: Oxford University Press, 1962), pp. 83-84.

[9] *America,* p. 137.

[10] *Ibid.,* p. 150.

odistic" had some Lutherans become that, to Schaff's horror, they accused his colleague, John Nevin, of Romanizing tendencies in his doctrine of the Lord's Supper, even though Nevin was trying to expound the eucharistic doctrines of John Calvin.[11] It seemed to Schaff that the same Methodist influence was at work undermining the traditional "idea of objective baptismal grace." [12] One is constrained to speculate what Schaff's reactions would have been if he had seen how this idea of objective baptismal grace was set forth in the tract on baptism written by the Rev. Samuel Wesley and revised and published by John Wesley in 1756.[13]

As a consequence of this transformation of Christian traditions that originated in Europe, the spirit of American Protestantism has its own special characteristics, and in many ways there is more affinity among American churches than there is between any one of them and its British or Continental counterpart.[14] This American spirit, the despair of the traditional German taxonomy that classifies the churches according to their confessions,[15] constitutes an ecclesiastical establishment uniquely our own. Ironically, the free churches, which began as a "second Reformation" directed against the establishments that had emerged from the sixteenth century, have shaped the definition of the Christian gospel among the American descendants of these establishments. Schaff himself saw the complexity of the relation between Reformed or Lutheran Pietism and American Methodism:

Methodism and Pietism have in common an earnest interest for subjective experimental [i.e., experiential] religion, repentance, conversion, regeneration. . . . Yet, after all, there is a very considerable difference between Methodism and Pietism, founded in the difference between the English and German national character. Methodism lacks throughout the German depth, and inwardness, the contemplative turn for the mystical, and a vigorous, fruitful, and profound theology; while on the other hand, it far surpasses Pietism in energetic outward activity, going forth to conquest. They are related in this respect like Martha and Mary, Peter and John.[16]

During the century since he wrote those words, the Pietist churches,

[11] Cf. Nichols, *Romanticism in American Theology*, pp. 84-106.

[12] *America*, p. 144.

[13] See Colin W. Williams, *John Wesley's Theology Today* (Nashville: Abingdon Press, 1960) , pp. 115-22.

[14] Cf. Jerald C. Brauer, *Protestantism in America* (Philadelphia: Westminster Press, 1953) , p. 8.

[15] Jaroslav Pelikan, "Foreword" to Werner Elert, *The Structure of Lutheranism*, tr. Walter A. Hansen (Saint Louis: Concordia Publishing House, 1962) , pp. vii-viii.

[16] *America*, pp. 139-40.

whether Lutheran or Reformed, have in many ways learned to imitate Methodism even more, as have the Puritan churches.

This free church establishment means that the history and character of Methodism in the United States cannot be assessed through a consideration of this church alone, but must be viewed in the framework of all of American culture. The closeness of the affinity between Methodism and the American spirit has come into dramatic evidence during the past century, as the growth of Roman Catholicism and Judaism in the United States has transformed this nation from a Protestant to a pluralistic one. By a corollary, the Roman Catholic "threat" to America conjured up by Protestant nativism was in actuality a threat to the ethos of a free church establishment. Yet it is a tribute to the inner vitality of the American free churches, including The Methodist Church, that many of their spokesmen have taken the lead in attacking the myth of Protestant hegemony and in urging that Americans of all persuasions—Protestant, Roman Catholic, Eastern Orthodox, Jewish, and secular humanist alike—recognize the fact of pluralism and come to terms with it.[17] To a degree that cannot be measured but must be intuited, however, even this pluralistic America continues to show its free church ancestry. Roman Catholicism in America, like the Methodism of which Schaff wrote, "lacks the German depth, and inwardness, the contemplative turn for the mystical, and a vigorous, fruitful, and profound theology; while on the other hand, it far surpasses [European Catholicism] in energetic outward activity, going forth to conquest." Martha is its patron saint, too.

Frontiers Old and New

On July 12, 1893, Professor Frederick Jackson Turner delivered a lecture on "The Significance of the Frontier in American History," by which he shaped a generation of historians of the United States.[18] It is not without significance that two of the pioneers of American church history during this century, Peter Mode and William Warren Sweet, deliberately related their interpretations of American Protestantism to the Turner thesis. It is certainly important that both of them found substantiation for the thesis in the history of American Methodism.

[17] Cf. Franklin H. Littell, *From State Church to Pluralism: A Protestant Interpretation of Religion in American History* (Chicago: Aldine Publishing Company, 1962).

[18] Frederick Jackson Turner, *The Frontier in American History* (New York: Henry Holt and Company, 1953) reprints this programmatic essay, together with later refinements and adaptations of it.

Sweet assembled documents to describe the history of several churches on the frontier.[19] But it was pre-eminently as a historian of Methodism in various areas that he adapted and revised what Turner had suggested about the vision of the beckoning frontier as a clue to American history.[20] For the understanding of this aspect of American church history, Turner's proposal was a fruitful and accurate, if not a complete, explanation.

It would appear impossible to interpret Methodist history without some such "frontier thesis," and long before Turner, Philip Schaff observed that Methodism in the United States was "particularly fitted for breaking the way in new regions, for aggressive missionary pioneer service, and for laboring among the lower classes of the people." [21] Much of the history of Methodism between the American Revolution and the Civil War, the very period Philip Schaff had in view as he spoke, was influenced by the needs of the frontier. To be sure, the influence was never unilateral. In the area of worship, for example, it would be an oversimplification to claim that frontier conditions alone were responsible for the indifference of nineteenth-century Methodism to the niceties of liturgical observance; as we shall see, there were indigenous factors within the history of Methodist worship itself that moved it to react as it did to the frontier. Still, the frontier did provide ideal ground for the Methodist understanding of worship to take root.

On the frontier the ties of tradition, whether religious or cultural, were loose. Yet those who had left their old ways behind them still needed and wanted what was essential in the tradition, stripped of the frills and accretions but renewed in its vigor and presented with power. A church that had been forged in the heat of one man's search for such vigor and power and in his rediscovery of the essence of evangelical Christianity was ideally suited to the demands of the frontier. And so "the westward movement of the frontier created over and over again a social and religious need to which [Methodist] revivalism ministered." [22] Here men found the Christian message of judgment and grace addressed to their

[19] Peter George Mode, *The Frontier Spirit in American Christianity* (New York: The Macmillan Company, 1923); see pp. 123-37 on Methodism. William Warren Sweet, *Religion on the American Frontier*, Vol. 4: *The Methodists* (Chicago: University of Chicago Press, 1946). Earlier volumes, the first of which was published in 1931, dealt successively with the Baptists, the Presbyterians, and the Congregationalists.

[20] Sweet, *Circuit-Rider Days in Indiana* (Indianapolis: W. K. Stewart Company, 1916); *Circuit-Rider Days Along the Ohio* (New York: Methodist Book Concern, 1923); *Men of Zeal: The Romance of American Methodist Beginnings* (New York: The Abingdon Press, 1935).

[21] *America*, pp. 137-38.

[22] Elizabeth K. Nottingham, *Methodism and the Frontier: Indiana Proving Ground* (New York: Columbia University Press, 1941), p. 193.

lost condition. Methodist sermons and hymns created an awareness of the specific sins of a frontier society, and the decisions elicited by the revival made the faith of distant centuries an existential thing. Because the spirit of the frontier has been shared by colonists and settlers, pioneers and immigrants, the Methodist way of faith and obedience has become embedded in the American experience, as our preceding discussion has suggested. After all, it was not a Methodist president but the Roman Catholic John F. Kennedy who summoned his fellow citizens to commit themselves to the call of a new frontier.

The very phrase "new frontier," however, suggests some of the subtlety of the Turner hypothesis—a subtlety often lost in the less creative writings of his followers. For the history of Methodism it is important to note that the frontier was a sociological as well as a geographical phenomenon. Thus, when the geographical frontier had moved west and when it finally disappeared, the techniques of frontier religion did not automatically lose their relevance. Like their brethren in faith across the Atlantic, American Methodists concerned themselves for the silent in the land. The American proletariat and the American Negro, both before and after emancipation, were still on the frontier long after urbanization and industrialization had begun to reshape American society. If anything, it was the loss of the frontier spirit rather than its retention that gradually alienated Methodism from elements of American society that had been its traditional concern, and caused The Methodist Church to be replaced in their loyalties by forms of Christian witness and obedience that seemed to breathe more of a Wesleyan spirit than the respectable Wesleyans did. Such, at least, has been the judgment of Pentecostal and Holiness churches, which even in their opposition to Methodism represent a Methodist movement, and even in their urban setting belong to the spirit of the American frontier.

The Life of the Mind

The Methodist movement, like the Protestant Reformation itself, may be said to have been born in a university. Therefore it might seem to be committed to the life of the mind and to intellectual pursuits. In fact, however, as earlier chapters of this *History* make clear, the educational achievements of Methodism in the United States did not come without severe internal conflict and self-examination. That process of conflict and self-examination was going on as Schaff wrote. He summarized the situation and pondered its possible implications:

Formerly, appealing to the apostles and evangelists of the primitive church, [American Methodism] used to condemn learning and theology from principle, as dangerous to practical piety; and to boast, that its preachers had "never rubbed their backs against the walls of a college," and yet knew the better how to catch fish in the net of the kingdom of God. But in this respect, a considerable change has been, for some years, going on. The Methodists are now beginning to establish colleges and seminaries, to publish scientific periodicals, and to follow the steps of the culture of the age. But it is a question whether they will not thus lose more in their peculiar character and influence with the masses, than they will gain in the more cultivated circles.[23]

Phrases like "never rubbed their backs against the walls of a college" are common in early Methodist language, even in the printed memoirs and diaries of frontier preachers; they must have been even more frequent in sermons and in conversation or debate. For a scholar like Schaff, of course, this attitude was hard to comprehend, smacking of a fanaticism and anti-intellectualism altogether foreign to his view both of culture and of Christianity. Even he had to admit, however, that the formalism and ritualism against which Wesleyanism was a valid protest had been closely connected with the training of the clergy in academic theology. Moreover, the anti-intellectualism of which he complains was seldom as unqualified as his words would suggest. It is possible, for example, to quote Peter Cartwright's pungent statement: "Really I have seen so many of these educated preachers who forcibly reminded me of lettuce growing under the shade of a peach-tree, or like a gosling that had got the straddles by wading in the dew, that I turn away sick and faint." [24] Yet even he was prepared, he said, to "thank God for education, and educated Gospel ministers who are of the right stamp, and of the right spirit." [25]

Alongside the anti-intellectual fulminations of a Cartwright it is necessary to place the heroic accounts of the Methodist ministers and laymen who labored to establish institutions of higher learning across the frontier. Contending against hostility outside the church and resistance within it, such men as John Carlisle Kilgo, the president of Trinity College, which was later to become Duke University, urged upon their fellow Methodists the necessity for specifically Christian colleges. "A pastor whose influence among his people is not sufficient to determine the selection of a Christian college instead of a secular institution," Kilgo maintained, "cannot hope to influence his people in the higher and graver principles

[23] America, p. 138.

[24] Autobiography of Peter Cartwright, Centennial Edition (Nashville: Abingdon Press, 1956), p. 64.

[25] Ibid., pp. 267-68.

of Christian faith." [26] Out of this work have come colleges and universities, many of which bear the unmistakable mark of their Methodist origins even when they are no longer subject to the discipline and support of The Methodist Church. In this sense the Methodist suspicion of the life of the mind, noted by Schaff, has certainly been outgrown.

Nevertheless, even in this respect Methodism embodies a deeply American characteristic that goes far beyond the borders of any one denomination. When American theologians of various denominational traditions participate in ecumenical discussions, they find that despite their deep and continuing differences they share a theological attitude that sets them apart from their European brethren. Even those whose theological scholarship is a match for any on the Continent are simply not willing to assign as much importance to such scholarship as European, and especially German, Protestants do. The corrosive effects of this American attitude are obvious to anyone who tries to be a theological scholar in the midst of a busy Protestantism that is cumbered about much serving, and Methodist theologians have had more than their share of suffering under the impatience of the church with the slow process of theological reflection. But at their best, the preaching, devotion, and action of The Methodist Church have also illustrated the positive value of a healthy suspicion about the importance of a conceptual interpretation of problems and issues in the life of the church. The problem remains, however, as Schaff saw, whether the evolution of a more sophisticated Methodism—and of a more sophisticated American theological scholarship generally—has not in fact deprived theologians of their effectiveness in addressing the churches, even while it has not succeeded in gaining any other audience for them.

The Methodist Share in the Great American Trial

Throughout this essay on Methodism's contribution to American culture we have been emphasizing the intimate connection between Methodism and the American spirit. But no event dramatizes this connection more forcefully than the split of 1844 over the question of slavery. Almost two decades before Fort Sumter, a divided church gave evidence of how divided the nation was. Writing about halfway between the Methodist schism and the national schism, Schaff attempted to explain to his German hearers that the split in the church had been brought on by what we now call "nontheological factors":

[26] Quoted in Paul Neff Garber, *John Carlisle Kilgo* (Durham: Duke University Press, 1937), pp. 62-63.

The Methodist Episcopal Church in the United States has been divided since 1847 into two almost equal parts, a northern and a southern. These have broken off all intercommunion, and have recently had a vexatious lawsuit about the division of the common property. The sole cause of the separation was slavery. The Methodists of the northern and western States are mostly abolitionists, and would not suffer that their brethren in the south should hold, buy, and sell immortal men as property.[27]

Part III of this *History* has provided a detailed account of the trauma of the schism, and of how it affected Christian faith and life at all levels of the church. It is highly regrettable that the commemoration of the centennial of the Civil War, which produced an entire library of books, did not seem to have provoked a comprehensive examination of the significance of the war for the history of American Protestantism. Christian students of the Civil War may be inclined to forget, therefore, the "not entirely holy and unselfish" [28] behavior of the churches. Secular readers of the sources, on the other hand, may dismiss the religious elements of the struggle as "the capacity for self-delusion of the Bible-drugged New England idealist." [29] But both Lincoln's conception of "the almost chosen people" [30] and the deep ambivalence in Southern Protestantism demand a far more sensitive interpretation of the place of Christianity on both sides before, during, and after the war. Perhaps the books inspired by the centennial will call forth such an interpretation sometime in the future.

Two issues in the interpretation of the church and the Civil War are of special interest to readers of this *History*. The first is the importance of the war in the history of the division and the reunion of American Methodism. Because of the role played by the Civil War in dividing the American churches, the ecumenical movement in the United States has been able to draw upon the national repentance over the war for some of its inspiration. The healing of the wound in Methodism was foreshadowed by the agreements formulated at the Cape May Conference in 1876, where the separated branches of the church were recognized as equally legitimate. Much of the ecumenical fervor in American Methodism during the past century has been directed to the cause of Methodist reunion. It must be admitted, in spite of Methodist contributions to

[27] *America*, p. 138.
[28] William Warren Sweet, *The Methodist Episcopal Church and the Civil War* (Cincinnati: Methodist Book Concern, 1912), p. 110.
[29] Edmund Wilson, *Patriotic Gore: Studies in the Literature of the American Civil War* (New York: Oxford University Press, 1962), p. 247.
[30] Cf. William John Wolf, *The Almost Chosen People: A Study of the Religion of Abraham Lincoln* (Garden City, N. Y.: Doubleday, 1959).

the Federal Council and the National Council, that the domestic Methodist question often did take precedence over the more general problem of Christian reunion. By contrast, the Methodist Church in Canada, which had not been divided as the American church had, took a leading part in the formation of the United Church of Canada.[31] The seriousness of the schism over slavery in Methodist history has been well summarized in a popular history of American Methodism:

Our Methodist fathers were citizens of these two areas [the North and the South] . . . ; and we of the twentieth century will never sympathize as we ought with the two sides unless we remember these powerful influences in the economic and social life of America. The unification of Methodism had to wait until the sad experiences of the War Between the States had been forgotten and the two sections were more nearly one in their ideals and hopes for the future.[32]

A second implication of the Methodist share in the great American trial that was the Civil War was its corroboration of the Methodist quest for a Christian society. Neither the reconstructionism with which American historians have begun to treat the abolitionists nor the tragicomic interpretation of prohibition in current American writing must be permitted to obscure the Christian zeal and idealism of the Methodist crusaders who believed that it was possible for man to progress morally and to do something about his condition on earth. The Methodist Social Creed of 1908, which was so decisive in the whole history of social Christianity in America, came from such zeal and idealism. It still remains to be seen whether the more sober theology of the past few decades will manage to inspire any similar dedication to the betterment of American life and to the cause of peace, or whether "biblical realism" will in fact prove to be a pious cynicism about the power of Christ to redeem this world. Without an answer to this question both in theory and in fact, the religious revival and the theological renaissance of the mid–twentieth century will not deserve the serious consideration of either the church or the world.

[31] See H. H. Walsh, The Christian Church in Canada (Toronto: The Ryerson Press, 1956) , pp. 288-307.
[32] Halford E. Luccock, Paul Hutchinson, and Robert W. Goodloe, The Story of Methodism (Nashville: Abingdon Press, 1949), p. 484.

2

Methodism and American Theological Thought

A Theology of Free Grace and Free Will

Even before the separated branches of American Methodism were re-united, they discovered no serious doctrinal differences among them. A little waggishly, Methodists sometimes suggest that the reason for the absence of doctrinal differences is an absence of doctrine. And in all candor it is puzzling for both the insider and the outsider to decipher the Methodist doctrine of baptism or the Lord's Supper or the relation between the states of humiliation and exaltation in the person of Christ.[33] One recent writer, an insider, has articulated this puzzlement in striking fashion:

The Methodist Church is thus in the anomalous position of prohibiting changes in standards of doctrine which are supposedly established but the nature of which no one knows! The fact that the Church is not at all embarrassed by this situation is strong evidence that it regards precise doctrinal statements as relatively unimportant. . . . Methodists apparently do not deem it necessary or desirable anywhere to state definitely and officially the theology which is everywhere assumed.[34]

Despite the puzzlement, there are emphases that are distinctly Methodist, within and beyond the great variety displayed in the chapters of this *History*. Perhaps the best formulation of these emphases is a phrase originally used in a somewhat different sense by its author: "a theology of freedom." [35] It is evident that Schaff was going too far when he said: "They are Arminian and teach, often even to the extreme of Pelagianism, the freedom and accountability of the human will, the possibility of resisting and losing the divine grace, and the possibility and relative necessity of repeated regenerations." [36] Yet he seems also here to have hit upon a feature of Methodism that unites it with the American spirit. A useful key to the theology of any individual is to in-

---

[33] On this last problem, see the very discerning comments of John Deschner, *Wesley's Christology: An Interpretation* (Dallas: Southern Methodist University Press, 1960), pp. 58-60.

[34] S. Paul Schilling, *Methodism and Society in Theological Perspective* (Nashville: Abingdon Press, 1960), p. 29.

[35] Karl Barth, *Evangelical Theology: An Introduction,* tr. Grover Foley (New York: Holt, Rinehart and Winston, 1963), p. xii.

[36] *America,* p. 139.

quire after the heresy into which he all but falls; that is, to ask: Toward which pole of the Christian dialectic does he incline, and from which does he turn away? Thus, in the polarity between freedom and destiny, George Whitefield would seem to have opted for destiny and John Wesley for freedom; therefore, Whitefield had difficulty avoiding Manicheism, while Wesley's emphasis could lead to "the extreme of Pelagianism" and to a subjective and moralistic interpretation of Christian faith.

As the experience of Jonathan Edwards after the Great Awakening makes clear, any theology that does not have an adequate doctrine of the religious affections and of free will has great difficulty facing up to the facts of a revival.[37] A predestinarian position like Whitefield's could speak about the freedom of God and therefore about grace as the free gift of God with great consistency and power, but this would not be relevant to the conversion experiences that did in fact take place as a consequence of Whitefield's preaching. The Wesleyan emphasis, on the other hand, sought to affirm the freedom of man's will to decide for or against grace, while at the same time refusing to curtail the freedom of God. Is this a fundamental inconsistency? So it has seemed to many interpreters, who have seen both Wesley and the Wesleyans as doctrinal amateurs and improvisers without a definite theological stance. Among others, however, Colin Williams has suggested a reasonable way out of this theological cul-de-sac. As Williams sees Wesley's thought, "the unbroken presence of Christ in the sacramental and liturgical life of the continuous visible Church" was a basic assumption of Wesley's ecclesiology. But Wesley put this into dialectical tension with an emphasis upon "the intrinsic holiness in the life of the [Methodist] ecclesiolae." With the separation of Methodism from Anglicanism, the latter emphasis became much more prominent than the former assumption. In short, as Williams summarizes, "It may well be that the lack of this polar balance, with the resultant overemphasis on the subjective, was the cause of much of the 'moralism' of Methodism and of her spawning of the riotously subjective holiness movements." [38]

Occasional and bizarre attempts to "Barthianize" Wesley notwithstanding, Williams' thesis seems to put Methodist theology into context more satisfactorily than others. It also illustrates how American the

[37] See John E. Smith's discussion of "Religion, Revivalism, and Religious Affections" in his "Editor's Introduction" to Jonathan Edwards, *Religious Affections, The Works of Jonathan Edwards,* edited by Perry Miller (New Haven: Yale University Press, 1959), II, 43-52.

[38] *John Wesley's Theology Today,* p. 154n.

Methodist emphasis is. For the very charge leveled at Methodism by Schaff—teaching, "often even to the extreme of Pelagianism, the freedom and accountability of the human will"—is the accusation that American theologians, even those who consider themselves Augustinians, had to hear from their Continental colleagues at the Evanston Assembly of the World Council of Churches in 1954, and since. When the dominant mood of the secular culture was to glorify man and his freedom, even at the expense of the freedom of God and the sovereignty of grace, the assertion of divine freedom may have required a limitation upon the doctrine of free will. But in a culture where most secular doctrines of man—whether Marxist, Freudian, or mechanistic—conspire to deny freedom and accountability, "free grace" and "free will" would seem to require each other. For either one without the other is heresy: this is what is valid about Wesleyan theology.

Revival or Liturgy as Means of Grace

Anyone who approaches the history of Methodism in America from the general study of church history should not be surprised at the absence of explicit doctrinal formulations in the Wesleyan tradition. In both the Eastern and the Western traditions of Catholic Christianity, many doctrines remained implicit for centuries before achieving dogmatic definition; some are still waiting to be defined. It is, however, more surprising to discover the liturgical indifference of the Methodist fathers. Wesley himself set down certain principles for the conduct of the public worship of the church, relating these to the proclamation of the Word of God and to the religious experience of the believers in a manner that a recent historian of the liturgy has interpreted in admiring terms.[39] Here again Wesley's saturation in the ecclesiastical tradition was a constitutive factor; conversely, the separation of Methodism as a church from the tradition meant, even in Great Britain, a loss of this liturgical substance.

But in the United States and especially on its frontier, where there was no ritualistic established church to preserve the "dead forms," the conventional means of grace and worship had little chance in competition with the prayer meeting and the revival. Schaff was, if anything, more horrified at the liturgical than at the intellectual and doctrinal state of Methodism in America:

[39] Horton Davies, *Worship and Theology in England from Watts and Wesley to Maurice, 1690-1850* (Princeton: Princeton University Press, 1961), pp. 143-209.

In worship, Methodism is not satisfied with the usual divinely ordained means of grace. It really little understands the use of the Sacraments, though it adheres traditionally to infant baptism, and four times a year celebrates the Lord's Supper, as a simple commemoration. It has far more confidence in subjective means and exciting impressions, than in the more quiet and unobserved but surer work of the old church system of educational religion. . . . These new measures have . . . nourished a most dangerous distrust of the ordinary means of grace, the calm preaching of the Word, the sacraments.

He described also how he had idealized the American prayer meeting when he was still living in Europe and how disillusioned he was by the reality. He was still prepared to recommend that the formalized churches of Germany consider the adaptation of the prayer meeting to their needs. Therefore he did not reject Methodist "new measures" out of hand, but believed that they "may, under wise direction, be very powerful means of awakening and promoting religious life." [40]

The history of Methodist worship after Wesley and since Schaff has both confirmed Schaff's hopes and borne out his fears. In 1864—just a decade after Schaff's *America*—the Methodist Episcopal Church revised the ritual, restoring the form of the committal to the service of burial and incorporating ceremonies for the laying of a cornerstone and for the dedication of a church. In 1896 the Methodist Episcopal Church adopted an order of public worship which was printed in the front of the *Hymnal*. (The Southern Church had carried its *Disciplinary* provision for public worship in its 1880 hymnal.) Essentially the same order was then adopted by both the Northern and Southern Churches as a common order of worship and appeared in the front of the joint hymnal of the two churches in 1905. This formal order of worship was widely used in Methodist churches. Even these minimal steps toward liturgical order, however, called forth protest. "The publication of this book [the hymnal] and the adoption of orders of worship caused a storm in many Methodist churches. It not only smacked of formality—it *was* formality. The older generation wondered what the church was coming to." [41] What the church was coming to was the recognition that "the only alternative to liturgy is bad liturgy," [42] a recognition that has accompanied the evolution of American culture from frontier to city.

Yet this liturgical development is not all on the plus side of the ledger.

[40] *America*, pp. 142-43.
[41] Nolan B. Harmon, "Methodist Worship: Practice and Ideals," in William K. Anderson, ed., *Methodism* (Nashville: The Methodist Publishing House, 1947), p. 234.
[42] Cf. Jaroslav Pelikan, "Luther and the Liturgy," *Martin Luther Lectures* (Decorah, Iowa: Luther College Press, 1958), II, 45.

Like the urbanization and suburbanization of American life, to which it belongs, the formalization of Methodist worship may be accused of destroying the genius of this church's life under the pretext of merely altering its forms. Just at a time when the so-called liturgical churches are seeking to eliminate elements of unnecessary ceremonial from their worship and to restore a simpler and more primitive rite, some of the so-called free churches have taken over these very elements of ceremonial. The freedom, informal spontaneity, warmth, and capacity for commitment for which Americans have a world-wide reputation were built into the patterns of Methodist worship. One of the crises of Protestant life in America today is the loss of these characteristics, which Protestantism has traditionally shared with America and imparted to it. When a pietistic evangelicalism is recognized to be no longer adequate—as it must be— does it not still have some positive contributions to make to an ecumenical church that seeks to be both reformed and catholic? American Methodism can continue to make a significant contribution to American thought and culture if it discovers a way of keeping some of the spirit of the revival within the forms of the liturgy.

A Hierarchical Church in a Democratic Society

Observers of American Methodism have often had occasion to note that this most American of churches is quite out of keeping with the American pattern in one respect—its polity. As Schaff commented, this polity is "in principle entirely hierarchical, and is so far in remarkable contrast with the political republicanism of the United States." [43] Chapter 13 of this *History* has described the impact of the democratic spirit upon Methodism and the formation of the Methodist Protestant Church as a consequence of the protest against the authority of the bishops. But Chapter 20 has shown that despite this protest, the Methodist Protestant Church itself had to reconsider the question of centralized authority. Thus, issues of church polity, together with such social issues as slavery, prohibition, and peace, have dominated the attention of Methodist churchmen.

In this respect, also, Methodism is representative of American Protestantism. The great debates of colonial Congregationalism were over the constitution of the church. When the meaning of baptism came up for vigorous argument, the issue was not principally baptismal regeneration but the validity of the halfway covenant in relation to the polity of the covenanted community. Even the conflict with Unitarianism, which

[43] *America*, p. 140.

dealt with the doctrine of man at least as much as with the doctrines of Christ and the Trinity, came down to the issue of who should be permitted to occupy a congregation and who had the authority to depose. Thus, the Methodist preoccupation with polity at the cost of theology stands in the American tradition, to which even denominations such as the Lutherans, who had usually slighted polity and concentrated upon theology, have conformed when they arrived on the American scene.[44]

What was unique about the Methodist polity among the free churches was its hierarchical character. Dr. Nottingham has designated Methodism a "clerical aristocracy," noting:

In spite of what might be called the element of democracy in Methodist organization, namely the amount of initiative allowed to lay members such as the local preachers and class leaders, the effective government of the Methodist societies was vested solely in the hands of John Wesley and his preachers. Looked at from that point of view the Methodist government was a clerical aristocracy.[45]

The zenith of the authority of this clerical aristocracy, or perhaps even autocracy, may perhaps be seen in the career of Francis Asbury, whose correspondence contains these moving and remarkable words: "I sit on a joyless height, a pinacle of power, too high to sit secure and unenvied, too high to sit secure without divine aid." [46] Earlier chapters of this *History* have shown that not every Methodist bishop had such power, and that not every one of them feared its consequences as much as Asbury did.

The evolution of the Methodist episcopacy has, however, seriously modified this situation. In a manner that seems to one historian to have mirrored the development of American society generally, the Methodist bishop gradually became more an administrator than a ruler.[47] That change has accompanied the growth of a professionally trained ministry and of a better educated laity. Although the complaints about the centralization of authority are as persistent and as sharp in the church as they are in the state, Methodism has achieved a balance between a hierarchical church and a democratic society. It has done so not through theological reflection upon the questions of faith and order, apostolic succession, and the nature of the episcopate—of this there has been very little,

---

[44] Cf. Carl S. Mundinger, *Government in the Missouri Synod: The Genesis of Decentralized Church Government in the Missouri Synod* (Saint Louis: Concordia Publishing House, 1947), pp. 199-214.

[45] *Methodism and the Frontier*, pp. 114-15.

[46] *Letters*, to Thomas Haskins, October 17, 1806.

[47] Robert Wesley Goodloe, "The Office of Bishop in the Methodist Church" (Unpublished dissertation, The University of Chicago, 1929).

probably too little—but by a pragmatic adaptation of the structures of the church to new needs and problems. Even in the least American aspect of its total structure, its church government, therefore, American Methodism has made a meaningful contribution to the development of American thought and culture, and it has done so in a thoroughly American way.

chapter 35

AMERICAN METHODISM: AN EXPERIMENT IN SECULAR CHRISTIANITY

THE GENERAL CONFERENCE OF 1864 OF the Methodist Episcopal Church sent an address of sympathy and appreciation to Abraham Lincoln. In reply, the president called the Methodist communion the most important church in the United States. With a politician's caution he avowed that he was making thereby no invidious comparisons. It was not the Methodists' fault that they had sent more soldiers to the front, more nurses to the hospitals, and more prayers to heaven than any other. Their contribution was the consequence of their greater numbers.

Is Methodism's significance merely a function of its size? That it has grown into one of the largest denominations is a meaningful fact. But categories of quantity are ill fitted for application to spiritual concerns. Methodist influence is related to other factors as well as magnitude. Its distribution—geographically, socially, and economically—is quite as important as its size. Speaking historically, its mobility is as significant as its numbers. After a late start, by virtue of its itinerant system it was able to be present wherever history was in the making, because it was where people were. Further, the chief scene of its operation was the frontier, which the modern historian has come to regard as the most decisive single influence on American life in the nineteenth century. Methodism's appeal, as Charles A. Beard observed, was to the "hewers of wood and drawers of water who were to count heavily in the conquest and government of this continent." [1] In the later days

[1] Charles A. and Mary Beard, *The Rise of American Civilization* (New York: The Macmillan Co., 1927), I, 451.

Methodism identified itself with the middle class, whose vote and mores have been so determinative in our democracy. There can be little question that Methodism in one way or another has exercised an influence on American life.

But to define spiritual force in a heterogeneous culture like our own is not easy. For the effect of a church is rarely of the trigger sort, except as in the crusade of Methodism for the Eighteenth Amendment or of the Protestants to block the appointment of an ambassador to the Vatican in 1951. A religious influence is more like a solitary chemical element in the soil. Who can say how much a pinch of nitrogen has added to the blush of a rose? Or, more aptly, a Christian influence in a nation is like the effect of a remembrance or a hope entertained by an individual. It is unquestionably present, but its moment can only be estimated, not computed.

The thesis of this chapter is that American Methodism represents *a colossal experiment in secular Christianity*. The forms it assumes in our history, the influence it exercises on American life, the success it enjoys, and the instruction it offers for the student of religious development flow alike from this fact.

By "secular Christianity" we mean a religion that takes the world for its medium and measures its success by the degree that it changes the individuals who comprise the world. The medieval church distinguished between the "regular" clergy under the rule of one of the religious orders —devoted to contemplation, special missions, the institutional care of the young, the poor, and the sick—and the "secular" clergy, who lived not under the rule of a religious congregation but "in the world," giving themselves principally to the spiritual uplift of workaday people. In the broadest sense, Methodism represents a secular movement within Protestantism. It expresses itself in activity in the temporal order: "I look upon all the world as my parish," said John Wesley. And while this utterance was originally addressed as a counterclaim against those who would exclude Methodist preachers by episcopal authority from Anglican dioceses, it expresses the essential genius of Wesleyan Christianity.

Field preaching, which was the trademark of original Methodism, was a going forth of Christian evangelists to reclaim men and women in the mines and factories of the profane order, rather than waiting for men to come into the sacred precincts of the church. Methodism in the days of its most rapid growth had a minimum of professional leadership; it was largely a lay enterprise. It evolved a polity which for efficiency would rival a business corporation with its quotas and chain of command. Methodism's avowed aim has always been to spread scriptural holiness, leavening the human lump with righteousness. It tests its success by moral fruits. "The most prevailing fault among the Methodists," John Wesley once observed in a famous letter, "is to be *too outward* in religion." [2] Fault or not, Methodism is a mighty exhibit in American history of Christian extroversion.

When we label Methodism as "Christian secularism," this is not to be confused with "secular" secularism, the malady from which the Western world suffers in our time. Secularism is the organization of life apart from God. It is what the New Testament denounces as worldliness, devotion to and delight in Mammon for its own sake. Secularism is the antithesis of Christianity, though Christian secularism is always in moral danger of losing its qualifying adjective. Christian secularism goes into the world, not primarily for the world's but for Christ's sake.

Christian secularism is to be distinguished from monastic Christianity, which draws a line between the sacred and the secular and proclaims mutual aloofness, with the result that each governs its own affairs by standards of its own. While the most impressive example of this sort of Christianity is the religious communities of the Middle Ages, Protestantism too has had its monks. Its ranks are full today of persons who grow angry if the church "meddles" with politics, economics, or education. In contrast, historic Methodism has had a concern for the world: in its noblest exemplars it may have cared little *for* the world, its prizes and praise, but much *about* it, its transformation into a place where righteousness dwells. While Methodism began in England as a pietistic movement, an essay in vertical religion, in America it has busied itself horizontally as well. John Dewey once remarked that "while saints are engaged in introspection, burly sinners run the world." Methodism is more interested in the sinners— either their conversion or their defeat—than in its own introspection.

Christian secularism of the Methodist variety differs radically from totalitarian Christianity, whose supreme European illustration is medieval Catholicism, and which finds its noblest example in America in the Puritan theocracy in New England. These were, of course, concerned with the world. But they were one-dimensional. Their purpose was to control society for ecclesiastical ends. The state was but an arm of the church. They boldly affirmed the right of religion to rule over the whole life of men. The Puritan fathers did not migrate to the shores of Massachusetts to build a democracy. Their goal was a theocracy, where the civil authorities were intended to be handmaidens of the church, where clerical control shadowed the entire institutional life, and where the purpose, as Cotton Mather stated it, was a godly commonwealth, "as near as might be to that which was the glory of Israel, the peculiar people."

---

[2] *Letters*, to John Valton, November 12, 1771.

But Methodism has never aspired to dominance of the state, though the liquor forces were to accuse the church of conspiracy in the days of the temperance struggle. Its avowed goal has never been to reduce the institutions of society to vassalage. Its purpose has been not to erect a theocracy but to leaven the secular order through the conversion to the Christian life of the men who make it.

Jason Lee, the famed missionary of the Oregon Trail, is an illustration of Methodist secularism. He set out in 1834 to take the Bible to the Flathead Indians—a foray into the world with the gospel. But very soon he saw, as have the most successful missionaries, that to Christianize the Indians "you must teach them to read; before you can teach them, you must get them to settle down by the schoolhouse; . . . you must wean them from their hunting; before you can wean them from their hunting, you must teach them other ways of getting the necessities of life,—chiefly by farming." [3] In a few months what began as an evangelistic enterprise broadened into an experiment in applied Christianity—a school, an agricultural station teaching animal husbandry and household arts, sawmills and gristmills. Lee himself took an active part in urging the Congress to set up a provisional government for the Oregon country "as the germ of a future state." Thus, an enterprise sparked and sustained by a Christian motive took upon itself flesh, not only to witness to Christian truth and grace but to make practically effective the principles regnant in it. The Lee mission is but one chapter in the oft-repeated appropriation by Methodism of worldly means for spiritual ends.

American Methodism is an amalgam of three forces. It is the gospel of Jesus filtered through the activistic temperament of John Wesley and habituated to the American frontier. Jesus' own religion was pre-eminently secular; it was exercised amid daily tasks and trials. His teaching drew upon secular life for illustrations—the sowing of seed, the patching of a garment, the losing of a coin, the building of a tower. His appeal was not to the professionals but to the common people, who heard him gladly. And how many of the Master's days were spent simply in doing good!

This corpus of teaching and example came to John Wesley, a voluntarist by nature, who preached faith but insisted that faith's best evidence is good works. His emphasis was transplanted to America, where it found a soil most congenial to it. Wesley's own high appraisal of the practical met its perfect mate in the pragmatism so characteristic of American thought and life. While Methodism never lost regard for the warm heart, its mysticism in the American scene has been increasingly muscular. While

---

[3] Richard M. Cameron, *Methodism and Society in Historical Perspective* (Nashville: Abingdon Press, 1961), p. 125.

it began, and has continued (at its best), as an evangelistic movement, it has aimed to save men in the world, not out of it. Validly Christian in motivation, its field of operation has been the workaday world.

The Accomplishments of American Methodism

Methodism's secularism was no small factor in its success. Oriented to the world, it accommodated itself to situations that baffled churches which looked to the Bible or tradition exclusively for guidance. It met effectively the problems created by the high mobility of a population moving frontierward. The communion that stressed a settled ministry was hard put to supply the needs of its people. Methodism mounted its preachers on horseback and linked its societies together in sprawling circuits under an itinerancy that guaranteed the Methodist Church the advantages of priority in most every settlement. The problem of securing proper men for the sparsely settled communities almost sank denominations like the Anglicans, who had to bring men with English ordination to their parishes. The meager salaries of a frontier parish, the insecurity of tenure, and the want of cultured response made it so hard to find proper clergy that the vestry of one parish church in Lancaster County, Virginia, declared that they would be glad to take any pastors who offered, "Let their lives be never so licentious or their qualifications so unfit." [4] Unbound by centuries-long traditions the Methodists met the need for clergy in pragmatic fashion. By their circuit system they added enough parishes together to guarantee a livelihood, and their polity assured that every church would have a minister and every minister a church. They atoned for the cultural lack by moving their preachers often, so that their ministry was fresh and vital if it could not be learned.

Again, the Methodists matched in an unusual practical fashion the democracy required by frontier life with the authority that effective churchmanship requires. The love of the Anglo-Saxon for self-government finally defeated the Puritan theocracy. The insistence on conformity to English custom and adherence to the apostolic succession nearly quenched the Anglican light in the southern colonies. The Methodists united democracy and efficiency in rare fashion. Francis Asbury, who was Wesley's appointee and in the bona fide tradition, insisted that he could accept the leadership of the American Church only *if he were elected by the American conference*. Thus, the centralized authority which made

[4] Thomas J. Wertenbaker, *The First Americans* (New York: The Macmillan Co., 1927), p. 129.

for Wesleyan success in England was mated with the right to choose their own leaders which American frontiersmen demanded.

Methodism not only met successfully the problems of polity, but it effected its own practical adjustment to the thought climate of its time. The eighteenth century was a period of naturalism. Its skepticism threatened the foundations of Christianity. But Methodism did not endeavor to answer the assaults of David Hume. As Bishop Francis J. McConnell once observed, Wesley did not refute Hume's logic but set England to singing. The songs, pouring from the throats of thousands who had been raised from sin to righteousness, from despair to hope, swept doubt before them.

In the nineteenth century the antireligious polemic took the form of evolutionism. Methodism, in the person of Boston University's Borden Parker Bowne, perhaps the ablest philosopher of religion in American Methodist history, did grapple with the foe at an intellectual level. But still, Methodism's most effective response was its appropriation of the concept of growth in the religious life; whatever may have been the origin of the species, God in his grace is able to raise his creatures through faith into perfection of love.

The unusual capacity of Methodism for accommodation to the world issued in phenomenal success, judging after the manner of men. While Barratt's Chapel was being erected in the 1780's, a gentleman in the neighborhood wished to know what use was to be made of it. Upon being told that it was a place of worship for Methodists, he observed that such a building was unnecessary. By the time the War of Independence was over a corn-crib would hold them all! [5] But this sect whose prospects seemed so meager was the largest denomination in the country by 1850; the census of the same year revealed it the wealthiest church in the nation as well.

Methodism's success was more than institutional self-aggrandizement. The Methodist Episcopal Church was a factor in preparing Americans in the formative years for their democratic responsibilities. Space permits discussion of only a few of the contributions Methodism made to government of, by, and for the people.

First, Methodism helped to break the hold of Calvinism on American life, replacing it with faith in the common man. Calvinism has received its full due for its part in the triumph of democracy. Unquestionably its faith in the divine sovereignty has been an ax laid at the root of every tyrannic presumption. But, from the standpoint of humanity, Calvinism is a doctrine of privilege with its eternal distinction between the

[5] J. M. Buckley, *A History of Methodism in the United States* (New York: The Christian Literature Co., 1897), I, 227-28.

saved and damned. Men are not really free in the Calvinistic scheme. It has not high regard for the individual in himself. He is a means to God's glory. It is difficult to build self-respect in a deterministic system. The unhappy fate of Jonathan Edwards and Puritanism in New England is an indication of the inherent enmity between Calvinism and democracy. Calvinism in itself could not generate the optimism essential to the building of a new world. Perry Miller, Puritanism's most distinguished chronicler, has pointed out that Calvinism had success in America only as it transformed itself into "an operational Arminianism." [6]

Methodism has had high esteem for the common man, manifested if in no other way by the effort it made to redeem him. Theologically Methodism has been sanguine about human nature. It has witnessed to the redemption possible for the least of the sons of men. It has raised its leadership from common men, alumni of "Brush College," as they proudly called themselves. The Methodist faith in the James Finleys and Peter Cartwrights spilled over into political life and formed the basis of a democratic electorate.

Second, Methodism did much to civilize the lawless men of the frontier. There was always the threat of a plunge into barbarism when men crossed the Appalachians. Many of the frontiersmen were in flight from the scene of moral transgressions in the colonies or the Old Country. There was little in the back country to encourage reform. Restraints were off. The conditions of life were savage. The adventurer was well represented. Gambling, brawling, drunkenness, murder, thievery, sexual license, and counterfeiting were prevalent. Peter Cartwright called Logan County, Kentucky, "Rogues Harbor."

The Methodist circuit rider endeavored to bring moral discipline to the unruly frontier. His main thrust was, of course, evangelism, the attempt to win men to righteousness of life. He proclaimed the evil of liquor, dishonesty, sexual looseness, and violence. Backed by the chastisements prescribed by church law, he sought to impose order upon the chaos of the frontier. He prepared men for response to the moral appeals, later on, of Lincoln, Cleveland, Woodrow Wilson, and the temperance advocates. Methodism sought to evoke that modicum of decency on which democracy depends.

Third, Methodism informed the masses. Democracy means discussion, and discussion is bootless unless it is informed. People must have facts at their disposal, facts in a form they can understand. They need not only facts but a framework of interpretation, within which they can view

[6] James W. Smith and A. Leland Jamison, eds., *The Shaping of American Religion* (Princeton: Princeton University Press, 1961), p. 362.

the facts and evaluate them. In other words, democracy depends on the dissemination of truth and value, which calls for skill in communication in its many forms.

From the first, the Methodist Episcopal Church was an educator of the masses. Every circuit rider carried a library of popular literature in his saddlebags. The *Christian Advocate* had by 1828 the largest periodical circulation in the world—30,000—of which a large part was in the West. The Sunday schools developed into discussion groups that translated public problems into moral issues. The Epworth League supplied the first lessons in public speaking to hosts of young people. Scores of colleges founded by the church swung open the doors of culture, and the Chautauqua movement, pioneered by a Methodist bishop, educated those unable to finance a higher education.

Fourth, Methodism helped to create a sense of democratic solidarity. Popular government rests on social unity. A democratic state can endure the sharpest differences as to means, but it disintegrates if there be disagreement as to ends, or if there is mutual intolerance. The dictator easily rises to power where there is a great deal of hostility residual in a population, ready to be channeled into violence. Any social force that makes men aware of their fundamental oneness of interest is on the side of democracy.

Here was another contribution of the Methodist movement. As the Beards, themselves not prejudiced in favor of the Methodists, phrase it in their monumental history of American civilization, "If the sermons and hymns of Methodism jarred on Jefferson's skeptical ears, its emphasis on self-expression as against authority and its appeal to the humble as against the mighty contributed to the swelling stream of mass consciousness that made republicanism secure, beyond the possibility of reaction." [7] Quite as potent as its songs and sermons in promoting unity among the masses was the quiet sharing by the Methodist clergy, from bishop to circuit rider, of the frontiersman's life. For while the Methodist system may have been Hamiltonian in its ideals of authority and efficiency, the personnel who made it go were Jeffersonian in their sympathies and willingness to sacrifice for the people.

They furthered freedom of speech by its exercise. Liberty, of course, is the air democracy breathes. Many forces worked to produce freedom— the heterogeneity of peoples, the breadth of the ocean that separated America from European tyrannies, the immensity of the continent, and the love of freedom of many who had suffered persecution in the Old Country. But none of these will preserve freedom if men are afraid to

[7] *The Rise of American Civilization,* I, 449-50.

exercise it. Only courageous speaking guarantees the right of speech. There are no processes of government that can assure freedom to men who allow their opponents to scare them. The McCarthyism of the modern period never legally enjoined anyone from speaking, but it silenced dissent by fear as effectively as by law.

The Methodist preachers for a century and a half have helped to keep freedom alive in America simply by refusing to be intimidated. Peter Cartwright once told Andrew Jackson in a public Methodist meeting that unless he were converted, God would damn his soul to hell as quick as he would a Guinea Negro. The incident is not recorded in the anthologies of freedom. But this—and utterances of a similar spirit by religion-inspired men—helped more than we can calculate to spare America from the rule of tyranny.

Finally, Methodism helped to build what Ralph H. Gabriel has celebrated as the supernatural foundation of democracy.[8] Popular government implies a theory of reality, a moral order supporting society and guaranteed by a Creator. Historic experience shows that where relativism prevails, where there are no cosmic sanctions for truth and righteousness, the stronger gets his way by force.

Methodism has undergirded democracy by offering "the higher law" and thus lifting men's eyes to standards above the purely expedient. Methodism has sought a perfection like God's—a perfection, be it noted, that consists in treating all men, the unjust as well as the just, impartially, a democratic virtue. Methodism has proclaimed a kingdom vaster than that bounded by the two great oceans and sanctions for right-doing beyond immediate consequences. So it has built into the American consciousness the supernatural dimension which foreign observers have long noted as the characteristic of our national life and the best earnest of its continuance.

The Roman Catholic Church has long been known as the civilizer of the Middle Ages. Within a briefer span, and to a more limited extent, the Methodist Church with its world-pointing piety and polity was the civilizer of the American frontiersman, making him ready for democratic responsibility.

Problems of the Past and Present

The history of American Methodism is not, however, unshadowed success. If the first century of its existence on these shores has proclaimed

[8] *The Course of American Democratic Thought* (New York: Ronald Press, 1940), p. 14.

the virtues of secular Christianity, the second is bringing to light some of its intrinsic shortcomings.

To begin with, while Methodism did much to civilize America, it failed to socialize the country. By this we do not refer to a system of social organization. We mean that while Methodism did much to lift masses of individuals to decency of life, it has not transformed the social presuppositions of American thinking. It has had relatively little influence in molding institutions. Methodism's great thrust toward social control—the prohibition experiment—was given up in about two decades. It would be false to say that it has not contributed to social betterment. But its efforts were ameliorative *of a condition it found*. It went along with slavery—at one time Methodists owned no less than 200,000 slaves [9] —supported two wars, and as a whole has lagged behind even baseball on the racial integration issue. Granted that social needs always outrun society's provisions for meeting them, Methodism has as much created the problems as supplied the answers.

Some of the reasons for Methodism's social backwardness are plain. For one thing, like their Protestant brethren generally, Methodists were handicapped by their individualistic premises. They conceived of sin largely in terms of personal transgressions—profanity, drinking, card-playing, dancing, worldliness in general. A Puritan concern for the moral conversion of individuals took precedence over social programs. The Methodist strategy of changing the individual was valid, but it did not change him enough so as to include his social attitudes. The church aimed at making individual Christians rather than changing the habitual actions of the whole society. It swallowed uncritically the moldy fallacy that if we develop Christian individuals society will thereby become Christian—as though it were not possible to build a crooked wall out of straight brick! The conversion of slave owners did not end slavery. Methodism, following the lines of Wesley's famous advice on money, "Gain all you can, save all you can, give all you can," promoted frugality and benevolence; but it failed to restrain avarice or to inquire closely how men got their money, or to ask seriously as to the rules of the money-making game in general. Its solution for social problems, until comparatively late in its history, was neighborly charity rather than social justice. Methodism's record is certainly no worse than other communions; but its social awakening has been too little and too late.

A second reason for Methodism's lack of a social gospel was that— as is the danger with a secular Christianity—the hand becomes the color of the dye in which it works. The church became so involved in society

[9] A. C. Cole, *The Irrepressible Conflict, 1850-1865* (New York: The Macmillan Co., 1934), p. 258.

that it found prophetic judgment difficult. Of course, Methodism has had its prophets, like Francis J. McConnell in the steel strike of the early 1920's, Ernest Fremont Tittle on the peace issue, and G. Bromley Oxnam before the House Un-American Activities Committee. It has inspired social utterances to its credit—for example, the pioneer Social Creed and the biting indictment of the business order in the Episcopal Address of 1932. But generally speaking, Methodism has identified itself with the middle class on social issues. President Theodore Roosevelt once privately remarked that he would rather address a Methodist audience than any other audience in America: "You know for one thing that every one there is an American." He was paying tribute to its representative character, but the very fact that it has eschewed extremes has denied to it a prophetic stance. On the racial question Methodism has been so hobbled by division in its own household over the Central Jurisdiction that it has not spoken with one voice to the nation. Methodism has not solved what has been called "the dilemma of the church"—the fact that to save the world it must identify itself with the world, but in so doing compromises with the world. "My desire," wrote Francis Asbury, "is to sit loose to every created object";[10] but to do so is to give up one's purchase on those very objects. The church must risk either irrelevance to the world or contamination by the world. Methodism has chosen the latter. The consequence is that it is a nice question whether Methodism has influenced the world as much as the world has shaped Methodism.

Again, a secular Christianity is subject to the shortcomings inherent in the pragmatic point of view. Pragmatism shuns speculations about the whole; it tackles its problems spot-wise. It has about it the air of improvisation—the initiative, therefore, being with the situation. Methodism has been so busy handling emergencies on the social scene that it has not had the time to work out a coherent social philosophy. Further, to the pragmatist the most practical consideration in any situation is self-preservation. Hence, a pragmatic church is ever in danger of "assuming that whatever makes for its institutional growth and security is for the glory of God." [11] The pragmatist is inclined to be calculating rather than idealistic: "Idealists are all right in their place, but this is a job for practical men!" Pragmatism majors, therefore, in short-term success. The pragmatist depreciates nonutilitarian considerations—theology, for instance. American Methodism has yet to produce a Calvin or a Schleiermacher. The most urgent speculative problem of the twentieth century has been the adjustment of science and religion, with its crucial bearing

[10] *Journal*, October 3, 1772.
[11] Walter G. Muelder, *Methodism and Society in the Twentieth Century* (Nashville: Abingdon Press, 1961), p. 409.

on the Scriptures. Methodist scholars have taken an honorable part in the discussion, but not leadership. Worship is another value that bows before Methodist practicality. We are not distinguished for liturgical excellence. Our Akron-plan churches, prized for their usefulness, have kept us out of the van of architectural advance. Superb in organization, strong in program, skillful in raising money, resourceful in meeting emergencies, Methodism has fallen behind its sister communions in those areas of experience where the practical has no primacy.

A Look at the Future

What of the future? What is the next stage in the Methodist pilgrimage? The future is hidden, but the most assured prediction would be that Methodism will become increasingly involved in the Ecumenical Movement. For this is the growing edge of Christianity in our time. Methodism is destined to pour its treasures into the bosom of the coming One Church. Its history will merge with that of the Church Universal.

Methodism will offer its outgoing spirit. The followers of John Wesley have been ecumenicists in principle from the day their leader wrote: "I desire to have a league offensive and defensive with every soldier of Christ." [12] Methodists have always been willing to offer a friendly hand to those whose heart they felt was as their heart.

Methodism will offer its practical experience with church union. The unification of the three Methodist branches in 1939 is the largest to be consummated on the American scene. If what Methodism has learned may temper the enthusiasm of those who see in church union a specific for Christianity's ills, what Methodism has undergone will also help to guide the larger church into the forms of association most viable.

In the coming One Church Methodism will represent the practical emphasis. The theologians—mostly of a doctrinaire sort—have captured the Ecumenical Movement. Its premises are hopelessly biblicistic; most of the communions, especially those from beyond our shores, are unwilling to venture beyond a scriptural warrant. The idiom of the ecumenicist is a speaking with tongues to the average Protestant. One of the sorest needs of the Ecumenical Movement is for someone to ask, "So what?"—not a theological term, to be sure, but relevant! What real difference do the matters which bulk so large in Faith and Order discussions make? The church needs someone to insist—as we believe John Wesley would do—that the ecumenical tree be judged by its fruits. There is no form

---

[12] *Letters*, to Henry Venn, June 22, 1763.

of church union, polity, order of ministry, or sacrament that is intrinsically superior. Each is to be tested by whether it furthers or retards the kingdom; and where the consequences are indistinguishable, we may say that the forms of faith and order are immaterial. If the One Church is to witness to life as well as unity, the practical Wesleyan emphasis will be needed.

The secular piety of Methodism, it is to be hoped, will keep the church faced toward its world. Granted, as we have seen, that Methodism's encounter with the world has not been an unbroken success, still, it has not retreated into an irrelevant pietism. Its conscience has been troubled by the problems of world peace, economic justice, racial fair play, even though its achievements have fallen below its pronouncements. Methodism will help to ensure that the "faith and order" of the Ecumenical Church do not swallow up "life and work" in the world.

Again, Methodism has a polity to offer the larger church, the most effective form of church government in Protestantism. It makes provision in an unusual way for the secular ideals of efficiency and democracy. The first is ensured by the centralization of appointive authority in the bishop and his administrative arms, the district superintendents. The second is guaranteed by equal representation of the laity with the clergy in all policy-making bodies of the church. The Methodist system did not come down from God out of heaven, adorned as a bride for her husband—as the proponents of some forms of church order would have us believe about their own. The Methodist polity was hammered out in encounters with the world, disciplined by the defection of O'Kelly in 1792 and the Methodist Protestants in the 1830's, matured by a century of experimentation that sought the best combination of centralized leadership with democratic control. It is a flexible, efficient, finely tempered instrument for kingdom purposes.

By the providence of God the church is moving toward unity. In that one body, of which Christ is the head, perhaps the Methodists will help to supply the bone and sinew, which the church perforce must have if it would stand erect and grapple victoriously with the powers of the world.

Appendix

AMERICAN METHODIST HYMNODY:
A HISTORICAL SKETCH

LOUIS BENSON IN HIS MONUMENTAL WORK *The English Hymn, Its Development and Use* (1915, reprinted by John Knox Press, 1962), offers the only complete and reliable discussion of Methodist hymnody to date. The substance of his work on American Methodist hymnody appears also in Robert G. McCutchan's *Our Hymnody* (Abingdon Press, 1937). The chapter "Antecedents of The Methodist Hymnal" provides a listing and brief annotation of hymnals prior to the 1935 edition. The need for the following chart was prompted by McCutchan's writing and is provided here as a guide rather than an authoritative discussion.

John Wesley's first hymnbook, *Collection of Psalms and Hymns*—the "Charles-town Collection," printed in South Carolina in 1737—was reprinted in England but found little use in America. Whitefield brought to his American meetings the Wesleys' *Hymns and Sacred Poems* (1739) and had it reprinted in Philadelphia in 1740. The Irish lay preachers, Philip Embury and Robert Strawbridge, undoubtedly made use of Wesleyan hymns and hymnbooks in their American work. By the year 1781 the wide use of these hymns in preaching services and worship prompted the Philadelphia printer Melchior Steiner to bind together, for use in St. George's Church, the three Wesley hymn collections: *Hymns for Those That Seek and Those That Have Found Redemption* (1742); *A Collection of Psalms and Hymns* (1741); *Hymns and Spiritual Songs* (1753). This practice of reprinting Wesley hymns was evidenced ten years earlier (1771) in the production of the exact same material by Isaac Collins in Burlington, New Jersey. Collins reprinted the collection again in 1773, and this later activity may have been the result of the influence of Francis Asbury. There is no indication, however, that Asbury did any editing at this time. *Hymns for Those That Seek and Those That Have Found Redemption* was reprinted by James Adams in Wilmington, 1770.

The chart of hymnbooks provides a superficial record of the "authorized" hymnals of the three main branches of American Methodism. Three English publications head the list, and their importance and influence is traced by dotted and solid lines.

The first and earliest publication, *A Collection of Hymns for the Use of the People Called Methodists,* commonly called the "large hymnbook of 1780," was not to influence American hymnody until after the 1820's, and more fully in 1849. The second collection, the hymns that were bound with the 1784 *Sunday Service,* never found popular use and soon fell into oblivion. The third seems to have had the most influence on the first forty years of the young church's life. This was the "renigade" collection of 1781—*A Pocket Hymnbook,* compiled by Robert Spence. This last fact goes far to explain the apparent lack of interest on the part of early Methodism for the definitive 1780 collection and, by virtue of this, the bulk of Wesley hymnody, which proved to be the mainstay of British Methodists for almost one hundred years.

The Methodist Episcopal Church was quick to make use of the Spence *Pocket Hymnbook* (1781), and various editions and variations of this basic publication sufficed until 1821. An interesting sidelight is seen in a comparison of the preface to Wesley's 1780 hymnbook (first American reprint, 1814) and Asbury and Coke's preface to the 1790 edition of the Spence *Pocket Hymnbook.* Wesley maintained that English Methodists needed a collection that was "neither cumbersome or expensive." The bishops felt that the Wesley collection was too large and expensive for American use, and thus justified the reprint of the smaller *Pocket Hymnbook.* No doubt the bishops' rejection of both the 1784 collection (*Sunday Service*) and Wesley's 1780 larger book needs to be studied along with the rejection by the young church of other direct Wesley influences.

The 1780 collection was studied in detail by the compilers of the 1821 hymnbook, and the next generation saw more use of basic Wesleyan hymnody. These additions are reflected in the 1836 and 1849 editions.

A study of hymnbooks of the Methodist Protestant and the Methodist Churches points up the practical problem of a "separatist group" in establishing and maintaining its own brand of hymnody. Harrod's collection (1830) proved of value in affording the Methodist Protestants with a popular collection of their choosing, but it does not reflect their editorial work. Stockton's work on the 1837 book was the first serious effort by this group to compile a unique hymnbook of their own. The content of this collection, as well as the 1780 "large hymnbook," is reflected in all three of the books produced by the two divisions within the Methodist Protestant ranks. When the church reunited, the adoption of the Tourjee hymnal (1882) served as a stopgap until the next, and last, definitive collection in 1901.

Four hymnbooks, dated 1847, 1874, 1880, and 1889, were authorized by the General Conferences of the Methodist Episcopal Church, South, before the joint hymnal of 1905. The text and tune edition, 1874, was authorized by the 1870 General Conference and is not accounted for by either Benson or McCutchan. The two editions of *Songs of Zion,* 1851 and 1873, had semi-official approval and enjoyed a wide use; these are listed among the authorized hymnals since they were actually supplements to the official hymnal. The problem of confining, or attempting to confine, the wide hymnic interests of Methodists to one volume was not peculiar to the nineteenth century. The church's effort to meet the needs of all its people through the publication of "unauthorized" hymnals and songbooks, in addition to the approved hymnal, continues to this day.

In the Northern Church a strong reaction against the great size of the 1849 edition (really an anthology) culminated in the authorization in 1876 of a book containing fewer hymns. In consequence, the number of Wesley hymns was drastically reduced, and has been reduced in each succeeding edition.

The musical aspects of hymnody so important to John Wesley, as reflected in his famous 1780 preface, were not fully perpetuated by first-generation American Methodists. There was limited use of the Wesley *Foundery Collection* (1742) and Butts, *Harmonia Sacra* (c. 1753, reprinted at Andover in 1816). In addition, the names of the tunes appropriate for each hymn began to appear in hymnbooks as early as the 1790 *Pocket Hymnbook*.

A bold attempt to produce an authorized and standardized book of hymn tunes, *David's Companion,* part of which was printed in 1807, was given tacit approval by the 1808 General Conference. Reflecting the musical activity of John Street Methodist Church in New York City, it was revised in 1810 and 1817, but never enjoyed official sanction. The chaotic situation was somewhat improved with the publication of *The Methodist Harmonist* in 1821. This tune collection, revised in 1833 and 1837, cross referenced to the 1821 hymnal.

Other tune collections with some degree of official approval were *The Devotional Harmonist* (1849); *Hymns for the Use of the Methodist Episcopal Church, with tunes for congregational worship* (1857); and *The Wesleyan Hymn and Tune Book* (1859), used with the Southern Church's 1847 hymnal. The work of Rigdon M. McIntosh as music editor of the Southern Church's 1874 hymnal is especially noteworthy. The Methodist Protestant Church never produced a tune book, but cross referenced to as many as a dozen collections in a tune index in the back of the 1859 hymnal.

After the publication of the 1874 hymnal of the Southern Church, all three branches of Methodism made provision for placing the tunes on the page with the texts. This development culminated in the publication of the 1901 Methodist Protestant hymnal—the first Methodist hymnal to be printed in only the tune-text format. Today, in the twentieth century, this tune-text format is standard in all denominational hymnals.

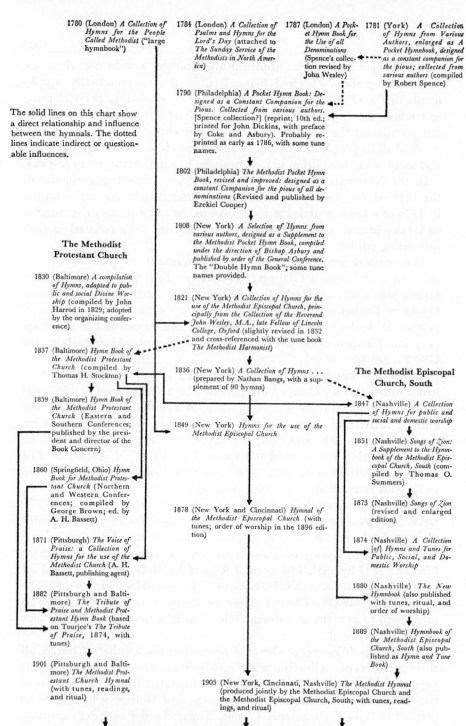

1780 (London) *A Collection of Hymns for the People Called Methodist* ("large hymnbook")

1784 (London) *A Collection of Psalms and Hymns for the Lord's Day* (attached to *The Sunday Service of the Methodists in North America*)

1787 (London) *A Pocket Hymn Book for the Use of all Denominations* (Spence's collection revised by John Wesley)

1781 (York) *A Collection of Hymns from Various Authors, enlarged as A Pocket Hymnbook, designed as a constant companion for the pious; collected from various authors* (compiled by Robert Spence)

The solid lines on this chart show a direct relationship and influence between the hymnals. The dotted lines indicate indirect or questionable influences.

1790 (Philadelphia) *A Pocket Hymn Book: Designed as a Constant Companion for the Pious. Collected from various authors.* [Spence collection?] (reprint; 10th ed.; printed for John Dickins, with preface by Coke and Asbury). Probably reprinted as early as 1786, with some tune names.

1802 (Philadelphia) *The Methodist Pocket Hymn Book, revised and improved: designed as a constant Companion for the pious of all denominations* (Revised and published by Ezekiel Cooper)

1808 (New York) *A Selection of Hymns from various authors, designed as a Supplement to the Methodist Pocket Hymn Book,* compiled under the direction of Bishop Asbury and published by order of the General Conference. The "Double Hymn Book"; some tune names provided.

The Methodist Protestant Church

1830 (Baltimore) *A compilation of Hymns, adapted to public and social Divine Worship* (compiled by John Harrod in 1829; adopted by the organizing conference)

1821 (New York) *A Collection of Hymns for the use of the Methodist Episcopal Church, principally from the Collection of the Reverend John Wesley, M.A., late Fellow of Lincoln College, Oxford* (slightly revised in 1832 and cross-referenced with the tune book *The Methodist Harmonist*)

1837 (Baltimore) *Hymn Book of the Methodist Protestant Church* (compiled by Thomas H. Stockton)

1836 (New York) *A Collection of Hymns . . .* (prepared by Nathan Bangs, with a supplement of 90 hymns)

The Methodist Episcopal Church, South

1859 (Baltimore) *Hymn Book of the Methodist Protestant Church* (Eastern and Southern Conferences; published by the president and director of the Book Concern)

1849 (New York) *Hymns for the use of the Methodist Episcopal Church*

1847 (Nashville) *A Collection of Hymns for public and social and domestic worship*

1851 (Nashville) *Songs of Zion: A Supplement to the Hymnbook of the Methodist Episcopal Church, South* (compiled by Thomas O. Summers)

1860 (Springfield, Ohio) *Hymn Book for Methodist Protestant Church* (Northern and Western Conferences; compiled by George Brown; ed. by A. H. Bassett)

1873 (Nashville) *Songs of Zion* (revised and enlarged edition)

1871 (Pittsburgh) *The Voice of Praise: a Collection of Hymns for the use of the Methodist Church* (A. H. Bassett, publishing agent)

1878 (New York and Cincinnati) *Hymnal of the Methodist Episcopal Church* (with tunes; order of worship in the 1896 edition)

1874 (Nashville) *A Collection [of] Hymns and Tunes for Public, Social, and Domestic Worship*

1880 (Nashville) *The New Hymnbook* (also published with tunes, ritual, and order of worship)

1882 (Pittsburgh and Baltimore) *The Tribute of Praise and Methodist Protestant Hymn Book* (based on Tourjee's *The Tribute of Praise,* 1874, with tunes)

1889 (Nashville) *Hymnbook of the Methodist Episcopal Church, South* (also published as *Hymn and Tune Book*)

1901 (Pittsburgh and Baltimore) *The Methodist Protestant Church Hymnal* (with tunes, readings, and ritual)

1905 (New York, Cincinnati, Nashville) *The Methodist Hymnal* (produced jointly by the Methodist Episcopal Church and the Methodist Episcopal Church, South; with tunes, readings, and ritual)

1935 (New York, Cincinnati, Baltimore, Nashville) *The Methodist Hymnal* (produced jointly by the Methodist Episcopal Church, the Methodist Episcopal Church, South, and the Methodist Protestant Church; with tunes, readings, and ritual)

Bibliography Volume, III

1. General Bibliography
2. Biography and Autobiography
3. Missions
4. Publishing
5. Education
6. Theology
7. Unification
8. Other Branches of Methodism
9. Official Publications
10. Periodicals

1. General Bibliography

Allen, Frederick Lewis. *The Big Change.* New York: Harper & Brothers, 1952.

Anderson, William K., ed. *Methodism.* Nashville: The Methodist Publishing House, 1947.

Asbury, Francis. *The Journal and Letters of Francis Asbury,* ed. Elmer T. Clark, J. Manning Potts, and Jacob S. Payton. 3 vols. Nashville: Abingdon Press, 1958.

Barton, Jesse Hamby. "The Definition of the Episcopal Office in American Methodism." Unpublished dissertation, Drew University, 1960.

Beard, Charles and Mary. *The Rise of American Civilization.* New York: The Macmillan Company, 1927.

Benson, Louis F. *The English Hymn: Its Development and Use in Worship.* New York: George H. Doran Company, 1915; reprinted Richmond: John Knox Press, 1962.

Buckley, James M. *A History of Methodism in the United States.* 2 vols. New York: The Christian Literature Company, 1897.

Cameron, Richard M. *Methodism and Society in Historical Perspective.* Nashville: Abingdon Press, 1961.

Carter, Paul. *The Decline and Revival of the Social Gospel: Social and Political Liberalism in American Protestant Churches.* Ithaca, N. Y.: Cornell University Press, 1956.

Christian Faith in Action [Constitution and Proceedings of Constituting Convention of the National Council, 1950]. New York: National Council of Churches, 1951.

Cole, A. C. *The Irrepressible Conflict, 1850-1865.* New York: The Macmillan Company, 1934.

Davis, Lyman Edwyn. *Democratic Methodism in America: A Topical Survey of the Methodist Protestant Church.* New York: Fleming H. Revell Company, 1921.

Denny, Collins. *A Manual of the Discipline of the Methodist Episcopal Church, South.* Nashville: Lamar and Whitmore, 1931.

Drinkhouse, Edward J. *History of Methodist Reform . . . with Special and Comprehensive Reference to . . . the History of the Methodist Protestant Church.* 2 vols. Baltimore and Pittsburgh: Board of Publication of the Methodist Protestant Church, 1899.

Du Bose, Horace M. *A History of Methodism* [Vol. II of McTyeire's *History of Methodism*]. Nashville: Lamar and Smith, 1916.

The First Assembly of the World Council of Churches. New York: Harper & Brothers, 1949.

Fitzgerald, O. P. *Sunset Views.* Nashville: Publishing House of the Methodist Episcopal Church, South. 1906.

Gabriel, Ralph H. *The Course of American Democratic Thought.* New York: Ronald Press, 1940.

Goodloe, Robert Wesley. "The Office of Bishop in the Methodist Church." Unpublished dissertation, The University of Chicago, 1929.

Harmon, Nolan B. *The Organization of The Methodist Church.* 2nd rev. ed. Nashville: The Methodist Publishing House, 1962.

Haygood, Atticus G. *Our Brother in Black.* Nashville: Southern Methodist Publishing House, 1881.

Herberg, Will. *Protestant, Catholic, Jew.* Garden City, N. Y.: Doubleday, 1955.

Hofstadter, Richard. *The Age of Reform.* New York: Alfred A. Knopf, 1955.

Holt, Ivan Lee, and Clark, Elmer T. *The World Methodist Movement.* Nashville: The Upper Room, 1956.

Hurst, John F. *The History of Methodism.* 6 vols. New York: Eaton and Mains, 1902.

Lay Leaders and Ministers Look at the General Board of Temperance of The Methodist Church. Evanston: Bureau of Social and Religious Research, The Methodist Church, 1958.

Leete, Frederick D. *Methodist Bishops.* Nashville: Parthenon Press, 1948.

Leiffer, Murray H. *Role of the District Superintendent in The Methodist Church.* Nashville: Parthenon Press, 1960.

————. *A Study of Retirement and Recruitment in the Methodist Ministry.* A Report to the 1944 General Conference. Chicago: The Methodist Publishing House, 1944.

Link, Arthur S. *American Epoch.* New York: Alfred A. Knopf, 1955.

Luccock, Halford E.; Hutchinson, Paul; and Goodloe, Robert W. *The Story of Methodism.* Nashville: Abingdon Press, 1949.

McCutchan, Robert Guy. *Our Hymnody: A Manual of the Methodist Hymnal.* 2nd ed. Nashville: Abingdon Press, 1937.

MacKenzie, Kenneth M. *The Robe and the Sword: The Methodist Church and the Rise of American Imperialism.* Washington: Public Affairs Press, 1961.

McTyeire, Holland N. *History of Methodism.* Nashville: Southern Methodist Publishing House, 1884.

Methodist League for Faith and Life. "The Occasion, Basis, Growth, and Purpose of the League." Pamphlet, n.d.

The Methodist Yearbook. Published by the Methodist Episcopal Church annually, 1880-1933.

Meyer, Donald Burton. "The Protestant Social Liberals in America, 1919-1941." Unpublished dissertation, Harvard University, 1953.

Minear, Paul S., ed. *The Nature of the Unity We Seek.* St. Louis: Bethany Press, 1958.

Mode, Peter G. *The Frontier Spirit in American Christianity.* New York: The Macmillan Company, 1923.

Mott, John R. *Methodists United for Action.* Nashville: Board of Missions of The Methodist Church, 1939.

Muelder, Walter G. *Methodism and Society in the Twentieth Century.* Nashville: Abingdon Press, 1961.

Nail, Olin W. *The History of Texas Methodism, 1900-1960.* Austin: Capital Printing Company, 1961.

Neely, Thomas B. *The Governing Conference in Methodism.* New York: Hunt and Eaton, 1892.

Nichols, James Hastings. *Romanticism in American Theology: Nevin and Schaff at Mercersburg.* Chicago: University of Chicago Press, 1961.

Niebuhr, H. Richard. *The Kingdom of God in America.* Torchbook ed., New York: Harper & Brothers, 1959.

Nottingham, Elizabeth K. *Methodism and the Frontier: Indiana Proving Ground.* New York: Columbia University Press, 1941.

Proceedings of the Oecumenical Methodist Conference . . . 1881. London: Wesleyan Conference Office, 1881.

Proceedings of the Seventh Ecumenical Methodist Conference. Nashville: The Methodist Publishing House, 1948.

Reed, Andrew, and Matheson, James. *A Narrative of the Visit to the American Churches.* New York: Harper & Brothers, 1835.

Roberts, George C. M. *Centenary Pictorial Album: Being Contributions of the Early History of Methodism in the State of Maryland.* Baltimore: J. W. Woods, 1866.

Schaff, Philip. *America: A Sketch of Its Political, Social, and Religious Character,* ed. Perry Miller. Cambridge: The Belknap Press of Harvard University, 1961.

Schilling, S. Paul. *Methodism and Society in Theological Perspective.* Nashville: Abingdon Press, 1960.

Shaw, Beverly F. *The Negro in the History of Methodism.* Nashville: Parthenon Press, 1954.

Shelton, Arthur Edwin. "The Methodist Church and Industrial Workers in the Southern Soft Coal Fields." Unpublished dissertation, Boston University School of Theology, 1950.

Shippey, Frederick A. "The Methodist Church Since Unification." A Report to the 1960 General Conference.

Simpson, Matthew, ed. *Cyclopaedia of Methodism.* Rev. ed. Philadelphia: Louis H. Everts, 1880.

Skelton, David E. *History of Lexington Conference.* Lexington, Kentucky, 1950.

Smith, James W., and Jamison, A. Leland, eds. *The Shaping of American Religion.* Princeton: Princeton University Press, 1961.

Statistics of Church Finance. New York: Department of Stewardship, National Council of Churches, 1960.

Stevens, Abel. *History of the Methodist Episcopal Church.* 4 vols. New York: Carlton and Porter, 1864, 1867.

Sturm, Roy A., and Wilson, Robert L. "Methodism's New Churches, 1950-1958." Multilithed report. Philadelphia: Department of Research and Survey, Board of Missions of The Methodist Church, 1960.

Sweet, William Warren. *Circuit-Rider Days Along the Ohio.* New York: The Methodist Book Concern, 1923.

———. *Circuit-Rider Days in Indiana.* Indianapolis: W. K. Stewart Company, 1916.

———. *Methodism in American History.* Rev. ed. Nashville: Abingdon Press, 1953.

———. *The Methodist Episcopal Church and the Civil War.* Cincinnati: The Methodist Book Concern, 1912.

———. *Religion in the Development of American Culture.* New York: Charles Scribner's Sons, 1952.

———. *Religion on the American Frontier, Vol. 4: The Methodists.* Chicago: University of Chicago Press, 1946.

Tigert, John J. *A Constitutional History of American Episcopal Methodism.* 6th ed. Nashville: Publishing House of the Methodist Episcopal Church, South, 1916.

Turner, Frederick Jackson. *The Frontier in American History.* New York: Henry Holt and Company, 1953.

Visser 't Hooft, W. A., ed. *The Evanston Report.* New York: Harper & Brothers, 1955.

Weatherford, Willis J. *American Churches and the Negro.* Boston: The Christopher Publishing House, 1957.

Weisberger, Bernard A. *They Gathered at the River: The Story of the Great Revivalists and Their Impact upon Religion in America.* Boston: Little, Brown, 1958.

Wertenbaker, Thomas J. *The First Americans.* New York: The Macmillan Company, 1927.

Wesley, John. *The Letters of the Rev. John Wesley, A.M.,* ed. John Telford. Standard Edition. 8 vols. London: Epworth Press, 1931.

Whedon, D. A. *Essays, Reviews, and Discourses.* New York: Phillips and Hunt, 1887.

Woodson, Carter G. *The History of the Negro Church.* Washington: The Associated Publishers, 1921.

Woodward, C. Vann. *The Strange Career of Jim Crow.* Galaxy Book ed., New York: Oxford University Press, 1957.

Yearbook of American Churches, 1933, 1961. New York: Annual publication of the National Council of Churches.

2. Biographies and Autobiographies

Bristol, Frank Milton. *The Life of Chaplain McCabe.* New York: Fleming H. Revell Company, 1908.

Clark, Robert D. *The Life of Matthew Simpson.* New York: The Macmillan Company, 1956.

Crooks, George R. *Life and Letters of the Rev. John M'Clintock.* New York: Nelson and Phillips, 1876.

Dabney, Virginius. *Dry Messiah: The Life of Bishop Cannon.* New York: Alfred A. Knopf, 1949.

Du Bose, Horace M. *Life and Memories of Reverend J. D. Barbee.* Nashville: Publishing House of the Methodist Episcopal Church, South, 1906.

Homer Eaton. A memorial volume published by the Methodist Book Concern. New York and Cincinnati, 1913.

Fisher, Galen M. *John R. Mott, Architect of Co-operation and Unity.* New York: Association Press, 1952.

Fitzgerald, O. P. *John B. McFerrin*. Nashville: Publishing House of the M. E. Church, South, 1889.

———. *Dr. Summers, a Life Study*. Nashville: Southern Methodist Publishing House, 1885.

Garber, Paul N. *John Carlisle Kilgo*. Durham: Duke University Press, 1937.

Green, William M. *Life and Papers of A. L. P. Green*. Nashville: Southern Methodist Publishing House, 1877.

Holt, Ivan Lee. *Eugene Russell Hendrix*. Nashville: Parthenon Press, 1950.

McConnell, Francis J. *By the Way: An Autobiography*. New York and Nashville: Abingdon-Cokesbury Press, 1952.

Mains, George P. *Francis Asbury*. New York: Eaton and Mains, 1909.

———. *James Monroe Buckley*. New York: The Methodist Book Concern, 1917.

Martin, Isaac P. *Elijah Embree Hoss, Ecumenical Methodist*. Nashville: Parthenon Press, 1942.

Moore, David Hastings. *John Morgan Walden*. New York: The Methodist Book Concern, 1915.

Moore, John M. *Life and I* [autobiography]. Nashville: Parthenon Press, 1948.

Palmer, Walter C. *Life and Letters of Leonidas L. Hamline*. New York: Carlton and Porter, 1866.

Pierce, Alfred M. *Giant Against the Sky: The Life of Bishop Warren Akin Candler*. New York and Nashville: Abingdon-Cokesbury Press, 1948.

Smith, George G. *The Life and Times of George Foster Pierce*. Nashville: Hunter & Welburn; Sparta, Ga.: Hancock Publishing Company, 1888.

Tarkington, Joseph. *Autobiography of the Reverend Joseph Tarkington*, ed. T. O. Godwin. Cincinnati: The Methodist Book Concern, 1899.

Vincent, Leon H. *John Heyl Vincent*. New York: The Macmillan Company, 1925.

3. Missions

Annual Reports of the Board of Foreign Missions of the Methodist Episcopal Church, 1907-39.

Annual Reports of the Board of Home Missions and Church Extension of the Methodist Episcopal Church, 1907-39.

Annual Reports of the Board of Managers of the Woman's Home Missionary Society of the Methodist Episcopal Church, 1881-1920.

Annual Reports of the Board of Missions of the Methodist Episcopal Church, South, 1845-61; 1870-1939 [there were no reports 1862-70; from 1919-39 the reports were published as *The Missionary Yearbook*].

Annual Reports of the Missionary Society of the Methodist Episcopal Church, 1820-1906.

Annual Reports of the Woman's Home Missionary Society of the Methodist Episcopal Church, 1890-1910; 1921-40.

Annual Reports of the Woman's Foreign Missionary Society of the Methodist Episcopal Church, 1870-1921.

Annual Reports of the Woman's Board of Foreign Missions of the Methodist Episcopal Church, South, 1878-1928.

Annual Reports of the Woman's Missionary Council of the Methodist Episcopal Church, South, 1911-39.

Baker, Frances J. *The Story of the Woman's Foreign Missionary Society of the*

Methodist Episcopal Church, 1869-1895. Cincinnati: Cranston and Curts, 1895.

Barclay, Wade Crawford. *The History of Methodist Missions*. New York: The Board of Missions of The Methodist Church, Vol. I, 1949; Vol. II, 1950; Vol. III, 1957.

Brummitt, Stella Wyatt. *Looking Backward: Thinking Forward. The Jubilee History of the Woman's Home Missionary Society of the Methodist Episcopal Church*. Cincinnati: W. H. M. S., 1930.

Butler, Mrs. F. A. *History of the Woman's Foreign Missionary Society, M. E. Church, South*. Nashville: Publishing House of the M. E. Church, South, 1904.

Butler, William. *From Boston to Bareilly and Back*. New York: Phillips and Hunt, 1885.

Cannon, James. *History of Southern Methodist Missions*. Nashville: Cokesbury Press, 1926.

Diffendorfer, Ralph E., ed. *The World Service of the Methodist Episcopal Church*. Chicago: Council of Boards of Benevolence, the Methodist Episcopal Church, 1923.

The Ecumenical Missionary Conference, Vol. I. New York, 1900.

Findlay, G. G., and Holdsworth, W. W. *The History of the Wesleyan Methodist Missionary Society*. London: Epworth Press, 1921.

Garber, Paul N. *The Methodists of Continental Europe*. New York: Board of Missions of The Methodist Church, 1949.

Harper, Marvin H. *The Methodist Episcopal Church in India*. Lucknow: The Lucknow Publishing House, 1936.

Haskin, Sara Estelle. *Women and Missions in the Methodist Episcopal Church, South*. Nashville: Publishing House of the M. E. Church, South, 1920.

Hollister, John N. *The Centenary of the Methodist Church in Southern India*. Lucknow: The Lucknow Publishing House of The Methodist Church, 1956.

Howell, Mabel Katharine. *Women and the Kingdom: Fifty Years of Kingdom Building by the Women of the Methodist Episcopal Church, South, 1878-1928*. Nashville: Cokesbury Press, 1928.

Isham, Mary. *Valorous Ventures: A Record of Sixty and Six Years of the Woman's Foreign Missionary Society, Methodist Episcopal Church*. Boston: W.F.M.S., 1936.

John, I. G. *Hand Book of Methodist Missions*. Nashville: Publishing House of the M. E. Church, South, 1893.

Journal of the First Annual Meeting of the Board of Missions and Church Extension of The Methodist Church. New York: Board of Missions, 1940.

Lacy, Walter N. *A Hundred Years of China Methodism*. New York and Nashville: Abingdon-Cokesbury Press, 1948.

Latourette, Kenneth Scott. *A History of Christian Missions in China*. New York: The Macmillan Company, 1929.

Mathews, James K. *South of the Himalayas*. New York: Board of Missions of The Methodist Church, 1955.

Mid-Century Report: Division of Home Missions and Church Extension of The Methodist Church. New York: Board of Missions, 1950.

Paik, George. *The History of Protestant Missions in Korea, 1832-1910*. Pyengyang: Union Christian College Press, 1929.

Pickett, J. Waskom. *Christian Mass Movements in India*. Cincinnati: The Abingdon Press, 1933.

Richter, Julius. *A History of Missions in India,* tr. Sidney H. Moore. Edinburgh: Oliphant Anderson & Ferrier, 1908.

Schmidt, Martin. *The Young Wesley: Missionary and Theologian of Missions,* tr. L. A. Fletcher. London: Epworth Press, 1958.

Tomkinson, Mrs. T. L. *Twenty Years' History of the Woman's Home Missionary Society, 1880-1900.* Cincinnati: The Woman's Home Missionary Society of the Methodist Episcopal Church, 1903.

Van den Berg, Johannes. *Constrained by Jesus' Love: An Inquiry into the Motives of the Missionary Awakening in Great Britain in the Period Between 1698 and 1815.* Kampen: J. H. Kok, N.V., 1956.

Wasson, Alfred W. *Church Growth in Korea.* New York: International Missionary Council, 1934.

——. *The Influence of Missionary Expansion upon Methodist Organization.* New York: Commission on Central Conferences of The Methodist Church, 1948.

Wheeler, Mary Sparkes. *First Decade of the Woman's Foreign Missionary Society of the Methodist Episcopal Church, with Sketches of Its Missionaries.* New York: Phillips and Hunt, 1881.

Wunderlich, Friedrich. *Methodists Linking Two Continents.* Nashville: The Methodist Publishing House, 1960.

Year Book of the Woman's Foreign Missionary Society of the Methodist Episcopal Church, 1922-40.

4. Publishing

Archibald, F. A., ed. *Methodism and Literature.* New York: Phillips and Hunt, 1883.

Batten, J. Minton. *The History of the Methodist Publishing House.* Nashville: Personnel and Public Relations Division of the Methodist Publishing House, 1954.

Centennial of the Methodist Book Concern and Dedication of the New Publishing and Mission Building, a memento volume. New York: Hunt and Eaton, 1890.

Fifteen Years and an Idea. A Report on Cokesbury Press. Nashville: Cokesbury Press, 1938.

Jennings, H. C. *The Methodist Book Concern: A Romance of History.* New York and Cincinnati: The Methodist Book Concern, 1924.

Roberts, Millard George. "The Methodist Book Concern in the West." Unpublished dissertation, The University of Chicago, 1947.

Stoody, Ralph. "Religious Journalism: Whence and Whither?" Unpublished thesis, Gordon College of Theology, 1939.

Whitlock, W. F. *The Story of the Book Concerns.* Cincinnati: Jennings and Pye, 1903.

5. Education

Baker, James C. *The First Wesley Foundation.* Nashville: Parthenon Press, 1960.

Bullock, Henry M. *A History of Emory University.* Nashville: Parthenon Press, 1936.

Cummings, A. W. *The Early Schools of Methodism.* New York: Phillips and Hunt, 1886.

Dannelly, Clarence Moore. "The Development of Collegiate Education in the Methodist Episcopal Church, South, 1846-1902." Unpublished dissertation, Yale University, 1933.

Galpin, W. Freeman. *Syracuse University, Vol. I.* Syracuse, N. Y.: Syracuse University Press, 1952.

Gross, John O. *Methodist Beginnings in Higher Education.* Nashville: Board of Education of The Methodist Church, 1959.

Hancher, John W. *The Educational Jubilee.* Cincinnati: The Methodist Book Concern, 1918.

Handbook. Department of Educational Institutions of the Board of Christian Education of the Methodist Protestant Church, 1916.

Hubbart, Henry Clyde. *Ohio Wesleyan's First One Hundred Years.* Delaware: Ohio Wesleyan Press, 1943.

Irby, Richard. *History of Randolph-Macon College, Virginia.* Richmond: Whittet and Shepperson, [1899].

Johnson, Henry M. "The Methodist Episcopal Church and the Education of Southern Negroes, 1862-1900." Unpublished dissertation, Yale University.

Massengale, R. G. "Collegiate Education in the Methodist Episcopal Church, South, 1902-1939." Unpublished dissertation, Yale University, 1950.

Mims, Edward. *History of Vanderbilt University.* Nashville: Vanderbilt University Press, 1946.

Mitchell, H. G. *For the Benefit of My Creditors.* Boston: Beacon Press, 1922.

Morgan, James Henry. *Dickinson College: The History of One Hundred and Fifty Years, 1783-1933.* Carlisle, Pa.: Dickinson College, 1933.

Price, Carl F. *Wesleyan's First Century.* Middletown, Conn.: Wesleyan University Press, 1932.

Second Quadrennial Report. Department of Educational Institutions of the Methodist Protestant Church, 1936.

Snyder, Henry Nelson. *An Educational Odyssey.* New York and Nashville: Abingdon-Cokesbury Press, 1947.

Speare, E. Ray. *Interesting Happenings in Boston University.* Boston: Boston University Press, 1957.

Sweet, William Warren. *Indiana Asbury-DePauw University.* New York: The Abingdon Press, 1937.

Tewksbury, Donald G. *The Founding of American Colleges and Universities Before the Civil War.* New York: Bureau of Publications of Teachers College, Columbia University, 1932.

Thompson, Bard. *History of Vanderbilt Divinity School.* Nashville: Vanderbilt University Press, 1958.

Wallace, David D. *History of Wofford College.* Nashville: Vanderbilt University Press, 1951.

Ware, Estell Frances. *The Story of Northwestern University.* New York: Dodd, Mead, and Company, 1924.

Watson, Elmo Scott. *The Illinois Wesleyan Story.* Bloomington, Ill.: Illinois Wesleyan University Press, 1950.

Wicke, Myron F. *A Brief History of the University Senate of The Methodist Church.* Nashville: Board of Education of The Methodist Church, 1956.

6. Theology

Beckwith, Clarence Augustine. *The Idea of God.* New York: The Macmillan Company, 1922.

Betts, George H. *How to Teach Religion.* New York: The Abingdon Press, 1919.

Brightman, Edgar S. *The Finding of God.* New York: The Abingdon Press, 1931.

——. *An Introduction to Philosophy.* New York: Henry Holt and Company, 1925.

——. *Is God a Person?* New York: Association Press, 1932.

——. *The Problem of God.* New York: The Abingdon Press, 1930.

Burtner, Robert W., and Chiles, Robert E. *A Compend of Wesley's Theology.* Nashville: Abingdon Press, 1954.

Carnell, Edward J. *The Case for Orthodox Theology.* Philadelphia: Westminster Press, 1959.

Cole, Stewart. *The History of Fundamentalism.* New York: Harper & Brothers, 1931.

Deschner, John. *Wesley's Christology.* Dallas: Southern Methodist University Press, 1960.

DeWolf, L. Harold. *The Case for Theology in Liberal Perspective.* Philadelphia: Westminster Press, 1959.

——. *The Religious Revolt Against Reason.* New York: Harper & Brothers, 1949.

——. *A Theology of the Living Church.* New York: Harper & Brothers, 1953.

Dillenberger, John, and Welch, Claude. *Protestant Christianity.* New York: Charles Scribner's Sons, 1954.

Drawbridge, Cyprian L. *Common Objections to Christianity.* New York: Samuel R. Leland, 1931.

Faulkner, John Alfred. *Modernism and the Christian Faith.* New York: The Methodist Book Concern, 1921.

Ferm, Vergilius, ed. *Contemporary American Theology, First Series.* New York: Round Table Press, 1932.

——. *Contemporary American Theology, Second Series.* New York: Round Table Press, 1933.

Furniss, Norman F. *The Fundamentalist Controversy, 1918-1931.* New Haven: Yale University Press, 1954.

Harkness, Georgia. *Conflicts in Religious Thought.* New York: Henry Holt and Company, 1929.

——. *The Recovery of Ideals.* New York: Charles Scribner's Sons, 1937.

——. *The Resources of Religion.* New York: Henry Holt and Company, 1936.

Henry, C. F. H. *Fifty Years of Protestant Theology.* Boston: W. A. Wilde Company, 1950.

Hocking, William Ernest. *The Meaning of God in Human Experience.* New Haven: Yale University Press, 1912.

Hordern, William. *The Case for a New Reformation Theology.* Philadelphia: Westminster Press, 1959.

——. *A Layman's Guide to Protestant Theology.* New York: The Macmillan Company, 1955.

Knudson, Albert C. *The Doctrine of God.* New York: The Abingdon Press, 1930.

——. *The Doctrine of Redemption.* New York: The Abingdon Press, 1933.

——. *Faith and Ethics.* The Evanston Series, 1935-36.

——. *The Philosophy of Personalism.* New York: The Abingdon Press, 1927.

——. *The Validity of Religious Experience.* New York: The Abingdon Press, 1937.

Lee, Umphrey. *John Wesley and Modern Religion.* Nashville: Cokesbury Press, 1936.

Lewis, Edwin. *A Christian Manifesto.* New York: The Abingdon Press, 1934.

——. *The Creator and the Adversary.* New York and Nashville: Abingdon-Cokesbury Press, 1948.

——. *God and Ourselves.* New York: The Abingdon Press, 1931.

——. *Jesus Christ and the Human Quest.* New York: The Abingdon Press, 1924.

——. "Main Emphases in the Theology of Karl Barth." Pamphlet, "A Lecture Delivered in the Chapel of Drew University, October 27, 1932."

——. *A Manual of Christian Beliefs.* New York: Charles Scribner's Sons, 1927.

——. *A Philosophy of the Christian Revelation.* New York: Harper & Brothers, 1940.

Luccock, Halford E. *Christianity and the Individual in a World of Crowds.* Nashville: Cokesbury Press, 1937.

McConnell, Francis J. *John Wesley.* New York and Nashville: Abingdon-Cokesbury Press, 1939; Abingdon Apex Book edition, 1961.

——. *Public Opinion and Theology.* New York: The Abingdon Press, 1920.

McCutcheon, William J. "Theology of the Methodist Episcopal Church During the Interwar Period, 1919-1939." Unpublished dissertation, Yale University, 1960.

Michalson, Carl. *Christianity and the Existentialists.* New York: Charles Scribner's Sons, 1956.

——. *The Hinge of History.* New York: Charles Scribner's Sons, 1959.

Our Faith in Series (God, Christ, the Bible, Love, Prayer, Immortality, the Holy Spirit, the Kingdom of God). Eight booklets published by the 1949-50 Advance for Christ and His Church.

Outler, Albert C. *The Christian Tradition and the Unity We Seek.* New York: Oxford University Press, 1957.

——. "The Methodist Contribution to the Ecumenical Discussion of the Church." Mimeographed paper, n.d.

——. "Methodist Doctrine." Mimeographed lecture, Yale Divinity School, 1950.

——. *Psychotherapy and the Christian Message.* New York: Harper & Brothers, 1954.

Piette, Maximin. *John Wesley in the Evolution of Protestantism,* tr. J. B. Howard. New York: Sheed and Ward, 1937.

Pringle-Pattison, A. Seth. *The Idea of God in the Light of Recent Philosophy.* New York: Oxford University Press, 1920.

Rall, Harris Franklin. *Christianity.* New York: Charles Scribner's Sons, 1941.

——. *The Coming Kingdom.* New York: The Methodist Book Concern, 1924.

——. *A Faith for Today.* New York: The Abingdon Press, 1936.

——. *The Meaning of God.* Nashville: Cokesbury Press, 1925.

——. *The Teaching Ministry and Evangelism.* Evanston Series, 1933.

——. *A Working Faith.* New York: The Abingdon Press, [1914].

Ramsdell, Edward. *The Christian Perspective.* Nashville: Abingdon Press, 1950.

Rowe, Gilbert T. *The Meaning of Methodism.* Nashville: Cokesbury Press, 1926.

———. *Reality in Religion.* Nashville: Cokesbury Press, 1927.

Scott, Leland H. "Methodist Theology in America in the Nineteenth Century." Unpublished dissertation, Yale University, 1954.

Sloan, Harold Paul. *The Christ of the Ages.* New York: Harper & Brothers, 1928.

———. *Historic Christianity and the New Theology.* Louisville: Pentecostal Publishing Company, 1922.

Smith, Gerald Birney, ed. *Religious Thought in the Last Quarter-Century.* Chicago: University of Chicago Press, 1927.

Smith, H. Shelton. *Changing Conceptions of Original Sin.* New York: Charles Scribner's Sons, 1955.

Sorley, William Ritchie. *Moral Values and the Idea of God.* New York: The Macmillan Company, 1918.

Tillett, Wilbur Fisk. *The Paths That Lead to God.* New York: George H. Doran Company, 1924.

Tittle, Ernest Fremont. *The Foolishness of Preaching.* New York: Henry Holt and Company, 1930.

———. *A Way to Life.* New York: Henry Holt and Company, 1935.

Welch, Claude. *In This Name: The Doctrine of the Trinity in Contemporary Theology.* New York: Charles Scribner's Sons, 1952.

———. *The Reality of the Church.* New York: Charles Scribner's Sons, 1958.

Williams, Colin. *John Wesley's Theology Today.* Nashville: Abingdon Press, 1960.

Williams, Daniel Day. *What Present-Day Theologians Are Thinking.* Rev. ed. New York: Harper & Brothers, 1959.

7. Unification

Garber, Paul N. *The Methodists Are One People.* Nashville: Cokesbury Press, 1939.

Joint Commission on Unification of the Methodist Episcopal Church, South, and the Methodist Episcopal Church. 3 vols. Nashville: Publishing House of the Methodist Episcopal Church, South; New York: The Methodist Book Concern, 1918.

MSS correspondence—Bishops Edwin Mouzon, Earl Cranston, John M. Moore, and Dr. John F. Goucher—1917-25. Archives of the Historical Society of the Baltimore Annual Conference, Lovely Lane Museum.

Moore, John M. *The Long Road to Methodist Union.* Nashville: The Methodist Publishing House, 1943.

Prospectus of the Discipline of The Methodist Church, Submitted to the Uniting Conference by the Joint Commission on Interdenominational Relations and Church Union of the Methodist Episcopal Church, Methodist Episcopal Church, South, Methodist Protestant Church. Printed for the Joint Commission under the Supervision of the Publishing Agents of the Uniting Churches, 1939.

A Record of All Agreements Concerning Fraternity and Federation Between the Methodist Episcopal Church and the Methodist Episcopal Church, South, and The Declaration in Favor of Unification Made by the General Conference of the Methodist Episcopal Church, South. Nashville: Publishing House of the M. E. Church, South, 1914.

Straughn, James H. *Inside Methodist Union.* Nashville: The Methodist Publishing House, 1958.

A Working Conference on the Union of American Methodism, Northwestern University, Evanston, Illinois. New York: The Methodist Book Concern, 1916.

8. Other Branches of Methodism

Centenary Yearbook of the Free Methodist Church. Winona Lake, Ind.: Free Methodist Publishing House, 1960.

Clark, Elmer T. *The Small Sects in America.* Rev. ed. Nashville: Abingdon Press, 1949.

Corbett, Lynn. *What, Why, How?—History, Organization, and Doctrinal Belief of the Southern Methodist Church.* Greenville, S.C.: Foundry Press, 1956.

Howland, Carl L. *The Story of Our Church.* Winona Lake, Ind.: Free Methodist Publishing House, 1940.

McLeister, Ira Ford. *History of the Wesleyan Methodist Church of America,* rev. by Roy Stephen Nicholson. Marion, Ind.: Wesleyan Methodist Publishing Association, 1959.

Marston, Leslie R. *A Living Witness* [Free Methodist Church]. Winona Lake, Ind.: Light and Life Press, 1960.

Mead, Frank S. *Handbook of Denominations in the United States.* 2nd rev. ed. Nashville: Abingdon Press, 1961.

Minutes of the General Conference of the Southern Methodist Church. Memphis, 1958.

Minutes of the General Conference of the Wesleyan Methodist Church, 1959.

Quadrennial Report of the A.M.E. Zion Church, 1960.

The Spirit and Emphasis of Free Methodism. Official leaflet published by the Free Methodist Publishing House, n.d.

The Wesleyan Methodist Church of America—Interesting Facts for Interested Friends. Official pamphlet published by the Wesleyan Methodist Publishing Association, 1959.

What Is the Department of Foreign Missions of the A.M.E. Zion Church? Pamphlet; New York: Department of Foreign Missions of the A.M.E. Zion Church, 1960.

9. Conference Journals, Minutes, and Other Official Church Publications

Commission to Study and Recommend Action Concerning the Jurisdictional System, "Report to the 1960 General Conference."

Constitution and Discipline of the Methodist Protestant Church (usually published following the General Conference; last edition in 1938).

Decisions of the Judicial Council of The Methodist Church, Nos. 1-175, 1940-1960. Nashville: The Methodist Publishing House. (Between sessions of the General Conference the decisions of the Judicial Council are printed in the *General Minutes.* They are issued in permanent clothbound form following each General Conference.)

Doctrines and Discipline of the Methodist Episcopal Church (usually published following the General Conference; last edition in 1936).

Doctrines and Discipline of the Methodist Episcopal Church, South (usually published quadrennially following the General Conference; last edition in 1938.)

Doctrines and Discipline of The Methodist Church (first edition in 1939; beginning in 1940 published quadrennially following the General Conference).

Minutes of the Annual Conferences of the Methodist Episcopal Church (published annually; from 1878 through 1939 the Minutes were published in two sections—Minutes of the Spring Conferences and Minutes of the Fall Conferences).

Minutes of the Annual Conferences of the Methodist Episcopal Church, South (published annually; from 1923-24 through 1939-40 published as *The General Minutes and Yearbook of the Methodist Episcopal Church, South*).

Minutes of the Annual Conferences of The Methodist Church (published annually; beginning in 1940 the Minutes were published in two sections—Spring Conferences and Fall Conferences; in 1948 these were combined and published as *The General Minutes of the Annual Conferences of The Methodist Church*).

Journal of the General Conference of the Methodist Episcopal Church (published as a separate volume, quadrennially, 1840-1936).

Journal of the General Conference of the Methodist Episcopal Church, South (published quadrennially, 1846-1938).

Journal of the Uniting Conference, 1939.

Journal of the General Conference of the Methodist Protestant Church (published quadrennially, 1880-1936; see Vol. II of this *History* for earlier editions).

Journal of the Fifth Northeastern Jurisdictional Conference of The Methodist Church, 1956.

Journal of the Rock River Annual Conference, 1921.

Journals of the General Conference, 1796-1836 (New York: Carlton and Phillips, 1855).

Minutes of the Book Committee, Methodist Episcopal Church, South, 1854.

Minutes of the Maryland Annual Conference of the Methodist Protestant Church, 1904, 1924, 1929.

Quadrennial Reports: Reports of the Boards, Commissions and Committees of The Methodist Church to the General Conference, 1960. Issued by authority of the Commission on Entertainment.

Report of Debates in the General Conference of the Methodist Episcopal Church, Held in the City of New York, 1844. New York: Lane and Tippett, 1844.

Sanford, Arthur Benton. *Reports of the Committee on Judiciary of the General Conference of the Methodist Episcopal Church.* New York: The Methodist Book Concern, 1924.

10. Periodicals

The Arkansas Methodist. (Methodist Episcopal Church, South). Established 1881; continued after unification as the periodical of the Little Rock and North Arkansas Conferences; still published 1963.

The Arminian Magazine, 1787 (published in England by the British Methodists).

Central Christian Advocate (Kansas City, Kansas, Methodist Episcopal Church). Published from 1852-1929 under this title; became in 1929 the Central Edition of the *Christian Advocate;* absorbed into the *Christian Advocate* after unification.

The Christian Century (Chicago, nondenominational), March 22, 1933; November 3, 1937; February 15, March 1 and 15, June 14, 1939.

Christian Education Magazine (Nashville, Methodist Episcopal Church, South). Began publication 1911; continued after unification.

Christian Student (New York and Chicago, Methodist Episcopal Church). Published 1900-1940.

Church History (nondenominational quarterly), September, 1958; December, 1959; March, 1960.

Daily Christian Advocate of the Methodist Episcopal Church. Published daily during sessions of the General Conference.

Daily Christian Advocate of the Methodist Episcopal Church, South. Published daily during sessions of the General Conference.

Drew Gateway (published by the Theological School of Drew University), April, 1933; January, 1934; Winter, 1961.

Garrett Tower (published by Garrett Theological Seminary), January, 1933; November, 1934; November, 1936.

Information Service of the Methodist Federation for Social Service (published in New York by the Federation for Social Service for several years around the 1920's).

Journal of Southern History, August, 1956.

The Methodist Protestant (Baltimore, the Methodist Protestant Church). Published under this title from 1834-1929; as the *Methodist Protestant-Recorder,* 1929-40. Absorbed into the *Christian Advocate* at unification.

The Methodist Review (New York, Methodist Episcopal Church). Published earlier as *The Methodist Magazine* (1818-28), *The Methodist Magazine and Quarterly Review* (1830-41), and *The Methodist Quarterly Review* (1841-85); discontinued in 1932.

The Methodist Quarterly Review (Nashville, Methodist Episcopal Church, South). Published 1903-6 and 1908-1930 under this title; discontinued in 1930. Earlier published under several titles: *Quarterly Review of the Methodist Episcopal Church, South* (1847-61; 1879-86; 1889-94); *Southern Methodist Review* (1887-88); *The Methodist Review* (1895-1903; 1906-8); not published 1862-78.

Missionary Seer (Washington, A.M.E. Zion Church). Began publication 1900; still published 1963.

Nashville *Christian Advocate* (Nashville, official paper of the Methodist Episcopal Church, South). Published 1832-1940; became property of the Southern Church in 1845. Absorbed into the *Christian Advocate* at unification.

New Orleans Christian Advocate (New Orleans, Methodist Episcopal Church, South). Published 1850-1946.

New York *Christian Advocate* (New York, official paper of the Methodist Episcopal Church). Began publication as the *Christian Advocate and Journal,* 1826; absorbed into the *Christian Advocate* at unification.

North Carolina Christian Advocate (Raleigh and Greensboro, Methodist Episcopal Church, South). Began publication 1855; continued after unification as the official organ of the North Carolina and Western North Carolina Conferences.

Northwestern Christian Advocate (Chicago, Methodist Episcopal Church). Published under this title 1852-1929; became the Northwestern Edition of the *Christian Advocate* in 1929.

Pacific Christian Advocate (Portland, Ore., Methodist Episcopal Church). Published under this title 1855-1929; published 1929-40 as the Pacific Edition of the *Christian Advocate.*

Primitive Methodist Journal (Shenandoah, Pennsylvania, monthly periodical of the Primitive Methodist Church). Began publication 1892.

Religion in Life (New York, Methodist Episcopal Church). Began publication in 1932 to replace *The Methodist Review.* Published after unification by Abingdon Press; still published 1963, in Nashville.

Southern Christian Advocate (Charleston, Methodist Episcopal Church, South). Began publication 1837; became property of the Southern Church in 1845; continued after unification as the *South Carolina Methodist Advocate,* official organ of the South Carolina Conference.

Wesleyan Christian Advocate (official paper of the Georgia Conference of the Methodist Episcopal Church, South). Began publication 1836; still published 1963 as the Georgia Conference paper.

The Wesleyan Methodist (the Wesleyan Methodist Church). Began publication 1843 at Syracuse, New York; moved to Marion, Indiana, 1957.

Western Christian Advocate (Cincinnati, Methodist Episcopal Church). Published under this title 1834-1929; became Western Edition of the *Christian Advocate* in 1929.

Zion's Herald (Boston, Methodist Episcopal Church). Official paper of the New England Conference; began publication 1823; still published 1963.

Index, Volume III

Abbey, Richard, 172, 181
Abe, Yoshimune, 87
Abingdon Bible Commentary, 284, 305, 314
Abingdon-Cokesbury Press, 536
Abingdon Press, 149, 188, 536
abstinence: see temperance and prohibition
academic freedom, 236-37, 248-49
accreditation of schools, 206, 217-18, 229, 237, 544-45
Adeline Smith Industrial Home, 13
admission to conference membership, 523-26
Adrian College, 203, 240, 242
Adult Bible Class, 284
Adult Bible Class and Teacher-Training Monthly, 154
adult educational work, 531
Adult Student, 154
Advance for Christ and His Church, 316, 509, 519, 540
Advance Specials, 506, 509, 520, 540
Africa, 15-16, 29, 62-64, 66, 70, 79, 103-9, 114, 125, 339, 350, 369, 490
African Methodist Episcopal Church: see A.M.E. Church
African Methodist Episcopal Zion Church: see A.M.E. Zion Church
African Union Church, 595
African Union First Colored Methodist Protestant Church, Inc., 595
Aggrey, James E. K., 584
Ainsworth, W. N., 439, 450-51
Akron plan, 157, 626
Alabama, 14, 144, 162, 174, 177, 178, 439: Anniston, 594; Birmingham, 120, 583, 586; Boaz, 214; Huntsville, 210; Tuscaloosa, 193
Alaska, 123
Albion College, 203, 221
Albricias, Francisco, 83
alcoholics, 549
Aldersgate experience, 291-92
Aleutian Islands, 123
Alexander, Will W., 366

Algeria, 480, 541
Algiers, 109
Allan, A. J., 572
Allegheny Church, Pittsburgh, 443
Allegheny College, 65, 77, 185, 203, 221, 276
Allen, Ray, 590
Allen University, 583
Allen, Young J., 73-74, 90
A.M.E. Church, 364, 427, 493, 570, 572-73, 581-83, 595
A.M.E. Review, 583
A.M.E. Zion Church, 11, 570, 576, 581-82, 584-85, 595
American Bible Society, 90, 101, 496
American Council of Churches, 593
American culture, Methodism in, 599-614, 616-23
American University, 215-16, 220, 497, 545
Ames, Edward R., 54
Amsterdam Assembly, 569-71
Amstutz, H. B., 572
amusements, 162-63, 340-41
Andersen, Arlow W., 143
Anderson, Bernhard, 322
Anderson, William, 356
Andino Institute, 101
Andrew Chapel, Savannah, 176
Andrew, James O., 25, 28, 47, 52, 429
Anglo-Chinese College, 74, 90
Angola, 103, 105-7, 539
annual allowance of ministers, 7-8
Annual Conference: evolution of, 43-45; powers of, 45, 462; organization of, 45, 462 (see Mission Annual Conferences)
Annual Conferences: Angola, 107; Atlanta, 14; Baltimore, 27, 416, 464; Belgium, 84; Bengal, 91; Bengal-Burma, 92; Brazil, 97; California, 119, 124, 348; Cincinnati, 187; Central Alabama, 14; Central West, 14; Colorado, 57; Delaware, 14; East Tennessee, 14-15; Florida, 14, 102; Genesee, 16, 183, 590; Georgia, 176, 191; Holston,

Annual Conferences—*cont'd* 180, 226, 465; Kentucky, 13; Korean, 446; Lexington, 13-14, 160; Liberia, 16, 106; Louisiana, 14; Malaysia, 92, 94; Maryland, 197, 199, 246; Michigan, 367; Minnesota, 187; Mississippi, 14, 25; New England, 465; New Jersey, 11, 270; New York, 190-91; New York East, 186, 191, 383, 404, 555; North Carolina, 14-15, 75; North Georgia, 465; North Sumatra, 93; Northwest Mexican, 98; Norway, 83; Ohio, 28, 65, 356; Oklahoma, 116; Philadelphia, 11, 27, 54, 67; Philippines, 94; Pittsburgh, 377; Polish, 84; Rock River, 56, 194, 196, 211, 246, 352, 383; Savannah, 14; South Carolina, 15; South Florida, 15; South India, 91-92, 105, 110; Southeast Indiana, 54; Southern California, 215, 464; Southwest, 15; Southwest Missouri, 465; Sumatra, 541; Sweden, 83; Switzerland, 83; Tennessee, 14-15, 54; Texas, 15; Troy, 25, 185, 190; Upper Mississippi, 15; Vermont, 54; Virginia, 38; Washington, 14-15, 160; West Texas, 15, 98, 117, 465; Wisconsin, 101; Wyoming, 464
Anti-Saloon League of America, 335, 337
anti-Semetism, 350-51
Aoyama Gakuin School, 87
Apex books, 537
Apostles' Creed, 481
appeal of appointments, 21, 37, 52
Appenzeller, Henry G., 89-90
appointment of ministers, 9-10, 477, 514
apportionment of funds, 506-7, 540
architecture, church, 543, 560-61, 626, plates 11-14
area system, 26, 31-36
Arecibo, 124

651

Argentina, 84, 96-97, 101, 541, 567
Arizona, 115, 118, 213
Arkansas, 15, 177, 182, 196, 210, 237, 241: Little Rock, 13, 492; North Little Rock, 583
Arkansas Methodist, 350, 354-55, 369, 378
Arminian Magazine, 145
Arminianism, 291, 301, 608, 621
Arms, Goodsil F., 101
Arndt, Anna, 108
Articles of Religion, 271, 273, 455, 460, 554, 588
Asbury Church, Washington, D. C., 16
Asbury College, 81, 228
Asbury, Francis, 9, 18, 19, 21, 26, 29, 32, 51, 62-64, 145, 148, 158, 196, 201, 223, 243, 380, 389, 441, 486, 541, 613, 619, 625
Asbury Theological Seminary, 591
Asia, 63-64, 69, 72, 77-78, 84-95, 114, 125, 406, 433, 539
Asian immigration, 118-19
Assaf, Charles, 118
associate General Conference (proposed), 430, 433, 435
Association of Southern Women for the Prevention of Lynching, 366, 369
Atlanta Area, 449
Atlantic Coast Area, 491-92
Audio-visual materials, 528, 531-32
Australia, 79, 181, 411
Austria, 81-82, 346
autonomous Methodist churches (overseas), 112-13

Bahama Island Conference, A.M.E., 584
Baker Institute, 210
Baker, James C., 16, 196, 483, 545, 567-68, 571
Baker, Richard T., 472
Baldwin University, 189, 195, 203, 212, 221, 276
Baldwin-Wallace College 203, 221
Baltic and Slavic Mission, 84
Baltimore Area, 491-92
Baltimore Book Directory (M.P.), 136, 153
Bangalore, 79
Bangs, Nathan, 52, 65, 145, 149, 170-71, 186
baptism, 473, 600, 608: infant, 154-55, 611
Baptists, 19, 61, 66, 91, 96, 120, 226, 388, 493, 580
Barbee, David Rankin, 440

Barbee, James D., 178-79, 182
Barbieri, S. U., 567, 572-73
Barclay, Wade Crawford, 156
Bareilly, 45, 76-78
Barratt's Chapel, 19, 620
Barth, Karl, and Barthian theology, 279, 290, 293-95, 297-315, 318-22, 325
Barton, Bruce, 401-3
Barton, Hamby, 28
Bashford, James W., 74
Bassett, John S., 236
Batavia, 93
Baxter, Richard, 145
Baxter Seminary, 222
Baylor, Francis R., 464
Behaviorism, 262
Belem, 100
Belgium, 81, 84, 103, 106
Belgium Methodist Mission, 84
Bell, Joseph W., 530
Bench of Bishops, 40, 48
benevolence funds, 237, 498-99, 545
benevolence giving, 489-90, 501, 505-6, 520, 589-90
Bennett, Belle Harris, 71, 98, 123
Bennett College, Brazil, 98
Bennett College, N. C., 13, 123, 211, 221, 492, 493
Benson, Frank T., 199
Berean lesson helps, 154
Berry, Theodore M., 492
Bertocci, Peter, 321
Bethel Church, New York City (A.M.E. Zion), 584
Bethel Ship, 82-83, 117
Bethlehem Centers, 71, 116
Bethlehem Houses, 494
Bethune-Cookman College, 222, 492
Betts, George H., 267
Bible: in college curriculum, 205, 218, 546; in church school curriculum, 563-64; in seminary curriculum, 563; critical study of, 248, 261-62, 265, 563; divine inspiration of, 268, 270, 588; translating, 88-89, 108
Bible Companion, The, 271
Bible School Leaf, 153
Bible School Series (M.P.), 198
Bible Study Home Department Quarterly, 154
Biblical schools and institutes: see theological seminaries
Birmingham Area, 117
Birmingham-Southern College, 213
Bishop, C. M., 450
Bishops: in areas, 32-36; assignment, 482; authority, 513-14; board membership, 509; consecration, 27,

Bishops—*cont'd*
474, 482; control of course of study, 270-71; control of theological seminaries, 248-49; Council of, 463-64, 512; duties, 35-36, 513; election, 461, 482; the Episcopal Address, 512, episcopal visitation, 512-13; judicial power, 36-40; jurisdictional system, 482; retirement, 469 (*see* episcopacy)
Black Legion, 357
Blackmore, Sophia, 92
Blackwell, R. E., 430, 450
Blake, Edgar, 400, 428, 431-33, 449
Bledsoe, A. T., 137
Board of Bishops (M.E.), 16-17, 23, 35, 48, 53, 81, 368, 463
Board of Christian Education (M.P.), 241
Board of Christian Social Concerns, 497, 521, 527, 533, 557
Board of Christian Work in the Dominican Republic, 125
Board of Church Extension (M.E.S.), 115, 496
Board of Education (The Meth. Ch.), 465-66, 476, 496, 525, 527-28, 532, 534, 545
Board of Education (M.E.), 209, 217-19, 270, 493, 533
Board of Education (M.E.S.), 224, 231-32, 235, 237
Board of Evangelism, 496, 533-34
Board of Finance (M.E.S.), 467, 496
Board of Foreign Missions (M.E.), 66, 75, 81-82, 100
Board of Foreign Missions (M.E.S.), 68, 108, 112, 141
Board of Foreign Missions (M.P.), 71-72, 198
Board of Home and Foreign Missions (M.P.), 72, 86
Board of Home Missions (M.E.S.), 68, 131
Board of Home Missions and Church Extension (M.E.), 67, 121, 499
Board of Hospitals and Homes, 466, 476, 496, 546-47, 559
Board of Lay Activities, (The Meth. Ch.), 467, 476, 496, 533-34
Board of Lay Activities (M.E.S.), 532
Board of Managers of the Missionary Society, 65-66, 96
Board of Managers of the General Fund for Superannuates (M.P.), 467

Board of Missions (The Meth. Ch.), 465-66, 476, 496, 512, 530, 534-35, 541-42
Board of Missions (M.E.S.), 234, 468
Board of Pensions, 466, 476, 496
Board of Pensions and Relief (M.E.), 466
Board of Publication (The Meth. Ch.), 467, 476-77, 496, 509, 537
Board of Publication (M.P.), 198, 467
Board of Social and Economic Relations, 497, 521, 551-53, 555, 559, 563, 576
Board of Sunday Schools (M.E.), 284
Board of Temperance, 467, 497, 516, 521, 548
Board of Trustees: local church, 463; The Meth. Ch., 469, 476
Board of World Peace, 497, 521, 550: see Commission on World Peace
Boards: General boards of The Methodist Church, 36, 465-68; location of, 476, 496; membership of, 509, 517; origins and development, 4-6; work of, 516-17
Bodine Training School, 107
Bohemian (Czechoslovakian) Mission, 118
Bolivia, 96, 99, 101, 541
Bollinger, Hiel D., 577
Bolshevism, 385, 399
Bombay, 78-80
book agents, 135, 141, 144, 146, 171-73, 178-79, 181-82, 183-89, 468
Book Committee: (M.E.), 134, 145, 147, 185, 467; (M.E.S.), 132, 177-78, 467
Book Concern (M.E.), 130, 133-35, 138-39, 143-44, 148-49, 154, 170-71, 183-89
Book Concern (M.P.), 135-37, 198
book publishing, 130-52, 536
Book of Worship, 174, 536, 562
bookstores, Methodist, 537-38
Borneo, 91-94
Bosley, Harold A., 572
Boston University, 99-100, 211, 215-16, 220, 248, 274, 321, 492, 620
Boston University School of Theology, 221, 243, 248-49, 273, 276, 291, 317, 319, 323, 516, 572, 574
Bovard, William S., 266
Bowen, John W. E., 361, 491
Bowne, Borden Parker, 263-65, 268, 273-74, 276, 278, 284, 299, 301, 620
Boxer Uprising, 74, 397

Boyland Industrial Home, 13
Boys and Girls, 154
Boys and Girls Quarterly, 154
Bragg, Mrs. J. D., 524
Brazil, 72, 84, 95-98, 100, 112, 141, 181, 414, 539, 541
Brazilian Methodist Publishing House, 97
Brazilian Wesleyan Conference, 181
Bremen, 82
Brevard Institute, 123
Brewster Hospital for Negroes, 13, 123
Brightman, Edgar Sheffield, 273-76, 284-85, 295, 297-98, 315, 320-24
British and Foreign Bible Society, 90
British Guiana, 584
British immigration, 346-47
British missionary work, 60-63, 76
Brittain, Harriett, 86
Brooks, Mrs. Frank, 573
Brooks, Robert N., 491
Broomfield, J. C., 442, 453, 458
Brothers College, Drew University, 221
Brown, George R., 465
Brown, George Warren, 431
Brown, William Adams, 262
Browne, Eleanor Kent, 569
Brummitt, Dan B., 195-96
Brunner, Emil, 293-94, 300, 303-4, 314, 319, 321, 324
Bryan, William Jennings, 254, 337, 344-45, 353
Buckley, James Monroe, 29, 138, 192, 410
Buckner, J. D. M., 273
Buckner, Walter C., 464
Buddhism, 88, 346, 539
Buenos Aires, 96-97
Buenos Aires Theological Seminary, 96-97
Buitenzorg, Java, 93
Bulgaria, 81, 83
Bultmann, Rudolf, 293, 303-4
Burma, 91, 111, 541
Burns, Francis, 15-16, 29-30
Burtner, Robert W., 318
Butler, John W., 99
Butler, William, Dr. & Mrs., 69, 76-77

cabinet, bishop's, 41, 513-15
Cadman, S. Parkes, 7, 306, 385, 416
Calcutta, 79
California, 78-79, 98, 115-118, 124, 126, 176-77, 186, 197, 213, 257, 441: Berkeley, 247; Los Angeles, 16, 123, 216, 247, 254, 362, 385, 545; San Francisco, 78, 118-19, 139, 198, 348; Stockton, 203

California Oriental Mission, 119
California Wesleyan College, 213
Call to Colors, 271
call to preach, 522
Callao, 101
Calvin, John, 291, 293, 303-4, 600, 625
Calvinism, 61, 122, 159, 173, 190, 264, 281, 291, 293, 315, 327, 620-21
Cambine, 107
Cameron, Richard M., 168, 317
camp program, 531
Campbell, J. B., 472
Campbell, Josephine Peel, 90
Camphor, Alexander P., 104
Canada, 27, 64, 79, 324, 347, 591
Canadian Methodist Church, 181, 411
Candler, Asa, 232-33
Candler School of Theology, 247, 249, 444
Candler, Warren A., 36, 232, 265, 273, 358, 439, 448, 450
Cannon, James, Jr., 333, 339, 358, 385-86, 433, 568
Cannon, William, 317
Cape May Conference, 409-11, 418, 423, 606
Capers, William, 52, 486
capitalism, 167, 371, 373, 379, 386, 388, 404-6, 539
card playing, 162, 624
Carey, William, 61-62, 76
Carlton, Thomas B., 134, 172, 183-84
Carnegie, Andrew, 207, 374-75
Carr, J. H., 123
Carrow, G. D., 96
Carter, Paul, 332, 340
Carter, Randall, 368
Cartwright, Peter, 604, 621, 623
catechetical instruction, 136, 156
catechism, 413-14, 419
Catholicism: see Roman Catholicism
Cazenovia Junior College, 222
Cazenovia Seminary, 222
Cell, George, 291-92, 315
Centenary Biblical Institute, 209
Centenary College of Louisiana, 203
Centenary Collegiate Institute, 209
Centenary Educational Fund, 244
Centenary Junior College, 222
Centenary of Methodism (1866), 209, 219, 245, 247

Centenary Movement (1919), 237, 400-401
Centennial Conference of Methodism (1884), 410-11, 443
Central Christian Advocate, 196, 477, 494, 537
Central College, 203
Central Conferences, **30-31,** 42, 45, 69, 110-12, 462, 477, 510, 512: Central European, 112; Central and Southern Europe Provisional, 112; Eastern Asia (China), 111; Germany, 112; India, 111; India and Malaysia, 45; Latin America, 42, 112; **Northern** European (Scandinavia), 111; Philippines, 112; Southeastern Asia, 112; Southern Asia, 111
Central Council, autonomous churches, 112-13
Central Jurisdiction, 475, 477, 484-95, 511, 515, 552-53
Central Methodist, 440
Central Methodist Church, New York City, 7
Central Mission Press, 107
Central Tennessee College, 210, 246
Central Training School, Mozambique, 107
Central University of the M.E.S., 228 (*see* Vanderbilt)
Ceylon, 62, 76
Chadwick, John S., 439
Chandag (India), 78
Chao, T. C., 75
chaplains, 258, 398, 493, 557-59
Chappell, Clovis, 316
Chappell, E. B., 450
Chappell, Winifred L., 377
Chartered Fund, 461
Chattanooga Report, 420-22, 427
Chautauqua movement, 193-95, 622
Cheeloo University, 75
Chen, W. Y., 75
Chengtu, 73, 75
Chiang Kai-shek, 75
Chicago Deaconess Training School, 122, 223
child labor, 120, 372, 382-83, 386, 551
Childers, M. A., 465
Childhood Sunday, 531
children, work with, 136-37: religious literature, 152-57; religious education, 527-29; books for, 536
Children's Day, 199, 219
Children's Visitor, 154
Chile, 96, 99-101
Chiles, Robert E., 280, 318
China, 63, 88, 93, 108, 111, 124, 307, 350, 397, 403,

China—*cont'd* 413, 539; missionary work in, 70, 72-76, 86, 92, 125, 140, 414
China Advocate, 264
Chinese immigrants: missions to, 91, 94, 119; concern for, 348-50
Chitambar, J. R., 80, 111
Chosen Christian College, 90
Christ Hospital, Cincinnati, 122
Christian Advocate (The Meth. Ch.), 316, 477, 537 (*see* New York *Christian Advocate* and Nashville *Christian Advocate*)
Christian Century, 273, 300, 313, 377-78
Christian education: *see* religious education
"Christian Education Movement," 237
Christian Home, 157, 531
Christian Index, 586
Christian Methodist Episcopal Church, 493, 581, 585-86 (*see* Colored Meth. Epis. Ch.)
Christian perfection, 255, 330-31, 587, 623
Christian Recorder, 583
Christian World, 99
Christian Year, 562
Christliche Apologete, **142,** 162, 197
Christmas Conference, 20-21, 46, 62, 389
Chungking, 73
church building and property, 505, 521, 561
Church Conference, 463
Church Extension (The Meth. Ch.), 2, 466, 543 (*see* Board of Home Missions *and* Church Extension Society)
Church Extension Society (M.E.), 67, 115
church membership: growth, 6, 503-5, 560; meaning of, 564-65; orders for reception of members, 473-74
church papers: *see* periodicals
church school, 193-95, 527-31, 564, 622: literature, 133-34, 152-57, 193, 272, 527-28, 536; teaching materials, 138-39; teacher training, 528
Church School Herald, 584
Church Survey Commission, 4, 508-10, 517, 520, 524, 535, 551
Church World Service, 575
church and state relations, 256, 260, 554-55
Church of Christ in Japan, 128
Church of Christ, Scientist, 597

Church of England, 18-20, 43, 60, 76, 79-80, 91, 291, 562, 568, 580, 609, 615, 619
Church of Jesus Christ of Latter-day Saints, 119, 597
Church of North India, 580
Church of South India, 567
City Evangelization Union, 7
city missions: *see* urban work
civil liberties, 402, 554-56
civil rights, 362, 553-54
Civil War, 4, 11, 53, 73-74, 86, 97, 115, 117, 122, 137, 139-40, 147, 155, 158-59, 164-65, 170-71, 175, 179-80, 183, 191, 193, 202, 205, 208-9, 214, 224, 226, 243, 245, 348, 391, 394, 487-88, 492-93, 501, 599, 602, 606-7
Claflin College, 210-11, 221, 246, 492
Claflin, Lee, 211
Clair, Matthew W., Jr., 16, 491
Clara Swain Hospital, 78
Clark College (University), 13, 210-11, 221, 245-46, 492
Clark, Davis W., 12, 147, 210
Clark, Elmer T., 401, 578, 595
Clark, Walter, 412
Clarke, Vincent P., 465
class leaders, 23, 470, 582, 613
Classmate, 152-54, 529
class meeting, 23, 564
closely graded lessons, 154
Coffin, Henry Sloan, 400
Coke, Thomas, 19-20, 51, 61-64, 76, 148, 441
Cokesbury Bookstores, 537-38
Cokesbury College, 201-2
Cokesbury Hymnal, 149
Cokesbury Press, 142, 148-49
College of Bishops (M.E.S.), 23, 36-37, 48, 132, 141, 235, 408, 429, 438, 457, 463-64
College of Bishops (The Meth. Ch.), 483
College of the Pacific, 203, 213, 221
College of Puget Sound, 221
College of West Africa, 104
college students, 439, 529-30
colleges: (M.E.), 221-22; (M.E.S.), 238-39; (M.P.), 242; (The Meth. Ch.), 203, 492 (*see* higher education)
Collins, Judson, 73
Collins, Susan, 107
Collyer, C. T., 90
Colorado, 14, 115, 212, 216: Denver, 247, 254, 319, 372, 379, 385
Colorado Seminary, 216
Colored Methodist Episcopal Church, 15, 108, 113 116,

Colored M. E. Church—
cont'd
234-35, 360-61, 363, 368,
427, 435, 478, 570-71 (see
Christian Meth. Epis. Ch.)
Colombia (S. America), 593
Columbia College, 203
Combs, Dr. Lucinda, 74
Commission on Camp Activities, 497
Commission on Chaplains,
497, 557-59
Commission on Christian
Higher Education, 545
Commission on Christian
Social Concerns (local
church), 557
Commission on Courses of
Study, 468, 476, 496, 523
(see Commission on Ministerial Training)
Commission on Ecumenical
Consultation, 574
Commission on Education
(local church), 527
Commission on Evangelism,
468, 476
Commission on Faith and
Order, World Council, 572
Commission on Federation
(M.E.), 412, 414, 416-17,
422
Commission on Federation
(M.E.S.), 412
Commission on Interdenominational Relations of the
M. E. Church, 453-54, 459
Commission on Interdenominational Relations and
Church Union of the M.
E. Church, South, 454,
459
Commission on Interecclesiastical Relations of the
M. E. Church, 412
Commission on Interjurisdictional Relations, 495
Commission on Membership
and Evangelism, 504, 564
Commission on Ministerial
Training, 496, 523 (see
Commission on Courses of
Study)
Commission of Nine (M.P.),
418
Commission on Promotion
and Cultivation, 496, 509,
512, 515, 518-19, 520-22
Commission on Public Relations and Methodist Information, 496
Commission on the Revision of the Hymnal and
Psalter (M.E., M.E.S.),
473
Commission to Study the
Jurisdictional System, 484,
498, 513
Commission on the Study
of the Local Church, 526-
27

Commission on Union of the
M.P. Church, 454, 459
Commission on World Peace,
468, 476, 549-50 (see
Board of World Peace)
Commission on World Service and Finance, 468, 476,
506, 518 (see Council on
World Service & Finance)
Commission on Youth Crusade, 529-30
Commitment Day, 548
Committee on Christian Social Relations (local
church), 556
Committee on Fraternal Relations (M.E.S.), 408
Committee on Membership
and Temporal Economy,
Uniting Conference, 471-
72, 476
Committee of Nine, Joint
Commission on Federation, 418-19; report of,
419
Committee on Social and
Economic Relations (local
church), 556
Committee on Temperance
and Social Service
(M.E.S.), 386
Communion: see Lord's Supper
Communism, 169, 256, 366,
405, 479, 480, 539, 551,
556, 585
compulsory military training, 549-50
conference claimants, 139,
142, 178, 461, 466
conference membership, 43-
44, 243, 413, 462, 523, 525
Conference of Methodist
Laymen, 405
Congo, 74, 103, 105-6, 108-
9, 111, 480, 541
Congregational Methodist
Church, 594
Congregational Methodist
Church of the U.S.A., 594
Congregationalists, 19, 61,
69, 73, 79, 83, 94, 105-6,
113, 120, 124, 155, 157,
163, 167, 204, 211, 213,
271, 580, 612
Congress, congressional legislation, 116, 140, 169, 340,
346, 349, 377, 383
Connecticut, 280, 580: Middletown, 203; New Haven,
280
conscientious objectors, 258,
471-72, 550
Consecration of Bishops, 27,
43, 474
Consecration of a Deaconess,
474
conservatism (theological),
254, 263, 265, 267-73, 286-
87
constitution: The Meth. Ch.,
31, 40, 45, 433-38, 510-11;

constitution—cont'd
first proposed constitution, 434-36; second proposed constitution, 437-38;
M. E. Church, 25, 35,
45-50, 133, 271; M. E.,
South, 42, 50, 58; M. P.
Church, 50
Constitution Northwestern
Holiness Association, 595
constitutional amendment,
38, 45, 55, 67, 462
constitutional amendments:
IX, 491, 494-95, 510-11;
X, 498; XII (proposed),
484, 513, 522
constitutionality, 22, 38, 41,
273, 429
conversion experience, 155
Cooke, R. J., 412
Cooper, Ezekiel, 32, 170-71
Co-ordinating Committee,
Uniting Council, 474, 477
Co-ordinating Council, 497,
508, 514, 519, 520-22, 554-
55, 557
Copenhagen, 83
Corbin, J. F., 118
Cornell College, 203, 221
Correa, Juan, 97
correspondence courses, ministerial training, 271, 523-
24
Costa Rica, 96, 99, 101
Council of Bishops, 17, 68,
257, 319, 455, 463-64, 474,
482-83, 509, 512-13, 515,
517-22, 556-57
Council on a Christian Social Order, 387
Council for Clinical Training, 558
Council of Co-operation,
Meth. Ch. of Mexico, 112
Council of Secretaries, 514,
516-19, 521-22
Council on World Service
and Finance, 496, 499,
509, 518, 521 (see Commission on World Service
& Finance)
Course of Study, 148, 243-
44, 263, 270-71, 283-84,
468, 523-24
Cox, Melville B., 66, 103
Craig, Clarence T., 569-72
Cranston, Earl, 415, 419,
421, 423-24, 447-48, 450,
plate 15
"Creed of Jesus," 268-70
Crèvecoeur Michel-Guillaume Jean de, 597
crisis theology: see neoorthodoxy
Crusade for Christ, 518, 530
Cuba, 96, 102, 118, 168, 414,
480, 541
Cuban immigrants, missions
to, 102

Cumberland Methodist
Church, 594

Cumberland Presbyterian Church, 443
Cunninggim, Merrimon, 574
Cunnyngham, W. G. E., 182
Curriculum Committee, Board of Education, 527-28
curriculum materials, 152-57
Curry, Daniel, 53, 191
Cushman, Ralph S., 307
Czechoslovakia, 81, 84, 403
Czechoslovakian immigrants, 118

Daily Christian Advocate, 364, 410, 417
Dakota Wesleyan University, 221
dancing, Methodist stand on, 162, 624
Daniel Payne College, 583
Danish immigrants, 142
Darlington, U. V. W., 439
Darwin, Charles, 254, 261, 390
Daves, J. T., 98
Day, Albert Edward, 265, 294
Deaconess Board, Annual Conference, 122
Deaconess work, 122, 390, 543
DeBardeleben, Mary, 116
Decennial Missionary Conference (Bombay, 1892), 80
"Declaration and Basis of Fraternity," 409
Declaration of Plan of Union, 459, 475
dedicatory services, 474, 562, 611
Delaware, 14-15, 19, 117: Wilmington, 271
delegated General Conference, 48
Delhi, 76
Dempster, John, 245, 247
Den Kristelige Talsmand, 142
Denmark, 81, 83, 166
Denny, Collins, 39, 46-47, 49-50, 52, 273, 358, 425-26, 439, 450-51, 458
Department of Architecture, Board of Missions, 561
Department of the Christian Family, 530
Department of City Work, 542; (M.E.), 120
Department of College and University Religious Life, 545
Department of Home Missions (M.E.S.), 68
Department of Ministerial Education, 524
Department of Ministry of Music, 532
Department of Negro Work, 542

Department of Research and Statistics, World Service, 543
Department of Research and Survey, Board of Missions, 504, 542-43
Department of Rural Work (M.E.), 121
Department of Spiritual Life, Woman's Division, 564
Department of Stewardship & Finance, Board of Lay Activities, 534
Department of Sunday School Instruction (M.E.), 195
Department of Town and Country Work, 542; (M.E.), 121
Department of Work in Home Fields, Woman's Society, 543
DePauw University, 203, 221, 473
Depositories, Book Concern, 148
Deschner, John W., 318, 577
desegregation, 552-54, 585, 589
DeWitt, James L., 108
DeWolf, Harold, 321-22
Dhulia, 78
Dickey, James Edward, 439
Dickins, John, 170-71
Dickinson College, 203, 208, 221
Dieterle, Christian, 82
Diffendorfer, Ralph E., 567
Dillard University, 211, 221, 223, 492
Dillenberger, John, 322
directors of Christian education, 532
directors of music, 532
Disciples of Christ, 94, 97, 580, 597
Discipline, 34, 67, 112, 142, 147, 152, 158, 468, 507; editing and publishing of, 145, 174, 536; legislation and regulations, 30, 37, 50-51, 138, 155, 189, 463, 465, 467, 473-74, 526-27, 535, 551, 561
Disciplines: 1792, 46; 1798, 20; 1801, 46; 1804, 46; 1808, 50; 1816, 8; 1844, 7, 10, 24; 1846, 24; 1900, 50; 1912, 248; 1924, 248; 1936, 471; 1938, 549; 1939, 4, 5, 459, 526; 1940, 243, 477, 523, 526, 530; 1952, 556; 1960, 586
District Board of Church Location and Building, 561
District Board of Lay Activities, 533
District Conference, The Meth. Church, 462

district schools of stewardship, 534
district superintendent, 8, 10, 462, 469, 477, 514-16, 520, 527, 541 (see presiding elders)
District Superintendents' Conference, 520
Division of Educational Institutions, Board of Education, 466, 468, 493, 524, 530, 545
Division of Foreign Missions, Board of Missions, 466, 540 (see Division of World Missions)
Division of Home Missions and Church Extension, Board of Missions, 466, 541 (see Division of National Missions)
Division of the Local Church, Board of Education, 466, 493, 528-29, 530, 532
Division of National Missions, Board of Missions, 497, 499, 533, 541-43 (see Division of Home Missions and Church Extension)
Division of World Missions, Board of Missions, 496, 499, 540-41 (see Division of Foreign Missions)
divorce, 470, 588
Djakarta, 93
Doctrines of Methodism, 608-10
"Dollar Money," 582
Dolliver, John P., 416
domestic missions: see missions, missionary work
Domestic Missions Society, Philippines, 520
Dominican Republic, 124-25
Downey, David G., 433, 449
Drake, Benjamin M., 25
Drees, Charles W., 99, 124
Drew, Daniel, 245
Drew Seminary for Young Women, 222
Drew Theological School, 92, 209, 221, 249, 263, 267-68, 284, 294, 322-24, 472, 568-69
Drew University, 196, 272, 313, 317, 319-20
Drinkhouse, E. J., 136, 197-98, 443
Du Bose, Horace M., 131, 265, 273, 294, 358, 411, 431, 450
Duke, Benjamin N., 233
Duke, James B., 233
Duke University, 75, 203, 233, 247, 249, 287-88, 444, 604
Dukes, O. A., 86
Dulles, John Foster, 259
Duncan, James A., 409
Duncan, W. W., 412
Dyaks, 92-93

Dye, J. H., 412
Dyer, John L., 163

East Greenwich Academy, 222
Eastern Asia Christian Conference (1949), 571
Eastern Index, 586
Eastern Orthodox Church, 570, 601
Eaton, Homer, 185
economic issues, 384, 404-5, 539, 551-52
Ecumenical Methodist Conferences: *1881*, 410, 423, 578; *1891*, 180; *1901*, 411; *1931*, 453; *1947*, 570; *1951*, 565
Ecumenical Methodist Council, 475, 578 (*see* World Methodist Council)
Ecumenical Missionary Conference (New York, 1900), 78
ecumenical movement, 145, 326-27, 565-81, 605-7, 626-27
Editorial Division, Board of Education, 466, 529, 532, 536
editors, church papers and book publishing, 171-77, 179-83, 189-99, 537
education: *see* religious education, higher education, secondary education
Educational Association (M.E.), 220
Educational Commission (M.E.S.), 235
educational jubilee year, 219
educational program, local church, 526-32
Edward Waters College, 583
Edwards, Jonathan, 61, 609, 621
Ehnes, Morris W., 108
Ehrenstrom, Nils, 574
Eiselen, Malcolm R., 439
elders: *see* ministry
election of bishops, 426-27, 483, 511
election of conference delegates, 45, 55, 462
Electoral Conference (M.E.), 55-56
El Evangelisto, 96
Eliot, Charles William, 205
Eliza Dee Industrial Home, 13
Elizabeth Gamble Deaconess Home and Training School, 122
Elisabethville, Congo, 108
Ellen Thoburn Cowen Memorial Hospital, 78
emancipation of Negroes, 209, 361, 487, 603
Emory and Henry College, 180, 203
Emory College, 227, 233

Emory, John, 43, 52
Emory University, 90, 203, 233, 247, 369, 444, 450, 493
endowment of schools, 209, 214, 218-23, 238-40, 242, 249
England, 51, 60-61, 63, 73, 75-76, 79, 83, 91-92, 103, 107, 145, 165, 173, 196, 201, 339, 446, 558, 569, 586, 597, 600, 610, 617, 620
Ensley, F. Gerald, 316, 574
episcopacy: authority of, 18-21; area system, 31-36; development of, 17-29; 613-14; episcopal residence, 33; itinerancy, 32; jurisdictional system, 482-83; nature of, 25-27, 40, 42-43, 459-60; term episcopacy, 24, 40-43; in The Meth. Church, 511-14
Episcopal Addresses: *1864*, 4, 12; *1882*, 227, 272; *1906*, 385; *1908*, 381; *1922*, 386; *1928*, 349; *1932*, 625; *1948*, 570; *1960*, 316, 495, 555, 565
Epworth Era, 154
Epworth Herald, 153, 157, 196
Epworth League, 153-54, 188, 365, 369, 374, 413, 622
Eskimos, mission to, 123
Essentialist, The, 272
Estonia, 81, 84
Ethiopia, 103, 403
Europe, 18, 79, 95-96, 103, 253, 290, 350, 375, 397-98, 406, 479, 550, 566, 600; immigrants, 163, 346-47, 353-54; Methodist work in, 81-84, 125, 195, 433
Evangelical Congregation Church, 587
Evangelical Methodist, The, 594
Evangelical Methodist Church, 592-94
Evangelical Union of the Philippines, 94
Evangelical United Brethren Church, 125, 580 (*see* United Brethren)
Evangelisk Tidende, 142
evangelism, 257, 468, 564
Evans, John, 216
Evanston Assembly, World Council, 572-73, 610
Evanston College of Preachers, 284
Evanston Collegiate Institute, 222
Evansville College, 221
every-member canvass, 534
evolution, 236, 261, 288, 588, 590, 620
Ewha Woman's University, 89-90

Exhibition Bible, 150
existentialism, 290, 322-23

Fairbanks, Charles W., 449
Faith and Order Movement, 568-69, 572-73, 578, 613, 626, 627
family, Meth. emphasis on, 157, 530-31, 537
Faulkner, John Alfred, 263, 267, 269-70
Federal Council of the Churches of Christ in America, 255, 394-95, 389, 471, 502, 574-75, 607 (*see* National Council)
Federal Council of Methodism, 415, 423
Ferré, Nels, 330
Ferrum Training School, 122
Finland, 81, 83
Finley, James B., 65, 621
First Colored Methodist Protestant Church, 595
First Methodist Church, Evanston, Ill., 456, 572-73
Fisher, Frederick Bohn, 334, 385
Fisk, Clinton B., 210, 408
Fitzgerald, J. N., 412
Fitzgerald, O. P., 175-77
Flemming, Arthur S., 576
Fletcher, John, 145, 147
Flint, C. W., 569
Flint-Goodridge Hospital, 212, 223
Flint Medical School, 212
Florence B. Nicholson Bible Seminary, 94
Florida, 14-15, 102, 117-18, 123, 442, 594: Daytona Beach, 492; Jacksonville, 13, 123, 583, 595; Key West, 118; Tampa, 118
Foochow, 74
Ford, Henry, 350-51
foreign missions: *see* missions and missionary work
Fosdick, Harry Emerson, 262
Foundry Methodist Church, Washington, 413
Fowler, Charles H., 175, 408
France, 81, 83, 95, 103, 339, 391, 479
fraternal delegates, 407-8, 410, 443-44
fraternal relations, establishment of, 408-9
"Free Church Establishment," 599-601
free grace, 608-10
Free Methodist Church, 589-92, 594
free will, 608-10
freedom of speech, 622-23
Freedmen's Aid Society, 11-13, 116, 186-87, 209-11, 214, 245-46, 359, 361, 363, 487
Freeman, Mark, 93
French, J. Stewart, 465

French Reformed Church, 83

French-speaking people, mission to, 117-18

Freud, Sigmund, 399-400

Frey, Lulu E., 90

frontier influence, 601-3, 615-16, 618, 621

Fukien, 93

Fukien Christian University, 75

Fundamental Methodist Church, Inc., 595

fundamentalism, 254-55, 261, 271-73

Funk, Robert, 322

Galloway, Charles B., 13, 157

gambling, 162, 340, 548-49

Gamboa, Conrado, 99

Gammon, Elijah H., 211, 246, 492

Gammon Theological Seminary, 221, 246, 249, 492-93

Garber, Paul N., 409-10, 446, 569

Garland, Landon C., 409

Garrett Biblical Institute (Theological Seminary), 221, 223, 243, 249, 272, 280, 283, 317, 320, 324

Garrettson, Freeborn, 52, 145

Gary, Elberg H., 385

General Commission on Budget (M.E.S.), 468

General Conference, 50, 460: control of schools, 230-31, 244; duties and authority, 522; election of delegates, 55-56, 462; membership, 46; places of meeting, 497-98; powers, 47-48, 460-61, 527; relations with episcopacy, 24-26; restrictions, 455, 460; women admitted, 56-58; laymen admitted, 54-56

General Conferences: Methodist Episcopal Church 1784, 20-21, 46, 62, 389; 1792, 48; 1804, 9; 1808, 9, 22, 38, 45, 47; 1816, 134; 1820, 22, 202, 213, 223; 1824, 23; 1828, 32, 152; 1836, 9, 67, 145; 1844, 23, 25, 65, 243; 1848, 11, 177; 1852, 11; 1856, 15, 30, 155; 1860, 44, 133; 1864, 11-12, 33, 67, 77, 116, 153, 209, 615; 1868, 33, 45, 172, 217; 1872, 12-13, 54, 66, 69, 134, 162, 184; 1876, 408; 1880, 70, 72, 136, 214, 410; 1884, 28, 67, 70, 105, 111, 411; 1888, 41, 56, 72, 105, 122, 234, 412; 1892, 7, 56, 153, 217, 444; 1896, 57, 104, 148, 154; 1900, 56, 360, 362, 375, 380, 390, 414;

General Conferences—cont'd 1904, 35, 124 138, 188, 362, 379; 1908, 67, 188, 230, 255, 341, 342, 363, 381, 391, 393, 416, 471; 1912, 107, 219, 338-39, 342, 395, 421, 455; 1916, 338, 362, 422, 452; 1920, 16, 30, 270, 340, 400; 1924, 138-39, 266, 271, 340, 349, 354, 434, 438; 1928, 271-72, 367-68, 452, 454, 473; 1932, 16, 139, 403, 454; 1936, 456

Methodist Episcopal Church, South: 1846, 68; 1854, 37, 244; 1866, 10, 38, 68, 130, 131, 172-73, 224, 228, 244; 1870, 38, 131, 228, 244; 1874, 132, 226, 407; 1878, 172; 1882, 172, 175; 1890, 71, 182; 1894, 140, 154, 235; 1898, 140, 235, 379, 396; 1902, 141, 178-79, 182; 1906, 230; 1914, 57, 231, 237, 247, 422, 455, 471; 1918, 39, 57; 1922, 57, 369; 1924 (special session), 438; 1926, 401, 439, 440; 1930, 473; 1934, 339, 454; 1938, 39, 456

Methodist Protestant Church: 1834, 71; 1884, 246, 443; 1892, 444; 1896, 444; 1900, 163; 1908, 416; 1916, 240, 471; 1932, 454; 1936, 455

The Methodist Church: 1940, 469-70, 474-77, 497, 507, 514, 530, 550; 1944, 31, 67, 497, 503, 517-18, 523-25, 558, 562; 1948, 507, 517, 519, 524, 525-26, 558, 570; 1952, 503, 508, 525-26, 530, 535, 537, 540, 551, 555; 1956, 58, 243, 484, 494, 518, 537, 545, 554, 555, 557, 562; 1960, 319, 490-91, 494, 497-98, 500, 510-11, 519, 521-22, 530, 534, 543, 549, 553, 555, 565, 574

general superintendents: see bishops

Genesee College, 216

Geneva, 566, 569, 572

George, Enoch, 22, 26, 27, 32

George O. Robinson School for Girls, Santurce, 124

Georgia, 14, 25, 60, 122-23, 210, 439, 450, 594: Atlanta, 13, 36, 70, 74, 203, 210-11, 232-33, 247, 453, 482, 492, 583; Augusta, 116, 492-93, 586; La-Grange, 203; Macon, 116, 191, 203; Savannah, 176, 191, 424, 428-29, 433; Thomasville, 123; Warm Springs, 458

Georgia Female College, 191

German-American Methodist work, 65, 81-82, 117, 122, 142, 162, 166, 196-97, 208, 246-47

Germany, 61, 68, 248, 253, 274, 280, 325, 346, 397, 403, 611; Methodist work in, 73, 81-82, 166; immigration, 346-47; theology, 600-601, 605

Ghana, 584

Gibson, Otis, 119

Gilbert Academy, 222

Gilbert, John Wesley, 108

Gines, Nannie B., 87

Ginling College, 74-75

Gladden, Washington, 388

Gold Coast, 584

Golden, Charles F., 491

Golden Hours, 133, 153

Golden Text Cards, 154

Gompers, Samuel, 353, 371, 376

Good Samaritan Hospital, Guanajuato, 99

Goodfellow, William, 96

Gooding College, 213

Goodsell, D. A., 12

Goodwill Industries of America, 120, 166, 542

Gospel Advocate, 142

Goucher College, 449

Goucher, John F., 50, 87, 89, 412, 416, 419-20, 423, 432, 447, 449, plate 15

Gowdy, John, 111

graded lessons, 139, 154, 156-57

Graded Sunday School Magazine, 157

Graham, Edwin R., 188-89

Granbery College (Institute), 97-98

Granbery, John C., 97, 412

Grant, Ulysses S., 194

Greek Orthodox, 346

Greeks, missions to immigrants, 117-18

Green, A. L. P., 177

Green Mountain Junior College, 222

Greene, S. L., 569

Greensboro College, 203, 238

Greenwich Plan, 580

Gregg, J. A., 576

Gross, John O., 576

Guanajuato, 99

Guatemala, 587

Guerrero, Marcellino, 99

Gulfside Assembly, 494

Guthrie, Elizabeth M., 71-72

Hall, Rosetta Sherwood, 89

Hall, William J., 89

Halsted Street Mission, 7

Hamilton, J. W., 12, 56, 448

Hamlett, James A., 568, 571, 576

Hamline, Leonidas, 24-25, 27-28

Hamline University, 203, 212, 221
Hammett, William, 47
Harding, Warren G., 253, 399
Hargraves, C. P., 576
Hargrove, R. K., 412
Harkness, Georgia, 295-96, 571, 574
Harland, Gordon, 322
Harmon, Nolan B., 310
Harnack, Adolf, 268, 274, 276, 295
Harrington, Francis M., 101
Harris, A. W., 433
Harris, Marquis L., 491
Harris Memorial Deaconess Training School, 94
Harris, S. R., 419
Harrison, Benjamin, 78, 187
Hart, Ray, 323
Hart, Vergil C., 74
Hartman, Lewis O., 31, 456
Hartzell, Jennie Culver, 70
Hartzell, Joseph C., 12, 70, 104, 106-9, 210
Hartzell Methodist Church, Luanda, 107
Havana, 102
Haven, Gilbert, 12
Hawaii, 119, 124, 164
Hawk, Jonathan B., 309
Hawley, John W., 452-53
Hayes, Lucy Webb, 70
Hayes, Rutherford B., 70
Haygood, Atticus G., 211
Haygood, Laura, 74
Heathen Woman's Friend, 69
Hedding, Elijah, 27, 32, 52
Hedström, O. G., 82
Heim, Karl, 305
Helm, Lucinda B., 70
Helms, Edgar J., 120
Hendrix, Eugene R., 230, 395, 450
Hennepin Avenue Methodist Church, Minneapolis, 319
Henry, W. G., 465
Herberg, Will, 322, 324, 347
Hering, J. W., 417
Hernandez, Alejo, 98
Hervey, James, 60
High Point College, 240
higher education, 201-49, 604-5: M.E., 208-13, 214-23; M.E.S., 223-25, 227-39; M.P., 239-42; The Meth. Church, 544-46 (see colleges, universities, theological seminaries)
Highroad, 157
Hildebrandt, Franz, 317
Hillman, J. L., 452
Hirosaki, 87
Hiroshima Jo Gakuin School, 87
Hiwassee College, 122
Hocking, W. E., 295, 305

Hoffa, James, 371-72, 387
Hofstadter, Richard, 333, 393
Hogg, W. Richey, 567
Holden Hospital, 123
Holiness Methodist Church, 595
Holiness Movement Church of Canada, 591
Holt, Asa, 412
Holt, Ivan Lee, 568, 571-72, 575, 578, 580
Home Department Quarterly, 154
home missions: see missions and missionary work
homes: for aged, 390, 466, 494, 546-47; for children, 466, 543, 547
Honda, Yoitsu, 87, 113
Hong Kong, 73, 125
Hood Theological Seminary, 584
Hoover, Herbert, 357-58
Hoover, James M., 93-94
Hopper, Stanley, 323
Hordern, William, 324
Horton, Douglas, 290
hospitals, 390, 466, 474, 541, 546-47, 558, 591
Hoss, Elijah E., 179-80, 412, 419, 422, 442, 450
Hough, Lynn Harold, 190, 265, 294, 355, 472, 550, 568-69
House Un-American Activities Committee, 480, 551, 556, 625
Howard, Dr. Lenora, 74
Hu King-eng, 74
Huancayo, 101
Hughes, Edwin H., 356, 451, 475, plate 16
Hughes, W. A. C., 491
Hungary, 81-82
Hunt, Albert S., 408
Hunt, Sandford, 185
Huntsville Normal School, 210
Hurst, John F., 29, 45, 412
Huston-Tillotson College, 492
Hwa Nan College, 74
Hyer, R. S., 431, 433, 450
hymnals, 145, 147-50, 174, 413-14, 441, 473, 536, 562, 611, 634
hymns and hymnology, 151, 562, 603, 631-33

Ibans (Sea Dyaks), 94
Iceland, 558
Idaho, 213
Iliff School of Theology, 221, 247, 249, 254, 276, 280
Iliff, Thomas C., 119
Iliff, William Seward, 247
Illinois, 14, 70, 123, 187, 194, 467: Batavia, 492; Bloomington, 203; Carbondale, 123; Chicago, 7, 13, 117, 120 139, 150,

Illinois—cont'd
156, 159, 188, 194-95, 247, 283, 333, 367, 372, 385, 454, 476, 496-98; East St. Louis, 367; Elgin, 78; Evanston, 203, 216, 243, 246, 405, 439, 446, 454-55, 571-73; Freeport, 194; Fremont, 187; Galena, 194; Lebanon, 203; Rockford, 194; Urbana, 206; Wheaton, 203
Illinois Wesleyan University, 203, 221
Illustrated Berean Lesson Quarterly, 154
Illustrated Lesson Paper, 154
immigrants, missions to, 117-19, 343-59; concern for, 165-66, 347-54, 357; problem of, 343-46; publishing for, 142-43; sources of, 346-47
Independent A.M.E. Church, 595
Independent Methodist churches, 113
India, 61-63, 69, 99-100, 120, 350, 539, 572; Indian immigrants, 119; Methodist work in, 44, 72, 75-81, 110-11, 122, 125, 541
Indian District, Burma Mission Conf., 91
Indian Mission Conf. of Oklahoma, 116
Indian Missions in America, 60, 64-65, 116, 123, 172, 234, 400, 542, 618
Indiana, 14, 54, 96, 195, 204, 472: Greencastle, 203; Indianapolis, 195, 586; Marion, 588; Upland, 203; West Lafayette, 240
Indiana Asbury University, 191
Indonesia, 63, 480, 539, 572
Industrial Workers of the World, 376, 378
Ing, John, 87
Inge, William, 305, 343
Interagency Committee on Research, 543
Interboard Commission on Missionary Education, 496
Interboard Committee on Christian Vocations, 496, 524
Interchurch Center, New York City, 497, 584
Interchurch World Movement, 377, 385
Interdenominational Student Conference (Evanston, 1926), 439
Interdenominational Theological Center, Atlanta, 492-93
Intermediate Quarterly, 154
International Council of Religious Education, 575, 589

International Human Relations Conference (Dallas, 1959), 553
International Missionary Council, 565-67, 570-71
International Sunday School Convention (Indianapolis, 1872), 195
International Sunday School Lessons, 136, 153, 195
International Uniform Lessons, 154, 156
Interpreter's Bible, 536
Interpreter's Dictionary of the Bible, 536
Interseminary Committee, 575
Interseminary Movement, 577
Iowa, 14, 83, 472; Indianola, 273; Mount Pleasant, 203; Mount Vernon, 203
Iowa Wesleyan College, 203, 212, 221
Ipoh, Malay, 92
Iquique English College, 101
Irish Methodism, 76, 411
Isabella Thoburn College, 78
Israel, 589
Italian immigrants, missions to, 117, 346, 351, 383
Italy, 81, 83, 118, 346, 403
Italy Conference, 83
itinerancy, 7-9, 18-19, 21, 51, 460, 619, 621-22
Ivey, T. N., 450-51

Jackson, Mrs. Abbie Clement, 576
Jackson, Andrew, 161, 623
Jackson Theological Seminary, 583
Jacoby, Ludwig, S., 82
James, J. A., 572
James, William, 278, 399
Janes, Edmund, 15-16
Japan, 63, 89, 108, 110, 124, 128, 397, 472, 539, 572, 580; Methodist work in, 71-72, 74, 84-88, 111, 113, 413-14, 541
Japan Methodist Church, 86-88, 113
Japanese immigrants, missions to, 118-19, 348-50
Java, 91-93
Jenkins, Benjamin, 73
Jennings, Henry C., 144, 146-47, 187-88
Jennings, M. L., 419
Jennings, S. K., 52
Jennings Seminary, 222
Jesse Lee Memorial and Industrial Home, 123
Jewish immigrants, 165, 346, 350-51
Jews, 337, 350-51, 356, 359, 589, 601
Johannesburg, 107

John A. Patten Community Center, 122
John Street Church, New York, 486
John Wesley Seminary Foundation, 591
Johnson, Andrew, 172
Johnson, Eben S., 108
Joint Commission on Federation, 412-15, 418-19, 420, 423
Joint Commission on Methodist Union (1934), 454-55, 459, 475
Joint Commission on Missionary Education, 576
Joint Commission on Unification (1916), 415, 421, 423-34, 437, 448-52
Joint Section of Education and Cultivation, Board of Missions, 496
Jones, David D., 456, 493
Jones, E. Stanley, 80-81, 149, 294, 316, 349, 367
Jones, Edwin L., 578
Jones, R. W., 412
Jones, Robert E., 16, 367, 431, 449, 491, 494
Joseph, Oscar L., 294-95
Joy, James R., 193, 433, 449
Juarez, Sosthenes, 98
Judicial Council (The Meth. Ch.), 429-35, 464-65, 491-92, 510, 514
Judicial Council (M.E.S.), 39-40, 457, 464-65
Junior Lessons, 154
Jurisdictional Conference, 451, 455, 461-63, 474-75, 489, 517
jurisdictional system, 461-62, 481-85; beginnings of, 419-20, 425-26

Kachins, 91
Kagawa, Toyohiko, 149
Kahn, Ida, 74
Kambove, 108
Kansas, 14, 186-87, 196, 212, 451, 472; Baldwin, 203; Enterprise, 247
Kansas City National Training School, 223
Kansas Wesleyan University, 221
Kapanga, Congo, 108
Karens, 91
Kaung, Z. T., 75
Kee, Howard, 322
Keener, John C., 98
Kelley, William V., 189-90
Kelly, Edward W., 491
Kelsey, George, 322
Kennedy, Gerald, 482, 560
Kennedy, James F., 97
Kennedy, John Fitzgerald, 344-45, 371, 603
Kent Industrial Home, 13
Kents Hill School, 222
Kentucky, 13-14, 123, 182, 210, 450, 612: Barbour-

Kentucky—*cont'd*
ville, 214; Carrsville, 356; Covington, 13; Lexington, 228; Louisville, 68, 115, 131, 182, 407, 424, 434, 440, 454-55, 496; Wilmore, 228, 591, 594
Kern, Paul B., 265, 568
Keys, Pliny, 107
Kidder, Daniel P., 146, 193
Kidney, Elmer L., 433
Kierkegaard, Søren, 290, 293, 313, 320, 321
Kilgo, John C., 353, 374, 410, 441, 604
Kimball, Henry D., 247
Kimball School of Theology, 247
kindergartens, 528-29
King, Lorenzo H., 491
King, Martin Luther, 371
King, Willis J., 491
Kingswood School, England, 225
Kirkland, James H., 181, 229, 235
Kittrell College, 583
Klein, F. C., 72, 86
Knoff, Gerald E., 576
Knudson, Albert C., 276-80, 284-85, 297-99, 300-301, 305, 315, 319, 321, 323-24, 569
Kobe, 86
Kolar, 78
Korea, 63, 84-85, 88-91, 124-25, 128, 539, 541, 572
Korean immigrants, missions to, 119
Korean Methodist Church, 112, 446
Korean War, 479, 558
Ku Klux Klan, 353-57, 365, 399
Kuala Lumpur, 92, 572
Kwansei Gakuin School, 87
Kyodan, 128, 580

labor movement, Methodist relations with, 166-68, 371-87, 559
laboratory schools, 528
Labrador, 558
Lacklen, Jesse, 306
Lacy, Edith, 78
Ladies' Repository, 137, 191
LaFetra, Ira H., 101
LaGrange Female College, 203
Lake Junaluska Assembly, 482-83
Lamar, A. J., 141, 424, 429, 431, 450-51
Lambuth, J. W., 73-74, 86
Lambuth, Mrs. J. W., 70, 86
Lambuth, Walter R., 74, 86-87, 108
Lanahan, John, 134, 183
Landon, Alfred M., 472
Lane College, 585
Lane, Isaac, 585

La Paz, 101
"Large Minutes," English Methodism, 18
Large Picture Cards, 154
Larson, John Peter, 83
Lastrico, Carlos, 97
Latin America: *see* South America
Latourette, Kenneth S., 63
Latvia, 81, 84
Lausanne, 568, 572
Lawrence College, 203, 212, 221
Lawson, Martin F., 465
Lay Conference (M. E.), 55
lay representation: Annual Conference, 55, 439, 442, 455, 498, 533; General Conference, 51-56, 442, 455, 462; Jurisdictional Conference, 455
Layman's Organization for the Preservation of the M. E. Church, South, 592
laymen: first elected book agents, 184; lay leaders, 467; lay preaching, 534; organizations, 467; work of, 532-36
Laymen's Day, 534
leadership training classes, 528
Leaf Cluster, 154
League of Nations, 259, 406
Lee, Jason, 65, 135, 618
Lee, Leroy, 38
Lee, Umphrey, 292, 315
Leete, Frederick D., 449, 451
Leningrad, 82
Leonard, Adna W., 307, 558
Leopoldville, 106
Leper Colony, Chandag, 78
Lesson Leaf, 154
Leuring, H. L. Emil, 92-93
Lewis, Edwin, 272, 284-87, 297, 304-7, 309, 311-15, 320, 323
Lewis, Spencer, 74
Lewis, Thomas H., 246, 416-19, 444-45, 451-52, 458
Li Bi-Cu, 74
Li Hung-Chang, 77, 88
liberalism, 254, 261-67, 273-89, 295-96
Liberia, 15-16, 30, 45, 65, 67, 103-5, 125, 128, 490-91, 541, 583-84
licensing to preach, 462
Life and Work Movement, 568-69, 627
"Light and Life Hour," 591
Lillian Harris Memorial Hospital, 89
Lima, Peru, 101
Lincoln, Abraham, 216, 224, 343, 606, 615, 621
Lincoln Street Community Church, Chicago, 120
Linn, Paul H., 433
literature: *see* publishing
Lithuania, 81, 83

liturgical practices and trends, 174, 473-74, 561-62, 610-12
Livingstone College, 584
Livingstone, David, 63, 105, 108
local church, 462-63, 466, 526-28; boards, 526; commissions, 527, 557; committees, 556 (*see* Division of the Local Church)
London, 79, 81, 410, 423, 578
Lord's Supper, 473, 481, 608, 611
Lore, Dallas D., 96
Louisiana, 14, 104, 117-18, 210, 241, 527: Alexandria, 430; New Orleans, 13, 70, 117-18, 130, 133, 210, 492; Shreveport, 203
Love, Edgar A., 491
love feast, 411
Lowe, Titus, 307, 310
Luanda, 105-8
Lumber River Annual Conference of the Holiness Methodist Church, 595
Lund, 569, 572
Luther, Martin, 281, 304
Lutherans, 96, 194, 196, 334, 503, 599-601, 613
Luzon, 94
Lycoming College, 204
Lydia Patterson Institute, 118
Lynch, James, 76
lynching, 332, 362-63, 365-67, 369

MacDonell, George G. N., 412
MacDonnell, George N., 102
MacMurray College, 221
McCabe, Charles C., 6
McCarthy, Joseph, 255, 480, 551, 623
McClintock, John, 154
McConnell, Francis J., 149, 264, 292-93, 310, 315-16, 356, 372, 379, 385, 395, 456, 547, 569, 575, 620, 625
McCulloh, Gerald O., 324
McCutchan, Robert G., 473
McDowell, William F., 31, 367, 433, 437, 448, 452
McFerrin, John B., 130-32, 140, 170-73, 186
McKendree Church, Nashville, 177-78, 182, plate 11
McKendree College, 203, 221
McKendree, William, 22-23, 26-27, 32, 47, 175
McKinley, William E., 163, 168, 343-46, 353, 371-72
McMurray, William F., 356, 453
McTyeire, Holland N., 4, 162, 172, 175, 226, 228-29
McTyeire School, Shanghai, 74

Maclay College of Theology, 247
Maclay, Robert S., 86, 89
Maddin, Percy D., 433, 450
Madeira Islands, 109
Madras, 78-79
Magee, J. Ralph, 33
Maine, 117
Mains, George P., 185
Malacca, 92
Malange, 106
Malaya, 91, 541
Malaysia Message, The, 92
Malaysia Mission, 93
Mallalieu, Willard F., 12
Manchuria, 403
Manila, 94, 540
Mark Twain, 176
Marquez, Felipe, 95
Marston, Leslie R., 592
Martin, William C., 565, 572-73, 577
Marx, Karl, 344, 401
Mary J. Johnston Memorial Hospital, 94
Maryland, 14-15, 163, 173, 177, 198-99, 212, 240, 280, 417, 467; Abingdon, 223; Baltimore, 16, 68, 71, 87, 136, 163, 196-98, 209, 389, 410, 416-18, 421-24, 428, 443, 446, 476, 496; Street, 594; Westminster, 240, 246, 444
Massachusetts, 26, 190, 617: Boston, 7, 69, 117, 119-21, 124, 385, 428, 542, 570, 576; Pittsfield, 190; Springfield, 438, 570
Mather, Cotton, 617
Mathews, James K., 567
matrimony, order for, 474
Mead, Charles L., 452-53
Mead, Samuel J., 106
Mead, William H., 106
Medan, Sumatra, 93
medical missions, 64, 69, 74, 89, 123
Meharry Medical College, 210, 212, 223, 492-93
Mekkelson, Josephine, 106
Melle, Otto, 82
membership training, 473-74, 564
Memphis Convention (1872), 228, 231
Menchen, H. L., 191, 332, 336
Men's Brotherhood movement (M.E.), 532-33
Merrill, Stephen M., 49-50, 412
Methodist Church of Brazil, 112
Methodist Church of Canada, 86, 111, 113, 411, 607
Methodist Church of Mexico, 99, 112
Methodist Church of Southern Asia, 580

Methodist Circuit Riders organization, 551
Methodist Commission on Church Union, 580
Methodist Committee for Overseas Relief, 496
Methodist Deaconess Hospital (Rapid City, S. D.), 123
Methodist Deaconess Sanitarium (Albuquerque), 123
Methodist Federation for Social Service (Action), 255, 284, 350, 365, 368-69, 377, 384, 395-96, 405, 551, plate 1
Methodist General Biblical Institute, 243
Methodist Hospital, Brooklyn, 192
Methodist Hymnal, The, 473, 536, 562
Methodist Layman, 534
Methodist League for Faith and Life, 271
Methodist Men clubs, 533-34
Methodist Nanking University, 75
Methodist New Connection, England, 411
Methodist Protestant Church, 52, 478: higher education, 239, 242, judicial procedure, 465; mission work, 78, 86, 125-27; missionary organization, 71-72; publishing, 135-37, 197-99; role in unification, 416-18, 421, 424, 434, 443-44, 452-53; Social Creed, 471; Sunday school literature, 136, 153
Methodist Protestant, The, 52, 136, 153, 163, 197-99
Methodist Publishing House, 142, 150, 170, 461, 467, 476, 494, 533, 536-38 (*see* Book Concern, Publishing House)
Methodist Quarterly Review (M.E.), 137, 154
Methodist Quarterly Review (M.E.S.), 280, 288
Methodist Recorder, 136
Methodist Review, The (M.E.), 137, 139, 189-91, 268, 270, 295, 300
Methodist Story, 509
Methodist Student Movement, 530, 545-46, 577
Methodist terminology, 597-98
Methodist Theological School in Ohio, 525
Methodist Union Theological Seminary (Korea), 90
Methodist Young People's Convention (Memphis, 1926), 440
Methodist Youth Conference (1947-48), **530**

Methodist Youth Fellowship, 496, 529-30
Methvin, J. J., 116
Metropolitan Temple, New York, 7
Mexicans, missions to, 234, 589
Mexico, 77, 84, 101, 118, 128, 397, 539; Methodist work in, 96, 98-99, 102, 112, 141, 414, 446, 541, 593
Michalson, Carl, 323-24
Michigan, 14; Adrian, 203; Albion, 203; Detroit, 13, 291, 385, 401; Traverse City, 423-25, 428, 430
Mieyama, Kanichi, 119
Miles College, 586
Miller, Robert T., 412, 419
"Million Movement" (M.E.S.), 90
ministerial education, 134, 243-49, 523, 604 (*see* course of study, theological seminaries)
ministry, the, 522-26, 619: appeal of appointment, 21, 37, 52; appointment, 477, 514; conference membership, 43-44, 243, 462, 522-23; licensing to preach, 462; local preachers, 523; ministerial regulations, 470; ministerial sovereignty, 46, 51, 613; ministerial support, 7-8, 461; ordination, 462; pensions, 133, 146, 498, 536; recruitment, 524; retirement, 477; supply pastors, 523-25; time limit on appointment, 8-10, 469-70; women as ministers, 525-26
Minnesota, 14, 188, 212: Minneapolis, 319, 595; St. Paul, 203, 247
Mission Conference, 44-45, 67-68, 77, 82, 462
Mission Conferences: Austria-Hungary, 82; Bulgarian, 83; Burma, 91; Central American, 102; Central Mexico, 98; Congo, 106, 108; East Central Africa, 107-8; German, 117; Germany, 45; India 44-45; Malaysia, 92; Mexican Border, 98; Netherlands Indies, 92-93; North African, 109; North Sumatra, 93; Portuguese East Africa, 107; Rhodesia, 108; Southeast Africa, 107; Sumatra, 93; West Central Africa, 107; Yugoslavia, 82
Mission Press, Mexico, 99
missionaries, 64, 68-69, 83, 100-101, 113-14, 125-27, 539-41

missionary bishops, 15, 24, 29-31, 67-68, 105
Missionary Seer, 584-85
Missionary Society (M.E.), 59, 63-66, 69, 76-77, 83, 86, 101, 104, 106, 119, 135 (*see* also Board of Managers)
Missionary Society (M.E.S.), 68
Missionary Tidings, 591
missions, missionary work, 59-128, 141, 538-44; beginnings of, 58-66; ecumenical missions, 567; foreign missions, 65-66, 72-109; national missions, 113-25, 543; organization, 66-72, 462, 466; schools, 234; self-supporting missions, 234; unification of, 414
Mississippi, 14-16, 119, 210, 213, 237, 241, 439: Decatur, 594; Holly Springs, 13, 210, 492, 586; Vicksburg, 159; Waveland, 494
Mississippi Industrial College, 586
Missouri, 14, 182, 237, 467: Fayette, 203; Kansas City, 52, 71, 117, 196, 234, 241, 257, 457-58, 497, 525; St. Louis, 135, 424, 432, 437, 496; Springfield, 595; Warrenton, 247
Mitchell, H. G., 248
Mode, Peter, 601
Monrovia Area, 491
Monrovia College, 583
Monrovia Seminary, 103-4
Monroy, Epigmenio, 99
Montana, 14, 115: Billings, 213; Helena, 213
Montana Wesleyan College, 213
Montevideo, 96-97
Montpelier Seminary, 222
Moore, John M., 31, 264, 273, 358, 409, 431, 438, 447, 449-51, 453-54, 457-59, 475, 569, plate 16
Moore, Noah W., Jr., 491
Moreland, J. E., 571-72
Morgan Christian Center, 212
Morgan College, 212
Morgan Memorial Church, Boston, 7, 120, 542
Mormons, missions to, 119-20
Morningside College, 221
Morrell, Thomas, 47
Morris Brown College, 583
Morris Harvey College, 228
Morris, Thomas A., 443
Morristown College, 13, 222, 492
Mota, J. E., 89
motive, 317
Mott, John R., 80, 565-66, 568-69, 571, 573, 577, 579, plate 9

Mount Union College, 203, 221

Mouzon, Edwin D., 31, 265, 273, 356, 358, 423, 427, 437, 447, 449-50, 454

Mozambique, 103, 105-7, 125, 541

Muelder, Walter G., 572-74

Müller, Christoph Gottlieb, 81-82

Murray, Thomas H., 412

Music Ministry, 532

Muslims, 93-94

Mutual Rights, 52

Nagoya, 86

Nanking, 75

Nashville *Christian Advocate*, 130-31, 164, 171, 173-77, 179-80, 182, 226, 234, 348, 355, 364-66, 370, 386, 391, 396, 402, 404, 450-51

Nashville-Birmingham Area, 491-92, 494

Nast, William, 65, 81-82, 196-97

National Association of Evangelicals, 587, 591

National Conferences of Methodist Men, 534

National Conference of Methodist Youth, 530

National Council of Churches, 255, 259, 496-97, 530, 574-77, 582, 589, 592-93, 607 (*see* Federal Council)

National Council of Meth. Youth (M.E.), 365, 369, 529

National Family Week, 531

National Fellowship of Methodist Musicians, 532

National Industrial Relations Conference (1958), 552

National Methodist Theological Seminary: *see* St. Paul School of Theology

national missions: *see* missions, missionary work

National Student Christian Federation, 577

nativism, 353-59

Nebraska, 14, 257, 451: Aurora, 273; Omaha, 217, 444

Nebraska Wesleyan University, 221

Neely, Thomas B., 29, 35, 50, 56

Negro Annual Conferences: M.E., 11-17; The Meth. Ch., 455, 461, 491 (*see* Central Jurisdiction)

Negro bishops, 16-17, 367, 489-90

Negro education, 209-12, 214, 487, 492-93

Negro missions, 116-17

Negroes: concern for, 160-61, 359-71, 485-88, 553-54; status of membership in

Negroes—*cont'd*
united church, 420, 422, 425, 427-33, 478, 488-89

Nelson, J. Robert, 572, 574

Nelson, Justus, 100

Nelson, Reuben, 184

neo-orthodoxy, 290, 293-95, 297-315, 319, 321-22, 563

Neo-Wesleyanism, 317-19

Nevada, 162, 213

Nevin, John, 600

New Congregational Methodist Church, 594

New England, 27, 120, 210-11, 486, 586, 617, 621

New Hampshire, 183: Concord, 243

New Jersey, 14, 191-92, 194: Atlantic City, 434, 469, 476, 497; Cape May City, 409-10, 421, 441; Madison, 192, 245; Maplewood, 191; Newark, 194; Ocean Grove, 418; Passaic, 377

New Jersey Conference Industrial Home, 13

New Mexico, 98, 115, 118: Albuquerque, 123

New Orleans Area, 491-92, 494

New Orleans Christian Advocate, 162

New Orleans University, 211

New York, 14, 27, 116, 162, 185, 387, 431: Albany, 9, 15, 357; Brooklyn, 118, 192; Buffalo, 14; Chautauqua Lake, 156, 195; Lima, 216; Newport, 186; Onandaga, 190; Ravenswood, 190; Saratoga Springs, 422; Stony Point, 567; Syracuse, 588

New York *Christian Advocate*, 29, 53, 138-39, 149-50, 160, 164-65, 168, 175, 184, 188, 191-93, 263, 268, 296, 310, 351-52, 355, 363, 376, 378, 383, 391, 394, 401, 435, 439, 449, 472, 622

New York City, 7, 14, 65, 78, 82, 100, 105, 117-19, 133-35, 139, 145-46, 149, 170, 172, 183-84, 186, 188, 191, 193-94, 211, 358, 372, 385, 476, 496-97, 499, 569, 583-84, 589

Newark Wesleyan Institute, 194

Newbury Biblical Institute, 245

Newman, J. P., 12

Newman, Junius, 97

Nichols, D. Ward, 573, 576

Niebuhr, Reinhold, 264, 297, 312, 324, 334, 387

Niebuhr, Richard, 389

Nigeria, 584

Ninde, W. X., 412

Nippert, Ludwig, 82

North Africa Mission, 109

North Carolina, 14, 16, 120, 123, 176, 210, 378, 456, 595: Asheville, 230, 358; Charlotte, 584; Durham, 203; Greensboro, 13, 123, 203, 492-93; High Point, 240, 242; Kittrell, 583; Lake Junaluska, 578; Salisbury, 584; Wilmington, 75

North Carolina Christian Advocate, 355

North Carolina Holiness Group, 595

North Central Jurisdiction, 475, 490, 504, 515

North Dakota, 595

North, Frank Mason, 380, 389-90, 395

Northeastern Jurisdiction, 475, 483, 490, 504, 534

Northwestern Christian Advocate, 158, 161, 169, 196, 333, 350, 355, 366, 378, 383, 402

Northwestern University, 187, 203, 215-16, 220, 267, 446, 572

Norway, 81, 83, 166, 573

Norwegian-Danish Theological Seminary, 246

Norwegian publications, 142

Norwood, Frederick, 317

Nova Scotia, 61-62

Nuelsen, Heinrich, 82

Nuelsen, John L., 82, 568

"O For a Thousand Tongues to Sing," 473

Official Board, local church, 463, 526-27, 556

Ogata, Sennosuke, 87

Ohio, 14, 77, 180, 187, 189, 196, 240, 344, 417, 525: Alliance, 203; Berea, 203, 247; Cincinnati, 70, 98, 122, 133, 145, 183-88, 191, 196-97, 245, 419, 437, 469, 476, 487, 537; Cleveland, 424, 433, 437, 444, 575-76, 621; Columbus, 368, 476, 496; Dayton, 82; Delaware, 203; Gambier, 196; Richwood, 189; West Lafayette, 458; Wilberforce, 583

Ohio Northern University, 221

Ohio Wesleyan University, 70, 180, 203, 221, 475, 576

O'Kelly, James, 21, 47, 52, 627

Okinawa, 88

Oklahoma, 15, 116, 241: Oklahoma City, 231, 247, 422

Oklahoma City University, 221

older people, work with, 531, 546-47

Oldham, William F., 79, 91-92

Olin, Stephen, 66, 154
Olivet Picture Cards, 154
Order for the Administration of Baptism, 473
Order for the Administration of the Lord's Supper, 473
Order for the Baptism of Youth, 473
Order for the Burial of a Child, 474
Order for the Burial of the Dead, 474, 557
Order for Receiving Children and Youth into the Church, 473
Order for Receiving Persons into the Church, 473
Order for Receiving Persons as Preparatory Members, 477
Order for the Reception of Probationers, 473
Order for Solemnization of Matrimony, 474
Order of Service (worship), 413-14, 441, 562, 611
Orders of Common Prayer, 546
ordination: bishops, 27-28, 42-43; deacons, 474; elders, 46, 462, 474
Oregon, 115-16, 135, 213, 441, 618: Salem, 203
Oregon Indian Mission, 65
Oregon Institute, 212
Oriental immigrants, missions to, 348-51
orphanages, 77-78, 108, 390, 494
Our Children, 153
Our Little People, 154
Our Morning Guide, 153
Our Teachers' Journal, 153
Outler, Albert C., 325-27, 572-73
Oxnam, G. Bromley, 316, 483, 512, 555-56, 569-71, 573, 575, 580, 625, plate 10

Pacific Christian Advocate, 355
Pacific Coast, Methodist work on, 118-19, 142, 176, 244, 247
Pacific Japanese Mission, 349
Pacific Japanese Provisional Annual Conference, 119
Pacific Methodist, 176
Pacific Methodist College, 224
pacifism, 406
Paine College, 108, 116, 234, 492, 586
Pakistan, 541
Palacious, Augustin, 99
Palembang (Sumatra), 93
Pan American Institute, Panama, 102
Panama, 96, 99-102
Paraguay, 97

Parish, Rebecca, 94
Parker, A. P., 90
Parker, Edwin W., 77, 110-11
Parker, Mrs. Edwin W., 69
Parker, Franklin N., 287
Parlin, Charles C., 556, 573, 578
parochial schools, 260, 359, 555
parsonages, 10, 535, 561
Pastoral Relations Committee, 477
pastors' schools, 271, 523-24
Paul Quinn College, 583
Payne, C. H., 217
Payne Theological Seminary, 583
peace, Methodist stand on, 549-51
Pearce, Liston H., 417
Peck, Jesse T., 24-25
Peck School of Domestic Science and Art, 13
Peking, 73-74
Peking University, 75
Pelagianism, 608-10
Penang, 93
Penn, Irvine G., 427, 431-32
Pennington, Chester, 319
Pennington School, 222
Pennington Seminary, 190, 192
Pennsylvania, 7, 14-15, 193, 208, 295, 377, 387, 583: Carlisle, 203, 208; Chambersburg, 208; Gouldsboro, 587; Meadville, 203; Mercersburg, 596; Philadelphia, 52, 54, 117, 119, 197, 394, 449, 486, 496-97, 583; Pittsburgh, 71-72, 120, 136, 385, 416, 443, 452-54, 476, 496; Shenandoah, 587
pensions, 133, 146, 498, 536
Pentecostal groups, 96, 403, 603
Penzotti, Francisco G., 97, 101
People's Central Institute, Brazil, 97
Pepper, John R., 450
periodicals and church papers, 136-37, 139, 142-43, 147, 153-54, 157-69, 191, 477, 537
Perkins School of Theology, 249, 444, 572, 574
personalism, 264, 276-78, 284-85, 295, 297, 299, 316, 320-21, 324
Peru, 96-97, 99-101, 541
Petersen, Ole, 83
Pfeiffer, Henry, 211
Philander Smith College, 13, 222, 492
Philippines, 63, 91, 94-95, 102-3, 111, 124, 169, 539, 541, 572
Phillips, John M., 184-85

Phillips School of Theology, 493
Picture Lesson Paper, 153-54
Pierce, George F., 25, 245
Pierce, Lovick, 408
pietism, 61, 600, 617, 627
Piette, Maximin, 291-92
Pilgrim Holiness Church, 589
Pilgrim Magazine, 157
Pilmoor, Joseph, 486
Piper, Arthur L., 108
Pittman Center (Tennessee), 122
Pittsburgh Book Directory (M.P.), 135, 153
Plan of Separation, 48
Plan of Union, 17, 31, 45, 50, 211, 369, 446, 475, 488-89; adoption and content, 455-58
Poland, 81, 84, 328, 346, 403
polity, 1-58, 442, 612-14, 616, 619-20, 627
Polytechnic - Intermountain College, 222
Ponce (Puerto Rico), 124
Pontianak, 92-93
Pope, Liston, 378
Port Arthur College, 223
Porter, James, 53
Porto Alegre, 97
Porto Alegre Institute, 98
Portugal, 63, 75, 95, 103, 106
Portuguese immigrants, missions to, 118
Prautch, W. A., 94
prayer cells, 564
prayer meeting, 610-11
preparatory membership, 503
Presbyterians, 19, 61, 66, 88-90, 94, 96, 109, 113, 120, 123, 125, 155, 173, 190, 194, 213, 226, 241, 580
presiding elders, 9, 147, 414, 469-70; length of appointment, 10, 24; elective presiding eldership, 21-22, 47, 49, 52 (see district superintendent)
prevenient grace, 280-81, 327
Primary Teacher, 154
Primitive Methodist Church, 446, 586-87
Primitive Methodist Journal, 587
Pringle-Pattison, A. Seth, 284, 305
printing, 130-31, 149-50 (see publishing)
prize fights, 162, 340
progressivism, 392-94, 396
prohibition, 161, 255, 330-43, 358-59, 399, 549, 624 (see temperance)
Prospectus of the Discipline of The Methodist Church, 459, 465

Protestant Episcopal Church, 120, 123, 167, 334, 503, 580
Protestants and Other Americans United for Separation of Church and State (POAU), 554-55
Provisional Central Conferences, 111
psychotherapy, 325-26
public school system, 226, 553, 555
publishing, 129-200, 536-38, plates 2-8: book publishing, 145-46, 148-49, 174; distribution, 143-44, 146-49; overseas publishing, 77, 80, 92, 95-97, 99, 107, 140-41, 413-14; printing, 130-31, 149-50
publishing agents, 537 (see book agents)
Publishing House (M.E.S.), 130-33, 140-42, 148, 154, 171-83
Puebla (Mexico), 99
Puerto Rico, 124, 414
Pyengyang, 89
Pykett, George F., 93

Quadrennial Commission on Christian Higher Education, 545
Quadrennial Committee (The Meth. Ch.), 535
Quadrennial Conferences, proposals for, 419-20 (see regional conferences)
quadrennial emphases, 514, 518-20
Quarterly Conference (The Meth. Ch.), 462-63, 504, 526-27, 556-57
Quarterly Conference (M.E.), 8, 51
Quarterly Review (M.E.S.), 137, 169, 173
Quarterly Review (A.M.E. Zion), 584
Quayle, William A., 33, 367, 435

race relations, 353, 360-71, 552-54, 585, 593
Race Relations Sunday, 211
Radio and Film Commission, 531
Raines, Richard C., 572
Rall, Harris Franklin, 149, 272, 280-84, 297, 301-3, 309, 315-16, 320, 569
Ramke, Heinrich, 82
Ramsdell, Edward, 324
Randolph-Macon College, 203, 223-24, 450, 571
Randolph-Macon College for Women, 236
Rangoon, 91
Rankin, Lochie, 70
Rankin, Thomas, 18
Ranson, Charles W., 565, 567

Rauschenbusch, Walter, 167, 388
Reconstruction, 5, 160, 170
Redford, A. H., 131-32, 172
Reed, Mary, 78
Reeves, E. C., 424, 450
Reformed Methodist Union Episcopal Church, 595
Reformed New Congregational Methodist Church, 594
Reformed Zion Union Apostolic Church, 595
Regional Conferences, proposals for, 425-27, 430, 432-35, 437, 449 (see Jurisdictional Conference)
Reid, C. F., 90
Reid, Emily J., 440
Religion in Life, 295, 303, 307, 537
religious education, 136, 138-39, 155-57, 266-67, 466, 527-32
Restrictive Rules, 37-38, 47-48, 460-61; Second, 54, 57; Third, 21, 30, 35, 41; Sixth, 133, 143, 146
retirement: bishops, 469; ministers, 469-70, 477
revivalism, 603, 609-10
Reynolds, A. L., 417
Reynolds, J. H., 449-50
Rhodes, Cecil, 107
Rhodesia, 103, 107-8, 125, 541
Rice, Merton S., 265
Richards, Erwin H., 106-7
Richmond Christian Advocate, 168
Rio de Janeiro, 97
Ritschl, Albrecht, 263, 268, 279, 295
Ritual (M.E.), 27, 611
Ritual (M.E.S.), 28
Ritual (The Meth. Ch.), 27, 473-74, 477, 562
Roberts, Benjamin Titus, 590
Roberts, Robert R., 22, 26-27, 32
Robinett, Gusta A., 541
Robinson, J. E., 91
Rockefeller Foundation, 212, 493
Rockefeller, John D., 206, 238, 374-75
Rodriguez, Trinidad, 99
Rogers, Henry Wade, 48, 431, 449
Roman Catholics, Roman Catholicism, 61, 84, 281, 503, 562, 617, 623; in America, 118, 165, 260, 334, 345-46, 358, 507, 546, 603; in Latin America, 95-96, 99; in India, 75, 79-80; in the Orient, 85, 94; Methodist relations with, 165, 338, 601
Roosevelt, Franklin D., 398, 404, 458, 558

Roosevelt, Theodore, 168, 344, 353, 392, 398, 625
Rosario (Argentina), 96
Rowe, Gilbert T., 287-89, 297, 303-4, 315
rural missions, 121-22
rural work, 390, 542
Rusling, James F., 374
Russia, 81-82, 88, 256, 339, 346, 351, 397, 402-3
Rust College, 13, 210, 222, 492
Rust Industrial Home, 13
Rust, R. S., 210
Ruter, Martin, 65, 171
Ryukyu Islands, 88

Sabbath observance, 163
Sabellianism, 278, 322
Sacco-Vanzetti case, 402
sacraments: see Baptism, Lord's Supper
St. George's Church, Philadelphia, 486
St. Louis Area, 491-92
Saint Paul School of Theology, 525
St. Paul's Church, Wilmington, Del., 271
St. Petersburg (Russia), 82
Saints' Everlasting Rest, Baxter, 145
Salmans, Levi B., 99
Samford, T. D., 450
Samuel Huston College, 13, 222
San Juan (Puerto Rico), 124
sanctification, 263, 330, 587-88, 590
Sandebudet, 143
Santiago College, 101
Santo Domingo, 125
São Paulo, 98
Sarawak, 91-94, 540-41
Scandinavia, 81-82, 111
Scandinavian immigrants, missions to, 117, 166; publications for, 142
Scandinavian language conferences, 246
Scarritt Bible and Training School, 71
Scarritt College for Christian Workers, 71, 234, 287
Schaff, Philip, 596-97, 599-600, 602-6, 608, 610-12
Schilling, S. Paul, 321, 563
Schleiermacher, Friederich, 263, 268, 290, 292, 295, 299, 313, 625
Scholar's Quarterly, 153
scholarships, seminary, 525
schools: see higher education, secondary education, colleges, theological seminaries, universities
Schwartz, Henry B., 88
Schweitzer, Albert, 283, 290, 295
Scopes trial, 254, 273
Scott, Leland H., 262-63
Scott, Orange, 587

Scranton, Mary F., 89
Scranton, William B., 89
Scudder, Ida, 78
Second Delegated Conference
  of the M.E. Church in
  India, 110
secondary education, 201;
  M.E., 213-15, 222-23;
  M.E.S., 226-27
secret society membership,
  588, 590
Section of Church Extension,
  543
Section of Home Missions,
  542
Section of Ministerial Educa-
  tion, 524
secularism, 616-19, 624-25
segregation, 258-59, 360,
  363, 368-69, 456, 498
self-supporting missions pro-
  gram, 100, 104-6
Senior Berean Lesson Quar-
  terly, 154
Senior Quarterly, 154
Seoul, 88-89
Sepoy mutiny, 76-77
Serampore, 76
Sesqui-centennial of Meth-
  odism, 446
settlement houses, 122, 390,
  529
Severance Union Medical
  College, 90
Seys, John, 15
Shanghai, 73-74, 90, 140
Shans, 91
Shaw, Alexander P., 16, 491
Shaw, Beverly F., 12-13
Shaw University, 210
Sheldon, Henry Clay, 276
Sheldon, William, 369
Shellabear, William G., 92-
  93
Sherwood, Rosetta, 89
Shinn, Asa, 52
Shipman, William 273
Shizuoka, 86
Shorter College, 583
Shorter Junior Lesson Quar-
  terly, 154
Shutleff, S. H., 307
Sibley Memorial Hospital,
  123
Sierra Leone, 62
Silver Shirt Legion, 356-57
Simon, John, 291
Simpson, Alexander, Jr.,
  431, 449
Simpson College, 222
Simpson, Matthew, 53-54, 99
Singapore, 91-93
Singh, Lilavati, 78
Singkawang, 93
Sinkinson, Charles D., 434
Skelton, David E., 13
slavery, 12, 63, 159-60, 359,
  486-87, 605-6, 624
Sloan, Harold Paul, 270-73,
  286, 306, 310, 472
Small, John B., 584

Smith, Alfred E., 337, 357-58
Smith, Boie, 83
Smith, Charles W., 420
Smith, David M., 141, 181-
  82
Smith, Eugene L., 540, 567
Smith, Rembert G., 405
Smith, Roy L., 265
Smith, W. A., 37-38
Snead College, 214
Snead Junior College, 222
Snead Senior High School,
  223
Snethen, Nicholas, 47, 52
Snyder, Henry Nelson, 231,
  431, 449-50
social concern, 160-69, 255,
  388-92, 538, 546-57, 617-
  18, 624-25
Social Creed of Methodism,
  167, 255, 363, 381, 386,
  395, 471-72, 547-48, 550-
  52, 554, 607, 625
Social Creed, Federal Coun-
  cil of Churches, 167, 395
social gospel, 167, 254, 331-
  32, 360, 388-97
Social Service Commission
  (M.E.S.), 355
Sockman, Ralph W., 355,
  571
Soerabaya (Java), 93
Soochow, 73
Soochow University, 75
Soong, Charles J., 75
Soong, T. V., 75
Soper, Edmund D., 475, 569
Soule, Agnes, 123
Soule, Joshua, 22, 27, 32,
  49, 52, 175
South America, 65, 72, 79,
  95-102, 105, 125, 433, 539,
  567, 573, 584
South Carolina, 15, 210,
  234, 439: Aiken, 593;
  Charleston, 152, 210; Co-
  lumbia, 203, 583; Orange-
  burg, 210, 246, 492; Spar-
  tanburg, 120, 203
South Carolina Christian
  Advocate, 130
South Central Jurisdiction,
  475, 482, 497, 504, 534
South Dakota, 14, 123: Mad-
  ison, 307; Rapid City, 123
Southeastern Jurisdiction,
  475, 482, 484, 490, 497,
  504, 512
Southern Association of
  Schools and Colleges, 229
Southern California School
  of Religion, 247
Southern Christian Advo-
  cate, 244
Southern Ladies' Compan-
  ion, 137
Southern Methodist, 440
Southern Methodist Church,
  592-93
Southern Methodist College,
  593

Southern Methodist Uni-
  versity, 232, 247, 249, 287,
  444, 450
Southern Review, 137
Southwestern Christian Ad-
  vocate, 16, 133, 171, 431,
  449, 494
Southwestern Christian Re-
  corder, 583
Southwestern College, 222
Southwestern University
  204, 450
Soviet Union: see Russia
Spain, 63, 81, 83, 94-95, 124,
  168, 290, 328, 396, 403
Spanish-American War, 102,
  164, 328, 396
Spanish Christian Advocate,
  99
Spanish-speaking immi-
  grants, missions to, 118
Spaulding, Winifred, 94
Spencer, Claudius B., 431
Spencer, Peter, 595
Springer, John M., 108
Stahlman, E. B., 141
Star of Zion, 584
Stevens, Abel, 144, 146
stewards, 51
Stewart, John, 65, 400
Stidger, William L., 265
Stockton, William S., 52
Stone, Mary, 74
Straughn, James H., 52, 416,
  451-52, 458, 475-76, 478,
  480, 568, plate 16
Student Loan Fund, 217-20
Student Volunteer Move-
  ment, 205, 577
Stuntz, Homer C., 94
Sue Bennett College, 123
Sumatra, 91-93
Summers, T. O., 131, 173-
  75, 226
Sunday morning service, 561
Sunday school: see church
  school
Sunday School Advocate,
  152-54
Sunday School Board (M.
  E.), 428
Sunday School Institute, 194
Sunday School Journal (M.
  E.), 152, 154, 156, 195
Sunday School Journal (Free
  Methodist), 591
Sunday School Magazine,
  154
Sunday School Standard, 157
Sunday School Union (M.
  E.), 152, 155-56, 194-95
Sunday School Visitor, 153-
  54
Sunday Service of the Meth-
  odists in North America,
  27, 562
supply pastors, 491, 523, 525
Sun Yat-Sen, 74
Swain, Clara, 77
Sweden, 81, 83, 166

Swedish immigrants, work with, 82, 143
Swedish Theological Seminary, 246
Sweet, T. B., 412
Sweet, William Warren, 1, 257, 445, 601-2
Switzerland, 45, 81-82, 294, 574
Syracuse University, 215-16, 220
Syrians, missions to, 118

Tagg, F. T., 198-99
Taiwan, 125
"Talk-back" programs, 532
Tamils, 91-92
Tarboux, J. W., 97, 112
Tarkington, Joseph, 146
Taylor, Charles, 73
Taylor, Prince A., Jr., 491
Taylor University, 203-4
Taylor, William, 66, 77-79, 91, 96, 99-106, 108, 110-11
Television, Radio, and Film Commission, 496, 531-32
Telugus, 91
temperance, 161, 329-43, 548-49; Board of, 467 (see prohibition)
Tennessee, 14-15, 122, 172, 177-80, 210, 254, 442, 583, 594: Athens, 214-15; Chattanooga, 214, 419-20; Jackson, 585-86; Knoxville, 179; Memphis, 228, 440, 450, 593; Morristown, 13, 492; Nashville, 68, 71, 130-31, 142, 150, 171-72, 177-82, 210, 212, 228, 230, 234-35, 246, 469, 476, 492, 496-97, 537, 582-83
Tennessee Indian School, 70
Tennessee Wesleyan College, 214-15, 222
term episcopacy, 24, 40-43
Texas, 15, 98, 117-18, 173, 204, 241, 442, 547, 594: Austin, 13, 206, 492; Brownville, 98; Dallas, 140, 232, 247, 553; El Paso, 118; Marshall, 492; Tehuacana, 241; Tyler, 586; Waco, 583
Texas College, 586
Texas Mission, 65
Thayer Industrial Home, 13
theological seminaries, 221, 244-49, 492-93, 525, 574 (see ministerial education)
theology, 254, 261-327, 605, 608-10, 621: conservatism, 254, 263, 265, 267-73, 286-87; doctrinal controversy, 271-73; ecumenical theology, 325-27; existentialism, 290, 322-23; fundamentalism, 254-55, 261, 271-73; liberalism, 254, 261, 262-67, 273-89, 295-96,

theology—cont'd
388-89; neo-orthodoxy, 290, 293-95, 297-315, 319, 321-22, 563; personalism, 264, 276-78, 284-85, 295, 297, 299, 316, 320-21; 324; major theologians: Brightman, 273-76, 297-98; De-Wolf, 321-22; Harkness, 295-96; Knudson, 276-80, 299-301; Lewis, 284-87, 304-15, 320; Rall, 280-84, 301-3, 320; Rowe, 288-89, 303-4; Tillett, 287-88; Wesleyan theology, 255, 263, 281, 291-93, 317-19, 327, 609-10
Thirkield, Wilbur, P., 12, 356, 367
Thoburn, Isabella, 77-78, 80, 122
Thoburn, James M., 66, 77, 80, 91-92, 94, 110, 122
Thomas, Frank M., 419, 433, 450
Thomas, W. G. M., 419
Thompson, John F., 96
Thomson, Edward, 12, 44
Thomson University, 210
Tigert, John J., III, 20, 22, 26, 51, 182-83
Tillett, Wilbur Fisk, 287
Tillich, Paul, 290, 324
Tilton Junior College, 222
Tilton School, 223
time limit of appointments: ministers, 8-10, 470; district superintendents, 469
Tippy, Worth M., 395
Tittle, Ernest Fremont, 265, 294, 355, 367, 405, 456, 550, 625
tobacco, Methodist stand on, 340, 470, 549, 588, 590
Tocqueville, Alexis de, 596
Together magazine, 537
Tokyo, 87
Toombs, Lawrence, 322
TRAFCO: see Television, Radio, and Film Commission
Transit and Building Fund Society of Bishop William Taylor's Self-Support Missions, 105
Transvaal, 107
Transylvania University, 228
traveling connection: see ministry, conference membership
Treider, Christian, 143
Tremont Street Church, Boston, 69
trial of church members, 401, 470
Trimble, Lydia A., 74
Trinity Methodist Church, Chicago, 194
Trinity Methodist Church, Cincinnati, 70

Trinity College, 233, 236, 353, 604 (see Duke University)
Troy Conference Academy, 191
Tsinan, 75
Tsuda, Sen, 87
Tucker, H. C., 97
Tunisia, 109
Turner, Frederick Jackson, 601-3
Turner School of Theology, 493
Twentieth-century Fund (M.E.S.), 235-36

Umtali Industrial Mission, 107-8
Unalaska, Aleutians, 123
Underwood, Horace G., 89-90
unification, 257, 407-78, 606-7; est. of fraternal relations, 407-11; period of federation, 412; first union proposals, 416-23; first proposed plan and its defeat, 423-38; forces working for union, 439-48; leaders, 449-52; final plan adopted, 455-57; Uniting Conference, 457-76; structure of The Methodist Church, 460-76; problems and adjustments, 500-501
uniform Sunday school lessons, 194 (see International Uniform Lessons)
Union American Methodist Episcopal Church, 595
Union Biblical Institute (Korea), 90
Union Church of Africans, 595
Union College (Kentucky), 214, 222
Union Evangelical Bookstore (Argentina), 96
Union Evangelical Theological Seminary (Buenos Aires), 97
Union Normal School (New Orleans), 210
Union of South Africa, 103
Union Theological Seminary (Manila), 94, 540
Union Theological Seminary (Mexico City), 99
Unitarians, Unitarianism, 159, 167, 263, 271, 334, 612
United Brethren, 94, 241, 417 (see Evangelical United Brethren)
United Church of Canada, 607
United Methodist Church of England, 411
United Nations, 259, 570
United Student Christian Council, 577

Uniting Conference, 52, 196, 257, 444, 457-76, 497, 548
Universalists, 159
universities: M.E. 215-16, 220; M.E.S., 232-33, 238; The Meth. Ch., 492
University of Alabama, 227
University of California at Berkeley, 176
University Center at Atlanta, 211
University of Chattanooga, 214, 222, 246
University of Denver, 212, 215-16, 220, 448
University of Illinois, 206, 545
University of Nanking, 75
University of North Carolina, 227
University of North Dakota, 222
University of the Pacific, 213
University Senate, 204, 215-18, 249
University of Southern California, 220, 247, 249, 545
Upper Iowa University, 203-4
Upper Room, The, 564
urban work, 6-7, 120-21, 390, 542
Uruguay, 96-97, 101
Utah, 119, 213: Salt Lake City, 119
Utah Mission, 120
Uttar Pradesh (India), 80

Valderrama, P. F., 99
Van Cleve, J. W., 425
Vanderbilt, Cornelius, 228-31
Vanderbilt University, 75, 90, 173-75, 177, 179-82, 228-35, 245, 247, 287, 324, 444, 451
Van Deusen, Henry R., 464
Van Dusen, Henry P., 289-90
Vashti Industrial School, 123
Velasco, B. N., 99
Vellore Christian Medical College, 78
Vermont, 185, 191: Newbury, 245; Poultney, 191
Vermont Junior College, 222
Versteeg, John, 309
Vidnesbyrdet, 142
Vincent, John H., 155-56, 193-95
Virgin Birth, 268, 272, 285, 312
Virginia, 7, 14-15, 26, 37, 122, 173, 198, 210, 223, 359, 430, 439, 595, 619: Ashland, 203; Emory, 203; Jamestown, 354; Richmond, 433
Voice of Methodism, 594
Voice of Missions, 583
Von Langenau, Baroness, 82

Wade, Raymond J., 568
Walden, John M., 12, 186-87, 210
Walden University, 210
Wallace, John J., 431, 433
Walls, W. J., 576
Walton, M. L., 419, 450
Wang Chih-P'ing, 111
war, Methodist stand on, 166, 396-98, 549-51
war claims payment, Southern Publishing House, 140-41, 178-80
War-Work Commission (M.E.S., M.P.) 398
Ward, A. Dudley, 576
Ward, Harry F., 356, 373, 379, 395, 405
Ward, William T., 93
Warren, Elizabeth Iliff, 247
Warren, Henry W., 12, 247, 416, 492
Warren, William Fairfield, 216, 248, 492
Washington, 247: Seattle, 247, 385
Washington, Booker T., 364, 371
Washington, D. C., 15-16, 123, 180, 198, 216, 395, 413, 453-54, 467, 496-97, 545, 556, 559, 583-84
Watchman, The, 594
Watkins, A. F., 450
Watts, Martha H., 98
Waugh, Beverly, 52, 443
Waugh, James W., 77
Webster, Alonzo, 210
Week of Dedication, 509, 520
Welch, Claude, 325
Welch, Herbert, 307, 326, 395, 452-54, 510
Wembo-Nyama, 109
Werner, Hazen, 306
Wesley Chapel, Cincinnati, 6
Wesley Church, Los Angeles, 16
Wesley College, 222
Wesley Community Houses, 71
Wesley Foundations, 206, 266, 466, 545
Wesley, John, 51, 161, 165, 225, 255, 259, 303, 329-30, 341, 380, 389, 441, 478, 487, 547, 562, 564-65, 588, 592, 600, 611, 613, 616-18, 624, 626: influence on American theology, 268, 271, 280-81, 289, 291-93, 315, 317-19, 609-10; missionary work, 60-63; stand on episcopacy, 18-21, 27-28; writings and publishing, 144-45, 147, 151, 174, 197
Wesley Memorial Church, Atlanta, 247
Wesley, Samuel, 600
Wesley Society, 317, 319

Wesley Theological Seminary, 249 (*see* Westminster Theological Seminary)
Wesleyan Christian Advocate, 162, 168, 355
Wesleyan College, 203, 236
Wesleyan Methodist, 588-89
Wesleyan Methodist Church (Connection) of America, 204, 240, 587-90, 595
Wesleyan Methodist Church, England, 446
Wesleyan Methodist Missionary Society, England, 63
Wesleyan Missionary, 588
Wesleyan Repository, 52
Wesleyan Service Guilds, 535
Wesleyan theology, 255, 263, 281, 291-93, 317-19, 327, 609-10
Wesleyan University, 186, 189-92, 203, 222
Wesleyan Youth, 588
West, Benjamin F., 92-93
West China Union University, 75
West Indies, 62, 79
West Indians, 102
West Lafayette College, 458
West Virginia, 15-16, 212, 439: Charleston, 228
West Virginia Wesleyan College, 222
Western Book Concern, 133, 135, 145, 148, 184-88 (*see* Book Concern)
Western Christian Advocate, 134, 147, 159, 162-67, 184, 191, 197, 244, 355
Western Jurisdiction, 482, 490, 504, 534
Western Maryland College, 199, 240-42, 246, 416
Westminster College, 213, 240-41
Westminster Theological Seminary, 198-99, 242, 246, 249
Wheaton College, 203-4
Whedon, Daniel D., 146, 189-90
White, H. H., 425, 430, 433, 450
White, Moses, 73
Whitefield, George, 609
Whitlock, W. F., 137, 147, 151
Wicke, Myron F., 217
Wieman, Henry Nelson, 278, 298
Wilberforce University, 583
Wilberforce, William, 76
Wilbraham Academy, 223
Wiley College, 222, 492
Wiley, Isaac W., 28-29, 210
Wilkins, J. Ernest, 492
Willamette University, 203, 212, 222, 247
Willard, Frances E., 56, 161, 333-35

Willerup, Christian, 83
Williams, Colin, 318, 609
Williams, M. O., 567
Williamsport-Dickinson Academy, 204
Williamsport-Dickinson Junior College, 222
Williamsport - Dickinson Seminary, 223
Wilson, Clarence True, 271, 334
Wilson, Luther B., 356, 412
Wilson, Woodrow, 391-92, 398, 621
Wisconsin, 14, 212, 394: Appleton, 203
Wise, Daniel, 193
Wofford, Benjamin, 224
Wofford College, 203, 224, 227, 450
Woman's Board of Foreign Missions (M.E.S.), 70, 102
Woman's Board of Home Missions (M.E.S.), 71, 116, 119, 234
Woman's Board of Missions (Congregational), 69
Woman's Christian College (India), 78
Woman's Christian College (Japan), 87
Woman's Christian Temperance Union, 161, 335
Woman's College, Baltimore, 416
Woman's Department of Church Extension (M.E.S.), 70
Woman's Division of Christian Service, Board of Missions, 466, 494, 496, 506, 518, 524, 533, 535, 541, 543
Woman's Foreign Missionary Society (M.E.), 69, 74, 77-78, 86-87, 89, 91-92, 96, 99, 101, 106, 109
Woman's Foreign Missionary Society (M.E.S.), 70

Woman's Foreign Missionary Society (M.P.), 72, 86
Woman's Home Missionary Society (M.E.), 13, 70, 119, 123-24, 211, 214
Woman's Home Missionary Society (M.E.S.), 71
Woman's Home Missionary Society (M.P.), 72
Woman's Medical Institute (Seoul), 89
Woman's Missionary Advocate, 70
Woman's Missionary Council (M.E.S.), 71
Woman's Missionary Friend, 69
Woman's Missionary Recorder, 583
Woman's Parsonage and Home Mission Society (M.E.S.), 71
Woman's Society of Christian Service (The Meth. Ch.), 481, 490, 506, 525, 535
Woman's Union Missionary Society, 69, 71
women: admitted to conference membership, 58, 525-26; as missionaries, 68-69, 125-26; granted equal lay rights, 56-58, 442; ordination of, 57-58, 471; work of Woman's Division, 535
Wood, Elsie, 101
Wood, Thomas B., 96, 101
Woodson, Carter G., 11, 13
Woolever, Harry E., 459
Woolley, John G., 166
Working Conference on the Union of American Methodism, 446
World Council of Churches, 259, 325, 566, 568-72, 574, 578, 582, 589, 592, 610
World Methodist Council 578, 582

World Missionary Conference (Edinburgh, 1910), 87, 104, 567-69
World Service funds, 490, 499, 506
World War I, 59, 81-82, 84, 88, 96-97, 102, 104, 109, 118, 120, 128, 142, 205-7, 253-54, 299, 337, 346, 350, 363, 365, 396-98, 401, 445, 501, 549
World War II, 84, 88, 111, 128, 254, 258-59, 320, 328, 501, 524, 528, 539, 544, 549, 551, 555, 557-58, 567
World's Student Christian Federation, 566, 577
worship: see liturgical practices, ritual, order of service
Wright, John E., 101
Wu I-fang, 75
Wunderlich, Ehrhardt, 82
Wunderlich, Friedrich, 82
Wyoming Seminary, 223
Wysner, Gloria, 567

Y.M.C.A., 205, 275, 398, 566, 577,
Y.W.C.A., 577
Yang, Y. C., 75
Yenching University, 75
Yokohama, 86
Yonsei University, 90
Young Harris College, 122
Young, W. J., 433, 450
Youth in Action, 591
youth work (The Meth. Ch.), 529-30
Yugoslavia, 81-82
Yun, T. H., 90

Zamora, Nicolas, 94
Zapata, Eduardo, 101
Zaring, Elbert R., 395
Zentmire, Cora, 106
Zion's Herald, 34, 160-62, 166, 301, 350, 355, 367, 384, 404, 456